"A lovingly assembled, translated, and annotated collection of intimate letters, full of sometimes dishy gossip, from two of the most fascinating personalities of the twentieth century, . . . *Speak Low* is a record of momentous events refracted through a love as complex as it was intense."

—JOHN ROCKWELL

"I found *Speak Low* fascinating. This massive correspondence appears to come from the same voice. As the years pass, people who love each other do have the same voice, and these two surely loved each other, without perhaps being 'in love.' The collection is lavishly and definitively informative about the highest show-biz milieu of the period. These letters are intimate without sentimentality, intelligent without literary pose, gossipy without slander, informedly opinionated without deviousness, and businesslike without toughness. I deeply admire the skillfully caring annotational glue provided by the editors."   —NED ROREM

"I couldn't stop reading. Even though I knew Weill and Lenya for fifteen years, their private side, as unveiled in these letters, is a revelation. I remember one day Kurt and I were chatting on his porch on South Mountain Road, and I noted that his life seemed to be settling down. He said yes, and he was glad because he knew, given time, that he'd have Lenya all to himself. This is an exhilarating correspondence, which is also a panorama of the golden years of theater and music in the twentieth century."

—BURGESS MEREDITH

"I spent a lot of time with Lenya during her last days. One day near the end she looked at me with those searing eyes and confessed, 'I've always envied you because you were able to sing Lulu.' I countered, 'But Lenya, you are Lulu.' And now that her revealing autobiographical fragment and these gripping letters are published, her portrait emerges in colors as vivid as Lulu's. Lenya and Weill remain unique and essential for the art of our time."

—TERESA STRATAS

"An impressive and enormously engrossing read about two of this century's greatest artists. If you love the theater, you will love knowing more about Kurt Weill and his enchanting Lenya. I certainly did."

—FRED EBB

"Kurt Weill and Lotte Lenya were an indispensable theatrical couple, and this exchange of letters is an indispensable record of their relationship. It is also a record of great musical achievement both in Europe and the United States."

"Behind the legends of a legendary relationship, this invaluable compendium of the extant correspondence reveals layer upon layer of fascinating reality. Readers of every kind will be grateful to the editors for their inspired research and brilliant detective work."

"Because Weill and Lenya were ardent and explicit letter writers and seem to have met everyone working in music and theater, there are fascinating insights into the lives of the masters of the first half of this century. Vividly and entertainingly organized by Kowalke and Symonette, *Speak Low* is invigorating! It was impossible to put down."

SPEAK LOW
(WHEN YOU SPEAK LOVE)

The publisher gratefully acknowledges
the generous contribution provided
by the Director's Circle of the Associates
of the University of California Press,
whose members are

Evelyn Hemmings Chambers
June and Earl Cheit
Edmund J. Corvelli, Jr.
Lloyd Cotsen
Susan and August Frugé
Harriet and Richard Gold
Florence and Leo Helzel
Raymond Lifchez and Judith Lee Stronach
Ruth and David Mellinkoff
Thormund A. Miller
Ann and Richard C. Otter
Joan Palevsky
Lisa See and Richard Kendall

SPEAK LOW
(WHEN YOU SPEAK LOVE)

· · · · · · · · · · ·

The Letters of Kurt Weill and Lotte Lenya

EDITED AND TRANSLATED BY
Lys Symonette and Kim H. Kowalke

UNIVERSITY OF CALIFORNIA PRESS

Berkeley   Los Angeles

The publisher gratefully acknowledges the generous contribution provided by the Roth Family Foundation toward the publication of this book.

University of California Press
Berkeley and Los Angeles, California

Acknowledgment is made for permission to reprint lyrics from the following songs as epigraphs: For Part I, "There's Nowhere to Go but Up" (Maxwell Anderson, Kurt Weill), © 1938 by DeSylva, Brown & Henderson, Inc.; for Part II, "Speak Low" (Ogden Nash, Kurt Weill), © 1943 by Chappell & Co. Both copyrights renewed and assigned to Warner/Chappell & TRO-Hampshire House Publishing Corp. All rights reserved. Used by permission.

Library of Congress Cataloging-in-Publication Data

Weill, Kurt, 1900–1950.
    [Correspondence. English. Selections]
    Speak low (when you speak love) : the letters of Kurt Weill and
  Lotte Lenya / edited and translated by Lys Symonette and Kim H.
  Kowalke.
       p. cm.
    Includes English correspondence and translations of correspondence
  from German.
    Includes bibliographical references (p.) and index.
    ISBN 0-520-07853-5 (alk. paper)
    1. Weill, Kurt, 1900–1950—Correspondence. 2. Composers—
  Correspondence. 3. Lenya, Lotte—Correspondence. 4. Actors—
  Correspondence. I. Symonette, Lys. II. Kowalke, Kim H., 1948– .
  III. Title.
  ML410.W395A4   1996
  782.1′092′2—dc20
    [B]   95-40544
                                                      CIP
                                                      MN

Printed in the United States of America

9 8 7 6 5 4 3 2 1

MY WIFE

She is a miserable housewife, but a very good actress.
She can't read music, but when she sings, people listen as if it were Caruso.
   (For that matter, I pity any composer whose wife can read music.)
She doesn't meddle in my work (that is one of her foremost attributes). But
   she would be very upset if I took no interest in hers.
She always has a couple of male friends, which she explains by saying that
   she doesn't get along with women. (But perhaps she doesn't get along
   with women precisely because she always has a couple of male friends.)
She married me because she enjoyed horror, and she claims that this desire
   has now been fulfilled sufficiently.
My wife's name is Lotte Lenya.
   Kurt Weill, 1929

[MY HUSBAND]

Some people thought Kurt was arrogant. But he wasn't arrogant at all; he
was just terribly shy, and that shyness kept people away from him, like a
wall he built around himself. Nobody really knew Kurt Weill. I wonder
sometimes whether I knew him. I was married to him twenty-four years and
we lived together two years without being married, so it was twenty-six years
together. When he died, I looked at him, and I wasn't sure I really knew
him.
   Lotte Lenya, 1979

CONTENTS

Illustrations follow page 218

INTRODUCTIONS

WEILL AND LENYA

I believe we're the only married couple without problems.
Weill to Lenya, 21 April 1938 (Letter 198)

They would seem an unlikely couple. He was a German cantor's son: short, prematurely bald, with thick spectacles that she thought made him look like a mathematics professor. Cerebral, well-educated, and reared in a close but restrictive family, he was already recognized as one of the leading young composers in Germany when he met her. Two years older, she was an Austrian Catholic coachman's daughter, christened Karoline Wilhelmine Charlotte Blamauer: waiflike and far from beautiful, but always appealing to men. Uninhibited, ill-educated, she escaped abuse by an alcoholic father, first becoming a young prostitute, then a would-be dancer turned actress in Zurich. In Berlin during 1922 she auditioned for a role in his first stage work, but he was playing piano in the pit and she wasn't able to catch sight of him down there. Two years later her employer asked her to row across the lake to pick the young composer up at the tiny train station in Grünheide on the outskirts of Berlin. He was to be a weekend guest at the summer home of playwright Georg Kaiser's family, with whom she was then living as a domestic helper. According to one of her later colorful but dubious accounts, it was more than just love at first sight: in their passion, he lost his glasses overboard before they reached the opposite shore. Soon they were living together in his tiny apartment in Berlin, where he gave lessons in music theory and composition in exchange for butter and other comestibles. Much to his pious family's dismay, they married in 1926. In 1932 they separated, in 1933 divorced, in 1935 reunited in Paris and then went to New York, in 1937 remarried and together applied for American citizenship. Except for brief periods of separation for professional reasons, they lived together until his sudden death at age fifty in 1950. Until the end, their relationship remained what it had always been—simultaneously tenacious and tumultuous, open to and always surviving many secondary romantic and sexual relationships.

This complex if otherwise unremarkable story about a couple whom a friend once characterized as "bourgeois bohemians" would hold little further interest if *he* hadn't been Kurt Weill and *she* Lotte Lenya, an artistic duo who are now seen almost to embody an entire era, Weimar Germany's legendary "Golden Twenties." It is hardly hyperbole to suggest that almost every major cultural and political event on two continents during the second quarter of the century impinged on their professional and personal lives. Despite an amazing array of stellar names among the dramatis personae of their private drama—

from Bertolt Brecht to Ira Gershwin, Marlene Dietrich to Mary Martin, Thomas Mann to John Steinbeck, Ferruccio Busoni to Charlie Chaplin, Joseph Goebbels to Paul Robeson—the two people with the leading roles were seldom upstaged. For Weill and Lenya were not merely two struggling artists who fell in love and married. Unlike certain other artistic duos, including such acquaintances as Franz Werfel and Alma Schindler, Moss Hart and Kitty Carlisle, or Helen Hayes and Charles MacArthur, Weill and Lenya needed each other on a "creative" level that transcended ordinary emotional, erotic, or professional bonds. It was surely this musicodramatic interdependence and empathy that bridged and fused Weill's and Lenya's otherwise conflicting biographical, intellectual, and psychological profiles. They maintained constant contact and continued collaborating even when seemingly irrevocably estranged on the personal level.

That mysterious but magnetic affinity was apparent from the outset: soon after he had met Lenya, Weill wrote to his parents that he was also now finding himself as a composer: "I have become noticeably more independent, more confident, happier, and less tense. Of course, living with Lenya again accounts for much of this. It has helped me tremendously. It's the only way I could put up with living alongside someone: a coexistence of two differing artistic interests, without domestic ties, each one helping the other on his own course. How long will this last? I hope a long time" (W–A&EW1, n.d. [1925], #221). Within the year, she was giving voice to his music, he was giving music to her voice. As Weill articulated in a letter to Lenya from 1926, their paths were separate but converged in song:

> When I feel this longing for you, I think most of all of the sound of your voice, which I love like a very force of nature, like an element. For me all of you is contained within this sound; everything else is only a part of you; and when I envelop myself in your voice, then you are with me in every way. I know every nuance, every vibration of your voice, and I can hear exactly what you would say if you were with me right now—and how you would say it. But suddenly this sound is again entirely alien and new to me, and then it is the greatest joy to realize how affectionately this voice caresses me. (Letter 15)

Despite her deprived educational background and lack of any musical training, Lenya's canny theatrical sensitivity and innate intelligence enabled her to become Weill's most trusted critic as well as his most famous interpreter. As such she became part of his work, subsumed in his music. And music was Weill's life: "I'm perfectly happy sitting in my study all day, composing," he told a friend (mem. FJ, p. 84). A role within Weill's inner ear, indispensable as it was, ultimately proved too limited for Lenya: "As soon as my feet hit the stage—I am safe," she told him (Letter 318). There she was in control and could subconsciously repair some of her early psychic damage. In 1927 she first appeared in one of Weill's works, as an eleventh-hour replacement for an indisposed opera singer at the premiere in Baden-Baden of the *Mahagonny Songspiel*. After the performance, Otto Klemperer saw her in the bar, slapped her on the back, and inquired in Brecht's (or Elisabeth Hauptmann's) pidgin English, "Is here no telephone?" The next year she created the role of Jenny in *Die Dreigroschenoper*. Her name had been inadvertently left out of the program, but the following morning Berlin's most powerful critic wrote that "she was good, she was very good." Weill's music had launched her career, and though never an ingenue type, for several years she worked steadily in leading roles in Berlin's foremost theaters.

But even the combination of an independent career and what Weill could afford to give of himself wasn't enough: "Lenya," he often told her when she protested his neglect, "you know you come right after my music." She needed more, both personally and professionally. She took lovers, and so did he. Some were famous; most were not. Hers tended to be more numerous and casual, less emotionally entangled. On the other hand, "Kurt didn't have many affairs, but they were rather serious," Lenya said, "because he was very emotional and honest in his love" (int. L3). In Germany her most ardent paramour was a tall, blond Austrian tenor whom she dubbed "the Flying Dutchman"; Weill cast him in both *Mahagonny* and *Die sieben Todsünden* so that he and Lenya could be together. Weill, in turn, fell in love with the wife of the famous set designer Caspar Neher, a onetime librettist of his, who remained Weill's good friend throughout. "That was a lovely affair," Lenya recalled without apparent bitterness. "She was a little sexy pony, one of those blonds, sturdy and witty. I could see why he would fall for somebody like that" (int. L3).

Weill and Lenya separated amicably in Germany during 1932 and divorced shortly after Weill fled Berlin for Paris the next year. Until her death Lenya maintained, contrary to all circumstantial and documentary evidence, that the divorce had been entirely strategic, designed to protect Weill's assets. She and her tenor did manage to smuggle some of his money out of Germany but apparently lost all of it at roulette on the Riviera. At the nadir of his career, Weill seemed willing to take her back at any point and on her own terms. He confided to a friend that he longed for the time when they could grow old together: "Then Lenya won't leave me anymore" (mem. FJ, p. 197). After her lover ran off with the proceeds from the sale of the house in Berlin and the affair had ended, Weill indeed welcomed her back. Most of their closest friends didn't even know they had divorced.

While he was in London for the first months of 1935, Lenya had her own "lovely affair," with Max Ernst in Paris. Nevertheless, Weill decided, against the advice of nearly all his friends, to take Lenya along to America with him. He boasted that "we've really solved the question of living together, which is so terribly difficult for us, in a very beautiful and proper way"—a way that would prove to be much like what he had described to his parents a decade earlier, and now echoed in his letter to Lenya: "Your qualities as a human being keep developing parallel to my own, so that (after ten years!) you are still giving me things that no one else can give me, things that are crucial. . . . I have a very good feeling about England and America as far as you and your work are concerned. We'll make it, won't we?" (Letter 133).

But in certain respects emigration to America was tougher on Lenya than on Weill, because her craft—acting—depended on mastery of a language that was not in any sense "international," where foreign accents limited a performer to exotic roles. Reviewing her first concert appearance in the United States, in December 1935, Marc Blitzstein prophesied that "Lenja is too special a talent, I'm afraid, for a wide American appeal." He was right. Whereas in New York Weill could still sit at his desk and compose music that usually succeeded in camouflaging his foreign accent, Lenya's "feet hit the stage" in America only rarely, and without much success until after Weill's death. After her role in Max Reinhardt's *Eternal Road*, she managed only a few weeks as a club singer at Le Ruban Bleu and a few months in a role Maxwell Anderson had written especially for her in *A Candle in the Wind*. In 1944, after seeing the musical *Follow the Girls*, she told Weill that she couldn't: "I saw . . . how very, very different it is, when they sing songs. I dont think I ever can learn that. Or somebody would have to teach me" (Letter 310). But she soon gave up on vocal instruction, too: "My singing lessons are pretty monotonous. I simply fail to see, how any one can spent a life time to make hi hi hi and oh-oh-oh for more than 2 month" (Letter 356).

They decided not to have children. Lenya's two abortions as a teenager in Zurich had left her unable to conceive. In her mid-forties, she offered to have surgery to correct the problem, as a last chance, but Weill dissuaded her: "I'm scared to death something would happen to you. I don't have the vanity that my name should live on through a son. I hope my name lives on through my music—or not" (int. L3).

The tensions that arose from the disparity between Weill's frenetic activity and success and Lenya's professional failure and subsequent enforced domesticity manifested themselves in self-destruction. As Weill worked himself toward an early grave, Lenya was no longer content merely to play canasta with Mab Anderson and the other wives of famous artists living on South Mountain Road in Rockland County. She shocked even the most accepting among them with both her choice of sexual partners and the flagrancy of her affairs with a young pilot and a Texan she called "Wild Bill."

For his part Weill, reportedly near-celibate while working on a show, enjoyed the attention of more than one would-be starlet during his periodic forays into the Hollywood film industry in the late 1930s and early 1940s. He and Lenya seemed to have reached an understanding, even joking about such "meaningless flings." And Lenya seemed not to mind the occasional periods of separation: "The only thing I hate to miss are those mornings when you sit at the piano and those wounderful tunes start to pop out of it" (Letter 336). But in 1944 Weill discreetly established a long-term liaison with an attractive and intellectually vibrant fellow-émigré living in Hollywood. "It was very civilized," but this time Lenya admitted to being jealous: "this one could turn out to be dangerous" (int. L3).

Yet Weill always returned to Lenya, his beloved Brook House, and the Broadway theater. After *Johnny Johnson* and *Knickerbocker Holiday*, the big success of *Lady in the Dark* and *One Touch of Venus* allowed him to embark on a series of experimental works with some of the foremost playwrights, directors, and designers in America: *The Firebrand of Florence*, an ill-fated operetta (with Ira Gershwin's lyrics) conceived as a vehicle for Lenya's comeback; the Broadway opera *Street Scene*, with Langston Hughes and Elmer Rice; the school opera *Down in the Valley;* the concept musical *Love Life*, with Alan Jay Lerner and director Elia Kazan; and Maxwell Anderson's antiapartheid "musical tragedy," *Lost in the Stars*. Weill seemed to take success and failure equally in stride: "It wouldn't be so much fun if it weren't so dangerous, so unpredictable" (Letter 369). As he approached his fiftieth birthday, he seemed on the threshold of a new phase of his career: "I've suddenly been promoted into the category of a 'classic' and they're even starting to talk about the 'historical significance' of my work" (W–A&EW1, 6 Sept. 1949). But Weill took to bed on his birthday, and a month later he died of a heart attack.

Although Lenya had appeared in a number of non-Weill plays and films in both Europe and America, during his lifetime her professional persona derived almost exclusively from his. Whereas the young Mrs. Weill had resented her husband's singular passion for his own music and sought companionship elsewhere, the middle-aged widow Weill monogamously devoted herself to his legacy, thereby assuaging her own guilt and at the same time succeeding under her second husband's guidance in building the international career she could never sustain while the first was alive. She recorded and performed far more than the five roles Weill had composed specifically for her, and in so doing ironically launched the posthumous Weill renaissance and established the mythology of the "ideal," gravelly voiced Weill singer. Although she never consistently pursued a career on stage or in film independent of her role as Weill interpreter, *The Roman Spring of Mrs. Stone* earned her an Academy Award nomination, and *From Russia with Love* brought her notoriety as the unforgettable stiletto-toed Colonel Kleb. Yet she seldom succeeded in entirely shedding associations with her husband's work; even her memorable portrayal of Fräulein Schneider in *Cabaret* seemed to derive from his inspiration. Outliving three more husbands, all of whom were predominantly homosexual in orientation, Lenya rarely wavered in her posthumous devotion to her first husband. On her deathbed in 1981, most of her last lucid moments still focused on Weill's legacy: Who would promote and protect his music? Would someone make sure that the right thing was done with the letters that documented her life with him?

THE LETTERS

Your letters are so sweet and you keep me so well informed
about everything, that I am practically with you.
    Lenya to Weill, Letter 336

There are 375 letters, 18 postcards, and 17 telegrams that survive—296 from Weill to Lenya, 114 from Lenya to Weill. The disparity is due in part to the fact that almost all of Weill's correspondence files were among the manuscripts, music, books, diaries, and notebooks that he left behind (and never recovered) when he fled Berlin on short notice in 1933. Therefore, there is no extant correspondence from Lenya to Weill prior to 1933. With characteristic disdain for the gaze of posterity, he apparently made no effort to save every letter thereafter either. It appears that, with few exceptions, the letters of Lenya's which have survived are either the ones addressed to him at home (where they did not have to take up room in a suitcase and be transported) or ones that Lenya herself may have retrieved when she visited him on the road. Accordingly, Lenya's 114 letters all date from 1933–35, 1938, and 1942–44.

Lenya, on the other hand, seems to have treasured Weill's letters, saving even the earliest notes and, throughout her many moves, preserving the collection as it grew in size. From the start she seemed to know instinctively that Weill was special; maybe not a Mozart, but a genius nonetheless. All but two of his extant letters have survived intact, without loss of text. As a result of her stewardship, the letters from Weill extend from shortly after their first meeting in 1924 until 1948 and thus provide a more complete, albeit one-sided, documentation of their lives apart. After 1944 Weill made fewer extended trips

[FIGS. 1 & 2]

to Hollywood and placed long-distance telephone calls more frequently, so the number of letters decreased substantially in the last five years of his life.

Of the 393 letters and postcards, 151 were written in Europe before 1935 and the remaining 242 after immigration to the United States. The fact that 212 of the items were nonetheless written in German (compared to 198 in English) is indicative of how long the two communicated privately in their native language after they had comfortably been using English on a daily basis with others. Weill's letters to Lenya from Hollywood in 1938 were still in German, although a telegram describing the Grand Canyon on his return trip was written in English. His next letter, during the Boston tryout of *Lady in the Dark* in January 1941, was in English; he later joked that after *Lady*'s enormous success he even dreamed and counted in English. Thereafter, except for salutations and sign-offs, he seldom used more than an isolated phrase of German. Lenya's first surviving letters after 1938 are also in English; they date from the start of her long road tour with *A Candle in the Wind* in January 1942. But her conversion was more gradual and less complete. She would often resort to German when exercised about something or when making fun of those who clung to the old country. Her idiosyncratic mishmash of mangled English and American-ized German often resulted in uniquely humorous formulations. In June 1944, for example, she wrote Weill that "I will help myself to bed and will have a divine sleep with heavenly dreams and heavenly *arschjucken von so viel* moskitobites." But she also observed in the same letter, "When I answered [Fritz] Stiedry in German, I spoiled about four pages before I got those few German lines together. That's good" (Letter 311).

When apart, even at certain times during their period of estrangement, Weill and Lenya seldom went more than a week without writing. "It makes me very nervous when I don't hear from you," he scolded her in 1935, and again two years later: "When I didn't have any news from you for several days, I surmised you weren't feeling well and was very worried until finally your letter arrived today" (Letters 139, 192). Often they wrote each other every day or two. Sometimes three letters carry the same date, as letters and replies crossed in the mail. Postal service in Germany assured next-day delivery, while mail from Los Angeles to New York in the 1930s and 1940s took no more than two days.

Their exchanges were uninhibited, intimate, and irreverent, with neither on the lookout to check if posterity was peering in. Occasionally Weill would jot down a melody with a risqué lyric, while Lenya would sketch a charmingly vulgar or erotic drawing. One finds matter-of-fact acknowledgment, if not acceptance, of the state of the other's current love affair. Weill's cryptic inquiry in May 1932, for example, "Is it nice in Hietzing? Is the hotel pleasant? Are the people nice to my little *Tütchen?*" almost conceals the painful wounds evinced in the oblique reference to Lenya's ongoing tryst with her "Dutchman." Especially during their uncertain first years in America, they gossiped, complained about colleagues and collaborators, railed at rivals, and griped about failed projects. They in-dulged petty jealousies, admitted to insecurities, and shared worries about money, family, home, the future. Not even Weill's closest friends, including Maxwell Anderson, were off-limits as targets. In July 1944, for example, Lenya reported to Weill:

> He [Anderson] left the party. He is sick. His beard is growing and as his beard
> grows longer his dullness grows with it. I feel sorry for him. He is just a victim of

his concit. He doesn't seem to get along with his play. How could he! He has nothing to say, what a good laxative couldn't do. He is a little bit like Darious. The way he can *cack* [shit] music Max can *cack* plays. (Letter 318)

Darius Milhaud was, in fact, virtually Weill's only composer friend. Whereas actors, singers, directors, choreographers, and especially playwrights and poets were potential collaborators, composers were either rivals—like Hindemith and Rodgers—or imitators—like Marc Blitzstein. Weill reserved his sharpest barbs for the cluster of artistic émigrés in Los Angeles and the mores of Hollywood:

Sunday afternoon I was at the Viertels'. He's an old fool, and she's a horrible witch. They won't see me again soon. In the evening I had dinner at Miriam Hopkins's; she is quite nice but terribly cold and superficial. It was a typical Hollywood evening, marvelous food on magnificent dishes, etc. Conversation exclusively about Hollywood and movies, on and on, until everyone was plastered, then they sang songs and told rotten jokes. And those were the NICE people! Gloria Swanson was there. She's still very beautiful, but it's a desperate beauty (here they mustn't get old, or they're as good as dead). (Letter 160)

The letters are also filled with artistic news, views, and aspirations, reactions to world events, reports on works in progress, reflections on the creative process and the émigré experience. In quick succession the reader gets a backstage view of German music and theater, the American musical theater in the late 1930s and 1940s, and the Hollywood studios. The register of names in the letters is a veritable Who's Who of the era. The composite offers a nonchalant cultural history, anecdotal in the best sense, alternately earnest and silly, self-centered yet observant of the larger world.

Lenya tended to be spontaneous, earthy, uncensored. Virtually free of pretensions or pomposity, she wrote as she spoke. As her vistas narrowed while at South Mountain Road or in hotel rooms on tour, she seemed more and more concerned with mundane matters of day-to-day existence, perhaps grasping for common ground with her husband, in whose professional life she figured less and less. Although they both surely felt the precariousness of earning a living without benefit of subsidies, commissions, or a teaching post, Weill was more measured in tone, almost paternal in his indulgence of her rebellions, and loath to share the burden of weakness or genuine unhappiness. Harold Clurman's assessment of Weill as "all theater, all mask" pertains even to his relationship with Lenya, as she herself noted. He seemed to compartmentalize his identities and reveal different aspects of his personality according to the reception he could expect from his various correspondents: in his letters to his brother Hans (mostly dating from 1917 to 1925), he discussed issues of literature and music in great detail; in those to his publisher Universal Edition (1925–33), he adopted a Viennese formality that cloaked underlying tactics of manipulation, as he charted his artistic course, plotted promotion, and negotiated a living. The rhapsodic expressions of idealism, love, and existential pain he rarely expressed to Lenya were instead directed to Erika Neher, and later, to a lesser extent, to a few others. (Publishing the Weill-Lenya correspondence in isolation, of course, privileges that relationship over the perspectives a comprehensive chronological sequence of varied addressees might offer.) In fact, after Weill's initial fawning declarations of devotion to Lenya in 1924–25, for which she rebuked him, neither seemed at ease either revealing or being privy to innermost thoughts and feelings. Paradoxically they finally settled into the relaxed intimacy of best friends, two profoundly lonely souls clinging to each other while intuiting that ultimately neither could be fulfilled thereby.

Almost as if they were attempting to veil endearments that might betray their need for the other, they developed a private language, derived in part from dialect and saturated with clever wordplay. They rarely addressed their letters to each other by their given names but rather used affectionate nicknames, sometimes patronizing, often puzzling, but almost always humorous in their connotations. Many are therefore virtually untranslatable: he called her *Blumenpflänzchen*, *Lilipe Lencha*, *Mistblume*, *Mordspison*, *Rehbeinchen*, *Schnäuben-Träubchen*, and dozens of other invented names, almost always in the diminutive. (A glossary of pet names and other invented or distorted words appears in Appendix A.) That so many of the names are related to flowers, blossoms, or plants may also be telling, for Weill tended to treat Lenya as an exotic but fragile creature, a perennial child in need of nurturing, even protection. Although this must have seemed stifling at times, Lenya frequently played along with the game by signing her letters to Weill *Blumi* or some variation thereof, or by drawing some sort of primitive flower in lieu of a signature. (We reproduce a few of these drawings with their respective letters.) She often countered with her own appellations for Weill—among them, *Fröschlein*, *Schnubschen*, *Schwänzchen*, and *Knutchen*—but often just settled for Kurtili, Weilili, or Weillchen. In virtually every case, we have left these pet names untranslated in the text of the letters, for their impact relies as much on sound as on sense; the list in Appendix A gives derivation and definition whenever feasible.

It was Weill who more frequently distorted spelling or pronunciation of ordinary words in a way that seems to have had meaning only for themselves. He may again have been playing the father figure, addressing his little (and often naughty) girl, who had spent her adolescence in Zurich, with diminutives formed in the Swiss fashion: *Blumi* instead of the conventional *Blümchen*, *Tröpfi* instead of *Tröpfchen*, for example. Weill furthermore had been born and raised in Dessau, where the often ridiculed Saxonian dialect is endemic (even Richard Wagner, born in neighboring Leipzig, was derided for his persistent Saxonian accent). Weill's idiosyncratic substitution of *i* for *e*, *ö*, and *ü*, as in *Birühmtheit* instead of *Berühmtheit*, was probably a parody of Saxonian dialect, a trace of which remained in his own speech. Whenever something had to be looked up, Lenya recalled, Weill would quote one of his elementary school teachers: "Da missen wir mal das Biiiechlein bifragen:" (*Da müssen wir mal das Büchlein befragen:* We'll just have to look this up in the little book). The element of surprise and affection engendered by Weill's and Lenya's private language animates their correspondence, and its etymology may challenge even bilingual readers. One of the most colorful recurring phrases, for example, juxtaposes stilted, outdated vocabulary with risqué colloquialisms: "Ich verbleibe in ausgezeichneter Hochachtung Dein ergebener Affenschwanz" (I remain in extraordinarily high respect, your devoted monkey tail; variants include "highly erect monkey tail" and "with monkey tail held high"). A list of recurring phrases, not readily translatable, concludes Appendix A.

You cannot know what is being left out of publications like this, which often turn out to be scandalous, full of silent omissions and bowdlerizations. Without access to the originals, one has to rely on the character and the qualifications of the editors. I hope they can be trusted not to falsify or bowdlerize.

Anonymous I, reader's report to the University of California Press

The present volume is a complete edition of the surviving letters between Weill and Lenya: Part I contains the German letters in English translation; Part II, the English letters in the original. (Those scholars who require access to the original language for all letters will be able to consult the forthcoming German-language edition in conjunction with this edition's Part II.) No letter has been omitted, abridged, or altered in any way, even in deference to persons still living. Letters and postcards have been ordered chronologically and numbered in one sequence. Telegrams have not been included in the count or the ordinary numbering; the designation *T* is preceded by the number of the most closely related contiguous letter or postcard. A header identifies the whereabouts of the author and of the addressee, as well as the date of the letter. Whenever the editors have supplied dates, they appear in brackets; when dating cannot be confirmed by circumstantial evidence, a question mark indicates its provisional status. A brief description of the physical object (such as the image on a postcard or the address on hotel letterhead) follows the header when appropriate. (Note that Weill often wrote on letterhead left over from hotel stays; this accounts for the discrepancy between his whereabouts and the hotel location. Each letterhead is given in abbreviated form after the first instance.)

The text proper of a letter includes editorial insertions, in brackets, only when necessary to make an otherwise incomprehensible or incomplete passage intelligible. Translations of the German letters (Part I) attempt to preserve the tone and timbre of Weill's and Lenya's idiosyncratic voices by avoiding literalness in favor of idiomatic equivalents, but they do not preserve or attempt to approximate errors in grammar, syntax, or spelling. Transliteration of proper names has been converted from German style to the standard English equivalents. In those instances where an English translation is inadequate to convey reasonably the meaning of a passage, the original German follows in brackets. Particularly sensitive issues of translation are discussed in the notes that print at the end of the letter. Because mastery of the new language was so coveted and so critical professionally and personally for both Weill and Lenya, all English-language letters (Part II) have been transcribed literally, preserving errors in spelling, grammar, punctuation, and syntax— without recourse to the use of *sic*. Readers are reminded that English was a second or third language for both, and the progress of their fluency may evince larger issues of assimilation.

In the letters written in German, phrases originally in English or other languages are italicized here; likewise, in the letters written in English, phrases in a foreign language (including hybrids) are italicized here. Underlining is reserved for those passages underlined by Weill or Lenya. All titles of literary, dramatic, cinematic, and musical pieces named in the German letters have been standardized and set in italic (for major works) or in quotation marks (for shorter works). Titles used in the English letters, often given in casual or abbreviated forms and without italic, appear as written. Nontrivial drawings and musical notations appearing in the letters are reproduced in their approximate location within the text of the letter.

Persons who play a recurring role in the correspondence are identified in the Biographical Glossary and listed in boldface type in the Index of Names. Others are identified, whenever possible, in a note on first appearance. When no additional information could be ascertained, incomplete names and titles are presented as they appear in the original. Explanations of context and documentation of particular events have been provided in notes to the letters or in the biographical narrative that precedes the larger chronological groupings of letters. Here, too, Weill and Lenya have been allowed to speak in their own voices, as we quote from interviews, oral histories, and their correspondence with other people. Thus, their letters to each other are set in relief against a broader background of issues, content, and style.

Parenthetical citations in both text and notes are keyed to a list of Sources Cited at the back of the book. Letters are cited by the initials of the correspondents and the date; interviews by the interviewee's initials preceded by "int."; memoirs by the author's initials preceded by "mem." Published sources are cited by author and page number only (unless there are multiple works by the same author in the Sources Cited, in which case the year is also given). Unless otherwise noted, all quotations of German-language sources in the text have been translated by the editors.

The overall organization of the edition hardly requires explication. The Prologue presents an autobiographical sketch of Lenya and a biographical portrait of Weill prior to their meeting in 1924, concluding with Lenya's account of that meeting. The letters themselves are grouped into two parts (German and English) of three chapters each, divided according to biographical and geographical considerations or hiatuses in the correspondence. Photographs, which are gathered in an insert, have been selected to illustrate the letters as specifically as possible; references to each figure print in the margins of the text. The Epilogue highlights Lenya's three decades of life as the widow Weill. Lys Symonette's "Afterwords" chronicle the provenance of the correspondence as well as the editors' involvement with it and its authors. The Acknowledgments are followed by two Appendixes: the first a list of pet names, described above, and the second a table of dollar equivalents for the different currencies referred to in the letters. After the Biographical Glossary for people most central to the correspondence and the list of Sources Cited, the reader will find three indexes, which present respectively a register of names, titles of Weill's works, and works by others. The two works indexes provide additional information about each entry, such as coauthors and dates, and English translations of the titles. We trust that the composite picture is at once a vivid panorama of the diverse cultural landscapes in which Weill and Lenya worked and an intimate profile of two fascinating artists.

Kim H. Kowalke
10 November 1994

Prologue
BEFORE THEY MET

KAROLINE WILHELMINE CHARLOTTE BLAMAUER

Among the papers found in Lotte Lenya's bedroom shortly after her death—some hidden between the mattress and box spring—were various attempts at autobiography, initially sketched during the 1950s at the cajoling of her second husband, George Davis, then resumed briefly a decade later with the assistance of David Drew, under contract from Little, Brown. The earliest layer of memoirs comprises annotated transcripts of interviews with Davis, artifacts of their aborted plan to write a biography of Weill. Other drafts convey Lenya's unmediated voice, evident from her handwriting or characteristically haphazard typing and her idiosyncratic English-language spelling and syntax. Those sections which evolved in "as told to" mode, with Davis or Drew drafting prose on the basis of interviews or notes from Lenya, tend to be more polished, but her voice is less recognizable. Although the sometimes overlapping layers of these surviving memoirs evolved over a period of nearly twenty years, those events and impressions preserved in several versions are remarkably vital and surprisingly consistent, and they evince little of the sense of "constructed myth" that characterizes Lenya's public statements about her life with Weill.

When asked why she seemed unable to go further with her autobiography, Lenya told her friend Lys Symonette: "My love for good language and great literature prevents me from writing bad English. German? I can no longer think in that language!" But in fact virtually every draft of her memoirs breaks off with her meeting Weill. In retrospect, no psychological sophistication is required to diagnose the cause of her writer's block. Although she could recount childhood trauma and terrors with equanimity and even black humor, she was unable to confront the truth about certain periods of her life with (and without) Weill that she had so long suppressed in her often rehearsed interviews. While cultivating a public persona unwavering in her devotion to Weill—building an international career as an interpreter of his music and taking her role as executrix of the estate very seriously—she was privately haunted by guilt for having abandoned him time and again.

To compensate to some extent for the lesser presence of Lenya's voice in the correspondence itself, we offer her own "pre-Weill" biography here. Many aspects of her complex personality can be observed in the following brief narratives we've selected, ordered, and edited from her various autobiographical fragments, some of which were drafted or edited by either Davis or Drew. In characteristically matter-of-fact fashion she recalls some of the grim realities of a poverty-stricken, abused child in turn-of-the-century Vienna, the tenacious opportunism of an aspiring actress in wartime Zurich, and the artistic ambitions of a young dancer in postwar Berlin. It was in these years of upheaval that Karoline Wilhelmine Charlotte Blamauer trans-

formed herself first into Lotte Blamauer and then, definitively, Lotte Lenja, or—as she preferred—simply Lenja (in English, Lenya).

The reader should note that our editorial practice here differs from that in the letters. We have corrected misspellings and conformed punctuation while leaving diction and syntax untouched. Because of the fragmentary nature of the sources and the multiple versions extant, the present narrative is a composite; omissions are not signaled by ellipses.

[FIGS. 3 & 4]

I was the third child born [18 October 1898]. The first one had died when she was four years old, and I was given her name, Karoline, "Linnerl" for short in Viennese. It was an unfortunate choice, this name, because my father adored the first child and never could look at me without resentment. My mother told me the reason he hated me. At the age of four the first Linnerl could sing the famous "Fiakerlied," and he, being one of the last *Fiakers* [coachmen] in Vienna, loved it. I had to learn to stay out of his way as much as I could in that crowded one room and kitchen we lived in until I left home for good. My brother, who was one year older than I, was not affected by my father's unhappiness about the death of his firstborn child. He was just another one who had to be fed. But it was always me who was dragged out of bed when he came home drunk (and drunk he was and stayed drunk until he died). And there I stood with my eyes full of sleep and tried to please him. I would sing for him the most stupid song he knew from his youth: "Wenn der Auerhahn falzt und das Rotkehlchen schnalzt" [When the grouse clucks and the red robin keeps time]. One night he got so furious at me for not remembering all the lines that he picked up the petroleum lamp and threw it at me as I stood trembling in the corner. The impact put the flame out and I was saved from burning to death. I tried to be as good as the first one was, tried desperately to turn my head the other way so I didn't have to smell his sour breath, until I was pushed back to bed to hear him say: "She is a 'Katzenkopf,'" which means Cathead. And there I was lying in my bed, trembling with fear that he would get me out again. But my mother, whom I loved, came to my rescue, putting the wooden board over the bed so he would forget about me.

It was just a wooden box, this bed of mine, with a straw mattress and a pillow, and during the day it was used as an ironing board. People sat on it; Mother used it for making noodles. But I felt secure under it. And under my wooden board I was away from my father getting up in the morning after a fearful night, screaming for his boots that he had taken off on his way home and lost. When he finally slammed the door to go to work, my mother took the board off my bed and gently said, "Linnerl, you can get up now." And then I crawled out, to go down to the basement to help my mother wash the laundry of her different clients until it was time to go to school. I couldn't help her much, but I could wash little things like hankies, kitchen towels, stockings, doilies. I loved those wash days, when I would be alone with her and could watch her through the steam-filled "Waschküche" [basement boiler room] with her strong peasant face, her beautiful gray eyes, and her incredibly delicate hands wrestling with those big sheets.

The house in which I spent eleven of my young years was located in Penzing, the thirteenth district of Vienna. There were three houses on each side of the street, the Ameisgasse. Those houses all looked alike and could be told apart only by their numbers.

There were thirty-four parties living on its three floors. At the entrance of the house was a huge wooden Christ hanging, and every so often, in a hurry for school, I forgot to make the sign of the cross and usually ran back to do so. The nice thing about the house was, being at the corner, our bedroom window faced the Neue Park (the new park—the old one was about five minutes' walk away from the house). From our kitchen window we could see across the field to the "Bier und Wein Stube" where my father spent most of his meager salary and from where I had to bring him beer in a stein. Because I ran across the street with the beer in order to avoid being hit by a car, I sometimes spilled some of it and handed the stein to my father fully prepared to be slapped in the face, which he did more often than not.

I was born with an allergy which no doctor ever could find out what caused it. In a way that was a blessing for me, because I could enter the hospital, which was in walking distance from the house at the Ameisgasse, at the first swelling of almost any part of my body, but which usually appeared on my lips, eyes, and neck. This harmless stigma gave me great troubles later on when I was an *élève* at the ballet school in Zurich. The doctors at that hospital knew every member of the Blamauer family. My brothers were there constantly with either broken arms or cuts in their feet from walking through brooks in the Halderbach, near Huetteldorf, where people carelessly threw beer bottles at the end of their picnics. My mother did not bother anymore to go with us. She knew we would be treated nicely, and I was especially treated nice, because the doctors liked me. I recited little poems for them during their lunch hour, and for that I was allowed to pick some strawberries in their garden, to the envy of the rest of their patients. The moment I checked into the hospital I was put to bed and put on a diet consisting of rice and applesauce. I loved both, and released after a few days, I prayed that my hives should show up soon again. At the age of twenty-one it suddenly disappeared and never returned.

From the sill of the kitchen window we could see all the way to Schoenbrunn and also look down on the two circus wagons stationed on the field throughout the year. It was a large family who ran that entertainment for the poor. Early spring they set up their source of income for the year, after long winter months building a stage twenty feet long and twenty feet wide, a little balustrade for the four musicians, and bleachers for about a hundred people. A wooden fence framed the stage and the bleachers, and the people on the outside of the fence paid a nickel, and the insiders, controlled by a little box office, paid a dime for the privilege to sit on those wooden benches. The entertainment consisted of dancing, acrobats, tightrope, and clowns. Among that audience was a little wide-eyed girl of five who never was asked for a nickel. Instead she was asked whether she would like to learn how to dance and walk the tightrope.

Having watched from my kitchen window for two years since the age of three, I was only too willing. My father could not care less, and my mother was happy for me, knowing how crazy I was about being in the "Theater." I was dressed in a Hungarian peasant dress with lots of ribbons flying around my head, a tambourine in my hand, and there I was, dancing to the tune of—I think it was Brahms (nobody ever could recognize it the way these three or four musicians played it). I learned to stand on my head; I had practiced that long before with my brother. But then the more difficult task was to learn to walk on a tightrope. It does not matter how high the wire was placed, it still worked on the same principle, which is balance. A wire was put up four feet above the ground, a little Japanese paper umbrella was placed into my hands for balance, and off I went. I fell many times but I did learn it, and I was a success with the audience, consisting mostly of neighbors.

One night they had hired a sensational attraction: a woman who slid down on a wire drenched in pink light, which was produced like one still uses with a certain powder around Christmastime for the fireplace, [wearing] a dress which opened like wings of a butterfly, hundreds of pleats. It was breathtaking. I went home, and the next morning after everybody had left for work or whatever, I took my father's suspenders, placed them on the hook my mother put up in the door frame between the kitchen for drying her laundry during the winter months, got up on a kitchen stool, placed the suspenders into my mouth and flew—with the result of losing two baby teeth. For the time being this was the end of my theatrical career.

In 1904, at the age of six, I entered the obligatory three years of "Volksschule" [public school]. The teacher, Fräulein Schwarz, was no more than five feet tall, black hair with here and there a thread of silver running through, eyes like black cherries, kind and lovable. The hunchback, which made her even smaller than she actually was, gave her a look like everything she had to carry was too heavy for those fragile shoulders. I still can hear her gentle voice asking me: "Blamauer, why don't you answer me? That's the second time I called you to the blackboard." I did not hear her. I was occupied with my feet, which were icy cold. I tried to squeeze out the water that came through the torn soles of my shoes. I started walking toward the blackboard through the giggling kids, because my shoes made a squeaky sound. When I arrived at her desk, tears were rolling down my face, partly of shame, partly from the cold. She saw me stepping from one foot to the other, leaving a little puddle of water under my feet. Lovingly she looked at me, made me take off my shoes, and wrapped my feet in newspaper for the rest of the hour. My shoes were put on the radiator to dry. She asked the girls to bring shoes and clothes for me the next day. Then she made it possible that I got a certificate for "community shoes." Those shoes I hated with a passion. They were so stiff, with thick soles as if made for eternity. Much too big, they gave me blisters the first day I wore them, and when it was not raining or snowing, I went right back to my old shoes in spite of all the holes.

Fräulein Schwarz's kindness never faded through the three years I was her pupil. It was she who found me the white dress for my first communion. She also was the first to encourage whatever dramatic gifts I have, praising me when I recited a poem. On the emperor's birthday there was always a celebration, and the best student in recitation was given the long poem honoring the emperor to recite, and that was usually me. It was discovered, too, that I had only to hear a song through once and I could repeat it perfectly. In that way I missed a certain formal training in music and was not encouraged to seek it. She gave me excellent marks which were needed in order to get into the Bürgerschule.

I was nine when I was transferred from the overcrowded schoolroom (thirty-five pupils) in the Diesterweggasse to the fashionable school for gifted children in Hietzing, am Platz, with only fifteen pupils in the classroom. As if to remind me that the friendly "Du" of my Volksschule years was a thing of the past now that I'd arrived in the Bürgerschule, and anyway to show me that she didn't like me, the principal, Fräulein Freyer, made an ugly hissing sound with the word "Sie" [formal *you*] whenever she addressed me: "Bla-mauer, Sssssssssie nehmen sich zuviel Freiheiten heraus mit Ihren Zeichnungen," she would say as she inspected some sketch of mine, "you take too many liberties—the carrot I gave you to draw was wilted on top but the one in your drawing has fresh greens." I was never given anything better than vegetables to immortalize. Fräulein Freyer was not lovely to look upon, yet she had the impertinence (or so I thought) to braid her hair in the style of our beautiful Empress Elisabeth. Beneath her coal-black beady eyes was a nose that seemed larger than it really was—first, because there was almost no chin to balance it, and secondly because her stiff white collar was therefore free to ride up over her mailbox slit of a mouth and emphasize the flair of her nostrils. Even from a distance she was unmistakable because of her peculiar gait—with thighs kept close together, as if to protect her virginity, although in fact it was never in the slightest danger.

During my summer school vacation, my father took me to his sister Aunt Marie, who had visited us many times, always bringing cookies and chocolate from her little store in Ottakring. The walk was a very long one, crossing the enormous field called "Die Schmelz," where all the refuse from the surrounding districts was dumped. I was frightened and unhappy to leave my friends behind, not knowing what would await me when arriving at my aunt. My father did not say a word all the way, which made the journey even more scary for me. It was getting dark, and I already missed my mother. I was not particularly fond of my aunt; I rather disliked her for taking me away from my home. She needed help to distribute the milk and rolls she sold. I had to get up at six in the morning. Off I went to different houses to place the milk and the rolls in front of the door, where people found them before going to work. It took me about an hour before I returned to the store. I loved this little "Milch-Geschäft" [dairy store] and after a while even grew very fond of my aunt. She used to take an afternoon nap, right after lunch, and that was the time when people looked in the window and came in when they saw me alone, knowing that I always gave them more than the scale indicated.

I was with my aunt for about a month when the whole picture changed. She made the acquaintance of a man, and he moved in pretty soon after. I could not sleep in the bed anymore with her but was put on a couch, which I should not have minded after having slept on a straw sack at home. But I was hurt being shoved around on account of this stranger. What made me dislike him even more was that when I sometimes had to cross the living room to get to the store when the bell was ringing, I saw my aunt putting some bandages around his privates, which frightened me. I never did find out what he had, and when I told it to my mother, she brushed me off by saying that he is a sick man and I would not understand it even if she would tell me. I grew more and more homesick. Nobody from my family came to see me, and one noon when he got Wienerschnitzel for lunch and I got a pair of frankfurters, my pride was so hurt that I took a nickel from the cash register and ran to the *Stadtbahn* [commuter line] which was close by and went home. I was not received enthusiastically. I did not cry.

At fourteen [1912] I graduated from the Bürgerschule, and that same week my mother took me to a small hat factory where I was to begin a four-year apprenticeship. It was operated by Gnädige Frau Ita, a shrewd but kindly old matriarch, and her two sons; they made hats only for men, the finest in Vienna. Each table had its own specialty, with one apprentice assigned to it. Particularly hateful to me were the priest's hats, for they had such stiff brims that I found it almost impossible to push a needle through them. So I often returned home with bleeding fingers that somehow, like stigmata in reverse, helped to strengthen my growing resistance to Roman Catholicism and everything to do with it. There was no garment-workers' union to protect a fourteen-year-old apprentice working fourteen hours a day. Although apprentices were not entitled to any pay until they had completed their four-year term, on my fifth Saturday Frau Ita slipped a coin into my hand when no one was looking. Three or four times a week I delivered finished hats to the Itas' retail shop on an elegant shopping street of the inner city. I generally made a small detour to the Kärntnerstraße to see the most beautiful shops and also the most attractive girls for sale, no matter what time of day.

It was during the summer of 1913 that my aunt Sophie came from Zurich, Switzerland, to visit my mother in Vienna. She'd been married three times, always to sickly husbands whom she had to nurse. How she had landed up in Zurich we never quite understood. But there she was, housekeeper for a retired doctor. Aunt Sophie was childless and now lamented that fact, and how comforting it would be to have the companionship of a daughter. (She made fun of my mother: "She has only to see a pair of pants on the washline and she's pregnant.") I worked all my charms on Aunt Sophie until she announced she was taking me back with her to Zurich. My father, thinking of the few Kronen I brought in, said, "She'll be a whore when she leaves the factory." To him that was the only alternative. My belongings were thrown together in a Pinkerl (the way vagabonds bundle their belongings and tie them to a stick), and off I went with Aunt Sophie to Zurich. I still remember my mother's smiling face at the Wiener Westbahnhof, and her goodbye: "Be smart, Linnerl, and don't come back if you can help it."

As the train got closer to Zurich, Aunt Sophie got increasingly panicky about the doctor's probable reaction to my arrival. He was to be told that I was there only for a short visit. The old boy did make a wry grimace at the sight of me; he was a stuffy old gent, with a goatee, heavy gold watch chain over his belly, who obviously was furious at this invasion of his privacy. When the doctor was in a good mood, my aunt would cook openly for me, but most often food was carried furtively into her room for me. My only amusement was a large straw trunk that held the remnants of her former grandeur: night-gowns, undies, linen sheets, fur pieces, all yellowing and smelling of camphor.

After a couple of extremely nervous weeks, Aunt Sophie made arrangements for me to stay with friends of hers, a photographer, which happened to be my good fortune, since he knew all the theater people in town. They were very sweet people without children and they liked me right away. Mrs. Ehrenzweig started the very next day to make me some clothes and fill up my wardrobe, which consisted of one skirt, one blouse, a few hankies, a much too big coat (which my mother got for me from one of her clients she washed laundry for), and a few odds and ends. Needless to say, I went through all the pictures of the artists he photographed, and when I came to the picture of a very beautiful woman and was told that she was the "Ballettmeisterin" (the head of the ballet corps) and a close friend of theirs, I didn't waste any time to beg them to talk to her to take me as her pupil. And she did agree to take me, for twenty-five francs a month—a sum that made my head spin, but my aunt agreed to pay a part and the Ehrenzweigs made up the rest.

In return, I made their breakfast, cleaned the studio before going to my morning class, came home to help with lunch, went back for a private afternoon class, and then back to help Frau Ehrenzweig with whatever she was doing—which was most apt to be pulling hairs from her chin, at which I developed a great skill.

I worked terribly hard that first year. I learned to stand on my toes (never with great pleasure), and I had already managed to get my first solo part in a Christmas fairy tale, as the prima ballerina's page boy. Of the twelve girls in the class, I was and remained the least talented on point. My body, feet, face, entire nature were against it, against all the attitudes of formal ballet. Instinctively I seized instead on pantomime, improvisation, free movement to give a sense of character. And in these I found myself. But the important event was that I was picked out by my later teacher to play little straight parts in the Schauspielhaus. Besides learning to act, I was also paid for it. In the evenings we were always busy in the theater. In this first season I was a page in *Lohengrin;* with three ballet girls I carried the Holy Grail across the stage in *Parsifal;* I saw Mary of Scotland's head chopped off in the third act as a torch carrier; I looked out of Mistress Overdone's windows as one of her girls in Shakespeare's *Measure for Measure;* I carried the gold of the Rhine on my shoulders as a dwarf in *Rheingold;* I danced to "The Blue Danube" in a ballet evening; I sat (for pure decoration) at the back of the stage as a flower girl in Gluck's *Orpheus and Euridice.* I was a gypsy dancer in *Mignon* and one of the sirens in the ballroom scene of *The Merry Widow.*

By the end of the first season I was a little homesick. My aunt was all for it that I should go back home. I didn't know then that she hoped I wouldn't come back. So she got me the money for the trip through the Austrian Consul, pretending that she couldn't afford to send me home. I got the money and went home. I came into a bad time. The whole country was in a state of terror of a possible war. My mother wasn't too happy to see me back and nothing had changed since I was gone, except my mother had separated from my father and had taken in two boarders in order to be able to support her children. We had only one bedroom and a kitchen and the place was crowded. I hadn't minded it before I had left, but I had gotten a glimpse of a better life and felt unhappy and was full of fear that I couldn't get back to Switzerland. I was supposed to be back by the first of September. Weeks and weeks passed and I didn't hear from my aunt. Finally she wrote me that she thought it would be better for me if I stayed home and gave up the idea about the theater. And she couldn't help me anymore either. I cried my eyes out, but my mother promised me to get the money for the ticket. She took on more laundry to wash, and I helped her as much as I could. But then the terrible thing that everybody was afraid of happened, and war was declared on 3 August 1914.

In order to get a passport I had to have a contract from the theater. I wrote a desperate letter to the intendant [Alfred Reucker] to send me one. (I was entitled to one only after three years of studying.) Thank God, he was very kind to me that first season, and he understood my problem and I got my passport. The train was by the time I could leave full with people who left the country and full with soldiers. I rode four days on that train, which was normally an overnight trip. When I crossed the border into Switzerland, I laughed and cried at the same time. I went straight to the theater (I was already two weeks late) to let them know that I was back. Then I went to see my aunt. She opened the door

[FIG. 5]

and I never saw a more surprised face in all my future life. She rushed me right into the room and whispered I couldn't possibly stay with her, she would lose her job. I had no intention to stay. But I had arrived without a cent and I needed a little money to get me through the first month. She did let me stay overnight. I was to make not a move, not a sound, until the next morning, when I would seek refuge with the Ehrenzweigs. As it turned out, the Ehrenzweigs were happy to have me back, and the old routine started again.

The second season was much better. I made about thirty francs playing at the Schauspielhaus; my fee for the ballet was reduced to fifteen francs. But it still wasn't enough to get me a room and live by myself. So when my aunt asked me whether I would help a friend of hers who ran a little store selling postcards, I was only too glad to go there every weekend and whenever I had time. I didn't know then that Emil, who ran the store, was my aunt's boyfriend. He was a nice man, about fifty, and had a passion for catching flies. There he sat with his big cigar catching the flies, putting them under glass, blowing smoke in the glass, and watching them get dizzy. I never found out what he finally did with them. I couldn't look.

I saved every penny I made and after a month I could accept the offer of Greta, one of the dancers, to move into her mother's big apartment. She rented out rooms. But only to people in the theater. She was enormously fat, very Semitic looking in spite of her blond, pretty hair, with a golden cross dangling on a black velvet ribbon on her big bosom like a landmark. "It's been in the family for centuries," she insisted. Her husband was a shy little man with thick glasses who worked for a printing shop and was shut up by her before he could ever say good morning. We all had breakfast together, which was announced by Mrs. Edelmann by running her fat fingers in a glissando over the piano, her prized possession. Greta was more like her father. She had nothing of her mother's brassiness. But she had a passion for men. She had a boyfriend (called a "fiancé" by her mother, who insisted on Greta being a virgin—which she wasn't—until the day she would marry). He was a Serb, a dreary guy, who was very proud of his country I knew nothing about, except that the archduke Franz Ferdinand was shot there, which started the war. Greta was constantly in trouble, being pregnant practically every other month. But it wasn't all his fault. He just happened to be the official one. But they did take me out to nightclubs, which were filled with war profiteers and their lavishly dressed girlfriends. During the war years Zurich was fantastically prosperous, with rich foreigners in the great hotels, students from all over the world; and of course I never in all that time saw a really poor Swiss. Every second house, it seemed, was a bank.

The theater was wonderful at that time. I remember the first rehearsal with Richard Strauss conducting his *Salome* with Marie Gutheil-Schoder. He was an extremely elegant-looking man. The orchestra had a tough time with him. They weren't used to such a controlled way of conducting. He hardly raised his baton, and when the musicians couldn't get the right sound for chopping off Jochanaan's head, Strauss stopped and said in his [Bavarian] accent: "Aber meine Herren, 's ist doch ganz einfach, g'rad so wie im *Lohengrin*" [but gentlemen, it's very simple; just like in *Lohengrin*]. One morning we were called to rehearsals for Busoni's *Turandot*. When I arrived, Busoni was already sitting at the piano, and he played for the whole rehearsal. After it was over, he sat down on the floor and started talking about his opera. I remember very clearly how he held his feet close to his body: a Persian posture perhaps, but rather stiff, as if it wasn't an altogether easy position for a man of his age. He rocked back and forth slightly and answered with a humorous smile the questions of the poor little rehearsal pianist.

Alexander Moissi played his famous "Living Corpse," Max Reinhardt brought his Berlin Ensemble to play Ibsen, Strindberg, and [Gerhart] Hauptmann. Fokine came with his Russian ballet, Baklanov sang Mephistopheles. I watched every single performance when I was free. I listened to every opera. Elisabeth Bergner (then unknown) became a member of the Schauspielhaus. I had a little part in one of the plays she played the lead in. I was holding a champagne glass in my hand and my little finger was sticking way out—I thought that was an extremely elegant way of holding a glass—when I saw her crossing the stage, stopping in front of me, pushing my finger back, and saying with that enchanting lisp of hers: "Das macht man nicht in feiner Gesellschaft" (one doesn't do that in elegant company). She got a big laugh with that improvised line and kept it ever after.

My second season was hardly begun before something wonderful happened to me. Herr Richard Révy, Oberregisseur of the Schauspielhaus, called me in for an interview. He was a pudgy, moonfaced man, high-strung, vital, with a profound knowledge of theater and a growing reputation as a director. He told me that he had been watching me, that he was confident that I had a real talent for acting, and that he was willing to take me as a private student without payment. The next day my lessons with Herr Révy began. The Viennese lilt in my voice he said could stay, the accent must go. He guided my reading and exercises in speaking, breathing, and articulation. Together we studied the Greeks, Goethe, Schiller, Strindberg, Ibsen, Chekhov. [Lenya dubbed Révy "Vanja," and he in turn, inspired by the character Jelena (Yelena) in *Uncle Vanya*, invented the nickname "Lenja." In her Zurich program credits "Lotte," short for Charlotte, sometimes displaced Karoline, but the surname Blamauer outlasted Lenya's time in Zurich, at least professionally.]

The beginning of the third season we got a new Ballettmeisterin, Fräulein Ruvina, who imposed less ballet, more Dalcroze and pantomime, with an occasional full evening of dance, and solo parts for me. Our prima ballerina didn't like that new regime and left soon after. But I was in heaven. I could use all my acting I had learned in the meanwhile and combine it with this new way of dancing. I got my first contract as a full-fledged member of the ballet with three hundred francs salary, and I could leave Emil and his flies behind me.

Greta was still my best friend. Her "Serb" was replaced by another official fiancé, this time a Frenchman who was in the jewelry business and provided her with nice clothes and a few pieces of his merchandise. She never approved of my boyfriend, who tried to make a living as a sculptor [Mario Perucci]. During the summer months, when our theater was closed, Greta and I worked at the Corso Theater, where they played nothing but operettas. She did the choreography, and I danced and sang whatever part I got. No big parts. One day we had a command performance for the king of Greece [Konstantin, 1868–1923] and his mistress. They sat in a box all by themselves and watched *Die Czardasfürstin*. We were all very envious of the mistress.

On the top floor of the theater was a nightclub, and there I sat one night with Greta and her Frenchman, looking at a rather good-looking young man with heavy dark glasses,

[FIG. 6]

surrounded by a noisy crowd of people, evidently his guests. I saw the star of the program rushing to his table, throwing her arms around him. I wondered who he was. He was Czechoslovakian and one of the richest men in town. Greta's boyfriend knew him, and after a while he left his table and sat with us for a while. He seemed bored with his company. He was very nice and seemed to enjoy every remark I made about his loud, heavily drinking friends. Next day I got my first flowers, the first big ones at the theater. I was rather embarrassed. After the show, I met him at the nightclub, thanked him for the flowers and asked him not to send any more.

And here starts the old, familiar rich man–poor girl story. He didn't stop sending me presents. He asked me to move to his villa on the lake, which I did. It was too tempting. I wanted to know how it feels to have everything, to be driven to the theater by a chauffeur, to have beautiful jewelry and not a worry anymore. I almost fainted when I discovered the secret behind his heavy dark glasses. He suffered from thyroid and his eyes stuck out like two bubbles on a stick children blow with soap water, but I got used to them, like I got used to the sudden wealth. But soon I started to miss Mrs. Edelmann's glissando for breakfast, missed my walks along the lake to the theater, and I felt lonely. I didn't like the way I left him—sneaking out at night without explanation. He was so good to me, but there was nothing I could say. He sent me all my things I left behind, and a year later, a year before he got married, he asked me for the last time to come back to him. I wished him luck and stayed at Mrs. Edelmann's. Greta never could understand what got over me to make such a foolish decision—as she put it.

Though by contract I was still in the corps de ballet, thanks to Révy I was playing more and more acting parts. With the war over, and everybody talking about the sensational theater developments in Berlin, Révy himself was obviously restless and finally resigned in the spring of 1921, telling me that if I decided to try my own luck, he would do everything to help me. (Révy took with him his protégée Conchita Clarens, a boyish flapper who had been Bergner's rival at the theater. He took a chance, made the rounds with theater agents, stayed in a pension while his wife and two kids stayed at her family's country place near Munich.) When I confided this to Greta, she was all aflame to make the flight and suggested that she and I put together a ballet evening. All that summer we spent every spare minute in a little rehearsal hall, with the *Korrepetitor* [musical coach] banging away at the piano. Révy designed our costumes, his wife sewed them, and we made up our own choreography. In one number I was a faun and Greta a nymph, in another I was Pierrot and Greta Columbine; we were Scotch lassies in another; Greta had a Hungarian czardas, and I had "The Blue Danube" as a solo à la Grete Wiesenthal. All in all a corny mishmash of ballet, Dalcroze, Isadora Duncan, the Sakharovs. We were certain we would take Berlin by storm. Mama Edelmann was rather less sure, convinced that if anything was stormed, it might be Greta's virginity. But finally she gave her blessings, we said our goodbyes to our envious ballet colleagues, and we were off to Berlin.

Early in the fall of 1921, we were met at the station by my teacher, and I was brought to the rooming house in the Lützowstraße. Greta had made previous arrangements to live with a relative of her mother. When I walked into that gloomy-looking room with that one light bulb, I felt rather depressed. Zurich was such a clean city—like coming from a dry cleaner—and there was poverty-stricken Berlin with a daily rising inflation. I had great trouble to understand the ever-changing money. The food was almost inedible. But our trunks full of costumes stood in one corner of my room—like a reminder what we came to Berlin for. We spent weeks and weeks running from one agent to another to show them our pictures, to explain our program. Nothing happened. We could get single jobs—dancing a number or two in some obscure nightclub. But neither one of us liked the idea. Greta was a dancer only and not interested in anything else. I couldn't make her go and see plays. She didn't care to walk around and get the smell of the city. When she finally got an offer as a choreographer in Elberfeld, a small German city, I didn't have to urge her to accept it.

By that time I had lost faith in our project and was glad when she left. Now I didn't have to run daily from one stupid agent to another, and I was free to see all the great actors at that time. I had a passion for the Scala, the greatest variety theater in Berlin, where I saw the Fratellinis, Rastello, the great juggler Barbette swinging way out in the audience. It was my passion until I left Berlin in 1933. I saw my first wrestling matches in a Biergarten in Friedenau—mostly Polish wrestlers, walking in a long line through the garden toward the ring, accompanied by an incredible brass band playing the "March of the Gladiators." I loved to walk on Saturdays up to the corner of Tauentzienstraße and KDW [Kaufhaus des Westens], a big department store where you could see girls in the strangest outfits standing at the corner, some with whips in their hands, some with high, shiny boots on, indicating that they were equipped to fulfill every kind of human passion. It's a funny thing the way people think of Berlin in those days as a sexual paradise, or hell. But besides the famous corner of the KDW and the well-walked pavements of the Friedrichstraße, there were other places and other occupations. People did go to work in the morning and come home in the evening. They did—some of them—fight for the things that matter.

I still had enough to live on. I still had my jewelry I could sell. Then one day [in October 1922] Révy told me about the job he was offered to direct a pantomime and that they were looking for a young girl who could dance and act. God, dear God, help me to have my dream fulfilled to be a dancer on a Berlin stage. Help me to have them choose me for the part they were looking for, a part which required a young dancer who could also act for a children's pantomime. My heart was pounding hard while I was walking down the aisle and climbing up on stage, which was filled with people and children and mothers. It seemed to me that I was standing there for days to wait for my name to be called. Then somebody said, "I think it's you they want." I didn't hear them calling me. I wasn't used to that name, Lotte Lenja. Then the director said "Go ahead," and I must have looked completely lost until I heard a very gentle voice coming from the orchestra pit asking, "What do you want me to play for you, Miss Lenja?" And the director turned around and said: "Oh, this is our composer." I hardly saw him, he was half hidden under the awning of the orchestra pit. I asked him whether he could play "The Blue Danube," and I heard him say, with a slightly amused voice, "I think so." The moment I started dancing to that tune—a tune I had heard practically from the day I was born—all my fears disappeared, and as long as I didn't have to stand on my toes and could dance barefoot, nothing would have stopped me if the producer wouldn't have said "That's enough" after a few minutes, which seemed so short to me. He asked me what else I could show them, and I gave an imitation of a circus clown on a tightrope and sang a song as a street singer. This time without music from the pit. I still hadn't seen the composer.

I was told that I got the part and to come back the next morning at ten o'clock for rehearsal. I remember stumbling over a rug in a still-dark aisle, running into a mirror in the foyer of the theater, crossing the street, one of the most famous streets in Berlin, the Kurfürstendamm, not looking for traffic, just running across to the Kaffeehaus where I was to meet my teacher, who also applied for the same show as director and who didn't get the job. When I told Révy what had happened, he didn't seem to be pleased at all. Worse than that, he didn't want me to go back next morning. He thought it a bad idea to start without him. He kept on talking. I wasn't listening anymore. After a while I left and looked across the street, took one last glance at the poster in front of the theater, which announced *Zaubernacht* [Magic Night], a children's pantomime by Kurt Weill.

I walked back to the rooming house I lived in. It was one of those gray stone houses on the Lützowstraße (named after a German general) in a rather middle-class neighborhood. I lived on the top floor in a tiny corner room with a little stone balcony, where I raised cactuses in small pots. Over my desk hung a picture of Nijinsky, which I had cut out of a magazine and framed carefully. One lamp with a forty-five-watt bulb stood on my night table, barely enough light to read by. There was a constant exchange of people; only a Russian lady with her daughter and myself lived there on a monthly agreement, but paying rent daily on account of the almost by-the-hour changing course of currency. Lunch was the only meal served by my landlady and her daughter (a former actress). This was the only time when you saw who lived there. They were never the same people the next day. She made more money that way. Many times I tried to figure out what it was I was eating. It looked like "Königsberger Klopse," a dish I had eaten before in Switzerland, but they sure tasted different there. I once asked her what was in those Klopses and she said in that inimitable Berlin dialect: "'s ist keene Katze, die Sie da essen, und vajessen Sie nicht, Fräulein, wir haben den Kriech valoren" (It ain't a cat you're eating, and don't forget, lady, we lost the war). I never asked her again and ate her Klopse without a murmur.

It was her daughter who told me about a producer who had a little group of actors playing the suburbs of Berlin, doing Shakespeare's comedies. She arranged a meeting for me. He was a very gentle, middle-aged man who was full of idealism and not interested in making money. He was preparing *Twelfth Night*, and he gave me the part of Maria and asked me to come back in a few days to read for him. I could have read it right there; I knew Shakespeare well, and the part of Maria was a short and easy one. But I went home and studied it once more, just to make sure. He liked my reading and gave me a contract, just a few lines typewritten: Otto Kirchner pays Lotte Lenja three million marks, payable at the night of the opening, which was two weeks later [in spring 1923]. One had to spend the money fast, it changed so quick. One didn't even bother to count it. After I got that job, my landlady's Königsberger Klopse seemed to improve a little. They seemed less slimy and had a healthier color. We played a few weeks longer than expected, and my contract climbed into the billions. You looked at that paper money, it looked kind of pretty, and one never had to be afraid of losing it. It wasn't worth nothing. One just stuffed it in a drawer and tried to get rid of it. I kept on working with my teacher on my voice, learning new parts, hoping that one day I could use it.

One day while I was still playing Maria, Révy called me and said I should give a good performance, he is coming with Georg Kaiser. I knew who he was, I knew he was considered the top modern playwright of Germany. I wasn't as excited as the rest of the cast. As far as I was concerned, I thought I was always good; I didn't need special encouragement. I had too much fun acting, no matter who was out there. I met Kaiser after the performance, and he asked me to explain the plot to him. He didn't know what was going on. I took it quite serious and went right into the trap and explained the story of the play. He seemed amused by my eagerness to make him understand. This evening was the beginning of a long-lasting friendship. Later on, when I knew him better, I was surprised by his childlike belief in people. Any sob story people told him he believed, and his wife had a hard time to convince him not to give away so much when stories were obviously told for arousing pity. When I was through with my engagement and started again looking for a job, he came quite unexpectedly to my rooming house, threw a suitcase on my table, and said, "Here is some paper for you. We want you to come for a weekend to our house in the country. We pick you up." And out he went. When I opened the suitcase, it was stuffed with money. He told me later he had just gotten it from his publisher.

I didn't hear all week from him, and I surely thought he had forgotten all about it, [FIGS. 7 & 8] when the doorbell rang and a lovely, tall, slightly gray-haired woman said, "I am Margarethe Kaiser, and my husband asked me to take you with me to the country. And take a swimming suit along. We live on a lake." The trip out to Grünheide, where they lived, lasted about an hour on the train. When we arrived at the little station, she said, "We take the boat! It's such a nice quiet lake today!" She got settled and started rowing us toward the house, which took about forty-five minutes. It was a beautiful lake, and the house was already visible from the middle of the lake. When we landed, Kaiser and two of his children were waiting, and he said laughingly: "Welcome to His Majesty the Kaiser's estate." I felt at home almost at once. I became his son Anselm's property almost immediately when he discovered that I could ride a bicycle as fast as he could and play soccer (which I had learned in my early days in Vienna from my boyfriend, who actually later became a famous player). The whole weekend was dedicated to outdoor life, and theater wasn't mentioned once. I became great friends with Kaiser and his family, and for almost a year I lived with them in Grünheide.

KURT JULIAN WEILL

Kurt Weill left no memoir of his youth comparable to Lenya's. The earliest autobiographical sketch to survive dates from 1925. A single paragraph, it is little more than a list of compositions, beginning with Zaubernacht *and ending with* Der neue Orpheus. *Until 1987 what little was known about his personal life prior to 1925 had been gleaned from later interviews and oral histories. In 1987 the Kurt Weill Foundation for Music purchased the Hans and Rita Weill Collection from Weill's niece. In addition to a number of compositions previously unknown or thought to have been lost, the collection included 115 letters written by Weill to his family prior to 1925. Shortly thereafter a smaller collection of letters to his teacher Ferruccio Busoni also surfaced. Although a reliable chronicle of Weill's early professional life is therefore now accessible in recently published reference books and biographies, none presents a personal profile of the young man whom Lenya encountered in 1924 (see, however, Levitz, pp. 82–99). The following biographical sketch, based largely on Weill's early correspondence with his family, quotes from Weill as much as possible, as well as from recollections of his family and friends preserved in oral history interviews housed at the Weill-Lenya Research Center, New York.*

The Weill family could trace its genealogy to the small village of Weil, near Stuttgart, where one Rabbi Juda had been born in 1360. His son Jakob took the name of the village as his own; several of his rabbinical treatises were posthumously printed in Venice in 1532. There followed a long line of rabbis, serving in Ulm, Burgau, Donauwörth, Steuhlingen, and Kippenheim, where Albert Weill was born in 1867. He became a cantor rather than a rabbi, and in 1897 married Emma Ackermann of Wiesloch (b. 1872), whose father had in turn descended from almost as distinguished a line of rabbis. Emma's brother Aaron was widely recognized as the leading authority on Jewish liturgical music, an active proponent of its ability to raise the level of spiritual awareness.

[FIG. 9]

In 1898 Albert accepted the position of second cantor in Dessau, a city of fifty thousand and the capital of Anhalt, a duchy governed by the liberal duke Frederick II (1856–1918). The duke put great emphasis on the arts and took special interest in the court theater, which—after a visit in 1872 by Richard Wagner himself—proudly proclaimed itself the "Bayreuth of North Germany." In the first five years of marriage, Emma gave birth to all four of their children: Nathan (1898), Hans (1899), Kurt (2 March 1900), and Ruth (1901). When a magnificent new synagogue opened in 1908, Albert Weill was promoted to first cantor, and the family moved into the ground-floor apartment of the adjoining *Gemeindehaus* [parish house].

In such a pious, close-knit family within a middle-class, provincial environment, Kurt Julian's musical talent was recognized early on and nurtured by both parents. His mother recalled that every year she went home to celebrate her own mother's birthday, taking along one of the grandchildren:

> That particular year it was Kurt's turn, and he was a charming travel companion, so full of fun. But one evening during carnival time, the children of the small town stormed into our house with all kinds of masks and noise, and Kurt became upset. He was only three years old, so he got very scared and started to cry and carry on. When I got very angry with him, my mother burst into the room like a storm unleashed, took Kurt's hand away from mine, and screamed at me: "You are not to touch this child! He is something very special." (EW–L, n.d. [1954], #91)

At age six Kurt began public primary school and spent a few hours a week at the synagogue school learning the tenets of the Jewish faith, the Hebrew language, and biblical history. At the age of ten, he moved up to the all-boys' Herzogliche Friedrichs-Oberrealschule, where he remained until age eighteen. Although somewhat disengaged from the curriculum mandated by the Prussian Educational Reform of 1892—including English, French, mathematics, history, and science—he passed the *Abitur* to gain entrance to university-level studies. One of his classmates remembered that "Kurt was a very gifted student, but never very competitive. He managed to keep his fifth or sixth place for several years. That was good enough for him" (Schebera, p. 9). Weill's sister, Ruth, vividly remembered those years:

> School lasted from eight until one, when the children went home for the midday meal. He always did his schoolwork right after. Every afternoon, promptly at 5:30, was the *Bummel* for the teenagers, the afternoon stroll. Kurt never missed the Bummel. No matter how deeply he was absorbed in something else, he'd jump up, wash his face and hands, slick back his hair, and be off with Hans, the lady-killer in the family. Back and forth in front of the theater, boys walking with boys, girls with girls, flirting, giggling, trading sly remarks. When they came home, Hans and Kurt talked about this girl and that. Dates with girls meant walking with them in the parks of the Schloß, crossing the river on the bridge from which one looked down on the waterfall. Kurt belonged to a boating club, and once a week during the summer the boys, wearing white shorts and white T-shirts, would go out in shells, while the girls waited at the clubhouse and then made a picnic. (Int. RW)

[FIG. 10]

But nearly everyone in his family said that, already as a child, "Kurt lived only for music." Although his father first tried to teach him, piano and organ lessons were soon turned over to Margarete Evelyn-Schapiro and Franz Brückner. A classmate noticed that "while we were playing soccer or volleyball, he practiced three to four hours every day" (Schebera, p. 9). Lenya learned from her in-laws that Kurt used to disappear for long stretches at a time into the privacy of his tiny room under the rooftop to scribble down music, and that this earned him the family's nickname of *Dachstubenkomponist* (attic composer). In one of his first press interviews, Weill said that he had "filled many pages of manuscript paper with compositions from the age of ten onward, without any instruction" (Kastner, p. 454). Two such attempts (probably dating from 1913) have survived; one of them is a setting of a medieval Ashkenazic wedding psalm.

After their move to new quarters, the Weills bought a grand piano, and Emma was very proud of the impression her "little genius" made on visitors with his playing. He was taken to concerts and the opera regularly. "Sometimes he and his friends would come back to the public rooms of the parish house," according to Ruth, "and play the same music in their own way, discussing it for hours. One of the rooms had a small stage where plays were produced. All the Weill children acted in these plays, and it was Kurt who always chose music when it was needed, and then played the piano or led a small orchestra" (int. RW). Although he also occasionally gave recitals and appeared in concerts next door in the synagogue, liturgical music is never mentioned in any surviving correspondence. He composed for the school orchestra and later, he admitted with some embarrassment, "even wrote patriotic war songs" (Weill 1930, p. 50), one of which, from 1914, has survived. At a school recital in 1915, he played a Chopin Prelude and Liszt's *Liebestraum* no. 3. In his final year at the Oberrealschule, the director asked Kurt to reorganize and conduct the twenty-five-member school choir.

By then Weill had acquired a set of "second parents," Albert and Edith Bing. In 1913 the duke had appointed Bing—who had studied composition with Hans Pfitzner and conducting with Arthur Nikisch—first kapellmeister at the court theater. From 1915 to 1918, Weill met Bing two to five times a week for lessons in piano, harmony, sight-singing, orchestration, score-reading, and conducting, while Bing's wife, the sister of the expressionist playwright Carl Sternheim, invited the boy into their home for gatherings of artists and writers. Kurt was quickly drawn into their very different cultural orbit, that of cosmopolitan and assimilated Jews who sought religiosity in music and literature rather than ritual. The Bings' son Peter became a lifelong friend to Kurt. Although the lessons did not include composition per se, Kurt showed all his efforts to his new teacher: canons and fugues, a song cycle, a string quartet. Bing introduced Weill into the musical life of the ducal palace, and he was soon giving piano lessons to the duke's youngest daughter. Bing also opened the court theater's rehearsals and performances to Weill, who often followed performances with score in hand. And when war decimated its musical personnel, the seventeen-year-old even worked part-time as an accompanist for recitals and a coach for repertory productions of *Fidelio*, *Rigoletto*, and *Hamlet*, as well as newer works such as Eugen d'Albert's *Tiefland*.

Weill's "first" family was suffering from the war too. Nathan had been called up in 1916 and was serving on the western front as a medical orderly. Hans had also been drafted but was finally rejected because two of his fingers were fused since birth. With the cantorial salary greatly reduced, Albert and Emma had difficulty keeping the two children who were still at home fed and clothed, though their fierce pride precluded discussing hardships with anyone. Ruth remembered taking hikes with Kurt to small villages trying to find food, without success. "Kurt frequently fainted from hunger and eagerly looked forward to any invitation where there was some good, solid food to be had" (int. RW). As vegetarians, the Weills were not affected by the "meatless days" mandated by shortages, but nevertheless descriptions of the abundant food at postconcert receptions took up more space in Weill's letters home than did his account of the event itself. After a recital in Cöthen in which he had accompanied the distinguished soprano Emilie Feuge, for example, Kurt, still heady from the success of his professional debut, wrote to his brother Hans:

> The concert was well attended, and I received tremendous applause, especially for *Tristan* [the "Liebestod"]. After the Grieg they brought me a huge bouquet of flowers, and I had to return to the stage three times. The rest of the concert also garnered much applause, mainly, of course, for Frau Feuge, who got more flowers than any Dessau flower shop could muster up. Afterward there was coffee and cake and then wonderful champagne. We went home at midnight, where there was another supper waiting. On top of all that, I also got forty marks. . . . I went to bed at 1:30, got up at 4:45 (the first time that I did not sleep for one minute!), and caught my train at 5:45, because it was impossible to skip school again. (W–HW, 22 March 1917)

By the time Kurt himself was of draft age, his sister remembered, "everybody had come to think Germany was on the wrong side, they were bound to lose. When soldiers would march past the house, Kurt would shut the windows to blot out the martial music" (int. RW). Nevertheless, in 1917 he took trumpet lessons so that he could join a military band unit if necessary. But prior to his medical examination he resorted to more drastic tactics, swallowing enough aspirins to induce palpitations that would disqualify him. Shortly after his eighteenth birthday, following much discussion about his future, his two sets of parents agreed on a compromise plan: with Bing's recommendation, Kurt would apply for admission to the Berlin Hochschule für Musik, but also—to satisfy his parents—

would enroll for the summer term at Humboldt University, with the financial help of his uncle Leopold, as an undergraduate in liberal arts.

Weill's first letters home after his arrival in late April 1918 are signed "Kurt Weill, Stud. Mus. (Kriegsmus!) et Phil." They describe his classes at the university in modern literature, philosophy of art (with Max Dessoir), and Greek philosophy (with Ernst Cassirer), as well as organ lessons at the Hochschule from Walther Fischer, score-reading with Karl Heymann, music history with Carl Krebs, sight-singing with Max Stange, and conducting with Rudolf Krasselt. Officially enrolled as a composition major, Weill was surprised to find himself the sole student of Engelbert Humperdinck:

> I've already been to two lessons with old Humperdinck. . . . The master was still quite ill but had gotten out of bed only on my account, and he had a hard time breathing. The autograph full score of his new opera [*Gaudeamus*] was lying on the piano. He asked me about this and that, gave me some homework, and then I was dismissed. But yesterday he came to the Hochschule, gave me new assignments, and told me that in the next lesson I should show him a sketch of my string quartet. I immediately dug it out, and now I'm working on it again. It's purely an accident that I got to Humperdinck. They got me mixed up with somebody else who had inquired whether it might be possible to arrange for lessons with him. . . . In any event, it really does mean something to have studied with Humperdinck. (W–HW, 9 May 1918)

By June Weill had become disillusioned. Disappointed by Humperdinck's neglect, he felt doubly victimized because his teacher's privileged position and wealth had inspired the jealousy of colleagues: "You musn't think I'm particularly proud to be 'someone who has been invited to the Humperdincks'.' Berlin has managed to dampen my enthusiasm completely." He returned to Dessau at semester's end in August but confessed to his brother Hans that he found its provinciality intolerable after four months in Berlin:

> I am completely incapacitated by the utter desolation of this place. . . . It's as difficult for me to get anything done in this environment as it was easy for me to work in Berlin. You see how dependent I am on inspiration from my teacher, from my fellow students, and from the opera and concerts in Berlin. Will I ever be able to create true art if I don't continue to be exposed to these influences? Sure, we both know I'll never be another Schubert or Beethoven; I think many others have suffered from the "sickness" of thinking they would be. (W–HW, 9 Aug. 1918)

Although dissatisfied with the conservative curriculum and faculty of the Hochschule, Weill decided to go back to Berlin. He arrived just in time to witness the abdication of the kaiser and the "November Revolution":

> The great revolution broke out on Saturday with such elemental force and such fabulous speed that one can hardly comprehend it if one lives outside Berlin. . . . On Saturday I stayed close to the Reichstag all day and saw them force their way into the barracks and form the workers' and soldiers' councils. I witnessed the parades, the speeches of Liebknecht, Hoffmann, and Ledebour, among others, and finally the fierce fighting that night in front of the royal stables. (W–HW, 12 Nov. 1918)

Sometimes I just can't believe that there really is a cease-fire now, that so much is changed and I no longer have to fear that dark something called the draft, which used to haunt my future, and that I can no longer become a royal Generalmusik-direktor. (W–HW, 15 Nov. 1918)

The impressionable eighteen-year-old soon found himself engaged in political action. He wrote of his worries about a dictatorship of the proletariat, his opposition to the Spartacists, and his work with the student commune at the Hochschule in its fight against rising anti-Semitism:

If they don't insist energetically on a convocation of the national assembly (which will not turn in favor of the Independents) and on the moderates' participation in the government, we can expect Russian conditions—and pogroms. Under pressure, every party is using the Jews as an effective means of distracting attention. . . . The mob is just waiting for the call to revolt and pillage, and their favorite target will be the Jews. (W–HW, 15 Nov. 1918)

With the events of the revolution continually threatening to close both the university and Hochschule, Weill's musical studies were disrupted, and he confessed to his brother that "to think about working productively is, of course, impossible" (W–HW, 27 June 1919). Although he managed to complete an orchestral suite—"more a study than an opus"—which he first mentions in November, he even considered abandoning composition:

I had already definitely decided to give up this scribbling [*Schreiberei*] altogether and throw myself totally into the conducting business [*Kapellmeisterei*]. We Jews are simply not productive, and when we are, we have a destructive rather than constructive effect. And if the young movement in music views the Mahler-Schoenberg line as being constructive and heralding the future (as I, alas, do too!), then that movement must consist of Jews, or Gentiles with Jewish accents. No Jew could ever write a work like the Moonlight Sonata. The mere idea of pursuing this train of thought is enough to force the pen out of one's hand. (W–HW, 27 June 1919)

Conflicted on several levels, Weill described himself to Hans as "dangling between two worlds," "in danger of sinking into an abyss." He thought that only love had the potential to affect him as powerfully as Beethoven's music: "Just once I would like to fall madly in love so I could forget about everything else. . . . It would be wonderful to get married as soon as possible, if only one could find a suitable partner" (W–HW, 27 June 1919). But in protracted analyses of the various types of candidates, Weill told Hans that he preferred the "brainless":

I must confess that these types of girls are quite preferable as far as females in general are concerned. The other kind, with whom I can converse more or less intelligently, I consider to be more like comrades, like-minded people. What I require of a woman, what everyone, we artists perhaps the most, needs of a woman—not only in the sensual but also in psychological and spiritual aspects—is what Goethe raised to its highest incarnation with his "ewig Weibliche" [the eternal Feminine], the very thing that one rarely finds in intelligent girls. The Dessauers seem to have a monopoly on the less-than-intelligent species. And where can one find the woman who offers a happy medium between the two? (W–HW, 15 May 1919)

A month later he expressed similar yearnings to his sister, Ruth:

In my neighborhood there are several young girls who sing all kinds of folk songs in harmony every evening. I love that kind of fresh, unspoiled, girlish voice. Isn't there by chance someone marriageable for me among your pupils? My terms: extremely pretty, very stupid, unmusical, with a dowry of a million marks. (W–RW2, n.d. [June 1919])

For a while Kurt thought he had found her in Martha Gratenau, whom he took for long walks in the Tiergarten and rowing on the lakes of Berlin before her parents broke up the relationship.

To support himself, Kurt also "dangled between two worlds." To supplement a small stipend from the Felix-Mendelssohn-Bartholdy Stiftung at the Hochschule, he took several synagogue jobs, the first of which, in Friedenau, paid 250 marks a month to train and conduct the choir. "It's an incredible job to guide the completely ignorant choir and the even more ignorant organist, to whom I must indicate every entrance, through all the intricacies of the Jewish service, especially when I myself am not that sure of the rather free practice here in Berlin." But despite his own hardships and impoverished living conditions in a tiny, unheated room next to the streetcar line, he found words of encouragement for his brother: "Remember Goethe, remember Shakespeare and Beethoven and Feuerbach, remember *Faust* and *Hamlet* and the Ninth Symphony and *Iphigenia*—then you will feel fine" (W–HW, 4 Sept. 1918).

Indeed, it was Berlin's cultural life that sustained Weill during his second and third semesters at the Hochschule: at the Berlin Philharmonic, a "shattering" performance of Beethoven's Fifth Symphony under Arthur Nikisch, Bruckner's Fourth Symphony, Mahler's "Resurrection" Symphony; at the opera, Pfitzner's *Palestrina*, Schreker's *Die Schatzgräber*, *Der Rosenkavalier*, Strauss himself conducting *Salome*, as well as *Figaro*—"the ultimate bliss, for the first time in my life I really understood what Mozart is all about" (W–HW, 9 May 1919). At the Hochschule he declared a double major in conducting and composition, concentrated on orchestration with lessons from the masterful Paul Juon, and threw himself into Schubert research with Max Friedländer. But most of all, Weill sought to understand "modernity": "I am not yet a person with a thoroughly modern sensibility. . . . I stink of provincialism" (W–HW, 21 Feb. 1919). In search of his own style, he sought to understand what was "new":

I notice that a "modern" clique has developed around me at the Hochschule, strangely so, because the teachers themselves are definitely not modern: Humperdinck—well, maybe in his bold carelessness in contrapuntal voice-leading. Koch is a stiff contrapuntalist, as a composer an ultramodern much-noise-about-nothing type; and Kahn—he's a truly naive Mendelssohnian, for whom every augmented triad is like a box on the ear. But in the midst of this a small circle of students has formed a group in which you have to feel ashamed if you don't know all the music of Richard Strauss and Reger, and also Korngold, Debussy, Schreker, Bittner, and Marx, etc. That is of course very exciting. (W–HW, 7 Dec. 1918)

In his final semester at the Hochschule his studies led him away from the "affected modernism" of Strauss, through Bruckner to Mahler (who offers "the richest prospects for the future"; W–HW, 20 Aug. 1919) and then on to the newly discovered Schoenberg:

> Think of everything in Strauss that is false, trivial, whitewashed, farfetched, and replace it with the ultimate in modernity—in Mahler's sense—with the deepest conviction of a great personality: then you have Arnold Schoenberg, as I'm getting to know him from his Gurre Lieder. (W–HW, 27 June 1919)

During the spring transportation strike he composed fourteen hours a day, completing a tone poem based on Rilke, but he found even that "an embarrassment": "I need poetry to set my imagination into motion; and my imagination is not a bird, it's an airplane. It's only a small consolation that the young composers around me are no better, often even worse. But they don't aspire to such heights as I do" (W–HW, 27 June 1919). He found himself more and more estranged from what he encountered at the Hochschule:

> Why aren't I as dull and apathetic as the others who consider it their greatest fortune to attend the Hochschule for five years or more—to whom it never occurs that there is music that they don't know, that they would never understand? Thank God I seek what is new and I understand it. (W–HW, 27 June 1919)

> Today I heard that one of the candidates for the job of director of the Hochschule is one of the most modern of modernists: BUSONI. Of course, the teachers and students at the Hochschule, that herd of old Teutonic, behind-the-times, idiotic goats, protest this with all their might. But he'd be healthy for this old dump, although I don't know if he's the right composition teacher. Anyway I think it's out of the question he'd be accepted. They're already spreading a rumor that he's a Jew, and when a student says something like that about you, then God help you. (W–HW, 18 Feb. 1919)

Tortured by his circumstances and artistic frustrations, he sought advice and received wildly divergent opinions from teachers he respected. Bing recommended that he study privately with Hermann Wetzler and Hans Pfitzner, Krasselt that he continue to study conducting at the Hochschule. But Hermann Scherchen said, "There was, of course, only one teacher from whom a talented person could still learn something: Schoenberg" (W–HW, 20 June 1919). After Weill wrote to Schoenberg and received in response "a very nice card offering to help me any way he could" (W–HW, 14 July 1919), his financial situation worsened. Albert Weill had lost his cantorial position in Dessau and in autumn 1919 would move to Leipzig to direct the B'nai B'rith orphanage there. Private study with Schoenberg then indeed seemed out of reach:

> Again and again I pore over it in my head: Should I stay here? And the answer that always comes is To Vienna! And then every time the same disappointment: to realize such a plan right now would be impossible for me. . . . If I had a job and would not have to be a burden on father's purse, I could console myself and wait until next fall, especially since by then I'd be considerably more mature and could better assimilate the gigantic impressions of Vienna and the studies with Schoenberg. I'm already seriously thinking about working at the Dessau theater anyway this winter. Then I could learn whatever is necessary for the profession of a conductor, it wouldn't cost

anything, and I could finish some compositions in peace. But would I then be able to go to Vienna with the same feelings I have now? (W–HW, 27 June 1919)

At semester break in August 1919, after conducting jobs in Munich, Cologne, and Tilsit had fallen through, Weill went back to Dessau to serve as an opera coach under Bing and the new music director, Hans Knappertsbusch. Despite work at the opera house that frequently lasted from 8:00 A.M. to 11:30 P.M., he still found time to compose a few songs and present a recital at the ducal palace in November, which his mother described in detail:

> The cream of society, all the nobility and Their Highnesses were present. And then little Kurt and Elisabeth Feuge [Emilie's seventeen-year-old daughter] took over, starting Kurt's compositions with that enchanting Lied "Die stille Stadt." After that the applause just wouldn't stop. Both of them were immediately asked to come to the duke's box and enjoyed compliments rarely given to such youngsters. The younger princes who had known Kurt already for some time were especially enthusiastic. (EW–RW, n.d., #91)

In December 1919, largely because Knappertsbusch had become a rival for Elisabeth Feuge's affections, Weill resigned and accepted the position of second conductor with a small municipal theater in Lüdenscheid, a city half the size of Dessau. There, in a makeshift theater in a converted ballroom, he rehearsed every day from 9:00 to 7:00, and five days a week conducted performances of operettas, including *Die Fledermaus, Martha, Der Zigeunerbaron,* and even *Cavalleria Rusticana*—often after just one rehearsal with the cast and orchestra. The day the new conductor arrived, the local newspaper reported that "the young man was rather surprised to learn on his arrival, late in the afternoon, that he should conduct a performance of *Martha* the same evening" (Simon). Weill wrote his brother that he not only had to conduct but also sometimes worry about the staging, sing little parts, and reduce orchestral scores for the small ensemble employed by the theater. Although years later he admitted that Lüdenscheid "was where I learned everything I know about the stage" (Weill 1938), at the time he complained constantly about the job: the "operatic garbage" got on his nerves, he felt "up to his ears" in operetta, and the unproductive life was driving him mad. Yet he took pride in a job well done: "I feel so sure of myself as a conductor that I'm not afraid of anything" (W–HW, 26 April 1920). "After every performance the director assures me that whatever operetta it was has never sounded better" (W–RW1, 16 Jan. 1920). He confessed to his sister that the musical theater, where "music can best express the unspeakable," would "probably turn out to be my life's work," although, he added, "I will not find many people who will understand me." He lamented, "But right now there isn't the slightest chance of composing anything at all," and confided that "nobody could possibly imagine how I suffer because of it" (W–RW1, 28 Jan. 1920):

[FIG. 11]

> I have been here all alone in my room the past few days. I've sought this solitude, for it alone brings me satisfaction, allowing me to savor the moment and listen as the rain of time slowly falls. Life is short, and one minute is more precious than a thousand dollars. There is so much to imbibe, so many inner problems to grapple with, for which no book can provide answers. So here I sit in my half-dark room, sensing such an intimate bond with all those who have sought solitude in their little dens away from the noise of the crowd in order to perceive more clearly the murmuring

hymns of the stars. And all of them, all of them are praying for frenzied humanity.
(W–RW1, n.d. [spring 1920], #265)

Nearing the end of the season, Weill decided to return to his composition studies: "The routine theater business leaves me more and more unsatisfied the longer I stay in it. I am positive about my decision to go to Vienna next winter, no matter what it costs. Only this prospect will enable me to put up with operetta for the next few months" (W–HW, n.d. [April/May 1920], #205). But in June 1920, after including songs and the "Vorspiel zu einem Drama" by Franz Schreker in a recital arranged by his brother Hans in Halberstadt, Weill decided instead that he would return to Berlin to study with Schreker, who had been named the new director of the Hochschule. After briefly visiting his parents, who had now relocated to Leipzig, Kurt spent the summer conducting operetta at the Spa Theater in Norderney (a resort island in the North Sea). With the promise of an allowance of fifty marks per month from his father's brother Leopold, he left once more for Berlin in the fall of 1920. He gave lectures, conducted a choral society, accompanied, and composed once again. He hoped for a commission to compose music for a play by Johannes Becher; when that didn't materialize, he salvaged some of his ideas in a symphonic poem, now known as Symphony no. 1.

[FIG. 12]

He never reenrolled at the Hochschule. Instead, in November Kurt reported to his father that, armed with a recommendation from the influential critic Oskar Bie, he had succeeded in getting an interview with Ferruccio Busoni, who was choosing his master class in composition at the Academy of Arts:

> You wouldn't believe how difficult it is to get close to Busoni; the doorman has orders to send everyone away. Nevertheless, I spent a tremendously interesting afternoon with him. . . . I have not achieved anything yet for sure. He is amazed at my youth; he kept my compositions but doesn't want to decide, because such big shots have already applied that there is almost no space for such a young fellow as me.
> (W–AW, 29 Nov. 1920)

Although the master class did not officially begin until the following July, by January 1921 Weill was visiting Busoni regularly, attending his concerts, and already writing to thank him for his support:

> This afternoon, in my surprise, I could only hastily stammer my thanks that someone should so enthusiastically take an interest in me, and someone, at that, whom I hold above all others in such glowing esteem. . . . Let me assist you in whatever you might need me for in the future that I might be able to do. I would be very happy to be thought of always as your sincerely devoted *famulus*. (W–FB, 20 Jan. 1921)

In describing his first four master students the following July, Busoni confirmed his close relationship with Weill, whom he dubbed "a very fine little Jew (who certainly will make his way and is already something of a factotum around the house)" (Busoni, p. 344).

Weill had found the mentor and friend he had been searching for. His three years of study with Busoni confirmed Weill's own human and musical inclinations: to devote himself to the stage and attempt to renew opera; to move toward a simpler style; to think critically about political events, social problems, and philosophical issues; to temper his quest for modernity with respect for the classic, especially Mozart; to synthesize the old with the new in a *junge Klassizität* [new classicism]. By introducing his pupils to such non-German influences as Stravinsky, Debussy, and above all, the Italian Renaissance, Busoni showed them a way toward new harmonic and melodic means of expression outside the post-Wagnerian tradition. Weill supplemented the largely nontechnical course of study under Busoni with intensive contrapuntal lessons from Philipp Jarnach. By the time he completed his three-year course, Weill had displaced Jarnach as Busoni's closest pupil. Busoni gave Jarnach a frank appraisal of Weill's talent:

> Considering his reserved vein and painstaking efforts, this young man's productivity is surprising. He has any amount of "ideas"—as you say—but they are concealed or implied, so that only "the likes of us" can discover and admire them. He does not seem to be conscious of when he has arrived at the right place; instead, he passes over it as if over sand and rocks among which beautiful individual flowers grow, which he neither tramples nor plucks, and over which he does not linger. His wealth is great, his selectivity still latent. One envies him and would like to help. But he will come to the right thing of his own accord! (Busoni, p. 373)

Although still barely subsisting on what he could earn from teaching harmony, playing, and conducting, Weill remembered this period as the happiest and most productive of his life. In November 1922 *Zaubernacht* premiered at the Theater am Kurfürstendamm. The next year, at the peak of the most devastating inflation in history, the Berlin Philharmonic programmed both Divertimento, op. 5, and the *Fantasia, Passacaglia, und Hymnus*, op. 6. Through his membership in the November Group Weill had gained the support of such important conductors as Hermann Scherchen and Fritz Stiedry, who conducted the Berlin premiere of *Frauentanz* in February 1924. This cycle of medieval love poems was dedicated to Nelly Frank, a distant Swiss cousin with whom Weill had fallen in love. Temporarily living in Berlin with her wealthy husband and two young sons, Nelly was three years older than Kurt, cosmopolitan and worldly. In spring 1924 she and Kurt trysted in Davos, a posh resort in the Swiss Alps, and she financed an extended tour of Italy—Weill's first. He heard Toscanini conduct at La Scala in Milan, admired the architectural sublimity of Bologna, rhapsodized about the intensity of beauty in Florence. His report to Busoni from Rome seems to confirm all that he had learned from his teacher:

[FIG. 13]

> I'm experiencing the Vatican's art treasures. Every day I visit three places: the Sistine Chapel, Raffaello's *stanze*, and his ornamentations of the Villa Farnesina, and again and again I fall on my knees before this perfection. I'm far too overwhelmed by all this to find the right words, but I know full well there must be some explanation for this deeply stirring aftereffect—that these people were incredibly able craftsmen, and that their sentiments were of the kind of purity that in itself would justify their presentation of divine subjects in human terms. The relations to the music of Bach and Mozart are many, extending to formal and melodic details; but to whom are such analogies as familiar as to you? Understanding the sculptures was more difficult for me. At first I looked upon them as an astonishing accomplishment; I was amazed at the know-how, the built-in momentum of the composition, but I could not penetrate the depth of this art—yes, I was about to deny the presence of spiritual expression in it. But confronted with the smile of a Roman girl, the soft irony of a fistfighter,

the total abandon of a dancing girl, I began to understand that this period had the same human context as our own, that only the format was restrained, veiled, condensed. . . . That means a great deal to me, filling a gap within me that at times had been painful. . . .

I'm glad that some of my ideas are at one with your own. Sometimes I believe that just these few weeks in the sun of the South have brought out things in my development that have long been dormant within me; in any case I'm experiencing an enormous desire for action, and I'm full of plans. I do so hope to find you feeling better. (W–FB, 15 March 1924)

After a final stop in Venice, Weill headed back to Berlin, but Busoni was not better. His condition continued to deteriorate, just as Weill's career was really taking off. Acting on Busoni's recommendation, Emil Hertzka, the director of Universal Edition in Vienna, offered Weill a ten-year exclusive contract and accepted for publication both *Frauentanz* and the op. 8 String Quartet. Although the arrangement had little or no immediate impact on his financial circumstances, the twenty-four-year-old composer now had a publisher, and his name joined a house roster that included Bruckner, Mahler, Schreker, Schoenberg, Berg, Webern, and Bartók. Of equal importance, Weill's next stage work was to be a collaboration with Georg Kaiser, the foremost German dramatist of the day, to whom Stiedry had introduced him. But Weill let his parents know that this success had not gone to his head:

My work has made such demands on me, and outside obligations have been increasing as well. Two movements of the Violin Concerto are finished, but for three days now I've been stuck—so my plan to have the whole thing finished before my visit with you can't be realized. But it's going to be great! Kaiser still hasn't delivered the end of the libretto. But that doesn't bother me, because I've got an infinite number of plans. . . . Now much—if not all—of my future development depends entirely on me. I've got to work enormously hard in the next few years in order to take advantage of the favorable launch I'm experiencing right now. (W–A&EW1, 29 May 1924)

Weill also reported that he had been offered the post of Berlin correspondent for the weekly program magazine of the German radio; his essay on Richard Strauss had appeared in the periodical *Anbruch*, in distinguished company; his efforts on behalf of Busoni's *Doktor Faust* had opened the door for production of his own work in Dresden; and *Frauentanz* had been accepted for the chamber music festival of the International Society for Contemporary Music in Salzburg.

The performance in Salzburg that summer marked Weill's transition from master student to a composer of some stature. One critic noted:

The cycle, wonderfully interpreted by Lotte Leonard, made Kurt Weill's name famous. Here, with the most reduced musical means, the most extremely fluid expression is found in the most compressed form. . . . Weill has invented his own melodic shape and impregnated the poetic content with his music. (Kastner, p. 455)

His personal life was also in transition. Nelly's husband had refused her request for a divorce, and the family left for an extended visit to the United States; Kurt's affair with an older, sophisticated woman was over. Weill confided to his sister:

> As a rule I'm against adages like "just cross it out and keep on going," because that inevitably leads to a certain superficiality. But there comes a time in everybody's life when one can't escape this sort of thing. Doesn't everybody believe to have found "his or her person," or "his or her lifestyle," or "his or her work," or "his or her God"? At some point everyone has to learn that "this person" doesn't belong to him or her, that their paths will be crossed by others, that the world wasn't created for us but we were created for the world, and that God does not love us but perhaps loves our good deeds. And that each May, spring will span the sky, the eternal sunrise will pour its gold over the horizons, and that during every hour of the day something will be created out of love: a child, a work, or a deed. . . . You seem to think that I simply let all unpleasant things slip by me. Not at all; I simply drain the cup to the dregs, because it's part of the times into which I was born, and it points the way to "beauty," which flourishes today just as it always did. Wherever I discover a feeling—whether beautiful or ugly—I grab it and empty the goblet without deliberating what may become of it all. And each time, I discover that even the bitter aftertaste of an unpleasant experience is worth more than the flat taste of indifference. (W–RW2, n.d. [1924], #262)

A few weeks later he reported to Ruth that "Busoni is deathly ill and none of us know where our heads are. It would be easier to suffer oneself than to watch another human being suffer so terribly. When I'm not with him, I have to bury myself in work in order to forget what he looks like." But he found comfort in a new mentor, a new surrogate family: "I visited the Kaisers last week in Grünheide; they've become dear friends and will probably be the only ones who can replace a small part of what I'm going to lose in Busoni" (W–RW1, n.d., #15).

LENYA: "THE ROWBOAT"

Georg Kaiser had a passion for music, and one of his best friends was the conductor Fritz Stiedry. I think it was Stiedry who introduced Weill to Kaiser. Kaiser had a weird assortment of paddleboats, sailboats, rowboats, scullboats, and so on. It was on one of those boats that I first met Kurt Weill. He was coming to discuss *Der Protagonist* with Kaiser. One Sunday morning Kaiser said, "Lenja, there's a young composer for whom I'm writing a libretto. Would you mind picking him up at the train station?" There were two ways to go to that station: walking through the woods or taking a rowboat. I said I'd take the boat; it was shorter and I like lakes anyway. I asked, "How will I recognize him?" and Kaiser said, "Oh, it'll be very easy. Composers all look alike."

It was a little, deserted station; on a Sunday there was nobody there. But I saw a little man with one of those typical musician's hats on his head and thick glasses. A blue suit and a little blue tie. Five feet, three and a half inches tall—an inch taller than I—with his hairline already receding. I asked him if he was Mr. Weill, and he said he was. "I'm here to meet you," I said, "and bring you to Mr. Kaiser. Would you mind stepping into that boat? That's our transportation." I started rowing and he kept staring at me. "You know, Miss Lenja, I think we've met before." "Where?" "You didn't come back for the rehearsal of the ballet." "Oh—yes." "I'm the composer of *Zaubernacht*."

When I met Weill, Busoni was suffering his last illness. He died in July 1924, and Weill was very shaken. There had been a deep sympathy between them. But I don't think Weill felt Busoni's death as an end, partly because he had just met Georg Kaiser. And that was a beginning.

Part I

LETTERS TRANSLATED
FROM THE GERMAN

. . . .

Winners lose
    And losers win,
Put your money down and watch
    The planet spin.
All good fortune changes hands.

Maxwell Anderson, "There's Nowhere to Go but Up,"
Knickerbocker Holiday *(1938)*

I · BERLIN: 1924–1933
Letters 1–38

Weill and Lenya after their wedding on 28 January 1926 in Berlin.

1924–1925

After their meeting during summer 1924, Weill and Lenya corresponded only when one or the other stayed with the Kaisers; a bit later, they wrote when Weill left Berlin to attend performances or productions of his works or when Lenya was on vacation. None of Lenya's responses to Weill's early letters has survived. We know little about their early months together, as Lenya seldom went much beyond the rowboat anecdote in her interviews. She did recall one of her first visits to Weill's apartment in Berlin, at the time he was finishing Der Protagonist, *late in 1924 or early in 1925:*

He had a charming little apartment, and that's when he was working on *Der Protagonist*. And he asked, "Would you like to hear a little bit of it?" I said, "Oh, yes. I would like very much to hear." And he said, "Well, my brother [Hans] hated it, but I wonder what your reaction would be." Strangely enough, as atonal as it was, I loved it. I said, "Well, Mr. Weill, I don't know why, but I really, really love that music." And he was so happy that he said, "May I make you some tea?" Of course, there was no refrigerator, so from the windowsill he got a little butter wrapped in paper and a little bread. And I had such a hard time to get that butter down, because it was so rancid—which he didn't even notice, because they were used to it; he went through the war, you know. So I didn't say anything; I ate it. (Int. L2)

1 WEILL IN BERLIN TO LENYA AT THE KAISERS' IN GRÜNHEIDE, [SUMMER/FALL, 1924]

Linerl,[1]

It's true that you need a human being who belongs to you, because there has to be someone to whom you don't need to lie. It's also true that this someone has to be me. But then how will you answer? Such a step would not be possible for me without a strong commitment of what you call—with a shrug of your shoulders—"feeling" and in which you'd gladly believe, since you don't know what it is. But right now you couldn't have such feeling for me. Are you willing to wait? ? ? ? ? ? ? ? ? ? ? ?

I think of you often and always happily. And I wished we could stay right where we were at the end of this evening. ? ? ? ?

Do come soon. Please.

> Your
> Kurt Weill

1. *Although Weill addresses Lenya by her nickname "Linerl," an affectionate Viennese diminutive of Karoline, he maintains the formal second-person, Sie, and signs his full name.*

2 WEILL IN BERLIN TO LENYA IN GRÜNHEIDE, [1924]

Written on two scraps of paper.

Dearest,

Today the most beautiful wish of my life has been granted. I never dreamed that I would experience something like this. Are you surprised that I'm pensive and lost in thought?[1] I can't rejoice out loud—the joy lies too deep.

> Entirely yours

Be grateful for all this happiness, my adored LIFE!

1. *Weill now uses the informal second-person, Du.*

3 WEILL IN BERLIN TO LENYA IN GRÜNHEIDE, [DECEMBER 1924]

Adieu, my worshiped life,

Be happy: physical separation has been overcome. I'm always with you in spirit. You'll have to be happy within my rapture of love. *Addio, addio—*

> Your
> Jésus-Boy[1]

1. *Weill seems to be indulging in a multilingual play on words: German Christkind, or Jesuskind, becomes Jésus-Boy (French-English). The signature implies a date near Christmas, because in the German tradition the Christkind (Christ-child) brings gifts and lights for the tree on Christmas eve.*

Please don't carry any anger in your heart either, *Tobili*. This too is only a beginning. I just have to get to where you want me to be without idolizing you any the less.

> Be loved,
> Dany

Monday evening

Muschelchen,

The memory of your blowup today is not painful. You were very beautiful—and you were right. I was to blame. My attitude was still wrong. But now—finally, finally—I've understood exactly where you want me to be. And now I also know that it isn't so hard after all. A shift, not even a weakening, of my feelings—that's all. How passionately I love you—today more than ever—is entirely my own private affair. The expression of this feeling can't be obvious to others; it must be perceived only by you—just as your love still radiated to me even during today's blowup. For you were right in everything, except in saying you never really "liked" me; too often you've proven the opposite is true (and written that you are tougher on me than on others). This makes me glad, because often such an outburst is the strongest proof of your affection. But you must still believe one thing: these little arguments are not the end; they are the insignificant frictions of the beginning, which are caused solely by my inexperience. That's over now. Today I give you a present: me. You may take this present without qualms; it will bring you only good things. Let me be your "pleasure boy" [*Lustknabe*], more than a friend but less than a husband. I'm in the world for you—that is self-evident, and you don't need to feel obligated. You'll now sense it. Give me just a small sign that you will accept the present. Please.

Caption: "The supplicant and the dancer." Let's be happy!

> Jésus

On Saturday you're invited to dinner with me at Lello and Hide's [Rafaello and Hide Busoni]. Lello intended to invite you formally, but I said I would tell you. Let me know if you don't feel like going, so I can cancel.

New Year's Eve the whole gang is going to Zadora's.[1] You really must come. It'll be a lot of fun. Perhaps the Kaisers will come too?

Just now I received your letter "per Sie." But that doesn't matter anymore.[2]

---

1. *Michael von Zadora (1882–1946), a Polish-American pianist and composer born in New York, had studied with Busoni and, like Weill, had been a member of his "inner circle" in Berlin.*

2. *Reversion from the intimate* Du *to the formal* Sie *is indicative of the strained relationship. It is the last nonironic occurrence of this mode of address in the correspondence. Neither Weill nor Lenya attended Zadora's party on New Year's Eve. Rather, Weill wrote his mother: "Considering that you'll be alone this evening, you should at least have a little fun when you get this letter tomorrow morning. Console yourself, because I'm staying home on New Year's Eve too. In the afternoon I have rehearsals [for the Berlin Philharmonic's performance on 22 January 1925 of* Das Stundenbuch, *a song cycle for*

baritone and orchestra on texts by Rainer Maria Rilke], and I won't be able to squeeze in Grünheide" (W–EW, 31 Dec. 1924).

6 WEILL IN LEIPZIG TO LENYA IN GRÜNHEIDE, 13 FEBRUARY 1925

Postcard: photograph of two lovers silhouetted in the lamplight of a salon, with a rhyming inscription: "Your heart speaks through your gaze; just tell me it's true, and do not lie!" Addressed to Fräulein Lotte Lenja, née Blamauer, and written in Saxonian dialect.

[FIGS. 14 & 15]

Lilipe Lencha,

Now I'm in Leipzig, but it's too bad nothing here's as nice as the weather. Tonight I'll be in Berlin again. How about you? I'll call tomorrow noon because I have to tell you something. About Cis-Schwein.¹ I am looking forward to being in my own place tonight.

> Yours always,
> Weill

1. *Weill's parents had moved from Dessau to Leipzig in 1919. Cis-Schwein was a well-worn, corny musical pun:* Cis *is C-sharp, enharmonically equivalent to D-flat, in German* Des. *A female* Schwein *(pig) is a* Sau. *Thus,* Cis-Schwein *is equivalent to* Des-Sau, *the name of Weill's home town. The composer Paul Dessau sometimes called himself by the enharmonic version of his name.*

7 WEILL IN BERLIN TO LENYA IN GRÜNHEIDE, [12 MARCH 1925]

Dear Lenja-Benja,

Lello [Rafaello Busoni] was here just now and wants me to tell you he's very upset that you have not been to see him for so long, and you should come see him Friday evening in any case. Otherwise he will be angry. Therefore, O my soul mate—Vote the Marxist Slate!¹

Claudio Arrau is no longer pretty.² He now tries to wear his hair like a man, sports a mustache, and looks very American. Fie upon Krex[?]! But even in his composition lesson he won't be parted from his boyfriend but brings him along:

Castor and Pollux
David and Goliath
Hermann and Dorothea
Hermann and Froitzheim³

Nothing has come of the Violin Concerto because nobody has any money. Besides all that, it's cold. ("No matter how much spring threatens, winter can't be far behind.")⁴

Therefore once more a heartfelt toast: Fie upon Krex! I bid greetings to the imperial [*Kaiserliche*] family as well as to Stretzel[?].

> To you, my greetings!
> Your
> Kurt Weill

1. *Friedrich Ebert (1871–1925), the first elected president of the Weimar Republic, had died on 28 February. The right-wing hero of the lost war, Paul von Hindenburg, was elected as Ebert's successor on 26 April.*

2. *Internationally acclaimed Chilean pianist Claudio Arrau (1903–91) studied theory and composition with Weill 1923–25, as did Maurice Abravanel and Nikos Skalkottas.*

3. *Hermann und Dorothea* is an epic poem by Goethe. Hermann and Froitzheim were famous German shoe manufacturers.

4. *A reversal of the well-known German verse, "Und dräut der Winter noch so sehr, es muß doch Frühling werden."*

8 WEILL IN BERLIN TO LENYA IN GRÜNHEIDE, [1925]

Muschi, süßes,

Now I'll tell you anyway what this letter will be about. And pass over our misunderstanding in silence, because silence will tell you best how your look tore me apart when we said goodbye to each other. Weariness? Oh no! But this occasion is too important to dwell on that—and my feeling for you so tremendous that no everyday event can possibly compete with it. There must be nothing petty between us, because one lifetime is not enough for two human beings to explore the cosmos that lies between them.

What I wanted to tell you is that I desire nothing more passionately than to be allowed to be endlessly good to you. I know that ugliness must disappear from your life for you to be able to believe that a very kind hand might wipe the pain away. I also know that nobody possesses what you're longing for as much as I do, because a thousand centuries and twenty-five years have been shaping me.[1] I would like to lavish on you all of what I <u>am</u>. Because I <u>have</u> nothing. Is it love? Is it kindness? I don't know. But you should take it with both hands. It is not a present from me, because it lives only for you; but it could become your present to humanity. It is independent of space, time, or matter. You just have to know and believe strongly that it is there—then it's already yours. Do you want it?

And do you understand how it hurts when you call me a fool [*Tschumpel*], and I look at you in disbelief that this word could come from you; and how afterward I'm dazed and helpless when you ask me for the smallest, simplest thing? You know that I'm not good natured, that I've always been a boor and not well liked, and that I am not "good." But there has to be somebody with whom I can let go; otherwise I will choke on my own optimism. You are something wonderful to which my faith clings. I savor the fact that you're alive. And it's incomprehensible that you might be able to love me. That I may love you is bliss enough.

> Very much yours,
> *Äppelheim*

1. *Weill turned twenty-five on 2 March 1925, but the date of the letter cannot be precisely determined.*

9 WEILL IN BERLIN TO LENYA IN GRÜNHEIDE, [1925?]

Liebili,

How I'd love to spend a quarter of an hour of my day imagining a little love package for you! May I do that?

What I'm allowed to do for you is too little. You should accept more of my love; there is so much of it!

Your Dany

10 WEILL IN BERLIN TO LENYA IN GRÜNHEIDE, [APRIL 1925?]

Seelchen:

Today I know who you are: You are Alpha and Omega, revelation from above and words of a child, sunrise and dusk of evening. For this is the equation: white is your soul, white is your body.

You are everything good. All the beauty of the clouds and the earth is within you, and the abyss, when it possesses you, becomes more heavenly than all the heavens. What was I when I stood before you? What am I now that your word is decisive for me? I have one destiny: to sink into you, to disappear into your life, to drown in your blood toward a new existence. I see myself within you—and for the first time I sense what I am, because I am allowed to be within you, like a reflection in a spring. Now as one anticipates death as an inexplicable gift, as the grace of a final submersion, so do I look forward to these days of May.[1] They shall bring a union that could only be yearned for by others—which we can create because you shall only be You. My tenderness and my strength belong to you. I am aglow in your hands; forge me according to your will. It's not paradise we are expecting, but hot, burning life. The Merciful One and her prophet — — —

I know these words can't express what has to be said. Let me say it again and again in different languages that can better capture you. You have to hover near everything I achieve, but no one will recognize you—because you are so far removed from all of them.

DANY

1. On 11 May, Weill wrote his publisher that his new address was Luisenplatz 3, bei Hassfort. Lenya moved there with him, and anticipation of their living together may have inspired Weill's Tristan-like outpourings.

[FIGS. 16 & 17] *By May 1925 Lenya and Weill were living together in Kaiser's tiny, gloomy apartment at Luisenplatz 3, which they nicknamed "Pension Grüneisen" after the most prominent funeral parlor in Berlin. The bed was so narrow, Lenya recalled, that they had to sleep in the same position throughout the night because one couldn't turn around without nudging the other out.*

11 WEILL IN DESSAU TO LENYA IN BERLIN, [28 OCTOBER 1925]

My *Tobby Engel,*

The first rehearsal [of the Violin Concerto] is over now. For the time being it still sounds horrible, and I'm afraid that tomorrow it will also leave much to be desired. Hoesslin is actually quite incompetent.[1] He can neither conduct nor rehearse; it's awful. People laugh and play wrong notes all the time (which he doesn't even notice), and there is not a speck of discipline. I can't get mad at him. I feel sorry for him. Because he takes on too much. He neither is disposed toward new music nor can interpret it; but he nonetheless believes he can make a career of it.

I was stupid to give this somewhat rough, abstract, completely dissonant piece to the Dessauers, who are the most ignorant and philistine of all. It will be unanimously rejected. One has to have already digested a portion of Schoenberg with all good will before one can understand this music.[2] The cynical attitude of the orchestra and the impotence of this conductor make me quite nervous—and I yearn to hear your clear, golden voice, which has the power to make everything seem better. I am ever so lucky that all the bad hours can now melt into the radiance of your presence. This alone makes me able to bear such situations. And if I didn't know I'd be seeing you tomorrow, I would be totally unhappy.—Now I'm going to rehearse with the xylophone player. He's a catastrophe, and it's a sure thing that he'll wreck the second movement.

Holy Linerl, help!

Come only if you feel well. Otherwise I will storm into your arms that evening. To the very last vein,

Your *Didi*

1. *The German premiere of Weill's Concerto for Violin and Winds took place in his home town of Dessau on 29 October 1925, with Stefan Frenkel as soloist. Franz von Hoesslin (1885–1946) was a pupil of Max Reger and Felix Mottl who later became musical director of several prominent opera houses; he directed the Bayreuth Festival for six years. On the envelope of the following letter, Lenya was to record, in the 1950s, that one critic had written: "We saw a pregnant woman in the audience; hope her milk won't turn sour over listening to this music."*

2. *Arnold Schoenberg (1874–1951) was, with Igor Stravinsky, one of the two most prominent and influential composers of the twentieth century. Early on, Weill had hoped to study with Schoenberg in Vienna, but insufficient financial means prevented it. A postcard from Schoenberg to Weill confirming his acceptance as a student has unfortunately been lost. He nominated Weill for election to the Berlin Academy of Arts on several occasions prior to the success of* Die Dreigroschenoper, *which represented a definitive break between their two aesthetic orientations. Thereafter he is said to have confessed that Weill's was the only music in which he could find no quality at all.*

12 WEILL IN BERLIN TO LENYA [WHEREABOUTS UNKNOWN], [1925?]

Diden,

When I tidied up my books I found these three little volumes of sketches to *Zaubernacht*,[1] which I'm giving you as a present today to precede me—because I simply have to send something along for you.—I'll probably be in Friedrichshagen tomorrow at 5:30. If I can get there earlier, I'll call. I still have to speak with Jochi [Felix Joachimson] at noon. Today I really worked. Now I'm going to Vox House.

Your *Didi*

1. *Weill's one-act children's pantomime, with a scenario by Wladimir Boritsch, had been produced at the Theater am Kurfürstendamm in Berlin on 18 November 1922.*

1926

In the surviving correspondence with his family, Weill does not mention Lenya until October *1925, and he links their relationship to a stylistic breakthrough in his music:* "Now it has seized *me again. I'm buried in this new opera* [Royal Palace], *and I leave the house only to take care of the most necessary everyday matters. I must master a type of expression that is still new to me. To my satisfaction, I can now say that—as I had already discovered in* Der neue Orpheus—*I'm gradually forging ahead toward 'my real self'; my music is becoming much more confident, much freer, lighter—and simpler. This is also linked to the fact that I have become noticeably more independent, more confident, happier, and less tense. Of course, living with Lenya again accounts for much of this"* (W–A&EW1, n.d. [1925], #221). *During this period he also reported,* "I'm working half the night. I'm in a constant fever, afraid it just might die out if I let it cool off" (W–A&EW1, 19 Nov. 1925). *In his birthday greeting to his mother in 1925, Weill wrote that he was going with Kaiser to the premiere of* Wozzeck, *by Alban Berg:* "Even the dress rehearsal caused a scandal. In three months I will be ready for one too" (W– A&EW1, 14 Dec. 1925).

On 28 January 1926 Lenya and Weill were married in Charlottenburg in a civil ceremony with three witnesses. Lenya recalled, "The only reason we got married was because of the neighbors: 'She's not married!' So I said, 'Come on, Kurt, let's get married. What the hell. You know, what difference does it make?' And when the registrar asked Weill if he would 'love, honor, and obey,' Kurt put his hands on his sides and said, 'Jawohl!' We laughed about it many times afterward. That was his only sign of militarism, that day when we got married" (Newman, p. 11). That month Weill also completed his one-act ballet-opera Royal Palace and

[FIG. 18]

then awaited the premiere of Der Protagonist (the published score of which he dedicated to Lenya) on 27 March 1926 in Dresden. Without false modesty, Weill reported to his publisher: "The success of Der Protagonist was not one bit less than that of Wozzeck; critical response was just as sensational; and everywhere modern operas are discussed, both works are mentioned in the same breath. Everyone who was there can confirm that there has never been such a successful first opera by a twenty-five-year-old" (W–UE, 29 April 1926). He admitted to his parents how exciting it was "to have THE big operatic success of the season" and "to become a world celebrity overnight." The letter ends, for the first time, with "Best regards from Lenya" (W– A&EW1, 1 April 1926). A week later, he signed both their names to his letter; she added her first coda to one of his letters on 26 June. But she later recalled, "The family was violently against me. My God! They didn't talk to me until they saw me for the first time on stage.

[FIG. 19]

Later on I became their favorite daughter-in-law" (int. L3).

On alternate days Lenya was playing Fanny in George Bernard Shaw's Blanco Posnets Erweckung [The Shewing-up of Blanco Posnet]. Weill wrote his parents: "She really looks sassy on stage, wears an old skirt, a green blouse, a yellow vest, a red scarf, and torn stockings, and already at her first entrance she receives loud bursts of laughter. . . . I'm very glad she's now found such a rewarding role after all. Next season she'll be having a premiere of her own" (W–A&EW1, 24 April 1926). After the play closed in June, they went to Zurich, then vacationed in Milan, Genoa, Alassio, and Cannes.

13 WEILL IN BERLIN TO LENYA IN GRÜNHEIDE[?], [26 MAY 1926]

Friday

Dearest *Spätzlein,*

Before I start to write, let me give you a quick but most affectionate greeting. The court proceedings, which finally began after a two-hour wait, were very funny. They had to do with Mrs. Berger's boarder, who broke into her room at night and stole money.[1] Naturally he accused me. The prosecutor asked me if by any chance I was the well-known K.W. That did it. He got six months, but with probation.

Last night I was at home. Strangely, when you're away, I have an insurmountable urge for solitude. I think that if you had not taken pity on me, I would be the perfect hypochondriac by now.

Yesterday Caña called twice and invited me for dinner on Saturday night.[2] I'm not sure yet whether I'll go. Last night I went bicycling in Grunewald [a forested suburb of Berlin] from six to seven o'clock. But now the front wheel is gone too. Today Bronsgeest got hold of me and invited me to dinner.[3] It was great fun. Tonight I'm going to the opera.

What do you think about this marvelous weather? I'm so happy for you. Work is going brilliantly again and without headaches. So don't worry about me. Relax and enjoy yourself.

> Take care.
> And keep loving
> your *Didi.*

REGARDS TO ALL.

1. Mrs. Berger was the landlady at Weill's previous rooming house on Winterfeldstraße.
2. Caña (whose full name is unknown) was one of the witnesses at the Weills' marriage.
3. Cornelius Bronsgeest (1878–1957) was a bass baritone at the City Opera in Berlin.

14 WEILL IN BERLIN TO LENYA IN GRÜNHEIDE, [19 JULY 1926]

My *Bubili,*

This morning I got off at Friedrichstraße and finished my work on the issue [of the radio magazine *Der deutsche Rundfunk*] right in the copy editor's office. On the way back I spent half an hour with Vogel, who has had an operation on his nose.[1] I'm going to meet him in the café on Wednesday at three o'clock. And now, the Weißmann mess.[2] After his devastating judgment of Schoenberg, his remarks about me are just malicious enough so as not to endanger my musical reputation. I'm quite pleased about it. I was tickled to death by Kaempfer's letter.[3] Arrau called; I've been invited to a musical "salon" at Mrs. von Nostitz's tomorrow night.[4] This, too, will be an experience.

I'm still not quite ready to start working. I haven't gained enough distance from things yet. But I just cleaned up my desk, and now I'm going to the post office. I've been thinking about why many of my relationships are so strained, and I realize that I have to become much more reserved and reticent. Since I don't take part in all the lying that goes on, it's probably better to remain outwardly passive than always to do what seems appropriate. Amid all that, do you understand how beautiful it is that you exist? So Hallelujah—in spite of everything! Farewell, my sparrow.

[*Komm wieder, wenn alles vergessen ist, Komm wieder, wenn du willst . . .*]

[Come back when all has been forgotten; come back, if you wish . . .]

Behave yourself! Take care of your little fingers! Take a nap at noon! Say hello to everybody!

K – i – s – s – e – s × 100,000

Completely yours, Didi.

1. The Russian-born composer Vladimir Vogel (1896–1984) had been a classmate of Weill's in Busoni's master class, 1921–24.

2. Adolf Weißmann (1873–1929) was the music critic for the BZ [Berliner Zeitung] am Mittag *and wrote for several music periodicals. He reviewed Weill's Violin Concerto negatively in the August 1926 issue of* Die Musik.

3. Walther Kaempfer (1900–1991) was a close friend of Weill in Berlin. After studies with Arthur Schnabel and Carl Friedberg and a short career as a concert pianist, he became an organist, holding positions in Paderborn, Essen, and Berlin.

4. Helene von Nostitz, a member of the Hindenburg family, was president of the Berlin chapter of PEN, the international literary society then headed by John Galsworthy. She was married to the prominent diplomat Alfred von Nostitz-Wallwitz.

15   WEILL IN BERLIN TO LENYA C/O DR. NATHAN WEILL IN KLEIN STEINBERG B/BEUCHA [NEAR LEIPZIG], [JULY 1926?]

My *Pummilein,*

Just one week ago we sat on the Piazza Signori in Verona and slowly discovered how beautiful it was there. As I think back now, I begin to feel a powerful yearning for you—so no more reminiscing! Anyway, I'll be seeing you the day after tomorrow. This very same thing has happened to me before: when I feel this longing for you, I think most of all of the sound of your voice, which I love like a very force of nature, like an element. For me all of you is contained within this sound; everything else is only a part of you; and when I envelop myself in your voice, then you are with me in every way. I know every nuance, every vibration of your voice, and I can hear exactly what you would say if you were with me right now—and how you would say it. But suddenly this sound is again entirely alien and new to me, and then it is the greatest joy to realize how affectionately this voice caresses me—it's almost like those first weeks, when I considered just thinking about you to be presumptuous. The wonderful thing is that I still have that same reverence toward you as I did in the very first hour, which makes it seem almost miraculous that you've come to me and all has turned out so beautifully. And now—just as it was on that first day—I'm no longer sad that somewhere else your voice resounds, and I'm not close by.

And now, a general report: Monday evening Jochi was here (alone) and later Kastner also came.[1] We sat on the balcony until 1:30 A.M. and gossiped. The day before I had gone on a long bike ride to Pichelsberg. The evening at Mrs. von Nostitz's was funny. Two entire floors at the Lützowplatz, with furniture fit for a castle, very beautiful antiques, valets, and everything that goes with that. Amid all of it, this middle-aged lady, the wife of a diplomat, dabbling in aesthetics and literature, a board member of the PEN club, acquainted with every conceivable international literary or political celebrity. Her collection of luminaries lacked young musicians, and so I had to fill that void. Besides Arrau and myself, there were the former (imperial) intendant of the Wiesbaden opera and two young literati (one a hysterical Jew, the other a monocled Aryan), as well as Liszt's very last lady student, who played the piano in a fantastically antediluvian style. Later on they talked about "Goethe's breakthrough" or "Stravinsky's body temperature" and "the mysterious power of Catholicism." I acted the worldly-wise raconteur, neither spilling my glass of lemonade nor burning anything with my cigarette; instead, approximately every half hour I dropped a well-pointed witticism. Whereupon Her Graciousness expressed her hope that I might come to see her again next fall. With a correct bow I bid my adieus. The valet got a one-mark tip. Amid a lively discussion about the totally unexpected results of the latest tennis matches (a real surprise for me, that's for sure!), we stepped out into the street. You see—I have become quite a man of the world.

At Jochi's it was really nice. He's a talented fellow and a decent person. Ihering knows about everything through Jarnach and is beside himself.[2] As for me, I've shoved that entire mess away from me, as of today. To me a thing like this is like an abscess that has to break; from then on, it lies behind me. At the same time, the ice is broken for my work. I hope that I can now glide back into it, and after I do, all I can say is "you poor suckers."

Frenkel has shown me about sixty write-ups from Zurich, which together represent a decisive critical success [for the Violin Concerto].[3] He's going to perform it again on 11 October, at a right-wing music festival in Halle. Hertzka is "stewing."[4] He can —— [kiss my ass], but twice!!!!

My Dideldum—may all the angels be with you!

I am terribly in love with you. And very happy that I'll be seeing you in a couple of days.

Be good and nice (to me).

The head of every note in *DER PROTAGONIST* is a *B-u-s-s-i* [little kiss] for you.

    Didi

I'll write you one more time.

1. *The prominent music critic Rudolf Kastner, who wrote regularly for the* Berliner Morgenpost, *had published one of the first biographical sketches of Weill: "Kurt Weill: Eine Skizze," Anbruch 7 (October 1925): 453–56.*

2. *The dramaturg Herbert Ihering (1888–1977) held positions at the Volksbühne in Vienna (1914–18) and the Deutsches Theater in Berlin, among others. The German composer Philipp Jarnach (1892–1982) was an ardent disciple of Ferruccio Busoni, whose opera* Doktor Faust *he completed upon the older composer's death. On Busoni's recommendation, Weill had studied counterpoint with Jarnach to supplement the instruction in Busoni's master class.*

Weill wrote his parents: "My friend Jarnach used my four weeks' absence to let loose a storm of intrigues against me.

Since they can't get me on artistic grounds, they now depict me as an unprincipled racketeer and try to influence all decisive professional circles accordingly. Every day I hear new gossip-mongering against me, and all of it goes back to that one source. It would be senseless to do anything about it. One has to let them yap until they're tired of yapping" (W–A&EW1, 22 July 1926).

3. *The Polish-born violinist Stefan Frenkel (1902–79) had studied with Adolf Busch and Carl Flesch and served as concertmaster of the radio orchestra in Königsberg and Berlin. Weill's concerto remained in Frenkel's repertoire throughout his solo career. In 1929 he arranged seven songs from Die Dreigroschenoper as virtuoso showpieces for violin and piano. When he emigrated to New York, the Metropolitan Opera engaged him as concertmaster.*

4. *Dr. Emil Hertzka (1869–1932) was the director of Universal Edition, Weill's publisher in Vienna. At the turn of the century Hertzka had taken over the faltering publishing house and negotiated contracts with Mahler, Schoenberg, and Schreker. Later he added Bartók, Berg, Webern, Milhaud, Janáček, Křenek, and Weill, making UE the foremost publisher of contemporary music.*

16 WEILL IN BERLIN TO LENYA IN GRÜNHEIDE,[1] 23 JULY 1926

Written in Saxonian dialect.

Dear Linerl,

On the way home I saw that I forgot to give you money, pig that I am. Still, you don't have to write my mommy again right away, you ol' tattletale.

Bye-bye,

Respectfully,

KNUT GUSTAVSON

1. *The envelope is addressed to "Frau Lotte Lenja-Weill, Notenquetschergattin"; "wife of the note-squeezer" alludes to a witty book of verse about a so-called child prodigy who squeezes the notes out of the keys when he practices (Alexander Moszkowski, Anton Notenquetscher [Berlin, 1906]).*

[FIGS. 20 & 21]

1927

On 2 March, Weill's twenty-seventh birthday, Erich Kleiber conducted the premieres of Der neue Orpheus *and* Royal Palace, *both with texts by Iwan Goll, at the Berlin State Opera. The first mention of Bertolt Brecht in any of Weill's surviving correspondence occurs on 24 March 1927. In his role as chief critic for* Der deutsche Rundfunk *Weill had favorably reviewed a production of Brecht's* Mann ist Mann *on 18 March.*

Shortly thereafter the city of Essen commissioned Weill to write music for an "epic piece" that would portray the industrial complex of the Ruhr district in words, music, stage action, and film, and Baden-Baden asked him for a one-act opera for the Festival of Modern Music. He was just finishing a two-act comic opera, Na und?, *with a libretto by his friend and erstwhile pupil Felix Joachimson. Universal Edition declined to publish it; the manuscript subsequently disappeared, and thus it was the only completed stage work that remained unperformed during Weill's lifetime. On 7 April Weill reported that "Kaiser is writing a new libretto for me, intended as a companion piece for* Der Protagonist" [Der Zar läßt sich photographieren] (W–AW, 7 April 1927). *In May Weill decided to link Brecht's Mahagonny poems into a "Songspiel" for Baden-Baden, and for the first time, Lenya became involved in the production of a Weill work, the sole non–operatically trained singer in a cast of six. Lenya recalled the first orchestra rehearsal: "The other five singers stood there with their partiturs and sang. Irene Eden told me to look at the score. I said, 'It doesn't mean much to me to look. I don't read music.' But I was the only one who didn't make a mistake" (int. L1).*

With Weill composing seven dramatic works (and five more incidental scores for the stage) within a three-year period, the newlywed Lenya—as she was to tell friends and interviewers in later years—frequently found herself left entirely to her own devices for weeks on end, with Weill showing up irregularly at meal times. "What's the matter? I hardly ever see you. Don't you love me anymore?" Totally surprised by her question, he answered incredulously: "But darling, you come right after my music!" (int. L5).

Occasionally Lenya landed jobs of her own in suburban theaters. Weill told his parents that she substituted as "Kukuli" on Sundays [perhaps in the obscure play Der Wundervogel*]. And as understudy to Grete Jacobsen as Juliet at the Wallnertheater, near Alexanderplatz, Lenya played the Shakespearean role, opposite Ernst Deutsch, more than sixty times. Many evenings Kurt delivered her to the stage door, left a bottle of May wine for her to share, and later returned to escort her home. But in his unpublished biography of Weill, Joachimson recalls one night when he and Weill attended the Berlin State Opera together:*

We went out for a smoke and he lit his pipe. I asked how Lenya was. "She's fine." He drew on his pipe. "Why don't we pick her up after the theater?" I asked. He shook his head. "Why not?" "She likes to go home by herself. Sometimes she goes out with the others for a drink. . . . It isn't easy to be married to me." "It isn't easy to be married, period," I said. "It's hard on Lenya." "What is?" "Well—I sit in my study all day and work. And I'm perfectly happy. I don't need anybody and I don't miss anybody." "Lenya is a professional herself. She understands that," I said. "Of course she does. But a woman . . . ," he didn't finish. The word remained suspended in the air. "Is she unhappy?" I asked. Again a pause. "No." He said, "I wouldn't blame her." "Blame her for what?" He didn't answer that but looked at me. There was a lot of hurt in his eyes. And then he said, "There is no one like Lenya" (mem. FJ, pp. 82–84)

Weill's former student and lifelong friend Maurice Abravanel recalled that he once "came right out and told her that she really ought not to be cheating on Kurt so much. Lenya replied matter-of-factly, 'But I don't cheat on Kurt. He knows exactly what's going on' " (int. MA1).

17 WEILL IN BERLIN TO LENYA IN GRÜNHEIDE, [24 MARCH 1927]

Dear *Tütchen*,

I'm in a hurry, but I just wanted to ask you to translate the enclosed review, since I don't know English. I'm glad that you are well and relaxing in the sun. Last night I worked here until one o'clock, while outside the incessant demonstrations paraded by.[1] That was something to warm my revolutionary heart. Today again I've been sitting at my desk since eight this morning. Tomorrow afternoon I have to go to Jochi's once more, because we still aren't finished. Tomorrow night there's a meeting at the radio station. The poor orchestral score [of *Na und?*]! I got an enthusiastic letter from Schulz-Dornburg.[2] Baden-Baden is pressing me about the one-act opera.[3] Reucker had Ehrhardt let me know that he wants to have the first option on *Na und?*[4] Now I have to go see B [Bertolt Brecht].[5] *Addio!* Be loved, *Schwämmi*!

from your *Didi*

1. *In January 1926 the Socialist/Communist coalition had proposed confiscation of all aristocratic properties to benefit the unemployed, disabled veterans, and victims of inflation. Before taking effect, the law was to be ratified by plebiscite. For two weeks in March 1927 supporters organized mass demonstrations to marshal support for the measure.*

2. *Rudolf Schulz-Dornburg, the music director of the municipal theater in Essen, had approached Weill to write music for the "Ruhrepos." See letter 20.*

3. *Weill wrote his publisher that he was considering scenes from* King Lear *and* Antigone *as possible sources.*

4. *Dr. Alfred Reucker (1868–1958) had served as intendant of the Zurich State Opera from 1902 to 1922, during which time Lenya was employed there. In 1927 he headed the Dresden State Opera, where he remained until 1933. Dresden had premiered* Der Protagonist, *as well as Busoni's* Doktor Faust.

Otto Ehrhardt (1888–1963) was a prominent stage director in Dresden.

5. *Lenya recalled that "it was Weill who first had gone to see Brecht, early in 1927. . . . He had read poems by Brecht that had stirred him deeply, and which said in words what he was increasingly drawn to say in music" (Lenya 1964, p. vi).*

18   WEILL IN NUREMBERG TO LENYA IN BERLIN, 4 MAY 1927

Postcard: etching identified as "König Ludwigsbahn, Nürnberg-Fürth (1835)"; Weill's writing on the picture side reads: "Be loved a thousand times by your Buster."

Tütchen,

I just arrived, having slept and traveled well. The city shimmers rosily as I look through the window of the railroad station. To judge from the people and the newspapers, this does <u>not</u> seem symbolic to me.[1]

1. *Weill was in Nuremberg, later a center of Nazi party activity, to attend a performance of* Der Protagonist. *In a postcard to his parents, he had written of Nuremberg's acceptance of the opera but warned, "Don't write anything to our relatives yet, because I have to be careful on account of Bavarian anti-Semitism" (W–A&EW1, 20 Dec. 1926).*

19   WEILL IN NUREMBERG TO LENYA IN BERLIN, [6? MAY 1927]

Letterhead: Grand Hotel Nürnberg

My *Didilein,*

I just had lunch with Wetzelsberger.[1] Now I'm terribly tired, but I still want to drop you a line before I get a little sleep. The rehearsal was gratifying. The opera has been rehearsed brilliantly, and the performance often comes close to the Dresden one. The Protagonist [Fritz Perron] is good, the Sister [Margarethe Ziegler] bad. Wetzelsberger is excellent and a charming fellow. He's from Salzburg, and thus has all the good and none of the bad characteristics of the Viennese.—Once again the opera has an extraordinary impact. But they're expecting a scandal. Well, so be it. I haven't seen the clan [*die Mischpoche*] yet. I hope to arrive in Berlin Friday at 7:49, otherwise at 9:30. I'm looking forward to that. I'll get the money. Tomorrow I have another in-depth rehearsal. *Addio Addio Addio.*

Kisses for all your little limbs.

Your *Frosch*

1. *Bertil Wetzelsberger (1892–1967), conductor.*

Berlin, Friday

My *Tütilein*,

At last I have time to write to you at length. In Essen that was out of the question. But now I can give you a blow-by-blow account, so you'll have some idea of what I've been up to. The flight was magnificent. One actually feels amazingly safe, and much less nervous than on a train. The most beautiful moment is when the airplane very slowly lifts itself into the air. On Monday afternoon we [Brecht and Weill] had a preliminary talk [with the Essen officials], and in the evening when we walked every which way through the factories, some overwhelming acoustic impressions suddenly gave me an entirely new concept of sound for the play. Tuesday we drove ten hours through the entire Ruhr region up to the Rhine. Koch knows the territory very intimately and could comment on everything.[1] Coming out of the poisonous fumes of the Ruhr valley to the Rhine we immediately thought: Never go back into the poisonous gases! And we realized how beautiful it would be to recreate the colorful liveliness of this river instead of the gloomy gray factories that lie beyond it. The next day by noon we again emerged from the mines into daylight; then it became clear—the terrible horror down there, the boundless injustice that human beings have to endure, performing intolerably arduous labor seven hundred meters underground in complete darkness, in thick, smoldering air, just so that Krupp can add another 5 million to their 200 million a year—this needs to be said, and in such a way, indeed, that no one will ever forget it. (But it will have to come as a surprise, otherwise they'll shut our mouths!) We spent four hours in the mines, six to seven hundred meters deep; we walked for two hours, then climbed on all fours through two levels, then down ladders a hundred and fifty meters into the depth—and afterward went pitch-black into the bathtub. All my bones still hurt today. Thursday we took another plane ride over the Ruhr region, then we spent hours in the Krupp steelworks. This was quite refreshing and soothing after those terrible impressions. In between we went to city hall, to Bochum and Duisburg, to museums and archives. We have drafted a very favorable contract; let's hope it will happen. We get paid 5,000–7,000 marks (each), but the play will belong to us. The title probably will be "REP" (Ruhrepos, Essen Documentarium). They have paid decently for expenses; I still have 30 marks left over.[2]

Today Brecht and I returned by train in a sleeping car; in the morning I stopped by the editorial office [of *Der deutsche Rundfunk*]; then I saw "Guiloclo" [one of Weill's students]—and now I'm writing to my little sweetheart. You have arranged everything so nicely for me, but nothing can take the place of you yourself—or even just a part of you. I am so glad you're having nice weather; you will surely get your strength back. You also are a real goodie-goodie [*Bravi*], because you write me so diligently. For that there will be a great reward. But, little sparrow, I'm not coming to Leipzig. As of tomorrow I will again be working like a slave on the Kaiser opera [*Der Zar läßt sich photographieren*]. If that isn't ready in two to three months, I will have slipped up completely. The latest possible performance date in Essen is at the beginning of March! I'm not going to Grünheide.

Addio, my *Seelchen*. I'm looking forward to Tuesday. Regards to everybody who is good to you. And many kisses on your little *B...lein*.

Your Kurti

[*Auf dem Monde sind fünfzehn Sterne, die lieben sisch u. misch, die lieben sisch u. misch*]

[On the moon there are fifteen stars, which love themselves and me, which love themselves and me]

Will you take care of informing the Poniatowskis, without causing a fight, that I'm not coming?[3] Then I'll write just a postcard: that it's impossible, as you already know; moreover, crowded trains, and so on.

1. *Karl Koch was a photographer who married the silhouette artist and filmmaker Lotte Reiniger (1899–1980). According to Weill's correspondence with Universal Edition, he filmed the original stage production of* Die Dreigroschenoper *in Berlin. Brecht introduced him to Jean Renoir, with whom Koch later collaborated.*

2. *The* Ruhrepos *(Ruhr epic) project collapsed before Weill set any of Brecht's song texts to music.*

3. *The Polish general Prince Joseph Poniatowski (1762–1813) was named maréchal de France by Napoleon; Weill's parents lived on the street named for him, at Poniatowskistraße 20. Sometimes Weill substituted an address for the surname of people he knew well: thus his brother Nathan, who lived on Täubchenstraße, became "die Täubchenstraße."*

[FIG. 22]

The Mahagonny Songspiel *premiered on 17 July in Baden-Baden; set in a boxing ring, it opened with a gunshot and ended with the actors waving crudely designed placards. Lenya's was inscribed "For Weill." The spectators jumped to their feet and demonstrations started. Anticipating a scandal, Brecht had distributed whistles to the actors, who defiantly blew them at the protesters. The play was the hit of the festival, which had also included Berg's "Lyric Suite."*

21 WEILL IN BERLIN TO LENYA IN PREROW, [1? AUGUST 1927]

Berlin, Monday

My *Tüti*,

Only now can I tell you properly how happy I was about your letter—that it's so beautiful there, that you'll get a good rest there, and that you love me.[1] If the weather stays like this and you relax, when I get there next week you'll be a brown, round, fat little dumpling.

It was wonderful in Grünheide. I swam, lounged around, read, worked very little, and thought much about how I can make life beautiful for my beloved little spirit. That's at least a reason for being, isn't it?

This morning I drove into town, had a hell of a lot to do in the editorial office; Mami [Margarethe Kaiser] was here for lunch, and this evening I'll drive out [to Grünheide] with her again—unfortunately only until Wednesday, because of my mother's visit. Papi [Georg Kaiser] said that *Mahagonny* would be brilliant for the Haller-Revue.[2]

He immediately telephoned Wurm[?], whom I visited just now. It's underway, but I doubt very much it'll work out.

Papi now has a marvelously bold and striking title for the opera: "Der Zar läßt sich . . . ."[3] I think it's great, so I immediately wrote to Vienna [Universal Edition]. The enclosed letter came from Brecht just now. So in any case, next Tuesday I'll come to see you (because I can't stand it any longer), then we'll see whether I can go there again at the end of the month. Is that all right?

You don't need to be jealous of [Helene] Weigel. Basically Mami can't stand her. Papi insists that it's absolutely certain that Mami and Anselm [Kaiser] will come along, but you know how that goes.

I've talked it out with Mrs. Hassfort [their landlady]. I really buttered her up. She's stupid, but very useful. Mami also says that we won't find another place like this.

May God keep you, my sweet. Be good, so you stay healthy, because you are the great joy of my life. Many thousand *Bussi* on your little bosom [*Busi*].

Your *Frosch*

1. *Emil Hertzka, the director of Universal Edition, had been so captivated by Lenya's performance that he sent her a check enabling her to take a holiday in Prerow, a quiet resort on the Baltic coast.*

2. *Hermann Haller (1871–1943) was the producer of the most lavish musical revues in Berlin.*

3. *"Der Zar läßt sich . . . ." brings to mind the infamous quotation from Goethe's* Götz von Berlichingen, *"Sag deinem Hauptmann: Vor Ihro Kaiserliche Majestät hab' ich, wie immer, schuldigen Respekt. Er aber, sag's ihm, er kann mich im Arsch lecken" (As always, I have due respect for His Imperial Majesty. But as for your commanding officer, tell him he can kiss my ass). The quotation was long considered too offensive to be cited in full, so all that was said was "er kann mich. . . ." "Der Zar läßt sich . . . ." implies the same thing: the czar permits his ass to be kissed. Just before the premiere, Weill wrote Universal Edition again, to ask if there was still time to change the title back to* Der Zar läßt sich photographieren, *as both he and Kaiser had been persuaded that the abbreviated title might be going too far.*

22 WEILL IN BERLIN TO LENYA IN PREROW, 6 AUGUST 1927
Postcard

My *Tütchen,*

A few quick lines before I go to the editorial office. Everything is OK with the Hassforts. When I came from the railroad station, she was demure and friendly as a dove and he, of course, didn't come to see me in the evening. All that because of ten marks. I think that's cheap.—I've called [Karl Heinz] Martin. He was terribly nice, and we'll be seeing each other at the beginning of next week. My father called on his way to Leipzig. My mother is passing through on Wednesday, and they've asked me if she can stay overnight. I said you were in Grünheide and would leave for the Baltic Sea at the beginning of the week to pitch your tent.—At the Kochs' it was exceptionally nice this time. We had a lively conversation until three o'clock. Küpper is very intelligent.[1] He said—to Koch's astonishment—that it was the music of *Mahagonny* that made the strongest impression by far on him. In haste, a thousand kisses, have beautiful weather, regards to all who are good to you.

Your *Frosch*

1. *Hanns Küpper (b. 1912) became a collaborator and friend of both set designer Caspar Neher and Brecht.*

Postcard

Liebchen, I just got your two letters. At least that's something, though a very poor substitute for yourself. I've wired you again just now to confirm that I don't expect my mother until Sunday, since Saturday I have a meeting about a movie; after that you won't be alone for long. If at all possible, I'd like to come as soon as Monday. I can leave at 2:00 and will arrive in Prerow at 8:57 in the evening (20:57), hopefully with Mami and Anselm. I hope I'll make it. Then I could be with you one whole night earlier . . . ! So if you don't hear anything further from me, expect me Monday evening.— Martin is coming to see me today; I have to play *Der Protagonist* for him. He wants to bring *Mahagonny* into a revue that Saltenburg is presenting at Christmas time.[1] In addition, Saltenburg might also want an opera (operetta) for performances in a straight run. I'm quite undecided whether I should offer *Na und?* for that. In any case, you see that I'm extremely busy again and so I can't be away for long. There's going to be a lot of trouble with the radio this time. But I'm so full of crazy anticipatory joy that I can't sleep anymore at night. 100,000 little kisses on your *b...* from the *Bubü.*

1. *Heinz Saltenburg produced revues and operettas in Berlin; he had produced Franz Lehár's* Paganini *in 1926 with Richard Tauber and Vera Schwarz.*

Berlin, Thursday

My beloved *Negerkindl,*

Yesterday I got two letters from you: in the morning I got the one forwarded to Grünheide, and the other one I found here in the afternoon. I'm ever so happy that you are already beginning to relax, because I was always a little afraid that you wouldn't take advantage of things there without me. But you are just my sensible little *Diderle.* I have such tremendous longing for you that I wish I could drop everything and leave on the spot to come to you; I can't possibly imagine how I'm supposed to stand this until Tuesday. All my days now consist only of the single-minded joy of looking forward to the moment when I can be with you again.

By the way, you don't have to feel too sorry for me. After those few days in Grünheide I now feel very frisky, and I don't look quite as bad anymore.[1] I rather think that it won't take me long to recuperate entirely. It seems certain that Mami and Anselm are coming along. Mami really is a dear, and I like being with her just because she's so fond of you. The children are now all at a good age—nice, intelligent, and decent. Anselm is slender and attractive. Last night I was at the Wurms' to play *Mahagonny* for them. Salter and Papi were there.[2] Everyone was simply knocked out. I had to play it three times. They now want to put a lot of pressure on Haller, and Salter will try to get the "Alabama Song" away from U.E. [Universal Edition] for America, because he thinks he can do terrific business with it over there. It was quite nice. Only that wife of his . . . ! By the way, they are insanely jealous because we are always in Grünheide.

My mother is here today. She sits on the balcony and reads while I work. This time she is very quiet and pleasant. *Tüti*, she says you should have sour cream or buttermilk for breakfast. You can probably get that there. I will see Martin at six o'clock today. Dear, there is a wonderful American movie, *Die Rivalen* (I saw it with Mami).[3] I liked it because of its pacifist stance and its artistic realization. Farewell, my sweet life. Even the longing for you is wonderful. I will come quickly.

Your

Froschi

1. Throughout his life Weill suffered from psoriasis and was especially prone to outbreaks during periods of stress and exhaustion.

2. Hans J. Salter (1896–1994), a Viennese-born composer-conductor, had studied with Felix Weingartner and Alban Berg. He joined UFA, Germany's foremost motion picture studio, as composer-conductor in 1929. In 1937 he left Germany for Hollywood, where he scored such successful motion pictures as Scarlet Street *(1945) and* Beau Geste *(1960).*

3. The film Weill refers to was What Price Glory? *(1926), starring Victor MacLaglen and Edmund Lowe and directed by Raoul Walsh. The original play, by Laurence Stallings and Maxwell Anderson, had been produced in Berlin with Fritz Kortner and Hans Albers in the leading roles. The film was first shown in Berlin in August 1927.*

1928–1929

No letters between Weill and Lenya survive from the two years of most intense collaboration between Weill and Brecht. Enjoying their independent and shared successes, Weill and Lenya [FIGS. 23 & 24] *were extremely busy professionally and seldom separated for more than a few days at a time. They left Berlin only to attend performances in the provinces or to take working vacations on the French Riviera with the "Brecht collective." Lenya's memoirs of these years, especially on the genesis of* Die Dreigroschenoper *and* Aufstieg und Fall der Stadt Mahagonny, *were published in the fifties and have often been reprinted; her personal accounts now supplement what has become the best documented period of their careers. An unpublished draft of "Lotte Lenya Remembers* Mahagonny" *conveys some of the excitement of these years:*

We returned to Berlin [from Baden-Baden], and Kurt and Brecht set to work transforming their *Songspiel* into a complete opera. Often now I went along with Kurt to [FIG. 25] Brecht's studio in the Spichernstraße. There was always a phase of their work in which they invited us all to contribute our ideas—in that first duet between Jim and Jenny there are two or three lines that were my own contribution. Out of these prolonged, fantastic, and often hilarious discussions, Brecht and Kurt would draw what suited them. Speaking of these occasions with Elisabeth Hauptmann, Brecht's secretary, we agreed, now that all this is history and solemn critical essays and books pour out in increasing volume, who would know how much fun went into all this? Into the picture of *Mahagonny* went everything we had read or heard about the America of the 1920s—gangster films, newspaper accounts of the Sacco-Vanzetti trial, the Florida boom, the doings of such celebrities as Aimee Semple McPherson, Jimmy Walker, Al Capone, Peaches Browning, Ponzi. . . . Josephine Baker came to Berlin and Kurt and I did see her. Certainly at that time we were much too poor to frequent expensive cabarets. Kurt and Caspar Neher had immediately become great [FIG. 26] friends and used to go for an hour or two to the "Femina," a huge dance hall, and watch the beautiful taxi dancers and their customers, and listen to what was probably the best dance orchestra in Berlin. This orchestra undoubtedly played many American songs, along with the latest hits of Spoliansky and Holländer. In the late twenties a young American theater composer was brought to our house at his own request ... he was George Gershwin, and later we were to know him well in New York, but at that time Gershwin's name was completely unknown to us. The writing of *Mahagonny* was interrupted in the late spring and summer of 1928 by a rush job for producer Ernst Aufricht—*Die Dreigroschenoper*. (Mem. L2)

What began as a lark to be done "with the left hand," as a diversion from work on the full-length Mahagonny, *and was almost sure to be a flop turned out to be the greatest German theatrical success of the era. Over the protests of the producer, Weill and Brecht had written secondary roles for their wives; Helene Weigel's role as a brothel madam was cut when she was hospitalized with appendicitis, but Lenya's as Jenny remained, although her one solo number, the "Solomon Song," was cut at the dress rehearsal. And even though her name was inadvertently omitted from the program, the next morning Berlin's most powerful drama critic singled her out: "She was good—very, very good." Lenya would no longer have to understudy roles in provincial theaters. As Weill wrote to his former student Maurice Abravanel, "Lenya has become a famous actress and at the moment plays big roles at the State Theater one after the other" (W–MA, n.d. [Dec. 1928]). She appeared in* Oedipus *under Leopold Jessner at the State Theater and in Georg Büchner's* Dantons Tod *and Frank Wedekind's* Frühlings Erwachen *with Peter Lorre at the Volksbühne. In 1929 she was cast in Marie Luise Fleißer's* Pioniere in Ingolstadt. *She returned on occasion to the Theater am Schiffbauerdamm to play both Jenny and Lucy and recorded songs from* Die Dreigroschenoper *and* Mahagonny. *When Rosa Valetti did not show up at the recording session for the former, Lenya sang the part of Mrs. Peachum too, disguising her voice by singing an octave lower than written.*

[FIG. 27]

[FIG. 28]

After Threepenny *fever had swept through Germany, Weill no longer had to write weekly articles for the radio journal or accept theory pupils. The Weills bought an automobile (a small "Fiat-Wagen") and moved to a larger apartment on the Bayernallee in Charlottenburg. Furthermore,* Der Zar läßt sich photographieren *had been taken up by dozens of opera houses after its premiere in Leipzig in February 1928. By the end of 1929, the score of* Aufstieg und Fall der Stadt Mahagonny *was awaiting its March 1930 premiere, again in Leipzig, and somehow Weill also had managed to compose the* Berliner Requiem, Der Lindberghflug, Kleine Dreigroschenmusik, *as well as songs for Elisabeth Hauptmann and Brecht's ill-fated Salvation Army comedy* Happy End *and incidental music for a half dozen other stage productions. All was not well, though. The aftershocks of "Black Friday" on Wall Street in October 1929 rumbled through the German economy. As two and a half million people joined the unemployed roster, Heinrich Brüning succeeded Gustav Stresemann as chancellor, while the National Socialists occupied 107 seats in the Reichstag.*

1930

In Lenya: A Life, *Donald Spoto writes: "In January 1930, Lenya wrote to Kurt from St. Moritz, Switzerland, where she was on a holiday with a friend. She was learning a new game, she reported; she was gambling at cards, which henceforth became a lifelong pastime. . . . Kurt replied that on Sunday, 12 January, Lenya's new recordings were heard on Berlin Radio— songs from* The Threepenny Opera, *as well as 'Bilbao' and 'Surabaya Johnny' and 'Alabama Song,' which she had made for the Electrola and Orchestrola companies under Theo Mackeben's baton" (p. 94). There is no trace of these letters in any of the inventories of the Weill-Lenya correspondence; if they once existed, they have disappeared.*

25   WEILL IN BERLIN TO LENYA IN ST. MORITZ, SWITZERLAND, 27 JANUARY 1930

Berlin, 27 January 1930

Dear *Tütilein*,

It was really a fine surprise when you called from St. Moritz today, and I could hear you as if you were here. I'm very happy that you have found the right place and you feel well. Let's hope that soon you will also have better weather. Only be careful that you don't catch cold when you are hot from running. And don't venture out into deserted territory!

There is little to say about me. The first two days without you were a bit strange. But yesterday I was on the go the whole day: at noon at [Weill's brother] Hans's for lunch, then to the theater, where I spoke with [Igor] Stravinsky, then to the café with [Ernst Josef] Aufricht [the producer of *Die Dreigroschenoper*], and in the evening to a radio concert [of *Le baiser de la fée*], which Stravinsky conducted. He was really enthusiastic about *Die Dreigroschenoper* and said that in foreign countries it is the best-known and most talked-about contemporary German work of art. It's seen as a play that could have originated only on German soil, but just the same an entirely new mixture of Shakespeare and Dickens. The music, he said, is perfect. I'm supposed to send him all recordings and music immediately, because he wants the play to be with him always.

The little Neher-*Schnucki* carried on tremendously, because she was just about to leave for Paris, where [Hans?] Gutmann has arranged a cozy nest for her.[1] Apparently she's had a big success with the November Group.[2] But that was no big deal, because after two hours of stupid atonal music (according to [Hans] Curjel's report) people simply went wild when the songs came on. By the way, they played *Die Dreigroschenoper* in Café Wien the other day, and everybody hummed along.

Aufricht didn't make a good impression on me. He's still preoccupied by "who's with whom" and "whether she is really good . . ." etc. He now wants to take over a second theater (probably the Renaissance) as a purely commercial theater with the help of a group of financiers. But I think this will probably become his main theater (or his only one). He isn't going to pick up *Amnestie* because both the play and the performance are just plain bad.[3] By the way, he said it's definite that [*Das Lied von*] *Hoboken* will be mounted at the Volksbühne and [Karl Heinz] Martin himself will stage it. [Hermann]   [FIG. 29] Speelmann is supposed to play Sam. Rehearsals start 20 February.[4]

In the evening I spoke with the Hindemiths, who were very embarrassed and overwhelmingly cordial. I also talked to [Otto] Klemperer. He was truly embarrassed and overly nice (because of his guilty conscience).[5]

Now I am really working again. The little opera [*Der Jasager*] is progressing very quickly. Saturday I met with [Caspar] Neher and will meet him again tonight;[6] in the afternoon I'm going to work with Koch. I haven't heard anything from Leipzig and am somewhat disturbed because no one has answered my telegram. I'll probably just go there in the next few days.

Well my *Liebchen*, now you know everything. So here are many many kisses for your little body, from your

Weillili

1. *Carola Neher (1900–1936) was to have created the role of Polly in the original production of* Die Dreigroschenoper, *but she withdrew when her husband Klabund died during rehearsals. She did play the role later in the run and created the character of Lillian in* Happy End, *singing some of Weill's best songs. In 1933 she fled to Russia, where she died in one of the gulags.*

Although the music critic Hans Gutmann was a frequent contributor around 1930 to periodicals (including Anbruch, Melos, *and* Modern Music*) and to the* Berliner Börsen-Courier, *he has left no further trace.*

2. *Taking its name from the month of the Weimar Revolution (November 1918), the November Group comprised an informal association of expressionist artists in Berlin organized by Max Pechstein and César Klein. In 1919 the Group established Workers' Councils for Art and instituted public art exhibitions, lectures, film presentations, and concerts of new music. The Group did not officially admit musicians to membership until 1922, although Weill had become an associate soon after his arrival in Berlin in 1920.*

3. *Amnestie was a play by Karl Maria Finkelnburg (1867–?), produced by the Volksbühne in January 1930. A review of* Amnestie *appears in Ihering, pp. 408–11.*

4. *The production of* Das Lied von Hoboken, *by Michael Gold, with music by Wilhelm Grosz, opened on 31 March with Lenya playing opposite Hermann Speelmann (1904–60) and Albert Hoerrmann, prominent actors in Berlin.*

5. *Paul Hindemith (1895–1963) was the leading German composer of the post–World War I generation. He and Weill had collaborated unhappily on* Der Lindberghflug *in 1929; both composers then withdrew their material from the joint score. Weill thereafter did his own setting of the cantata, which was premiered by Otto Klemperer at the State Opera on 5 December 1929. Hindemith and Weill, longtime rivals, were soon at odds over the program of the 1930 Neue Musik Berlin festival; Weill withdrew* Der Jasager *from the program in protest after the festival's organizers (including Hindemith) rejected Hanns Eisler's* Die Maßnahme *on the basis of Brecht's text. Klemperer had reneged on his commitment to mount the full-length* Mahagonny *at the Kroll Opera in Berlin, where Hans Curjel was the dramaturg.*

6. *The set designer Caspar (Cas) Neher was not related to the actress Carola Neher; his wife's name was Erika.*

26 WEILL IN BERLIN TO LENYA IN ST. MORITZ, 28 JANUARY 1930

Berlin, 28 January 1930

Dear *Rehbeinchen*,

Today is our wedding anniversary. I deliberately didn't send you a telegram, because it might have made you sad. And you have no reason at all for that. This morning—when I saw the number 28 on the calendar—right away I reminisced a bit, thinking how beautiful these first four years have been. And then I worked for a long stretch, and very productively. Altogether I feel very cheerful, because I'm really working again, and because the little opera [*Der Jasager*] is taking on a very unique and lovely character.

Your letter arrived this morning. I'm so glad you're feeling well there, and that this time you've had a good trip.

Today Brügmann finally answered my telegram. So I'll drive to Leipzig tomorrow (Wednesday) morning with Neher and hope I can drive back Thursday afternoon or early Friday at the latest. These two days are crucial for the whole production, because Brügmann now has to be dealt with properly. I'm glad that Neher is coming along.[1]

(Stop! Now I've sent you a telegram, so you already know that I'm in Leipzig, and of course I had to add a kiss for you on our anniversary.)

Otherwise there's nothing new since my letter yesterday. Yesterday afternoon and evening I spent with the Kochs. Unfortunately my gymnastics lesson was canceled today. Next time Mackeben is going to work out with me.[2] Frankfurt Radio still hasn't answered the letter.[3] Oh well, the hell with it! The Sohns [Leo and Ruth, Weill's sister] called today. They know an executive at Aafa, and he calls them all the time.[4] He wants to do a film with you (apparently in order to get to me). I think we should talk to these people when you return. Aafa is at least as good as Südfilm-Gesellschaft, where La Neher [Carola] makes her films. By the way, this director [Richard] Löwenbein, with whom La Neher works, is supposed to be an impossible guy, who up to now has turned out only shit.

Lipmann called just now.[5] He's negotiating with various places and seems to be quite enterprising. [Caspar] Neher and I will be seeing him tonight.

Farewell, my sweetie. I love you very much, and I'm already looking forward to having you back here again.

> A trillion kisses
> from your
> Weillili

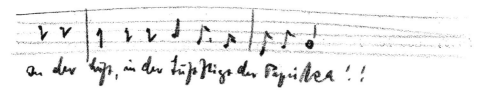

[*In der Luft, in der Luft fliegt der Paprika ! !*]

[In the air, in the air flies the paprika ! !]

1. Caspar Neher and the stage director Walter Brügmann were working with Weill on plans for the premiere of the full-length opera Mahagonny, which opened in Leipzig on 9 March 1930. Neher and Weill had coauthored the director's manual for the opera without Brecht's participation.

2. The German composer and conductor Theo Mackeben (1897–1953) played keyboards and served as musical director for both Die Dreigroschenoper and Happy End in Berlin. He also recorded many songs by Weill with the Lewis Ruth Band (1928–30).

3. Lenya had been invited to do four or five songs on a variety hour for Frankfurt Radio.

4. Aafa was one of many small film companies that struggled for survival; most failed.

5. Heinz Lipmann (1905–67) was a dramaturg for Leopold Jessner at the Berlin State Theater.

Berlin, early Friday

Beloved *Schätzilein,*

Yesterday I got back to *Berlliin* in good shape. The car wasn't running well on the way to Leipzig, so for two marks I had the carburetor and brakes adjusted there by a brilliant fellow (both had been totally neglected). Now it runs like never before. Neher knows a lot about cars, and he told me all kinds of things. Really, we sometimes treat the car a bit too carelessly. After it was fixed yesterday, Neher said that only then could he tell that it's the most beautiful auto he's ever seen. But the mechanical parts need better care.

I was so busy all the time in Leipzig that I could hardly spend an hour with my parents. We worked only with Brügmann. At first he seemed really dumb, so that first evening we were quite desperate. Then he suddenly got excited when the word "masks" came up. Finally he saw the light (insofar as he could, being such a jackass). The outcome: we'll play the entire piece with masks, completely rigid ones made to fit the facial form of each performer. Of course, that will be a great advantage. Since we're committed to going through with this, it could actually turn out to be the most modern theatrical performance; for years everyone has talked about using masks, but nobody has done it. And they will really hamstring those over-emoting singers. I had a marvelous idea right away: at the end, the "Gott in Mahagonny" must tear the masks off the men's faces. After that the revolution starts. (Isn't that beautiful?) By the way, the casting seems to be very good. [Marga] Dannenberg is doing Begbick; she's actually the biggest personality in Leipzig. Jim has also been well cast [Paul Beinert]. The set will look great.

I've been really happy about your news. Too bad the weather isn't so good. But you must truly relax, then you can rest even in less favorable weather. It's not all that important for you to get out and do sports. I thought right away that this Liedes woman[?] would be a washout. But don't worry about that, we'll be together again soon. You've been gone for one week already, so it won't be too long before you're with your sweetie again and will get many millions of little kisses over your entire little body and especially on your *Poo'chen.* That will be *primi!!!*

Well, Frankfurt Radio has put you down for a variety show on 8 February, at 9:15 in the evening. There are three other participants (among them Max Kuttner and Hans Reimann),[1] so you probably won't have to sing too much. Four big songs (two sets of two songs) would be enough. Rehearsal is supposed to be one hour before, beginning at 8:15. The contract just came, but there's no indication whether they have agreed to the program we've sent them. I'll write them back now (with your signature) and ask if the program is OK, whether you'll sing with piano or orchestra, and whether you may possibly have an additional short rehearsal Saturday morning. When I get an answer, I'll sign the contract right away with "Lotte Lenja" and send it back. But you should do it only if you won't get irritated. There's no reason to, because you can do this whole thing with your eyes closed. If these people don't have time for careful rehearsal, I would suggest you do it with piano. It's much simpler, and a good pianist is ever so much better than a bad orchestra that has never played these things. I'll prepare everything for you, so that, depending on the news from Frankfurt, the orchestra or piano music will be there on time. In any event I'll sign your name as if you were actually here. Your program could look something like this:

Heilsarmeesong ["Der kleine Leutnant," from *Happy End*]
Bilbao-Song [from *Happy End*]
Erst kommt das Fressen [second finale of *Die Dreigroschenoper*]
Surabaya-Johnny [from *Happy End*]
Nur nicht weich werden ["Das Lied von der harten Nuß," from *Happy End*]

Write me right away to say whether you agree, so I can get the music together. You would have to leave for Frankfurt on Friday evening by sleeping car. It's very possible you could leave for here after the concert, if you're not too tired.

There, my *Rehbeinchen*, farewell. Your telegram came just now, and I answered it right away. Physically and mentally I'm doing quite well, only both my soul and body have a longing for you (and my eyes are a little red from driving).

> Behave yourself, so that you will come back like a round full moon to your
> Weillili
> (who is ever in love with you!!)

Don't forget to write some postcards: Aufricht, Martin, Lipmann, and Leipzig, etc.

---

1. *Max Kuttner (1883–1953) was a light tenor who specialized in Lortzing operas. The German writer Hans Reimann (1889–1969) founded the literary cabaret Retorte in 1923 but was best known for his parodistic contributions to operettas and revues.*

28 WEILL IN BERLIN TO LENYA IN ST. MORITZ, 3 FEBRUARY 1930

Berlin, 3 February 1930

Dear *Schätzilein*,

I'm writing you just a few quick lines so that you won't be without news from me. Hardly anything newsworthy has happened. Frankfurt Radio hasn't answered my letter yet. If they don't respond by Wednesday, I think you should cancel.

Life is proceeding peacefully, but it is completely lackluster without you. Friday evening I was at the movies with Hans, Rita [Weill's brother and sister-in-law], and Lipmann to see a magnificent Asian film with a love dance by two Japanese dancers, which you would like very much. Saturday I strolled around with Neher, and we watched all the people going to costume balls; it was very funny (especially when Fehling drove by the zoo in a crazy outfit).[1]

Last night I had a date with Hesse and La Hauptmann,[2] who, for a change, are closely united once more. La H. hasn't taken a bath for at least three weeks and looked like puke. We kidded her terribly. I said that all anyone called her in Berlin was Royalties-Sadie, and that whenever she entered a theater, the dramaturgs would yell, "Hurry, put your plays away, La Hauptmann is coming to adapt them." Lipmann laughed himself sick. By the way, he had just talked to you, which made me very envious.[3] But I'll be calling you this week, too.

Brügmann is here today. He's coming for lunch with Neher, and then we'll work straight through until evening. He'll stay until Wednesday. That will give me a lot to do. And then another half a week will have passed, and it'll be only a few more days until you're here again.

Auf Wiedili, mein Rehbeinchen; I'm half-dead from joy in anticipation of your return.

> Your little
> Weillili

[Hans] Heinsheimer has already paid back the 100 marks.

1. *Jürgen Fehling (1885–1968) was one of Berlin's most outstanding director-producers.*

2. *Emil Hesse-Burri, Elisabeth Hauptmann, and Hans Hermann Borchardt were credited as collaborators on Brecht's* Die heilige Johanna der Schlachthöfe *in its first edition (1932). Hauptmann (1897–1973) was Brecht's most capable and devoted literary collaborator, responsible for the English-language "Mahagonny Songs" (1924), the German translation of* Beggar's Opera *that served as the basis for* Die Dreigroschenoper *(1928), the script for* Happy End *(1929; under the pseudonym Dorothy Lane), and the German translation of the Noh play that became* Der Jasager *(1930). Although she received credit for her translations, the full extent of her contribution to Brecht's oeuvre—including sole authorship of poems and stories attributed to Brecht—has only recently been recognized.*

3. *According to several of Weill's and Lenya's friends, Lipmann and Lenya were romantically involved at the time.*

1930–1931

[FIG. 30]

Describing the premiere Aufstieg und Fall der Stadt Mahagonny, *in Leipzig on 9 March 1930, the critic H. H. Stuckenschmidt wrote: "It has been a long time since the premiere of a new work has been awaited with such tense excitement.... It represents a climax in the operatic history of the present era.... Political opponents were already hissing during the first act. Toward the end, open tumult broke out. [Gustav] Brecher barely managed to bring the performance to a close. And thereupon started a quarter hour of the most violent disputation, such as has not been heard for many, many years" (pp. 75, 77). Several theaters canceled their plans to produce the opera. In October storm troopers forced their way into the second performance at the Frankfurt Opera and hurled stink bombs.*

After all three of Berlin's opera houses declined to stage Mahagonny, *Ernst Josef Aufricht leased the Theater am Kurfürstendamm from Max Reinhardt and produced the opera in De-*

[FIG. 31]

cember 1931, in a revised version featuring Lenya as Jenny and Harald Paulsen as Johann, with Alexander von Zemlinsky conducting. During rehearsals long-standing tensions between Weill and Brecht over artistic, aesthetic, and political differences exploded, with Brecht denouncing Weill as a "phony Richard Strauss" and finally withdrawing from the production, leaving Neher and Weill in control. It was one of the first contemporary operas to achieve a continuous run in a commercial theater—more than fifty performances.

After its premiere in June 1930, the Weill-Brecht "school opera" Der Jasager *was endorsed by the ministry of education and by 1932 had been produced in more than three hundred German schools. The much-publicized court case over the film adaptation of* Die Dreigroschenoper, *Weill and Brecht vs. Nero Films, ended in November 1930, with Weill winning control over the* treatment of his music in the film and a contract for several future film projects; Brecht lost his case for an injunction against the screenplay but accepted a monetary settlement. From August 1930 until October 1931 Neher and Weill collaborated on Weill's most ambitious stage work, the three-act opera Die Bürgschaft.

After Das Lied von Hoboken, Lenya appeared as an elegant courtesan in Paul Kornfeld's dramatization of Lion Feuchtwanger's novel Jud Süß and then recreated the role of Jenny for G. W. Pabst's film of Die Dreigroschenoper, in which she rather than Polly (Carola Neher) [FIG. 32] sang "Pirate Jenny." As soon as the film was finished, she appeared in Francesco von Mendelssohn's staging of Valentin Katayev's comedy Squaring the Circle. In June 1931 Lenya accepted Erwin Piscator's invitation to play the role of a sailor's whore in The Revolt of the Fishermen of St. Barbara, which was to be filmed in Russia as a cooperative venture with Germany. The cast and crew left by train on 28 July. Conditions were horrendous: Lenya recalled that in her hotel room chairs collapsed, faucets broke off in her hand, rats devoured food left untended. Months passed, but the set still wasn't finished and not a foot of film had been shot. No letters from this period have survived. Lenya recorded in her memoirs: "Kurt had written me that he would telephone on my birthday [18 October] at the hotel; and miraculously the call came through promptly, his voice as clear as though he were in the next room: 'Darling, I've bought you a house for your birthday.' The moment was so wonderful, but so unreal, that I kept croaking, 'Yes . . . yes . . . where is it?' Kurt told me that it was in Kleinmachnow [a fashionable Berlin suburb], that it was a modern house with a little garden. Then: 'Lenya, and the house is number 7 [Wißmannstraße], do you hear, 7! Our lucky number!'" (mem. L1). When Lenya [FIG. 33] returned to Berlin, she joined preparations for the Berlin premiere of Mahagonny.

1932

Amid the turmoil of the presidential elections, in which Hitler was running, on 10 March Die Bürgschaft premiered at the Berlin City Opera in a production conducted by Fritz Stiedry and directed by Carl Ebert. Three days later productions in Wiesbaden and Düsseldorf opened simultaneously. Lenya recalled: "I think it was one of Weill's happiest collaborations. They [Weill and Neher] had been very close friends since 1927 and completely understood each other. For Weill it was a kind of relief after the restraint of writing for untrained singers, children, and the special needs of Brecht. I remember him saying, 'Jetzt muß ich mich mal wieder ausmusizieren,' meaning that he wished now to let the music speak as fully as possible. The work is based on a parable by [Johann Gottfried von] Herder, the great classical humanist, and it is about justice in a primitive society and injustice in a totalitarian society" (Osborne, p. 50).

No other theater dared to follow through on production plans. The opera came under direct political attack, led by the Kampfbund für deutsche Kultur and supported by the Goebbels press. Subsequent events made such a parable even more topical. Franz von Papen, on the right wing of the Center (Zentrum) party, replaced Brüning as chancellor; before year's end, he in turn was succeeded by Kurt von Schleicher. Unemployment rose to 6.5 million, while the virtually senile Hindenburg seemed oblivious to the intrigues that surrounded his presidency. Weill wrote to his publisher that "one needed good nerves" to carry on. In his mailbox Weill found a warning: "What's a Jew like you doing in a community like Kleinmachnow?" (int. L3).

29 WEILL IN WIESBADEN TO LENYA IN BERLIN[?], [MID-MARCH 1932]

Tütilein,

I'm at the railroad station in Wiesbaden, so I can catch a train to Mannheim and leave right away again on Thursday. The weather is marvelous, and I'm in a very good mood. I attended the dress rehearsal [of *Die Bürgschaft*]. It was very interesting. The second act in the original version is much better than in Berlin. Rankl conducts it marvelously.[1]

I'm looking forward to the [new] house like crazy and even more to my little *Schnapspison vom Stölpcheneck.*[2]

> Farewell, my *Littichen,*
> accept a million little kisses
> from <u>your</u>
> Weilli

(and don't get my bed dirty)

1. *Karl Rankl (1898–1968), an Austrian conductor and composer, had been a pupil of Schoenberg's in the early 1920s. He worked at the Kroll Opera in Berlin and in December 1929 conducted the premiere of two workers' choruses by Weill. Rankl went to Britain in 1939 and served as musical director of Covent Garden from 1946 to 1951.*

2. *Lenya had written to her mother on 15 February that she and Weill "were very busy with the move" and that they planned to move into Wißmannstraße 7 by the middle of March.*

30 WEILL IN DÜSSELDORF TO LENYA IN BERLIN, [11 APRIL 1932]

Letterhead: Park Hotel / Düsseldorf

Tütilein,

The performance [of *Die Bürgschaft*] tomorrow night doesn't start until eight o'clock, so I would just barely make the night train. Therefore I'll be leaving on Wednesday, along with Horenstein, but I don't know yet on which train.[1] Probably I'll get to Berlin Zoo [station] at five o'clock. So if you don't hear otherwise, I'll be on the five o'clock train. If you have too much to do, you needn't come to the railroad station. I'll just call you at home.

It's very beautiful here. The performance should be a good one. The piece is marvelous. I've regained great courage once more.

> Farewell, my *Lila Schweinderl,* and be kissed by *Pünktchen.*

1. *Jascha Horenstein (1899–1973) had been appointed chief conductor of the Düsseldorf Opera in 1928. He was forced to leave Germany in 1933; he emigrated to America in 1940.*

[FIG. 34]

In April 1932 Lenya went to Vienna to sing the role of Jenny in a truncated version of Aufstieg und Fall der Stadt Mahagonny *at the Raimund Theater. Hans Heinsheimer, who directed the production, recalled Lenya's reaction to the twenty-nine-year-old blond tenor playing Jim: "She took one look at him [Otto Pasetti] and whispered to me: 'That's a nice looking boy!' I knew when I saw the gleam in her eye that here was trouble" (int. HAH). Pasetti, who sometimes* called himself *"von Pasetti"* and *"Dr. Pasetti,"* was married to Erna Marek, and they had a two-year-old son named Mario. A year before, he had moved from Innsbruck to Vienna, where he lived with his mother-in-law for a time, apparently to pursue a singing career. Accompanied by the pianist Alfred Schlee, in 1931 he recorded *"Muschel von Margate,"* a song from Weill's incidental score to Leo Lania's play Konjunktur. (Schlee was then a minor functionary at Universal Edition; in 1932 he took over the Berlin office of the firm and after the war eventually became artistic director.)

Weill attended the premiere of Mahagonny in Vienna on 26 April and stayed with Lenya at the Hotel Imperial for two weeks. He stopped to meet Caspar Neher in Munich before returning to Berlin. Shortly after Weill's departure, Pasetti moved from the Hotel Mariahilf into the Hotel Hietzing with Lenya.

31 WEILL IN MUNICH TO LENYA IN VIENNA, [22? MAY 1932]
Letterhead: Hotel Vier Jahreszeiten / Restaurant Walterspiel / München

Sunday afternoon

Dear *Tütilein,*

Here I sit in the hotel. Cas [Neher] sent a postcard saying he won't arrive until evening. The drive was wonderful and went by very quickly. In the Salzburg area, at some obscure stop, there was a "talkie" movie house next to the railroad station. What do you think they were playing? *Die Dreigroschenoper.* And who smiles cryptically at the passersby? Lotte Lenja (that picture where you are fixing your garter). A genuine little celebrity!

They're serving five o'clock tea here right now. I'm reading the newspapers, watching how they dance. But I'm already getting bored. Therefore I'm addressing myself once more in full confidence to my *Lila Schweinderl.* Since Cas is arriving so late, I'll take the last night train and be in Berlin tomorrow noon. I can hardly wait to be back in my room. I have nothing else in my head but to work again. I hope I can still do it. Each time I'm afraid it won't fly.

It will be really wonderful when you come. I'm already looking forward to seeing you. Come soon. Sweetheart, be so kind as to call Kalmus; I had tried to reach him and give my regards.[1] Get yourself money when you need it. Buy yourself a little perfume! There, that proves I'm not a miser. That was very mean!

Now I'm going to go for a walk. It's terribly sultry here. Right now they're playing a pop song: "Come with Me to Abbazia!"

Wild horses couldn't drag me!

Be loved, *Schätzchen*
Pünktchen kisses you

---

1. *Alfred Kalmus (1889–1972) was one of the principals of Universal Edition.*

Berlin, Tuesday morning

Dear *Tütilein,*

It was very nice of you to write me right away. But you see how it is with the *Doofi* when the *Klugi* is away! Let them really fix the car before you leave so you don't have any problems while you're on the road.

I waited a long time in Munich until the Nehers finally drifted in at 8:30. They had bad roads, tire trouble, etc., and were so exhausted that they went to bed right away, and we postponed our discussions until the next morning. Yesterday morning I talked with Cas in detail. He'll be away until the end of May, then we intend to work, at first on cantatas, then on an opera with very few roles, which could also be played in private theaters. Cas was very nice, and it was very important to have met with him because Brecht is employing every possible means to get him away from me. Erika [Neher] was very chic, in new clothes head to toe, her hair dyed rust-red, and Cas was very proud

[FIG. 35]

of his elegant wife. I left Munich yesterday at noon on a marvelous express train, which arrived in Berlin at nine o'clock in the evening. Then I landed on Wißmannstraße with six pfennig in my pocket.

It's wonderful here. The trees are not as far along as in Vienna; it's only beginning to get green and the most beautiful time is yet to come. But you still haven't missed anything. Today the weather is very bad, cold and rainy. I've called a few people (Curjel, [Heinrich] Strobel). But they are very grouchy and fearful. Things are more unhealthy and more tense than in Vienna. Nevertheless, it's better here. You'll be surprised how one can breathe again when one enters this beautiful, bright house. Harras [Weill's

[FIG. 36]

German shepherd] recognized me right away and was as happy as a kid. Polly [Weill's cat] awaits maternal bliss with resignation. There was a lot of mail, but all trivial. Very high gas and electric bills.

Please give the enclosed clipping from yesterday's *B.Z.* [*Berliner Zeitung*] to Heinsheimer. Have him make twenty copies to send to the most important theaters. *Die Bürgschaft* will be performed here again on the 12th and the 20th.

Otherwise there's nothing new. I'm happy to be home again and I'm already looking forward (very confidentially!) to my little *Weilliwüppchen.* I hope I'll soon slip back into working again. I wish for nothing more than a beautiful summer of work.

Is it nice in Hietzing? Is the hotel pleasant? Are the people nice to my *Tütchen?* How is *Mahagonny* going? From here I can now see how important it would be if *Mahagonny* could play in Vienna for quite a while and how important altogether Vienna could become for us.

Take good care of yourself, *Schätzchen,* be a *Klugi* or at least try, and be kissed a thousand times by your

Pünktchen

Berlin, Friday

Dear Weillchen,

I was very happy that you called yesterday, because all morning I was needing to hear your voice. It's too bad that your return trip had to be postponed again, because here in the house everything is getting lovelier (with very beautiful weather). But you're right, you could hardly have refused Heinsheimer those two days. Of course you'll have to organize your return trip in such a way that it isn't your "first day" [of her menstrual cycle], or you'll be too nervous. In any case, you seem to feel good there, and that's the main thing. What did you accomplish with Bach in regard to Mariederl's apartment and your own concerns?[1] How is *Mahagonny* going? I've written to Heinsheimer to see if he couldn't recommend a guest performance at the Munich Kammerspiele.

I wrote you a long letter on Tuesday and reported on my return trip, Munich, etc. It was addressed to Hietzinger Hof. I hope you got it. Not much has happened in the meantime. Most of the time I'm at home or I go for a walk with Harras. Tuesday I went to the movies with [Walter] Steinthal. We saw the Japanese movie that Koch adapted. Very much worth seeing. Afterward we met Maurus, the great star of the State Theater, engaged by Lederer for next year.[2] It was very nice. I had to set off for home at 11:30 in order to catch the last bus. Wednesday I was in the State Opera: a new production of *Ariadne* [*auf Naxos*]. What a magnificent opera! Yesterday I had the Strobels over for lunch. Toward evening Steinthal called and came out here to look at the house, which he liked very much. Then he showed me a house in Wannsee that he wants to buy, with a magnificent garden, quite near us. Then we went to Kutschera's.[3] So those are my adventures. Today is a magnificent day, so I won't drive into town at all. I still can't seem to work. But I hope that I'm close to being able to. Each time it's so difficult to start up again. Strobel has interesting stories about the clique. Herr Brecht ridicules *Die Bürgschaft*, calling it a *Spießbürgerschaft* and an *Avantgartenlaube*.[4] Clever, isn't it? It also seems to be common knowledge that Brecht and [Hanns] Eisler made a movie offer to Frau Stuckenschmidt one week before *Die Bürgschaft!*[5] Nebbish! Steinthal says he's just waiting for the day when he can clean out this cesspool.

I hope you will have used the time there to take advantage of your success and your connections, so you don't have to depend solely on Aufricht when you want to perform in the theater. Have you seen Martin again?

Tütilein, I thought those two weeks at the Imperial [hotel] with you were wonderful, and I think a lot about them. You too? Altogether I hold you <u>very dear</u>, and I'm dying to see you.

> Farewell, my beloved *Wüllichen*
> A kiss on your sweet little belly
> from your faithful
> *Pünktchen*

La Täubler called and has written you at Hietzinger Hof. I have a pleasant message for her: the brother of Frau Strobel, a rich young man, is having an affair with Adele Kern.[6]

1. *Probably David Joseph Bach (1874–1947), a pioneer in the Workers' Music movement and director of the arts section of the Austrian Social Democratic party; he had asked Weill to write a large-scale composition for the May Day festival, and they maintained contacts with regard to a Viennese production of* Die Bürgschaft.

Mariederl is the diminutive for Marie (Blamauer), Lenya's sister. While in Vienna, Lenya visited her family in Penzing and found her mother living with a brutal alcoholic, Ernst Hainisch, who had recently been released from prison.

2. *Gerda Maurus (1903–68) was best known for her performance in Fritz Lang's* Frau im Mond. *She was married to Robert Stemmle. The identity of Lederer is uncertain. It's unlikely that it was either Felix (1877–1957), a conductor, or Victor (1881–1944), a musicologist.*

3. *Franz Kutschera (b. 1909) collaborated with Brecht; he appears on the Wolfgang Rennert recording of* Die Dreigroschenoper *released in 1966 (Philips 6768700).*

4. *Spießbürger is a philistine; Gartenlaube is an arbor in the garden suitable for trysts, as well as the name of a family magazine popular with the lower middle class. In both puns, Brecht is ridiculing the appeal of his two former collaborators' opera.*

5. *Frau Stuckenschmidt was Margot Hinnenberg-Lefèbre, a singer who won acclaim for her interpretations of new music. Her husband, H. H. Stuckenschmidt (1901–89) achieved international stature as a freelance composer and writer about music, working for various periodicals and newspapers before he succeeded A. Weißmann as music critic of the* Berliner Zeitung am Mittag *in 1929. He reviewed* Die Bürgschaft *in Anbruch 14 (Nov.–Dec. 1932): 217.*

6. *Selma Stern Täubler (1890–1981) was a relative of Weill's. A historian and author of the novel* The Spirit Returneth *(Philadelphia, 1946), she was to become the archivist of the American Jewish Archives in Cincinnati. Adele Kern (1901–80) was a prominent coloratura soprano.*

34 WEILL IN BERLIN TO LENYA IN VIENNA, [28 MAY 1932]

Berlin, Saturday

Dear *Tütilein,*

Last night I received your express letter. It came exactly at the right time, because there was a terrible rainstorm and I spent the entire day in my room without being able to produce anything worthwhile. Some nice words from my little *Wülli* are very comforting at such a time.

There is nothing new at all since yesterday, and I'm only writing so that you can hear from me once more before you leave. Just take it easy driving. It's a fun drive up to Linz. It's supposed to be a beautiful old city. Find out about the road to Berlin or Leipzig from there. Always stay at the best hotels!

Please, darling, do me a favor and call U.E. once more before you leave (U.47585), and say your charming goodbyes to Kalmus, Winter, and Fräulein Rothe.[1]

The way Heinsheimer pours holy water over himself really got on my nerves too. I think he hurts himself a lot doing that, because no one takes him seriously. But that will take care of itself.

Yesterday I was in Zehlendorf to get newspapers. Kardan[?] was here because your bed has arrived (*primi* for two *Pisonen*!!, very suitable for *schliepeln* [sleeping] together!). He bored me with tales about Kohlkopf[?].

Tomorrow Kaempfer is coming to see me. Monday [Maurice] Abravanel. And then?

Then comes the star,
called *Tütchen*,
née Lila Schweindi
Good-bye, *Schätzchen*!

   Your Weilli

1. Hugo Winter succeeded Emil Hertzka as director of Universal Edition in 1932. Betty Rothe (1885–1966) was Hertzka's secretary from 1907 to 1932.

No other correspondence from 1932 has survived. Lenya's itinerary between 1932 and 1935 cannot be precisely reconstructed, because the pages containing visas and entry stamps for those years have been removed from her passport with such skill that the lacunae can be detected only with close scrutiny. Pasetti's travel documents indicate that he left Vienna with a spouse, "Karoline Pasetti," on 24 August 1932 for the destination of Bad Satzmannsdorf, Burgenland. The Aufrichts relate that Pasetti and Lenya went to the Riviera, where they gambled constantly in various resorts, especially Monte Carlo. Lenya's biographer reports that Lenya wrote Kurt for a loan in the autumn, and that "he immediately wired the first of several large payments to her" (Spoto, p. 106; there is no known archival documentation to support this claim, however).

Meanwhile, Weill had renewed his collaboration with Georg Kaiser, and in August reported to his publisher that he and Kaiser were making good progress on a new play, Der Silbersee. *In November he received a commission for an orchestral work from the princesse Edmond de Polignac (Winaretta Singer) and an invitation from the vicomte and vicomtesse de Noailles to present* Mahagonny *and* Der Jasager *in a semi-staged performance at Salle Gaveau in Paris. In an attempt to lure her away from the gaming tables, Weill invited Lenya to perform and even offered Pasetti the tenor role; they agreed. Maurice Abravanel conducted an expanded version of the* Songspiel, *and the concert attracted a stellar audience which included Igor Stravinsky, Jean Cocteau, Pablo Picasso, Arthur Honegger, André Gide, and Georges Auric. Darius Milhaud recalled that Weill took Paris by storm, and Lenya was the toast of the critics. Weill returned alone to Berlin on 14 December and informed his publisher that he definitely wanted Lenya to play the leading role of Fennimore in the Berlin and Vienna productions of* Der Silbersee. *Lenya and Pasetti stayed in Paris until the new year, then returned to Vienna.*

1933

During the first weeks of January Weill finished the score of Der Silbersee. *On 23 January von Schleicher asked Hindenburg for emergency powers enabling him to suspend the Reichstag temporarily. Hindenburg refused, von Schleicher tendered his resignation on 28 January, and on 30 January Hindenburg offered the chancellorship to Adolf Hitler. Soon thereafter, Weill prophesied to Universal Edition: "I think that what is going on here is so sick that it can't last longer than a few months, but I might be wrong" (W–UE, 6 Feb. 1933).*

Saturday, Zehlendorf

Dear Linnerl,

I only want to clear up a small misunderstanding: Fräulein Erika [the maid] received your little package in the same mail as my book—and she didn't tell me anything about it. For reasons unknown, she is so nasty again that I feel like kicking this hysterical goat in the ass. I'll have to tell her off—then she might behave again for a couple of weeks. The Leipzig premiere [of *Der Silbersee*] will probably take place on 18 February. It would be great if you could come.

This morning—when I was driving Rivière to the subway—I skidded on the ice and hit a tree.[1] The fender, hubcap, front axis, shock absorbers were all damaged—to the tune of sixty marks. But—as usual in such cases—I was lucky to have walked away from it.

All Berlin is laughing about those fine brothers Martin and Beer[?]. They're finished.

Otherwise I don't know anything new. I'm trying to make this kind of life bearable for me. But that is very, very hard to do, because it's so totally different from what I'm used to. I'm happy to have talked to you—and then again, not happy at all. I can only hope that you believe everything I've told you.

Much love and only good wishes for you. As always,

your Weilli

1. *The French musician and aesthete, later the director of the Musée de l'homme, Georges Henri Rivière had arranged the first "Weill Serenade" (December 1932) in Paris.*

Berlin-Zehlendorf, 9 January 1933

My Dear Linnerl,

All kinds of news to interest you. *Der Silbersee* is premiering in Leipzig on 18 February and at the same time in several other theaters (Magdeburg, Hamburg, Erfurt, perhaps Frankfurt). Berlin looks very bad, and at the moment there is no hope that the play can still be produced this season. The Volksbühne, too, is on its last legs and, in order to make money at the box office, lets [Emil] Jannings play just about any role.[1] All the other theaters are out of the question. Perhaps later on, in the fall, someone will do it.

Bidi [Bertolt Brecht] has pestered Aufricht for days to get me together with him. Finally I suggested that Aufricht should arrange it. That took place on Friday, but nothing really came of it. I was quite cool and restrained, while he was sedulous, submissive, shit-friendly. He wants to write a shorter play as a supplement to *Mahagonny*, with a wonderful role for you. He claims to have good material for that. After I got home, he called me at two o'clock in the morning with a proposition. Well, what do you think? You'll never guess: he wants to "dramatize" *Der Lindberghflug* for this purpose. Isn't that insane? Now he's calling me all the time; I should meet with him, but I don't want to yet. This time he will hear things from me that so far no one has ever told him. By the way, I've read his adaptation of *Measure for Measure,* which in part is very beautiful. I noticed right away that there's a wonderful role in it for you, and in fact he said he was thinking about you in that connection.[2] Perhaps Aufricht will do it.

Rivière was here for over a week. He was very nice, but it was a strain. Like everyone in Paris, he thinks that you could, of course, take tremendous advantage of your Paris success, if you would only go to the trouble. Are you actually learning French?

Now the latest: I have a big movie offer. Gab Frank is really a big wheel in the movies.[3] In just six months he has built up "Europa-Distribution," which already is the only rival of UFA. He suggested that I do four films with him in the next two to three years. I've made extensive demands to have a decisive voice, especially as far as the director, the property, the screenwriter, etc., are concerned. The first film is to be done right away, and indeed it's a subject I can accept in good conscience: *Kleiner Mann— was nun?* by Fallada.[4] For director they're negotiating with Gründgens, Berger, and [Berthold] Viertel.[5] It will be a big-budget, first-class movie, through which my name should develop such drawing power that afterward I'll be able to make musical films entirely according to my own ideas. I'm quite inclined to accept the offer. Waiting much longer with the film serves no purpose, especially in view of the present theater situation. I will hardly be able to get more favorable working conditions or a better subject. I have already asked for Cas [Neher] as a collaborator. I might be able to do the second film with René Clair. I'll try to push you through as "Lämmchen."[6] To be sure, the part is not at all your type, as you can already guess by the name. In any case, I will do everything to get you into the film. That goes without saying.

There are also personal reasons why I want to accept the film. In the last few weeks I've seen once again how I completely fall apart when I'm not working. This film, which is already supposed to be in the studio by March, together with the premiere of *Der Silbersee,* would throw me into such a whirl of work that I would no longer have time for bouts of depression.

How is it with you, *Tütilein?* I thought you might write to me after the telephone call. But most likely you're not allowed to. I've thought of you a lot these past days and wished so much for my sake that someday it could again be the way it used to be. But you probably don't want to hear that. In the house everything is in order; our house dragon [Erika] is nice again, Harras very good and devoted. The Catholic Church wants 334 marks in taxes. Can that be? I still have 887 marks to pay in taxes, besides the current payments. They're totally crazy. And all this time I'd been picturing the ski trip you said we would take together. But that, too, will have to fall by the wayside if I do this film.

Farewell, *Tütilein*. Take good care of yourself and please do not entirely forget

your
Weillchen

1. *Emil Jannings (1884–1950) was one of the most famous actors in Berlin; he played Professor Unrath in* Der blaue Engel.

2. *Brecht had been approached in November 1931 by the director of Gruppe Junger Schauspieler to make a new adaptation of Shakespeare's* Measure for Measure. *Although that production never materialized, Brecht did not abandon the project, but radically rewrote the play as* Die Rundköpfe und die Spitzköpfe *(1936), with music by Hanns Eisler. In 1939, Weill set "Nannas Lied," one of the songs from the play, as a Christmas present for Lenya.*

3. *Gabriel Frank was the husband of Nelly Frank, with whom Weill had been involved shortly before meeting Lenya.*

4. *Hans Fallada's novel* Kleiner Mann—was nun? *had become an international bestseller soon after its publication in 1931 and was eventually translated into twenty languages. Like* Der Silbersee, *Fallada's novel dealt with the consequences of economic depression.*

5. *Gustaf Gründgens (1899–1963) was one of Germany's greatest actor-directors (later the subject of the film* Mephisto). *Ludwig Berger (1892–1969) was also an outstanding actor-director.*

6. *In the novel, "Lämmchen" is the wife of the unemployed textile salesman Pinneberg, who lives in an unheated garden-shed on the outskirts of Berlin.*

37 WEILL IN BERLIN TO LENYA IN VIENNA, 19 JANUARY 1933

Zehlendorf, 19 January 1933

Dear *Tütilein*,

I was very happy with your two letters and especially with the news that you're coming to the premiere [of *Der Silbersee*]. It'll be terrific to see each other again in private. I don't know yet how much earlier I'll arrive in Leipzig. It'll probably be an exciting time; it now looks like the movie [*Kleiner Mann—was nun?*] will actually become a reality, and the shooting in the studio might already start by the beginning of March, so you can imagine how hard I'll have to work. But that's exactly what I want. Probably I'll take the box of manuscripts with me to Leipzig and continue working there. Steinthal has negotiated brilliantly for me. I'm supposed to get a fee almost unheard of these days: 20,000 marks (nobody but you is supposed to know this). Three to four thousand is the usual fee for music today (Rathaus et al.).[1] And for the time being I'm a virtual dictator. So I refused the directors they've suggested to me, including Gründgens, after I saw parts of his film, which is really bad. Since I was able to push Cas [Neher] through, and since [Rudolf] Neppach, the director of productions and a former set designer, is an excellent man, I probably won't take any star director but rather a young person, with whom it would be easier to work. I'm especially thinking of [Henrik] Galeen, who did that beautiful film *Mitternachtsliebe*.[2] We haven't talked about casting yet. As soon as my contract is settled, I'll mount a grand attack about "Lämmchen"!

Tütilein, I have to make a quick run into the city now. These are just a few lines to you to keep you up to date. I'll write again soon. I sent the ski outfit.

All the very best for Linnerl!
Your Weilili

1. *Karol Rathaus (1895–1954) was a Polish composer who studied with Franz Schreker; he taught at the Berlin Hochschule für Musik until 1933, when he moved to London.*

2. *Henrik Galeen (b. 1882?) entered German films in 1910 as an actor, then in 1914 became a screenwriter and director of important films, including* Der Golem *(1914),* Das Wachsfigurenkabinett *(1924),* Der Student von Prag *(1926), and* Alraune *(1927).*

38 WEILL IN BERLIN TO LENYA IN VIENNA, 28 JANUARY 1933

Zehlendorf, <u>28 January 1933</u>

Dear *Tütilein*,

Life is funny: seven years ago today at about this time we met [Martha] Gratenau, Lind, and Caña in front of city hall in Charlottenburg.[1] Now Gratenau is a happy housewife and mother, Lind probably has become an old woman, and Caña is dead; you're far away from me, and I sit in my little house and brood over whether someday love will bloom again for me too.

How are you, Linerle? Are you well and happy? When I don't hear from you for such a long time, I just can't imagine whether you actually think about me or, even more, about the two of us. When are you coming? I'm so delighted that you'll be coming to Leipzig with me. I imagine I'll be staying there from approximately the 14th [of February] on. It's funny that people from France are asking all the time about the Leipzig premiere. Rivière is coming, and yesterday [Vicomte Charles de] Noailles wrote from Hyères to Leipzig that his wife [Marie-Laure] will come to Berlin one week before. By the way, I keep forgetting to write you that a very beautiful big purse came from Noailles, dark blue with a thick twisted chain. I can't send it to you, because it would cost too much duty. But perhaps you could write him a little picture postcard sometime with thanks for the present: Vicomte de Noailles, Saint-Bernard, Hyères (Var), France.

There are a lot of complications with the film. By the middle of the week I was ready to chuck the whole thing, for the first time. Without even asking me, they simply engaged Thimig, after I had told them that very day that this sort of casting would be out of the question for me.[2] We had a huge fight, and now the atmosphere is charged. I gave them an ultimatum: if by the end of next week no director has been engaged that meets my specifications, I'll resign. Of course they want to delay things as usual, so that at the last moment it can all be done the way they want it. It's always the same. Only [Gabriel] Frank is behaving decently and is completely on my side. And since they all have to depend on him, I can still try to push through a few things before I throw in the towel.

What's more, on the day the big fight took place, a big car crashed into my Citroën in the middle of Fehrbelliner Platz. The whole left side is ruined. I'm fine, except for a few harmless bruises. You'll probably have a terrible fit, but it wasn't my fault. I've given the whole thing over to Rabau,[3] so that I can get back at least part of the expenses. Now I'm without a car, which is not too unpleasant for me because it's so much healthier. Have you received the ski things? Are you taking a lot of walks in that beautiful winter weather?

> All good things for you, *Tüti-Pison,*
> from your
> Weilli

1. *Witnesses at Weill and Lenya's wedding on 28 January 1926. Emil Lind (1872–1948) and his wife were close friends of the Kaisers.*

2. *Hermann Thimig (1890–1982) was a member of one of Vienna's oldest theatrical families. His brother Hans and his sister Helene, who married Max Reinhardt, were both actors.*

3. *The* Jüdisches Adressbuch für Groß-Berlin *lists an attorney in Charlottenburg named Dr. Alfred Rabau.*

For the most part Weill sheltered Lenya from his depression, but he confessed his despair to Erika Neher in a letter written on 29 January:

I've been absolutely desperate again for several days, because once more things are going badly for me, and I was in such a miserable state of mind that I thought I'd never break out of this streak of bad luck. But then, after a few days, things began to look a bit more hopeful. It's strange what an important part HOPE can play in such difficult times. It takes the toughest kind of hard knocks to make a human being lose courage; given the slightest ray of hope, we blossom all over again, make new plans, and see everything in a rosy light. You know, angel, I do believe that at some point in time all that I'm going through right now will be important for my further development. Because I'm always alone and can't often talk to you about it, what I'm experiencing now is something like taking lessons in human degradation. Having to face all of this alone, I'm slowly starting to feel a tremendous distance from things and people. This could of course be a real danger, as I'm too young to become so embittered and so afraid of people. But you protect me from that, my good angel. . . . This honest and great passion, this certainty that there is still such a thing as beauty, truth, and love. . . . I also believe that the only way to achieve any kind of inner development in times like these is to become a stoic, but not to lose that great emotion within your heart. That's why I am always filled with gratitude toward you, my dearest, sweetest, most tender, richest little angel, because without you I could never have survived all this but would have perished by now. (W–EN1, 29 Jan. 1933)

The director of the Leipzig production of Der Silbersee, *Detlef Sierck, recalls that he had been "advised" not to open the play, but rather "to fall ill and postpone the opening for a couple of weeks, and then everything could be dropped" (Halliday, p. 28). He refused, and officials did not yet have the power to cancel the productions. Therefore, on 18 February,* Der Silbersee *premiered simultaneously in Leipzig, Erfurt, and Magdeburg. Lenya and Weill attended the Leipzig performance, which took place without incident. One observer remembered the event vividly: "Everyone who counted in German theater met together for the last time. And everyone knew this. It was the last day of the greatest decade of German culture in the twentieth century" (Hans Rothe, quoted in Halliday, p. 33). The piece garnered the most unequivocal critical praise that Weill had ever experienced, but Nazi organizations issued a common manifesto denouncing the "mindless, inferior, sick" work and demanding its immediate withdrawal. Nazi demonstrations disrupted the second performance in Magdeburg on 22 February, and Weill was the focus of anti-Semitic abuse. On 26 February Weill's publisher remarked that "no one believes that things can go on much longer as they are" (UE–W). He was right: Weill had been asked to withdraw from the film project, but Lenya did go through with her recording of several Silbersee songs for Electrola in Berlin, with Gustav Brecher conducting. The next day the Reichstag burned. Hitler blamed the Communists and used the event as an excuse to suspend civil liberties, enabling authorities to search homes and arrest suspected Communists. Brecht fled for Prague. On 4 March officials closed all three productions of* Der Silbersee.

Walter Steinthal telephoned Weill on behalf of Fallada, who had already been arrested, warning that Weill should leave Berlin and await somewhere else the outcome of the 23 March balloting on the "Enabling Act." While Weill was waiting at Café Wien, Lenya and the photographer Louise Hartung hurried to Kleinmachnow to pack some of the most important belongings. (A few days earlier they had "cleaned" the house of letters from theater managers, directors, and conductors who had spoken favorably of Weill's music.) Then they picked Weill up and drove straight through the night to Munich, the next morning checking into Hotel Vier Jahreszeiten, where nearly the entire Berlin intelligentsia seemed to have assembled.

Weill's almost daily correspondence with his publisher had stopped abruptly on 1 March. On 14 March Weill reported to UE that he had returned to Berlin to continue "film negotiations" and "arrange my affairs." The letter betrayed the extreme tensions of the moment:

I get the impression you've already thrown in the towel and, probably under the influence of the numerous Berlin alarmists you've met there, have fallen into a lethargy which is unwarranted, especially now. I find it quite wrong and indefensible to have you all sitting in Vienna and moping instead of doing the only thing possible under today's circumstances: to go abroad and explore all the possibilities for finding new markets for your works; to establish new contacts, track down or create new performance opportunities. Why aren't you in Paris now, dear Dr. Heinsheimer? You have seen how the enormous success I had there hasn't been exploited at all, as there's no one really working on it there. . . . It's a real shame that the incredible opportunities that Paris now offers me (and no doubt Křenek and Alban Berg, as well) have remained entirely untapped. I myself am doing what I can. For months now I've been carrying on negotiations instead of saving my nerves for my work. (W–UE)

Weill concluded by volunteering to go to the United States to promote his own music, if the Broadway production of The Threepenny Opera *turned out to be a hit (it turned out to be a disaster, closing on 22 April, after just twelve performances).*

On 21 March Weill packed a small suitcase and drove with the Nehers in their car toward the border. His passport confirms that the next day he crossed the border at Lunéville, south of Luxembourg, with five hundred francs of restricted foreign currency for the purpose of "travel in France during the month of March." Contrary to the myths she invented with expert coaching from her second husband, George Davis, Lenya had no idea how Weill eventually escaped the country. In 1953 she wrote Caspar Neher, "as you probably remember, at the time Kurt left Germany, I was not with him. . . . I continued on to Vienna [from Munich], and Kurt returned to Berlin. What happened after that? Did he return to the house in Kleinmachnow? When did he decide to leave Germany? What did he take along? Were you with him?" (L–CN, 5 Oct. 1953).

2 · PARIS, LONDON: 1933–1935
Letters 39–148

Weill backstage and Lenya on the set of the original production of
Die sieben Todsünden, Paris, June 1933.
(Photos by George Hoyningen-Huene; see Letter 41)

1933

Weill arrived in Paris on 23 March and checked into Hôtel Jacob. A week later he moved to
Hôtel Splendide and met with Alfred Kalmus, who insisted he sign a new contract with Universal
Edition that would drastically reduce his monthly advance. He asked for the firm's assistance
in transferring ten thousand marks from his German bank account to Austria via a risky and
complicated maneuver involving laundered business accounts: "If I tell you that this is the only
money I have at this point, you may be able to understand my concern" (W–UE, 9 May
1933). On 15 May, Weill was informed by Universal Edition that the attempt to transfer funds
to the "Firma Weill" had failed.

In early April Weill resumed his regular correspondence with his publisher in Vienna and
reported that "in the ten days I've been here, I've already accomplished all sorts of things. . . .
The best and youngest dancers of the Ballets Russes have been assembled from the remnants of
Diaghilev's troupe and his former students into a distinguished company under the direction of
George Balanchine, with Boris Kochno as their business manager. . . . Yesterday an English
financier, Mr. [Edward] James, the husband of Tilly Losch, suddenly appeared. He wants to
fund the whole undertaking, but only if I write something. . . . I've insisted on collaborating
with a poet of equal stature, as I've a plan for which I must have a good text, since in no case
will I write an ordinary ballet. I've proposed Cocteau." When Jean Cocteau declined, Weill
reluctantly agreed to James's insistence on Brecht and enthusiastically endorsed the idea of
asking Lenya, whose resemblance to his own wife James found striking, to play Losch's singing
"double," Anna I. After meeting Weill in Nancy on 5 April, Lenya said yes. Pasetti would

[FIG. 37]

sing in the male quartet. Lenya also informed Weill that Pasetti wanted to have a child with her. She recalled in one of her last interviews, "Kurt looked at me and said, 'But that would hurt me very much.' That was that. I said, OK, I won't have it. That was the relationship we had" (int. L3). Brecht, who was then staying in Switzerland, arrived around 10 April and left a week later, when he and Weill had finished the text of Die sieben Todsünden. *Weill began composition on 16 April and moved from his hotel to the Noailles' home so that he could work undisturbed. He finished the piano score on 4 May and began the orchestration immediately.*

Meanwhile, Weill had sent the libretto to Neher, who had agreed to design the production. When he received it, however, he informed Weill that the text was "literary trash," and therefore he could not participate. In an undated letter to Erika Neher from May 1933, Weill expresses his dismay over Neher's decision and uncharacteristically lays bare his emotional state:

The worst thing is the fact that neither of you (how terrible that I have to include you both in this) has any confidence whatsoever in me; otherwise you'd realize that every text I've set looks entirely different once it's been swept through my music. . . . But no, darling, let's be honest. The reasons lie elsewhere. C. has been holding me at bay for weeks because of his indecisiveness. You have now confirmed by telephone (and in writing) something I had suspected all along, that for completely understandable reasons, Cas is now reluctant to work with B. and myself. . . . This is the same Cas who *never* dared to say anything against B., who kept quiet whenever there was a complaint, who left me completely in the lurch in my battle against B. during the Berlin *Mahagonny,* who always got together with him even after B. and I had become enemies. . . . Little angel, dearest, most beloved, sweetest angel, don't be angry that I'm writing all this. But I do have to carry this burden alone. Since six o'clock yesterday I've been pacing this room, brooding over the matter, and now your letter has arrived. . . . I'm in one hell of a situation. I have to find another designer, right when I'm working day and night on the full score—to say nothing of my problems with the divorce lawyers, problems with the Dresden bank, problems with the ballet rehearsals, and the continuing aftereffects of the serious dizzy spells I suffered on Sunday afternoon. But I should not close this letter without telling you that, despite everything, the thought of you makes me quiet and happy, and my thoughts of you are sad but very beautiful. (W–EN2, n.d.)

Caspar Neher soon reconsidered and rejoined the production team of Les Ballets 1933, which included Maurice Abravanel as conductor and Balanchine as choreographer. The first of Lenya's surviving letters dates from this time.

39 LENYA IN VIENNA TO WEILL AT THE NOAILLES' IN PARIS, 8 MAY 1933

8 May 1933

Dear Weillchen,

Unfortunately I couldn't come to the phone just then because I was having cramps. I think the contract with [Edward] James sounds really good. I just wrote him a few lines and asked him for the contract. I'm all for treating these contractual matters as strictly business. I'm really very happy to earn this money, plus I'm so looking forward to this work. Pasetti is very glad to be in it too. It's also great for him to sing a little bit again. L. W. [*Lieber* (dear) Weill], I've taken the liberty of remitting 81 and 23 marks from your account for my car insurance and car registration, respectively. I only have 100 marks here, so I couldn't pay them both. Personally I don't have any more money in D [Germany]. So I'll send you 100 marks and 30 francs from here; that's approximately the total, 104 Reichs-Marks. I hope you won't be angry. I'm not going to ask how you are, because I know how it is when you're writing piano score and orchestrating.

The weather here is still lousy, and there's not much sun. But that doesn't matter. I've already thought about a beautiful costume for the practical girl from Louisiana [Anna I]. Won't it be wonderful to stir things up a bit again? I'll sing like a songbird. But how all this is going to turn out without [Helene] Weigel and Brecht is sure a mystery to me. Have you heard anything from him? I hope not. Sometimes I really do miss Cäschen [little Cas (Caspar Neher)]. He's always the same nice Cas. I wonder what he's doing, and whether a little national flag is already fluttering from his Hanomag. Have you seen the *Berliner Illustrierte?*[1] That's really something. It gives you the feeling that this is going to go on for decades. Now good luck, Weillchen, and see you soon. I'll be staying at the Splendide [hotel] again. It's so conveniently located.

> All good things,
> Linnerl

I've dropped the *Lotte* from my name and want to write it like this instead: L. Marie Lenja. Isn't that better?[2] The *Lotte* is so like a Kraut.

---

1. *The Hanomag was a small, inexpensive car popular in Germany. The* Berliner Illustrierte *was the most popular illustrated weekly magazine (in newspaper format) in Germany. Lenya's feeling was accurate: two days later Berlin lit up with the book burnings, Jews were banned from all cultural activities, Jewish bank accounts were frozen, and mail to and from all "disruptive elements" was monitored and sometimes censored.*

2. *Lenya may be taking a jibe at the vicomtesse de Noailles, Marie-Laure, with whom Weill was rumored to be romantically involved.*

[FIG. 38]

On 1 June, Weill gave Brecht a progress report: "It's the usual chaos. Of course, a small clique has developed out of the devotees of the old Ballets Russes, for whom ours isn't 'ballet' enough, not enough 'pure choreography.' Because of that there have been tremendous fights for the past few days, and I succeeded in getting one of them 'put on ice.' Though Balanchine is swaying between two factions, he's worked well and has found a style of performance that is very 'balletic' but still realistic enough. Lenya and the Family will be very good, as, of course, will the set by Cas and the music. . . . Of course, we'd all be delighted if you could come. James has already half-promised to pay for your trip if you can come, and I think I can squeeze a thousand francs out of him" (W–BB).

The premiere of Die sieben Todsünden *on 7 June was attended by what Tamara Toumanova called "the best elite of la société française, l'élégance du théâtre, du grand monde" (Toumanova, p. 51). Weill had sent Brecht a thousand francs so that he could attend the premiere, but Brecht described the piece to Weigel as "pretty enough but not very important" (Brecht, pp.*

165–66). Weill, on the other hand, thought it "the finest score I've written up to now" (W–UE, 29 June 1933). Although reports indicate that it was applauded vigorously, critical notices were decidedly mixed. The same day Universal Edition informed Weill: "As things now stand, with the collapse of the German market for your works, the income from your compositions has been reduced to a minimum scarcely worth mentioning. . . . We would have been happy if, in spite of your current circumstances, you had shown some understanding of the publisher's situation and allowed the contract to continue for the next few months without monthly payments. If you are not prepared to accept this solution, we propose that we return to you the full rights for all your works for one year" (UE–W, 7 June 1933). A week later, exhausted, suffering from an outbreak of psoriasis, and on the brink of nervous collapse, Weill vacationed in Italy: Alassio, Positano, Rome, and Florence.

40   LENYA IN PARIS TO WEILL IN ALASSIO, ITALY, [16 JUNE 1933]

Friday

Dear Weilili,

Many thanks for both your postcards. Thank God you're by the sea. And it's nice that you just happen to be in Alassio. Now take it easy and make good use of the time (because it slips by). There's a lot going on here. I'll describe the matters one at a time:

1. Enclosed automobile tax has to be taken care of. You have to send the registration form (for the car) to Erika [the maid], and she will get it renewed for you. I've sent her the money (and with it her 80 marks, which you most likely have forgotten). That's that.

2. Strauß, the attorney, called. The date for the divorce has been set for Monday. I immediately wrote to Täubler and wired Hartung that her expenses should be reimbursed right away.[1] I hope they're both in Berlin, otherwise it'll have to be postponed, and that costs money. Dr. Strauß has asked for 250 marks for the second attorney. I told him that I didn't have your address yet, and that I'd let him know as soon as I have it. This is not so urgent.

3. The director of Ultraphon called. I met him (an especially slimy, completely ignorant schlemiel). They want to record [Marlene] Dietrich, and apparently Dietrich has asked to do songs of yours. But it seems she wants you there to play piano, etc. I've given him the address of Universal Edition, so they can have the music of the *Happy End* songs, "Surabaya" and "Matrosen-Tango," sent to them. They insisted on knowing where you were and casually hinted at how important it would be for you if Dietrich would sing your songs. I said that this surely would be interesting for you, but it would be even more important for their company. Besides that, it would also be a question of money. If they pay for your trip, your living expenses, and a big fee (I did not say that, only *you* can demand that), perhaps you will interrupt your vacation for a week. You can't be arrogant enough, Weillchen. They haven't got a clue—they didn't even know that your *Sieben Todsünden* was running—and if Dietrich hadn't asked for you (which I assume to be the case from the conversation), they wouldn't have the slightest idea. I'll give them your address in a few days, so as not to look too eager. Perhaps you can

write to Dietrich (she's probably staying in Versailles again) that Ultraphon has approached you, etc. This thing seems to be very important for them. If you want to call me, you can reach me every morning until 9:30 at Etoile 1456. I'll give your address to Ultraphon tomorrow.[2]

4. London is definite. James is doing the [English] translation with me, since the other one is unusable. It's a big job for me. He hasn't negotiated a fee yet, but I'll bring that up now. The London season begins on 27 June, and it'll be our turn to open on 3 July. They've done a stinking thing to Abravanel. James (because of the intrigues of the Russians, and especially Nabokov)[3] has engaged an English conductor for London and canceled Abravanel.[4] It happened last night. I overheard James telling him at the next table while I was there working on the translation. I told James I didn't think it was a good idea for someone else to try to do your music. But you know how it is. I called Abravanel and told him he should call in sick for five days. Tonight just happens to be the premiere of *Hiob*. He did that first thing this morning, and fifteen minutes later Nabokov came to see him and assured him how <u>wonderfully</u> he does his shit. Then there was a phone conversation with James, so now it'll be like this: Abravanel will conduct your work, the dances by Nabokov, and the Schubert, if they can't come up with any more dirty tricks to pull on him.

So that's all for today. Write me soon—let me know how much the automobile registration fee is and how long to renew it for, and I'll send the money to Erika right away out of my own funds for the time being, and we'll figure it out later on. Now enjoy, Weili, swim a lot and bake yourself in the sun, if there shineth one. This letter should be sent off quickly. All good things for you, my Weillchen, and greetings to Hans.

> Greetings,
> Your *Kleene*

Please send me <u>everything</u> that has to be taken care of.

1. *Weill's relative Selma Stern Täubler and Lenya's friend Louise Hartung represented them in the divorce proceedings in Berlin. Very few of Lenya's and Weill's closest friends knew that they divorced in 1933. Late in life Lenya acknowledged to a few friends that she and Weill had separated during this period, but she maintained that the divorce had been a matter of necessity to protect their assets in Germany. After World War II, Louise Hartung sometimes served as an intermediary between Alfred Schlee, a director of Universal Edition, and Weill.*

2. *David Drew reports that Weill and Dietrich met during the summer and suggests that Weill's song "Der Abschiedsbrief" (with lyrics by Erich Kästner) was intended for Dietrich's recording project (p. 249).*

3. *Nicolas Nabokov (1903–78), a cousin of the novelist Vladimir Nabokov, had studied with Busoni and Paul Juon in Berlin in 1922–23, concurrently with Weill. Les Ballets 1933 presented his ballet Hiob; in 1939 he became an American citizen.*

4. *The conductor was Constant Lambert (1905–51), a composer-conductor-critic akin to America's Virgil Thomson. Reviewing the London performance of the Todsünden, he wrote that "Lenja can get into the word 'baloney' a wealth of knowingness which makes Mae West seem positively ingenue." He also wrote very perceptively of Weill: "Weill symbolizes the split that is taking place not between highbrow and lowbrow, but between highbrow and highbrow.... He and Alban Berg represent the two extremes of Central European aesthetic, and in their widely different ways are the most successful exponents of their respective styles."*

Friday, 5:00 P.M.

My dear Weillchen, you *Pi,*

Many thanks for your sweet letter and the lovely scented herb from Alassio. Of course I remember the village, especially the washerwomen.[1] There was a long wall and farther on a cemetery. So on Tuesday [20 June] we did *Mahagonny,* and again it was a huge success, although the performance was terrible. [The singers] Peters and Fuchs were so sloppy, and Mrs. Abravanel was terrible (can't sing at all).[2] Abravanel himself was bad too. I had a big argument with him the next day and told him, among other things, that you weren't very well served by such a "Kálmánesque" performance.[3] He rushed it to death. Once again all the concentration had to come from me. Overall it's a tremendous strain to bring something to the performance when the rest of it is lousy. Pasetti really sang very beautifully that evening, and Gretler was as dependable as ever.[4] But everything else was awful. "Alabama" and "Denn wie man sich bettet" had to be repeated after thunderous applause. But I wasn't happy that evening. Don't write anything to Abravanel. I've already given him a piece of my mind, and for London he'll be on his toes.

Thursday morning Pasetti flew to Vienna; he comes back on Saturday. The thing with the money didn't work out quite right. His father let himself be influenced somewhat by Dr. [Hugo] Winter and didn't do the job entirely in the way Pasetti had instructed him to. He wired me today that everything is OK now.[5] He also stopped by Universal Edition to take care of *Mahagonny.* Universal had asked 15 pounds (!) for a single performance of *Mahagonny* (for that lousy performance material, half of which was simply missing and which James has had redone for the London performance). For the Milhaud, James is paying only 5 pounds. He said he could do *Mahagonny* only once in that case. So P[asetti] was at U.E. and negotiated with them (on your behalf—I hope this is all right with you). Now they will take 4 pounds per performance, for a minimum of four performances. That's more feasible. In an hour I'm going to see James, who came back from London today, and I'll tell him.

I went to James's agent for my contract. For the three weeks he'll pay me 230 pounds (guaranteed), with five performances per week, which amounts to around 3,000 marks. That's really wonderful. He wanted to pay me less, but the *Mahagonny* success softened him up. I have to be in London on the 26th. The first public dress rehearsal of *Die sieben Todsünden* is on the 28th; the performance in German for the press is on the 30th. The first English-language performance is on the 5th, if it hasn't bombed by then. But I'm really nervous about "My young sister and I" [the opening line in the English version, *Anna-Anna*]. He'll also definitely do *Mahagonny.* First he wants to do it on the radio. He doesn't want this Mrs. Abravanel, but rather Rosenthal.[6] That's also much better for me. "Alabama Song" is far more effective if there's a pretty girl standing behind me and not such a klutz. She really should be cooking instead.

There were lots of people again at the *Mahagonny* performance. Only Marie-Laure didn't make it. (I think I'll make a stink about that one.) I think it's quite likely that you yourself are the eighth deadly sin. As for me, the duchess of Clermont Tunerre (I think I spelled it wrong) attended the performance, and this no longer entirely youthful lady was so enthusiastic about *Mahagonny* and me that she came into the dressing room and absolutely demanded to see me.[7] She called the very next morning, and in the afternoon I went over to have tea with her. All by herself, with no company. She was really charming. She wants to write an article about me. Then she showed me her house (which is on rue du Raynard). In the music parlor she confessed to me that she plays "the flute." Hee, hee, I almost said, like old Fritz [Frederick the Great (Friedrich II, der Große, later called Alte Fritz)], and probably as poorly, too. But I held my tongue. After an hour I took off. By then it had become too genteel for me, but nowhere near so *ur-gemütlich* as at the Biene's[?]. She asked what she could do for me in England. Today she sent me letters of introduction for two different ladies in London. I should go there. Well, in a word: I've been at a duchess's. I really fancied myself like Eliza Doolittle in *Pygmalion*. There's something of that in this whole thing. But people were crazy for *Mahagonny* again. That's much more fun than anything else.

There hasn't been much mail. Take care of these few things. Everything else I've done already. After London I'll go to Kleinmachnow for sure. I also think it's the right thing to do. But Weillchen, don't <u>you</u> even think of going back to Germany. Don't let yourself be enticed by Cas. It would be terrible. I haven't heard anything about the divorce. I'll call Strauß before I leave. We can meet you at the end of August, and then we'll fix you up an apartment in Paris. Everything is OK with the house. The clipping from *Melos* should be very interesting for you.[8] Mr. and Mrs. David from Düsseldorf have been pestering me since *Mahagonny* to get together with them.[9] So I'll meet them for dinner tomorrow. That's the quickest way to get it over with.

Francesco [von Mendelssohn] saw *Mahagonny* and was very nice. He stayed on just for that and left the next morning for Venice. I haven't heard another thing from Steinthal. They really are strange people. You were absolutely right to leave immediately after the premiere, because I find the clique here even worse than the one in Berlin. In Berlin at least once in a while somebody spoke the truth. But here everything is that slimy "*merveilleuse.*"

Now farewell my Weili, drive nice and careful, and don't expose your shiny little head to the sun too much or you'll get dopey. My London address is Theatre Savoy, Strand. Give my kindest regards to Cas—and if Erika is along, to her also—and for you, as always, all good things from

    Your *Kleene*

X—I finished this letter at 7:00 P.M. But then Scherchen called and came to the hotel for dinner.[10] He wanted to talk to you to tell you that he is going to do the *Lindbergh-flug* in Strasbourg on 7 August. He was so boring, and so was I. Naturally I let him pay for his own dinner. Then James came with the signed contract, thank God, but Sch. kept on sitting there until James left, and then he started acting quite the lonely one, whereupon I flew to my room in a flash. *Vogue* has taken pictures of me, and I just showed them to James. He was so enthusiastic that he ordered three big ones for the lobby in London and thirty-six more (!!) for the newspapers and publicity. Just caught him at a good time. Besides, the pictures are very beautiful. Very Parisian. But good.[11] Hans Hess's girlfriend said that [Elisabeth] Hauptmann had to get out of Brecht's apartment (his car, manuscripts, etc., have all been confiscated), because she couldn't stand the constant police raids anymore.[12] Brecht (whom I cautiously did not invite to *Mahagonny*) is supposed to be saying all the bad things he can about Hauptmann. She couldn't hold out to the end.[13] Well, it's too disgusting. So Weilli, I'm going to sleep now. I have to be at James's by 9:00 A.M. tomorrrow for the translation. I'm going at it like Blücher.[14] Now farewell again!

1. Weill and Lenya had stayed in Alassio during their trip to Italy in July 1926.

2. The concert on 20 June at Salle Gaveau featured the "Paris version" of Mahagonny, which had been a triumph (with Lenya and Pasetti in the cast) the previous December, and Kleine Dreigroschenmusik. Albert Peters and Erich Fuchs, a bass baritone from Berlin, were also singing in Die sieben Todsünden; Friedel Abravanel (b. 1905) sang under the professional name Maria Schacko, misspelled in the program as Marie Chacko.

3. Emmerich Kálmán (1882–1953) was a Hungarian composer of operettas, including Die Csárdásfürstin (1915) and Gräfin Maritza (1924).

4. The prominent Swiss actor Heinrich Gretler (1897–1977) had played a role in Donizetti's La fille du régiment at the Theater am Schiffbauerdamm in 1930.

5. On 6 June, Weill informed UE that "Baron Florian von Pasetti Friedensburg [Otto's father, a colonel in the Austrian army] will be coming to see you concerning the Leipzig money. I hereby ask you to dispose of the money in the manner Mr. von Pasetti will request." On 14 June Universal Edition wrote Weill that "according to Mr. Pasetti's instructions, we have asked Hofmeister to transfer RM 3,300 to the address he has given us. Mr. Pasetti has instructed us to exchange the rest of RM 6,700 into Austrian schillings through the Länderbank. The Länderbank has informed us that so far they have been unable to comply with this request, but that they would keep trying" (UE–W).

6. Hilde Rosenthal would also sing the secondary female role (Bessie) in the Rome performance of Mahagonny later in the year.

7. Elisabeth, duchesse de Clermont-Tonnerre, appears several times in Count Harry Kessler's diary. A member of Natalie Barney's feminist literary group, L'Académie des Femmes, she wrote her memoirs under her maiden name, Elisabeth de Gramont.

8. The May/June issue of Melos, a periodical about contemporary music published by Schott Verlag and edited by Dr. Heinrich Strobel, included a review of Edward J. Dent's biography of Ferruccio Busoni, as well as an essay by Kurt Zimmerreimer entitled "Stoff- und Textfragen der neuen Oper," which identifies the libretto of Weill and Neher's Die Bürgschaft as "a particularly complicated case."

9. Hanns W. David had conducted the first production of Die Dreigroschenoper in Düsseldorf.

10. The conductor Hermann Scherchen (1891–1966) established his career as a champion of new music with the concert tour of Schoenberg's Pierrot lunaire in 1911. He founded the Neue Musikgesellschaft in Berlin, as well as the progressive journal Melos. Having encouraged the nineteen-year-old Weill to study with Schoenberg, Scherchen later conducted Weill's "Berlin im Licht," for military band, in 1928, and the Hindemith-Weill Lindberghflug in 1929 and 1930.

11. Lenya was photographed by the famed George Hoyningen-Huene (1900–1968), who was based at the Paris Vogue from 1926 to 1935.

12. Hans Hess, a former pupil of Hindemith, was the son of the wealthy Erfurt art collectors Alfred and Thekla Hess. A private printing of their guest book contains autographs of Lenya and Weill, as well as original watercolors and drawings by Paul Klee, Lyonel Feininger, and Wassily Kandinsky. An introductory note by Hans Hess includes: "Kurt Weill had his first local success at the civic theater not entirely without the help of my father, who had ordered several hundred tickets and invited all his friends. Modern music was as difficult to understand as modern painting, but the Protagonist was performed with great success" (p. 41).

13. Two years later, in recommending Hauptmann, Brecht stated, in contrast, that "after Hitler's takeover she stayed on in Berlin for one more year. . . . She had to endure more than twenty house searches and was arrested. She succeeded in gaining her freedom, as there was no proof of any wrongdoing. . . . She is one of the most dependable and capable human beings I know" (Bertolt-Brecht-Archive 654/90, 18 Aug. 1935).

14. The idiom refers to Gebhard Leberecht von Blücher (1742–1819), the famous Prussian general who helped Wellington defeat Napoleon at Waterloo.

Positano, 28 June 1933
Casa Cosenza

Dear Linerl,

In Naples I got all my mail and found your two long letters. Many thanks for your detailed report. I'm very happy that London is going to materialize after all, and under such favorable conditions for you. Your *Mahagonny* success, and everything that went with it, has made me very happy too. People like this duchess are really important for you. I'm convinced that you could have a big career in Paris now, if we handle things just halfway cleverly, because what you do would be an unexpected feast for the Parisians, who simply have a natural appreciation for the subtlety of this kind of art. In London, too, you must take advantage of every possible contact. I've already written from Alassio to the director of London Radio that he should plan something for you. His name is Clark.[1] I'm very curious to see how things will go in London and how these "insular people" are going to react.

Our trip was marvelous. You can't spend more than two days on the Adriatic coast (Rimini, etc.). It's very much like Binz [a lower-middle-class summer resort by the Baltic sea]—exactly the same type of people. We drove on immediately through the Apennines—where we stayed in a very beautiful spot (Popoli). Naples is a surprisingly beautiful, big, and lively city. And Positano is an ideal place for relaxation. A fishing village hewn into the rocks, with a tiny beach. You don't see any people there, because they all get lost in their houses, each of which is set apart from the other. There isn't a soul on the beach. I'm happy to be here, although of course I would have liked to help in London. But right now I do need the rest. It's very pleasant to be with the Nehers. Erika and Georg [the Nehers' son] are here too. They have an apartment next door. I have a magnificent room with a huge terrace directly above the ocean. Of course, it's very primitive, but after 9 July we'll have electricity. And I'm glad not to be in a hotel for a change.

We'll probably have to pay the fee for Strauß's other Berlin lawyer. I had written to you that Erika [the maid] was supposed to pay it from the GEMA money.[2] Did you take care of that?

I will slowly take care of all my mail from here. I'll also write to you again very soon. "Break a leg," you busy bee (I'm always envious when other people work)!

All the best to you and warmest regards to Pasetti, whom I thank again for all he has done in that money matter.

Your Weillchen

---

1. *Edward Clark (1888–1962) was a British conductor and writer on music who had studied with Schoenberg in Berlin. A champion of new music, he headed the music department of the BBC, where he programmed unfamiliar works of Bartók, Busoni, Stravinsky, Schoenberg, and many other contemporary composers.*

2. *GEMA, Gesellschaft für musikalische Aufführungs- und mechanische Vervielfältigungsrechte, is the German counterpart to ASCAP; it collects royalties for musical recordings and performances and distributes them to authors, composers, and publishers.*

Positano, 4 July 1933
Casa Cosenza

Dear Linerl,

I've subscribed to a London clipping service, and today I already received the first reviews of the London dress rehearsal. You must have had a huge success, and it seems that you've beaten little Tilly [Losch] by a horse's length. Well, congratulations! I'm terribly happy. From these first reviews I can't really tell much about the work's success. Anyway, the reviews are devoted almost exclusively to it, and it seems that we have again kicked up quite a bit of dust. I'm keeping all the reviews for you.

You really should dig up a French and German publicity agent to make sure that your London success gets mentioned in the Parisian, German, and Viennese papers. That would be very important right now! You should also hire a manager, if you can find a good one.

I should have heard from you by now, because I already got answers from people I had written to earlier. But you're probably terribly busy.

There isn't any news from here, except that I'm slowly but steadily recuperating. I'm going to take a two-to-three-day boat ride with Cas this week to Capri, Pompeii, etc. It is, as always, very beautiful and relaxing here. I got a very nice letter from Kaiser and one from my parents, who write me that for the first time in a year they received a letter from you. Little by little I'm taking care of the rest of my mail.

> For today, all the very best
> from your
> Weillchen

Regards to Pasetti

Positano, 16 July 1933

My dear Linerl,

I spent two days with Cas in Capri (where it's very beautiful) and was a little disappointed not to have any news from you when I got back. But I can imagine that you've got a lot to do and can't get around to writing. But just the same I'm always worried when I don't hear from you for more than a week and don't know how you are. I'm also very anxious for news about the *Mahagonny* performance. I've received new reports about *Die sieben Todsünden* (from London), all very good and again very favorable for you. I'm keeping everything and will bring it along for you. The reports about *Die sieben Todsünden* from Germany are shameless and mean. They're simply making up lies about a failure and maintain that Paris, too, does not want to hear any more about these botched pieces of work, which the "new Germany" rejected long ago.[1] In retrospect I've come to realize that Paris too has quite an active anti-Weill contingent and that they are agitating against me furiously. Sometimes I wonder whether I really need to put myself into a another witch's cauldron and use up my nerves fighting this dung heap of intriguers. If I move to Paris, I'll certainly live way out of the city and do nothing but work. Or maybe it would be better to live very simply somewhere in Ticino, Lake Garda, or some place like that and go to Paris only when it's necessary.

You see, I'm slowly getting well, and the more my strength returns, the more these questions again come to the fore: what's going to happen, where should one be working—and on what? We'll have to talk about all that in detail, won't we? What do you intend to do next? Are you going to Berlin? And when could we meet? It's terribly hot here right now. My rash has as good as disappeared, and also the psoriasis is receding. If it gets any hotter here, I think I'll leave in approximately a week and drive slowly north, for a little bit of Rome, a little bit of Florence, then perhaps a little bit of the mountains. Tomorrow I'm meeting Ruth and Leo [Sohn], who are leaving for Palestine.

Now, *Kleene,* be sure and write your *Kleenen* about what your plans are and whether you're carryin' on with your successes, and take a little kissy from your

Weilli

1. By July 1933 most of the musical press had been brought under control of the new ministry of culture. The June issue of the monthly periodical Die Musik, *for example, featured photographs of the new cultural leaders of Germany, including Joseph Goebbels, Bernhard Rust, Hans Hinkel, Paul Graener, and Max von Schillings. The issue began with an epigram by Goebbels: "Wenn die Kunst die Zeit formen will, dann muß sie sich auch mit ihren Problemen auseinandersetzen" (if art aims to have an impact on its time, it must come to grips with its problems).*

45   LENYA IN OSTEND, BELGIUM, TO WEILL IN ARABBA, ITALY, [22 JULY 1933]

Saturday, Ostend

My dear Weili,

Thanks for your sweet letter. I didn't know the German papers were writing about *Die sieben Todsünden.* Hartung told me her brother had written that they were playing *Die Dreigroschenoper* in small movie theaters again.[1] If that's true (which I'll find out right away when I get there), then this newspaper claptrap by some overanxious people is not all that important. We already know they're vicious. That's the way they treated you long before this. Only now they let loose all their hatred. Of course it's very difficult to tell what you should be working on and where. You'll probably know the "what" very soon. I'm thinking along the lines of Shakespeare or perhaps a [Frank] Wedekind pantomime. *Die Kaiserin von Neufundland* would make an enchanting ballet piece.[2] I believe there's already a rotten setting by Holländer.[3] But that's no reason not to do it again. I'll send you everything by Wedekind and whatever else might be interesting for you; only you'll have to tell me where to send it and whether I might have to use a "code" address. Maybe you'll let me know what *you* might have in mind. Shall I send you some Nestroy? Traven has some new books out.[4] I'm wondering whether or not you might want to live in Vienna. But the whole atmosphere there is so hopeless. With some skill and the right connections you could avoid the anti-Weill contingent in Paris. I suppose this is the fate of all the chosen ones. I wouldn't bother my head for one second over any of this. And Paris is still a wonderful city to live in. And you already have some good friends there. But we can talk about all this in person. In any case, you're already going to be seeing Marie-Laure in August (and don't you let them force you into their customary formal wear—rather go on strike against it your very first evening there)—and afterward we'll meet you wherever you want. Of course I'll help you with your apartment in Paris.

I'm really quite curious about Germany. [Walter] Gropius and his wife came to the last *Sieben Todsünden* performances in London, and I spoke with them afterward.[5] They had terrible tales to tell. They said their only remaining pleasure was the *Dreigroschen-oper* recordings and that you were already considered one of the classics. Here's what happened with *Mahagonny:* Cas's pictures with a letter from you—dated the 7th—arrived on the evening of the performance—which was the 18th. I don't know what happened to them. They came too late, anyway. James had not advertised at all. He had lost a lot of money, had big fights with the Russians, and probably no longer gave a damn. Because of this, I wanted to cancel; so on the evening before the day of the performance I took seven sleeping pills. Of course, I was almost unconscious the next morning, and James came immediately with the doctor, who gave me something to counteract them. But at 5:00 P.M. I just felt I had to get on that stage, so I staggered into the theater. That I did a terrific job despite all this (Pasetti is very critical of such things, and everyone else said so too) is a complete mystery to me, especially because after the performance I totally collapsed and they had to take me home. I was raging like a bull because that louse James had the nerve to stand in front of the curtain and "introduce" the piece only on the evening of the performance. Tilly was in the theater. She says she just could have died watching the preceding program: some pieces by Markevitch (supposedly beautiful—I didn't hear them); then Gusso sang four Lieder badly; in between there were endless pauses because the lighting never worked; then Allanova(!) came and danced—and then it was our turn.[6] The theater was one-third full and, even though there were so few people, it was still a great success. But there's no chance of repeat performances. Tilly said she first noticed during that performance how badly everything else had been organized. That, however, doesn't really have much impact on us. From the newspapers you can see that ours was the most important piece. I don't know how the *Mahagonny* press will turn out (I don't believe that any reviewers came).

The next day James showed up and demanded the full score of *Die sieben Todsünden.* He insisted it belonged to him because he had paid for it. I declared that he had a right only to the lithograph full score, and I would have this score copied in Berlin and then forwarded to him. He insisted on having this done in England (he wanted to give an open-air performance of *Anna-Anna* on his farm, and he supposedly needed the full score for that). What do you say about this half-wit? Well, in any case, I haven't let the score out of my hands. As a result, he didn't give me the royalties that are due you and said he would send them as soon as I sent him the copy. You can be sure that we'll get that money for you. It won't be much, anyway. I've given him the two pictures by Cas. Cas has given all the drawings (which rightfully belong to James, he says) to Kochno,[7] and now I've given up the two *Mahagonny* drawings. But if Cas wants them back, I'll write James that he should pay for them because Cas asked me for their return. On top of all that, he insisted that Pasetti and I would have to make good in November or December for that one week we lost because of the early closing (our contract was supposed to run until the 27th). He guaranteed us a round-trip. So we agreed to that. The main thing was that he paid us our money. If he wants to do something more of yours again in November, I'll gladly be at his disposal. He insisted we should stay at his farm for a week. But I was no longer in the mood, and besides I was really pretty sick about this *Mahagonny* experiment. But now I must stop doing this amateur claptrap. I just have to be very careful as far as the copying is concerned. Who in Berlin can do it? You didn't write me either whether that U.E. thing is true, i.e., if they've sent you the 5,000 francs. Perhaps you can drop me a line about that. On the last day here the system for roulette arrived, and we've already tried it out. But it didn't work. Maybe we were doing something wrong, which is possible because we had little time to figure it all out. It's brought us luck anyway. When we found out that the system didn't work and we had already lost 3,000 Belgian francs, Pasetti got so furious that he got up and gambled here and there until he had won 6,000 francs within twenty minutes. In the evening he won again, 3,000 francs, but then we were too dumb and gambled it away again. But we did save 3,000. Now he's trying to figure out this system, and if it works we'll stay until tomorrow and leave Monday morning, visit with Hans and Rita [Weill], and slowly burrow our way back to Berlin. We should get there by Thursday.

Now, Weilili, I've told you everything I know. I'm really happy that you're doing so well, and that your rash has almost disappeared. You'll see how much more relaxed you'll be after you've had a good rest. How long is Cas going to stay with you? And will you always let me know where you'll be and when you'll be traveling around? And take good care of yourself! I need a rest, too. I weigh 103 pounds (which I like), but I'm pale and haggard-looking, and that is not at all nice. I doubt I'll be able to recuperate in Germany. I'm only doing it for Erika and also to see for myself what it's like there now. Weillchen, you won't believe how scared I am to go into that house without you. I guess it might get better later on; it's not sentimentality on my part either. I don't know what it is. Just thinking about it brings tears to my eyes.—I'll bring back with me whatever you want. If I find that it's hopeless for you to think about going back there within the next few years, we should try to sell the house. If not right away, then later. Don't you think so too? I simply could not live in it permanently. I just don't want that. And I believe you'll understand that too. This upheaval will last a long time. And I'd rather live in your immediate vicinity—the most beautiful house could not keep me from that. I'm very much looking forward to seeing you again. I probably won't be able to recuperate fully before that. Now my *Glätzchen,* fare thee well for now and answer the two questions I've underlined. I'm very tired and am going to bed now! Perhaps that system will really work, and then you won't have any more money worries either. That would be wonderful! I'll use the time in Berlin to learn only French. English will come easily. But first I want to learn French. That Hartung woman who always insisted in Berlin that she could speak every language in fact knows none. But that really isn't important. I wanted to get you a pipe in England, but I felt so sick that I had to take the train, and therefore I didn't have a chance to buy one anymore. But in Berlin I'm sure to find something nice for you. Now good night, my dear little, good Weili, don't you carry on so because you are "so brown" (do you remember "God, how brown you are"?) and write soon. You don't have to write me long letters; I know how it is when nothing new is happening. But you can always write me a little postcard. That's not strenuous, and it would make me happy as a monkey.

All the very best to you from
Linderl

1. *Lenya had asked Louise Hartung to come to London to play a small role. Hartung, who went to Ostend with Lenya and Pasetti, later recalled that they lost all the money they had earned in London.*

2. *Die Kaiserin von Neufundland was a two-act pantomime first performed in 1902, with Wedekind himself announcing the various scenes, in the manner of a Moritat street singer.*

3. *The German composer Friedrich Holländer (1896–1976) was associated with Max Reinhardt in Berlin. His song "Ich bin von Kopf bis Fuß auf Liebe eingestellt" from* Der blaue Engel *(1930) brought him international fame. He later scored many Hollywood pictures, among them* Desire *(1936), a film starring Marlene Dietrich and Gary Cooper, for which Weill had hoped to provide the music.*

4. *The Austrian actor and playwright Johann Nestroy (1801–62) wrote more than sixty plays, many of them satirical. The identity of B. Traven (1882?–1969), a novelist and short-story writer, is still debated. He lived most of his life in Mexico, where he wrote one of his most famous books,* The Treasure of the Sierra Madre. *Will Wyatt suggests in* The Man Who Was B. Traven *(New York: Doubleday, 1980) that he was Albert Otto Max Feige, later known as Ret Marut.*

5. *Walter Gropius (1883–1969) was a prominent German architect and the founder of the Bauhaus, an institution of great significance in the development of modernist design and architecture.*

6. *The program on 18 July included* Kleine Dreigroschenmusik, *Igor Markevitch's* Les Hymnes, *Darius Milhaud's* La Mort d'un tyran *danced by Alanova, Fernando Gusso singing airs by Scarlatti and Pergolesi with piano accompaniment, and a staged production of the Paris version of the* Mahagonny Songspiel. *(Gusso had appeared with Tilly Losch in the Les Ballets 1933 production of* Valses de Beethoven, *with music orchestrated by Nicolas Nabokov.) Reviews of the evening were almost uniformly scathing, as can be seen in this remark from the* London Evening News, *19 July 1933: "They say that every country and every age gets the amusement it deserves. It is hard to believe that even modern Europe deserves Igor Markevitch and Kurt Weill."*

7. *Boris Kochno (1904–90) was a director of the Ballets Russes and a dancer in the troupe; he was also Sergey Diaghilev's lover.*

46 LENYA IN BERLIN TO WEILL IN POSITANO, ITALY, [26? JULY 1933]

Dear Kurti,

I sent you a long letter from Ostend (that was on the 23rd). Up to now I haven't had any news from you. We arrived here in good shape. Otto by car and I by train. It's very beautiful here, and everything in the house is OK. The mortgage payment is due to Teltow Savings Bank—262 marks. Apparently Walter[?] hasn't been paying them anymore. I was trying to get money out of the account at Dresdner Bank, which does not present any difficulties. I only need confirmation from the tax bureau that all the taxes have been paid (Zimmermann [notary?] will take care of that for me) and an affidavit from the police that we have our residence here. I've already gotten that. Teltow Savings Bank has given me until 3 August to pay. So that's taken care of too. Please send me Abravanel's address immediately or send it directly to [Edward] James, London W1, 3 Wimpole Street. He asked me for it by telegram. Tilly wrote me that her entire Ballet

1933 will probably go to New York. <u>She</u>, not James, is negotiating with the manager, and that's much better. She'll write me again when she knows something more definite. Otto has to be in Vienna for two days. His wife [Erna] is remarrying, and he has to go because of the child. He wants to leave for Vienna by the middle of the week. Please send him your address: <u>Wien 1, Hotel Meissl und Schader</u>, Neuer Markt 2. Perhaps he'll bring back Mariedl [Lenya's sister], whom I want to invite for eight to ten days because it rained the whole time she was on vacation. By now Otto has worked through that system, and this Fischer[?] seems to be a little crazy. With that system we would have lost our shirts. Otto gambled again for half an hour in Spa when we were driving through there, and he quickly won another 4,000 francs—therefore, we're very well off now. Erika will be getting money from us now. So you won't have to worry about that anymore. How are you, Kurtchen? Are you feeling any better? I'm eagerly awaiting your letter to find out what you're doing now. When are you meeting the vicomtesse [de Noailles]? I saw Curry [Hans Curjel]. He's doing fine. He's busy with a film right now: *Wilhelm Tell*. Then he wants to take some time off. After he finishes the film, he has a vacation coming. That's when he would like to see you, if you're well again by then. Now fare thee well, my little one, and write us quickly how you are doing and don't forget to send your address to Otto. Regards from Erika. Harras recognized me the minute he heard my voice. He's wonderful. I'm anxiously waiting for news from you, how you're doing healthwise at this time. How do you like Rome, Florence? Here it's very hot, and the city is quite dead. What's Cäschen doing? How long will his vacation last? Best regards to him. For you, always the very best from your

    Linderl

I'm going to forward the printed stuff to you. Maybe it'll interest you. Otherwise, there's no mail.

47   WEILL IN ROME TO LENYA IN BERLIN, [28 JULY 1933]
Letterhead: Hôtel Victoria / Roma

Friday

Dear Linerl,

I've been in Rome since Tuesday, and after four weeks of Positano dreck, I'm enjoying a decent hotel room with a private bath for a change. This city is magnificent; I'm running around all day long by myself, because the Nehers are with Küpper, whom I don't want to see.[1]

I'm leaving tomorrow and will stay near a lake between Rome and Florence (Hotel Roma) through this Sunday, and Tuesday or Wednesday I'll be driving north. The next address will be Trento (Italy), poste restante. I'm curious to see what you'll write.

The situation for me is getting clearer and more obvious all the time. The only question is how to shrink the monthly budget as much as possible. Did you get the letter I sent to Ostend, and what do you think of that plan?[2] Before I come to a definite decision about the house and Erika, you both should write to me or meet me somewhere.

Possibly Pasetti could come alone first so we can discuss everything. The performance of M. [*Mahagonny*, in Rome] will be on 29 December. Otherwise I know of nothing newsworthy. I'm feeling very well. I hope you are, too, in our little house by Lake Michigan.

Regards to Pasetti, Erika, Harras!

The very best to you from your
Frosch

1. *According to an interview conducted late in her life, Lenya recalled that at one time Hanns Küpper had had an affair with Erika Neher.*

2. *Weill's crucial letter addressed to Lenya in Ostend, in which he outlined his plans for the future, has not survived, if indeed she ever received it.*

48   LENYA IN BERLIN TO WEILL IN TRENTO, ITALY, 29 JULY 1933

Saturday
July 29

Dear Kurti,

I just now got your letter from Rome. I had written to you in Positano only this morning (I forgot to enclose the accounting), and I also sent you some printed matter that perhaps might interest you: *Anbruch, Der Scheinwerfer, GEMA* magazines, etc.[1] Did you get my letter from Ostend yet? Please have them forward such things to you. Since I still haven't gotten your letter to Ostend, I don't know what your plans are. In any case Otto will be in Vienna on the 6th in the evening (he has to go there because his wife is getting married, and he has to take care of some things concerning their child), and he will stay for three days. He would like to meet you after that and suggests— since he wants to visit his parents in Toblach anyway and since you will be in the mountains nearby—to meet in Cortina d'Ampezzo (that's a place, and not a made-up word!)[2] or in Gardone, Grand Hotel Fasano. If you mention Otto's name, Gardone will be cheaper, whereas Cortina is <u>very</u> expensive during the summer.

In any case, he could meet you in South Tyrol on the 11th or 12th. He asks you to write him with the details in Vienna (from the 6th until the 8th), <u>Hotel Meissl und Schader</u>, Wien 1, Neuer Markt 2.

Everything else I've already written to you in Positano. Please have them forward all your mail. I'm doing fine. Everything in the house is OK. Erika sends you her best regards, and you make sure you get well very soon. We've got to run to the Anhalt railroad station so that

[The letter breaks off here.]

1. Anbruch *was the music monthly published by Universal Edition;* Der Scheinwerfer *was the leading German-language theater journal.*

2. *"Das ist kein Ort, denn Mahagonny—ist nur ein erfundenes Wort" (that isn't a place, for Mahagonny—is only a made-up word) is the closing line of the* Mahagonny Songspiel.

4.8.33

My dear Linscherl,

In Trento I found everything you sent, and I thank you very much for all your sweet letters. Now I'm pretty well informed about everything, but you'll have to tell me a lot more in person. It's a shame you had to get so upset about that *Mahagonny* performance. I do so hope that by now you can recover from all this aggravation. And above all, see to it that you put on some weight! You know I don't like you to be such a skinny little sparrow. So eat a lot, and don't be so fidgety.

We had a wonderful trip: Orvieto, Siena, Florence, the Apennines, Rovereto, and finally—in radiant sunshine—a wonderful drive through the Dolomites. These mountains can really be unbelievably beautiful. Now we've landed in a charming little hotel. The Nehers are going to meet Erika's father [Professor Johannes Heinrich Tornquist] from Graz. In a week they'll drive back. I'm going to stay here until the 11th, and I just wrote to P. [Pasetti] in Vienna that I'll meet him in Toblach (which is very close by) or here on the 11th or 12th.[1]

For the moment I'll be happy to discuss with him what might have to be done now in Berlin. I think if he does go back to Berlin, I will pay that promised visit to Marie-Laure, who by then will be in Davos, and after that we two could meet. I'll talk it all over with P., and I'll tell you the rest in person.[2]

Give my regards to Cury [Curjel] and tell him I'll write him in the next few days and that the Rome performance will be on 29 December. Whether or where I would meet him depends on our travel plans. The business about that 5,000 [francs], of which U.E. informed you, is OK. You can let them make a copy of the full score only if James pays for it, otherwise under no circumstances. The bill must go directly to James. You can have it done at Wohlauer's (I believe they are on Ansbacherstraße). It's really terrific that the Dresdner Bank will release that money. The money with Walter will probably go down the drain. Well, he can't do anything about that.—I have all kinds of plans, prospects, offers. We'll make it, don't worry! I'll write to you once more before leaving here. In any case we'll be seeing each other soon! Do get that beauty rest! Give my regards to Harras and Erika. The very best to all of you and a tiny little kiss!

I don't have Abravanel's address. His father lives in Villemomble, near Paris. Perhaps he's at his brother's in Montreux.

The printed matter has not arrived.

1. *Pasetti's travel documents indicate that he left Vienna on 10 August with a destination of Italy.*
2. *Aware that his letters to Lenya were probably being monitored by the secret police, Weill wrote discreetly, often using cryptic language or references.*

50 LENYA IN BERLIN TO WEILL IN ITALY, [7? AUGUST 1933]

Monday, 11 A.M.

My dear Kurtili,

Many thanks for your telegram. Otto left yesterday for Vienna. I hope he'll arrive safely in the new car (which is beautiful). He'll take a little more time, since he can only go forty kilometers per hour. Yesterday I was invited to lunch by the [Gustav] Brechers. I had met him in the street by chance. They are really charming. He's leaving for a few weeks' rest in Switzerland and would love to see you. (He wrote a letter to you yesterday.) Perhaps you can drive over to visit him. I had no idea he was Czech. He would love to conduct the performance [of *Mahagonny*] in Rome. His fees are very modest. He'd probably do it just for expenses. He would have loved to do *Die sieben Todsünden* too under the same terms. But of course now it's too late for that. This would be one way to get rid of that sloppy Abr. [Abravanel]. Of course, I don't know what you have in mind for there [Rome], but Br. [Brecher] would certainly be an asset. I'm so glad you're doing well. You're really recovering with a vengeance. That way it will last. I'm eager to hear what Otto will have to say. Now I'm out here alone with Erika, and it's very beautiful. Yesterday Erika was crying her heart out because you're not here. She is more attached [to you] than a dog. I read a lot. I've taken up the *Divine Comedy* again, and already the very beginning is so beautiful! Did they forward the mail to you? Also the printed matter? Friday was the premiere of *Kleiner Mann—was nun?* That's just what it was: little man, what now?—Was that ever awful! It was a big flop. If you had done the music, it would have been like Mozart writing music for *Kyritz Pyritz*.[1] The music was by a certain Böhmert.[2] [Rudolf] Neppach didn't appear either, nor was Cas mentioned anywhere. Anyway whatever he contributed was not very notable. That's about all I can report about "art." Today there was yet another summons, and I took Louise [Hartung] and Helkia[?] along, and now I'm waiting for them. I also saw the lawyer in Potsdam. The final court session [for the divorce] will be on 18 September, when the whole thing will be settled. He (Dr. Hahlo) has sent me another bill for 300, which I won't pay right away. How much did you agree upon with Strauß, and how much did he already get? Otto should write all this down. He'll let you know about the other payments. I'm beginning to recuperate nicely. I saw Kardan today. He looks like a living corpse. Both his parents have killed themselves. The father poisoned himself, the mother threw herself out a window, and he's about to starve to death. It's terrible. Now both of the girls are here, and I'm going to close. Things are going according to plan. Write me a few lines and receive the very best regards and some kisses from your

Old Linderl

1. *Kyritz Pyritz, a burlesque by H. Wilken and O. Justinius, was first produced in 1881 at the Belle Alliance Theater in Berlin, with Guido Thielscher as the pharmacist.*

2. *Probably not Böhmert, but Harald Böhmelt, a minor composer later assigned by the Nazis to change the locales of operetta plots to German territories.*

51 WEILL IN ZURICH TO LENYA IN BERLIN, 25 AUGUST 1933
Picture postcard: Restaurant Roseggletscher mit Sellagruppe

Dear Linerl,

The Noailles were not in Davos—instead, Marie-Laure is in French Switzerland, and he's in Salzburg. They couldn't stand it in Davos, and I too drove on immediately; now I'm up here (two thousand meters altitude) at Br.'s [Brecher?], who has found out about a fabulous place. Then I'm going to leave for Zurich, where I'll meet Curry [Curjel], and from there I'll drive either directly or through French Switzerland to Paris. I'll write in detail as soon as there's something to write about.

> Much love to you and lots of tiny greetings,
> Your *Frosch*

It really looks just like this over here!

52 WEILL IN MERANO, ITALY, TO LENYA IN BERLIN, [27 AUGUST 1933]

Merano
early Sunday

Dear Linerl,

Shortly after Davos it began to snow, and the snow was falling so high up on the Flüela Pass that it was hard to keep going, because the windshield was so covered with ice that the wipers no longer worked. At 5:00 I arrived in Zermatt, where I had to have water taken out of the carburetor; at 6:00 I left, then the Ofenpass was very easy; at 7:30 I was at the border, and from there a miserable road to here. I arrived at 10:00. Today I'm glad I drove straight through, because there's beautiful sunshine here and now I'll have a leisurely drive to Arabba. Today I feel fine. I hope the weather there will be nice too. Then everything will look brighter. Be happy and diligent so you'll be a fine pussycat, and so I won't have to get angry when I see you. *A bientôt!*

> Your Kurt

53 LENYA IN BERLIN TO WEILL IN PARIS, 30 AUGUST 1933

Wednesday, 30 August

My dear Weillchen,

Yesterday Curry called because he wanted to see me. But I couldn't get into town soon enough because the car is in Spandau. Now I'll meet him tomorrow. I've talked to Cas. But he couldn't tell me much of what's new. He is very upset because nobody has offered him anything yet. But he maintained that it didn't matter to him, that he's never been worried about money!! Today I got a long letter from Dr. Strauß. That's because I had written to him, when Dr. Hahlo (the attorney who's not admitted to court) and his representative asked for 300 and 200 [marks] respectively. Now Strauß writes me that he had sent 200 for your attorney and mine on 1 May 1933. But I had already been to see my lawyer (Dr. Vogt, who is Hahlo's representative) before Strauß's letter arrived, in order to find out what was really going on. Strauß also writes that I have to pay Dr. Vogt 150. Strauß doesn't mention what happened to the other 250. Because as far as I remember, you had sent 500 in advance for the lawyers and 250 for Strauß himself. Is that right? In either case, I'll only pay Vogt, and if Hahlo gets in touch with me because of your lawyer, I'll go see him personally. That's always better. The main thing is that the 18th will have passed. Then they can wait for the payments. Strauß wanted to know your address, since the agreement we had drafted at the time has not yet been certified by a notary. Now, as far as I'm concerned, I don't think it's necessary.

I know you realize that I'll do only what's good for you too. And we can save the expense of a notary. What do you think? I haven't done anything further about the matter with Walter, since P. told me you were not much in favor of it. The contract is at the lawyer's, with the receipt, but it can be declared void at any time. I've given the declaration that was requested to Zimmermann. Because the money hadn't been declared in 1931, it had to be declared with the current tax assessment (because of this latest "treason against the people" law). This also has been taken care of. It's OK. Zimmermann is very decent and capable. I told him the money is at Walter's, and he thought that if you wanted to get at that money, you should hire a good lawyer. Because Walter himself can't do a *thing*, and wouldn't get anything either. Now you have to figure out exactly what you want to do. If you like, you could assign the money to me or whomever else you choose, and then we might get in touch with these people directly. This has to be done soon anyway, because the second 10,000 payment was due on 4 August (I believe). Write soon to tell me what you want to do. I'll go to the bank and bring them the State Revenue Department's ruling, which is quite favorable to you. By the way, is there still something in the safe-deposit box besides the account? Apparently the mortgage payments have been made, because nothing more has come from Teltow. Everything with the taxes is OK. Did you already withdraw my power of attorney over your account? P. said you had intended to do that. If it hasn't been done yet, I'll see that a few things get taken care of. The following items have to be paid:

[The letter breaks off here.]

54   LENYA IN BERLIN TO WEILL IN PARIS, [SEPTEMBER 1933]

Thursday

Dear Kurtili,

Many thanks for your lovely letter. I just wanted to answer you right away. Today I'm going to meet Suse[?]. As she had told me at the time, the thing had a purely practical value. But if it doesn't under these circumstances, she'll probably let it go. I'll find out today if I can make the mortgage payments from Eri's [Erika's] money. Or do you want to pay it yourself for some reason? Please write me a line about that. I've been paying a few things from this money, including the attorney, the garden fence, etc. I'll send you an exact accounting. I saw the attorney Engelhardt. The plaintiff has asked for two weeks' time. In any case, they do want to keep the newspaper going.[1] And Eug. [Eugene Meyer?] thinks they will certainly pay. That really would be great for my baby. If Julian [Kurt] can find someone better than Eri, I would almost go for it. Of course, she's also too expensive. Perhaps Deta [Strobel] might know of someone. Otto thanks you very much for Holland [a planned performance of *Mahagonny*]. He'll write to them. I'm keeping my fingers crossed about the matter with the publisher.[2] That would really be very, very good. Even if you only get 300, that alone would be a relief. Life really is not so expensive over there. Too bad nothing came of that thing with Marlene [Dietrich]. There were big headlines here: "Marlene's film booed in Paris."[3] That's too bad. I feel sorry for her. With growing fame in Hollywood, they all seem to get hysterical. I'm looking forward to the recording. The divorce matter is in order. There's no longer any need to rush it (I don't think). It's good enough for now. I only hope that you'll find something soon, so you'll have your peace and get out of those hotel rooms. Whenever you're ready, I'll find the time to help you. Nothing else is new. I, too, think it best to let a real estate agent handle the house. It's really hard to rent it. You have no idea how many houses are on the rental market. And even if you can get someone, the house will always be difficult to sell, because you don't know how it will look afterward, and it would cost a lot to have it renovated. I'll do whatever can be done to get rid of it as soon as possible. You can imagine it won't be easy. You mustn't worry that I am too fidgety. I only wrote that I'm too nervous to work. Do you understand? And I also didn't feel like it. Brecher will go see you tomorrow. He's staying at the Majestic [hotel]. He'll probably call. That should be all for today. Things to answer right away: there's only the mortgage—and not really that either. It hasn't arrived yet, and after it does there will still be a few days' time. In the meantime I'll probably have found out from the tax bureau what's actually going on. I've talked to [Eugene] Meyer. He thinks that if they haven't answered you by the end of this week, I should go there again, something they already suggested to me before. I'll take care of this matter too. So, my *Pünktchen*, that's about it. As far as the furniture is concerned, if something should happen in the next few days, I could always have it sent to Munich and leave it in storage until an apartment has been found, or is it better to wait until things are definite?[4]

Mother sent me the pictures for you. You didn't write to me about your winter things. Do you need them right away or in two weeks?

> All the very best for today,
> Your Linerl

As always, best regards to W.[?]

Does the Musikverein need to be paid? I have the money order form right here.

1. *Lenya is referring to Steinthal's* 12 Uhr Blatt. *After the Nazis came to power in early 1933, many of the Jewish-owned newspapers found it expedient to sell their assets to Eher Verlag, the Nazi party's official publishing firm. However, they had to act fast, since there would soon be no other market open for such a sale. After the passage of the Reich Press Law on 4 October 1933, all newspaper owners and editors had to be of "Aryan" descent. As reported by Ernst Aufricht in his memoirs, Walther Steinthal had hoped to be paid some sort of indemnity through the German Embassy in Paris before this law was to be enforced. It is rather doubtful that his efforts had any success. Consequently Weill, who apparently had invested some money in the* 12 Uhr Blatt, *did not receive any compensation either.*

2. *On 3 September 1933 Weill had protested to Universal Edition by registered letter that "for five months now you haven't paid me the monthly installments to which you are obligated by our contracts" and demanded the payment of the delinquent 500-mark monthly stipends. Universal Edition pointed out in its reply of 21 September that "the income from your works has virtually ceased, performance of your works in Germany (the country that was by far your largest source of income) has been made impossible; so you cannot ask us to continue to make these payments. . . . You yourself know very well that the bulk of your oeuvre is written for the stage and that outside Germany there are almost no performance possibilities of any consequence." After Weill and Alfred Kalmus met in Paris, a compromise was reached: UE agreed to make the back-payments, and Weill released them from their contracts and agreed to pay them a percentage of future income derived from works assigned to other publishers. On 31 October 1933 Weill signed a new publishing agreement with Heugel in Paris.*

3. *The film was* The Song of Songs, *directed by Rouben Mamoulian for Paramount.*

55 LENYA IN BERLIN TO WEILL IN PARIS, [OCTOBER 1933]

Sunday

Dear Kurti,

Thanks for your letter. I'm terribly sorry that this business with the publisher is at a stalemate. It would have meant such peace of mind. Right now I'm mad as hell. Your mother called; she's staying with Ruth for a few days. She asked how things were going, and I told her all about the publisher. She said, "Well, it doesn't really matter, and it isn't all that bad." They, too, care only about their own troubles. My old lady is not one iota better. It'd be best if we could come into the world as orphans. Now my *kleines Fröschlein*, write me right away and tell me what the house looks like, approximately how big the rooms are, and whether there's lighting. If not, I'll send some lamps along as well. And whether you might need a kitchen table. I have one here, too. For the time being, only Julian's [Kurt's] things are being sent. They'll leave here on the 8th and will be in the house in Munich [Paris] on the 13th–14th. Shall I send garden furniture for the terrace? Please answer these few questions right away. Furthermore, what's to be done about Eri? It'll be all right if you don't need her for the time being. Perhaps Deta knows someone. Still, in many respects Eri is really first-rate. Well, we've got time to deal with this problem before we see each other. I'm leaving on the 10th or 11th; when I arrive depends on how the trip goes. Does that suit you? The cancelation of your registration [at the police precinct] has been taken care of. Yesterday I paid another 39.50 for property tax. I must meet with Zimmermann to talk about all of this. I hope Deta will come soon. I'm also sending some linens. The winter things will arrive together with Walter's coat on the 10th through [Nathan Weill's wife] Leni's brother-in-law. We've seen Cas just once, and I might as well tell you that he left me with a very unpleasant impression. He was so full of shit (as always when he's especially insecure), talking about "his" opera that premieres in January.[1] So what, that's all you can say about that. I left early. I have a tremendous longing to hear the music of *Die Bürgschaft*. It would be like a purifying bath in the River Jordan or the Ganges. You know Cas is simply squirming. And that is so unpleasant. Now keep well, my Weili. By the way, what should I do with all these clippings? Pack them in a box and keep them? That would be best. I was at [Hans Curjel's wife] Jella's. She packed up all her junk and she's going to live in a furnished place as of the first. I don't know anything else to tell you. I've heard absolutely nothing from Suse. I'm under the impression that she's "inclined from head to toe" toward her mother (in reaction against her father).[2] I will get the P. from W.[?]. All the very best to you. Perhaps there is already a letter from you on the way.

Your Linerl

1. *Karl Böhm conducted the premiere of Rudolf Wagner-Régeny's* Der Günstling, *with a libretto by Neher, in Dresden on 20 February 1935.*

2. *"Inclined from head to toe . . ." is a reference to Marlene Dietrich's famous song from* Der blaue Engel: *"Ich bin von Kopf bis Fuß auf Liebe eingestellt."*

56 WEILL IN PARIS TO LENYA IN BERLIN, [OCTOBER 1933]

Wednesday

Dear Linnerl,

Many thanks for your letter. The way you've arranged things is very good. The lady who owns the house near Munich [Paris] has turned down the offer. In order to put an end to this senseless search, *Frosch* will rent a nice studio in a quiet neighborhood in or outside Munich. When you're ready to send the furniture there, do send along some lamps, and also a small kitchen table and the little brown table from the dining room, and possibly the blue carpeting, if you think that it's still usable, as well as some books, which are essential—as you say—to make a home feel like a home, and then some music (as much as the limited inventory will allow), some bed and household linens, a few dishes, etc. It will probably be a large studio, which could be set up as a combined work and dining area, with one or two additional rooms, a kitchen, and a bathroom. I'm sure that *Frosch* will find something like that in the next few days. If you think that the blue carpeting is useless, you'd better just leave it there. The prospective buyer might like that. Also send me the *Kühlerhaube* and the little stove—perhaps the garden furniture as well, if that doesn't add much to the moving costs, since one can always use it.[1] At the moment I can't think of anything else—but you know more about these things than I do anyway.

It's great that you'll be coming to help me decorate the place. It's about time I got back to work. Can you send me—or bring with you—*Uncle Tom's Cabin* (a thick Reclam edition; it's probably lying on top of my little closet upstairs) and the Multatuli?[2] As far as Eri is concerned, I agree that we should discuss this before we decide what to do. Until then, you'll probably let her stay in your house? Put the reviews into a box—all of them—finis. Don't get upset when they come to get the furniture. It's for the best. Munich will be nicer than Berlin. I guess you'll get here around the 14th. Goodbye!

Your K——

I never got Otto's letter from Prague!

1. *Since* Kühlerhaube *means the hood of a car, this is undoubtedly more code—perhaps what they agreed to call Weill's piano.*

2. *In 1932 Weill had suggested to Erik Charell four possible projects, including a musical adaptation of Harriet Beecher Stowe's novel, which he envisioned as a simple* Volksoper: *"moral tableaus from the age of slavery (which is one of my most important topics for an opera)" (W–UE, 15 June 1932; see Drew, pp. 389–91). Multatuli was the pseudonym of the Dutch writer Eduard Douwes Dekker (1820–87), whose central work was* Max Havelaar, *a denunciation of colonialism. References to Multatuli remained on Weill's project lists until the late 1940s.*

Apparently Pasetti and Lenya had separated, at least temporarily, at this time; documents indicate that his official residence was Baumgartenstraße 91, Vienna, and that he and Erna had divorced sometime between May 1932 and September 1933. Pasetti's papers show his address on 31 October 1933 as merely "Germany." In early November, Weill's "La grande complainte de Fantomas" was broadcast on Radio Paris, and that month Weill moved to 9 bis, place Dreux, Louveciennes, signing a three-year lease on a first-floor apartment in a simple house. By then Lenya and Pasetti were reunited at the roulette tables, in the resort town of San Remo on the Italian Riviera. Staked, it seems, by some of Weill's money that they had managed to get out of Germany, they bought from a Mr. Krauss or Kraus another surefire system for winning at roulette. Years later, Lenya told the following colorful account of these months:

"I got as much folding money as I could, in very large bills, and folded it into the palm of a glove. I took the car, having already made up my mind to go to Monte Carlo. I had every cent that I could lay my hands on in this one glove. When I arrived at the border, I was determined, if the guards made any trouble, to gun the car and force my way through. Fortunately nothing happened. My papers were examined, and I was waved through. And off I went to the casino." (Int. MA)

57 LENYA IN SAN REMO, ITALY, TO WEILL IN PARIS,
[LATE NOVEMBER? 1933]

Saturday

Dear Weilli,

I'm a little late with my answer to your lovely letter. I've got a bad cold. A lot of things have happened this week. Krauss is gone. It was impossible to work with this man. We're winning 200–250 lire each day with a small investment of capital. We'll talk about everything in Rome. It's too involved to write it all. We've looked around for living quarters. The average price is 400 lire per month. Houses are much more expensive. I'm still hesitant to settle down here. First, I don't like the Italians, and second, there's no beach because the railroad passes through. So there aren't any apartments near the sea, only up in the mountains. Maybe for the time being we'll stay here, until Erika comes, and then later go to Rome to take care of everything. There isn't enough time before that. Imagine, yesterday seven crates (weight 460 kilos!!) packed full of books and music arrived here.[1] The shipping agent mixed up the crates, and instead of the linens, blankets, carpets, etc., these crates arrived. Isn't that idiotic? This shipment cost 230 marks!! It's crazy. It's no use getting irritated about it; we're just lucky we were still able to get something out of the house. Now I've written Erika asking her to send me an exact inventory of the things that are still in Berlin. Some she will bring along with her here; the rest could still be forwarded. It won't be so heavy anymore and therefore not expensive either. Right now I'll leave all of the unnecessary odds and ends here at the hotel and send you the most important things. Schnabel [the shipping agent in Berlin] has no money left after this shipment, since apparently he has not yet sold the modern furniture. That's why he hasn't sent the money to your parents yet. However, there are still 800 marks with Notary Busch (for possible capital gains tax), which will be free on 31 January. If the thing with your parents can wait until then, I'll have it taken care of with this money; otherwise I'll send it from here. It really isn't my fault that this thing is so mixed up. It's obvious that these things can't all go smoothly when everything lies in alien hands, and one has to rely on people like this Schnabel, etc. Erika is going to bring Harras along. He's in a kennel, where he's doing fine. That costs 30 marks per month. I've taken care of all that. I had the 20 marks sent to Zimmermann (I take it you forgot it anyway). In Rome I'll return 1,000 of the 2,000 francs you advanced me in Paris; the second half I'll pay back at the end of January. The fire insurance has to be canceled. You'll have to do that, because it's in your name. I would sell the frozen bank account as soon as possible if I were you, rather than paying the court cost. I won't pay it either. They can kiss our a . . . Have you received the divorce certificate from your lawyer yet? I have mine already, i.e., it's with Notary Busch in Berlin. Please send that letter to Engelhardt for me. Read the letter from Saminghausen[?]. I've given Deta's address, because I don't want those people to know where I am. I'll be very glad when I can straighten things out.

This roulette makes me very nervous. That too will be better once Erika is here. Then I won't have to be there all the time. But I don't want to sit alone in the hotel either. I'm very happy that you're well. I hope the thing with [Erik] Charell will work out. I had a funny dream about that. I told him that deep down inside he thought the music "Das gibt's nur einmal," etc., was still more beautiful than Weill's, only he was afraid to admit it.[2] Well, I hope it won't be as bad as all that. I think it's very smart to keep up your relationships with your few French friends. The others are totally unimportant. Is the thing with the car working out? Don't forget to send the song to Dietrich.

I'm very curious about [Robert] Vambery's subject matter. With you collaborating, he'll surely do something worthwhile. Whatever he conceives by himself would be far less good. What is Bidi [Brecht] doing? Is he still in Paris? [Hans] Hess, that swinish bully, has never been heard from again. Well, by now I really have had enough. That's why I've had no qualms about telling Krauss to shove off. All of them are only in it for their own gain. I'm cured now. Your house is really wonderful. It strikes you all the more as you look around. In a word, really cozy. What have you heard from Cas? This Stemmle is very talented, don't you think?[3] A little phony, but that doesn't matter. Well, my *Mahagonny* things have not arrived, but I must put something together. Do you think I'll be able to get a hat like that in Rome? I suppose so. Please give us the name of a hotel in Rome. We'll be there on the 26th. When are you coming? We're not sure whether we'll go by train or by car. Curjel volunteered to pay 500 Swiss francs. We had asked for 800 for me. Won't there be any more left over? I'm not being greedy; I just don't think one should give in to those people. But I leave it up to you, whatever you think would be right. Now Weili, write me about the hotel and where the rehearsal is. That's all for today. If possible, please mail the letter to Engelhardt before the year is up. Now stay well, my Weili. I hope your rash won't be so stubborn (as Karlweis says).[4] Are you still seeing the doctor? Last night it hailed here. But now it's warm again. *Auf Wiiiiiiidisehn*

> Your old snotty-nosed Linerl

(Last night I went to see *42nd Street*. An enchanting movie. Unfortunately dubbed in Italian. The audience was really stupid. They laughed and whistled all the time. Imagine what we are going to be in for! We'll have to make it clear that we're presenting a German work and won't be trying to "make like Italians." But they are so dumb . . .

If you get to Rome earlier, we'll come too.

Should we be there for Christmas?

1. These crates, sent "by mistake" to San Remo, apparently then never made it to Paris. They probably contained some of Weill's music manuscripts, as well as his library. David Drew's hypothesis concerning the fate of Weill's musical effects (pp. 436–39) does not seem to take this information into account.

2. Werner Richard Heymann's "Das gibt's nur einmal" was a hit song from Erik Charell's film Der Kongreß tanzt.

3. Robert Stemmle (Robert Adolf Ferdinand, 1903–74) was a film director, married to the actress Gerda Maurus.

4. Oskar Karlweis (1894–1956) was a prominent actor; in 1944 he would play Jacobowsky in the New York production of Franz Werfel's Jacobowsky and the Colonel.

58 WEILL IN LOUVECIENNES, FRANCE, TO LENYA IN SAN REMO, [29? NOVEMBER 1933]

Wednesday

Dear Linerl,

I'm glad to have news from you. I can imagine how it bugs you that those bourgeois people are now living in that beautiful house. I feel the same way, but then I tell myself that it would have hardly been possible for you to live in that environment, and nothing that we gave up there is irreplaceable. You can see what they're doing to the likes of us: without cause GEMA [the German performing rights society] has reduced me from 125 points to 5, which means from 4,000 marks to 150. This is practically expropriation; one could also call it highway robbery.[1]

I think it's very sensible for you to take a small apartment soon and have Erika come. That'll be much nicer for you. Perhaps it would be still better if you'd do that right away in Menton. In any case, it's smart to get out of the hotel soon. I find the sale of the house financially not unfavorable; it's actually more than we ever expected to get. What you've done about the money for my father is OK. I hope someone can pick up Harras from the Society for the Protection of Animals soon. That poor creature!

My health is better. The rash (which has not spread any further) looks much better as of yesterday, and I hope it will gradually heal. I've had a very upsetting experience: the three songs [from *Der Silbersee*] were a great success at the concert. Caesar ["Ballade von Cäsars Tod"] had to be repeated, because a French composer, Florent Schmitt (approximately as talented as Butting), got up and screamed: "Heil Hitler! Enough music by German refugees," etc.[2] The audience acted quite decently and soon shut him up, and the song was sung once more and was again a success. But almost the entire French press is on the side of this "French master" against me. The same people who a year ago jumped with enthusiasm for *Mahagonny* are now cool and reserved. [Darius] Milhaud is being remarkably decent. This matter seems to be going entirely too far for him. For a few days I was very angry, although it shouldn't matter to me, because my publisher [Heugel] told me this Schmitt is a lunatic and completely irresponsible.

Everything else is going well. Charell seems to be serious about wanting to do the Stemmle material. The film deal is moving forward; I met with Marcel Achard, whom I like quite well.³ Once again all of Paris was talking about me for two days. You see, not a day without some fun. The symphony is coming along. La [princesse de] Polignac has already paid me 5,000 francs.⁴ I hope things are going well for you. I'm keeping my fingers crossed for the roulette.

> Your Weillchen

1. *In a letter of 28 February 1934 to Universal Edition, Weill requests a complete index of his works to present to the Italian performing rights society (SIAE), which had accepted him as a new member; GEMA had confirmed in writing to Weill that it had released him from membership, effective 30 September 1933.*

2. *The composer Florent Schmitt (1870–1958) had won the Prix de Rome (on his fifth try, in 1900), served as music critic of* Le Temps *(1919–39), and in 1938 was to be elected president of the Société Nationale de Musique Indépendante. Max Butting (1888–1976) had been one of Weill's associates in the November Group.*

3. *Marcel Achard (1899–1974) was a successful French playwright and poet (*Jean de la Lune*).*

4. *Weill had begun the Second Symphony in Berlin as a commission from Polignac; the first movement is dated January 1933, whereas the full score of the finale is marked "Louveciennes/Februar 1934."*

59 WEILL IN LOUVECIENNES TO LENYA IN SAN REMO, [8 DECEMBER 1933]

> Louveciennes
> Friday

Dear Linerl,

I was very happy with your long letter and enjoyed your detailed report. It's sad that the Krauss system isn't working, after the two of you had put so much faith in it; so now it turns out that it doesn't work at all the way you've always insisted it would—namely, as effectively in the casino as when you're figuring it on paper beforehand. I think it's fine if you try another system, without risking too much money, provided you immediately put a stop to it if you find that it doesn't work either. Should that prove to be the case, I would suggest that you turn all your energy to learning French and English and that Pasetti take up singing lessons again. But you should think about whether you want to do this here or in the South. (Supposedly there are good singing teachers in Nice or Monte Carlo, in connection with the opera house.) Of course, you can live more cheaply in the south of France, especially if you send for Erika, which I think would be very good, especially since I'm quite impressed that she voted NO.¹ Dr. Walter ("Fridolin")[?] paid 350 francs per month for a charmingly furnished little three-room house in Cannes, and were he to have rented it for a couple of years, it would have cost only 300. And that during the summer season! You could certainly earn a living, if you would extend the tour [of *Mahagonny*] somewhat, and whatever you need you'll get from me, because I don't want you to take even a penny out of the little emergency fund you presently have. The moment you speak French you can get work here. Just the other day Achard asked me whether you can already act here. Therefore you must not be anxious at all. If the [roulette] system works—*tant mieux*. If not, we'll make it just the same.

All's well with me. The house is wonderful; most of the time I'm outside and don't want to see anybody. They're all a bunch of pigs, gossipy lowlife rabble. For a week they had something to talk about again, with that incident at the concert. Since almost everywhere composers like Schmitt write for the newspapers, they've thrashed me wildly, the same newspapers that hardly a year ago couldn't contain their enthusiasm. I'm staying quite calm and remain absolutely secure about my work. For all this there is only one answer: just keep going. The symphony will be very beautiful; I hope to be finished with the sketch in eight to ten days. La Polignac has already paid one-third, and that's given colossal wings to my imagination.

Milhaud is behaving very decently (since he's an old enemy of Schmitt); the Aufrichts and Steinthal are nice, as always; Charell is also very cordial. He's now decided to produce the last play that Stemmle told us about (the story about the boys and the teacher), only he can't commit to a date but is willing to explain to my publisher that he'll do this thing with me for sure. In the meantime, he'll try to get me an important film, either here or in Hollywood, and if I get another theatrical piece, he'll help to place it. Vambery now has a charming subject from the old English theater for some sort of folk play with music; I believe it's what I need at this moment. If my publisher is agreeable, I'll start work on it immediately.[2]

My rash is already quite dry, but it's still very obstinate and doesn't exactly look pretty. But I don't care one way or the other, because I see only a few people. Sunday noon I gave a little *déjeuner* with Marie-Laure, Charles [de Noailles], and Monnet.[3] It was very nice, with first-class food. This Sunday the Deutsches are coming for lunch,[4] and in the afternoon Charell. I have news from Curjel. You have to be in Rome by the evening of 26 December, since the rehearsals are on the 27th and 28th, and the performance is on the 29th. Probably Hildchen [Hilde Rosenthal] will be the second girl, I hope. The other men are coming from here.

I hope to be able to push through at least 500 Swiss francs for you and 300 for Pasetti; that's considerably more than for all the others, who are being paid only travel and living expenses. If Spain would work out, you could make good money.

Otherwise I can't think of anything at the moment. Today I'm going to meet a manager at Citroën about my car. I hope it'll work out so I can get rid of that lemon.

Now farewell, little Linnerl, take good care of yourself so that you look nice in Rome, because

all Romans
have hot blood in their veins![5]

Auf Wiedersehen! Regards to Pasetti.

Your Weilli

The house question was resolved very well—and just in time, because who knows if they wouldn't have confiscated it by now, after the incident [with Schmitt], which caused quite a big to-do in the German papers.

1. *The last democratic election in Germany, giving the Nazis a small majority in the Reichstag, took place on 5 March 1933. On 14 July a new law decreed that the Nationalist Socialist German Workers' Party henceforth would constitute the only political party in Germany. To consolidate his newly won power, Hitler called for a plebiscite on 12 November 1933, the day after the anniversary of the 1918 armistice, a black day that still rankled in German memories. Hindenburg added his support in a broadcast to the nation: "Tomorrow, show your firm national unity and your solidarity with the government." The response was almost unanimous, and it took much courage to abstain or to cast a negative vote.*

2. *Vambery later recalled that he had suggested to Weill a musical adaptation of an Elizabethan play,* The Poor Devil; *Weill submitted Vambery's French synopsis to his publisher, Heugel, who found the idea appealing.*

3. *Henri Monnet (b. 1896) was a French financier and amateur musician. A cofounder of L'Orchestre symphonique de Paris, he was also a member of the French Senate.*

4. *Mrs. Gustav Brecher was a daughter of Dr. Felix Deutsch, an enormously wealthy and prominent director of AEG (Allgemeine Elektrizitäts Gesellschaft) in Berlin. They had a great deal of money invested in UE. The Deutsches mentioned in several letters are probably related to that family.*

5. *Quotation from "Ballade von Cäsars Tod" in* Der Silbersee.

60 WEILL IN LOUVECIENNES TO LENYA IN SAN REMO, [16 DECEMBER 1933]

Saturday

Dear Linerl,

I'm waiting for news from you, hoping I'll get some soon. Since you haven't written, I assume that the new system doesn't work either. Well, next week we can discuss what finally will have to be done.

I've written to Curjel that you must have 500 francs (Swiss francs!), Pasetti 300. I hope he'll agree to this.

What do you think about the following proposal: we meet in Florence toward evening on the 24th, spend Christmas Eve together; on the 25th I'll show you Florence (something I'm already looking forward to); on the 26th you two go by car to Rome and I'll take the train. That would be really nice, wouldn't it?

I'm doing all right. The rash is getting better, but slowly; I now have another doctor, since the son of the *Pußta* [Hungarian] didn't help me. Cäschen won't come to Rome, because it might be harmful to him after what has happened here, which has been played up big in the German newspapers. Once again he couldn't make up his mind, because he didn't want to say no to me, until I myself wrote to him that I couldn't take on that responsibility.[1]

Yesterday I finished the sketch of my symphony, and I'm very happy that I can also do something like this better than the others. Now I'll start on that stage work with Vambery. We'll write a role for you in it.

Otherwise there's little news. I almost went to America with [Max] Reinhardt for a huge Jewish theater work. But the date they wanted it for was too soon. Perhaps we'll do it in the fall.

Let me hear from you soon, also about the Christmas plans; stay healthy (is it as cold there as it is here?). Regards to Pasetti and for you a thousand greetings

from your Weilli

1. *After the performances of* Die sieben Todsünden *in Paris and London, Neher had received a temporary* Berufsverbot *(revocation of his work permit) from the Nazis. Waiting in vain for other offers outside Germany, he had to choose between*

emigrating and taking his chances in Germany. He opted for the latter; in November 1933 he designed the scenery for Friedrich Schreyvogel's Tod in Genf *at the Berlin Volksbühne.*

1934

After attending the well-received Mahagonny *performance featuring Lenya and Pasetti at the Accademia di Santa Cecilia in Rome on 29 December, Weill visited his parents in Carlsbad, Czechoslovakia, and then returned to Paris. Shortly thereafter, Hitler signed a ten-year non-aggression treaty with Poland, and Chancellor Engelbert Dollfuß suspended parliamentary government in Austria.*

61 WEILL IN LOUVECIENNES TO LENYA IN ITALY,
11 JANUARY 1934

Louveciennes

11.1.34

Dear Linerl,

Now that I've happily made it back here, I'm a bit disappointed that I haven't had any news from you. Abravanel said the two of you drove to Naples. You could have at least written me a postcard from there.

It was very enjoyable at my parents'. They were terribly happy that I'd come. They're really nice once they are away from the rest of the family. They're quite content and don't complain at all. For a mere 100 marks I had a very attractive winter suit made. In addition, a Carlsbad doctor gave me a bloodletting to cure that rash. It's completely gone from my head and almost all gone from my hands, but there's still some on my body. Now I don't know what actually helped: the diet, the tea, the injections, the ultraviolet rays, the ointment, or the bloodletting. Probably none of it. In any case, I'll stay on the diet, because I notice that it's better for me.

I was in Vienna for only a day and a half. When you see the refugees hanging around there, you're really glad you're not one of them. I find it all the more unpleasant because the worst mob of literati has simply clumped together there, which is so totally unproductive. I had made an appointment with [Karl Heinz] Martin, and there they were, all huddling together: Pallenberg (the most repulsive of the lot), the Polgars, the Martins, Bois, and all the other hypocrites.[1] They're complaining and wailing, but they're still far too well off. They all harbor a hatred for Paris, because there's no use for them there. By contrast, thinking about how nice and jovial it was when we were all together in Rome, I realize that we've done the right thing after all. Of course, they all send their regards to you. The nicest of the bunch was [Fritz] Stiedry, who had just come back from Russia. He saw [Georg] Kaiser in Berlin; things are terrible.[2] He's completely at his wits' end and talks only of suicide; Stiedry seriously believes it might end in catastrophe if they don't get him out. Do you think I should invite him here? I heard from Cas. He's going to Düsseldorf and wants to come see me, perhaps for a few days next week. According to what I've heard in Vienna, he is behaving very well and is in no way thinking along the party's lines. I saw Heinsheimer, whom I treated with condescension. He's nothing but an ugly little asshole now. Even he couldn't get anywhere with his brownnosing. Only "little Herbie"[?] has made it: he's landed in the ministry of propaganda—with a monthly salary of 200 marks.

Now farewell, little Linerl. When are you coming back? Write soon; regards to Pasetti, and again, a thousand thanks for everything.

> Your Weillchen

Write me soon about you've decided, whether and where you will take an apartment and whether you will have Erika come. And think about studying French!

1. *Max Pallenberg (1877–1934), the great Czechoslovakian-born actor, played Mephistopheles in the 1933 production of Goethe's* Faust *at the Salzburg Festival. Alfred Polgar (1875–1955) had been a theater critic for* Die Weltbühne *and returned to his native Vienna in 1933. The actor Curt Bois (1901–88) appeared in Konjunktur in 1928, for which Weill had written the score. Bois immigrated to the United States in 1934 and thereafter appeared on Broadway and played character parts in many Hollywood films. He returned to East Germany in 1950 and played the lead role in* Herr Puntila und sein Knecht Matti *with the Berliner Ensemble under Brecht in 1952. His wife, Hedi Ury, was an actress.*

2. *After the* Silbersee *premiere, the Nazis accused Kaiser of "cultural bolshevism" and included his books in the burning on 10 May 1933. Goebbels ordered Kaiser's plays removed from the repertoire of all theaters. Kaiser withdrew to Grünheide and openly attacked Goebbels: "Satan has gone crazy in this country" (Kaiser, p. 20). He unsuccessfully attempted to write under a pseudonym and finally left Germany in August 1938 and settled in Switzerland, where he died in 1945. His wife and children stayed behind in Germany.*

62 WEILL IN LOUVECIENNES TO LENYA IN ITALY, 12 JANUARY 1934

Letterhead: Kurt Weill / 9 bis, Place Ernest Dreux / Louveciennes (S.-&-O.) / Téléphone 128

12.1.34

My dear Linerl, aka *Zibelyne*,[1]

I'm very glad to have news from you. It makes sense that you drove around a little. I too was disappointed by Naples—only the sunshine is marvelous, but you probably didn't get to see much of that. Meanwhile, you must have received my letter. I'll send you the documents you need from here. If I were you, I'd try to get out everything that is still there. There is no way to be entirely secure against those looters. Those people will try anything, because they know you're far away, and there's nobody around to give a darn about these things. Pasetti will surely know what to do with respect to the money matter. But I would insist, with the threat of a lawsuit, upon payment of every last penny. In addition, I would try everything to get the carpets, the featherbeds, and especially the linens out of there. The linens are very important, because we need them so urgently. For such small items there must certainly be a way. Maybe it would be easier for you to turn this whole thing over to Leni [Weill]. She's happy to be able to do something for us, and I'm convinced she can get these things out. Kardan is really a schlemiel. I'd be satisfied just to know where those things actually were, or whether somebody hasn't already stolen them.

What you write about me is true to a certain extent. But the Křenek matter has already been settled for months and is quite insignificant. Our performance [*Mahagonny*] at Santa Cecilia was much more "official" and more important than such a music festival. Křenek now acts quite the great Austrian master, using Catholicism to make his way.[2] His Vienna premiere will probably be manipulated in the grandest style, in the presence of Dollfuß and the cardinals.[3] But where will it get him? Who's interested in that? For me only one thing is really important: to find a good libretto. Then everything else falls into place. But it's insanely difficult. I've now started to work with Vambery, but I don't know how that'll go. It would be a real blessing if someone could finally produce what I want. It makes me nervous to think of what one could accomplish instead of wasting one's strength looking for a libretto. In the meantime I'm writing the full score of the symphony, and of course I'll try to place it favorably. All the movie plans have gone the way of all flesh. Well—one mustn't lose patience. Perhaps everything looks particularly ugly today because it's been raining without stop.

The letter from "Grete" has just arrived. I had no idea that *Mahagonny* was given there [in Copenhagen], and I certainly didn't send a telegram.[4] I'd advise you to answer and to send a picture. May things go well for you—break a leg with your gambling!—and much love to you,

Your Weilli

1. *The novel* Zibeline *by the French author Philippe de Massa survived in the library at Brook House at the time of Lenya's death. The heroine Zibeline is described as follows: "Envying her rich furs, certain Parisian ladies gave her the name of Zibeline, that of a rare, almost extinct wild animal." Weill calls Lenya variations of the name for the next six months, spelling it* Zybeline, Zybelinerl, Zyberlinerl, Zibelinerl, *and* Zybelienerl.

2. *The Austrian composer Ernst Křenek (1900–1991) had written* Karl V *for the Vienna State Opera; the text extolled the universalism of Catholicism.*

3. *In fact this premiere never took place. On 25 July 1934, an SS group, dressed in Austrian army uniforms, assassinated Chancellor Engelbert Dollfuß (1892–1934), while others seized the radio station and broadcast the news that Dollfuß had resigned. Because it was a twelve-tone work, the rehearsals of* Karl V *were stopped, and the opera was not staged until 22 June 1938 in Prague.*

4. *Brecht's associate Margarete Steffin (1908–41) was living in Denmark at the time. A private theater in Copenhagen had presented what turned out to be the last prewar production of* Aufstieg und Fall der Stadt Mahagonny, *between 30 December 1933 and 10 January 1934. One of the leading newspapers (Dagens Nyheter) reported on 2 January 1934 that Weill, who supposedly was living in Vienna and had heard the performance on the radio there, had sent a telegram to the opera company: "It came off well. The music was exactly as I had imagined it should be. Marvelous artists." It is clear from Weill's response that the composer's stamp of approval was bogus—perhaps a publicity ploy by the theater.*

63 WEILL IN LOUVECIENNES TO LENYA IN ITALY, [17? JANUARY 1934]

Wednesday

Dear Linerl,

A thousand thanks for your long letter. I'll answer it right away. P. [Pasetti] will certainly know what needs to be done. But do it cautiously and think it through beforehand, so you won't get into any unpleasant situations. I'm curious whether the [roulette] system is going to work out this time. It certainly is okay that you both are earning your money that way, so that you'll be able to continue working in peace later on. When I saw how your beloved colleagues in Vienna were sitting around moaning, I thought to myself, my dear *Zybeline* is far more clever. The only one among that whole bunch of hypocrites who is doing it right is Bergner, who's had an enormous success in London.[1]

That tapeworm problem isn't serious, it only comes from your naughtiness. But you must do something about it; there are a lot of remedies. Just to be on the safe side, though, I'd see a doctor to get rid of it. When I write to Nathan [Weill], I'll ask him.

I'm feeling well again. I'm working on the full score of the symphony; that's fun.

There's another thing going on locally about a libretto (in addition to the Vambery play, which might turn out very well); I'll write you about it in detail. Now I've got to rush off to Paris. Saturday I'm taking my driver's test, so I can finally drive around in my first-class Max.² I'm glad that Erika is coming and that Harras can be with you then. [FIGS. 39 & 40]

> In haste all good wishes for you,
> for Pasetti, and for the worm,
> whom we shall call Adolf,
> if that's OK with you.
>
> Your Weilli

1. *Elisabeth Bergner's first big success in London came in the role of Gemma Jones in Margaret Kennedy's* Escape Me Never, *a role she also played on Broadway in 1935.*

2. *Weill referred to any luxury automobile as a "Maxwell" or "Max." The Maxwell, an American luxury car that ceased production in 1925, was made famous by Jack Benny on his radio program, where he continually commanded Rochester to "get the Maxwell ready." Hans Heinsheimer recalled: "I have never seen a man enjoy his first automobile—a Graham-Page—more than Kurt Weill, and I will not forget the exuberant, relaxed, boyish pleasure with which he drove the car, with Lenya, me, and a lovely lady of my choice from Vienna, over the mountains toward Italy. A short stretch of the dreadful pre-Autobahn road was in splendid condition, and as he gave the American car all it had, Weill improvised a childishly primitive doggerel, singing with his famous veiled voice: 'Ja, so ein Sträßchen / Ja, das macht Späßchen' " (Heinsheimer, p. 139).*

64 WEILL IN LOUVECIENNES TO LENYA IN SAN REMO, 25 JANUARY 1934
Letterhead: Kurt Weill

Thursday, 25.1.34

Dear *Zyberlinerl*,

Many thanks for your postcard, which pleased me very much. I'm always happy when I know you're all right. It's great that your calculations look so good, but you'll have to see what happens when you try to put them into practice [at roulette]. What about your living quarters? Did you take the place for 500 lire? Or haven't you decided yet whether you might prefer to go to France? And what about your visa? Right now you most likely want to wait for the possible success and first fruits of your new system before you make further decisions. I heard from Cas. He has accepted a good two-year contract in Frankfurt and will move there during the summer. I'm very happy for him, since this certainly will be for the best in view of his predilections. He wants to visit me from the 9th to the 20th of March, as he'll be working in Düsseldorf anyway at that time. Do you want to come here as soon as February or at the end of March instead? You can arrange it whatever way is best for you.

I'm doing very well. I stayed out here all last week and got a lot of work done. The full score [of the Second Symphony] is two thirds done. This week I'm busy with some very important negotiations that are almost settled (knock on wood). Here's what they're about: Jacques Deval, the season's most in-demand and most frequently performed French playwright, whose play *Tovarich* is the biggest international theatrical hit of the year, wants to do his new play with me. We want to dramatize his most successful novel, *Marie Galante*. An excellent, <u>serious</u> subject: a French peasant girl runs off with a man and ends up somewhere in Panama, but once there she wishes only to go home again; she earns money in a whorehouse, and when she has saved up enough and has already bought her steamship ticket, she dies. If at all possible, the play is supposed to open as soon as May at the most beautiful theater in Paris, the Théâtre Marigny, and then in the fall in London and New York. It looks as if this might be the big international opportunity I've been waiting for. The publisher is enthusiastic. As soon as the contract is settled we'll get started, and for a few months I'll have to work <u>very hard</u>. But that's exactly what I want. The Vambery thing is also coming along quite well. He's really <u>very</u> talented. My publisher likes the Vambery material so much that he's giving him an advance on which he can live in peace for four months. So you see, lots going on! Unfortunately I'm still without a car. The date for the driving test hasn't been set yet. Now farewell, Linerl. Write again, be healthy and happy, and figure the odds diligently. Regards to Pasetti! For you a little kiss.

As always, your Weilli

65 WEILL IN LOUVECIENNES TO LENYA IN SAN REMO, 20 FEBRUARY 1934

20.2.34

Dear *Zyberlinerl*,

Many thanks for your letter. I'm glad you're well and that it's so pleasantly warm there. The weather has been awful here, but now it seems to be improving. I was in a miserable mood last week. The events in Austria are really terribly depressing for anyone who has some sense of justice left.[1] Animals are more merciful than these people. Politically we have come to a most dangerous turning point. Not since 1914 have we been as close to war as we are now. I for one don't believe that it'll come to that, but the wartime spirit is growing more and more, and those vandals won't rest until they finally have their way. Well, it's best not to think about it but rather enjoy every day that one can still spend in peace.

It's a shame the [roulette] system isn't working to your satisfaction. That means we'll soon have to look around for a different way to make a living. But it might turn out as we've discussed. I've had lots of irritations lately. I haven't seen Deval since his visit a week ago Sunday. He was supposed to come over today, but he canceled again—supposedly because he's sick—and postponed it until next Sunday. I no longer believe that this project will work out by spring. As in other domains, it's just another case of a damned lack of focus. So now I'm sitting around waiting. After you left here, I finished the symphony as planned. Sunday I'm invited to La Sandrock-Polignac's, and I'm ready to string her up on one of the pipes of her organ if she doesn't give me my money.[2]

[FIG. 41]

I've sent the checks to Leni [Weill], the family finances have been taken care of, and today I'll be speaking to someone about the bank account. Max asked me to thank you for the compliment. He's got a new bulb for his headlight and yellow fog gels (since then there's been no more fog in Paris). I've been in bed for a day, bad diarrhea with a fever; no idea what it's from, because I've always eaten at home. I'm still not over it, can't eat anything at all. Vambery keeps working, and I'm starting to busy myself with materials for this operetta.[3] Best regards to Pasetti. "Break a leg" as far as the system is concerned.

Lots of love from your Weilli

1. In the first months of 1934 the Austrian Nazis, with weapons and explosives furnished by Germany, had instituted a reign of terror, blowing up railways, power stations, and government buildings, and murdering supporters of the Dollfuß regime. Several thousand troops, Hitler's "Austrian Foreign Legion," camped along the Austrian border in Bavaria, ready to cross over and occupy the country at an opportune moment.

2. Weill's reference to the princesse de Polignac alludes to Adele Sandrock (1864–1937), an actress who in the "golden years" of UFA became famous for her portrayals of dragonlike, bossy old ladies.

3. Weill and Vambery had abandoned their plans for a musical play based on The Poor Devil *and instead began work on the "satirical operetta"* Der Kuhhandel.

66 WEILL IN LOUVECIENNES TO LENYA IN ITALY[?], [26? FEBRUARY 1934]

Monday

My dear Linerl,

Many thanks for your letter. I wouldn't give you two cents for [Weill's sister-in-law] Rita's nonsensical babble. I'd like to have her problems! Today I'm going to write Frankenberg that he should send the money to Lipschütz.[1] Write to Kardan that he can dispose of that amount. I received the enclosed reminder from the Potsdam tax revenue department; it was forwarded to my Paris address. Have you already seen to the payment? If not, I'll send it from here. Kardan actually seems to be working out well. I'm really looking forward to seeing the dog. That will be quite a scene when he arrives. As far as Erika is concerned, it would, of course, be best if she'd get a job so you could be rid of that burden. Today I heard from Leni [Weill] that the transaction with the checks worked out, and I'll ask her to send me 200 marks every month from now on. The sale of my Berlin bank account seems to be difficult.

I'm glad that the system is going better. I'm curious as to the final results. Don't trouble yourself about the books and the music; there's no hurry for that, and perhaps I can take them with me when I come to visit you occasionally. The recording from Mariederl [Hubek] arrived, but it's still at the railroad station. I'll pick it up today.

I'm doing fine. I haven't seen Deval for two weeks; he's sick. I'm now occupying myself with the operetta, which might turn out very beautifully. I've already done three numbers, which are quite effective, especially the one that starts like this:

Once I owned a cow;	*[Ich habe eine Kuh gehabt,*
I don't own that cow anymore.	*Ich hab die Kuh nicht mehr.*
Instead—	*Ich hab dafür,*
God help me—	*Gott helfe mir,*
I now own a machine gun.[2]	*Jetzt ein Maschinengewehr.]*

I have great expectations as far as this play is concerned, because working on it comes so easily—more easily than I've experienced in a long time. Vambery works well, but very slowly. A lazy bunch, these writers. On Wednesday I spent the entire evening with [Max] Reinhardt. This big biblical thing seems to be progressing. [Franz] Werfel is already at work on it. It would be a giant task for me, since it's a real oratorio. It's supposed to premiere at London's Albert Hall. It was very nice at Polignac's, but that beast hasn't given me my money, not yesterday either when I visited her at her nearby country estate. At her dinner party I met a very beautiful lady, some marquise or other. I wanted to flirt with her, but she only raved about you and asked me to send you her regards. She didn't want anything to do with me.

[FIG. 42]

I've been seeing Natasha quite often.[3] Deval is terrible to her because she won't sleep with him. Isn't that disgusting? She's in London right now. Now farewell, little *Zybeline*.

          Your Weilli

I'm going to see Mimi[?] today.

1. Paul Frankenberg, a banker in Berlin (Burgstraße 27), answered Weill on 3 March: "Before I execute your request of the 27th of last month, I must kindly ask you to let me know whether you are still a resident of Germany living only temporarily in a foreign country. Should you reside permanently in a foreign country, your bank account will be frozen and can be used only by permission of the agency for foreign currencies, according to the new laws governing all foreign currencies. Despite the small amount involved, a payment to Mr. Lipschütz can be forwarded by me only with special permission from the agency for foreign currencies" (letter forwarded to Lenya by Weill; returned to him with Letter 68).

2. "Ich habe eine Kuh gehabt" is the tenor aria in act 2 of Der Kuhhandel.

3. Natasha (later Natalie) Paley (1905–81) was a stage and screen actress. A Russian princess in the Romanov line, the daughter of Grand Duke Paul Alexandrovich and Olga Karnovich, she received the title of Princess Paley by decree in 1915. For a time she was married to the French couturier Lucien Lelong and was Marie-Laure de Noailles's closest friend.

67 WEILL IN LOUVECIENNES TO LENYA IN SAN REMO, [3–6 MARCH 1934]

          Saturday

Dear *Zybelinerl,*

Many thanks for your lovely letter. The package of books came today; a thousand thanks for everything. The chair for the garden hasn't arrived yet; I'm quite curious about it, and I thank you in advance for such a nice present, but I really wouldn't want you to spend so much money on me, do you hear? I only sent you the Potsdam reminder to find out whether you had already paid it. Of course I'll pay it. Please do write to tell me if there's anything at all I can take care of for you so that you don't have to touch your own money. I'm in a very good mood because yesterday, on my birthday, spring arrived, and because Harras is here. That really gives me pleasure. He won't leave my side, and even when I'm working, he stays in my room. He arrived in a huge crate, and there was a big crowd because everybody wanted to see him. Once out, he had to pee for five whole minutes. He recognized me immediately by my voice. The first night he howled constantly, and I didn't sleep because I kept running downstairs to console him. But now he has adjusted completely and is pleased as punch. I go for a lot of walks with him. That's very healthy for me too. The weather is heavenly, and I am quite another person because it is so beautifully warm.

The Vambery play [*Der Kuhhandel*] is coming along. I've done a very beautiful bar-carole, sung by the President, the General, and the Secretary while gazing on the sleeping Santa Maria ["Schlafe, Santa Maria"]. The belt you gave me is fabulous, and the tobacco pouch too. You sure know how to make me happy; I think it's all very nice of you. But you've spent an awful lot of money on me. Gilbert is coming now to read me his play.[1] Goodbyyyiie!

Sunday evening

Today was an exciting day. Last night I got a call asking me to wire my address to Marlene [Dietrich], which I did right away, and by this morning there was the following telegram: "Would you be interested in coming here and working with Sternberg and me on a musical film. Time required approximately six months. Wire me whether you want to and whether you can. Everything else taken care of by Paramount. Warmest regards. Marlene."[2] Now you're raising your eyebrows. You're surprised, aren't you? I'll call tomorrow morning to talk with you about it. I think one can only say yes to this, no? Sternberg and Marlene and six months of work—that doesn't come up often. Tomorrow I'll go to my publisher [Heugel] and postpone the Deval thing [*Marie Galante*] until fall. The thing with Reinhardt [*Der Weg der Verheißung*] will be harder. I would not like to give it up. But I must tell myself: (1) all those Reinhardt plans will probably keep dragging on, and (2) with whom should he do it if not with me? Besides, I definitely think that both things can be combined, that over there I can also work on the Reinhardt. I'm curious what you'll have to say tomorrow morning. If I really do go over there, you should think about whether you both would want to have the house while I'm away. Then you could live very cheaply, since I'll be paying the rent and Mrs. Berthon [the housekeeper] anyway.

Now something else important: Steinthal called me. [Rolf] Nürnberg has again become business manager of the *12 Uhr Blatt;* they want to make a settlement with Steinthal and pay all the creditors. Now Nürnberg maintains that we voluntarily lowered our claim to 4,999 marks. As I understand it, that was only to be the case if they actually paid the 4,999 marks in cash. Since they haven't done that, the agreement is not in effect. Or has Engelhardt handled this as idiotically as he has everything else? I would like to ask you to help me in this matter. We'll share the booty equally. You can accept it without a second thought, because you have both had so much trouble over this affair—and my business is really going well, knock on wood.

Now good night, Linerl. I'm excited because of Hollywood, but I'd better not count the chickens yet. Tomorrow morning I'm going to my publisher. The garden chair is at the railroad station. I'll get it tomorrow. Many regards to Pasetti, and again a thousand thanks for everything.

As always, your Weilli

Tuesday

Linerl, I was very glad to have spoken to you. Today I got a telegram from Sternberg: "Dearest Weill, I would like it if you could let me know your conditions so I can forward them to my firm. I have long wanted to have you here, and I am sure you will like it. Greetings—Sternberg." I've answered that the studio should first make me an offer, because that will give me a negotiating advantage, and that they should inform me of the dates, because I have no idea when they're planning this thing. Possibly you could come here first, and we could go to London together to get me some suits made. That would be great.

In haste once more, all good things,
Your Weilli

1. *The reference to Gilbert is ambiguous: Robert Gilbert (1899–1978) was active as a composer and librettist of musical comedies and operettas in Europe, where he collaborated with Oscar Straus, Ralph Benatzky, Robert Stolz, and Werner Richard Heymann on some forty odd productions. Jean Gilbert (1879–1942) wrote the score for the famous operetta* Die keusche Susanne *(Magdeburg, 1910).*

2. *Josef von Sternberg (1894–1969) had settled in Hollywood in 1924; in 1930 he directed the first German "talkie,"* Der blaue Engel, *which initiated a long association with Dietrich.*

68 LENYA IN SAN REMO TO WEILL IN LOUVECIENNES, [8? MARCH 1934]

Thursday morning

My dear Weili,

Many thanks for your lovely long letter. (Why don't you use the typewriter? That would be so much less time-consuming for you.) That telephone call with the news was really some surprise! Did all of this happen after your birthday? If only things would keep moving along like this. I'll be terribly happy for you if this film project works out. Mainly, of course, for your own sake, but then again because of these other vermin. Wouldn't that be some triumph! Perhaps it really was a good thing that you sent [Dietrich] that song ["Der Abschiedsbrief"]. She probably didn't answer sooner because she was deep in work. Of course it's best to have Paramount suggest a fee. Through Sternberg and Marlene they'll get the right picture of you and won't underestimate your value. I'm really curious what they'll offer you. Hollywood is very expensive. How much does the trip cost? They would have to pay for it. But of course they'll do that.

Since Deval won't be ready in time, it all looks very good. And Reinhardt certainly will drag on. I agree that you could be doing something else in between. The main thing is for Hollywood to work out. Imagine the faces of Charell, Brecht (who—once it's all settled—will hear it from me through Steffin . . .),[1] and all those people in Berlin. And what a project! A musical film with Sternberg and Marlene! It's unbelievable how great that would be. Then you could make use of all the ideas you've gathered throughout the years you've been waiting for a film; if it really works out, you could get a good contract. In any case, your publisher will know what such a contract ought to look like. And how is my little Weill going to look? Really grand. Naturally, this is going to do some damage to your character, because you'll probably get terribly cocky, but I'll just have to overlook that.

Well, everything has worked out with Harras. It's amazing that he still recognized you. Just keep him around you all the time, even during meals; he probably had to stay with stupid people, and now it will do him good if you talk sensibly to him again. Can Mrs. Berthon handle him all right? He doesn't need rice and bones every day. He can eat potatoes and mixed vegetables as well. You must give him milk bones. You can get those anywhere. The other things—carpets, beds, linens, etc.—have already been sent to Innsbruck. We're waiting for confirmation from P.'s parents that they've arrived. I'm going to let everything stay there for now, until it's been decided whether you're going to Hollywood; so for the time being I won't send you those things but keep them in mothballs with P.'s parents. Then when you come back you'll be able to get everything. This Schnabel [the shipping agent]—together with P.'s father-in-law [Marek]—has actually embezzled the 450 we were still supposed to receive. But it doesn't matter. P. won't pay his wife any child support until the 450 has been recouped. She can go to her father, and he can give her the 450. That way it'll stay in the family. So for once Mr. Marek had someone else put one over on him.

I've heard nothing from Erika since we've shown her that she overcharged the account for 102 marks. She seems to be all mixed up. And always to my disadvantage. I wrote her very nicely and brought it to her attention. Now she seems to be offended again. Well, that's probably the last thing I'll have to do with this Third Reich. Should you find a nice American who'd marry me right away for an American passport—keep me in mind. Of course, I could come at any time should you need me. You'll need some new clothes if you go over there. You won't have to pay Mrs. Berthon during that time, or do you have a contract with her? If not, you should pay only part of her wage—maybe 200 francs; she can't insist on it either. But we'll discuss all these things in detail. Now about the *12 Uhr Blatt*. The reduction of the debt to 4,999 naturally was intended only if it were paid off in monthly installments of 300, beginning 15 November 1933. Otherwise the debt was to revert automatically to 10,000. Because the lien was assigned to me, I believe this wasn't even legally binding, since at the time Saminghausen did say to P. that he'd have to determine the legal validity of his (P.'s) power of attorney, as well as the assignment to me in case of a settlement, i.e., payment of the 4,999. Since such a settlement never took place, it's probably true that they don't know about the assignment to me. Think about what you want to do with the money (in case you get it). Accordingly we will have to see whether an assignment to me is preferable to your claiming title. If not, do have the assignment to me declared invalid at Engelhardt's. I suggest you take care of this, if at all possible, without Engelhardt, because he's too stupid and slow. Anyway, it's very good that Nürnberg is back in the picture. He can get on top of things. I'll do whatever is in my power to help, and without a share, of course. I don't have to tell you that I'm happy to do anything for you.

I think that's all for today. Keep after the *12 Uhr Blatt* in any case, despite the Hollywood prospects, since perhaps something can be salvaged. Now farewell Weillchen; if you should need something, write right away. Also to let me know how things are progressing. I'll be very excited to hear how everything works out. Greetings to Harras. And for you all good things.

> As always,
> your *Zybe*

[Letter from Paul Frankenberg enclosed.]

1. *Margarete Steffin had joined Brecht's circle in 1932 and then followed him into exile. After a period in Denmark, Steffin was denied a visa for Sweden, Finland, and the United States because of her active tuberculosis. She did gain admittance to Russia, but soon landed in a hospital. Brecht left her there alone; she died at age thirty-three.*

69 WEILL IN LOUVECIENNES TO LENYA IN SAN REMO, [12 MARCH 1934]

Monday morning

My dear *Zybelinerl*,

Many thanks for your lovely letter. It's really remarkable what good and sure instincts you have. Last week exactly the same thoughts kept haunting me, namely that it would make no sense silently to play the offended one, and so Saturday afternoon I drove to Paris and sent the following telegram:

> Dear Sternberg, I now have the definite possibility of postponing theater obligations here; therefore would appreciate report on how the matter of our movie is progressing. Cordially, your W.

When I came home, your letter was there. So you see how right you were, and I thank you very much because you're such a big *Klugi*. Perhaps the telegram I sent was a bit risky from a negotiating point of view, because on the basis of it—if they'll negotiate at all—they'll make me an even lower offer. But one can always haggle to raise it. Besides, I'm well aware that the first film I'd be doing over there wouldn't bring me a fortune but rather offer me a singular chance to stake out a claim. If it even comes to negotiating, of course I should maintain that I'm very expensive, but I shouldn't let it get wrecked because of that. I now know intimately the quite pitiful conditions under which Werner Heymann went over there (for the Charell film).[1] He gets nothing at all for the film; instead he has relinquished the publication rights to the movie company and in exchange gets an advance of $7,000, as well as the paid trip and a living allowance of $250 per week. Now I'm very curious about Sternberg's answer. Up to now, Monday morning at 11, nothing has come yet. This waiting is terrible. Nothing will come anymore today, because telegrams are always dispatched during the night and arrive in the morning, and yesterday was Sunday. If I still don't get an answer, I'll send the following telegram to Marlene as the conclusion to this affair:

There once lived two royal children	*[Es waren zwei Königskinder,*
who loved each other dearly.	*die hatten einander so lieb.*
They could not get together,	*Sie konnten zusammen nicht kommen,*
the ocean was much too deep.[2]	*das Wasser war viel zu tief.]*

It's too bad that all the calculations with the Krauss system were in vain. But you know that I've always been very skeptical. Actually I don't understand much about these things, and of course I don't want to discourage you, but I believe you'll have to give up this big fortune hunt at some point and consider this new possibility that Pasetti has found as a last experiment. It would be quite wonderful if this new thing goes the way you hope. But if it doesn't, it would really prove that—as everyone says—no system is truly effective at winning in the long run. And then we have to think seriously about what you two want to do. Maybe I can arrange to come down there for a little while to talk it all over with both of you. In any case, you must know that there's no reason whatsoever for you to be discouraged or depressed, and you mustn't think that you wouldn't know how you two could survive, or anything along those lines. You know you can count on me at any time and in any way. An old Jew is always happy if he can take care of someone, and you know that you won't have any worries as long as I can earn something. I think it's sufficient to have a certain sum secure, to make it through the coming war on either shore. Other than that, one should worry as little as possible. Therefore, we'll wait for the results of your new experiment and then hold a serious war council on what should be done.

It's a little inconvenient that Kardan is arriving so soon, but then at least you'll be done with it. You can tell him when he comes that you'll be seeing me in ten days, so this lovely visit of his will be somewhat limited. By the way, I absolutely insist that we share the cost of this visit, because most of what Kardan has done is for me. Please don't be stupid, and do tell me what my share is. At the moment it's much easier for me than for you.

Harras is doing splendidly. He's made friends with the entire Berthon family and takes tremendous advantage of this friendship. They're crazy about this dog. I'm with him a lot. He sleeps in the guest room, and when I come home at night, there's great joy at seeing each other again—especially because of the milk bones he usually gets then. By the way, I now see that Erika treated him all wrong. He's much gentler now and understands every word when I speak to him. He's terribly playful, and when I'm in a bad mood, he can cheer me up immediately.

The weather here is bad all the time—rain, sleet, cold. Not a sign of the famous French spring. I already have nine numbers for the operetta, among them two big hits.

Unfortunately, Vambery has to go back to Budapest by the end of the month, because he can no longer afford to stay here. I hope he'll keep on working.

In one of the newspapers here it said that [Otto] Klemperer had died in America. But I don't know whether this news is correct.

I get a letter from Cas every week. Most of the time they're very funny stories, which really make you laugh if you know the people. He has a lot to do, two plays at the State Theater, since [Gustaf] Gründgens is intendant there now. In June he wants to drive with me to Algiers again.

Otherwise, there's nothing else new today. As soon as I hear something, I'll let you know. Don't be nervous. "Break a leg" with the new experiment! Regards to Pasetti and much love to you,

Your Weilli

1. *Werner Richard Heymann (1896–1961) had studied with Paul Juon (as had Weill) and worked in Berlin theaters as a conductor and composer of incidental music. He became one of UFA's top composers, for films including* Die Drei von der Tankstelle *(1930) and* Der Kongreß tanzt *(1931), then emigrated to Hollywood in 1933. He would later serve as musical director for the motion picture version of* Knickerbocker Holiday *(which included little of Weill's score for the play).*

2. *A stanza from a well-known German folk song.*

70 WEILL IN LOUVECIENNES TO LENYA IN SAN REMO, [13 MARCH 1934]

Tuesday

Dear *Zibelinerl*,

I just wanted to dash off a few lines to let you know that I haven't received any reply to my last telegram which I sent off a week ago and in which I asked Sternberg to have Paramount make me an offer first. So I'm afraid this beautiful project too has gone the way of all flesh. During the first few days when no answer was forthcoming, I thought they were using those tactics to keep me hanging. But now, after a week without news, I believe that the thing has fallen through. Either someone has raised some stink about me, or the whole thing isn't being done at all. Who knows? It would be a pity if this thing were buried, because it really was a big chance, and it would've been great fun for me, as you can imagine: the beautiful trip, the new surroundings, and last but not least, the highly interesting work—to say nothing of the faces of all those who are green with envy. Can you make sense of this whole affair? First such enthusiasm that Marlene turned Paris upside down from Hollywood in order to get my address, then the enthusiastic telegram from Sternberg, and then—when they were supposed to get serious about negotiations, etc.—not another word. Of course, it would be a grave mistake tactically if I were to telegraph once more. I simply have to wait. And there's no use banging my head against the wall.

Otherwise I'm fine. I've already composed seven numbers for the Vambery operetta, all of which have turned out extraordinarily well, in a very beautiful, new style. My creative juices are really flowing, it's going remarkably easily, and I have a lot of ideas. So I'm almost always at home and at most drive to a movie sometimes. Thursday I was invited to a party at the Deutsches'. Deval is in Prague and maintains that he's working on the play there. Natasha [Paley] is in London and is playing a part in the Don Juan movie with Douglas Fairbanks [*The Private Life of Don Juan*]. I've gone to the theater some; I saw a charming old operetta, newly adapted, and an excellent play by Bourdet, *Les temps difficiles*, very decently acted.[1]

You haven't written anything about the system. Isn't it working?

> For today all the best for you and many regards to Pasetti,
> Your Weili

Concerning the *12 Uhr* matter, I immediately wrote the gist of your letter to Steinthal, who's in Prague and meeting with Nürnberg there.

---

1. The Difficult Times was a play by the French dramatist Edouard Bourdet (1887–1945), who was best known for his comedies of manners, including La prisonnière *and* Le sexe faible.

71 WEILL IN LOUVECIENNES TO LENYA IN SAN REMO, [23 MARCH 1934]

Friday

Dear Linerl,

Last night I got back from Normandy [visiting the Aufrichts] and finally found a telegram from Sternberg here. In it two things are clear: first, that it actually hurt his pride that I didn't communicate my conditions to him personally; he seems to have interpreted that as lack of confidence in him. But apart from that he's still a very slick businessman and was simply letting me wait a bit. Here is what he wired me:

> Dearest Weill, I can't talk to Paramount without you personally giving me some idea of the minimum conditions you would accept to come here, since this whole thing can only be an experiment. Stop. Even if you were willing to come for nothing, I would still seek the best terms for you. Greetings, Sternberg.

The completely vague sentence about the experiment is most likely a pressure device, as he probably wants to let me know that I'm still an unknown quantity for the American movie industry. Now I'll wire him some sweet talk, how grateful I am to him for negotiating for me, etc., and will tell him my conditions: travel expenses, $250 per week for living expenses, no more than a six-month work period, and a fee of $6,000 (15,000 marks). Then they'll haggle, but I won't go for less than $4,000 (10,000 marks). Even if I tell myself that money doesn't matter so much on a first film over there with the best people available (which inevitably leads to other things), I still don't want to sell myself short, because it will only be possible to work with them if they truly need me, and there is no better measure of that than what they pay me. Now it will probably be another two weeks before they answer, but at least I'm content that the negotiations are proceeding.

It was very nice at the Aufrichts. The estate is fabulous, and I think it's great what they're doing there. Yesterday I was in Deauville and went for a walk in the sun by the ocean. It really is a marvelous beach.

Today a "second notice" came from the finance office in Potsdam for 72.81 marks. I'll answer them that I'm unable to pay it and that the threatened foreclosure would yield no results via diplomatic channels, but that I invite them to pay it from my blocked account if they can get it unblocked.

Otherwise there's nothing new. Write again soon to tell me how you are, and accept many greetings, *Doofi*, from your

Weilli

72 WEILL IN LOUVECIENNES TO LENYA IN SAN REMO, [29 MARCH 1934]

Thursday

Dear Linerl,

Although there's nothing new, I still want to write you a few lines so you'll have some news for Easter [1 April]. Many thanks for your last letter, which crossed mine. Saturday I sent a very clever telegram to Sternberg:

Dear Sternberg, am very grateful that you want to negotiate on my behalf, am convinced that you'll achieve the best possible results, stop. Propose following terms: all travel expenses, weekly expenses of 250 dollars, limitation on length of time of work. My customary asking price would be 6,000 dollars, but leave to you the commitment of obtainable fee from 4,000 upward. Most cordially, your W.

By the end of the week Marlene will also get a nice letter, which I wrote last week. I probably won't hear anything more before Easter. But I'm not holding my breath at all, because in any case it all depends on pure chance—and also on whether they really want to have me, and that must now be revealed.

It's starting to get very beautiful here, although sometimes it's still a little cold. I haven't been to Paris all week. That skunk Deval is finally back from his trip; tomorrow I'll have dinner at his place. If my publisher hadn't paid him such a high advance, I would tell him I'm no longer interested in this thing. I now have ten excellent numbers for the operetta, among them a real hit, "Auf Wiedersehn!", a "National Anthem of Santa Maria," two songs for the young man, etc. In the bordello the old general sings an old, stalwart drinking song:

Forty-nine bottles!	*[Neunundvierzig Flaschen!*
The first bottle was wonderful.	*Schön war die erste Flasche.*
But more wonderful is the second.	*Aber schöner ist die zweite Flasche.*
Holy Joseph pray for us.	*Heiliger Joseph bitt für uns.*
Forty-nine bottles!	*Neunundvierzig Flaschen!*
The second bottle was wonderful,	*Schön war die zweite Flasche.*
But the third one is more wonderful.	*Aber schöner ist die dritte.*
Holy Joseph, pray for us, etc.	*Heiliger Joseph bitt für uns. usw.]*

After each verse everyone stands up, as a sign of being "solidly committed to the native soil." Then they carry the totally drunk general off while singing the national anthem.

If only that Vambery didn't work so terribly slowly. I'd be able to write down the whole piece at a single stroke, but I always have to wait for days until I get a few more lines. These writers are a real cross to bear! A lazy bunch.

Your story from the *Wiener Journal* is marvelous. By the way, are you following the Stavisky and Prince affairs?[1] It's all terribly exciting, a pure gangster story. What do you think about the events in Germany? Hitler now admits that the Jewish boycott is bringing the finances of the Reich to the brink of ruin, because the export of German merchandise has stopped entirely. Now they're begging people to buy their wares again, but the entire world answers: As long as you move against the Jews, we will not buy from you. This movement comes from America. Of course the Reich will overcome these difficulties too, but *das Volk* are being "proletarianized" in the proud conviction that they are the greatest people on this earth. Cas writes very unhappily that he probably can't come to Algiers because the frontiers most likely will be closed. You can only feel sorry for the poor devils in there, and when I hear something like that, I'm overjoyed that we're out. In this spirit I wish you a beautiful Easter holiday!

> Your *Frosch*

1,675 lire in two days is terrific, but how did it go after that? You know that this is absolutely the last experiment! After that you have to learn French and English—or there'll be trouble!

Greetings to Pasetti, the Columbus of roulette.

1. Nothing is known about the "Prince affair." Serge Alexandre Stavisky (1886–1934), a French Jew born in the Ukraine, had been accused of fraudulent financial dealings and bribery of high governmental officials in France in December 1933. He was found dead shortly thereafter, an apparent suicide. The scandal reached into the highest circles of the government, and it was widely suspected that he had been murdered. In January 1934 there were demonstrations in the streets of Paris, and on 6 February a mob led by quasifascist groups tried to storm the Palais Bourbon. Police opened fire, wounding some three hundred and killing eleven. In the ensuing political crisis, Prime Minister Edouard Daladier was forced to resign. He eventually returned to a cabinet post, however, and in 1938 he again became prime minister. With Neville Chamberlain he shared the blame for the capitulation to Hitler at Munich in September 1938.

73 WEILL IN LOUVECIENNES TO LENYA IN SAN REMO, [6 APRIL 1934]

Friday

Dear Linderl,

How're you? Did you have a nice Easter holiday? Do you still have visitors? How is the new system going?

With me everything is at a standstill. Sternberg isn't answering again; tomorrow it will be two weeks since I wired him with my conditions. These movie rascals are all the same; they're enough to make you throw up. The worst thing is that I can't make any plans so long as I don't know anything definite about whether this matter is taken care of. But probably I'll never really know, and the moment I've made my work plans for the summer they'll suddenly begin to send telegrams again—and it will again come to naught.

I'm having a lot of trouble with Deval. He's the worst yet of all the literary swine

I've met, and that's a bunch. He came back from his trip and assured me he'd start to work immediately, that he didn't have anything else in mind and could concentrate completely on *Marie Galante*. If I go to Hollywood, he said he'd go with me, because he could work there very well. But he would oblige me in all respects. Today I phone him, and now he tells me he's leaving in two weeks—for Hollywood! Which means, in other words, he'll never write the play; he's cashed in on the advance and that's the end of it. You can imagine how embarrassing this is for me with [Paul] Bertrand; the first theatrical venture I wanted to undertake with him is a total failure, because the 25,000 francs he's given to Deval are as good as lost. Even Brecht could still learn something from Deval!

Yesterday I called [Heinz] Herald. A week ago he got some important news for me from Reinhardt, but didn't think it necessary to call me. Reinhardt's quite enthused about what Werfel has already done on the biblical oratorio and wants to know if I too could possibly come to Vienna when Werfel goes there. I said I'd come only if R. officially asks me to, that is, if the whole thing is already in a state that would warrant my making the trip. I'm thinking about whether this trip—if I undertake it—could possibly be combined with a visit to you. What do you think? I'd like to go by car, but that takes too much time. In any case, I'm quite sure we can see each other in the course of this month and then can also talk about what your plans are next.

Vambery has left, after I made a big scene in order to get him to work in Budapest. I hope he'll finish the piece now. Of all the projects, it's the one most ripe for a decision and also the one with the most potential. I'll now try to see if we could possibly do it in London. Of course, I'll have to do all this myself, since Bertrand won't move a finger. [Henri] Monnet asked me to go to London with him for a few days. We can stay with a friend of his who's on very good terms with [Charles] Cochran. Maybe I'll do that if I don't go to Vienna. All of this, of course, would be far simpler if the Hollywood thing had materialized, because then I would have suddenly had an identity in the industry. But I won't lose my calm over Sternberg's stalling tactics. If he wanted to, he could easily get less expensive people.

Now the weather is very beautiful. I've been to Paris only once this week, because there's nothing going on in that city, there aren't even any good movies.

Linerl, if that Kardan is still there, please be kind enough to ask him what's happened to the Nehers' white wicker chair. In his last letter Cas asked about it again, which is very embarrassing for me. If those philistines have gotten it too, you could perhaps say there'd been a mistake, that the chair did not belong to us at all. Maybe then we could get it back.

You might have gathered from this letter of mine that I'm in a rather bad mood. But that actually doesn't happen very often. Most of the time I'm cheerful. But this *Schweinerei* today has made me so mad.

Bidi [Brecht] is writing an operetta with Eisler! They'll probably use everything I've told him about musical theater in it. But that just leaves me cold. What kind of an operetta could that dried-up herring possibly write, and especially with that nutcracker?

I saw Deta [Strobel] again, for the first time in a long while. She was really very nice; she's a poor devil. Otherwise there's nothing else new. Let me hear from you soon again.

With monkey tail lifted high [*mit hochgehobenem Affenschwanz*],
Your *Froschi*

The little flower is from my garden. The lilacs already have tiny buds. Harras is doing splendidly.

74 WEILL IN LOUVECIENNES TO LENYA IN SAN REMO, [15? APRIL 1934]

Sunday

Dear *Zybelienerl*,

Many thanks for your call. I'd be very happy if you were to come here for a bit, or if we were able to drive to Vienna together. Unfortunately I haven't yet been able to reach [Heinz] Herald this morning, and out here the telephone doesn't work after 11:00 on Sundays. Therefore, I have to go into town and see if I can hunt him up somewhere before I send this letter. I'm afraid, though, that he won't have heard anything from the magician [Reinhardt]. Everything is so tedious with these jerks. I was thinking you could leave there around Tuesday or Wednesday (I think via Genoa) to arrive in Basel the next morning, where I would be waiting for you at the train station with the car, so we could take off. It's a much shorter trip for me to Basel than to [San Remo], and it would be on my way when I drive to Vienna. When I've finished in Vienna, you could drive here with me and then stay on a little bit. Of course, I only want to make this trip to Vienna if it's really worth it. If I don't go, you could leave there Tuesday evening and be here early Wednesday. At the moment I don't have much to do. Vambery won't send any new lyrics for another eight or ten days, and Deval is already leaving for Hollywood this week.

So look: if I do reach Herald now and find out something from him, I'll include it in this letter. If I don't hear anything more today, I'll send you a wire on Tuesday morning to say whether I'll await you in Basel or in Paris and when. Everything else I can tell you in person.

Cordially,
Your *Froschi*

I've now spoken to Herald. It still seems quite uncertain when I'm supposed to be in Vienna, in no case before the end of the week. Therefore, it would be more practical (should you not wish to wait for the decision) if, for the time being, you were to come here first, so you could arrive on Wednesday or early Thursday. By the way, there's now also a *couchette* from Nice, which is almost like a second-class sleeping car but ever so much cheaper—in case you want to save money. So send me a telegram to let me know when you're arriving, with the exact time if possible.

Auf Wiedersehen!

If I have to go to Vienna, we might possibly go there by car from here.

Weill's passport indicates that he spent a few days in London in early May. In a letter to Universal Edition on 5 May, he reported the "very big success" that Lys Gauty had with his song "Complainte de la Seine" and indicated that he might be going to America as soon as the summer.

75 WEILL IN LOUVECIENNES TO LENYA
[WHEREABOUTS UNKNOWN], 17 MAY 1934

17.5.1934

Dear Linerl,

Many thanks for your detailed report. I just got your letter of Tuesday, and I want to send a quick reply, so you'll still receive it. I'm very glad that everything with those matters is working out well. I haven't received a notice about the package, but it's not certain yet whether Cas is coming. Of course, it would be great if you two didn't have to go to San Remo, but be careful that nothing happens with the money. I'll find out at the bank tomorrow whether one can buy marks here and at what exchange, or wait— I'll call my bank before I mail this letter, so I can let you know about the exchange rate. That thing of P.'s with Germany would, of course, be fantastic, but it sounds so unbelievable that I'm afraid there's a trap behind it somewhere. Sure, it's possible that it's really as you seem to think, that the man wants to do this thing again. I'd strongly advise you against it, as well as against making the trip altogether. If you could really get a third or even a fourth of it without the trip, I'd take it and not do anything further. That would be terrific indeed. Since he agreed to it, he should have to pay it, even without P. having to come to him. Please handle this matter with greatest care and with all possible distrust. P. must make the trip only if he has taken precautions against all possibilities. In any event, that man can do very little since his hands are tied. But one can't be careful enough in such matters.

For my part, the ignition seems to be working again, knock on wood. It was marvelous in London. It's a magnificent city. I walked around a lot and saw a lot; I'll be writing you about it. There's surely more for me to do there than here, and I'm thinking I might let you two have my house for the fall while I settle down in London for several months or stay at [Edward] James's farm. He's offered it to me in such a cordial, friendly way that I can accept without hesitation. Surprisingly, everything's worked out well with my appointments. [Eric] Wollheim had wired me in London from here [Paris] that he'd be in his office on Monday morning. And so I saw him there Monday and Tuesday. He was very nice; he thought I would be tremendously well liked in London and that I was exactly the man Cochran needs right now. For the time being he wants to make sure that Cochran commissions two or three scenes from me for a big revue he will probably start in the fall. He was really enthused about the story of the operetta [*Der Kuhhandel*], which I had related to him, and wants to talk to Cochran about that as well. It's definite that I'll meet with Cochran here between the 5th and 7th of June. Meanwhile, it came out that Jed Harris was back in London at the same time as I. I spent a great deal of time with him on Saturday evening. He's a Galician Jew, very young, very smart, very pompous, and conceited. He told me that the music of *Die Dreigroschenoper* was a tremendous success in New York, and everybody was of the opinion it was a new path at last, that they were tired of all that jazz music, including [George] Gershwin, and that my music would be the only sort that could take its place. He'd be terribly happy to work with me. He had already talked to the most important dramatic authors in New York (Ben Hecht, Kaufman, and also the author of the biblical Negro play that was such a huge success),[1] and all were to be had instantly for a collaboration with me. I played a lot of the operetta [*Der Kuhhandel*] for him, and he was terribly enthusiastic. Then, at 2:30 A.M., he went home. And never was seen again. But Black (the friend of Monnet's) will try to talk to him further and arrange a new rendezvous.[2] I visited Tilly [Losch] in her little house. She doesn't look well and is nervous because of her lawsuit. I was in Elstree with Natasha and talked with [Alexander] Korda. A repulsive guy. I believe this time I was quite clever: I invited Natasha out several times to the restaurants where all the theater and movie people sit around, and they were whispering all around us. It was very expensive, but terribly chic. Once I went out with a Lady Abdy, who lives at James's place. James told me afterward that she had fallen in love with me, whereupon I quickly departed.

I got back Tuesday night and found a letter from Sternberg:

Dear Weill, thanks for your kind letter. I have not yet submitted your letter to the company, because I still don't have a property at this point, and your minimum demands are too high to push toward something still in doubt. By the way, I never did intend to negotiate on your behalf, as I never do anything like that. I leave the negotiating to others. But I had the great desire to work out a big new musical film, which would bring you more than enough if it was a success. But your attitude toward this experiment prevents me from pursuing it at this time. I hope that the future will offer us a project so we can more favorably arrange to collaborate. My best wishes, and hoping we'll see each other soon . . .

Ergo, offended liverwurst. But this means nothing at all; especially after I saw that horrible Catherine movie [*The Scarlet Empress*] in London, I'm not sure one could accomplish anything with this megalomaniacal schmuck. I'll answer him today that he can be sure he could very quickly come to terms with me financially once he has a property. I find the situation, after this letter and after his flop with Catherine, very favorable.— And now a miracle: Vambery's working. He's already sent three completed, very good scenes with new text, so that I can work, thank God. Hein told me that Bertrand has completely taken me into his heart, because I took care of the gramophone matter for him so promptly, and consequently 6,000 francs will go into my account.[3] I'm quite a perfect gentleman, a cavalier, etc.

I'm in a good mood and have regained all my self-confidence. Look for something really nice for yourself for this summer, where you can work and vacation at the same time, and where P. can also work. You both should look around once more, so you'll find something pleasing and practical. Write soon. Thanks for everything. Greetings to P.

All good things for you.

Your Knudchen

And: in exchange for marks the bank would have paid 5.88 today, but there's no guarantee how much they'll pay next week.

1. *George S. Kaufman (1889–1961) was an extremely successful playwright who collaborated frequently with other writers throughout his career, among them Marc Connelly, Edna Ferber, and especially Moss Hart. He won a Pulitzer Prize for his work with George and Ira Gershwin on* Of Thee I Sing *(1931). The unnamed author Weill refers to might be Marc Connelly (1890–1981), who won the Pulitzer Prize in 1930 for* The Green Pastures. *Set in a small black church in the South, the play relates the stories of Adam and Eve, Cain and Abel, Noah, Moses, and on up through the crucifixion of Jesus. The reference is less likely to Paul Green (1894–1981), whose* In Abraham's Bosom *had won the Pulitzer Prize in 1926.*

2. *George Black (1891–1945) was a prominent English impresario whose shows were noted for their rapid pacing. As managing director of General Theatre Corporation (1928) and Moss Empires Ltd. (1933), he controlled forty halls, including the famous Palladium.*

3. *Otto Hein was the director of Coda, a publisher of light music. Weill's songs "Je ne t'aime pas" and "Complainte de la Seine" were published by his company.*

76 WEILL IN LOUVECIENNES TO LENYA IN ARABBA, [24 MAY 1934]

Thursday

Dear *Zybelinerl*,

Many thanks for your express letter. I'm curious how you like it in Arabba. It's really perfect for learning French, because you can work there in peace. The old innkeeper will be a lot of fun. And behind the church, where the forest begins, there's a spring with marvelous water. Do you both want to stay there for the time being, or do you want to go somewhere closer to Vienna, where P. can work and where you can take better care of the money matter? The main thing is that you both stay put somewhere where you can work. What's happened with the other money matters?

The package arrived already on Saturday, without any problems, at Abr.'s [Abravanel]. Thanks for everything. I'm very happy with the beautiful quilt, but Mrs. Berthon can't understand at all how one could sleep under something like that.

Jäger[?] writes that as of now the debt is 608 marks, but more notes are due on 1 June, 1 July, and 1 August, and the entire debt will be 1,040. For the time being I'll pay only the 608. They think that they'll be able to come to an agreement with the bank.

Otherwise there's little news. I'm working on the new lyrics that V. [Vambery] sent. It's coming along very well. Gilbert sent the new version of "Anybody," which is charming.[1] I'll busy myself a little with that too. Reinhardt is coming here on Saturday. Tomorrow I'm invited to La Polignac's and Monday to Bertrand's; then Bertrand comes here on Wednesday. Cas will probably turn up here one of these days. Mrs. Berthon bought a giant leather sofa at an auction for 75 francs, including delivery and tip, which one can turn out and make into a real bed.—Now be diligent, write again soon and get yourselves that money.

> All good things,
> Your Knuti

1. *"Anybody" probably never materialized, or it appeared under a different title. The Gilbert referred to is most likely Robert Gilbert, the well-known lyricist of* Im weißen Rössl, *who worked closely with Charell.*

77 WEILL IN LOUVECIENNES TO LENYA IN THE PIEVE DI LIVINALLONGO, ITALY, 28 MAY 1934

Louveciennes, 28.5.1934

Dear Linerl,

Many thanks for your long letter. The idea of going to the Aufrichts isn't a bad one, and it could probably be easily arranged (though I'm not completely convinced you could stand it there for a longer period of time). But if you're trying to save, it doesn't seem quite right for you to make this expensive trip to Normandy now and have Pasetti make the same trip by car two weeks later. Wouldn't it actually be smarter for you to come to Vienna for a week as well and wait there until everything's taken care of, and then the two of you drive together? By the way, it's very likely that we could meet each other during that time. I spoke with Reinhardt yesterday, and it's almost definite that we'll meet with Werfel after 5 June either in Salzburg or Vienna. However, I did ask him not to make the appointment before 8 June, because I'm supposed to meet with Cochran on the 5th or the 6th. I'm pretty sure that this trip to see Reinhardt will happen, because Lord Melchett, too, wants to meet us at that time, and Reinhardt wants to make sure he pays Werfel and me an advance.[1] That's another reason you should wait those few days in Austria—preferably in Vienna, and you could come for a bit to Salzburg too, if I don't come to Vienna.

Aside from that, I think it's out of the question for you to spend the summer in Normandy, because it's incredibly expensive. For 10 schillings (30 francs) you can't get anything at all there, for 40 francs only something awful. Of course, no place is as cheap, and at the same time as good, as in Austria. But if you don't want to or cannot stay there, I'd advise you to look for something on the French Riviera, where it's easier to find something good that's affordable. You could, of course, learn French there wonderfully, and in the meantime I could look around for an apartment here. It takes a very long time to find something suitable. I could line some places up for you over the summer, so you won't have to choose until after you get here.

The Reinhardt thing really seems to be taking off now; he absolutely wants a premiere shortly after Christmas, which means I'll have to work insanely over the coming months. I had just started to work productively again, when suddenly Cas and Erika arrived. This disturbance makes me a bit nervous, but they're very nice and tell tremendously funny stories. Also, they'll only be here until the end of the week. They are staying upstairs in my room, and I'm staying downstairs on the new bed. Cas's mood is better than I had anticipated. Yesterday we took a car ride up close to Normandy. It was very beautiful. But I saw again how expensive it is there.

So now I'll see that I get my trip organized as quickly as possible, and then I'll immediately let you know. In any case it would be idiotic for you to come here on the 5th, right when I go to Austria. For the time being, arrange it so that you go with P. to Vienna, at which point you will get further news from me.

Of course you'll receive a copy of the lost purchase document from Jäger when the debts have been paid. I still feel that P. should refrain, if at all possible, from making a trip to Germany and above all should stay away from new enterprises and instead try with every means possible to get the 50,000 lire and the money from Pereleny[?]. He should be satisfied with that, since you can live on it for a year while he finishes his studies. Cas, for instance, knows about the Ahrendt[?] matter, and I say to myself, if Cas already knows something, it's no longer a secret. Therefore, don't take any chances.

Did you get my letter sent to Arabba? I've written to Jäger that I'll pay the 600 marks for the time being. I already wrote you that the package arrived without any difficulties.

Now I think that we'll soon see each other in Austria. You'll hear from me immediately, possibly by wire, when I know more details. Please do always give me your address, so I know where I can reach you.

Regards to Pasetti. Much love to you, and give my regards to the Pordoi [a mountain pass in the Dolomites]!

Your Knut

It's quite possible that I'll meet Vambery after the meeting with Reinhardt, which may last about a week, and that I'll either take him back here with me by car or work with him somewhere in Austria.

1. *Lord Melchett was an ardent Zionist millionaire whose father had employed Chaim Weizmann (1874–1952) as a chemist in his factory in Frankfurt am Main.*

78 WEILL IN LOUVECIENNES TO LENYA IN THE DOLOMITES[?], [4 JUNE 1934]

Monday

Dear *Zybelinerl*,

This morning I got your telegram, and I'm glad that my letter arrived. It's good that you didn't go to Aufricht's. He was here and said that a whole tribe of Mendelssohns is there. Herald called me this morning and told me that it's as good as certain that Reinhardt will expect me in Salzburg toward the end of the week. By Wednesday I'll have definite news. I've heard from Wollheim in London that he's coming to Paris tomorrow and is expecting Cochran here on Wednesday or Thursday. He'll try to arrange my appointment with Cochran as early as possible, preferably on Wednesday, so I can leave by car on Thursday. But if I can't meet Cochran till Thursday or Friday, I'll take the train to Salzburg (I think it now has third-class sleeping cars). As soon as I know something definite, I'll send you a telegram. But I believe it would be simplest for us to meet in Salzburg directly. I'll probably stay with Max. If so, we could find something nice for you close to Salzburg. Maybe Pasetti has already told you where to stay in Salzburg. If so, please write to me. If by some chance we should miss each other, send news to me in Leopoldskron, will you?[1] I'll try to have Vambery come to Salzburg, so I can work with him. He's actually finished the play except for the purely musical things, and I'm very pleased with his work. If I come by car, perhaps I'll bring him back with me.

The Nehers have left now. We had some nice days, though a bit strenuous, since when one has visitors, one always has the feeling they're bored and that one must entertain them. Cas is really a fine fellow, with a truly sympathetic manner. He painted me a very pretty picture and framed it for my music salon. He's quite enthusiastic about my new works, especially the symphony, but also the operetta. He says I've developed tremendously during this year. You can imagine how enthusiastic he was about the house and about my whole way of life here.

Wednesday I had Bertrand Sr. and Jr. and Hein here for lunch. They got a very good meal. Then I played them the operetta. Bertrand was completely beside himself and is now very big on me.

It's sensible that you stayed up there and that you're waiting there until I come. I hope you won't get too bored. Is Forgler's[?] son going to drive you to the train? Then it's not a long trip to Salzburg at all.—Now keep your fingers crossed diligently for my talks with Cochran. If I have a little bit of luck, I won't give a hoot about the Reinhardt thing.

Come to think of it, in case I go by car, maybe we could meet in Innsbruck on the second evening of my trip and from there drive to Salzburg together. I'll wire you in detail about that.

I'm very happy that I'll see you by the end of the week. I hope it all works out.

Much love, your Knut

1. Reinhardt's castle, a mile and a half from Leopoldskron, had been built in the mid-eighteenth century as the private residence of Archbishop Firmian. Norman Bel Geddes recalled that Reinhardt ran his castle in a grand manner that would never be seen again. He described the enormous house and grounds: "The main floor was a flight above ground level, gained by a magnificent marble staircase which corkscrewed upward for three majestic flights. Above the main entrance hall was another great hall one hundred feet long by seventy wide and three stories high. . . . The rest of the house was equally remarkable. Its inner walls had been built sufficiently thick to accommodate service corridors through which domestic help could move unseen. Logs, eight feet long, could be brought through these corridors and placed in the fireplaces in every room without disturbing the occupants. Walls and ceilings throughout the house were encrusted with rich allegorical relief in plaster, and mirrors were everywhere. Reinhardt had reputedly spent more than a million dollars on plumbing, electricity, and repairs. In front of the house was a private lake, a mile long and a half mile wide. The grounds were beautifully landscaped: one grove of trees and shrubs a hundred yards in depth ran the length of the lake. There were a number of guest cottages within walking distance of the main house. The stables and surrounding yards could not have been crowded into Rockefeller Plaza. The household staff numbered thirty" (Geddes, p. 282).

[FIG. 43]

79 WEILL IN LOUVECIENNES TO LENYA IN ARABBA, [10 JUNE 1934]

Sunday

Louveciennes

Dear *Zybelinerl,*

I received your telegram this morning and therefore am writing you directly in Arabba. It's too bad that it didn't work out for Salzburg, but now Max has postponed the meeting because he's doesn't want to stay in Salzburg, probably because of the bombing there.[1] He phoned Friday night to ask me to be in Venice in about ten days; Werfel and Lord Melchett, the main sponsor, will also come. I assume that this time there will be a meeting, since Max has a directing job in Venice then anyway. By the way, he wants to nail everything down to some extent, in order to ask Lord Melchett for an advance for Werfel and me, and I'm taking the stance that I must have that, because otherwise I'll have to accept other things to earn money. Actually I'm quite happy that the matter has been moved to Venice, because I can take the opportunity to swim a bit and burn my hide. It will be my only opportunity this summer anyway, since—as it seems—I'll have an enormous amount of work. In any case, I've asked Francesco [von Mendelssohn] to look for a quiet little hotel on the Lido for me.

Wollheim is behaving well; I spent two hours with him and Cochran yesterday and played them the operetta. He [Cochran] liked it very much. Of course he's afraid it's not popular enough for the broad masses and that the subject might be too "satirical." But he really went for the music, and at least I've managed to get him to ask Wollheim to have a rough English translation of the libretto made, and after that he will make his decision. Wollheim told me afterward that the whole thing looked very good; Cochran had told him again and again that I was the man he needed, in particular with regard to the revue he wants to open in the fall, for which I should do a few numbers. Most of all I'm supposed to bring him new ideas. It's also a good sign that he wants to see me again tomorrow, even though he's only here for three days. That's when I'll present a series of proposals that I worked out today. By the way, he spoke very enthusiastically about *Die sieben Todsünden* and about you, and I'm convinced that there'll also be a possibility for you here, once I've established myself.

Besides that, in the next few days I'm also going to try to show the operetta to an American impresario who's here.[2] Then I'll be finished here and can take off by car (around Wednesday or Thursday). I wrote to Vambery to see if he could come to Venice, so I could also work with him while I'm there. If he can make it, I might possibly have him come as early as Saturday or Sunday and let him stay for two weeks in order to finish the entire libretto of the operetta, because that is the most important thing for me at the moment.

Now I'm curious as to what your plans are. Of course I could meet you somewhere on the way to Venice, in Bolzano or Fasano, so we could talk about everything. I'll spend half a day in Zurich to play my symphony for Bruno Walter. Do you want to ride along to Venice and wait there for Pasetti? Once Reinhardt is there, you won't see me very much, but up to then it would really be swell. But if your decision to go to France still holds, there really isn't much point for you to travel around a lot. As soon as P. is ready, you two can drive here to my house and then look for an apartment. It's entirely possible that I'll still have to go to London after Venice. If, after that, I have to set to work, you two could go to the beach somewhere near here. I believe that would be the most sensible arrangement. What do you think?

By the way, it's also possible you could have Abravanel's apartment if you want it, because they might go to Australia from 28 July until next March, where he's supposed to become the director of a touring opera company. The matter will be decided in the next few days. They already have another interested party, but Friedel [Mrs. Abravanel] would rather let you have it, if you want it. I think that's very promising.

It's probably very beautiful in Arabba now. The air up there is so soothing and probably will be very good for you. Your longing for the house is only because of the gypsy life you lead. Once you settle down again somewhere, it will pass quickly. It's gorgeous here now. I had myself a most comfortable Sunday—worked a bit, rummaged around a bit, lay around in the garden on your lawn chair, and ate with Harras in the little restaurant at noon, because Mrs. Berthon is off today.

Now, little one, listen: if my present plans don't go out the window again (as I hope they won't), I'll send you a telegram by the middle of next week to tell you when I am leaving and when and where we can meet each other. By that time I'll probably have some news or other from you as to what your intentions are. I hope this time it will all click.

> Much love and little kisses,
> Your Knuti

Monday morning. Just now your letter of Friday arrived. I'm very happy you're so diligent and that Pasetti will be there until Friday. Then he should quickly get his affairs in order, so you two can drive here. Thursday morning I'm going to play the operetta for that American, so I could leave in the afternoon. But I think it would be smarter for me to take the train, since that is much cheaper for traveling alone. Preliminary plan: depart by train on Thursday afternoon. Friday in Zurich; resume the trip in the evening, possibly meeting you somewhere (Lake Garda), where we would stay over Sunday or continue directly to Venice, where you'll be coming. Think about this and send a telegram. In Zurich I'll stay at the Bellerive apartments.

> Much love, and thanks for the gentian flower.

1. Even before the murder of Chancellor Dollfuß in July 1934, Austrian Nazis, with weapons and dynamite furnished by Germany, had instituted a reign of terror, blowing up railways and government buildings.

2. The "American impresario" was the Russian-born Sol Hurok (1888–1974), a legendary and powerful prototype of the old-style great impresarios. (In a letter of 14 January 1935 to Heugel, Weill reports that he had a telegram from Hurok asking whether the operetta was still available for America.)

On 21 June, the Copenhagen newspaper Aften-Avisen published an interview with Weill conducted in Paris by Ole Winding: "Naturally Paris must become my new home. I know that *here new battles await me, battles that at home are already old hat but still have to be waged here, and I feel I'll be able to do some good. It's hard but at the same time nice to begin anew with such an about-face. In my heart of hearts I have never left Germany." Weill spent most of the summer traveling. His passport indicates that he arrived in Basel on 14 June and Zurich on the following day, and then spent 16–25 June in Venice, where Lenya met him. Pasetti seems to have gone to Vienna; he informed her of "passport trouble" and the failure of various efforts to smuggle Weill's money out. Weill returned to Louveciennes on 27 June; Lenya left San Remo for a short stay at Weill's house and then secured an engagement at the Corso Theater in Zurich. On 5 July Weill left for a ten-day stay in London. He spent the first two weeks of August in Italy, then five days in Austria, before returning to Louveciennes on 20 August.*

80 LENYA IN SAN REMO TO WEILL IN LOUVECIENNES, [26 JUNE 1934]

Tuesday

My dear Weili,

Once again I've waited an entire day. Nothing. Yesterday there was an express letter from Pasetti, which was mailed Sunday morning. He has been reported to the police anonymously because of "political machinations," and they've taken away his passport as a result. He can tell me about it only in person. He thinks it may take days to get his passport back, and he has to be glad that they let him run around loose. Which pig turned him in like that can't be determined for the time being. He thinks that <u>he</u> must make a report in San Remo, since the money was deposited in the bank there under his name and the transactions were also under his name. He writes that if the accounts are gone, we won't get anything anymore; if they're still there, there's some hope yet. Also that then they will wait awhile before doing something with that money. He's absolutely desperate. He suggests I come to Vienna if he can't get away anymore this week, so I can make a written complaint to San Remo, and then we would stay in Vienna until the fall, living off the sale of the antiques, which he has had appraised at approximately 2,000 schillings, and then go to Paris and sell the stamp collection there. We can surely get the money out through Peresleny, but it will take some time. In no case do I want to go to Vienna. That would be terrible for me. I sent him a telegram yesterday that I'm anxiously awaiting him here. I do so hope he'll arrive here in the next few days. I don't want to lose my nerve now, although this waiting is awful. I'll write you immediately when I hear something from him. Were it not for you, I really don't know what I would do now. But this bad luck has to stop soon. I accompanied Vambery to St. Mark's, then came back here again. I've canceled the cabin, as I don't need one just for myself. I hope you had a good trip and arrived safely. If only you'd have some luck in London. I'll go mail this letter now. If only something would arrive tomorrow.

Now farewell my Weilili. Whenever I think of you, tears come to my eyes, because you're so good to me. If only I could pay you back for all of this some day. I'll write you as soon as I hear something. Farewell, *Fröschlein.*

All good things,
Your Linerl

Please don't get nervous; somehow everything will turn out all right.

81 WEILL IN LOUVECIENNES TO LENYA IN SAN REMO,
[28 JUNE 1934]
Letterhead: Kurt Weill

Thursday

Dear Linerl,

I actually got to the Nehers' in Verona and spent half a day with them, because they pestered me so. The trip back was very uncomfortable, because I couldn't afford a sleeper (it would have cost more than 150 lire from Milan to Paris).

Here I found all kinds of interesting stuff: a telegram from Deval saying that *Marie Galante* will be ready by the end of July(!); a charming telegram from Edward [James] (with the familiar *Du*) insisting I stay with him; an overwhelmingly cordial letter from Charell announcing that he's coming to Paris at the end of July with new, important propositions for me; a letter from a big London theatrical agency, whose head is coming to Paris this week to negotiate with me.

So you see, plenty of action! In any case, you mustn't have any pangs of conscience because you're taking advantage of a bit of help from me right now. One of these many projects is bound to materialize and consequently keep my business booming. Besides, I do need to know that all is well with you, and that you are without worries, if I'm to be able to work in peace—so it's pure selfishness on my part.

I've still had no news from London, but given the invitation from James, I firmly intend to go there in any case, because it won't cost me much and I can accomplish a lot more if I'm on the scene.

I'll keep my fingers crossed for you in San Remo. But don't get worked up if it all falls through. It can happen to anyone, and you two don't need to reproach yourselves. I'd advise you two not to go to Vienna but rather directly to Paris to find an apartment there, so this gypsy life can finally come to an end. But first get all your affairs in order, so you won't have to travel all over the place again. Especially in the Arendt matter, you must try very hard right now to get all the money that's coming to you, because otherwise this man might no longer care to get this thing over with. And don't do any- thing without a lawyer! If you two see an opportunity to sell your things in Vienna and could actually get 2,000 schillings for them, and at the same time insist that this Peres- leny matter get settled, you could both return to Vienna for eight to ten days (but with- out the car), i.e., if they let P. in (if he can pass through the border controls). In any case, see to it that everything has been taken care of before you end up here, so you'll be able to work in peace. If you still need money to settle certain matters, don't hesitate to write me; I'll be glad to lend you whatever you may need in order to find peace and quiet for your work, as well as to get started here in Paris.

Once you've taken care of everything, you both can stay here at my house while you look around for something nice for yourselves. I'll try to line some things up for you.

So keep your chin up, *Kleene*. All my love to you and P.

Always, your Knutchen

82 WEILL IN LONDON TO LENYA IN LOUVECIENNES, 14 JULY 1934
Postcard

Saturday morning

Dear Linerl,

I'm very nervous about that telephone conversation. Of course, there are lots of reasons why it could be impossible for him [Pasetti] to send a wire. It was the tensest of days because of that speech Adolf delivered in the evening.[1] Let's hope you'll have some news today. If anything is awry, we should immediately get in touch with Brandenstein (whom we met in Venice).[2] Maybe P. didn't want to send a telegram and wrote you instead. Or perhaps there won't be any news at all until he's gotten out. I definitely hope to be in Paris tomorrow night.

All my love! Knut

Melchett's telephone: ROMSY 40

1. *In his speech to the Reichstag on the evening of 13 July, Hitler referred to events that had forced him to purge some of his closest associates (including Ernst Röhm) from the storm troops. Hundreds of Hitler's followers, as well as several army generals (von Schleicher among them), were killed in the "blood purge."*
2. *Baron von Brandenstein was a close friend of the Mendelssohn family.*

83 WEILL IN ARABBA TO LENYA IN ZURICH, [7? AUGUST 1934]

Arabba, Tuesday

Dear Linerl,

I got your letter this afternoon. I think the insurance matter is of little importance, because most likely he won't pay the 74 schillings due every month but rather assumes you'll pay it—and that is out of the question. I'll bring the document with me to Zurich. To Dinkhauser[?] I'd answer only very briefly that the party with whom Dr. Otto P. spoke over the phone in Bolzano is unknown to you, since you were not present during the call.

I'm terribly happy that you're feeling so well and that everything is going so beautifully.[1] You surely will like it when you live in the country. The Curjels are really very nice, and the work will be fun for you. The little song by [Mischa] Spoliansky could be very nice,[2] and you'll certainly do my song marvelously ["Je ne t'aime pas" or "Complainte de la Seine"?]; I've been singing it all day long. It'd be a good idea to address the second refrain to the audience, with a gest similar to that of the second refrain of

"Wie man sich bettet," yet not tragically, but delicately resigned and blossoming out toward the end!

Things are going well for me. The weather yesterday was wonderful, and we went for a long hike. Today we took a five-hour walk up the Col di Sangue. Now it's raining. The Nehers are nice; I'm relaxing and devouring dumplings. Today I got a telegram from Herald: "Propose work session with Werfel in Salzburg starting Sunday, finalizing of contract assured." This suits me fine, since the Nehers, too, will be leaving for Germany on Monday. Perhaps we'll go to Lake Garda on Friday for two days if it continues to rain here. My coming to Zurich depends on how long I have to be in Salzburg. But you won't need me for the rehearsals, will you? You can do that all on your own now! I'll write to Rieser and will ask Werfel to write him as well.[3] Be nice, merry, and sedulous.

> All my love for you,
> Your Knut

1. *The newly renovated Corso Theater had reopened in July with a variety show and a big reception, attended by Thomas Mann and Max Ernst, who had painted a mural for the Mascotte Bar in the building. In August Lenya played the role of Pussy Angora opposite Otto Wallburg in the operetta* Lieber reich aber glücklich *by Arnold and Bach, with music by Walter Kollo. Her song in the last act, "Ein bißchen Liebe," was, according to one critic, "of a totally different style than the rest of the farce, an artistically interpreted, welcome interlude that forced even the most laughter-hungry audience into quiet meditation"* (Neue Zürcher Zeitung, *19 Aug. 1934).*
2. *The Russian-born composer Mischa Spoliansky (1898–1985) had gained fame in Berlin for his cabaret songs and film scores.*
3. *Ferdinand Rieser (d. 1947) was the manager of the Zurich Schauspielhaus and the Corso Theater. He employed many distinguished refugee actors but was asked to resign in 1938 because of threats by the National Front, a nationalistic Swiss antiforeigner organization.*

84   WEILL IN BOLZANO, ITALY, TO LENYA IN ZURICH, 10 AUGUST 1934

Postcard

Dear Linerl,

Today we drove to Bolzano because it was too cold up where we were. The weather here is magnificent. Now we'll leave for one day at Lake Como. I'll be in Salzburg on Monday. Write to me poste restante. I hope you are well and all will work out all right at the theater.[1] Perhaps I'll be finished in time, so I can be in Z. [Zurich] on the 16th. I'll try. All good things for you. Little kisses from your

> Knut

1. *In Zurich Lenya once again crossed paths with her mentor Richard Révy; in an undated letter from 1934 addressing him as "Wanja," Lenya reported: "It's been relentlessly hot here lately, and the theater's been empty. My song is getting better and better and the people are applauding less and less. . . . In the swimming pool I saw Fritz von Beust [a wealthy former lover; see p. 20], somewhat gray with a slight paunch, angry because I was sitting in the restaurant with three handsome men and did not look at all down and out. What can I do? Farewell, Wanja" (L–RR).*

85 WEILL IN SALZBURG TO LENYA IN ZURICH, 15 AUGUST 1934

Letterhead: Hotel Stein – Salzburg

Wednesday morning

My dear Linerl,

I arrived here yesterday morning, after a miserable drive through rain on bad roads; the evening before I could manage to get only within fifty kilometers of Salzburg. I found your letter at the post office. The things with P. [Pasetti] are simply disgusting, but there's no sense dwelling on them anymore. You mustn't react in any way! We'll talk about it in detail sometime.—It's really wonderful that you're having fun with your work. I don't think the song needs to be cut. It's certainly not too long; people just can't imagine how you can carry off something like that. If you can somehow make [Max] Roth [the conductor] understand, without making him feel resentful, I'd see how it goes without the cut on the 16th.

I've found the situation entirely changed here. Max [Reinhardt] has already signed a contract for the work to premiere in New York between 15 February and 15 March. Werfel, who made a grand entrance here with wife [Alma Maria] and two publishers, had wangled the larger share of the authors' royalties for himself during my absence, and the advance was also ridiculous. At eleven o'clock I declared I was leaving; by four o'clock I had ensured that the royalties would be divided equally between Werfel and myself; at nine o'clock in the evening I got them to the point where they were willing to try to raise my advance to 1,000 pounds. If I achieve that, the conditions will be more attractive than I had ever expected. The division is so favorable that just a moderate success could bring me 1,200 dollars a week. I hope it will now be definitively settled. I'll have to work like a fiend in order to meet the deadline. I'm moving to Leopoldskron, where it's wonderfully beautiful. I hope to be able to leave toward the end of the week. Unfortunately I can't be there on the 16th, but you can get through this by yourself now, can't you? Keep well. Break a leg! Little kisses from

[FIG. 44]

Knut

I'm writing to Rieser now and also will talk to Werfel.

86 WEILL IN LOUVECIENNES TO LENYA IN ZURICH, [21 AUGUST 1934]

Tuesday

My dear Linerl,

Just a quick note to say that I arrived here quite safely. In this beautiful weather the drive was mere child's play. I found everything here very nice and clean. Harras got bitten on the nose but is happy as can be.

My worst fears have come true: *Marie Galante*, completely finished, was lying here waiting for me. How I'll get it done is a real puzzle. It's a big thriller (bombshell of a role!!!) with nice musical possibilities. I could certainly do it very well. But when? Right now I feel as if I'll never come up with any ideas again. I'm really glad that you have it so good there and that you're content. Be shrewd about the matter of the car. Be a cutie-pie, write soon, and take a thousand greetings from your

   Kurti

87 WEILL IN LOUVECIENNES TO LENYA IN ZURICH, [26 AUGUST 1934]
Letterhead: Kurt Weill

Sunday evening

My dear Linerl,

   Many thanks for your long letter. I'm so glad you're feeling well and are content. It would be very nice if you could get the car and drive with Jella [Curjel] for a bit to the south of France and come here afterward. By then I hope to be a little further along with my work. Can't the thing about the car be done in Germany? I'm afraid that this too will be loused up again, if P. [Pasetti] has his fingers in it. In any case you have to watch out. (I believe about a quarter of everything he's told us and now, as before, consider him a swindler who is apt to do almost anything. Therefore don't get yourself involved in <u>anything</u>, do you hear?)

   I told Curjel that *Marie Galante* will go to the theater that casts you in it. Therefore he should see to it that the thing with *Kiki* works out, because otherwise I'll press for a contract with Rieser for *Marie Galante*. Of course he won't want that. He should mount *Kiki* in February and in March *Marie Galante*.[1] Besides that he should talk Blum into letting you sing your own chansons in November.[2] I think that these three things can be achieved if you get after them a little bit. It would be a shame if this cabaret thing didn't work out; you'd certainly have great success, it would be money earned easily, and you could learn English wonderfully.

   I'm working nonstop. Today I did two songs for *Marie Galante:* a lullaby she sings to the old Negro and the song she sings before she dies; she's shot before the last words. For the Bible thing I already have two excellent numbers and all kinds of preparatory work. I'm diligently studying the original liturgical music that my father sent me, but it can't really be used, or at best only for the recitatives.

   Today I played the operetta for Charell and his brother. I never saw such enthusiasm. He understood it completely, has brilliant ideas, and will give me a contract immediately. But he has said that so many times!! It's supposed to be "the most beautiful music of the century," but he also thinks the libretto is great.—Letter from Bruno Walter: he wants to do the symphony in New York and Amsterdam! I fear "the envy of the Gods."[3] *Addio,* Linerl, I'm going to *schliepeln* [beddy-bye]. Stay cute and take a kiss from your

   Knuti

I'm absolutely in favor of your keeping the car until I give you my Ford when I buy myself a Buick (fresh, ain't I?).

1. Kiki *was a 1921 musical version of* The Glad Eye *(itself an adaptation of* Le zèbre*), with lyrics by Reginald Arkell and music by Herman Finck. In 1931 Mary Pickford had starred in the film* Kiki.

2. *Swiss composer and conductor Robert Blum (b. 1900), who had been Weill's classmate in Busoni's master class in 1923, conducted* Der Jasager *in Rome in December 1933 and was active in Zurich in 1934.*

3. *"Mir grauet vor der Götter Neide / Des Lebens ungemischte Freude / Ward keinem Irdischen zuteil" (I fear the envy of the Gods; the privilege of untroubled happiness is not for mere mortals to enjoy) is a quotation from Schiller's* Der Ring des Polykrates.

88   WEILL IN LOUVECIENNES TO LENYA IN ZURICH, [6? SEPTEMBER 1934]

A rectangular piece of the upper left-hand corner of this letter has been cut off, but no text appears to have been excised.

Thursday afternoon

Dear Linerl,

Just a few quick lines. From your letter: my first reaction to the Nelson matter was very favorable, because in his own field Nelson is an excellent man.[1] Of course, I can't judge from here whether his name is really that bad in Zurich, but frankly Dr. W. is not entirely authoritative in this, since he is the competition.[2] Not much can happen to you in any case, if you see to it that your three chansons and the sketch are really first-class. At worst they could only say you hadn't been properly cast. The pay is excellent, and I believe the contract is in order, if you can still push the points in question through. But to be entirely safe, you can show it all to someone like Hegeler, so that you're legally protected in any eventuality.[3]

I'll talk with Rotter right at the beginning of next week about the song "Romeo und Julia" with the refrain "Willst du schon gehn, der Tag ist ja noch fern, es war die Nachtigall und nicht die Lerche."[4] That could become a song like "Surabaya Johnny." Or do you know someone else who could write a lyric like that? Mehring is in Zurich as far as I know.[5]

And how about for the third one a text by Wedekind? For example, "Das Lied vom armen Kind," a little bit like a *Moritat*, with many acting possibilities (the blind child, the old spinster, the mangy dog, the poor poet, etc.).

It will be difficult to find a sketch. I haven't heard a thing from Vambery for weeks. The thing with Charell, which looks very favorable because he's completely enthused about the music, is up in the air, since I still haven't received the libretto. Charell has latched onto the weak points of the action with a sure grip, especially toward the end, and has very good suggestions for changes. He would start it in London in the fall of 1935, probably with his own money!

I'm now making pretty good progress with the Bible piece, knock on wood, since I'm slowly working myself into the style. We would want to arrange your visit here—which I'm happily looking forward to—so that it wouldn't coincide with the time when Deval arrives, because that is the most ticklish moment. I'll write or wire you about that later.

I'm very glad that things are going ahead smoothly for you. I hope the whole thing will work out.

In haste, just two little kisses,
Your Weilli

1. *Rudolf Nelson (1878–1960) founded the German cabaret Chat Noir in 1907 and the Metropol-Kabarett in 1910. He greatly expanded the role of the informal narrator, or* Conférencier, *and wrote many hit songs and the music for several operettas. Having toured with his troupe until 1932, he fled to Amsterdam in 1933. His extremely successful revue* Der rote Faden *premiered in 1929 and included several actors from the original cast of* Die Dreigroschenoper.

2. *Probably Dr. Oscar Wälterlin (1895–1961), who led the Zurich Schauspielhaus into international prominence after 1933; he engaged many important émigré actors and actresses in his ensemble. His Basel address appears in Weill's French address book from the period.*

3. *Probably not Hegeler but Henggeler, a well-known attorney in Zurich at the time.*

4. *Fritz Rotter (1900–1984) had been a lyricist and producer in Vienna and Berlin who later worked in Hollywood. Weill apparently hoped to get permission to set Rotter's lyric; the Shakespearean refrain he quotes is "Wilt thou be gone? It is not yet near day: it was the nightingale and not the lark."*

5. *Cofounder of Berlin's dadaist movement, Walter Mehring (1896–1981) was also a cabaret performer, poet, and playwright. In 1944 Weill would adapt his own French chanson "Je ne t'aime pas" to accommodate Mehring's poem "Wie lange noch."*

89 WEILL IN LOUVECIENNES TO LENYA IN ZURICH, [11 SEPTEMBER 1934]

A rectangular piece of the upper left-hand corner of this letter has been cut off; some sentences on the verso are therefore incomplete. Bracketed ellipses denote missing copy.

Tuesday evening

Dear Linerl,

Just a few quick lines for you; after that I must go *schliepeln*, because I have to set to work again early tomorrow. It doesn't mean a thing that the Nelson matter fell through. There's really no need for you to louse up your name just for the money (which you very possibly might not even have received). Something else will surely turn up. I'm really looking forward to your coming here at the end of the month. By then I must have the entire *Marie Galante* and half of the Bible thing finished. With the Bible thing I'm hitting my stride, and it might well be very beautiful. Deval is coming this week, and after that I'll do *Marie Galante* in one stretch alongside the other thing. Now as before, Charell is beside himself with enthusiasm about the music [*Der Kuhhandel*] and tells everybody that a hundred years from now they'll still be singing it. But he has a lot of objections to the libretto, most of them, unfortunately, not without reason. But he exaggerates a bit, because for my part I don't care two hoots for his [. . .] he should make a contract—and with that he is again in no hurry whatsoever.

Hey, do tell Curjel that I know an excellent man for him: his name is Front (like a front soldier); he was the assistant director to Ebert at the City Opera [Berlin], is a highly qualified and likable person, and is surely what he's looking for.[1] He's situated somewhere in Italy, I can find out his address through Cas. He will be inexpensive and will do everything you ask him to.

Aufricht was here. Apparently he's not very happy being in the country and would love to do theater again. I'll ask him to produce *Marie Galante* in Switzerland, Austria, and Holland with you and a first-rate ensemble (with Ginsberg as the Japanese man, a wonderful role for him), starting it at the Corso Theater in Zurich purely as a guest performance, then Vienna, etc.[2] I think this is a good idea. Translation by Vambery, musical direction by [Theo] Mackeben. Now good night, *Pilouchen*. I'll still read my *Gi* ["gizette" for "gazette"], and then I'll trundle off! Bertrand has invited me for dinner again. Fast friends. Little kisses!

> Your Knut

Can you find out what to do with the [. . .] It's best if a shipping agent does the moving so that one can get everything in [. . .] and that for that [. . .] But maybe it's possible that you [. . .]

Once you're here, you'll get the best *Sächelchen* for the winter.[3] Bertrand will give me almost half of the Reinhardt advance, that's 30,000 francs. The rest will be credited to my account [. . .] The Reinhardt thing alone will bring in more than B. [Bertrand] would pay me in five years.

---

1. *Theodore Front (b. 1909) later immigrated to Los Angeles, where he now operates a large music store. Carl Ebert (1887–1980) had directed* Die Bürgschaft *in 1932.*

2. *The Swiss actor Ernst Ginsberg (1904–64) was often typecast as the young revolutionary in leading Berlin theaters in the 1920s. A leftist and an intellectual, he fled in 1933 to act with the Zurich Schauspielhaus.*

3. *Weill's unusual use of the word* Sächelchen *("Wenn Du kommst kriegst Du primi Sächelchen für den Winter") alludes to the scene in Goethe's* Faust *where Mephistopheles speaks of the* Sächelchen *he has placed in the magically secured jewel box in order to bedazzle and win over Gretchen. Translation as "little things" or "trifles" does not convey the vivid image of the original formulation.*

90 WEILL IN LOUVECIENNES TO LENYA IN ZURICH, 16 SEPTEMBER 1934

Written on back of envelope: "I've paid off Jäger completely."

Sunday evening

My dear Linerl,

Just so you don't think I've forgotten it, I do want to write you a few quick lines after our telephone conversation, which I enjoyed very much. But these last few days have been frightfully busy. I often have to see Deval (he has no car), and as soon as I'm back, I immediately set to work again. Musically this Bible thing is becoming very beautiful and very rich. It actually makes me notice how far I've developed since *Die Bürgschaft*. It's just as serious, but in expression much stronger, richer, more varied—Mozartian. I have a couple of brilliant things for *Marie Galante*. Only it's so difficult in my present condition to be working on something that ties me down so I can't let off steam. And it's not easy to compose both things side by side. I'm hoping to be so far along with *Marie Galante* in two weeks that I'll have only to orchestrate it. Then I won't be so nervous anymore when you come. Besides that, I'll be finished with part 2 of the Bible by then. Then I'll be able to see the other side of the mountain that lies in front of me. This week I was offered the biggest movie to be shot in London this year, with an American director and Clive Brook in the lead role.[1] I declined the offer by asking for 1,200 pounds (90,000 francs). What if they accept? Well, I'll let things take their course. You know that Bruno Walter wants to do the symphony. It could be he'll do it in Amsterdam as early as this October. At that time I probably couldn't even go there, or at best I'd go back and forth quickly by plane. In any case, it will be really wonderful if he actually does it. Because he's now the biggest international conductor here, having had greater success in Salzburg than Toscanini! I'm calling the work "Fantasie für Orchester (Sonate, Largo u. Rondo)."—I'm really looking forward to your visit. Jella [Curjel] should come with you. We'll find her a room here, and she can eat with us. Then we can talk about your chansons. Perhaps I'll do one for you also. Now good luck with the Cornichon and with the car.[2] Write me if you need money.

Little kisses! Knuti

1. *Clive Brook appeared in* Loves of a Dictator, *shot in London and released in the United Kingdom in 1935.*

2. *After Erika Mann's "Pfeffermühle Cabaret" had left Zurich, the Cornichon became the city's resident antifascist cabaret. It soon came under attack by the Swiss National Front because of the preferred employment of German exile artists, which may explain why Lenya's proposed engagement at the Cornichon did not work out.*

91 WEILL IN LOUVECIENNES TO LENYA IN ZURICH, [23 SEPTEMBER 1934]

Sunday

Dear Linerl,

Many thanks for your letter and postcard. Meanwhile I hope you've gotten the car matter under control and have made it back to Zurich. It probably would be more sensible to leave the car somewhere in Zurich that doesn't cost much, since here you'll hardly ever need it. This week I worked like crazy again, have written three terrific numbers for *Marie Galante*, among them a big and very beautiful chanson. By the end of the week I want to have the entire score for *Marie Galante* (in sketch) and the second part of the Bible thing finished. Today I'm somewhat down, have terrible headaches and can't work. But I hope I can get started again tomorrow.

It's too bad the Cornichon thing has fallen through, if only because it would have been good for you to stay active professionally. But it's also very important, of course, for you to study English at full steam. Once you're here we'll see whether it would be smarter for you to take a room in the city. We should find an English teacher to work with you every day.

We have to find out two things about Ginsberg: (1) whether he can sing, and (2) whether he knows English.

Florelle is going to play Marie Galante.[1] That's a brilliant choice for here, because she's a box-office draw and will sing the chansons decently (by local standards). Inkijinoff (from *Sturm über Asien*) will play the Japanese man, and for the third lead we want to have Harry Baur.[2] That would be a fantastic cast.

Everything else in person. Write when you'll be arriving.
(Ouch, my skull! Bye-bye!)

      Weilli

    1. *The famous French actress-singer Odette Florelle (1901–74) had played Polly in the French-language version of Pabst's film* Die Dreigroschenoper *(*L'opéra de quat' sous*).*

    2. *Inkijinoff did indeed play the role of Tokujiro Tsamatsui, the cosmopolitan Japanese merchant serving as an American espionage agent in the Canal Zone. The cast did not, however, include the distinguished French stage and screen actor Harry Baur (1880–1943).*

92   WEILL IN LOUVECIENNES TO LENYA IN ZURICH, [27? SEPTEMBER 1934]

                                         Thursday

Dear Linerl,

    So I'm expecting you in Louveciennes on Saturday evening. I'd advise you to leave early, so you'll have the whole day. You'll probably first drop Jella off at a hotel in Paris. Naturally you'll have to pick up the tab for the trip.

    The enclosed letter came from [Rudolf] Nelson. I have the impression he would immediately engage you for something else if I write and suggest it to him. Don't be so concerned with the prestige of your engagements. First the people from Cornichon offered you 1,200 and then suddenly 750. Why? Couldn't you make a deal? What about 850 or 900? You do want to go on performing, and one thing leads to another. In any case, I'll write that Nelson a nice letter, because I don't want you to be on the outs with such people. And I'd also advise you to meet with the Cornichon people once more before you leave, so that these connections are not simply cut off. So if I don't hear anything further from you, I'll expect you Saturday evening.

      Bye-bye!
      Weilli-Knut

On 6 October Weill gave a progress report on "the Bible thing" to Max Reinhardt:

Ever since I returned from Salzburg I've been working literally day and night on our project with an enthusiasm I haven't known for quite some time. I believe (and so does everyone else to whom I've shown some of it) that it's the best music I've written up to now. Most important, I think I've succeeded in solving the technical questions, in that I've been able to create large-scale musical forms—interrupted by spoken dialogue—without changing any text. Thus the whole thing gets the scaffolding it needs, and the danger that it all might melt away (which frequently comes to mind when you read the libretto) is eliminated. . . . I am using original Jewish motifs only sparingly, i.e., only when there's a connection to the liturgy. The Jewish liturgy is rather poor in melodies—it's mostly composed of melodic turns and short motifs, which at times could serve as background to the rabbi's readings. . . . Werfel has sent me all four parts of the work now. I greatly admire what he's done. . . . I'm most pleasantly surprised with the end of the piece. The vision of the Messiah has true greatness in its genuine naïveté and simplicity, and all questions about the work being tendentious have thus been laid to rest, since a light has been shed upon its full meaning. . . . I'm convinced more than ever that it'll be necessary to cast some of the roles with singers, but those singers of great stature that you had in mind. You will hardly find actors able to forget that 'naturalism' and to act in 'elevated' style, whereas singers are accustomed to acting in elevated style, and it will be easier to wean them from their false pathos than actors from their naturalism and false pitches. . . . I think it's essential that we bring a conductor with us, one who understands this kind of musical theater, who can get to work immediately and without long discussions and will collaborate enthusiastically with devotion to the project. I think Jascha Horenstein, the most talented and committed among the young German conductors and also known in America, is the ideal man for the job. (W–MR)

Weill then left for Amsterdam for the final rehearsals and premiere by Bruno Walter and the Concertgebouw Orchestra of the symphony commissioned by the princesse de Polignac.

93 WEILL IN AMSTERDAM TO LENYA IN PARIS, [10 OCTOBER 1934]

Wednesday

Letterhead: Amstel Hotel / Amsterdam

Dear Linerl,

Just a quick note. The rehearsal [of the Second Symphony] was wonderful. Walter does it marvelously and everyone is really enthusiastic, especially the <u>entire orchestra!</u> It's a good piece and sounds fantastic.

The assassination of Barthou is a catastrophe.[1] Now the last man resisting the Huns is gone. (We are lucky that you didn't come here, because you wouldn't have been able to get back.)

It's very beautiful here, but expensive. I want to leave on Friday at 10:00 and, if you don't hear otherwise, I'll be back Friday afternoon at 4:55 at the Gare du Nord.

Behave yourself, or I'll write to your mommy!

> *Yours Sincerely*
> Kurt

The people here are absolutely crazy about me—interviews, etc. . . . [2]

1. *As minister of foreign affairs, the French author and statesman Jean Louis Barthou (1862–1934) had sought to strengthen France's ties with Russia, Great Britain, and the Danubian states. Having gone to Marseilles to escort Alexander I, king of Yugoslavia, to Paris, Barthou was murdered, together with the king, by Fascists with the approval of Mussolini.*

2. *Weill's optimism was premature. He reported to Maurice Abravanel on 21 January 1935: "It was a great success with the audience—catastrophic press ('banal,' 'disjointed,' 'empty,' 'Beethoven in the beer garden,' etc.). . . . Not one friendly word. Apparently this piece has unleashed against me in the most determined manner those factions that have always been latent up to now" (W–MA). The critical response after Walter conducted it with the New York Philharmonic in December 1934 was little better, and Weill completed no further instrumental works for the concert hall.*

Picture postcard: Hotel Touring-Garni / Ochsengasse 2 / Basel

Dear Lenscherl,

It's quite nice here, but boring. The hotel is exactly like the Bellerive in Zurich. I'm leaving here early Wednesday and will be at the Gare de l'Est in Paris at 2:30 in the afternoon. Best regards from my parents. Little kisses,

Knut

1935

Marie Galante had opened at the Théâtre de Paris on 22 December; Marc Blitzstein reported that it lasted less than a week but suggested that several of the songs "might pick up and have a career of their own" (Blitzstein 1935, p. 132). Indeed, Weill later claimed in an interview that "J'attends un navire" became a defiant theme song of the French Resistance during World War II. Weill's passport indicates that he had arrived in Basel on 30 December 1934, apparently in order to meet his parents, who were still living in Germany. On 22 January he landed at Newhaven, Sussex, with a visa stipulating that he take no employment and remain in the United Kingdom no longer than one month. He was working simultaneously on the satirical operetta Der Kuhhandel *and the biblical spectacle* Der Weg der Verheißung.

95 LENYA IN PARIS TO WEILL IN LONDON, [23 JANUARY 1935]

Wednesday

My dear Weili,

Yesterday at 5 P.M. I took your car to Louveciennes. At the [place de l']Etoile the bumper fell off, and I managed to tie it back on with the belt of your raincoat, which was lying in the backseat. When we got out there—Moni[?], M. Ernst, and I—Berthon was busy repairing all the chairs.[1] Harras is fine. His illness didn't turn out to be much of anything. We had coffee out there, then we left again. I hope you arrived safely and without getting seasick. I'm keeping all my fingers crossed for London. It will be very difficult; I can't imagine where you'll ever begin. Yesterday at 3:00 I went with Moni to the lady doctor. An extraordinarily nice person. Even speaks German. She examined me and found my belly completely healthy (not a trace of a tumor, etc.). This thing is purely external and is not connected with the bladder either. It's a type of growth that no one knows where it comes from—like warts. It has to be removed right away, because otherwise it will keep growing. She herself won't do it, but she recommended a good doctor. She beamed when she found out I was Lotte Lenya, knew me from the movies, etc. She gave me a referral for the doctor so he'd give me a good price.* But it'll still cost a few hundred francs. It will be removed under local anesthetic (electrically). Maybe I'll go to the doctor on Monday. I'll telephone today and have it done right away. I'll have to stay in bed for a few days, and she thinks there's absolutely no danger. Moni will stay with me. When you come back, I'll be well again and without the little tip [*Zippi*]. . . . My [English teacher, Mme] Charan has tonsillitis. M.E. [Max Ernst] will definitely leave tomorrow. Last night we were at Strecker's (the painter) with Mrs. Sternheim and Mops.² He was quite delighted. Had been in Germany. I wanted to pump him a little about Hindemith, but he was very careful. Furtwängler is said to be acting quite stupidly, humbling himself before the cross. How disgusting all this is!³ Your *Dreigroschenoper* music is being played quite openly everywhere, Strecker says. Nobody uses "Heil Hitler" as a greeting anymore. But he also thinks that all this doesn't help much. He was very nice, that's that. Nothing more has happened. Today I sent 200 francs to my old lady. So I'm done with that. The examination cost 40 francs. That's cheaper than Dr. d'Alsass [Jacques Dalsace]. I am very glad it's an external thing, and that my belly is healthy. Now, my dear Weili, farewell. I wish you the best of luck in London. Maybe it will really work out. That would be wonderful. Think of your Linerl on the 28th, the day you married the *Kleene* with a heel-clicking *"Jawohl."* Many little kisses for you,

> Your Pips

*Prix d'Amis—that's what they call it, she said.

The letter to Bravi has been sent.

1. *According to Max Ernst's biographer Patrick Waldberg, Weill had already known Ernst in Berlin. When Weill told* [FIG. 45] *them of the painter's troubled financial situation, Charles and Marie-Laure de Noailles acquired for their collection the first* Monument to Birds. *Lenya had met Ernst in Zurich when she appeared in* Lieber reich aber glücklich. *Their affair in fall 1934 to summer 1935 is documented in a substantial collection of colorful letters; in one of them, from February 1935, Ernst asks Lenya to persuade Weill to recommend his paintings to Monnet. In his memoir* A-Not-So-Still-Life, *Jimmy Ernst remembers how impressed he was when—as a very young boy during a visit to his father in Paris—he met the woman whose voice he knew so well from her recordings of* Die Dreigroschenoper. *However, when he noticed his father petting the lady's knees and she in turn whispering sweet nothings into his ears, he asked to be let out at the next métro station.*

2. *The painter and scenic designer Paul Strecker (1900–1950) was a brother to Ludwig and Willy Strecker, the owners of Schott Verlag, the publisher of Paul Hindemith. He lived in Paris but returned to Germany in 1944. Thea Sternheim (b. 1883), the first wife of dramatist Carl Sternheim, was the sister of Edith Bing, the wife of Weill's first theory teacher.*

3. *In November 1934 the Reichsmusikkammer had announced a boycott on performances of Hindemith's music. Wilhelm Furtwängler defended the composer in an article published on 25 November, and that evening an ovation for him at the Berlin State Opera delayed the downbeat for twenty minutes. In December, Furtwängler was relieved of his conducting and administrative posts, and Goebbels made a personal attack on Hindemith at a Nazi rally. In January, Hindemith was forced to take a six-month leave of absence from the Berlin Hochschule. The relationships of both Furtwängler and Hindemith with the new regime were highly conflicted and ambivalent.*

96 WEILL IN LONDON TO LENYA IN PARIS, [24 JANUARY 1935]

Thursday

Garlands Hotel

Dear Linerl,

Before I start running around again, I just wanted to write you a few quick lines. Yesterday I had no less than seven big meetings. A whole lot of things have been initiated, but it will be terribly difficult to get some results. Right away everyone asks for an English translation of the libretto. It costs 700–800 francs to have a rough translation done here. How could I explain that to old Bertrand? Tomorrow afternoon I'll play

[*Der Kuhhandel*] for a very big manager and at the end of the week I'll see Korda (who, however, is supposed to be completely unmusical). Instead of my operetta, Cochran is doing *Liebelei* by Oscar Straus and the new operetta by Cole Porter, which is a huge success in New York.[1] That Mrs. Deutsch is very useful, because she runs all over the place making publicity for me.

Afternoon. I found someone to do the rough translation. With that I'm one step further along. Now that I've paved the way for everything, I simply need a little bit of luck. Last night I visited Tilly [Losch] in the theater. She complains bitterly because she has no prospects in sight. When my affairs advance a little, I'll start looking around for you. That will be much easier. How are you? Have you seen the doctor? Are you being nice and neat? I'm living in a charming old hotel, very English. The boardinghouse was unbearable, and I immediately moved here, where Vambery used to live. Write soon. Kiss,

Knuti

1. *The Viennese operetta composer Oscar Straus (1870–1954), best known for* Der tapfere Soldat, *published* Liebelei *in 1934 (Doremi Musikverlag, Basel). Cole Porter's* Anything Goes *opened at the Palace Theatre in London on 14 June 1935.*

97 LENYA IN PARIS TO WEILL IN LONDON, [26 JANUARY 1935]

Saturday

My dear Weilili,

I sent a detailed letter about my *Zippi* thing to you at the boardinghouse. Didn't you get it? I've been to a good lady doctor, it simply has to be removed, not at all dangerous. But it must be done right away, because otherwise it'll keep growing. Monday I'll go to a doctor whom the lady doctor recommended, and it probably will be done on Tuesday. Then I just have to stay in bed a few days. I wrote all of that to you in detail. When you come back, I'll be quite fine again. Many thanks for your sweet letter. My God, Weilili, if only you would get lucky. This Cochran seems to be an old half-wit who doesn't want to take any risks. But I still believe that if you'd had a finished libretto at the time of those first negotiations, he would have done it. Don't you think so too? Now it must be terribly hard for you to get this thing going again. I beg you, Weili, leave me out of things entirely for the time being. The operetta is really the most important thing now. For if that takes off, so will I. Have you thought of Jessner?[1] Maybe it would also be useful to get together with him. Just so one more person will be talking about you. Moni told me that today in the *Pariser Fremdenblatt* (is there such a thing?) there was a very good review of *Marie Galante*, in which they compare you to Offenbach. Perhaps I can still dig it up. Vambery certainly can't help you at all. And Tilly? That one will be only too glad just to find something for herself. Her influence can't be all that great, or she wouldn't be wailing like that. But she probably knows a lot of people. I'm curious as to what's going on with Korda. Have you heard anything about that Lubitsch-Dietrich thing?[2] I still think that if Lubitsch knew the operetta, he'd do it. Up to now Curjel hasn't answered me either. Well, not much can be expected from that corner anymore. Tomorrow I'll have another lesson. The old lady [Mrs. Charan] has been sick. I visited her once. Have you heard anything about *Die Dreigroschenoper?* Brecht has left London again anyway, I heard through Herta Wärcher [*sic*], whom I saw yesterday and who had just come from London.[3] She's a bit of a communist. Had been with Eisler. But had nothing important to tell. But maybe you can also accomplish something through that Hohenberg, if you promise her Polly for later on.[4] Weili, I really don't know if all this is even necessary. Don't you worry about rooms, etc., for me right now. I can get all that through Lucia Moholy, who is very clever about such things.[5] That Herta Wärcher will arrange it for me. Now I'm going *schlippeln.* Tomorrow morning I'll send this letter off via airmail. Perhaps then you'll still get it by Sunday. In case you come before the middle of the week, I can't meet you at the train station, because I have to stay in bed a few days. But you won't be returning that soon. Don't worry about me. This thing is really not dangerous, and it's being done under local anesthetic. I've written to Leni and told her that Fritz [Nathan Weill] can come if he wants to, as soon as you get back from London (around February 5—so you'll have a little breather if he does come). Now she'll have to answer. Is it warm in your room? The weather here is miserable. Now farewell, my good little Weili, I think of you a lot and hope you'll get lucky so you don't have to run around for nothing. All good things and a little kiss for you,

     Your *Kleene*

1. Leopold Jessner (1873–1945), the intendant of the Berlin State Theater from 1919 to 1930, had subsequently limited his work there to directing, with more than forty productions to his credit. His 1929 Ödipus (Sophocles), which featured Lenya, was admired by Brecht, who considered the staging to be "epic." Leaving Germany in 1933, Jessner came to the United States via Rotterdam and Tel Aviv and spent the last years of his life in Hollywood. His daughter Lottchen was rumored to be enamored of Weill.

2. During this period Marlene Dietrich was involved in a dispute with Alexander Korda over $100,000 that he allegedly owed her for Knight without Armor. Famed director Ernst Lubitsch (1892–1947) became Paramount's production manager in 1935 and produced both Desire and Angel for Dietrich in the United Kingdom.

3. According to Ruth Berlau's memoirs, Hertha Walcher was a former secretary to the communist activist Clara Zetkin; Jacob Walcher, a trade unionist, was a close friend of Brecht's.

4. Hohenberg had been a secretary to Ernst Josef Aufricht at the Theater am Schiffbauerdamm in Berlin.

5. Lucia Moholy was the wife and collaborator of László Moholy-Nagy (1895–1946), a painter and designer of Bauhaus fame. Walter Gropius engaged him for the Bauhaus in 1923. In 1928 he designed sets for Erwin Piscator in Berlin. In 1934, after brief stays in the Netherlands, England, and France, he immigrated to the United States. He was appointed the director of the New Bauhaus in Chicago, renamed the Institute of Design in 1944.

98   WEILL IN LONDON TO LENYA IN PARIS, [26 JANUARY 1935]
Letterhead: Garlands Hotel / Suffolk Street, Pall Mall / London SW1

                                        Saturday

Dear Linerl,

    Many thanks for your letter. I'm very glad you saw the doctor and that it's only an external thing. I'm also in favor of having it removed right away. But afterward you have to go to bed immediately and keep very quiet and by no means go out too soon, okay? According to what you write, it's quite harmless, thank God. Moni will take care of you when you're in bed. Or would you rather wait until I get back?

I'm slowly making headway here. This afternoon I meet with Korda, who has already been nudged from various sides. Early next week I'll see two very important managers; the translation of the libretto will be ready on Tuesday; Cochran is coming back from New York on Thursday. I think I'll have to stay here until the end of next week. As long as things are progressing, there's no point in leaving. I'm saving quite a bit of money on my meals, so I can stay in the hotel, which is a bit expensive but very pleasant. I should buy myself a hat, because mine blew away on the boat. And I also should treat myself to a coat, because I can't be seen in the old one anymore. I'm going to do that now with the Aufrichts, who popped up here yesterday and want to go back to France. But I want to persuade them to rent a little house here, which would be good for us, because housing conditions are so tough here. Now take it easy, *Kleene,* keep the *Zippi* fresh for the meatballs! A kiss for the 28th.

> Knuti

99 WEILL IN LONDON TO LENYA IN PARIS, [27 JANUARY 1935]
Letterhead: Cumberland Hotel / Marble Arch / London W1

> Sunday

Dear Lenscherl, *Pison,*

I've moved because it was too cold and uncomfortable in my hotel. Now I'm in a hotel exactly like the Bellerive in Zurich, first-rate, with private bath, and cheaper than the other one! The Aufrichts will tell you how things are going here. I'll stay here regardless until I either have achieved something or see that it won't fly. I would rather be in my little house, but I must see this through. I'm quite content with the way things have gone up to now. Sutro wants to help me start my own theater.[1] Today he invited me to lunch. At the next table was Anna May Wong, who had asked to be seated next to me![2] She's very nice, but too "Hollywood." Not cute like my sister or that other person with the little tip [*Pison mit Zippi*]. Please tell Mrs. Berthon that my mail should still be forwarded until she's told otherwise. Address: Cumberland Hotel, London W1. This week I'll start to look into your affairs. If my plans succeed, I'll take a small apartment. I hope that all is well with you. Once you're entirely well again, would you like to move to Louveciennes?[3] We could arrange it however is most convenient for you. Do you need money? Then write me accordingly. Be a cutie. Many little kisses from

> Knuti

I bought myself a fantastic overcoat at Dunno's—drop-dead chic. You'll be surprised. All the debs are ogling me.

---

1. *John Sutro (1903–85) was associated with such literary figures as Evelyn Waugh and Graham Greene and involved in motion pictures (J. Arthur Rank Ltd.).*
2. *Anna May Wong (1907–61) starred in a number of Oriental mystery films in the late 1920s, as well as the Sternberg-Dietrich* Shanghai Express *(1932).*
3. *During this period Max Ernst addressed his letters to Lenya at the Hôtel de la Paix.*

100 LENYA IN PARIS TO WEILL IN LONDON, [LATE JANUARY 1935]

Letterhead: Hôtel Madison Élysées / 52, rue Galilée / Paris

Dear Weili,

I just came from Louveciennes. I'll forward your mail from here and include the package with the pajamas. I was just at Mrs. Aufricht's. Please don't leave there, Weili, until you know what's going to happen. You know that time you ran away from Cochran and the whole thing fell through. In Louveciennes everything's OK. Harras is healthy and barked like crazy when he heard the car. Mrs. Berthon is a nice old hen. Otherwise there's nothing new. Farewell my Knuti! Everything good to you. Your mail will go directly to the Cumberland. I've given the address to the post office. Many little kisses,

> Your *Kleene*

Best regards from Mrs. Aufricht and Wolfi [Wolfgang Aufricht]

101 LENYA IN PARIS TO WEILL IN LONDON, [30 JANUARY 1935]

Letterhead: Le Select / 99, Boul. Montparnasse (coin rue Vavin) / Paris VI

Wednesday

Dear Weilchen,

I just saw Dr. Dalsace (who is really an enchanting old Jew). So, he says this thing has to be removed, but it's definitely not dangerous. Now I must decide: Either I can go to the hospital, in which case the operation won't cost anything, but the stay is 50 francs per day, and I'll have to stay in bed for approximately three to four days after the operation. Or I can have it done in a private clinic, in which case the total cost would be 1,000 francs. He asked me whether that was too expensive; I hesitated a bit. He thought I could just as easily have it done in the hospital, since he'd be there during the operation, but after that I'd stay in a ward with others. I don't mind that at all, and we'd surely save approximately 600 francs. What do you think, Weili? I have an appointment with Dr. Dalsace and the doctor from the hospital on Saturday to find out when it can be done. Please write me right away what you think about this so I'll have your answer by Saturday. Now farewell, my Weili. I'm glad I have a good doctor and the thing is not dangerous. It's a simple polyp and has nothing to do with the insides. The consultation didn't cost anything (because I'm an artist!). Many little kisses,

> Your *Zippi*

102 WEILL IN LONDON TO LENYA IN PARIS, [30 JANUARY 1935]

Letterhead: Park Lane Hotel / Piccadilly / London W1

Wednesday

Dear *Kleene*,

I haven't slept for three nights because that hotel was like a railroad station. Finally, after the third sleepless night, I was so utterly exhausted and nervous that I quickly decided to take a beautiful, quiet room here at the Park Lane. It's not even that much more expensive, and however much more it costs I can save by eating cheaply. That Cumberland is a pigsty. I had a room next to the elevator and nothing would convince them to give me something else. It's better for my negotiations that I live decently; the Cumberland has too bad a reputation. Things are going terribly slowly. The translation will finally be ready today. Maybe now we'll make better progress. Today I'm at Melchett's. Yesterday Poldi [Jessner] came to see me. He was charming, raved about you at length, and thinks you definitely should come to London. He will surely get you to perform here. Lottchen [Jessner's daughter] will call you in Paris. Last night I was at Spoliansky's, who's a real nice guy—the only nice colleague. Vambery's laziness is simply driving me to despair. It's now becoming obvious that the play is too long, something I've been telling him for half a year. He was supposed to cut it for the translation, so it would be easier to read, but he hasn't lifted a finger. Enough to make you throw up.

A thousand thanks for your letter and all the mail. The doctor seems to be an idiot. It's very smart that you're going to see d'Alsace. In any case, it's nothing bad, and that's the main thing. The mail can still be sent to the Cumberland, as I'll pick it up there. You'd like my room. I can finally work here too, now that I've caught up on my sleep. Keep working diligently on your English. My sister was seen in a Hollywood restaurant on Reinhardt's arm. You don't have anything like that in your family![1] Many little kisses,

Knuti

1. *A private, ongoing joke about their illustrious "families": in this case, Weill is referring not to his only sister Ruth but to Francesco von Mendelssohn's sister, Eleonora. In letter 104, Lenya picks up the joke with her "brother," Charles Lindbergh.*

103 WEILL IN LONDON TO LENYA IN PARIS, [31 JANUARY 1935]
Letterhead: Park Lane Hotel

Thursday

Dear Linerl,

I just now got your letter. I'm very glad that you've been to see d'Alsace and that it's nothing serious. But I'm adamant that you have it done in a private clinic. One should not scrimp on things like that, and 1,000 francs is actually less than I had originally anticipated. Besides, maybe you can get it done for a little less, because you can still bargain a bit. In any case, I'm <u>not</u> for a French public clinic and a community ward. In France that can't be very pleasant. But you must be aware, and also emphasize to d'Alsace, that it has to be a <u>very clean</u> private clinic, yes? I'm glad this d'Alsace is so nice to you and that you have confidence in him. It's too bad I won't be over there when it's done. Or do you want to wait until I get there? If not, do write me the address of the clinic, and then you'll receive a little letter from me every day. I'm glad to be in a beautiful hotel finally and able to sleep again. It was too awful in the Cumberland. I'm groping ahead slowly and sometimes am totally discouraged by the snail's pace here. But it would be bad to break off now, because I couldn't reestablish the various contacts. Today I saw [Karol] Rathaus with his wife and—Dolly Haas.[1] Thanks for the pajamas! Now Linerl, take care of yourself, be nice, with or without the *Zippi*. Write how much money I should make out a check for. The check from Italy (1,500 francs) has come. Moni will take care of you when you have to stay in bed. Under no circumstances should you get out too early, do you hear? Your financial accounting in your last letter was very cute. You really seem to be a great little miser. Now stay well, *Kleene*, write me right away about what's been decided, and whether you want to have it done now or after my return. Many little kisses from

     Knuti

1. *Dolly Haas (b. 1911) had been a movie star in Germany. She immigrated to the United States in 1936, where she married the caricaturist Al Hirschfeld.*

104   LENYA IN PARIS TO WEILL IN LONDON, [31 JANUARY 1935]

Thursday evening

My dear Kurtili,

   A thousand thanks for your lovely letter. I hope you now have finally settled down comfortably and can sleep well. This is <u>very</u> important for your negotiations. Please don't be nervous. Weili, you know that everything always goes slowly anyway. Before my lesson today I stopped in at the Aufrichts, who were just about to leave, and I had coffee with them at the Georges V [a fashionable hotel near the Champs Elysées]. He says that if you can't stay over there any longer and the negotiations have progressed to the point where they show some positive results, he'd be glad to relieve you and bring the matter to a conclusion. Do you think that would work? I really don't. (1) Because of the language, and (2) Probably nobody in London knows who Aufricht was and is. Vambery really is a pig for never working. What is he doing, anyway? After all, it's his play. Mrs. Aufricht thinks that if she were over there, he would undoubtedly work. But what kind of idea is that? Shall I redirect your mail to the Park Lane or are you picking it up at the Cumberland? In any case I will write a postcard to Mrs. Berthon, so she'll give your address to the post office. That's just a small matter.

   Tomorrow I'm having lunch with Lottchen Jessner, who called me right away the first evening. Today I met with Dr. Dalsace at Charan's; he now doesn't want me to go to the hospital (he thinks it would be embarrassing because so many interns would be watching). He has put me down for Saturday morning, 9:00 A.M., in the private clinic of a friend of his (who will also do the operation, because he's not a surgeon). This other doctor will examine me there, and maybe it'll be done right away. But I can go home, so I won't have to pay the clinic. M.E. [Max Ernst] is going to take me there and will wait for me, because I won't be able to drive afterward. In the evening he will definitely leave. He's gotten the money for his ticket together. But Moni will still be here until the 8th. So I won't be alone. I feel very secure with Dalsace, as I would with Nathan.

When you get back, write a postcard to Mrs. Berthon, so she can clean and heat the place in time. If you have time to see this Wiesengrund, you should do so. That one always has such good connections to the genteel, delicate aroma.[1] And he does beat the drums for you a bit—that is, when he's not too busy praising his own immortal creations.

There's nothing new here at all. Apart from my old lady [Mrs. Charan], I don't see anyone either. That's OK too. Letters are dutifully coming from Pasetti. After an audition at the radio, Schuschnigg—whom he has now seen in Vienna—wants to make him into *the* Austrian tenor.[2] Maybe he'll make it. I wonder if we would get our money back then?[3] —Now Weilchen, my eyes are falling shut. I too have heard from your sister about that thing with Reinhardt. But that's nothing to speak of. My brother (Charles Lindbergh) is now involved in a big lawsuit. Because they filched his little kid. And therefore we're always in the papers now. This is getting embarrassing for my family. Farewell my Knutchen, and don't get annoyed about your sister. She's really cute. But compared to my brother, she's just a blond goat.[4] Sleep well, and all good things from your Linerl.

My Knutchen, just now I got your nice letter. Don't worry about me, I'm in good hands with Dalsace. You can see that from the fact that he doesn't want me to go into a hospital, either. The private clinic is supposed to be <u>very</u> good. And if I can go home, it's really for the best. I'd rather have it done now, then it'll be over with. It's really nothing. The old lady will also visit me. I'm very glad that I can go home. Then I can say, the way your sister does, *I go hom. I want to be alone.*

Now I'll take a quick bath, then go eat with Lottchen. At 5:00 P.M. I have a lesson. I'm always thinking of you, hoping something will come through for you in London. And now I'm glad that you're living in a decent place and can sleep in peace. Which reminds me of Monnet's story about the parliament member who went home and, having had a good rest, made his speech early in the morning. If only it would be that simple for you.—It seems practically everyone is in London. I'm only waiting for Betti Stern to go there, then I'll go too. Because wherever she may go, there I too wish to go . . .[5] So farewell, my good little Weili. I still have money. I'm not a miser, I just don't like to spend anything. Many kisses,

       Your *Zippi*

(I hope that tomorrow it will be gone.)

1. The brilliant neo-Hegelian, semi-Marxist philosopher, sociologist, music critic, and sometime composer Theodor Wiesengrund Adorno had attempted to protect his university appointment by substituting his mother's Italian family name for his father's obviously Jewish name, by which Lenya refers to him. The content of a few of his articles in Die Musik (c. 1934) indicates that he also had tried to please National Socialist cultural politicians. Lenya is quoting the finale of the first act of Der Kuhhandel: "ein vornehmes, zartes Aroma."

2. Kurt Edler von Schuschnigg (1897–1977) had served in various capacities in the Austrian cabinet. He succeeded the assassinated Dollfuß as chancellor of Austria from 1934 to 1938. After trying to maintain Austria's independence, Schuschnigg was confined to a concentration camp from 1938 to 1945.

3. In an interview with Gottfried Wagner in 1976, Lenya admitted that Pasetti was "a crook, who sold the house and stole the money. . . . He was nothing, he was just shit" (int. L3).

4. Cf. letter 102, n. 1.

5. *Lenya alludes to the "Melodram" in* Die Dreigroschenoper, *where Macheath tells Polly, "Wo du hingehst, will ich auch hingehn." Salka Viertel identifies Betti Stern as a nouveau riche hostess in Berlin who was close to Marlene Dietrich.*

Otto Pasetti makes no further appearance in the correspondence. He apparently absconded with a large sum of Weill's money, as well as a car, and little is known about his activities thereafter. In October 1936 he stayed at the Carlton and Erzherzog Karl hotels in Vienna but gave his home address as Berlin, his profession as "opera singer." In January 1937 he was back in Innsbruck, with a profession now listed as "none." From there he left for Graz, then established residency in Zurich, once again as an opera singer. He left for Prague in 1937; his trail before the outbreak of the war ends there.

105 LENYA IN PARIS TO WEILL IN LONDON, [2 FEBRUARY 1935]

Saturday

My dear Weilchen,

No operation today. The doctor examined me. It's a polyp. But I'll have to have a light general anesthesia just the same; a local one won't do. The doctor makes a very good impression; the clinic is very clean. So it'll be done on Tuesday at 11:00 A.M. I'll feel mighty important being put under. But at the same time, I'll be glad when it's over. I can go home after just one hour. Moni will be coming with me, because M.E. is leaving tomorrow evening. Tomorrow afternoon we want to drive out to Louveciennes for dinner. I'll call there later to find out whether Madame Berthon will cook something for us. That's OK, isn't it?

Today I got no nice letter from you. How goes it with you, my Knuti? I had dinner with Lottchen [Jessner] on Friday at the Univers. First-class oysters, schnitzel, and a little coffee. Afterward her friend Weininger, with whom she's been for four years (and who paid the bill), came and joined us.[1] I don't think I ever met anyone more enthusiastic about your music than this man. He knows everything. Starting with *Der Protagonist*. Raves like a lunatic about the first act of *Die Bürgschaft*. He insists on meeting you in London. I told him you'd probably be there until Wednesday, and that he'd be able to catch you if he leaves here on Tuesday. I think he might be important for London; he knows everybody and is honestly enthusiastic. He's also a friend of Sutro's. In the old days he used to frequent [Georg] Kaiser and [Fritz] Stiedry. But anyway you probably know who he is. In any case, he's a really nice person (a bit of Viennese sentimentality—but you're surely used to that from me). They insist on "going out" with me again. Perhaps I'll do that on Monday. Only he can't stand Aufricht. He thinks he's totally incompetent. Anyway, I won't be by myself when I go to London. I'm very much looking forward to seeing Poldi [Jessner]. After hearing me speak two sentences in English, Lottchen was quite surprised by my particularly good pronunciation. I'm being very diligent now, and I've conversed a lot with my old lady, who told me her whole life story—it's got just about everything. There isn't a subject about which I couldn't converse in English. Lottchen told me what a good and successful book Lania has written.[2] I can't quite believe it. Successful, maybe, but good? Anyway, he's supposed to be making a lot of money. From Curjel I hear nothing, except that his health isn't the best. Maybe the milk didn't come directly from the cow. Perhaps he's not writing because I wrote to him I would be in Zurich early in February. But most likely he won't have anything to offer me. Well, Weillchen, that's all for today. Tonight we're going to a cabaret in which Kiki is appearing.[3] Moni, M.E., and I. As a farewell, so to speak, because he's leaving tomorrow. Which means I'll probably have to offer to pay for a round. Not very eagerly—but one shouldn't overdo it either. Now fare thee well, my Knutchen; it seems an eternity since you went away. I hope all is well with you. Are you eating decent food, and are you getting enough sleep? I love you very much and am concentrating all my thoughts on the hope that you may succeed in everything you undertake. I'm also very curious about that overcoat, which Aufricht described in glowing terms. Farewell, my Kürtchen, thank God I haven't heard anything further from that jackass Alatini[?]. Write soon.

Your Linerl

1. *Aufricht described Richard Weininger in the twenties as* "a Maecenas, an elegant bon vivant, married to a Czech from the family of the coal tycoon Petchek" (p. 57). *His brother Otto Weininger (1880–1903)was the author of the now-infamous* Geschlecht und Charakter (1903), *which asserted the intellectual superiority of men over women and deprecated the Jewish race. He committed suicide soon after its publication.*

2. *Leo Lania (1896–1961), born Lazar Herman, was the author of* Konjunktur. *In March 1928 Weill had written incidental music for Piscator's production of the play. Lania was also one of the screenwriters for Pabst's* Dreigroschenoper. *His* Pilgrims without Shrine *and* Land of Promise *both were published in 1935.*

3. *Kiki of Montparnasse was an artist's model much in demand in the 1920s and the mistress of Man Ray.*

106 WEILL IN LONDON TO LENYA IN PARIS, [4 FEBRUARY 1935]
Letterhead: Park Lane Hotel

Monday

My dear Linerl,

I got another little letter from you today. I'm glad this thing will finally be taken care of tomorrow and that you'll be rid of it for good. But you must definitely stay in bed for a few days and take good care of yourself, OK? It's really typical of that "high-born" family of thine that thou wouldst have a polyp there, of all places. But I've always told "my sister" just what kind of family this is, and "your uncle" from the Chatelet knows very well why he doesn't want to have anything to do with the likes of them.

I've had a terrible cold for three days now, and I can hardly see out of my eyes because of the congestion. Last week I was practically ready to give up doing anything over here, because there's no way to get ahead with the English. In order to get anything done you would probably have to sit here for half a year. Nevertheless, quite a few things did happen since then to give me a little hope again.

Everyone's told me that Mannheim has such good connections and money over here.[1] She called me on Friday, so I invited her for dinner. She's a nice person, not a hypocrite, but very honest and open. Her English boyfriend, whom she's been living with for seven years and is going to marry now, is especially nice and likable. She's completely crazy about the piece—finally just what she's been looking for. She's given it to her friends and advisers to read, and they're all enthusiastic. She's been taking voice lessons for a year and a half, because she wants to switch over to operetta to avoid treading on [Elisabeth] Bergner's turf. She'll give this project high priority. She's able to put up some of the money herself—besides, she has the Rothschilds behind her. She understood the play right away and realizes that the part of Juanita—although it's not a big role—has great possibilities, particularly for her. Yesterday afternoon she and her boyfriend picked me up to drive into the country for dinner. The road seemed very familiar to me—and suddenly we landed at Bushey Hall. It was very nice—the place is exactly the same as it used to be. On the way back we stopped in at Kortner's,[2] who's already a big shot over here. He's terribly interested in the project, and this afternoon I'll play it for him. Maybe the whole thing will get a boost now. It's certainly better to be dealing with people who understand what's intended than with agents, etc. It would be so wonderful if this thing would work out. Once one has had a success, there's an awful lot that can be done over here. I'm sure you could be doing things here too, but more so in your special field than in the theater, where there's an oversupply of German actresses.

I've made friends with [Mischa] Spoliansky, who's a charming fellow with a nice wife and three children! He's crazy about me and you too. I'll bet he'd collaborate on your repertoire. But I'll also propose that he feature you in a small revue he's preparing here. The way things look at the moment, I'll probably have to stay here the entire week and perhaps even longer. If all goes well, I'll be working here, and you could come over right away. Then I'd probably have to go to Paris for a few days to take care of things there and come back here with you. Today I'm going to see Lambert.[3] That Deutsch woman turned out to be a miserable bitch; thank God she's gone. I bought English money from the Aufrichts, including a ten-pound note for 750 francs; it turned out to be counterfeit. Isn't that a piece of bad luck? Today I already had a visit from someone from Scotland Yard. I hope I'm not going to have any problems. Now keep your fingers crossed, little Linerl. It would be so critical to get the operetta off to a good start here. It doesn't matter how that's accomplished, and I'd prefer to get it done through Mannheim than through [Eric] Wollheim, who's a con artist. I'll be thinking of you tomorrow morning with all my might, hoping it will all go quickly and successfully. Let me hear from you right away, will you? And don't let the anesthesia go to your head. Bye-bye and many little kisses from

> Knuti

Some years ago Weininger was a very rich crook. I'll still welcome him with open arms.

1. *Lucie Mannheim (1899–1976) had been a leading actress in Berlin. In 1933 she immigrated to England, where she played Nora in Ibsen's* A Doll's House.

2. *The Austrian actor Fritz Kortner (1892–1970) was one of the leading figures in German theater. In 1929 he appeared with Lenya in* Oedipus, *directed by Leopold Jessner. He fled Germany in 1933, first to Austria and England, and then in 1938 to the United States.*

3. The British conductor, composer, and critic Constant Lambert had conducted some performances of Les Ballets 1933 in London. In an appreciative review of Die sieben Todsünden (see letter 40, n. 4), he suggested that Weill was "undoubtedly the most successful and important of the Central European composers who have experimented with the jazz idiom."

107 LENYA IN PARIS TO WEILL IN LONDON, [7 FEBRUARY 1935]

Thursday afternoon, 6:00 P.M.

My dear Weilchen,

So today was my day in the clinic. I screamed like crazy when they gave me the injection, which hurt something awful. Just as I went to lie down on the table, I got my period (six days early). But now it's all over, and I'm relieved. I stayed in the clinic until noon and then went home. I've been sleeping, and now I feel fine. I'm going to stay in bed for a few days. Mrs. Aufricht is coming tomorrow. You don't have to worry, everything is OK. But there are nicer things in this world than operating rooms and these knife-wielding doctors. I won't write any more today because I'm too tired. Farewell, my man; "Once you're away from the spot, no more *Zippi* you've got."[1]

Your *Kleene*,
who has behaved as bravely as a trooper should

1. Lenya here echoes a popular couplet by the German humorist Otto Reutter (1870–1931) about his inability to keep track of his overcoat: "Geh' ich weg von dem Fleck / ist der Überzieher weg."

108 WEILL IN LONDON TO LENYA IN PARIS, [8 AND 9 FEBRUARY 1935]

Letterhead: Park Lane Hotel

Friday evening

Dear Linerl,

Just a few lines. I just got your short letter of last night, and I'm so glad that you've gotten this thing over with. I can imagine that the injection was very painful, you poor *Kleene*, but that *Zippi* just had to be done away with, no? Now I beg you to rest and keep quiet for at least a week, stay in bed and *schliepeln* and have them send up good meals. I hope Moni won't have to leave while you are confined to bed. Please tell her how grateful I'd be if she could stay until you're better.

This afternoon I have another very important meeting with some gentleman who wants to work for me. This contact came through Mannheim, who's no longer so keen on the operetta but instead is wavering something awful. The money she's supposed to have doesn't seem to amount to much either. I've spoken to Weininger. He's very nice, but I don't think he can do anything. Anyway, I'll keep trying that too. I don't have many illusions left.

But I'm under the impression that a lot can be done for you over here. Last night they played the entire *Dreigroschenoper* over the radio in an adaptation by some young people who want to bring it to the stage and who asked right away whether there was a chance you might play Polly. They praised you to the rafters. I'll meet them again at the beginning of next week and talk to them about your repertoire. At this very moment, Saturday morning, I'm reading the first review of last night's *Die Dreigroschenoper*—a terrible drubbing. It's supposedly just jazz music and is not to be taken seriously. Now, in my old age, I have to take this kind of panning for—of all things—*Die Dreigroschenoper*! I really don't know what will come of all this.[1]

I simply must concentrate on the possibility of doing a film with René Clair. Perhaps I can succeed with that. That would enable me to pursue all those other things while working on the film; at this point I don't see any possibility of getting the operetta started this spring (*Die Dreigroschenoper* with you would be more likely). Anyway I'll follow every lead to the bitter end, but I hope I'll finish by the end of the week so I can come home around Saturday. I had already played with the idea of asking you to come over here as soon as you're able to get out of bed, so I could "install" you here. But (1) first I want to see how serious that *Dreigroschen* thing is, and (2) I imagine you probably want to recuperate a little in Louveciennes before you come over.

About living accommodations here, I'm thinking that it's very important to live decently and to have a good address. That's expensive; but one can save in other ways. They have those charming *"flats"* over here: one room with a bathroom and a small kitchen, and I would suggest that as a rule you'd take care of your own meals, which is ever so much cheaper and better than having that restaurant fodder. That way you could live very comfortably, and by doing your own cooking, you'd avoid the extra expense. What do you think? Of course, everything would be simpler if I were working here in the spring. Now be nice and behave yourself. I hope that you're not getting too bored.

> Many little kisses from your
> Weilli

Do you need money?

---

1. *The radio production was directed by Denis Freeman and conducted by Edward Clark. The press was indeed extremely hostile; typical was Ernest Newman's review in the* Sunday Times: *"The 'Dreigroschen Oper' . . . is described by its authors as 'after* The Beggar's Opera *of John Gay'. It may be after that masterpiece, but it will certainly never catch up with it: these two dull dogs achieve the almost incredible feat of making even crime boring."*

---

109 LENYA IN PARIS TO WEILL IN LONDON, [9 FEBRUARY 1935]

Saturday

My dear Weili,

Many thanks for your nice telegram. I hope all goes well for you from now on. I'm staying in bed like a good girl and I'm being very nice. On Sunday I'll get up for a while. Yesterday Dr. Dalsace was here to check up on me. In the afternoon Aufricht and my old lady [Charan] were here. Mrs. Aufricht had to stay home with her son, who has had the flu for a week now. Aufricht says one has to be very careful with Weininger, who's supposed to be a big swindler. But you probably know that anyway. Aufricht is very bored, and it probably was stupid that he didn't stay in London. Because there is absolutely nothing for him here. On Tuesday I'll be moving to Louveciennes. Another week [in the hotel] will be up. Do you approve? Or should I wait until you come back? As far as the cost is concerned, it comes out the same, because in Louveciennes one has to pay for plenty of heat, since it's so cold there. I haven't paid the doctor; he's going to send a bill. Maybe it would be wiser to wait until you come, since I can't really travel around without my papers. And you probably won't be back until the end of the week. I've already paid the hotel through Tuesday. I still have 300 francs. Now I'll need a little more for taxis and the pharmacy. Otherwise I'm being very thrifty. Now farewell, my Knuti. Aufricht regretted not having stayed in Louveciennes while you were away. But one couldn't have known that you'd be gone so long. I'm very glad to have this thing behind me now. It's a great feeling to be without that *Zippi*. Now you can't make fun of me anymore. Fare real well, *Glätzchen*.

Your *Kleene*

110 WEILL IN LONDON TO LENYA IN PARIS, [10 FEBRUARY 1935]
Letterhead: Park Lane Hotel

Sunday

Dear Linerl,

Today you're getting another short letter so you won't get too bored. Yesterday I played the operetta for one of the biggest American film agents, who's also starting to get involved in theater. I've never in my life seen such enthusiasm. He wanted to hear everything twice, is excited about the libretto as well, and actually grasped completely what the work is all about. He is supposed to have a lot of moneyed people behind him. I'm going to meet him again tomorrow to find out what he has in mind. He brought along his son, a young man who works in a modern theater here, knows every note I ever wrote, and talks about you as if you were Duse.[1] Actually there's a circle of young people here who would love to do something for you. Today the future looks a little rosier to me again—although the most important English critic has just written of *Die Dreigroschenoper:* It is hard to say which is weaker, the text or the music; probably the music, which does not even contain any good secondhand tunes. There ain't nothin' to be done about it.

This hotel living makes me want to puke; the evenings especially are boring, and I'm in no mood to work. But I still have to stick it out. I do so hope that this thing will get going. Anyway this man could do a lot for me in motion pictures.—I hope you are feeling well, are being careful and resting. I realize more and more what sorts of possibilities you have over here.

Now farewell, comrade; write soon, eat well, study your English hard. Many kisses from your

Weilli

111 LENYA IN PARIS TO WEILL IN LONDON, [10 FEBRUARY 1935]

Sunday

My dear Knutchen,

Your sweet long letter arrived just now. It's simply dreadful that it's come to the point where they have to tear *Die Dreigroschenoper* to pieces. I'm very depressed. My poor Weili. It seems they're still clinging to their old *Beggar's Opera*, as far as *Die Dreigroschenoper* is concerned. But maybe the way I sing the *songs* could really help matters along. It would be one way to get people to understand them better. Only we must take care that the piece is presented in the right way. It would be very difficult for me to survive another flop. Cabaret is not quite as dangerous. I'm dying to play Polly. I'm much better suited to theater than to cabaret. I'm sure I'd be successful. Up to now it's always worked out. I've always had my doubts about that Mannheim deal. You know, she really wants to have a sure thing to launch her, something that would allow her to use all her tricks from Germany. Your operetta is something entirely new, especially for her. You'd probably need your own theater to produce it. And you know, Weili, I'm really not too surprised that they're tearing you to pieces now. Lord knows those yelping dogs can cause a ruckus. They've all been over there for quite some time now. I think it's terribly important that you stay there and try to get your feet on the ground, if you hope to get anywhere over there. In that case, if I were you, I'd rent out the house here and go back to pursue all the connections you've established now. Because if you're not there, they'll be gone in no time. There's nothing doing for you over here either, except that you're living comfortably. But as far as that's concerned, I would make it just as comfortable for you in London. You know I could do it quickly and without a fuss. That little bit of housework I can do with my left hand. I'd love to live in a flat and would of course do everything myself. There really shouldn't be any question about that. I'm going to move to Louveciennes after all on Tuesday evening. It's more practical, and I'll have just enough money. I'm driving out there tomorrow morning with Mrs. Aufricht, who wants to have her hot plate back, and I'll bring some of my things with me then. That should work out all right. That way I'll be saving 100 francs, because they won't give me a special rate if I don't stay at least a full week. And if you come as soon as Saturday, I would have to pay 25 francs for the room as of Wednesday, and God knows that wouldn't be worth it. I'm paid up until Tuesday. I'm managing this all right, Weilchen; you won't have to worry about it. I'm fine. Very well, indeed. I've recuperated quite nicely from all those injections and am waiting till I'm all finished with my period before I get up again. Moni is leaving for Nice. London didn't work out. Anyway I simply couldn't live with her. She's very nice and decent, but she gets on my nerves something terrible, forever talking about her kids, crying, and being unhappy. I don't need that right now. Besides I do everything much faster myself and I do it without having to wring out my soul because I have to wash a pair of stockings, all the while complaining how different things used to be. Do you understand? I'm just not cut out to be friends with "fine ladies." Now Weili, think it through about staying over there and how I could possibly help you. As of Tuesday evening I'll be in Louveciennes. A film with René Clair would be very good for you as a start. Have you heard anything about Marlene-Lubitsch? Not a thing's been said about that *Merry Widow* movie. It's playing here at the Madeleine. Monnet called yesterday, but I couldn't get to the phone. Now farewell, my Weili.

Your *Kleene* is always thinking of you.

The hotel didn't accept my notice, so I'll have to stay another week. Please write me there.

112 LENYA IN PARIS TO WEILL IN LONDON,
[11 FEBRUARY 1935]

Monday afternoon

My dear, good Weilili,

Many thanks for your letter. I'm pretty upset about the newspapers. Was that radio performance properly prepared? And did they have to do this? After all, this *Dreigroschenoper* goes back six years and—in the final analysis—doesn't give a proper impression of you. And you were so completely against coming out with *Die Dreigroschenoper* now. England is so important for you. You couldn't possibly have conquered the territory in the short time you've been there. Please, Weilchen, don't get impatient. It'll be worth it if you stick it out. Unfortunately the press hasn't been courted enough. So they have no idea who you really are. Just like when [Edward] James loused up *Die sieben Todsünden*. Please be careful about what happens next. A panning of *Die Dreigroschenoper* like this—on the radio yet, where you don't get anything for it—is so completely unnecessary. It's better to wait awhile and look out for your reputation. I implore you, Weilchen! Think of people like Elisabeth Bergner, who had as good a name in Germany as yours. It's taken her two years to find the right kind of start. I know it's difficult for you right now and that you're impatient. But after all, you do have that Bible thing in the fall. If these young people are very good and can present an outstanding performance, then one could take a chance. But in that case you'd have to stick around and devote your effort to it full-time. But I'm not telling you anything you don't already know yourself; still, I do know you better than anyone else does—your impatience and your aversion to hustling and bustling! But it's a new beginning for you over there, and that takes time. I'm meeting Aufricht this afternoon. He spends all his time playing bingo. I have an old aunt in Vienna; she's seventy years old, and that's what she does too.

I'm curious to see how this new fellow is going to help you. Perhaps, Weilchen, you should consider moving to England permanently. We could arrange to live there very inexpensively. As I told you before, I'm game for anything. It'd be so easy to do that little bit of housework. And you could be completely independent. I wouldn't disturb you at all. But you know that anyway. Over here there's nothing at all going on. Concentrate everything on England. In the fall they're planning a big surrealist exhibition there. M.E. [Max Ernst] has been at the Pony [Château le Pony in Jégun] for a week and is working and writing letters about how long the winter evenings are over there and how it's been snowing.[1] Last night I went out for dinner with Moni. I met Theodor Wolf (from the *Berliner Tageblatt*) there.[2] All of them are still waiting for Hitler's death. People like that remind me of walking mummies. I went home early. You have to give four days' notice if you want to cancel a room. I didn't know that. But it really makes no difference. I'm being very thrifty. But I do eat better food now, because this whole business has made me rather nervous. Otherwise I'm feeling fine, and I'm not bored at all. Today I have another lesson. That's a lot of fun. I'm reading six plays in English: "Famous Plays of 1934." Each one worse than the last. Unbelievable trash. I can read it almost as if it were a German play. So you see, Weili, your *Kleene* may look ditsy, but she's really not. I'm so looking forward to seeing you. My residence permit hasn't come yet. I think they must have forgotten about it. Now farewell, my Weilchen, many little kisses,

    Nibbi

Maybe you should come back now and try your luck again in a few weeks? Aufricht fervently begs you to consider not showing the operetta or auditioning it, but rather biding your time.

---

1. *Max Ernst wrote to Lenya on 8 February: "I'm riding around on horseback and in the evening I'm tired and hungry, sleeping well, and slowly getting my health back. Your deck of solitaire cards is helping me to survive those long winter evenings. It's been snowing and my* Popo *is sore from all that horseback riding. Dear Lenerl, forget me not" [ME–L]. On 11 February he wrote again: "The cat came into the dining room for lunch and threw up an entire mouse. That was very stimulating for the appetite, and I had to think of Germany. Beginning next week I'll have visitors from England, two ladies—one of them awe-inspiring, the other one somewhat less awe-inspiring. If possible, I'll withdraw even more eagerly into my gentile foreskin until that storm will have subsided. I love you very much and I'm always thinking about you. That's my main occupation" [ME–L]. He included a surrealistic drawing of a pig, captioned "Ich bin ein" (I am a).*

2. *The chief editor of one of Berlin's leading papers, Theodor Wolff (1868–1943) had once turned down the young Joseph Goebbels for a job.*

---

113   WEILL IN LONDON TO LENYA IN PARIS,
[11 FEBRUARY 1935]
Letterhead: Park Lane Hotel

                                          Monday morning
My dear Linerl,

    I had expected some news from you today, and I'm a bit worried that nothing came. I hope this thing is healing by now and that you're already feeling better. No doubt something like this takes a lot more out of you than you'd expect. Please be very careful and stay in bed for the rest of the week. I hope I can come back by the end of this week or the beginning of the next. And I do so hope that by then you'll be able to come to Louveciennes with me.

Yesterday I had another very important meeting. I played the operetta for the musical and literary staff of the film producer.[1] They were honestly enthused and said over and over how right this thing would be for London and what success it could have over here. They want to propose it to Dean as a *double production* (first on stage and then on film). Now I have to pursue this matter. Cochran is arriving this week too. Did I already write you that Charell showed up here with a ghastly circus piece, and in just two days he has palmed it off on Korda?[2] You have to come up with that kind of shit in order to get somewhere with these people.

Last night I saw a delightful movie starring Claudette.[3] She's very nice, but she still has a rather large *Zippi*, whereas you don't have one anymore at all, and therefore you're much nicer. I hope to be getting some news soon, otherwise it gets so nerve-racking to keep waiting. Why didn't you write anything about money? Most likely you don't have any left. Is Moni still there? Are you getting bored? Do you want me to come back sooner? Many little kisses from your

    Weilli

---

1. *Weill is referring to the advisers of Basil Dean (1888–1978), one of London's most important theater and film producers. He directed many of Noel Coward's successes and headed Entertainments National Service Association (ENSA) during World War II. His films include* Lorna Doone.

2. *Charell's expensive production of* The Flying Trapeze, *with a score made up largely from bits of Ralph Benatzky's music from shows unknown in Britain, lasted two months.*

3. *Claudette Colbert, born in 1905 in Paris, became one of Hollywood's most versatile leading ladies. Weill probably saw her Academy Award–winning performance in Frank Capra's* It Happened One Night *(1934).*

114 WEILL IN LONDON TO LENYA IN PARIS, [13 FEBRUARY 1935]

Letterhead: Park Lane Hotel

                                                 Wednesday

Dear Lenscherl,

Just a few quick words. I got all your letters. It seems those reviews didn't do me any harm, because they're by music critics who are known to be imbeciles. Aufricht should talk. Up to now his theory hasn't proven correct, and I don't have any faith in his abilities. I'm working in three different directions now: today I'm going to make a contract with this big American manager, who will then get in touch with important entrepreneurs. Wollheim is going to be here tomorrow and I'll start on the Basil Dean thing; and Tuesday I hope to be auditioning for Komisarjevsky, Cochran's most important collaborator and stage director.[1] I'll probably be in Paris on Wednesday and possibly return here the week after, if necessary. Things don't look too bad; one just has to stick it out. I'm very happy to have such good news from you, and you mustn't worry about me. I'll be sending you a check this week. Many little kisses,

    Knuti

115 WEILL IN LONDON TO LENYA IN PARIS, [14 FEBRUARY 1935]

Letterhead: Park Lane Hotel

Thursday morning

My dear Linerle,

Just a few quick lines. I'm in the middle of contractual negotiations. On Tuesday these people presented a draft that already looked quite respectable. Yesterday we worked out a response that we'll present to them. Since I'm slowly getting used to the tempo over here, I realize that it won't be ready for signature this week, especially seeing as I have to drag that old Frenchman from rue Vivienne [Paul Bertrand] along. Well, I'm glad that things have at least come this far. Wollheim is extremely capable and terribly nice—except that he moves at the same slow pace as the others over here. Well, one has to take it in stride. I'm working every free minute on the piano-vocal scores of both works! I'm also constantly looking for an apartment for you. But that's very difficult. Yesterday I saw something fantastic: small, very elegant, brand new apartments with a living room, bathroom, and kitchen and a marvelous view, but terribly expensive (almost 400 francs per week for a single person!). Today I'm going to ask again whether there's a vacancy in the house I told you about. That seems to be the best option. Naturally everything will be easier once I know for sure if and when you're coming, because then—if I should find something suitable—I could grab it then and there. I've also looked around for a cheaper hotel for myself, but haven't found anything passable. I completely forgot to ask you whether you might need some money and have no idea how much I left you with. Enclosed is 500 francs. Now be sure to keep your fingers crossed. I'm also negotiating for a translator (very difficult!) and a stage director. Now I've got to dash to Wollheim. I got a long letter from Kaiser. I have a little pimple on my nose—probably a legacy from you. Bye-bye!

Knut

116 WEILL IN LONDON TO LENYA IN PARIS, [15 FEBRUARY 1935]

Letterhead: Park Lane Hotel

Friday

Dear Linerl,

Your letter from last night already arrived in today's morning mail. I'm happy that you're doing well. So that American agent turned out to be a total flop. All he wanted to do was to straitjacket me with a general contract, but I was a real smarty not to fall into that trap. Weininger, too, has proven to be just what I had always suspected him to be: nothing more than a big mouth. (But be nice to him anyway when he's in Paris.) Despite all this, I'm not pessimistic right now. Wollheim's back here, and it's clear that of all of them he's the most capable and the most decent one around. Today I want him to meet with Sutro. Anyway, he has a letter from a wealthy Dutchman who wants to put up 1,000 pounds for the operetta, if I'm willing to let Heckroth do the scenery (and I'd be glad to, because he's very good).[1] So now I'll try with all my might to raise the rest of the money and produce it myself.

You have no idea what an excellent reputation you have over here. Yesterday Vambery was invited to a very fancy dinner party, where—unaware of the fact that he knew you personally—everybody was idolizing you with superlatives. So I'm wondering whether you shouldn't come over here right away so I could introduce you to people, etc. Or would you rather wait until I come back here later on? Think about it. If at all possible, I'd like to come over on Thursday, if only for a short time. Now, farewell, old pal, don't get too brazen, and carefully preserve that *Zippi* they snipped off.

Your Knuti

[Added by Lenya in pencil: "Don't say anything to Aufricht."]

1. The style of German stage designer Hein Heckroth (1902–70) was distinguished by his use of projections, often surrealist in character. He first became known through his contributions to the Kurt Joos ballet Der grüne Tisch (Essen, 1932). His emigration took him first to France in 1933 and then to England, where he worked with various companies and theaters, on productions including A Kingdom for a Cow (1935; the English adaptation of Der Kuhhandel). He lived in South America before returning to Germany in 1955.

117 LENYA IN PARIS TO WEILL IN LONDON,
[16 FEBRUARY 1935]

Saturday

My dear Weili,

Thanks for your letter and the check. It's great that the mail is so fast. As far as my coming over there is concerned, I don't know whether it wouldn't be better to wait until you're here again. First of all, it'll be hard for me to get out of the country as long as that matter of a residence permit hasn't been straightened out. I certainly will need an affidavit confirming that my application has been on file, since my visa has been expired for some time now and they could make trouble for me at the border. They told me at the time—that was on 24 January—that I would get this thing within two or three weeks. But you know yourself how long these things take. If I really wanted to leave, I would have to go there in person and try to speed up the process. I'm going to move to Louveciennes on Tuesday evening. It's all working out very well. I have given them notice here. We can discuss everything when you come.

Would Vambery be able to do lyrics to "L'inconnue de la Seine" [Weill's song, "Complainte de la Seine"] for me? I think something like that would be very good for England. It might make a good opening. A bit mysterious and serious—and after that I could sing something happy. Of course, that swine Brecht could write something wonderful for me. However . . . —Do you have any idea who could write lyrics for me in London? Yesterday I bought some records on boulevard Raspail. "Seeräuberjenny" and "Wie man sich . . ." and a record by Florelle, "J'attends un navire" (very beautiful).[1] I took Dr. Dalsace the two records of mine with a bunch of violets (because he's been so nice). He was terribly pleased and told me that he had heard *Die Dreigroschenoper* on London radio, but that it was a very poor performance. Sung so "properly" and melo-dramatically. Is that true? When you pass by a record store, please get the "Querschnitt aus *Mahagonny*."[2] Here it's out of stock, and they have to order everything from London. But that takes so long. If you don't forget, bring it along for me. Who is this wealthy Dutchman? I think it would be best to produce this thing yourself with the help of some moneyed people. This whole struggle with the operetta reminds me of the movie *Crime without Passion*, which at first nobody wanted to do either, and then it became a tremendous success.[3] I also have good vibes about that old Jew Wollheim. All the others just talk big. It's no great achievement to be enthusiastic about the operetta. Heckroth is terrific—especially since he copies Cas [Neher] so faithfully. All you need now is someone to put up 5,000 pounds. If only you could get Kiepura . . . him we'd take in a minute![4] I have a lesson at four o'clock, and then this letter will get mailed immediately at the railroad station. Maybe you'll get it tomorrow, even though it's Sun-day. Last night I went to the movies with that Aufricht woman and Wolfi. We saw the German version of the Renate Müller film *Victor und Victoria*.[5] It's a trouser role for Müller, and she's enchanting. She looks terrific in tails. The film is done amazingly well by Schünzel.[6] Before it started, they played some recordings in English, and I feel more and more that I could really make it, because my voice is so totally different from those recordings—which are very good, of course, but so different. That certain girlishness in my voice (without vibrato or *sexapeal*) might be the ticket—we have to capitalize on it. I'm so *ful of pep* (that means loaded with energy)—something I would be smart to take advantage of. In that store on Raspail I had to autograph a book, because I'm such a celeb. That was very nice. People must know that I don't have a *Zippi* anymore. Only that Claudette.—Weininger has a big mouth, but he's nice just the same. And I do need people like that in England. It's really funny that people there know me and are raving about me. From where and from what do they know me?

Aufricht is really out of it. He doesn't have any guts now. She would like to go to London in the worst way, but he won't go. But that's really not important. Maybe they would like to rent Louveciennes, if you decide to stay over there. That wouldn't be a bad idea, because it's awkward paying that Berthon woman all this time for doing noth-ing. But that will all be cleared up in a few days. Well, Weili, as of Tuesday I'll be in Louveciennes. Farewell, my Knuti, be the kind of *Klugi* you always have been and take many little kisses from your

Nibbi

---

1. "Wie man sich . . ." *refers to* "Denn wie man sich bettet," *which Lenya recorded in 1930 (Telefunken A371). Florelle had created the role of Marie Galante, and she recorded four of the songs, including* "J'attends un navire."

2. *The original recording, Electrola E.H. 736, has been rereleased on compact disc, Capriccio 10 347.*

3. Crime without Passion *was codirected and filmed by famed cinematographer Lee Garmes, who later won an Academy Award for his work on* Shanghai Express.

4. *The world-famous tenor Jan Kiepura (1902–66) made many highly successful motion pictures.*

5. *UFA's* Victor und Victoria *starred Renate Müller (1907–37), who had been trained by Max Reinhardt; she committed*

suicide rather than cooperate with the Nazis. She and Lenya had played rivals in Fritz Kortner's production of Der Boxer *at the State Theater in Berlin.*

6. *Reinhold Schünzel (1886–1954),* Tiger Brown in Pabst's Dreigroschenoper *film, remained in Germany until 1938.*

118 WEILL IN LONDON TO LENYA IN PARIS, [17 FEBRUARY 1935]

Letterhead: Park Lane Hotel

Sunday

My dear Linerl,

There's nothing much new today. I got a telegram from New York; this time directly from [Meyer] Weisgal (the producer). I'm supposed to have the piano score [*Der Weg der Verheißung*] copied at his expense because he needs it immediately. Well, seems like this thing will actually come off. Now I'm going full steam on the piano score, and I'll keep working nonstop in my hotel room.

On Friday I'm getting Sutro and Wollheim together. Wollheim is looking for a theater that's already in use, so that we wouldn't have to pay rent, lighting, heat, publicity, etc. If everything works out with that Dutchman, we would already have half the money in addition to what Sutro is willing to put up. Sutro is now going to approach one of London's richest families (they're Jews) and try to interest them. He wants to arrange for me to play the operetta for them. I hope to see Komisarjevsky on Tuesday, and on Wednesday I'm invited to a very important party. I'm hoping that by the end of the week I can come over there. Tomorrow I'll look for a room for you—the kind I wrote you about before. Today I won't have to see a single person. That's very pleasant for a cave dweller. Now I'm going over to Hyde Park to hear the Sunday soapbox orators, and then it's back to work some more. Do you know that Wessely is doing a new play by Kaiser in Vienna?[1] It's supposed to be a big success. Now farewell—I hope to see you soon! But only if you don't run and complain to your mama, you old tattletale!

Your Knuuuuti

1. *A leading actress in Vienna, Paula Wessely (b. 1908) starred in Georg Kaiser's* Adrienne Ambrossat.

119 WEILL IN LONDON TO LENYA IN LOUVECIENNES, [19 FEBRUARY 1935]

Letterhead: Park Lane Hotel

Tuesday

Dear Linerl,

Many thanks for your long letter. It's wonderful that you're in Louveciennes now. Go for a lot of walks, take good care of yourself, and recuperate completely. Things here are going at a snail's pace. Yesterday I was totally desperate because I got turned down by some very wealthy people in whom I had total confidence. Now I've written a rather clever letter to Melchett (with Wollheim's help) in which I describe my situation very openly and ask him if I might dedicate the Bible music to him. He simply must react to this one way or another. Mannheim obviously thought she would get that part even without bringing in some money. Now that she sees I'm moving on without her, she runs to Wollheim and offers him money again. In any case, her boyfriend seems terribly tight. Yesterday I had a long talk with Vambery about you. Everybody is sure that you could have a big career over here. But it would take a lot of patience and a great amount of energy to get started. Of course, if you get the right start, you won't have any more worries. We'll talk about all that. I would like to come over there by the end of the week, even though there are a lot of new things coming up here. Since I have a round-trip ticket, it would be worth it, even if I have to come back here next week. Please tell the post office not to forward mail anymore. I just got a call from [George] Black: Monnet is coming tomorrow with René Clair, and we're going to have dinner together. This Monnet is a real friend, isn't he?

Addio, my *Pisönchen*, regards to Harras and Mrs. Berthon. Little kisses,

Weilli

---

120 WEILL IN LONDON TO LENYA IN LOUVECIENNES,
[21 FEBRUARY 1935]
Letterhead: Park Lane Hotel

Thursday

Dear Linerl,

For four weeks I've been waiting for a meeting with these very important people, and now—wouldn't you know—it's been set for Friday. Just so I can be here that one day I have to exchange my round-trip ticket and have my visa extended. In any case, I'll leave by train at 10:00 on Saturday morning via Dieppe. Maybe it would be wiser to stay, because every day new possibilities are opening up. But it won't do any harm to take a break now and go back later on. At the moment I'm at my wit's end: René Clair told Korda that he wants to do this movie with me. The answer was: I've already decided that [Mischa] Spoliansky is going to do the film! Boom! Long live mediocrity! Down with the good people! I immediately threw all of them out with the garbage and declared that I had no desire whatsoever to enter into competition with people like Spoliansky; you've got to know at what level you want to work. On the other hand, a very interesting prospect for the operetta is opening up through René Clair. He's very nice. Many thanks for your letter and the mail. I'm looking forward to my little niche in Louveciennes. This thing about the scar tissue is very typical. I guess we'll have to put a little leech to work. So I hope to see you Saturday at 5:32 at the Gare St-Lazare.

Little kisses,
Knuti

Bummed around town last night: Clair, Monnet, [Anatole] Litvak, Sutro, Tilly [Losch], and I.

Sunday morning

My dear Weili,

Your telephone call was a nice surprise. Please stay over there as long as you need to. I'm very curious about what's going to materialize from all these various possibilities. It isn't particularly surprising that Korda prefers to make this film with Spoliansky. But maybe this will disabuse you somewhat of your conviction that there's such a thing as "nice" colleagues. I think they're all little pigs who think only of their own advantage, and you can hardly blame them for that. Just be careful. And don't do the wrong things just because you're impatient. After all, you still have that Bible thing—something that could be turned into a big event. Anyway, there's nothing whatsoever for you over here. So you really have nothing to lose by staying there. Only this thing with Mrs. Berthon has to be taken care of; it's crazy to be paying her 600 francs for doing nothing. Please drop a line to this "Marie Laura" [Marie-Laure de Noailles] (who has called you three times now). I slept at the Walchers last night—from Friday to Saturday—because I had to be at the Salpêtrière Hospital at 9:30 A.M. Dr. Charrier wanted to cut me open again, but Dalsace was against it and gave me a few things to try, which I'm doing now. He thinks a local treatment can get rid of it. Today I got the bill from the clinic, which I think is very decent. Please, Weili, write a check for them right away. The address is on the bill. Otherwise there's nothing going on here. I keep going to Charan's and working [on my English]. I'm waiting until the end of the month; then I'll go to the prefect's office to find out about my residence permit. Out of the 1,000 francs I've paid the following:

    200 hotel
    200 Charan
     80 permanent
    100 Berthon
     45 records for Dalsace
     60 garage, battery recharged
     50 medication
    ———
    735 francs

I still have 200 francs. I probably spent the other 65 francs on gasoline, oil, cigarettes, coffee, movies, ABC. I'm living very well and economically.

This afternoon I'm going to the Aufrichts for coffee at 4:30. It's raining cats and dogs here, and I'm getting a bit bored. But that's understandable. Weili, I'm always worried that we're spending too much money. Don't you want to ask at the bank again how much money you still have? Just for your peace of mind. Enclosed tax matter has to be straightened out by the end of the month (Friday the 28th). Maurice [Abravanel] has sketched it out for you. If you come back before the deadline, it'll be all right. If not, you have to fill it out and send it to the address printed in parentheses. That's all for today. Do you know your way around tax matters? Are you that much of a *Klugi?* Now farewell, my Weilchen. There's been no mail.

> Your *Kleene*

It's too complicated to send you these tax forms. If you're not here by Tuesday, Maurice will write them a few lines saying you're out of town and will take care of the matter as soon as you return.

If you think you could bring back a little something for me, that would be great (but only if there's enough money). It mustn't cost much. Please stay over there; it would be a shame for you to break things off after such a long time.

[A postscript by the Aufrichts follows.]

122 WEILL IN LONDON TO LENYA IN LOUVECIENNES, [24 FEBRUARY 1935]
Letterhead: Park Lane Hotel

Sunday

My dear Linerl,

I'm glad I was able to reach you by phone. I've had some stormy days. Thursday, quite by accident, I ran into a friend from Paris (Jean-Michel Frank, a friend of the Noailles'). In the afternoon he called me and told me that Madame Schiaparelli—the owner of the biggest fashion studio, and a very influential woman—wanted to meet me.[1] Shortly thereafter she called and invited me to accompany her to an opening that same night. I said: I have no tails. She replied: a genius doesn't need tails. That sounded quite promising. Later that afternoon Wollheim told me that he had met a gentleman who was the secretary of a Mr. Horne, one of the biggest theatrical entrepreneurs here, and that he had interested him in the operetta and made an appointment with him for Friday. In the evening I was sitting with Schiaparelli in her box along with—Mr. Horne, who happens to be her boyfriend! After the theater we all had dinner at the Savoy. Then Friday lunch at the Savoy with Sutro, Wollheim, and the secretary, and we made an appointment for an audition on Saturday. I invited Schiaparelli to this, as well as Frank and his friend, a young American. Great enthusiasm. I played from 12 to 1:30, and after that Mr. Horne invited us to Claridge's (as we entered the dining room, who should be sitting there but Korda? You should have seen the look on his face!). After lunch I played for another hour. The result: if a translator can be found, they want to do it as a big event, with stars! I'm still skeptical, because it's looked good so often before and then petered out to nothing. But it sure would be nice.—In the afternoon I went to see that revue with Tilly. God-awful. Tilly is too fat (like a dumpling), and her dancing is terrible. She's desperately looking for a rich husband but goes about it the wrong way and entirely without charm. She acts very decently toward me. I'd like to come over during the week if that's at all possible and stay through Sunday. I hope you can come back with me, if (knock on wood) I should have to go back.

Now farewell and be merry, take care of that little belly of yours and take a lot of walks, give my regards to Harras and the Berthon family. Tell them I'll take care of the money matters when I come. Many little kisses,

      Your Weilli

Did the French tax forms arrive? What do you think about that [Heinrich] Strobel?

1. *Jean-Michel Frank, a friend of Charles de Noailles, had decorated the Noailles house in Paris. The Italian-French couturiere Elsa Schiaparelli (1896–1973) was the niece of the famed astronomer Giovanni Schiaparelli. Born in Italy, she began her career as a scriptwriter and translator in New York. She moved to Paris in the 1920s, became a French citizen, and set up shop for designing and manufacturing sweaters. Soon she established herself in haute couture. Her friend Horne, who was to finance the production of Weill's* A Kingdom for a Cow, *appears nameless in her autobiography,* Shocking Life *(p. 80): "Now this year [1935] I had an English beau who followed me wherever I went, and he was an incorrigible dreamer. He had* la manie des grandeurs, *and persuaded me to open a house in London." She also recalls that Jean-Michel Frank had "revolutionized interior decoration. He invented a new style of furniture combining simplicity with considerable luxury. He was small in stature and had a terrific and desperate inferiority complex, but limitless wit."*

123 WEILL IN LONDON TO LENYA IN LOUVECIENNES, [26 FEBRUARY 1935]
Letterhead: Park Lane Hotel

                                        Tuesday

Dear *Kleene,*

Many thanks for your two long letters. I can only dash off a few lines to you because I'm totally kaput from these nerve-racking negotiations. I'm superstitious, so I won't say too much. But it looks promising. Horne seems to want to do it as soon as the end of April! (There'll be many a pleasant day before the hanging.) Tomorrow I have to audition for the owner of the theater, because he has to share in the costs. If he, too, is willing, the whole thing will be set. The conditions of the contract as we discussed them are favorable. But—as I said before—it still can all turn to naught just the same. I sent flowers to Schiaparelli today, together with a sketch of "Le Roi d'Aquitaine" [a song from *Marie Galante*], which I want to use in the operetta. Anyway I intend to come over this weekend. Don't forget to get your papers in order so you can come back with me. I saw a charming room for you today. We'll talk about all of this. Just keep your fingers crossed, and don't say a word to anybody yet! I'll send you a telegram—or rather, if you don't get a wire from me, I'll be at the Gare St-Lazare at 5:32 on Friday. I don't speak English well at all. You common folk probably speak it much better. Enclosed are two checks. Tonight I'm going to dine with [Darius] Milhaud, who happens to be in town (I think they're all awfully worked up over what I might be up to over here!). If only things would work out—if only for the sake of those yappers! Now be nice until Friday.

      Your Weilli

Weill's passport indicates that he arrived in Paris on 1 March, in time to celebrate his thirty-fifth birthday the following day. He returned to London on Tuesday, 5 March.

Letterhead: Park Lane Hotel

Wednesday

My dear Linerl,

Just a short note so that you don't wait in vain for some news. The crossing was terribly stormy. I got my reentry permit for one month without any trouble. There's nothing much new here. Everything hinges on Bostock, who can't be reached right now.[1] Nothing whatsoever happened during my absence, even though they know it has to be decided at once. Wollheim is going crazy with the Charell thing, which is supposed to open at the end of April. I called Schiaparelli—she was very nice; tomorrow I'm going to have dinner with her, and perhaps I can give things a little push. I'm going to see Bernstein—that's the one René Clair had recommended to me.[2] That's all for today.

The three days in Louveciennes were very nice. The only disappointment was that you hadn't preserved that *Zippi* for me. But I shall report this to the fairer-skinned branch of your family here.

I hope you're going to spend a lot of time in bed and live the high life so you can gain a little weight.

Now, *Kleene,* farewell.

Many kisses, your

Knuti, in the flesh

1. Probably the owner of the theater.

2. Henri Bernstein (1876–1953) was the author of popular light comedies and satires, one of which enjoyed great success in Vienna and Berlin under the title Baccarat.

Letterhead: Park Lane Hotel

Friday

My dear Linerl,

Many thanks for the mail. Right now it looks promising again. Yesterday I had dinner with Schiaparelli, and that seems to have gotten things moving again, because in the afternoon Horne's secretary called, and although—according to Wollheim—Bostock hasn't read the libretto yet, Horne is supposed to have decided to produce it anyway—regardless of Bostock—and the contracts will now be drafted! There was a telegram from Heckroth this morning saying he could hunt up 1,000–1,500 pounds. If that's the case, everything might be set. In the meantime the sacred weekend serenity has intervened, and nothing whatsoever can be done before Monday afternoon. Wollheim is convinced we've made it and that there's nothing to fear anymore. But I'm still skeptical. Anyway, tomorrow I'll look around for a cheaper room where I can work alternately on both piano-vocal scores in earnest—since I'll have to stay here until all questions have been settled. (I'm trying to get Eggerth.)[1]

How's the *Kleene* doing? I really hope that tomorrow it won't hurt so much anymore. I'd be so pleased if you'd go somewhere to recuperate. It would be great if you could go spend a few days with the Révys. So what if it costs a little. It won't cost much more than being in Louveciennes. But somebody should go with you, so you won't have to be alone. It's very cold here today. Now farewell, and have an ultracozy Sunday, with a little coffee and the movies. Many kisses, your

Knuti

1. *Marta Eggerth (b. 1912) was the reigning star of filmed operetta in Germany and Austria in the 1930s and 1940s. She and her husband, Jan Kiepura, appeared on Broadway with great success in* The Merry Widow.

126 WEILL IN LONDON TO LENYA IN LOUVECIENNES, [11 MARCH 1935]
Letterhead: Park Lane Hotel

Monday

Dear Linerl,

The mail is fantastic: Here it's 10 A.M., and I already have your letter from last night. We got another ticket, or rather you did, because you parked without your lights on after you took me to the train. (We'll say, of course, that I was the one driving the car.) I'll send it to the brother of the bedbug; please look up the address and send the enclosed letter along with the ticket: his name is Etienne Milhaud.[1] Mrs. Charan can also give you the address.

Did you send off the full score of *Die sieben Todsünden* that I left on my desk? If not, please do so right away. The address is: SKANDINAVSK TEATERFORLAG COPENHAGUE. NY VESTERGADE 13[II].[2]

Also, please call Provence 0835 (zéro-huit-trente-cinq)—this is the [Otto H.] Hein office—and tell him that my London address is still the Park Lane Hotel.

Another thing: please ask the lovely Eric [?] for the New York address of Ludwig LEWISOHN (pronounced *Lyuisson*) and send it to me.[3]

Heckroth sent a detailed letter, in which it sounds as if the thing is OK. Knock on wood. René Clair sent me a wire that he was coming. Saturday I went with him to see *The Beggar's Opera*—it was one of the most beautiful nights I've ever had in the theater, an incomparably more beautiful and more aggressive production than *Die Dreigroschenoper,* and much better performed.[4] Stylistically this was a theater of perfection such as I've previously encountered only with the Japanese. I'll go again with you. I'm also quite in favor of your coming over here soon. It's such an interesting city, and you will undoubtedly feel better here. You can still recuperate a bit, sleep a lot, and go for walks. Today I'll try to find out about the room I told you about. But in any case you can come here as soon as your things are in order, perhaps even this week. Take the train via Folkestone-Boulogne, second class, and stay on deck while aboard the ship.

I'm presently looking for a cheaper hotel for myself, but don't know of one yet. Bye-bye now, and I hope to see you soon!

> Your Knut Garbo

1. *Etienne Milhaud was the first cousin (and brother-in-law) of the composer Darius Milhaud.*

2. *Die sieben Todsünden was eventually produced at the Royal Theater in Copenhagen on 12 November 1936; withdrawn after the second performance in response to the German ambassador's protest, it was the last production of the work during Weill's lifetime.*

3. *Ludwig Lewisohn (1882–1955) had been chosen to do the English adaptation of* Der Weg der Verheißung.

4. *This new production had opened at the Criterion Theatre on 6 March 1935, with Charles Mayhew, Dennis Hoey, and Joan Collier in the cast.*

127   WEILL IN LONDON TO LENYA IN LOUVECIENNES, [16 MARCH 1935]
Letterhead: Park Lane Hotel

Saturday

Dear Linerl,

The contract has been finalized; I'm sending it off to Bertrand today. I'm sure he'll cause trouble because I've made no effort to take his personal interests into consideration. If he doesn't like it, then he'll have to keep on negotiating. The contract is very advantageous for me. They're paying me an advance of 400 pounds (20,000 francs), half of which Bertrand will have to let me have. The people here are extremely nice and actually do whatever you tell them to. They have agreed to Komisarjevsky as director—he's the best here, and one of the very best anywhere. Heckroth will do the set design. They want to engage a charming American soubrette (Gina Marlowe) for Juanita and to cast a star in the role of the General. Wollheim wants to see to it that they pay my expenses during the rehearsal period (these people actually initiated it themselves!). Now I'm working nonstop on the piano score. The opening is supposed to be at the end of May. That's a terrific time over here. Most likely I'll get a charming theater (the Gaiety). Of course, things are still up in the air—so I'm not saying a word to anyone yet. If only that old shithead [Bertrand] would sign soon. I'll simply have to stay here until all the roles have been cast, and the translation, conductor, etc. taken care of.

The traffic summons goes back to that old Bois affair, which only now is being dealt with. Please be so good as to send it to Milhaud or ask the bedbug to give it to him. Wollheim has invited me to come to the country tomorrow. I hope you're going to enjoy a real cozy Sunday. You seem to be living pretty high in my little castle. Bye-bye—

> Knut

We did an entirely new first scene, a love scene while trout fishing!

Letterhead: Park Lane Hotel

Wednesday

Dear Lottchen,

Today I finally got an answer from the old shithead. He has a few objections (out of principle), but he's being very sensible as far as the main points are concerned, and I think everything will be signed in a few days. I'm having lunch today with Komisarjevsky to talk about casting. For a few days I was afraid that the tense political climate (the situation on the Continent is extremely scary again) would cancel everything.[1] But nothing of the kind. People here don't bother much with politics. That's really very comforting.

Yesterday I went with Spoliansky to a revue that's very successful here but really very bad, although well acted in some instances. Douglas Byng plays almost nothing but old women—he's a young homosexual—but he's excellent. It reminds me again of the kind of success you could have over here. Spoliansky is convinced of it too and would be happy to write some songs for you. Besides, I'm realizing more and more that Wollheim could place you somewhere immediately—within three or four weeks—provided you have a good repertoire. He has marvelous connections—he's actually the one who arranges the programs for the best cabarets.

I've just seen a lovely room that looks out onto a very quiet garden, charmingly furnished—all new—with bathroom and kitchen, in a very elegant house owned by two old Jewish ladies. It's not cheap either, but I'll try to bargain them down to 200 francs per week. I think I'll take it as of Sunday. You can have it for two weeks while I go to Louveciennes to work there, and when I come back, we'll take one more room in the same house. We'll be able to afford it by then, since I'll probably get 15 pounds (1,000 francs) per week for living expenses. If you want to work here, you have to live in a decent place. And you can save a lot by having your own kitchen. The spring weather here is beautiful too. When do you want to come? Now I'm off to see Wollheim. Bye-bye! Kisses!

　　　Knuti

If you're coming soon, I'll take two rooms in that house. I'll stay there until all of the casting has been done, which means at least another eight to ten days. Then I'll go to Louveciennes to get the worst part of the work out of the way.

---

1. On 16 March 1935 Hitler had revealed the existence of a German Air Force and announced the reintroduction of compulsory military service, in open violation of the Treaty of Versailles.

Wednesday

Dear Lottchen,

Just a few lines to tell you I'm fine. The new apartment is charming [7 Brancham Gardens], very bright and clean and very quiet. Only it's not really warm here yet, and I always have to turn on the electric stove. In the morning I make myself a fine little tea with toast and marmalade. It's unbelievably cheap when you shop for yourself. I'm glad to be out of the hotel and not have to see anybody.

When I arrived here, I found a letter from Komisarjevsky refusing the offer. That was a big surprise to all of us, and we just can't figure it out. But I'm not exactly un-happy about it, because I feared a staging that would be all too Russian. What's more difficult is the question, Who next? Do you have any ideas? These people are willing to accept a non-Englishman, as long as he speaks English fluently. The real problems seem to be starting only now. But that was predictable. Today Wollheim wants to negotiate the reimbursement of my expenses. Otherwise nothing's new. How are you? You've been behaving yourself. But I won't write to your mommy anymore, because your fam-ily doesn't understand.

For today, your *Zappelfritz* sends all his love.

Please send me the white wool socks to wear at home.

Saturday

Dear Lenscherl,

I'm writing just a few lines so you won't be without news from me. I feel fine, be-cause I'm comfortable in this room and able to work very well. I'm almost finished with the piano score, and then I'll go on to the orchestra score right away. The other things are taking their course—again and again this slow pace drives one to desperation, be-cause every day we lose now we'll have to make up for later on. But there's nothing to be done about that. The translator question hasn't been resolved yet. Meanwhile, we're negotiating with two outstanding people (one of them is A. P. Herbert, whom Cochran had proposed); they're reading it over the weekend and will reach a decision by Mon-day.[1] The problem of finding a director looks promising too. We hope to get the fellow (his name is [Felix] Weissberger) who did staging for Reinhardt for years and has a very good name here. He's a very nice young man, with whom one can talk plain En-glish, in every sense of the word. He's in New York—we sent him a telegram, and he's already replied. Finally, we have optioned two very fine theaters—among them the Sa-voy, which I would really like because of its excellent name (especially for operettas) and also its very good stage.

Except for those negotiations, I'm almost always at home; just once I saw an operetta that featured Frances Day, who's charming (an Anny Ondra type, only much better).[2] It looks as if they'll pay my expenses only during rehearsals. But I'm living very inexpensively and pleasantly. Marie-Laure has invited me to Hyères and promised me a quiet room with a piano. It's very tempting, but I'm afraid I won't be able to go that far away.

How are you doing? How far along with your travel preparations are you? Let me know in time when you intend to come, so I can bargain the price for the other room. For the time being, everything is still vacant here, and the people are charming.

The write-up is from the *Frankfurter Zeitung*. Hans [Weill] just sent it to me. It's amazing what guts Holl has, isn't it?[3]

It's cold here; I always have to put on the electric oven, and at night my nose gets cold.

See you soon. Yours faithfully,

Glätzchen

1. *The writer Alan P. Herbert (1890–1971) had long contributed to* Punch. *An Oxford graduate and a former navy lieutenant and barrister, Herbert wrote the librettos for the operettas* The Blue Peter, Plain Jane, *and most notably,* Riverside Nights *and a new version of* La vie parisienne.

2. *Frances Day (1907–84) starred in* Jack and Jill *(1934), a musical comedy by Vivian Ellis and Desmond Carter (the latter would adapt the lyrics for* A Kingdom for a Cow*). Anny Ondra (1903–89) was the pretty blond star of Czech, Austrian, German, and British films who was married to the boxer Max Schmeling.*

3. *Karl Holl (1892–1972) succeeded Paul Bekker as the music critic of the* Frankfurter Zeitung; *he had reviewed premieres of many of Weill's works. In his review of the opera* Der Günstling *(Wagner-Régeny/Neher) from 27 March 1935, Holl courageously noted: "The work's overall bearing is not as absolutely new, not as singularly epoch-making as might be deduced from early reports. In reality—and this must be emphasized openly and in all honesty—we're dealing here merely with a continuation of experiments that had addressed the technical and social engagement of opera theater, advocated in theory and practically executed by Brecht and Weill, and ever since consistently developed by Weill and Brecht."*

131 WEILL IN LONDON TO LENYA IN LOUVECIENNES, [2 APRIL 1935]

Tuesday

Dear Linerl,

Just a few lines. I'm incredibly busy. Today I got both your letters. I'm expecting you on Saturday. Take the train at 10:30 from Gare du Nord via Folkestone-Boulogne. You'll arrive here at 5:20. (Find out about the change to summer time.) Buy a third-class ticket and pay the extra for second class from Paris to Boulogne (that train has only second class). On the boat you'll be in second class on a third-class ticket anyway, and in England one always travels (better) in third class. Passport inspection takes place on the boat; it will be quite harmless for you, since you haven't been here for some time. If they ask what you're going to do here, just tell them you're learning English because you're going to America this fall. As an address give them 7 Brancham Gardens. I'll send you a check for 8,000 francs. Give Mrs. Berthon 1,250 for the rent; I'll be paying her salary from here before coming back. Buy yourself whatever you need, and bring the rest of your stuff with you too. It's very cold here. Please bring me my warm socks and the new warm underwear, also a few neckties (the gray and the green ones and the bow tie). You'll have a room, and they'll give you a break on the price.

I hope that A. P. Herbert will do the translation. He's very enthusiastic. We probably will get the Palace Theatre, the best one in London (Cochran!).

I'm looking forward to the home-fried potatoes.

See you on Saturday at 5:20.

Have a nice journey, and be nice.

> Your Weilli

132 WEILL IN LONDON TO LENYA IN LOUVECIENNES, 4 APRIL 1935

Postcard

Dear Lottchen,

It would be great if you could bring along my winter coat. Or do you have too much to carry? The old one will do, and you can cover yourself with it on the train. If at all possible, do bring along hangers. You're getting a first-class room up where I am. I'm going to get 10 pounds (700 francs) per week as of 1 April, and when rehearsals start, 15 pounds! But <u>nobody</u> must know about this! That way I'll be able to buy myself a set of tails, and you can buy what you need too. Great, isn't it? See to it that Heckroth comes along with you. So long until Saturday. I have a headache!

> Your Knuti

[A. P.] Herbert has accepted.

Lenya's passport (with a number of pages missing for the immediately preceding years) indicates that she arrived in London on 8 April and apparently stayed there with Weill through June. Her British Registration Certificate, dated 12 June, was issued to Karoline Weill, as was a new German passport obtained on 30 August from the German Embassy in London.

In an English adaptation by Reginald Arkell, with English lyrics by Desmond Carter, the satirical operetta never completed as Der Kuhhandel *premiered as* A Kingdom for a Cow *at the Savoy Theatre on 28 June. Weill had revised a good portion of his original score and substituted several numbers closer in style to British music-hall idioms than the Offenbach models that underlay the rest of the work. Muir Mathieson conducted a cast that included Jacqueline Francell, Webster Booth, and George Gee. Reviews were mixed; the* Times *described it as "hovering uneasily between comic opera and musical comedy" and found it "a matter of some difficulty to tell when sentimental music is satirizing itself and when it is being itself. Weill writes a particularly nauseous kind of jazz with every beat of a bar of common time made into a strong beat, and his waltzes are more sympy than the old-fashioned kind." More favorable reviews appreciated the topicality of the play as the world entered another arms race and praised Weill's score for its craft and wit. But it closed after a run of just two weeks, a financial failure.*

After investing so much effort in its original conception, securing an English adaptation and production, and rewriting his score, Weill was very disappointed and physically drained from the ordeal. On 9 July he returned to Louveciennes; Lenya stayed on in London, and Weill

[FIG. 46]

addressed his letters to her care of Gerty Simon, a photographer whose portraits of Lenya taken in Berlin and London are now in the Weill/Lenya Archive, Yale University.

133 WEILL IN LOUVECIENNES TO LENYA IN LONDON, [10 AND 11 JULY 1935]

Wednesday

My dear Linerl,

The trip over was very nice; the Matrays brought me home.[1] The house here is beautiful as always, but there's an enormous number of things to be taken care of, and I'm in no mood at all to do any kind of work. Now my incredible fatigue is beginning to show. Harras is in great shape, and the Berthon family is proud of Emile, who has won five prizes at the school for locksmiths. I think of London only as far as you are concerned. Everything else I have to forget first. But I was especially pleased with you again this time; I think you are a grand *Pison* and that your qualities as a human being keep developing parallel to my own, so that (after ten years!) you are still giving me things that no one else can give me, things that are crucial. On my way back I was thinking that we've really solved the question of living together, which is so terribly difficult for us, in a very beautiful and proper way. Don't you think so? I have a very good feeling about England and America as far as you and your work are concerned. We'll make it, won't we?

Now I'm happily looking forward to my vacation. I have such a ringing in my ears at night. Don't know what it is. I've found a quite confusing letter here from Cas [Neher], and I can't make head or tail of what he actually wants.

Please be so kind as to tell Cahill three things: (1) I need a complete libretto of the operetta for America. (2) Mathieson is to make a complete *piano score* from all the materials and send it. (3) When they're finished, they should immediately send me my entire *Orchester-Partitur (full score)*.[2] It would be nice if they would mount the operetta in the provinces and then bring it back to London.

Farewell now, my little *Pison*. I'll write again tomorrow. Many little kisses from your

Weilli

It would be better to mail all these things directly to Heugel, 2 bis, rue Vivienne.

Thursday

I forgot to mail this letter, of course. I just got your letter. Only now do I understand the content of Cas's letter that I got here. It seems he's coming right away and that I'm to meet them at Lake Thun. I can't tell from either letter where they want to go after that, but it seems to Lake Garda, which would suit me very well.

Yesterday I was with Madeleine, who was very nice, as always.[3] The car is running; I'm having the ignition, brakes, clutch, and carburetor fixed. I hope it won't cost much. I still have 15,000 francs in the bank. Quite nice, isn't it? I'll be very careful with my spending on the trip and will negotiate in Salzburg so that the entire sojourn in America won't cost us anything. Then we can save that Heugel money for emergencies. Now

Francesco [von Mendelssohn] is coming to see me. The Matrays are coming for dinner. I just called Bertrand and gave him the soft soap. Still, he was very nice. He's going to leave tonight. I'm already feeling a bit better, and I'm beginning to look forward to our trip to America. You too? I'm going to dismiss Mrs. Berthon before that trip and send back the grand piano. Madeleine will try to find someone to rent the house. Maybe I'll sell the car. Neumann[?] is offering 7,000 francs.

I have to quit now. Be happy and take it real easy; I'll write once more before I leave. Don't tell Cahill that I'm leaving. Kommer either.[4] You can tell Cahill that I have to meet [Franz] Werfel to work with him. I'll write to him then that he should come to Salzburg.

> All my love for you,
> Your Weilli

1. *The German dancer and choreographer Ernst Matray (1891–1978), who had worked with Max Reinhardt at the Deutsches Theater in Berlin, had replaced Felix Weissberger as the director of* A Kingdom for a Cow. *Matray and his wife, Maria Solveg, followed Reinhardt to Hollywood, where Matray taught dance at Reinhardt's Hollywood workshop.*

2. *Frank Cahill had been hired by the financial backers of* A Kingdom for a Cow *as the production's business manager. The musical director was Muir Mathieson (1911–75), who would conduct for more than five hundred films during his tenure as musical director of London Films, which began in 1934.*

3. *Madeleine Milhaud (b. 1902), the wife of Darius, became a close friend of Weill's; their relationship is documented in correspondence spanning more than a decade.*

4. *The Rumanian-born Rudolf Kommer (1888–1943) worked himself up from humble beginnings as a cabaret artist in Vienna to Max Reinhardt's principal assistant. His nickname was Kätchen.*

134 WEILL IN LOUVECIENNES TO LENYA IN LONDON, [13 JULY 1935]

Saturday morning

My dear Linerl,

I'm shoving off! I'll take my time driving. Cas called me last night from Basel. I'm going to meet him at Lake Thun tomorrow. But he seems afraid to be seen with me! This abject fear and faintheartedness they get when meeting anybody from that country! It gives you a sudden satisfaction at having made the right choice.

I've taken care of everything over here. Francesco has talked to Max [Reinhardt], who sang a long hymn of praise about me. I'm looking forward to the sea. It's terribly hot here. Please drop me a line in Bolzano (Italy), poste restante. By the way, it's possible I'll be going to Venice, because I can talk to Max by himself there. Francesco suggested it. I'll always send you my address. And you must always drop me a line. Cahill called yesterday. They're closing the show (thank God), and it's supposed to reopen in the fall. I told him I've got to work with Werfel for ten days and would then meet him in Salzburg. Bye-bye, *Pison*! Many little kisses

> from your Weilli

135 WEILL IN MORAT, SWITZERLAND, TO LENYA IN LONDON, [14 JULY 1935]

Sunday

My dear Linerl,

The drive yesterday was marvelous; taking a leisurely trip by car is pure pleasure. The repairs, including lubrication, came to only 80 francs, and the license didn't cost anything because of the security deposit I gave them last year. Yesterday I drove up to Dijon (three hundred kilometers in five hours, but quite leisurely); there I relished a first-rate meal. Then I drove on and reached the border by six o'clock. I wanted to stay overnight at Neuchâtel, but it was awful there, so I drove on to Morat, where I slept wonderfully.

Now I'm having my little coffee, then I'm going swimming, and then I'm going to drive to Lake Thun. I'm curious what those roaming jailbirds will have to say about events back there. As soon as I know where I'm staying, I'll wire you my address, and then I want to hear from you right away. While I was driving I thought, I'll write out the "Mirjam Lied" [from *Der Weg der Verheißung*] for you in English so you can begin studying it already. Francesco thinks it's self-evident that you'll get the part. He came with [his sister] Eleonara, who was very nice, refreshing, and funny, and she sends her regards. She's also going to America. She says that New York is a theater city like Berlin in '28. I'm really looking forward to this America trip. You too? I hope it'll all work out. I shudder at the thought of the gigantic score I'll have to write. But right now I don't want to think about that. Now be nice, and take a kiss from your

Weilli

136 WEILL IN LUCERNE TO LENYA IN LONDON, [16 JULY 1935]

Dear Linerl,

At Lake Thun yesterday I met the Nehers, including Cas, who's very afraid to be seen with me. But he's really nice and his manner seems unobjectionable, as far as that's possible. The Nehers have left for Zurich, and I'll be following them slowly; a marvelous drive past Interlaken and Lucerne. Tomorrow it'll be the Dolomites, where we're going to meet Erika's father [Johannes Tornquist]. How are you? I hope to be getting some news in Bolzano. It's incredibly hot. But the car ride is wonderful. Many little kisses for you.

Your Weilli

137 WEILL IN BRAXEN, SWITZERLAND, TO LENYA IN LONDON, [17 JULY 1935]

Wednesday evening

My dear Linerl,

For two days now I've been staying in a wonderful hotel near a magnificent forest lake quite close to Toblach, where I saw the Grand Hotel of blessed memory.[1] Today we met Erika's father, a highly intelligent man with whom one can carry on a very good conversation. I'm already quite tanned and getting better, but I would really like to stay put someplace quiet for a week, probably at Lake Garda. I'm expecting some mail from you tomorrow, which I asked to have forwarded from Bolzano. I'm curious to see what kind of news you might have.

I'm slowly getting to the point where I can look forward to working again. But

If I think of London in the night,	[*Wenn ich an London denke in der Nacht,*
I find no sleep to ease my plight.	*Dann bin ich um den Schlaf gebracht.*][2]

This London flop was a heavy blow for me. But "just don't get soft, baby!"[3]

I hope you're well and are living it up the way I am. Be nice or I'll tell your mommy.

Write me at Verona, poste restante. Many little kisses,

Your Knuti

1. *See letter 48: in an effort to smuggle some of his money out of Germany, Weill was to have met Pasetti at the Grand Hotel in Toblach in early August 1933.*

2. *Weill is alluding to "Nachtgedanken," a very famous poem from Heinrich Heine's* Zeitgedichte, *written during his Paris exile.*

3. *A quotation from "Das Lied von der harten Nuß" (Happy End): "nur nicht weich werden."*

138 WEILL IN LEVICO, ITALY, TO LENYA IN LONDON, 22 JULY 1935

Picture postcard: "Barche e vele sul lago e monte Rovere."

Dear Linerl,

I'm sunburned, but otherwise I'm fine. For once I'm able to catch up on my sleep. Tomorrow I'm going to drive to Verona, where I finally hope to find some mail forwarded from Bolzano, because up to now I haven't received anything at all. After that I'm going to Venice for a few days and from there to the sea for a while, somewhere on the Adriatic coast. It's not exactly fun traveling with the Nehers, because they're so terribly scared. I'll write to you in more detail from Venice. All the best to you, and many little kisses from your

Knuti

Regards to Gerty [Simon].

Letterhead: Hotel / Terminus / Venezia

Tuesday

Dear Linerl,

Last night I arrived in Venice; today I went swimming at the Lido, and now I'm going to meet Max [Reinhardt] for dinner. I'm curious as to what he'll have to say, because up to now I've been without any news. As always, it makes me very nervous when I don't hear from you. But then—I didn't receive any mail forwarded from Bolzano; not in Verona and not here, either.

I'm feeling very well, but I've had enough of Italy and won't be coming here again for quite some time. Especially right now, it's really horrifying to be in this warlike atmosphere, full of soldiers, with "rah-rahs" blasting from every corner. The process of stupefying these people is making gruesome progress.[1] But then again—this city remains a miracle. Today I went to a Titian exhibition. He's not a first-class painter, but he's very interesting just because of that. I've had a lot of time to think about myself. I would be so happy to be able to do something big again, something right—without having to think about those dull-witted audiences of Europe's big cities. Maybe it'll be possible to build up something in America so that I can write my kind of operas again. But that Reinhardt thing—it's full of peril, and also very difficult.

I'd like to go swimming in the sea some more, because that's the best way to recuperate. Tomorrow I meet up with the Nehers again, and then we'll go somewhere near Trieste—some hundred kilometers from here. I'll wire you my address. I'll be in Leopoldskron [Reinhardt's castle near Salzburg] by the end of the week. I'll know more after tonight. I hope to hear from you soon that you're doing OK. Kisses from

Your Weilli

1. *Hitler and Mussolini had first met in June 1934; at about the same time the emperor of Ethiopia, Haile Selassie, applied to the League of Nations for protection against Italian aggression. In October 1935 Mussolini would invade Ethiopia.*

Postcard

Dear Linerl,

We made it here and found a magnificent beach; the water is wonderful for swimming, and I stay at the beach all day long. I'll be here until next Thursday, and then I'm off to Salzburg. I spent an entire evening with Max in Venice. Everything seems to be going all right, and he thinks [Meyer] Weisgal will also show up in Salzburg. Of course, that would be for the best. Max is a repulsive publicity hound, that much I've been able to find out. Tomorrow I'll be writing you in detail, after I finally will have gotten some mail here. All my love as always,

Your Weilli

Friday, 26/7/35

My dear Linerl,

I think I forgot to write you my address on yesterday's postcard. It's Novi, Yugoslavia, Hotel Slavia. But there's no point writing me there, because the mail takes a long time, and I'm here only until next Thursday. So write me poste restante in BOLZANO (Italy), where I'll be on Friday. I'm so eager to get some news from you at last. I imagine that the entire batch of mail from Bolzano and Verona will finally get here tomorrow. Wolfgang Reinhardt told me that he had seen you and that you're fine.[1] The old man made a very bad impression on me. But I won't trouble my head about him; I'll do my work and see to it that I achieve other things in America. I still haven't gotten over this London flop, and I stay awake at night brooding about it for hours. My only consolation is the Verdi letters, which I'm reading again. The analogies are startling. I'm thinking seriously of doing something with either Brecht or Cocteau this time. Cocteau could do *Alice* marvelously, so that you could play her.[2] With Brecht I'd like to do an opera based on the Chinese play *Die nördlichen und südlichen Provinzen* or the *Kreidekreis*, something very small and unpretentious.[3] This is the surest sign that I'm beginning to recuperate from that "*knock out.*" Also the ballet for the Grand Opéra would be a good thing now. It all depends on what's decided in Salzburg. I'm writing to Cahill today to see if he wants to come. You could find out whether he'll be going by car and whether you might drive with him (beware of that wife of his!). I hope you're making good use of the contacts over there and of the *succès d'estime* I undoubtedly have scored. Here it's wonderful, and the Adriatic is a marvelous sea. Be happy, and lots of little kisses from your

Knuti

1. *Wolfgang Reinhardt (1909–79), one of Max Reinhardt's two sons, became a screenwriter, producer, and director.*

2. *The multitalented French writer-artist Jean Cocteau (1889–1963) served as aesthetic spokesman for Les Six, a group of young composers strongly influenced by Erik Satie. After Cocteau had declined Weill's invitation to write the libretto for the ballet commissioned by Les Ballets 1933, they planned a Faust opera, but it was abandoned in the early stages of discussion. The reference to* Alice *remains obscure, as Lenya would be an unlikely choice for* Alice in Wonderland.

3. Kreidekreis *(1925) was the best-known play of Klabund (Alfred Henschke; 1890–1928), the husband of Carola Neher. Brecht eventually did base his* Kaukasische Kreidekreis *(1943–45) on it, but without collaboration with Weill. There is no surviving documentation of any contact between them until they met again in New York in November 1935, during Brecht's brief visit for the Theatre Union's production of* Die Mutter.

---

142 WEILL IN SALZBURG TO LENYA IN LONDON, 6 AUGUST 1935

Tuesday

Postcard

Dear Linerl,

Yesterday I drove [to Austria], then stayed overnight in a small place outside Salzburg and drove there this morning. I've seen [Heinz] Herald and Kommer, who both tell me it is essential that I go to America as soon as possible, because they don't want to cast without me. Now I'll drive to see Max, after getting the car thoroughly cleaned. I'm not going to stay in Leopoldskron but rather in Hotel Gablerbräu. It was frightfully difficult to find a room. I wrote to Cahill a long time ago (from Novi) and invited him to Salzburg, but he never answered. Please try to call him (Grov. 1428) and talk him into coming and give him the address. I'll stay until the beginning of next week and write you tomorrow. A thousand kisses,

Your Weilli

143 WEILL IN SALZBURG TO LENYA IN LONDON, [7 AUGUST 1935]

Wednesday

My dear Linerl,

I just got your telegram, and I'm surprised that you've been without news from me. Something is wrong here! You got last week's letter from Novi and sent your answer to Bolzano. Then I also wrote you a postcard from Novi. I remember very clearly that I stated on it that you were the neatest *Pison*, and I also wrote you something about Reinhardt. After that I wrote you an airmail postcard from Trieste. That was last Wednesday. Finally, I also wrote you a postcard from Bolzano, where I had to wait two full days for my money from Paris. But that very card I just found in my suit pocket, pig that I am! Poor Linerl, you had to worry again for no reason at all. I still don't understand why you didn't get those two postcards. But in the meantime you must have gotten my postcard from here. My trip was wonderful, but I'm glad to be starting work again. Just between you and me, that Neher family was beginning to get on my nerves with their constant angst. Besides—well, you know me. It's very pretty here. Yesterday Reinhardt was quite nice. Werfel will be here today, and then the real work begins. I've started pestering them about you. At this point it's impossible to figure out how long I might have to stay here. If I have to stay longer, I'll move to Leopoldskron. Cahill will be here tomorrow; that will be a lot of fun. Today I talked to Zuckmayer and Bruno Walter (who wants to do my symphony with the Vienna Philharmonic).[1] I think a lot about you and am so looking forward to seeing you. You simply have to come soon. Be happy. Farewell and be kissed many times by your

Knuti

My sister Greta [Garbo] was supposed to come to Leopoldskron, but I advised her against getting hooked up with such a family.

Regards to Gerty.

1. *The dramatist Carl Zuckmayer (1896–1977) was a good friend of Brecht's and wrote the screenplay of* Der blaue Engel.

Letterhead: Hotel-Restaurant / "Gablerbräu" / Salzburg

Sunday

My dear Linerl,

I'm up to my neck in work. Every night I go to Leopoldskron for dinner, and then we work until four o'clock in the morning. Werfel is about the most obnoxious and slimiest literati pig I've ever met. He's scared of every note of music, but he's easy game because he's a coward and immediately gives in, as long as one remains firm. Max behaves nobly, is very outspoken and unequivocally on my side, deciding all discussions in favor of the music. He understands completely what I want, and he's as crazy about the music as he is about me. In that respect the work is a lot of fun for me. He knows an awful lot and has brilliant ideas. Of course, he really does realize what he's got in me, and there's always a sort of quiet understanding between him and me. I hope that this Werfel beast will leave on Tuesday; then I still want to work alone with Max for one or two days. Right now it seems rather definite that we'll already be going to America in September, because Max wants me to be there right from the start. I'll talk to him about you only when I have him to myself. I can't imagine that he would refuse me.

Otherwise it's lovely here. I spent the entire day with Cahill, who's really very nice. Edward [James] is here, too, so the three of us had lunch together. Cahill had gone to see *Faust* the night before; today we'll see *Jedermann* together, and tonight we'll attend the dress rehearsal of *Entführung* with [Bruno] Walter.

Many thanks for your cute letters and the two little pictures, which I think are very good. The texts by Steindorff seem to be quite serviceable.[1] If all goes the way I hope it will, you should come over when I'm back in Louveciennes, so we can prepare for our trip together. Are you looking forward to it? Now farewell *Kleene*,

Always, your Knuti

Frank Cahill gives you his love.

---

1. *Probably Ulrich Steindorff (b. 1888), an expressionist playwright active in Berlin during the twenties.*

Wednesday

My dear Linerl,

Just a few lines so you won't be without news from me. We've now gone through the whole piece and they're all, even Werfel, enthusiastic about the music—most of all Max himself, who says over and over how happy he is to be working with me. There's now a steady exchange of cables with New York about a theater, something that hasn't been settled yet. Tonight we were on the phone with New York for almost an hour.

Right now it looks as if Max will be leaving on 1 September on an Italian boat, and he insists that I go with him. If that should be the case, you would have to come to Paris in a hurry. It seems I'll be getting paid enough to cover my stay there for the two of us to live on. But I'm afraid they won't pay for your trip—Kommer has flatly refused and proved to me that it's never done. Naturally, for the time being I'm sticking firmly to my demands, since the worst that can happen is that we'd have to pay for your trip ourselves. Kommer, who's really repulsive, also seems to be raising a stink about your getting a part (of course Tilly [Losch] is behind that), but I'm going to push it through via Max, once I have him to myself. I've succeeded in getting Francesco to come along—he'll be here tomorrow—which is worth a lot. Cahill is in Vienna. I'm rather tired because we've been working every night. I hope that by the end of the week I'll know something definite about everything, and then I'll leave for Paris immediately. Should we really be leaving on 1 September, I'll send you a telegram. I haven't had any news from you in a few days. I hope all is well. Lots of love from your

      Knuti

146 WEILL IN SALZBURG TO LENYA IN LONDON, [17 AUGUST 1935]

                                                  Saturday

My dear Linerl,

    Having prepared everything so I could leave tomorrow in order to take care of that matter in Innsbruck on the way, I just got a telegram from Weisgal saying he's on his way here and absolutely has to see me with Max. He's going to arrive on Saturday (24th); it therefore makes no sense for me to leave here now, because I definitely will have to be here when that man arrives. So I'll move to Leopoldskron, where I can work in peace on my piano score, and also do some swimming and take advantage of the opportunity to work with Max some more. Things are looking up for you since I've succeeded in excluding Kommer, and I hope I can push it through, especially now that I have Max to myself. Since according to the new plan I'll now be here until the 27th or 28th, it might happen that we'll have to sail very soon afterward—possibly even the first few days of September. So you'll have to have everything ready, and also find out about your reentry permit to France! Please send me the storage receipt for Innsbruck, and write a letter telling them I'll be there toward the end of the month to make the necessary arrangements for my things.[1] I'm happy about your letter today, because I hadn't heard from you all week. This place is swarming with people I know—enough to make you sick to your stomach. I'll be disappearing to Leopoldskron for a week, so I can get away from this scum. Many little kisses,

      In haste, your Knuti

---

    1. After the sale of the house in Berlin, a shipment of Weill's belongings had been sent to Pasetti's father in Innsbruck.

147 WEILL IN SALZBURG TO LENYA IN LONDON, [21 AUGUST 1935]

Letterhead: Schloß / Leopoldskron / Salzburg

Wednesday

Dear Linscherl,

Today Herald will tell you everything that's worth knowing. At the moment it looks like Reinhardt is going to do *Fledermaus* in London, and that I'll be going to New York with Herald in order to prepare everything. Herald wants to go on an English boat that leaves Southampton on 7 September. If we do take that one, you won't have to come to Paris after all. Herald (who's very nice and really wants you to sing Miriam) will help you get a visa. Be kind of nice to him; he's a decent schlemiel. The final decision will be made once Weisgal gets here, but Herald will be able to tell you before then, because he's seeing Weisgal on Friday. I think they'll pay me $100 (20 pounds) a week for my stay there. If we manage it right, we can both live on that, especially since it's cheaper there than in London, and prestige is no concern over there. I'll still try to squeeze the cost of your trip out of them, but on an English ship it won't be too bad. As soon as things have been decided, I'll send you a wire. On the way back I still want to see Hans [Weill], who has those *Sächelchen* for you. I have a beautiful room here and I'm alone all day long, thank God, something I'm enjoying very much. Only the work isn't going quite right yet. Salzburg is swarming with people I know, one more miserable than the other. I don't even bother to go into town anymore. I got the storage receipt. It's very good that you're working on your singing. I met a very important man from New York radio. Together with Steindorff we'll work up a repertoire over there. Farewell, *Pison;* I'm hopeful that everything will work out all right, also with your passport. Lots of love to you,

Your Knuti

148 WEILL IN SALZBURG TO LENYA IN LONDON, [26 AUGUST 1935]

Letterhead: Schloß / Leopoldskron / Salzburg

Monday

Dear Linerl,

We're in the middle of negotiations with Weisgal. The situation is difficult, because there's actually less money and the theater is smaller than we expected. But I believe it can be done anyway, with a modicum of goodwill. Max is opposing it, because he's lazy and evidently doesn't smell enough money (for quite a while now his veneration of money has made me feel like puking). He's also trying to talk us into giving this thing up altogether. He's trying to lure me into doing something else with him at Josefstädter Theater, with film etc., but I see through his schemes, and I'm thoroughly disgusted with this tired king of the castle. I'll tell you all about it in person. There'll be a decision this afternoon. If it comes out the way I hope it will, then I'm supposed to sail with Weisgal on the *Majestic* on 4 September. For the time being he'll pay me $100 per week, then $200 when rehearsals start and—if I agree to do the conducting myself—$250 while the show runs. That's very decent. Now we can start thinking about your trip. Naturally it would be great if we could sail together, and I've reserved a double cabin, just in case. But the *Majestic* is a very expensive ship, and your trip comes out of our own pocket. What do you think? I would suggest that you first come to Louveciennes. Then we can decide what would be best and come to a decision by the end of the week. I want to take off tomorrow and hope to be in Louveciennes by Wednesday evening. Do you want to come on Thursday? Are your papers in order? Weisgal is nice and thoroughly decent. Instead of Herald (who unfortunately is only a schlemiel), he wants to take Francesco with him, which is, of course, more to my liking. Together we're supposed to cast the show. Therefore, I'm sure it'll work out for Miriam.

As I said before, everything depends on what Max says or does this afternoon. If it doesn't work out, I'll send you a telegram; i.e., if by Wednesday afternoon you have no other news, come to Louveciennes, where we can discuss everything.

Yesterday I was in total despair, when it looked as if the whole thing would fall through. Then and there I decided to take matters into my own hands, and I discussed everything with Weisgal, Werfel, Francesco, and Kommer, and I realized that it could indeed work out; now it all depends on the old man. Please just tell Herald that I asked you to come to Paris and that you know nothing further.

Farewell, *Kleene,*
I'm looking forward to seeing you.
If only you haven't gotten too fresh!
Bye-bye

    Knut

If you can't or don't want to come to Paris, I'll prepare everything in Paris, come to London, and board in Southampton (instead of Cherbourg).

3 · NEW YORK, HOLLYWOOD: 1935–1938
Letters 149–212

The first publicity photo of Weill and Lenya taken in the United States,
1935. (© Louise Dahl-Wolfe; courtesy Staley-Wise Gallery,
New York. See Letter 203.)

1935–1936

The decision that Lenya would accompany Weill to America wasn't made until the last minute. Maurice Abravanel recalled that when Weill told him he was thinking of taking Lenya back, he asked, "'Kurt, are you crazy? I mean, you need a real wife!' Weill responded, 'Yes, yes, yes. But you know, in the Jewish tradition, the husband always forgives his wife.' And Kurt, in all those years—it was eleven years since I had met him—had never once mentioned anything about Jewish tradition! And I—an idiot—instead of realizing—ah, he wants her back and is looking for an excuse! Then he went to the Milhauds and said, 'You know I have to go to America, and it bothers me because even though Lenya's Catholic, I think she might have a very difficult time with the Nazis for having been with me.' He wanted the Milhauds to say what I hadn't said. But they didn't want to either, because they found Lenya's behavior toward Kurt horrible too" (int. MA1).

Lenya arrived in Paris on 2 September 1935, got her temporary visa from the American consulate the next day, and sailed with Weill from Cherbourg on the SS Majestic *on 4 September. They docked in New York on 10 September and checked into the St. Moritz Hotel, where they were planning to live for the next three months before "The Road of Promise" (*Der Weg der Verheißung, *ultimately titled* The Eternal Road*) opened and they could return to France. Lenya recalled that they had seen the famous skyline of New York so often in the movies that* when they arrived, "it was really like coming home." They did the town: riding elevators in the famed skyscrapers, going to movies and plays, hitting the jazz clubs. "We just dropped our bags and went straight down to Broadway into a movie theater and saw The Dark Angel, *I think it was Ronald Colman and Vilma Banky."* Unfortunately it was a revival of the famous silent film, so they laughed about their mistake and tried to understand the English intertitles (int. L4). In the clearest demonstration that the fictional America they had constructed in Europe didn't always match what they found, Lenya recalled that they took a cue from the Berlin blackface production of the misleadingly titled Das Lied von Hoboken (Günter Weisenborn's adaptation of the work of the American novelist Michael Gold [1893–1967]) and grabbed a ferry for New Jersey; there they learned it was Harlem they were looking for (Beams, p. 14).

Within a month, at Ira Gershwin's invitation, Weill had attended a rehearsal of Porgy and Bess and exclaimed, "It's a great country where music like that can be written—and played" (Welles). He would later identify the experience as pivotal in shaping his own perceptions of the potential of Broadway musical theater. Something of a minor celebrity, Weill gave numerous interviews, and in December the League of Composers sponsored a concert of Weill's music, but the welcome of many critics and fellow composers (of a modernist bent) wore out by intermission. Moreover, an end for The Eternal Road was still not in sight. Opening night had been postponed because of the enormous alterations necessary to accommodate Norman Bel Geddes's set at the Manhattan Opera House.

In January 1936 the company disbanded without having mounted the production. Max Reinhardt went to Hollywood and Franz Werfel went back to Vienna, whereas Weill and Lenya decided to stay, and Weill obtained a new passport from the German consulate. Weill's beloved German shepherd, Harras, stayed on in Louveciennes with Weill's French caretakers, the Berthons. Weill and Lenya left the St. Moritz for more modest lodgings at the Hotel Park Crescent on Riverside Drive and Eighty-seventh Street. Although Lenya had trouble with the language, Weill was quickly speaking fairly idiomatic, if heavily accented, English. At a party he met Harold Clurman, one of the three founding directors of the politically engaged Group Theatre, which had assembled an outstanding company of young actors. Clurman introduced [FIG. 47] Weill to the other two directors, Lee Strasberg and Cheryl Crawford, and they started thinking about a project that could occupy Weill until Meyer Weisgal would reassemble the Eternal Road company. Weill suggested either a "very American topic" or a musical version of Jaroslav Hašek's Good Soldier Schweik. The Group, in turn, proposed an Americanized Schweik, and [FIG. 48] Clurman suggested the project to playwright Paul Green, "the most American playwright" they could think of. In May Cheryl Crawford arranged a meeting in Chapel Hill; Crawford and a companion went by car, Weill by train. Paul Green remembered waiting, as instructed, for the appointed train, but Weill didn't get off when it arrived, so Green went back home. Then the telephone rang, and it was Weill, calling from a remote farmhouse. He had gotten off at a siding that hadn't been used as a passenger stop for years (Sanders, p. 226). After they finally got together, they started work, drawing "general inspiration" from Georg Büchner's Woyzeck and Carl Zuckmayer's Captain of Köpenick as well as Hašek.

149 WEILL IN CHAPEL HILL, NORTH CAROLINA, TO LENYA IN NEW YORK, [3 MAY 1936]

Letterhead: Carolina Inn / Chapel Hill, N.C.

Monday morning

Dear *Blume*,

It's wonderful here. I'm a completely different person when I'm away from the city. I slept quite well on the train; looking out the window this morning, I found myself in the midst of a really green summer landscape with a fragrance reminiscent of the south of France: the heat combined with the flowers. Sleeping Beauty messed up again. When I got off the train, there was no car, no village, no telephone, only a few dilapidated Negro shanties. Thank God I had read a newspaper interview with Cherill [Cheryl Crawford] that mentioned the name of the place I was supposed to go to. I finally talked a young man with a Ford into driving me there. America's oldest university is here. The whole place looks very English; you can see green trees and meadows from every window. I have a charming room with a shower, and I'm living the high life. This peace is heavenly. You see only young people here, and you realize for the first time what America is really like and how unimportant New York is for this country. Paul Green makes a very good impression: refreshing, young, easy-going, almost like Zuckmayer. I think he's going to be a good man for me. We've already worked very well all afternoon and evening. The two aunties [Crawford and her friend] didn't drift in until evening.

How's the gracious flower doing? You're probably puttin' on the Ritz in that apartment. But you definitely have to get away for at least two months this summer. It's the only possible way to live.

I'll be back on Sunday. See to it that Franz has the ballet ready.[1] Maybe Sofie can translate it?[2] I'd pay her for it. Be sure that nothing goes wrong with those many offers from [Arthur] Lyons, etc., while I'm away.

Bye-bye, you doll. Little kisses

1. *The Austrian writer Franz Hoellering had promised Weill the scenario for a ballet. Concurrently Weill had been commissioned for the American Ballet Company by Agnes Meyer, wife of the owner of the* Washington Post, *Eugene Meyer, for a ballet based on Frank Wedekind's* Kaiserin von Neufundland. *Neither project ever materialized.*

2. *Weill's second cousin Sofie Messinger (1901–88; her father and Weill's mother were first cousins) was one of the relatives who helped with the necessary affidavits for Weill's entry into the United States.*

150 WEILL IN CHAPEL HILL TO LENYA IN NEW YORK, [6 MAY 1936]

Letterhead: Carolina Inn

Wednesday

Dear *Blume*,

Just a few lines so you're not without news from me. I'm enjoying the peace, the warm weather, the wonderful air here very much. We're working outdoors all the time.

Paul Green is a strange fellow, and I'm not quite sure whether he's able to handle this project. But Cherill is terrific, and it's astonishing how much she understands. Anyway, it's interesting for me, and I think it's not impossible for something worthwhile to come out of this.

I still have no news from you, and I'm a bit upset that nothing has come from Franz yet. If only this ballet would work out! It would simplify everything so much. Please do cultivate Florence [Meyer]! I'll let you know exactly when I'll be comng back, probably Sunday evening.

Much love to you!

Knuti

151 WEILL IN CHAPEL HILL TO LENYA IN NEW YORK, 7 MAY 1936
Postcard

Thursday

Blumi,

I got your letter and the mail yesterday, but nothing from Franz has arrived so far. I'm glad you can spend some time outdoors. Yesterday we made great progress in our work, and if he writes it the way Cherill and I have laid it out, it could turn out to be a fabulous play. We're going to leave Saturday noon and get there late Sunday or Monday afternoon. So you can stay away over the weekend.

Kisses

[FIG. 49]

After a week, Weill and Crawford returned to New York with a scenario in hand. In early June 1936 all the collaborators went with the Group to their summer rehearsal quarters at the Pine Brook Club in Nichols, Connecticut. Crawford, Green, Weill, and Lenya shared an old house about two miles away on Trumbull Avenue. By the end of the summer, Lenya had claimed Green as her first American affair, and the Group had committed to a full-scale production of Johnny Johnson, *a title derived from the most frequently occurring name on the American casualty list of World War I. But with the company already falling apart, its members suspicious of rumored Communist cells within and choosing sides in disputes between Strasberg and Clurman, it was unable to cope with the musical demands of the play. Strasberg replaced Clurman as director, but by opening night on November 1936 almost half the score had been cut because it either didn't fit Strasberg's naturalistic staging or was too difficult for the actors to sing. Although everyone expected a disaster, it wasn't. Reviews were respectful, and despite the company's disarray, the play managed to run for sixty-eight performances in a Broadway house far too large for its character.*

1937

By the time Johnny Johnson *closed, in late January 1937, the biblical spectacle* The Eternal Road *had finally opened (on 7 January), to enthusiastic response from audiences and critics alike. Brooks Atkinson wrote, "Let it be said at once that the ten postponements are understood and forgiven. Out of the heroic stories of old Jewish history Max Reinhardt and his many assistants have evoked a glorious pageant of great power and beauty." But even sold-out houses could not cover the unprecedented weekly running costs of the huge production (with a cast of hundreds), and it closed in May, after 153 performances. Nonetheless, the composer had had two shows running on Broadway simultaneously for several weeks, and he was no longer a visitor but an émigré. After he and Lenya were remarried in Westchester County by a justice of the peace on 19 January, Lenya went back the same evening to her small but featured roles (as Miriam and the Witch of Endor) in the biblical pageant. A week later Weill set off for Hollywood, arriving on 27 January. His initial contacts had been arranged by his friends from the Group Theatre: Harold Clurman, Stella and Luther Adler, Elia ("Gadge") Kazan, Sylvia Sidney, Clifford Odets (then married to the Viennese actress Luise Rainer), and Cheryl Crawford (in whose New York duplex apartment in the East Fifties Lenya was then living). Odets had written the screenplay for a motion picture based on Ilya Ehrenburg's novel* The Loves of Jeanne Ney, *to be directed by Lewis ("Milly") Milestone, of* All Quiet on the Western Front *fame, and produced by Walter Wanger. Weill was to write the score for the film project, initially entitled "Castles in Spain."*

[FIGS. 50 & 51]

152T WEILL EN ROUTE TO HOLLYWOOD TO LENYA IN NEW YORK, 26 JANUARY 1937

Western Union: telegram in English

WONDERFUL TRIP THANKS GOOD NEWS SEND AFFAIRE JONES LOVE = *SCHNUBE*

152 WEILL EN ROUTE TO HOLLYWOOD TO LENYA IN NEW YORK, 26 JANUARY 1937

Letterhead: New York / Central / Lines / Twentieth Century Limited

Tuesday morning

Dear *Blumi,*

I had a first-rate dinner, read the newspapers for hours after that, went to bed at ten, snoozed a little, then woke up and had just sent for a bottle of beer when your telegram arrived. That was a pleasant surprise. It sounds as if you all were rather tipsy, but I'm happy that everything seems to be going all right as far as the apartment is concerned. Franci [Francesco von Mendelssohn] was really nice during those last few days. But not as cute as a certain *Blumi,* called *die Ameise aus 'Wüüüin'* [the ant from Vienna]. After that I slept through the entire night. I just got up because we'll be arriving in Chicago soon.

Please tell Charles [Alan] to send me a short weekly report about *The Eternal Road*—how business is doing, how the performances are going, and how audiences are reacting. Please buy a few copies of *Cue* magazine with the article about me and send one copy to my parents,[1] together with the big program book [of *The Eternal Road*], and the rest to me. Now farewell, *Blumi.* Many little kisses,

Your *Schnubi*

Chicago: It's freezing cold here, and I'm glad I brought along my coat, especially because I have a swollen tonsil. I just went to a hotel where I'll have a first-class breakfast (of course, never without a newspaper). This is a fantastic city; it looks just like in the early gangster movies.

1. David Ewen, *"Musical Modernist,"* Cue 5 *(23 January 1937): 6–7; 44. Weill's parents had fled Germany for Palestine the previous year.*

153T   WEILL FROM HOLLYWOOD TO LENYA IN NEW YORK, 28 JANUARY 1937
Western Union: telegram in English

WELL ARRIVED THINGS LOOK ALL RIGHT WRITING TOMORROW LOVE KISSES =
SCHNUBE

153   WEILL IN HOLLYWOOD TO LENYA IN NEW YORK, 28 JANUARY 1937
Letterhead: A Hull Hotel / Hollywood Roosevelt / Home of the Stars / Hollywood / California

28 January 1937

Dear *Blumilein*,

So I drifted in here yesterday, January 27(!). There was nobody at the train station except one of the agency employees, who took me straight to the Walter Wanger office, where Milly [Lewis Milestone] and Cliff [Odets] were waiting for me. I started working on the script immediately, and after one hour I had already succeeded in writing a song that will work into the story line brilliantly. It'll be a kind of revolutionary song, but at the same time a love song. Wanger, who is surprisingly nice and cultured, was enthusiastic about the idea and has great expectations for this song. What's more, I gather I'll be able to do all kinds of things in the film, because they've built entire scenes around the music. I was in the office the whole afternoon. Then I took a room at the hotel here; I'll look around for an apartment as soon as I can, but I imagine a small house would be best, because all the apartment houses and hotels are so badly built that you can hear every word from the adjoining room (and of course the radio!).

My first impression of this place is rather awful. It's a miserable village; you can't take five steps without meeting someone you know. The scenery is magnificent, with mountains in the background, like Salzburg. But what they've built into it! It looks exactly like Bridgeport—except New York is three thousand miles away. So far the climate doesn't agree with me. It isn't warm and it isn't cold, and I have constant headaches. But that's probably only for the first few days.

Yesterday I had dinner with Jack and Cheryl; we met Harold in the same restaurant (he has a job already) and Stella (who is not very likable), and [Elia] Kazan.[1] Charlie MacArthur was there, and I sat with him for an hour, which was a lot of fun. Florence's sister was there also.[2] I called Reinhardt, but he was out for dinner with Korngold.[3] Today I'm going to have lunch with Luise [Rainer] (who, of course, is already fighting with Cliff). Tomorrow there's a big gala premiere of her film *The Good Earth*.

I think I have great opportunities here, and it's entirely possible that I'll get a very big contract, because everyone says I have no competition, and they really need people like me. Jack is trying to get rid of the agent that Milestone forced on me and get another, much better one, whom I met this morning. But that will be difficult, because Berg and Allenberg now also have become aware of what they've got in me.[4] [Anatole] Litvak told Wanger that he wants to do *Wuthering Heights* with me, and today I'll see one of the leading MGM people, who seems to be very enthusiastic about me. I'll try to settle on something else while I'm still working on this film here. Because I'm afraid I'll have to spend approximately three months on this film (they still don't have a leading man and will hardly start shooting before another two to three weeks). But you can't get impatient here, that's the main thing. I'm not losing anything, since I can arrange for Chappell to keep paying.[5]

This morning I already got your letter from the day before yesterday, as well as the book. Cheryl is alone here, thank God. The pickax beast is in Palm Springs.[6] I'm happy that you seem to be living the good life, and I envy you our nice apartment by the river and the nice people there in New York. But I instead will be looking around for a little Max[7] this afternoon! I think we should keep the grand piano, no? Then you can practice too! Today marks eleven years since we married for the first time, and now you are a Weillchen for the second time. You just have to have everything double, you *Ameisenblume*. Your letter was very nice, and also the *Sächelchen* you packed together quite nicely; as usual you are most frightful/delightful.[8] Write again soon; regards to all, and take many, many little kisses from your

Schnubi

In case the [marriage] licenses from Armonk haven't come yet, you'll have to write them. In the *New York Post* there will be an interview with me; please send it. When the press clipping book comes back from the Wanger office, please send me [Brooks] Atkinson's write-up from the *Times*. Tell Charles that I talked with Sam Marx about him.[9] He seems to have made a good impression.

---

1. *Jack Wildberg was Cheryl Crawford's attorney. Harold Clurman (1901–80), a founder of the Group Theatre, had directed Clifford Odets's* Awake and Sing! *(1935) and* Golden Boy *(1937). His work after the Group Theatre disbanded included* All My Sons *(1947) and* The Member of the Wedding *(1950). A lifelong friend of Aaron Copland's, he also authored* The Fervent Years *(1945), a history of the Group Theatre. The actress Stella Adler (1902–92) was a member of the Group Theatre, as was her brother Luther; both had studied with their father, Jacob P. Adler. In 1935 she starred in* Awake and Sing! *In 1949 she founded her own acting studio in New York, the Stella Adler Conservatory, which later relocated to California.*

2. *Elisabeth Meyer, daughter of Eugene and Agnes Meyer and sister of Florence, married the filmmaker Pare Lorentz.*

3. *Erich Wolfgang Korngold (1897–1957), son of the eminent Austrian music critic Julius Korngold, had achieved fame as a composer while still a teenager. In 1920 his opera* Die tote Stadt *received unusual acclaim. Reinhardt brought Korngold to America to write the score for* A Midsummer Night's Dream *(1934). After 1935 he scored on average two films per year in Hollywood, including* King's Row.

4. *The agent Bert Allenberg (1899–1958) represented some of Hollywood's top talent.*

5. *The American branch of the English music publisher Chappell & Co. was established in 1935 with Max Dreyfus (1874–1964) as president. Virtually every great American composer of songs and musicals of the era was published by Chappell, and Max and his brother Louis (1877–1966), who had headed the London branch since 1929, were mentors to a generation of young talents, including the Gershwins, Jerome Kern, Cole Porter, and Rodgers and Hart. The two were among the founding members of ASCAP.*

6. *Weill is referring to Cheryl Crawford's companion Dorothy Patten (1905–75), who had been an actress with the Group Theatre; she came from a prominent Chattanooga family.*

7. *A car; see letter 63, note 2.*

8. *In Weill and Lenya's idiosyncratic private dialect, "wiede-niedelich" is a play on the words* widerlich *(repulsive)* and niedelich *(cute)*.

9. *Marx was a story editor at MGM.*

154 WEILL IN HOLLYWOOD TO LENYA IN NEW YORK, 30 JANUARY 1937

Letterhead: Hollywood Roosevelt

Saturday, 30 January 1937

My dear *Blümchen,*

Only a small daily report today. I feel much healthier now, so apparently I've already gotten used to the climate. Besides, yesterday was a glorious sunny day, and I must admit that this place looks truly magnificent when the sun shines. The day before yesterday I had lunch with Luise, who looks really miserable, old and ugly, and is awfully hysterical (Cliff must not have it very easy, but probably he doesn't make it too easy for her either). It's astonishing how these movie people treat such a star, like the lowest shit, talking down in exactly the kind of tone that so annoyed you with Sillman.[1] I think you would have one fight after another here. They're sweet as pie to me. Everyone wants to get to know me, everyone—without exception—knows of my successes (Atkinson's review [of *The Eternal Road*] had been reprinted in the most important paper here). Max Gordon (who six months ago wouldn't have said hello to me) jumped up from his table and ran over to me as if we were old friends. "It's too bad about people."[2]

In the afternoon I worked with Milly, who's very nice. We hope to have the *second draft* of the script finished by the beginning of next week. After that, all we need is a *leading man.*

Yesterday morning Luise drove me around a bit to look for an apartment. Everything is overcrowded. Maybe I'll move way out to the ocean. But that's a bit expensive. In the afternoon I visited Franchot Tone with Cheryl.[3] Of course, a star's house like that (with a *swimming pool,* etc.) is furnished very sparsely and with truly the most refined tastelessness. But he's a charming fellow. In the evening Luise gave me her tickets for the big Hollywood premiere of *The Good Earth.* I took the Queen[?], who arrived yesterday, along with me. The movie's extraordinary in its conception and in many details, and it's astounding that they're doing something like that over here, something so serene, grand, and philosophical. Luise is very good, but a bit monotonous and too conscious of technique, and since Muni is exactly the same, you never get really involved with either one of them.[4] But what a gala premiere! Well, it was the pits. A gathering of unattractive, jealous, ugly people: the men all Jews of the worst kind; the women *"alien girls,"* the very essence of whores, but all of them cold and superficial, just lying in ambush.

There's only one way to get on here: you have to take everything with a great sense of humor and make fun of it (to yourself, because you mustn't show it!), and just enjoy the beautiful scenery and make money. The night before last I was with Max and Helene [Reinhardt]. They're charming. They have a small two-seater that Helene drives herself. Max has wired Paul [Green] that he should send the draft for the film, and I've also sent him a telegram. Everyone tells me that Max runs around everywhere saying I've written the most beautiful music of our time.

Now Livia is coming to fetch me to look at apartments and cars.[5] In the afternoon I'll go to the races. You see I'm living it up. I hope you are too. Cheryl is flying back on Tuesday. I'm glad that you won't be alone in the apartment then. Just now I read that Stravinsky has declined to do *Amphytrion*. Now I'm curious whether they'll offer it to me. Have you already started to work on the *songs*? It's nice to hear that *The Eternal Road* is making such good progress. The only money we'll get out of that one will be your salary. They have not paid a cent of royalties to Reinhardt and refuse to even discuss the question at all. Naturally, they'll do the same thing to me. But at the moment it's more important to keep the show running.

Now farewell, *Blumi*. I guess I'll have news from you again today or tomorrow.

> A thousand sweet kisses from your
> *Frosch*

1. *Leonard Sillman (1908–82) was a well-known producer of Broadway revues, including* New Faces of 1934 *and* Who's Who, *both of which were showcases for new talent. Lenya probably had auditioned for* Who's Who.

2. *"Es ist schade um die Menschen" is a quotation from August Strindberg's* Ein Traumspiel *(A Dream Play; 1901).*

3. *Franchot Tone (1905–68) was a member of the Group Theatre who went on to stardom in films, including* Mutiny on the Bounty. *He was married briefly to Joan Crawford.*

4. *In 1933 Rainer had studied the role of Fennimore for the Deutsches Theater's planned production of* Der Silbersee *in Berlin. Rainer's costar Paul Muni (1897–1967; born Muni Weisenfreund) had appeared in Yiddish and Broadway theater but became a major film star after* Scarface *(1932). He won an Oscar for* The Story of Louis Pasteur *(1936).*

5. *Livia Castiglioni was the daughter of an actress married to the Austrian financier Camillo Castiglione, who at one time had "angeled" several Reinhardt productions. Meyer Weisgal wrote that Livia's job was "to follow Reinhardt about and preserve for posterity his every remark" (p. 123).*

155 WEILL IN HOLLYWOOD TO LENYA IN NEW YORK, [31 JANUARY 1937]

Letterhead: Hollywood Roosevelt

Sunday

Dear *Blümlein*,

Jack Wildberg is flying to New York today; he'll give you the letter tomorrow and tell you everything. Please mail the letter to my parents (11 cents); the Bremen is going to sail on Tuesday.

There's not much news since my letter of yesterday. I still haven't found a place to live. I've seen Francesco's house; it's simply heavenly, but will be vacant only as of February 21. Perhaps then I'll take it. You'll like it too, and you could lie in the sun all day long. I've seen a lot of little Maxes but haven't made up my mind. I'm not doing much work yet. Yesterday I went to see *Camille*. I think it's a very fine movie, and she [Greta Garbo] is wonderful in the death scene. I spent the evening with Cliff and Luise, who are having terrible fights already and who both are extremely neurotic. Perhaps Luise will fly to New York today too and call you then.

Blümlein, in case you haven't already started to paste in the reviews, do send them here instead, i.e., all of the clippings that are in the scrapbook. Then I'll prepare excerpts as I've done with *Johnny Johnson;* that'll be best.

I'll write you in detail as to what Hans should undertake.[1] Don't worry about "E.R." [*Eternal Road*]. Reinhardt told me he heard that Meyer Weisgal is trying to raise some more money. He doesn't think they will fire you, but he says it's possible the whole thing will collapse. (I don't believe it.) If they say anything to you, tell them you'll immediately wire Reinhardt, Mrs. Eitingon, and me.[2] Your position is very strong, because they simply have to maintain a good relationship with me. It's possible they'll fire others and then have you continue as Miriam or give you Ruth. In any case, don't let it bother you; even if it does close, it won't be all that bad, because then you can be with your Jewish flower, still the nicest place to be.

1. Hans, Weill's older brother, was still in Germany but was planning a trip to New York to explore the possibility of settling there.

2. Bess and Motty Eitingon had been generous patrons of the Group Theatre. A Russian Jewish immigrant, Eitingon had made his fortune as a successful furrier.

156 WEILL IN HOLLYWOOD TO LENYA IN NEW YORK, [1 FEBRUARY 1937]

Letterhead: Hollywood Roosevelt

Monday

Blumi,

I couldn't give Jack the letters to take along, because I went out to the Reinhardts' (who have a marvelous house high up on a hill with a magnificent view). I took a long walk with Max. He's worried about "E.R." They're acting like pigs; they haven't paid him a penny and won't even answer his telegrams. They really are a bunch of swine.

The sun's shining here, and it's like a spring day on the Riviera. Work on the movie is slow, but it's quite interesting to learn the techniques of screenwriting. So far I haven't had any inspirations; it's really an entirely new medium for me, and I still feel quite insecure.

You can hardly speak to Cheryl anymore, because all she can talk about are the fabulous offers she's getting and how capable she is. The Group people are furious with her, because she seems to be doing quite a bit of dirty dealing privately for herself and Dorothy. Well, I couldn't care less. I hardly see her, and I won't be going near the pickax beast.

It's so terribly difficult to find an apartment. Everything is overrun with people. Today I'm going to look around again. I don't think I'll take a house. If I could find a nice hotel, that would be much better for the time being.

It's possible that Jack will want to hang on to the reviews of E.R., but it would be better if you would send them to me and tell him I'll excerpt the most important ones, just as I did with *Johnny Johnson.*

Now farewell, *Blümchen*. Because of Hans I'll write again tomorrow.
Bye-bye, you *Pison*.

    Schnubinchen

157 WEILL IN HOLLYWOOD TO LENYA IN NEW YORK, 2 FEBRUARY 1937

Letterhead: Hollywood Roosevelt

2 February 1937

Dear *Blümchen*,

Yesterday I received your letter of Friday. You seem to be having a hell of a lot of fun in your dressing room. Please give the girls my regards.

It's very cool here again. I saw a marvelous apartment yesterday—in a large villa way up in the mountains for thirty dollars a month, absolutely ideal for me—but it had already been rented the day before. Now I want to wait awhile until I find something equally beautiful and inexpensive, because that would allow me to save a lot of money and at the same time be far away from the general scene. I haven't decided about a car either, only went for my driver's license. You can get that here in ten minutes, and it doesn't cost anything.

Hans will have arrived by the time this letter gets there, and I'm glad you will no longer be all by yourself. It's terrible that I won't get to see him at all. But perhaps those business connections he's developing will bring him a little closer to here, and I could meet with him then. They would probably let me go for two or three days. The most important people we could introduce him to would be Eugene Meyer and Motty [Eitingon] (who'll be back on the 9th). I'll be writing to Florence [Meyer] and Bess [Eitingon], and you surely can arrange for Hans to meet Bess even before Motty comes back. I've already talked to Strelsin; you can call him at the Gotham [Hotel] and make an appointment with him, a purely social one at first, for dinner or something like that. I'll write to Maurice Levine within the next few days.[1] You could also call his wife (who's very nice) and ask whether she'd be inclined to invite you over with Hans, so Hans would be able to talk to her husband. One could also ask Jack Wildberg if he has any connections in industrial circles. Motty should put Hans in touch with Bullowa[?]; he is tremendously influential. Most important of all, Hans should immediately send me a detailed letter about his plans, whether he was able to get money out [of Germany] and whether he wants to transfer his business, perhaps by way of an American branch. By the way, as far as I know, Rosamond's father is a very rich and important man; do you think you could talk to her about all of this?[2] That's about all I can think of at the moment. Hans himself will probably bring recommendations, have friends to see, etc. We'll have to arrange it so I can telephone you some night. Tell me an evening when you definitely will be home after the performance. Then I'll call you around ten o'clock local time, which is one o'clock at night for you.

I see very few people here, since they're practically all people I wouldn't want to see in Berlin, Paris, London, or New York either. Cheryl is staying a few more days; apparently she cannot tear herself away from her beloved.

> Bye-bye, my darling. Take care of yourself.
> Love and kisses,
> Knütchen

1. *The industrialist and arts patron Alfred Strelsin (1898–1976) was also one of the financial backers and coproducers of* The Eternal Road. *He purchased and revitalized a number of failing businesses, and Meyer Weisgal recalls that "he was always surrounded by a bevy of beauties" (p. 127). Maurice Levin, the owner of Hearn's department store, contributed $50,000 to the production of* The Eternal Road.

2. *Rosamond Pinchot played the Queen of Sheba in* The Eternal Road *and shared a dressing room with Lenya. In his memoirs,* Voices Offstage, *Marc Connelly remembers her as Jed Harris's production assistant in Thornton Wilder's* Our Town *(1938). After the dress rehearsal of that play she went to her Long Island home for a rest. The next morning she was found in a car in her garage, dead from carbon monoxide.*

158 WEILL IN HOLLYWOOD TO LENYA IN NEW YORK, 4 FEBRUARY 1937
Letterhead: Hollywood Roosevelt

4 February 1937

Dear *Blume,*

I bought a classy Max. After I had almost decided on a new Ford on the installment plan, I suddenly got the idea to take a look at used cars—in the price range of our Buick—which are much cheaper here, and I actually found a 1934 Oldsmobile in excellent external and mechanical condition, a green two-seater coupe, very elegant, with a fantastic motor. It rides like a Buick, and of course it will look much better here to be driving around with a gorgeous car—and it's also $350 cheaper than a Ford. I only paid $200 down and then it'll cost $30 a month, including insurance and taxes.

[FIG. 52]

Of course, life is beginning to look quite different now that this elegant Max is going to arrive today. Now, if only I could also find a nice apartment somewhere in the mountains, so that they could all kiss my ass. But it seems very difficult. There's still nothing in sight. If I don't find anything suitable in the next few days, I'll take a room for two weeks in the hotel here and then rent Francesco's house on the 21st, when it becomes vacant. Since it consists of two separate apartments, I could share it with somebody, which would make living very cheap. I'm thinking of someone like Gadge [Elia Kazan, also known as Gadget], who's very nice and is also alone here, or some other single gentleman. Please talk to Francesco about this, and ask him what he thinks. His house is the most beautiful and reasonable I've seen so far. Too bad it isn't available yet.

Lore[?] sent me a telegram. Please tell her that I recommended Forster right after my arrival here, but they're afraid of his accent and can't see him in this role, as they have someone like Gary Cooper or Frederic March in mind.[1] In any case, it would be too late for this film, because they'll want to start shooting in two weeks. Still, if they don't find anybody else, I'll talk to Wanger again and also look around elsewhere to see if anything can be done.

Many thanks for the mail, *Blümchen*. I was very happy with Paul Bekker's review, because it deals with things that should have been said a long time ago, and it's good that he mentions them, since he is one of the most important music critics in the world.[2] That "queer" party must have been really something. And you right there in the middle. Typical! Next Wednesday there's going to be an all-Gershwin concert, and I've been invited to a party afterward.[3] That will probably be my first Hollywood party. Today I'm having lunch with Gottfried and Salka Viertel.[4] The papers here are full of stories—Luise is supposed to have left Cliff already, just because she has gone to New York. This is the most bourgeois hick town I've ever seen: everyone's gossipy, narrow-minded, jealous. All these stories make Cliff very nervous. Have you seen Luise? She's staying at the Waldorf Astoria.

Please talk to Vannie[?] and see whether he's already gotten in touch with Mr. Oberstein from RCA. This is the man who is supposed to do the recordings of *The Eternal Road*, and I would like them to be done as soon as possible; Vannie should take matters into his own hands and put some energy behind it all. I will also write to him about this.

I imagine that Hans has already arrived, and I hope to be hearing from you today or tomorrow.

> All good things and many little kisses,
> your Knuti

1. *Rudolf Forster (1884–1968), Macheath in G. W. Pabst's film of* Die Dreigroschenoper, *tried his luck in Hollywood, but without much success.*

2. *Paul Bekker (1882–1937) had been the chief music critic of the* Frankfurter Zeitung *before becoming the intendant of the theaters in Kassel and then Wiesbaden. In 1934 he immigrated to New York and resumed his career as a critic for the German-language newspaper* Die Staatszeitung und Herald. *His review of* The Eternal Road *appeared on 31 January 1937.*

3. *The all-Gershwin concerts by the Los Angeles Philharmonic on 10 and 11 February were conducted by Alexander Smallens and featured Todd Duncan singing excerpts from* Porgy *and* Bess. *Both were sold out a week in advance. While playing the Concerto in F during the second concert, Gershwin blacked out for a short time—one of the first signs of his fatal brain tumor.*

4. *Gottfried Reinhardt, Max's son and an important film producer in his own right, was having an affair with the screenwriter Salka Viertel at the time.*

159 WEILL IN HOLLYWOOD TO LENYA IN NEW YORK, 7 FEBRUARY 1937

Letterhead: Hollywood Roosevelt

7 February 1937

Dear *Kleene*,

Was I ever happy when you called this morning! I was just wondering what you might be doing on Sunday, when the telephone rang. And right now—at 2 P.M.—your nice letter and the scrapbook arrived. It's marvelous that Kommer happened to be there when you met Marlene; that warms one's heart after all. Mr. Lubitsch has engaged Kaper and Jurmann for the Marlene Dietrich movie.[1]

You don't have to worry about me getting bored here. You ought to know that I never get bored and that I prefer to be by myself than with that bunch of swine. Of course, I'd love to be out of this hotel by now, and I wish Francesco's house were already vacant. It would be so nice if he could kick those people out. The car is heaven, and I'm driving around a lot. But the weather has been bad all week. Tomorrow I'll order a new suit and a tuxedo (a "*Dinerjaket*," like the one [Eric] Wollheim used to have), because I need both of them urgently, and since you are earning so nicely, I really can afford it, don't you think? Things like that are very important here, and I wouldn't dare go to the Gershwin party in that old tuxedo, when most likely all of Hollywood will be there.

The movie is going very slowly, and I've already found that it will be a tough battle insisting on the few things that show what I can accomplish in the film medium. They won't be much in any case, because it's a completely realistic film, and Milly doesn't have the slightest sensibility for original films that incorporate fantasy. But Cliff is very nice and will help me a lot. He wants to do a film for Luise with me at MGM, which I would like very much if they would let me write a few songs for her—which means, in Hollywoodese, if they pay me a lot of money. But I observe everything here very calmly and with great amusement, with the comforting thought that I can go back to New York and do a new show for Broadway. Last night, when Rouben Mamoulian couldn't wait to introduce me to all the Paramount people, I could see how favorable my position is. By the way, he's very nice.

Hans should use the time here to his best advantage and try everything possible to move to America. Did he already see *The Eternal Road?* He didn't mention anything about it on the telephone. Perhaps he could postpone his return trip and actually come out here for a short time, especially since he already has his return ticket. I really hope that he'll be able to accomplish something for himself. I'll also write to Florence and Levin. I've already written to Motty.

I imagine you're showing off something "aaaawful" with all those [Actors'] Equity meetings. I would love to watch you there just once. Do you make speeches too?

Now I'm going to the Viertels'—mainly for that wonderful drive by the ocean. Tonight I'll be at the Litvaks'.[2]

There's a chance that the movie will go more quickly. That is, they're trying to get Boyer, and if they do get him, they would have to wrap the film up very fast.[3]

Now farewell, *Kleene.* Cheryl won't arrive before Thursday morning (by *train*).

> Many sweet little kisses for you,
> *Frosch*

1. *Bronislav Kaper (1902–83) was a Polish-born composer of popular tunes and film music. Walter Jurmann (1903–71) was an Austrian-born composer and lyricist of popular songs. They began collaborating in 1929. The film made by Dietrich and Lubitsch in 1937 was* Angel, *with a score by Friedrich Holländer.*

2. *Tola Litvak and Miriam Hopkins; see letter 160, note 1.*

3. *The French actor Charles Boyer (1897–1978) became one of Hollywood's most popular leading men in the 1930s.*

Letterhead: Hollywood Roosevelt

10 February 1937

Dear *Ameisenblume*,

You seem to take me for a complete dummy if you think I haven't already bought myself a collar and a tie (I still have a shirt). The dinner jacket came just now; it fits fabulously and looks chic ($45!), the debs will feast their eyes. But I have no desire whatsoever to go to the party; I won't go to the Gershwin concert in any case, but rather with Cliff to the movies.

Sunday afternoon I was at the Viertels'. He's an old fool, and she's a horrible witch. They won't see me again soon. In the evening I had dinner at Miriam Hopkins's; she is quite nice but terribly cold and superficial.[1] It was a typical Hollywood evening, marvelous food on magnificent dishes, etc. Conversation exclusively about Hollywood and movies, on and on, until everyone was plastered, then they sang songs and told rotten jokes. And those were the NICE people! Gloria Swanson was there.[2] She's still very beautiful, but it's a desperate beauty (here they mustn't get old, or they're as good as dead).

I haven't seen anyone since Sunday, only Milly, Cliff, and Wanger. I've realized by now that I feel best here when I'm alone and can go for a walk, read, drive the car, and begin to think about my movie music. Today I rented Francesco's house, and I can move in already on the 18th or 19th (then my address will be 6630 Whitley Terrace, Hollywood). It's a darling house, and I'll surely feel better there. But I'm still reluctant to take in someone else. I had offered it to Gadge, but he came the next day and said he would have his wife come, and that is decidedly too much for me. I'll hire someone for only one or two hours in the morning to clean up and make breakfast. I'd rather eat dinner in a restaurant. That way I'll live more cheaply than in the hotel, even if I don't get anyone else for the house.

Today I got the letter from you and Hans. It would be so good if Hans's Pittsburgh project would work out. Perhaps he can quickly wrap things up in Pittsburgh and come here (as if it were that easy!). But he shouldn't fly. Yesterday another plane crashed here. Such is the land of technical perfection.

You know, when you see the work in the studios, you start to learn to respect Hollywood. It's really fabulous how calmly everyone does his work, and the expert knowledge in every department is fantastic. Yesterday we had a long meeting with Wanger, who really is charming. I made very good suggestions for improving the script and believe that now it will become quite decent, better than most. The song that recurs throughout can't be cut, as it has been built into the action brilliantly.

I wrote to Jed [Harris] today; you'll have to invite him over once (but without Cheryl). I think it's charming that he looks after you like that. I also got a letter from Kay [Swift?]. I don't see Reinhardt at all; he's working with Heinz Herald and Korngold![3]

Many regards to Hans and kisses for you, *Pflänzchen*.⁴

Schnubi

1. *A prominent actress of stage and screen, Miriam Hopkins (1902–1972) achieved stardom through her work with Lubitsch and Mamoulian, specializing in bitchy parts. She costarred with Bette Davis in* The Old Maid *(1939) and* Old Acquaintance *(1943). The third of her four husbands, to whom she was married from 1937 to 1939, was Tola Litvak.*

2. *Gloria Swanson (1897–1983), one of the most famous stars of Hollywood, was nominated for three Academy Awards during her career; Joseph P. Kennedy bankrolled her production company.*

3. *Korngold had adapted Offenbach's music for Reinhardt's adaptation of* La belle Hélène *produced in Berlin (1930) and London (1931). An American version played on Broadway in 1944, the year after Reinhardt's death.*

4. *Pflänzchen, a diminutive of* Pflanze, *literally means "little plant," but it was used to depict fast, sophisticated, young urban women of the 1920s.*

161 WEILL IN HOLLYWOOD TO LENYA IN NEW YORK, [13 FEBRUARY 1937]

Letterhead: Hollywood Roosevelt

Saturday

Dear *Blümchen*,

Many thanks for the mail and your little letter. Alma Maria [Werfel]'s letter is practically illegible. Those poor souls seem to think they'll make money from this show [*The Eternal Road*]. I received a long letter from Louis Nizer with "exact" figures.¹ Mind you, according to those, it really does look hopeless. Notwithstanding the management's terrible mistakes, one sad fact cannot be erased from the record—namely that last week the box office went down from 29,000 to 22,000, which to me is a true sign that there is no real interest in this kind of show on the part of the public. (Of course, one mustn't say this to <u>anyone</u>.) Nizer thinks it could still become a success. Of course he wants to cut the royalties (which they don't pay anyway). In my opinion the whole thing will collapse within a short time, unless new funds are invested and the weekly expenses cut drastically—then the show might have a chance to run until spring. The whole thing is *"deeply disgusting."* Reinhardt keeps behaving like a big flaming asshole. He's furious because he isn't getting any money, but of course he won't lift a finger. He lets Kommer do the negotiating. Since I've been here, I've seen him only once. He's stuck in the middle of a terrible clique ([Ronald] Button [his lawyer], [Ernst] Matray, Herald, Korngold), and it's better not to have anything at all to do with him. He spends his evenings with the Sokoloffs.² Well, to hell with him.

I've found out that the only thing to do is to keep to yourself here. I eat out all by myself every night, walk around a bit, go to a movie, and read my newspapers. This is always the best way for me to cope in such a setting, and it's the only thing that impresses them here, because they all just hate to be alone.

The Gershwin party was *"Hollywood at its worst."* There was a bar with Javanese hula-hula girls, another one with American whores, and one jazz and one Russian orchestra, both of which couldn't play because Gershwin insisted on playing his own compositions again, although everybody (except me) already had an entire Gershwin concert behind them.³ The whole Gershwin clan was very cool toward me, but Mr.

Smallens was overwhelmingly cordial.[4] Milly, Miriam, Lubitsch, Mr. and Mrs. Paley, Dick Goetz, etc., etc.[5] I was glad that I was well dressed, and toward the end I went into the street with the whole Gershwin family just as they brought up my slick Max. You should have seen their eyes pop out. That made it worth the trouble. By the way, here [George] Gershwin comes off as even more of a nebbish.

Thursday I had lunch with Boris Morros, the musical director and a very influential man from Paramount. He's a Russian Jew, very shrewd and not exactly likable, but quite nice to me. He tore *The Eternal Road* to shreds. It must be hell to have to depend on people like that. There's a much better atmosphere in our studio, because Wanger is a decent, cultured gentleman. Right now Cliff and Milly are fighting. The screenplay isn't ready yet. Cliff is making all kinds of difficulties, Milly would like to get started with the shooting—well, the usual stink. Part of the script is very good, but other parts are still weak. It will be a tremendous battle to try and push through a few really good things for me. For the time being I myself don't have any ideas about what I could do with all of this. But I'll think of something, and then there will still be time enough to start fighting for it. Wanger really likes me.

I've seen the screen tests of the Group actors. (By the way, Dorothy was in such a state of nerves that they had to send her home; she was talking crazy and was completely irrational. That seems to be a general Group ailment.) I find the tests very amateurish and believe that any Hollywood actor is better; only Gadge was good and, surprisingly, so was Bud Bohnen. But Wanger is enthusiastic about Luther (whom I find atrocious) and wants to give him leading roles.[6] In any case, they liked the tests, and the Group's contract will be finalized, which makes me happy for the people involved.

I've seen some very good films, which you must see: the [James] Cagney film *Great Guy* is wonderful, *The Plough and the Stars* is very interesting (with a marvelous Irish comedian); also very nice are the Sonja Henie film *One in a Million* and Claudette [Colbert]'s new film, *The Maid of Salem* (is she ever a better *actress* than Phoebe!).[7]

I met Steindorff[?] and mate in a restaurant. My, are they dreadful. I swear I got sick to my stomach—that's how disgusting they were.

Thursday I'm going to move into my house (6630 Whitley Terrace, Hollywood, Calif.). I'm really looking forward to that, and I'm sure it will be great there. I hope the weather will be better, so I can sunbathe on the terrace. It's been raining for days.

Blumi, I've asked the bank to deposit $1,000 in our special account, because that's our savings account. Then we still have over $800 in the current account, and by the middle of March there will again be the $750 from Chappell.—That means we still have $4,000 in the savings account. Are you getting along on the money, and did you save something to buy *Sächelchen*? Aren't you the big earner, with your $150 per week!

I would like to have my recordings here: the four *Dreigroschenoper* records, *Mahagonny*, Lys Gauty.[8] But if you can't get them, I'll borrow them from Cliff.

If you see Francesco's Harry[?], please tell him I went to see his car dealer some time ago, but he had nothing suitable for me and I had to buy elsewhere.

I'm very curious to hear what Hans has been able to accomplish. *Addio, Kleene.* A little kiss on your little beak.

> *Frosch*

Has Cheryl given you my little Valentine present?

1. *The prominent and flamboyant New York attorney Louis Nizer (1902–94) represented many celebrities, including Charlie Chaplin and Mae West, as well as 85 percent of television and film producers.*

2. *A veteran of the Moscow Art Theater, Vladimir Sokoloff (1889–1962) came to Hollywood in 1937, as a sort of male counterpart to Maria Ouspenskaya for Russian character roles.*

3. *George Gershwin loved to entertain at parties. George S. Kaufman quipped that George played material from his new shows so much at parties that by opening night, when the audience heard the overture, many of them must have thought it was a revival.*

4. *Alexander Smallens (1889–1972) conducted the premiere of Prokofiev's* Love of Three Oranges *in 1921, the American premieres of several operas by Richard Strauss, and* Porgy and Bess. *He was the leading conductor of the Lewisohn Stadium concerts for several seasons, as well as the music director of Radio City Music Hall (1947–50).*

5. *William S. Paley (1901–90) was the president of CBS. Dick [William] Goetz (1903–69) was the son-in-law of Louis B. Mayer and vice president of Twentieth Century–Fox at the time.*

6. *Roman "Bud" Bohnen (1894–1949) and Luther Adler (1903–84) were both members of the Group Theatre. Bohnen had played Grandpa Joe in* Johnny Johnson, *while Adler would coproduce and act in Ben Hecht's pageant* A Flag Is Born.

7. *Phoebe Brand (b. 1907) had played Minny Belle in* Johnny Johnson; *she married Morris Carnovsky (1907–93), a leading actor with the Group Theatre, who later played many roles on Broadway. Having played both the chief of the Allied High Command and the psychiatrist Dr. Mahodan in* Johnny Johnson, *Carnovsky was later on the Hollywood blacklist. When Jack Warner learned that Brand had also been blacklisted, he cut out her scenes from* Caged, *which was to have been her film debut, in 1950. She did not appear in film until 1994, in Louis Malle's* Vanya on 42nd Street.

8. *Lys Gauty (1903–93) was a French cabaret and opera singer, for whom Weill had composed "Complainte de la Seine" and "Je ne t'aime pas" in 1934. Her recordings of French versions of the "Barbarasong" and "Seeräuberjenny" had won the Grand Prix du Disque in 1933, while "J'attends un navire" became her greatest success. In 1936 Gauty had written Weill requesting him to write especially for her a song "with an easy refrain," for which she would then supply a lyric.*

162 WEILL IN HOLLYWOOD TO LENYA IN NEW YORK, 18 FEBRUARY 1937

Letterhead: Hollywood Roosevelt

18 February 1937

Dear *Blümchen,*

Just a few lines, because I'm moving today. Imagine, while I'm already busy packing, the owner of Francesco's house calls and says I can only stay there for six weeks, because she's sold it as of 1 April. So in a few weeks I'll have to start all over again to look for something else. Had I known this, I would have taken the other small house I saw, which—just yesterday evening—was rented by Morris and Phoebe. Oh well, such are the heavy blows of fate!—Wanger is providing me with a beautiful grand piano for my house. I engaged a fat Negro lady who comes for two hours in the morning, five dollars per week. I think it will be nice in the house, but it's so idiotic that I'll have to move out again so soon.

Otherwise, little news. As soon as I'm in the house, I'll begin to work on the music for the film. They'll start shooting as soon as they have a *leading man.* My agent insists he will have contracted a new film for me as soon as I'm finished with this *job.*—I'm dying to do *Liliom.*[1] If the Guild is unwilling, I'll try it with Burgess Meredith (don't tell Cheryl!!). It would be really terrific. [Erik] Charell has good ideas, but of course he won't do it, because there wouldn't be enough money in it.

I haven't seen Luise yet. On Monday I was at the Reinhardts for dinner with the Matrays and Sokoloff—obnoxiously boring. Farewell, *Blümchen*.

You seemed a bit impatient on the telephone, but that's only because you are such a gigantic little dumbhead—but niiiice [*nieeeedelich*].

> Many little kisses,
> Knuti

---

1. *Weill had seen Ferenc Molnár's* Liliom *in Berlin in 1928. The New York Theatre Guild had produced it on Broadway in 1921 with Eva Le Gallienne; when ultimately Weill was unable to acquire the musical rights, the Guild produced a revival of the straight play in 1940, starring Burgess Meredith and Ingrid Bergman, making her Broadway debut. Eventually Rodgers and Hammerstein obtained the rights for a musical adaptation:* Carousel, *directed by Rouben Mamoulian.*

163 WEILL IN HOLLYWOOD TO LENYA IN NEW YORK, [20 FEBRUARY 1937]
Letterhead: Hollywood Roosevelt

Saturday

6630 Whitley Terrace

Dear *Pflänzchen*,

It was just like you to send me a telegram to show off because of those *Sächelchen* you bought. You're carrying on as if you were the only new owner of such treasures—while I'm getting a new dinner jacket, and this week I'm also having a suit made (which I need as badly as daily bread, that's how threadbare my suits look).

Since I've been here in this house we've had glorious spring weather. I stay home all day, because the entire house is bathed in sunlight, and next to the room in which I work there's a beautiful terrace, where I go to take in the sun. I like the house very much and am glad to be out of that miserable village. By tomorrow I'll have a maid, and I'm doing everything myself, my bed and breakfast (but I messed up my little coffee today). Wanger has supplied me with a marvelous Steinway, for free. It's too bad I have to move out of this lovely house by 1 April. In some ways it resembles my house in Louveciennes, but its setting is much more beautiful, with a splendid view of the ocean.

Otherwise there's little to report. The script will be ready today. It's much better now, and I believe that musically I'll be able to do a few good things with it. Cliff will try to see to it that I do a movie for Luise with him. And my agent claims that Paramount has told him they'll have a new film for me as soon as I finish this one. Well, well, we'll see.

I went with Milly and his wife to [Otto] Klemperer's concert in Los Angeles (very bad) and afterward to a gambling club. Marlene [Dietrich] was there, but I didn't talk to her. There surely will be a better opportunity later on. In the greenroom with Klemperer was the wunderkind Korngold grown old. I put on my haughtiest face and stayed for only two minutes. All of them are abundantly disgusting.

Paul Graetz died suddenly of a heart attack.[1] After waiting so long, he had finally signed for a very good role in the next Garbo picture. Ironic, isn't it?

Last night I was at Morris and Phoebe's, who also have taken a cute little house. These Group people are still nicer than the others, and they're also the only ones here with whom you can get together once in a while. Only Dorothy is horrible—mean, morose, insecure, and terribly stingy. I firmly believe she's got a screw loose. She's going to a ranch today to rest up for the screen test. I got a very nice letter from Cheryl. Please give her my regards, and tell her I think it's impossible to perform *Johnny Johnson* with piano alone (as they apparently intend to do in Cleveland).

That'll be all for today, *Blümchen*. I'm in a very good mood, because I had to laugh this morning when your telegram about the *Sächelchen* arrived at 7 A.M.

> Little kisses on your little snout,
> Your *Schnube*

My telephone number is GRANIT 2798 (Hollywood)

---

1. *Paul Graetz (1890–1937) was an outstanding actor and cabaret performer who had performed in plays by Kaiser and Brecht in Berlin but was unable to establish himself in Hollywood.*

164 WEILL IN HOLLYWOOD TO LENYA IN NEW YORK, [25 FEBRUARY 1937]

Thursday

My *Blümelein*,

The *Sächelchen* arrived yesterday. The new shirt is fine, the tie is terribly chic, and the *pyjamas* fit well. Next week I get my new suit—a gray one. Won't you be surprised!

The weather is terrible again; it's been raining cats and dogs for two days, and it's ice-cold here in the house. I bought wood, and I sit by the fireplace and freeze, as in Louveciennes. I haven't seen anyone for a whole week. In the mornings I work at home; in the afternoons I go to the studio, then I eat in any old restaurant and go home. Last night I was at Morris and Phoebe's. Bud [Bohnen] did magic tricks, none of which worked. We laughed our asses off. Monday I was at the studio the entire day until four in the morning and watched how the musical director (who's very capable) recorded the music for a new Wanger film (*History Is Made at Night* with Charles Boyer and Jean Arthur, charming). I learned a lot. The atmosphere in this studio is marvelous: upbeat, matter-of-fact, no fights but lots of whiskey.

Terry wrote that she'll talk about the matter [*Liliom*] with her people this week and let me know right away.[1] If they won't do it, I'll try to get the rights myself and do it with Guthrie McClintic and Burgess Meredith.[2] (But mum's the word!)

It's really cute how you always write that I should tell you about Garbo. I don't see her either. You must think that stars are just running around here all the time. Sometimes you do get to meet them, if you frequent certain (especially horrible) restaurants and nightclubs. Karl Freund, the cameraman, has done *Camille* with her.[3] He says she's incredibly easy to work with; she's like a little girl in the studio, well-behaved and obedient, but she also has many ideas of her own.

Today I'll work all afternoon with Cliff, and in the evening there's a dinner with Milly. It's funny how you can live here completely cut off from everything if you arrange it that way right from the start. I'm a bit nervous that we haven't started shooting yet and still have no *leading man*. Next week we're supposed to get started for sure. But there's no use being impatient. Since this is my first time, I simply have to see it through to the end. It dawned on me that I never would have come here if I hadn't accepted this picture.

That's all for today. Be a good girl, love for Cheryl and Hans, kisses for you, and thanks for the Sächelchen.

Don't ever believe that Cheryl has no money. She has a special contract with Wanger and gets $100 per week!!

1. *Theresa Helburn (1887–1959) was a cofounder of the New York Theatre Guild. Her codirector, Lawrence Langner, described her as a "wild-looking woman with nerves like whipcord and power like steel" (Bordman, p. 333).*

2. *Stage director and producer Guthrie McClintic (1893–1961) was the husband and manager of the actress Katherine Cornell.*

3. *Karl Freund (1890–1969) was born in Czechoslovakia and became one of Germany's leading cinematographers before arriving in Hollywood in 1929. Famous for his special effects in Fritz Lang's* Metropolis, *he won an Academy Award for* The Good Earth *in 1937 (and later shot the television series* I Love Lucy*).*

165 WEILL IN HOLLYWOOD TO LENYA IN NEW YORK, [3 MARCH 1937]

Wednesday A.M.

Dear *Blümchen*,

Just a few quick lines, because I have to go to the studio right away. I got the package today; a thousand thanks for everything (the gray pants weren't in it, only the old linen ones from Bridgeport, but that's enough). The smoking jacket is very beautiful, only a bit too long. The weather here is divine, real summer weather, but we're having big trouble with the movie, because Wanger is creating difficulties and we're trying to do the whole thing with another studio (which, however, I believe will be very hard). Wanger says he can't spend as much money on the movie as Milly would like him to, because he thinks the film will be banned in most European countries. Well, it's all the same to me, because I'll get my money in any case, and (*between us!*) I'm not having such great fun working on this film anyhow. The most wonderful thing would be if they'd scrap it altogether, and I could do another movie right away. But they probably won't do that. I'm not getting the least bit upset but am taking a real holiday on my terrace. I'm looking around for a tennis coach and someone to lend me a racket, or I'll buy one.

Just now I got a letter from Francesco, asking whether Curt and Hedi Bois could stay with me for "one week."[1] I must say this is a terrible prospect. I have already refused to let the Group people (who are much nicer) stay in the house here. Besides, it wouldn't look good. Please call Francesco right away; say that I just called and told you I couldn't do it, because I'd just invited some of the Group people to stay in my house and no longer have room—or if you can think of a better excuse, I leave it up to you. He wanted me to send him a telegram, but I would prefer that you take care of it with him.

It was nice to have talked to you on the phone twice the other night. But your telegram said: *"Please call me tonight. . . ."* You seem to have been a bit *confused*. Probably from horseback riding. I think it's quite sensible of you, I mean the horseback riding, because it's probably very good for you. But be careful that you don't fall on your little *Bobo* and break off one of your ornaments.

Dorothy is staying in a sanatorium here until her people come to take her home. All the Group people say she shouldn't go back to Cheryl under any circumstances, because that one will completely ruin her.

> *Addio, Blumilein,* be nice and think of your faithful
> *Schnubi*

1. *See letter 61, note 1.*

166 WEILL IN HOLLYWOOD TO LENYA IN NEW YORK, [3 MARCH 1937]

Dear *Ameisenpflanze,*

What I wished for in my letter to you this morning has now promptly come true. Today Wanger decided not to produce the movie for the time being but to wait until he finds the right all-star cast. The whole production has been called off. You can imagine how upsetting this was—but not for this little smarty. I get all the money as soon as I deliver the music. Therefore, tomorrow I'll begin working out the music, scene by scene. I hope to have everything ready by 1 April. That will be advantageous for me, because payment corresponds to the length of time I work on the film. The agent is now trying to find another job for me after 1 April. If he hasn't found anything by the day I deliver my music, I'll leave right away.

I'm glad that I can now work systematically. I hope some ideas will come to me. It's not easy to write music for a movie that hasn't been filmed yet. But that's what a smarty is for.—Now I'm curious to see if I'll get another job. That would be the ticket, wouldn't it? But even if I don't find something right away, I'm glad that I don't have to spend three or four months on this film.

Milly thinks he wants to drive to San Francisco with Gadget and me over the weekend, but it's uncertain whether I can get away.

Of course, this thing is miserable for the Group people. The glorious contract Cheryl worked out seems to be a big washout. Morris will play Anatole France in Herald's Zola movie, Bud will do another film for Wanger, and Gadget will do another movie with Milly. Before doing anything else, Stella and Luther had their Jewish noses fixed. Herald's ass is sitting on ice; he's waiting to find out if Wanger will deep-freeze him.

Blumi, send me the *3Groschenoper, Mahagonny*, and Lys Gauty records as soon as possible. If you send them immediately, I'll have them early next week, so you don't have to send them airmail. I'll need them when I negotiate with other studios.

Farewell, you *Pison*. Many little kisses,

> *Frosch*

Please, *Blumi*, write a letter to my parents for once. I haven't written in a pretty long time. King George Street/House Wolfsohn

167 WEILL IN HOLLYWOOD TO LENYA IN NEW YORK, [8 MARCH 1937]

Monday morning

Dear *Blume*,

There's not much to report. I'm working diligently on the music for the movie, which most likely will never be shot. But I'm using this as an exercise to learn technique, and I've already found out a few things the others apparently don't know yet. Of course, I could write any old thing and deliver it and take my money. But you know how it is with me, I started to get interested and worked out a genuine and probably very good full score. In any case I'll work on it a great deal in the next few weeks, because I want to get it finished by the end of the month. I've definitely decided to come back by the beginning of April if I don't have a deal for something else by then. That's the only thing to do, because nothing impresses these people here more than someone who decides to leave on his own. However, there do seem to be several possibilities. Today I'm going to Paramount. Boris Morros, the music director there, called to tell me he might have something for me right away, something that would only take me a few weeks, because the movie has already been shot in its entirety. This week I'll also meet with Mervin LeRoy,[1] who's one of the most important producers of musical films, and Wanger, too, wants to talk with me about a new film (he's going to do a very beautiful film about Fifty-second Street from 1890 until now). I hope I get the *records* soon, and I hope Lys Gauty's *records* are among them, because they will be important here.

I'm happy you're doing so well and are enjoying horseback riding so much. Of course, I haven't started with tennis yet, but I feel fine and haven't gained any weight. One eats very little around here. I'm thinking a lot about what play, with a good part for you, we could possibly do in New York in the fall. That *Liliom* affair won't ever come about as long as it's in the hands of those senile mummies from the Guild. I haven't heard from Terry in two weeks, and I'm sure the thing is dormant again.

It surely won't get going before I'm back in New York. I don't give a hoot about Jed [Harris]'s twaddle. When push comes to shove, he'll end up doing some insignificant little comedy anyway. But if we had a property, I'm convinced we would find the money and a producer. Paula says you were a big success in *The Eternal Road*, that theater people are talking about you and you're very popular with the public.[2] By the way, she also said she had read a play with a wonderful part for you. She wants to get it for me.

Luise and Cliff are now acting like secluded lovebirds; you can't even get them on the telephone. What has God wrought! Saturday I had lunch with old [Berthold] Viertel (who's a nice gaga), and I took a walk along the *beach* with him, and whom should we run into, in a rather deserted spot, but Luise and Cliff on bicycles. Of course, they were furious to see me with Viertel, but that's quite all right. Unfortunately she's very disliked here; I haven't heard one person who's had a good word to say about her. But she's a big hit.

Yesterday I was home the entire day; I worked and read and sunned myself. Today I'll go see Dorothy, who is supposed to have lost her marbles completely. Time passes terribly quickly here. Milly is by far the nicest and most decent human being here. Maybe we'll drive to San Francisco over the *weekend*. If I do another film here, you should come over and stay a while; then we could go to the ocean for two weeks here and return by car via San Francisco. What do you think about that? But if you're bored right now, we could do it even if I don't have another movie.

Farewell, *Pflänzchen*. Regards to Cheryl, and tell her I've written to [Marc] Connelly. But she's probably still away.

> Many little kisses,
> Kurt Julian

1. *The director and producer Mervin LeRoy (1900–1987) established his reputation in the 1930s with Warner Brothers' gangster cycle featuring Edward G. Robinson. He produced the* Wizard of Oz *(1939) and received a special Academy Award for* The House I Live in *(1945).*

2. *Paula Miller (1911–66), the wife of Group Theatre director Lee Strasberg, was Marilyn Monroe's constant companion and mentor.*

168 WEILL IN HOLLYWOOD TO LENYA IN NEW YORK, [10 MARCH 1937]

Wednesday

Dear *Blumenpflänzchen*,

Many thanks for your letter of Sunday, which I received today. You don't have to worry about Hollywood. I think I'm being quite clever. I'm working on the music for the film as if it were being shot, so I can show these people what I imagine film music ought to be. Of course, I've caught fire, and I'm writing very good music. I'm convinced it'll cause a sensation, because it's much better than what the others are doing. I'm telling everybody what I'm doing, and they're all beside themselves with enthusiasm. For me it's a very good exercise in a field that's still new to me. For this kind of movie you have to write a much more "symphonic" type of music than for the theater. But I think I've already discovered things they don't know yet and couldn't execute if they tried, because they don't have the musical know-how. I'm working almost all day,

I'm enjoying it, and I have good ideas. Now that I'm at work I'm beginning to realize how good it is that I didn't develop a *social life* here. Because that's why most of the people here can't work.

The agent seems to be quite clever, and it's not impossible that I'll get a *job* at Paramount very soon. I spent the entire day there today and have seen the film in question, a gigantic movie with Gary Cooper that has marvelous images of a sinking ship, slavery, etc. They originally wanted Schoenberg for it (but that seems to be difficult);[1] but it seems I'm too expensive for them (that's actually a good thing). In any case they're very hot for me, and today they even talked about an arrangement whereby I'd work half the year with them and the other in New York (in theater), and they'd also be interested in my theater productions. But that's probably just talk. Wanger told the agent he wanted to do a musical film with me and that I should come to see him tomorrow. I'm waiting for the records, so I can play them for him. All of this looks quite good right now.

I know of nothing else new for today, since I haven't seen anybody. Just buy yourself pretty *Sächelchen;* you needn't put any money in the bank. If the *show* isn't running or you don't want to go on with it, just come here. The weather here is marvelous now.

I saw Antheil recently.[2] He has a hell of a lot of respect for me and apparently has made me a lot of publicity (which everyone has confirmed)—most likely because he wants to act the great Weill connoisseur. His wife—who, by the way, is pregnant—has opened a modern art gallery here, which is very much in style, since snobbery plays a big part around here (she's preparing a big Max Ernst exhibit and expects it to be a great success). As the first social event at their gallery they'd like to hold a reception for me, with a performance of the *Jasager* and a screening of the *Dreigroschenoper* film. I think that would be very good for me, because I'm still too little known here, and everyone would come to that. If you were here, you could do some songs, but it would be easy in any case to arrange a song evening for you.

I'll write Burgess Meredith directly on the *Liliom* matter, because those dopes from the Guild probably won't do anything. I also think it would be the ideal thing right now. Enough small talk. How's Charlie [Alan]? Regards to the girls in the dressing room, Margot[?], Rosy [Pinchot], Charlie, Francesco—and to your *Bobo.*

> Your
>
> *Schnutz*

Thursday morning. Nothing new. My new suit is great, especially with the wonderful shirt and tie from you. Last night I had dinner with the Group people, and then I saw *Maytime*, a charming operetta film. The agent has arranged a luncheon with Mervin LeRoy for today, and in the afternoon I'm going to see Wanger.

> Many little kisses

1. *In 1937, Gary Cooper starred in* Souls at Sea *and* The Adventures of Marco Polo. *Schoenberg had also proved too "difficult" to be commissioned for the score of* The Good Earth, *demanding "complete control over the sound, including the spoken words. . . . The actors would have to speak in the same pitch and key as I compose it in." For a vivid description of his meeting with Irving Thalberg (1899–1936), the head of MGM, on that occasion, see Viertel, pp. 206–8.*

2. The American composer and pianist George Antheil (1900–1959) won a certain notoriety in Paris in the 1920s with the self-consciously modern, machinelike style of his Airplane Sonata (1922) and Ballet mécanique (1925). His Transatlantic was probably the first American opera to receive a major production in a foreign country (Frankfurt am Main, 1930). He settled in Los Angeles in 1936 and wrote the "Film Music" column for Modern Music, as well as a lonely hearts column in the popular press and war analysis for radio. His autobiography, Bad Boy of Music (1945), became a bestseller.

169 WEILL IN HOLLYWOOD TO LENYA IN NEW YORK, [13 MARCH 1937]

Saturday

Dear *Blume*,

Your news about *The Eternal Road* sounds terrible, but Reinhardt has received a telegram from Kommer that looks even gloomier than your report, and I got a letter from Horner, who also is predicting an early end.[1] Reinhardt has decided to sue, and I think he's absolutely right. It's bad enough that these crooks won't pay us, but the way they're trying to get around it is really outrageous. I, of course, hear nothing at all. I've given my agent (Pinto[?]) explicit instructions as to the conditions under which I'd be willing to reduce my royalties from 2½ to 2 percent and have asked him to negotiate with Nizer. That was ten days ago, and I've had no response. Probably Nizer won't talk to anyone. I'll write to Pinto again today. Please don't tell anyone that Reinhardt is suing. He said I could join his suit, and I probably will. But it won't do any good. They've ruined the whole thing in an absolutely criminal way. The premature announcement of reduced ticket prices is the height of stupidity and nonprofessionalism. All Hollywood is laughing about it, and dear Weisgal better not show up around here. Kommer insists that it's a disaster right now but that there's hope it will go better after the 21st. I don't believe it, because a show can't catch up once it's been ruined like this. Well, to us it's all the same, although it would have been nicer, of course, to have a *long run* on Broadway, not for the money but for the prestige. Besides, you're earning nice money, and that's another reason I'm being very careful about deciding whether I should sue. I'm convinced that if I were in New York and could negotiate personally, I'd get my money. In any case I'd advise you not to get mixed up in all those things; just take your money and buy the *Sächelchen* you want, which is more important after all.

Thursday was an eventful day for me. At noon I had lunch with Mervin LeRoy, one of the biggest producers and directors at Warners and a very important man. (He's the one Cheryl claimed had offered her a job for $60,000 a year, but when I mentioned her name, he could barely remember her!) He was terribly nice to me and said—among other things: "*You will have no difficulties because you have the greatest reputation of all musicians.*" His wife (a Warner daughter) is crazy about the *Johnny Johnson* music and would like to do a *Johnny Johnson* film with, of all people, Charlie Chaplin. He's already talked to him about it, and Charlie is reading the play right now. But LeRoy says it takes him months and months to make any kind of decision. LeRoy will probably offer me a film called *The Great Garrick*, which he'll be doing in a few months. In the afternoon I was with Wanger; I played some recordings for him and was just starting to play some of the music for Cliff's film (which belongs to Wanger anyway), when the door opened and—in came Charlie Chaplin. He is truly the most enchanting person I've ever seen; you can sense his genius ten miles away. We hit it off right away. You can't imagine how enthusiastic he was about the music, jumping up all the time and saying, "play that again," and everything he said showed extraordinary understanding. He was beside himself about the opening of the film, where I start with some wild Spanish music with a lot of castanets which suddenly give way to the clatter of machine guns, while the wild music continues.[2] *"That's one of the greatest ideas I've ever heard,"* he said. We were together for an hour and a half, saw color tests for the new Wanger film (*Vogues of 1938*), and he talked only to me. You can imagine how that impressed Wanger. Before Chaplin showed up, Wanger was saying he didn't know whether I was American enough for the film *52nd Street,* but then when I was about to leave, he said, *"Let's get together on '52nd Street,' "* and yesterday he called [Bert] Allenberg and said I should get together with the man who's writing the script. All of this, of course, does not mean I'll get the film. I would really love to do it, because it's a real musical with a brilliant idea behind it and great possibilities. So keep your fingers crossed. Perhaps I could get the film *Souls at Sea* at Paramount, but they don't pay well. I'd do it anyway if I don't get *52nd Street,* because it would be a very brief commitment, so I could keep my weekly pay of $1,250, and the most important thing is that I do a film now, because no Broadway success helps around here if you can't say you've done this and that film. I'm in fact more expensive than all the others. Except for Steiner nobody gets more than $750 a week, so I'm doing quite well with my $1,250.[3] And if I could earn $5,000 in four weeks and have one of the biggest Paramount pictures with Gary Cooper to show off, I'd be very pleased.

Paul Bekker died—and in London, Flechtheim.[4]—*That's all, darling. Be a good girl, much love—*

> Knuti

1. *The Czech-born designer Harry Horner (b. 1910) came to the United States with Reinhardt. He designed the sets for both* Railroads on Parade *(performed at the 1939 World's Fair in New York) and* Lady in the Dark. *He won Academy Awards as the art director for* The Heiress *(1949) and* The Hustler *(1961).*

2. *The Spanish Civil War had started in July 1936. By October 1936 the Fascist insurgents had appointed General Francisco Franco chief of state. Thereupon Franco pleaded for and received help from both Hitler and Mussolini; the well-known bombing of Guernica is one example of the German response. Hitler told his generals, "A hundred percent victory for Franco is not desirable from the German point of view. Rather we are interested in a continuance of the war and in keeping up the tension in the Mediterranean" (Shirer, p. 409). By his continued support of the butchery in Spain, Hitler assured himself of Spain's eventual "benevolent neutrality" during World War II.*

3. *Max Steiner (1888–1971) wrote more than 150 film scores, including* King Kong *(1933) and* Gone with the Wind *(1939).*

4. *Alfred Flechtheim (1878–1937) had been a prominent art dealer in Berlin.*

Monday

Dear *Blume*,

I'm very *excited*. Just now I got a letter from Terry [Helburn]. She had written me quite some time ago, but the idiotic Roosevelt Hotel let the letter be returned to sender. They want to do *Liliom*, but they still have to resolve some difficulties with the rights, so nobody is supposed to know about it yet. She answered every question explicitly. We're trying to find the right person for the adaptation. Maybe we can find someone here. They'll try to get Mamoulian as director and Lederer for the lead (which would be brilliant casting as far as the audience is concerned).[1] But I'll also try to get Cagney. She asks what kind of *royalties* I want and whether a $500 *advance* would be *alright*. So they seem really serious. I hope there won't be any problem with the rights.

I had an interesting afternoon yesterday. From four to ten I was with Grover Jones, one of the finest and best-known *screenplay writers*. (He wrote that wonderful silent film *Virginia Post*—do you remember?—and many others; also *Bengal Lancers*, etc.) He's writing the script for *52nd Street* for Wanger, and it looks like it'll be brilliant. He's one of the most interesting and intelligent men I've ever met, which just goes to prove once again that they make better movies here because they have better people. This man knows the rules of filmmaking as intimately as I know music and Picasso knows painting, and it was exciting to see that those things we like so much in American movies are quite consciously derived from a genuinely philosophical worldview. This man is a typical American; he's fifty years old, has been to New York three times, has a magnificent estate close to the ocean where seventeen people are living—children, parents, uncles and aunts, friends—as well as sixteen dogs and all kinds of other animals, with three swimming pools, a printing press, etc., etc. It really was *"Hollywood at its best."* He would love to do the film with me and completely understands my ideas for musicals. But it seems Wanger has doubts whether I'm "American" enough for this picture. I responded that the "most American" composer, Irving Berlin, is a Russian Jew—and I'm a German Jew; that's the only difference.[2] But I'm not all that crazy about it. If the *Liliom* thing is going to work out, I'll still try to get that Paramount film, which I could do in four weeks, and then I'd be free for this beautiful work.

It's very cold here again; it's been raining all day. I heard from Pinto. He'll see Nizer this week.

> Farewell, *Blume*
> Little kisses,
> *Schnube*

---

1. *Francis Lederer (b. 1906) was a prominent Czech film actor who never reached similar star status in Hollywood.*
2. *The songwriter Irving Berlin (1888–1989) dominated American popular song for five decades. His stage works include* Louisiana Purchase *(1940),* This Is the Army *(1942), and* Annie Get Your Gun *(1946).*

FIGURES

habe ich nach Cäschen
Sehnsucht. Der ist doch immer
gleich nett. Was er wohl
macht. Ob auf seinem Haus-
map nicht doch schon ein
kleines nationales Fähnchen
weht? Hast Du die Berliner
Ztg. gesehen? Das ist schon
allerhand. Da hat man das
Gefühl, es geht Jahrzehnte.
Nun leb wohl Weillchen
und auf bald. Ich wohne
wieder im Splendid. Das
liegt so bequem.
Alles Liebe Linnerl
Ich habe von meinem Namen das Lotte weggelassen
und will statt dessen so schreiben: L. Marie Lenja

Ich das nicht kennen. Dieses Hotel ist so barvelig

1. The second page of Lenya's first surviving letter to Weill, 8 May 1933 (Letter 39).

May 8/42

XVII 31a

THE RITZ-CARLTON
BOSTON

ASSOCIATED WITH
THE RITZ-CARLTON···NEW YORK

Blumi,

I'm just thinking that, in case you don't want another sheep dog you could get one of Kingsley's police dogs. He will be glad to give you one. Moss was very nice and said immediately he would send you another one. He wanted to send you a wire but I told him that I had talked to you. I suppose you got already the

2. A page from Weill's first letter to Lenya written in English, dating from January 1941, when he was in Boston for the tryout of *Lady in the Dark*. The date in another hand in the upper left corner is incorrect; it was added after Weill's death, as was the inventory number by yet another hand. (Letter 213)

3. Lenya's mother, Johanna Blamauer, ca. 1900.

4. Lenya's father, Franz Blamauer, ca. 1900.

5. Lenya as a member of the corps de ballet at the Zurich Municipal Theater, 1916–20.

6. Karoline Blamauer, Zurich, ca. 1918. The photograph was perhaps taken by her mentor, Richard Révy, at about the time he dubbed her "Lenja," inspired by a character in Chekhov's *Uncle Vanya*. Lenya called him "Vanja."

7. Georg Kaiser, the foremost German playwright of the day and Weill's first librettist, 1925.

8. Weill, Lenya, and Margarethe and Anselm Kaiser in Grünheide, ca. 1925.

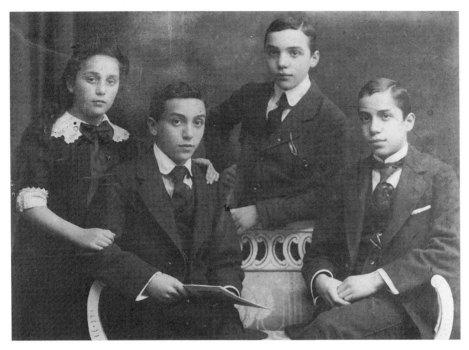

9. The four children of Albert and Emma Weill: Ruth, Hans, Kurt, and Nathan, ca. 1911. (Photo: P. Clasen Studio, Dessau)

10. The Weills were naturists. Kurt and two friends in the buff, ca. 1916.

11. Kurt in formal conducting attire in Lüdenscheid, ca. 1920.

12. Weill's composition teacher, Ferruccio Busoni, in Zurich, 1917.

13. Kurt and Nelly Frank on holiday in Davos, Switzerland, 1924.

Liebeswerben

Dein Herz aus Deinen Augen spricht,
Gesteh es nur und leugne nicht!

7117/18

14 & 15. Postcard from Weill postmarked 13 February 1925, addressed to "Frl. Lotte Lenja geb. Blamauer bei Kaiser, Waldeck 4, Grünheide (Mark) bei Erkner" (Letter 6).

Liebes Herrchen, wir bin'de in Leipzig, aber schön is wieder nichts als das Wetter. Heute abend sin'de wieder in Berlin. Sie oder? Morchen mit— tag seh ich mal an, weil ich Ihnen was erzählen muss. Von Lis— chwein. Ich freu mich auf meinu ... heut abend. Stets Ihr Weile

Fr. Lotte Kluge.
geb. Neumann
bei Kaiser, Wedding
Prinzliche Mark)
bei Berlin.

16. Luisenplatz 3, where Weill and Lenya moved in May 1925. (Photo: Brigitte Taylor, London)

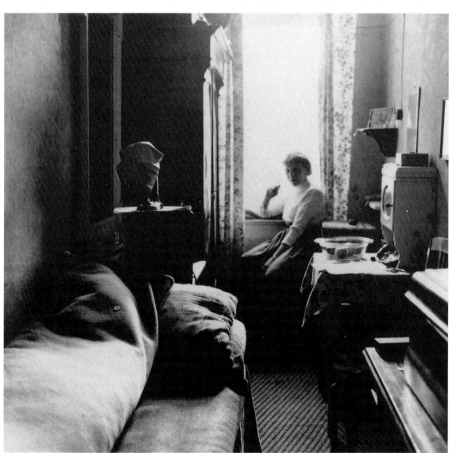

17. The interior of their apartment, nicknamed after a funeral parlor "Grüneisen."

18. The premiere of *Der Protagonist*, 1926: Kurt at the entrance to the Dresden Opera House, with the conductor, Fritz Busch; the intendant, Alfred Reucker; and the director, Joseph Gielen.

19. Lenya joins the Weill family: Emma and Albert Weill are in the front row; Kurt, Lenya, Rita (wife of Hans), and Leni and Nathan are in the back row.

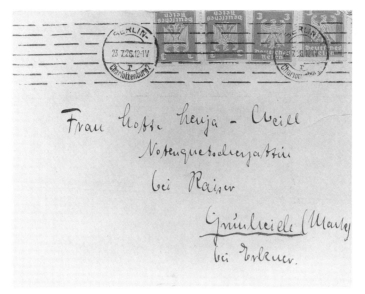

20. The envelope of Letter 16, from Weill, addressed to Frau Lotte-Lenja Weill, *Notenquetschergattin*, bei Kaiser, Grünheide.

Anton Notenquetscher.

——◻——

Ein satirisches Gedicht in vier Gesängen

von

Alexander Moszkowski.

Mit 23 Illustrationen von Philipp Scharwenka.

Vermehrte billige Volksausgabe.
(Zehntes bis fünfzehntes Tausend.)

————

Berlin SW.
Carl Simon, Musikverlag.
1906.

21. The title page of *Anton Notenquetscher*, a satirical poem by Alexander Moszkowski.

22. Lenya and the cast of the *Mahagonny Songspiel* in Baden-Baden, July 1927. Weill is at the far left; Lenya's sign reads, "Für Weill!"

23. Weill as photographed by Lotte Jacobi, ca. 1928. (Lotte Jacobi Archives, Photographic Services, University of New Hampshire)

24. Lotte Jacobi's portrait of Lenya, ca. 1929. (Lotte Jacobi Archives, Photographic Services, University of New Hampshire)

25. Brecht, Lenya, and Weill, ca. 1928, during rehearsals for *Die Dreigroschenoper*.

26. Caspar Neher, designer, librettist, and close friend to Weill, 1931.

27. Peter Lorre and Lenya in Wedekind's *Frühlings Erwachen*, 1930. (Photo: Zandor & Labisch, Berlin)

28. Lenya in the automobile that Weill purchased after the success of *Die Dreigroschenoper*, ca. 1929.

29. Albert Hoerrmann and Lenya in Karl Heinz Martin's production of *Das Lied von Hoboken* at the Berlin Volksbühne, 1930.

30. The conductor Maurice Abravanel with Weill, the director Jacob Geis, and the theater manager Max Berg-Ehlert after the performance of *Aufstieg und Fall der Stadt Mahagonny* in Kassel, March 1930.

31. Lenya as Jenny and Harald Paulsen as Johann in the December 1931 production of *Aufstieg und Fall der Stadt Mahagonny* in Berlin, which ran for fifty consecutive performances at the Theater am Kurfürstendamm. (Photo: Louise Hartung; Atlantic Photo, Berlin)

32. Lenya as Jenny in Pabst's film of *Die Dreigroschenoper*, 1930.

33. The house at Wißmannstraße 7, in the fashionable suburb of Kleinmachnow, which Weill bought as a birthday present for Lenya in 1931, but which they shared only briefly. (Photo: Brigitte Taylor, London)

34. The tenor Otto Pasetti, Lenya's lover, ca. 1933. Hans Heinsheimer recalled, "She took one look at him and whispered to me: 'That's a nice looking boy!' "

35. After Lenya and he were estranged in 1932, Weill and Erika Neher were romantically involved.

36. Weill and his beloved German shepherd, Harras, ca. 1933.

37. Lenya and Tilly Losch in the Paris production of *Die sieben Todsünden*. (Photo: George Hoyningen-Huene; Studio-Iris, Paris)

38. Man Ray's photograph of Marie-Laure, vicomtesse de Noailles, who had sponsored a concert of *Der Jasager* and *Mahagonny* in December 1932. In April 1933, after Weill fled to Paris, he stayed with the Noailles for several weeks while composing *Die sieben Todsünden*. (©Man Ray Trust, ADAGP/ARS, 1995)

39. Weill with his Graham-Page automobile, Salzburg, 1934. (Photo: Reimann)

40. Erika, Weill's maid who remained in Berlin, and Harras, ca. 1933.

41. A great patroness of contemporary music, the princesse de Polignac, *née* Winaretta Singer, had commissioned Weill to write a symphony. Weill wrote, "I'm ready to string her up on one of the pipes of her organ if she doesn't give me my money" (Letter 65).

42. Weill and Natasha Paley in Paris, 1934.

43. External view of Max Reinhardt's castle, Leopoldskron, outside Salzburg.

44. Franz Werfel, Max Reinhardt, and Weill meeting in 1934 to plan *Der Weg der Verheißung*.

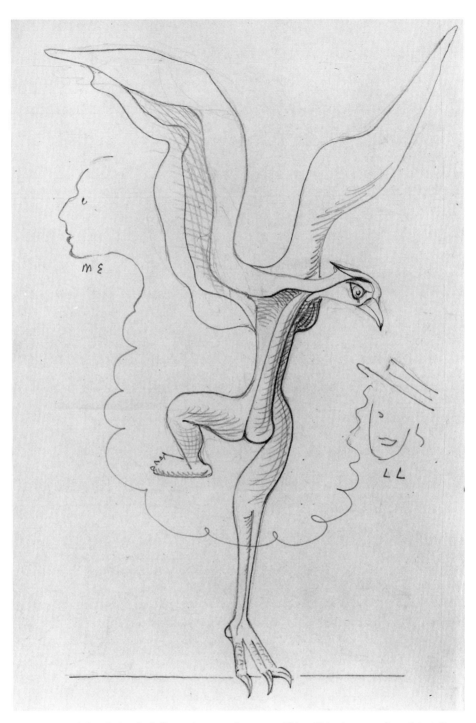

45. Max Ernst's inscription, including caricatures of Lenya and himself, in the copy of René Crevel's *Mr. Knife, Miss Fork* that he gave Lenya in 1935. The book, translated by Kay Boyle and illustrated by Ernst, was published in Paris by Black Sun Press, 1931. (©1996 Artists Rights Society [ARS], New York / SPADEM / ADAGP, Paris)

46. A portrait of Lenya taken in London by Gerty Simon, 1935.

47. Cheryl Crawford, Lee Strasberg, and Harold Clurman in 1932: the three founding directors of the Group Theatre, which commissioned *Johnny Johnson*. (Ralph Steiner Photograph)

48. The author of *Johnny Johnson*, Paul Green,
ca. 1935. (Photo: W. Moulton)

49. The Group Theatre at its summer workshop in Connecticut, 1931.

50. Lenya in the role of Miriam in *The Eternal Road*, 1937.

51. Lenya's friend Florence Meyer, probably portraying the Priestess of the Golden Calf, in *The Eternal Road*, 1937.

52. Weill and his "Max" in Hollywood, February 1937.

53. George Platt Lynes's photograph of Lenya's own "glamour dream," New York, ca. 1936. (Courtesy Estate of George Platt Lynes)

54. A photograph of Lenya from about 1941 that confirms Weill's argument against cosmetic surgery: "Your teeth lend character to your face just as they are and certainly enhance your personality on stage" (Letter 188).

55. Weill, Fritz Lang, and Boris Morros in the recording studio for *You and Me*, 1938.

56. The dancer Marie Eve, Lenya, and Herbert Jacoby, the owner of Le Ruban Bleu in New York, May 1938.

57. Margaret Dale, Danny Kaye, and Gertrude Lawrence in *Lady in the Dark* at the Alvin Theatre, 1941.

58. The success of *Lady in the Dark* allowed Weill and Lenya to purchase Brook House, an eighteenth-century farmhouse near New City in Rockland County, in the summer of 1941.

59. Weill and Lenya with Maxwell Anderson in the living room of Brook House, ca. 1948.

60. Lenya and Evelyn Varden in Anderson's *Candle in the Wind*, 1941.

61. Lenya and Mab Anderson in the Civil Defense Watch Tower, 1942.

62. Lenya's paramour "Wild Bill" Jones.

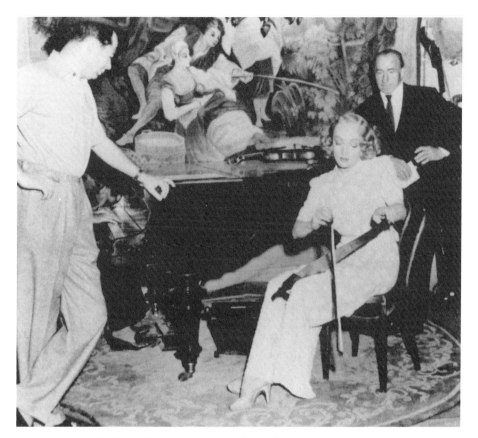

63. Marlene Dietrich playing the musical saw in Hollywood, 1942.

64. Mary Martin as Venus, 1943. (Photo: Vandamm; Billy Rose Theatre Collection, the New York Public Library for the Performing Arts, Astor, Lenox, and Tilden Foundations)

65. The authors and principal cast of *One Touch of Venus*, 1943. *Left to right, standing:* Kenny Baker, John Boles, Cheryl Crawford, and Paula Laurence; *seated:* Elia Kazan, S. J. Perelman, Weill, Mary Martin, and (probably) Ruth Bond.

66. Jo and Thomas Révy in Los Angeles, ca. 1944.

67. The *Firebrand of Florence* creative team, 1945. *Left to right:* Weill; Ira Gershwin, the lyricist; Edwin Justus Mayer, the playwright; and Catherine Littlefield, the choreographer.

68. The Duke and Duchess of Florence: Lenya and Melville Cooper, 1945. (Photo: Museum of the City of New York)

69. Lenya's entrance, *The Firebrand of Florence*, 1945.

70. Brecht and Ruth Berlau, ca. 1942.

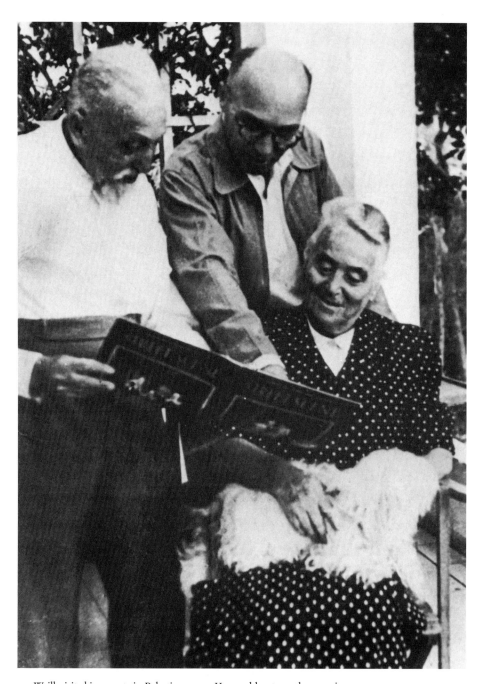

71. Weill visits his parents in Palestine, 1947. He would not see them again.

72. Weill on the beach in Palestine, June 1947.

73. Weill and the Palestine Orchestra.

74. Weill and Alan Jay Lerner working on *Love Life*, September 1948.

75. Lenya seated with her mother and sister, September 1948; Mab Anderson *(left)* and Rita Weill *(right)* stand behind.

76. Weill in his favorite white turtleneck pullover, in which Lenya buried him.

77. Weill's studio in Brook House after his death, 1950.

78. George Davis and Lenya, ca. 1952.

79. The final resting place of Weill and Lenya, in Mount Repose Cemetery, Haverstraw, New York. The musical notation on Weill's tombstone is "Bird of Passage," from *Lost in the Stars*. When ordering her tombstone, Lenya's executor Alfred Rice misspelled her third husband's name (Detwiler). (Photo: Irma Commanday)

Wednesday

Dear *Pflänzchen,*

Opportunities in this place are here one day and gone the next. Last week it looked as if I would get two jobs, and at the moment it seems I won't get either one. Paramount has offered such a ridiculous fee for *Souls at Sea* that the agent simply refused, although it's he who really wanted me to do it. They wanted to pay $3,000 for the entire job, and there's more music than in the Milly film, for which I'm getting $7,500. It's obvious I'm more expensive than all the others, and as long as I haven't shown them what I'm able to do, it will be difficult to get that kind of money. But $3,000 is such an insulting offer it's not even worth talking about it. I would have done it for $5,000. But this Russian Jew, Boris Morros, is trying to show his boss that he can get the best people for the least money. Deep down, of course, he was impressed that I refused. Wanger is inclined to give me the movie *52nd Street,* but he's a weakling, and somebody must have told him my music wasn't popular enough. He keeps going back and forth. At first he told the agent I was the one to do it. Then he was undecided. Then, after Chaplin's enthusiasm, he was in favor of it again, and finally he got scared once more. Then the scriptwriter, whom I saw on Sunday, declared that he wanted to have me, but at the moment he [Wanger] seems to be against it again. It's going back and forth like this, and at the last minute there'll be an arbitrary decision—for or against me. Next week the agent will get me together with other producers as well. If I don't get a job for now, I still hope to set things up so that I can do another film sometime during the year, which in effect would be the same thing.

I hope the thing with *Liliom* works out. The Guild announced in last Sunday's *Times* that they are planning a musical version of *Liliom* and that I am already working on the music. However, I'm a little scared that something like what happened with the Wedekind ballet might happen again. One never can be sure with that bunch of central European swine. I have very good ideas for *Liliom* and already have written down a few things. Do you think you could find a German copy of *Liliom* at Brentano's [New York bookstore] and send it to me?

How are you doing, *Blümchen?* As you will have noticed, I'm a little impatient at the moment, but that will pass, and besides there's no reason to be, because even if I don't do another movie now, we'll still have $9,000 in the bank. I've been very thrifty. A real miser. Only the Max gets the best of treatment, so it'll look sharp when you get to see it.

Many kisses
big and small, your
Schnube

Saturday

Dear *Blume*,

This has been a bad week. First the demise of the Gary Cooper film, then sudden doubts on the part of Wanger—and just now a letter from Terry with the news that Molnár had wired his agent (Dr. Pauker) that he did not wish to have an "opera" made of his *Liliom*.[1] At first Pauker thought Molnár had already given out the musical rights, but it's clear in a letter he just received that Molnár simply does not want *Liliom* set to music. I vaguely recollect that Molnár had the same attitude years ago when [Karl Heinz] Martin had negotiated with him.—This is a catastrophe. But I won't give up; instead I'll try everything to persuade Molnár. Can you think of anyone who has some influence with him?

These last few days Charell has been after me constantly because of *Liliom*. He offered to finance the whole thing, while still letting it run under the Guild's name. He seems very hot for it. But Terry wrote me that the Guild would not want to work with Charell. Now he's left for New York and told me he'd like to talk to Terry (of course, I haven't told him about Terry's disinclination). He says he's convinced that he could get the rights, especially since he's going to Europe on 21 April and could talk to Molnár personally. Now I'll try to get the two of them together (Terry and Charell), because I'm convinced it would all work out if they could agree with each other. It all depends on making it clear to Molnár that I want to do not an opera but a play with music. In any case, Charell will probably call you; please be nice to him (he thinks you don't like him, and he supposedly gets along better with me than with you). If Terry were willing, he could be extremely useful in this matter. In either case I'll work out a battle strategy in the next few days and figure out how to wage an all-out campaign against Molnár.

I just saw Wanger. It was so disgusting you can't possibly imagine; I wish one could afford to spit in the face of someone like that. He says: *"I'm afraid your music isn't popular enough for this picture."* I say: *"You heard what Chaplin said."* He: *"Yes, but Chaplin also said your music is distinguished and I don't want distinguished music."* I: *"What do you want?"* He: " 'Ich küsse Ihre Hand, Madame' *or* 'Zwei Herzen im Dreivierteltakt.' "[2] I: *"I can write you as popular songs as these, but better."* He: *"To hell with better, I don't want better."* What can you say to that? He's scared to death because of the Fritz Lang film, and now he only wants to cater to the very lowest denominator. He says he wants to talk to me one more time, and I'll dig out the worst things I've written and play them for him, but he'll probably end up with [Werner Richard] Heymann (who perhaps is behind all of this). As long as I can't find people who are really interested and want something a little bit better, there really is no use. I'll now do everything possible to get to know such people. My music for Milly's film is almost finished in sketch, and I think I can deliver it on 1 April. In any case I'll stay here for a few weeks after that, even if I haven't found anything, and devote my time exclusively to meeting people and working on them. This has always been the only way for me to achieve anything, and here I have to do it again. I believe that I can succeed here, but it will be the same struggle as everywhere else.

The idea that Cheryl should go it on her own comes from me. I wrote her that two weeks ago already. I'm convinced she could become one of the most successful producers in New York, and I would prefer to work with her—if she were left to her own devices and no longer dependent on that hysterical Group. Please tell her I absolutely would love to do a play with her. I'll write to her as well.[3] Perhaps you could talk about the *Liliom* business with her, too; she'll know about it anyway through the newspaper. She could be very helpful in keeping Terry's interest alive, and making it clear to her that we mustn't simply give up after the first try. But Terry should not get the idea that Cheryl is trying to butt in. Perhaps it's better to keep her out of the game. But Cheryl will understand how important this thing would be for me, and she wouldn't do anything that could do it harm.

I'm not at all discouraged by all these setbacks. My nerves are very well rested, thanks to the completely quiet life I've been leading here for weeks now, and of course the fact that we're financially secure for the time being makes one feel much freer and calmer. If I don't do a movie now, I'll work with all my might to prepare one or two theater projects and then return here later in the winter. One can always find some kind of job here.

How are things for the *Ameisenblume*? Are you careful when you ride horseback? Livia [Castiglioni] plus horse fell down a slope yesterday, but it's typical that the horse is dead while nothing happened to her.

Perhaps tomorrow I'll go see Milly, who lives two hours from here in the mountains.

> Farewell, *Pflanze*
> A thousand kisses, your
> Knute

1. Although *Liliom* was a failure at its premiere in Budapest in *1909*, ten years later it was widely performed and became the most famous work of the Hungarian playwright Ferenc Molnár (*1878–1952*). Dr. Edmond Pauker (*1887–1962*) was born in Budapest and came to the United States in *1922*; he served as the American literary agent for Molnár and Vicki Baum. He obtained the American rights for Die Dreigroschenoper *and in 1954 tried to stop production of the Marc Blitzstein version at the Theatre de Lys in New York.*

A notice in the New York Times (*9 May 1937*) reported: "Mr. Weill has also been keen to score a musical version of Liliom *and, so far as he knew last week, everything was settled between himself and the Theatre Guild. He had done a good deal of preliminary work on it, along the lines of* The Threepenny Opera. *But the unhappy news is that Ferenc Molnár does not want his play set to music and that is that.*" Weill had similarly had to abandon plans for a ballet based on Wedekind's Kaiserin von Neufundland *when the rights could not be cleared.*

2. "Ich küsse Ihre Hand, Madame" (I kiss your hand, Madame) *was one of Richard Tauber's signature songs, with music by Ralph Erwin and lyrics by Fritz Rotter. "Zwei Herzen im Dreivierteltakt" (two hearts in three-quarter time) was an extremely popular song by Robert Stolz (*1880–1975*), which became the operetta* Der verlorene Walzer.

3. Weill wrote to Crawford: "Don't worry. Hollywood won't get me. A whore never loves the man who pays her. She wants to get rid of him as soon as she has rendered her services. That is my relation to Hollywood (I'm the whore)" (Crawford, p. 99).

Monday

Dear *Blümchen,*

I just received your letter of Friday. How odd that there are no performances at all for four days this week. I've seen the ads they're putting out: seven hundred seats for $1, a thousand seats for $1.50—this looks suspiciously like bankruptcy. What they are doing is simply horrendous.

Yesterday I took a wonderful drive through the mountains with Herald. You go high up and suddenly the ocean lies before your eyes, and then you go down a magnificent road, as if you're driving from the Maritime Alps toward Nice. Herald was very nice. I talked to him at length about *Liliom.* He had a good idea: he would talk to Géza Herczeg, who is a good friend of Molnár's and certainly would help me.[1] Just now he called and said he had a long talk with Herczeg and that the matter looked hopeless. Molnár has turned down not only some of the lesser composers but also Puccini(!), [Franz] Lehár, and [Emmerich] Kálmán to compose *Liliom,* because he deems it his most important work, which is supposed to immortalize his name only. Herczeg thinks I should write to him (Molnár) directly in any case, but he didn't hold out much hope. It seems that once again we can bury a dream. But eventually I'll find something else. This week I'm meeting [Jacques] Deval, and perhaps he'll write something for me. Personally, I'm taken by a very wonderful idea for a play that I want to discuss with Irwin Shaw, who is very talented, I think (*Bury the Dead*).[2] I also want to talk to somebody about the idea of "The Goddess of Justice," something I had worked on before with Franz [Hoellering]. Then there are the two subjects that Cheryl has. Besides, I could also ask Terry whether she might find something among various plays that the Guild has done successfully, perhaps by [George Bernard] Shaw or maybe [Georg Kaiser's] *Von morgens bis mitternachts.*

There's nothing else new here. Now I'll go to see Allenberg and inform him that I'll give him until 15 April to find me something. If he doesn't find anything at all, I'll leave on 15 April. I'm now writing the *score* for the picture, and I think I'll be finished with it by 1 April. The weather has been very bad for two weeks now, and it's icy cold. The perpetual California sunshine seems to be a fairy tale. I wrote a nice letter to Cheryl. She's probably so depressed because of the Group, but there's no help for them. If I should find another *job* here (which I would like, now that *Liliom* isn't working out), you should probably come here with Cheryl. You'd like it here, it's gorgeous country.

I hope you can somehow recuperate from that not so very *"eternal"* road.

Many little kisses, your
Knut

1. *Ferenc Herczeg (Franz Herzog; 1893–1954) was the author of several plays and novels. Weill often referred to Hungarians by the generic "Géza" or "Béla."*

2. The works of Brooklyn-born novelist and playwright Irwin Shaw (1913–84) are marked by social awareness and dramatic intensity. Bury the Dead (1936) was his first successful play.

174 WEILL IN HOLLYWOOD TO LENYA IN NEW YORK, [25 MARCH 1937]

Thursday

Dear *Blümchen*,

Many thanks for your letter of Monday. I hope you've taken advantage of your days off to recuperate a bit. Today I read in the newspaper that two thousand people attended the Sunday matinee and that the show will be safe until the end of April because of a large number of benefit performances. Maybe they'll be able to drag it through the summer.

I'm doing fine. The sun is finally shining again today after it rained for days—and this place isn't made for that. You're right that it makes no sense to keep on fighting out here. Someday they'll probably come around, and at the moment I really don't need them. I think my attitude is the right one for this place. Evidently there's a lot of talk because I'm not being seen anywhere, and that seems to impress them. The agent says he's absolutely sure he can work out something for me, but he wants to wait until something really first-class comes along. But I won't waste my time or lose any sleep over it. I hope to be able to deliver my music by the end of next week, and then it will take another week until I get my money, so I'll be leaving on approximately 15 April, unless I've found something very good in the meantime.

At the moment I'm totally mesmerized by the events in Spain [the Civil War]. André Malraux is here.[1] He's the great French writer (*La condition humaine*) who went to Spain to fight on the side of the Loyalists and founded the air force, which just now has been decisive in winning a battle. The day before yesterday I went to his *mass meeting*, and yesterday Salka Viertel gave a party for him. It was exactly as it had been with Chaplin: he talked only to me. That is how people like us triumph here: water finds its own level. Of course, he knows every note I've written and said, "Just recently I heard your great masterpiece *L'Annonciateur* again." I said I didn't know what he meant, that that wasn't one of my works. Finally it turned out he meant *Der Jasager*, which he personally had translated with that brilliant word. He spoke of incredibly interesting things in Spain, and it gives you the urge to drop everything and go there and get involved. He has gotten quite a bit of money together here to get some medical help and to get the children out of Madrid.

I met Mamoulian at the party. He was enthusiastic when I told him about the *Liliom* idea and said we absolutely would have to get Molnár's permission. I haven't done anything further in that matter, but I think I'll send off a detailed telegram to Molnár.

But something else has happened that's very interesting. Sam and Bella Spewack, the authors of *Boy Meets Girl*, were there and came straight over to me. Only after listening to these people do you realize what kind of success I've had. They have fantastic offers for a musical in New York and want to do it with me. They have pretty high standards and—as they say themselves—are in that typical situation where their weakest play was their biggest success. If we can agree on a collaboration, they will start work on 15 April and refuse everything else. They have great respect for me because they asked Wanger whether he would engage me for their movie *Vogues of 1937*, and he told them there was no way I would do that, he wouldn't even dare to offer it to me. I'll see them the day after tomorrow. I think this is a big opportunity, because they've had a recent success—just as I have—and they're the up-and-coming figures, not the old Broadway hacks, which is probably why they want to work with me. Well, we shall see.

Friday I'm going to have lunch with Luise at the studio. Saturday lunch with Salka Viertel and Gottfried [Reinhardt]. I'm doing both of these because my agent insists that MGM is very interested in me, and they pay the most.

So now you know everything again, little *Blumenpflanze,* and I can go on painting my little notes of music. I have done a very good score for this film. I'm calling it *The Unrecorded Symphony.*[2]

> Many little kisses, your
> *Schnüberich*

I beg you to notice the distinguished linen paper, 25 cents a pad!

I'll move to a hotel when I have to get out of this house, probably to the Beverly Wilshire (where Marlene lives!).

1. The French writer, art historian, and politician André Malraux (1901–76) went on to become France's minister of culture in 1959.

2. In the studio copyist's final piano version of the score there are forty numbered entries. It contains borrowings from Der Silbersee, Der Kuhhandel, *and* Marie Galante.

---

175 WEILL IN HOLLYWOOD TO LENYA IN NEW YORK, [28 MARCH 1937]

Sunday

Dear *Blumenblümchen,*

How are you? I haven't had a letter from you for several days, and I imagine that maybe you took a little trip on your days off. According to everything one hears around here, the show seems to be doing very badly, and they think it will hardly last beyond the end of April. The so-called management insists on having Reinhardt come to the hundredth performance on 3 April. I don't know what good they can expect from that. Meanwhile, they owe me (i.e., Heugel and me) over $1,000, but of course they wouldn't think of paying it. The whole enterprise is a self-inflicted financial disaster.

There's a lot of news to report from here. On Thursday I drove with the Matrays to Santa Barbara, where the Reinhardts were spending a few days. It's a heavenly place by the ocean, set among hills, more beautiful than any place on the Riviera. In the evening we drove back in bright moonlight. On Friday I had lunch with Luise and watched her work for a little while. She really is quite talented, the way she notices right away what's good or bad for her and then insists they change things and rehearse until they get it right. She was shooting a scene with Powell.[1] In the evening I went to Klemper-er's concert with her. She talks only about her woes with Cliff, and to listen to her, it would seem theirs is a truly Strindbergian marriage. But you can only believe half of what she says, and anyway it's quite uninteresting.

Yesterday morning I got an unexpected call from Wanger, saying he wanted to see me. I went there, and he gave me the script to the movie *Vogues of 1937*, which he's shooting in color right now. The Spewacks wrote the script, and they seem to be very much after him to get me to collaborate on it. They want me to compose music for a big fashion show in revue form, which would take up approximately one-fourth of the film, as well as some parodistic music that would run throughout the entire film. Wan-ger was terribly nice because he heard that MGM is interested in me. This really seems to be true. Allenberg is convinced that we can sign with MGM. That would be good, because they pay the most and have the most wide-ranging possibilities. Besides, the Spewacks have told Wanger they want to do a musical with me, and he told them im-mediately that he would finance it.

Then I spent the entire afternoon and evening with the Spewacks. They're charming people; you'll like them a lot. The wife has something of Madeleine Milhaud. We worked out a wonderful plot, and all three of us are very enthusiastic: a play about the refugees. It starts in the Mannheim Opera during an opera rehearsal, which suddenly is interrupted by a Nazi who fires everyone because they are non-Aryans. They all immi-grate to New York, and we will show their adventures there, with a lot of humor, of course, but, for example, there's also a scene in which they receive a letter from one of their friends in Mannheim who is no longer alive when the letter arrives. In the end, one of their friends from Germany comes to tell them that everything has been ar-ranged so they can come back, but they tell him they do not want to return, and at the very end they perform the opera they once had rehearsed in Mannheim in a little movie theater in some small town in America. Isn't that a marvelous subject? I'm sure they can write in a part for you; that is, I would like to *team* you up with Curt Bois (whom they'd like to have in the show). And do a terrific song for you.

Of course, I'm all fired up about this. The Spewacks are going back to New York on 15 April and then would want to work with me. If I do get *Vogues*, I'll tackle it just the same, because it would be quick and easy money. But with Wanger it's very uncertain whether I'll get it. I'll try to get a contract for two films a year with MGM, which would enable me to do this play first.

What do you think, *Blumi;* if I do another film, wouldn't you want to stop perform-ing and come here instead? It all depends, of course, on whether you actually prefer performing. It probably will be very beautiful here now; we could live by the ocean, and you could relax and rest. Think about it, and when I know whether I'm doing the movie, we can decide. A thousand little kisses for you,

Your *Schnube*

---

1. *William Powell and Luise Rainer were filming* The Emperor's Candlesticks. *They had also costarred in* The Great Ziegfeld, *the MGM movie for which Rainer won her first Academy Award. She received her second Oscar for* The Good Earth *a year later, but then her career trajectory plummeted.*

Wednesday

Dear *Blümchen,*

There's not much to report. Wanger still can't make up his mind whether he wants me to do *Vogues.* I'll see him again today. He's a complete fool, and that's the way he is with everybody. Tomorrow I'm going to MGM with my agent, and by the end of the week I hope to find out where I stand. Tomorrow I have to get out of this house, and I don't know quite yet where to go. Probably I'll just take a room in a hotel or a small apartment in an *apartment house.* I spent an evening with Spewack. He said he felt very good about the play. Around the middle of April they'll go to New York and start getting their farm in Pennsylvania in order, and then they'll begin working on it. He really seems to want to do it, because he's telling everybody about it. But I must make sure to keep after him, since all the composers—especially Gershwin—want to work with the Spewacks. Gershwin seems to be shitting in his pants because of me. Yesterday there was a Hungarian goulash *party* at Herczeg's. The Reinhardts were there with their entire entourage. Day after day they're with the same people: Korngold, the Sokoloffs, Herald, the Castiglionis. Tonight I'm going to the Reinhardts' for dinner with Dieterle and the Buttons [Reinhardt's lawyer].[1] Herczeg thinks it will be impossible to get *Liliom,* but there may be other plays by Molnár just as suitable for me that he would be willing to give me right away. He told me the story line of *Heavenly and Mortal Love,* which seems to be very beautiful, and he suggested I also read *The Glass Slipper.*—I'm glad that Cheryl is working on the "Gentle Crafte"[?] project, because I think it's very promising. I got a letter from her too.—I'm now making the fair copy of the movie music, and my right arm is hurting from all that writing. It's so stupid that I have to get out of this house; naturally it won't be this quiet anywhere else. Reinhardt seems to want to go to that hundredth performance in New York. Weisgal called him and told him that Francesco is drunk all the time. In the event that I do another movie, you could come back with Reinhardt and bring along all the papers from Moses [immigration lawyer], so that we could immigrate from Mexico. A letter from Charles came, with a devastating report of the show's condition. Now farewell, *Pflänzchen,* and many little kisses for you. I'll wire you my new address.

1. *German-born film director William Dieterle (1893–1972) would eventually direct Wanger's film* Blockade *(1938), what "Castles in Spain"/"The River Is Blue" became after Weill's, Odets's, and Milestone's contributions had been rejected. Among his dozens of film credits are* The Life of Emile Zola *(1937) and* The Hunchback of Notre Dame *(1939).*

Western Union: telegram in English

MOVING THURSDAY TO HOTEL KNICKERBOCKER HOLLYWOOD LOVE AND KISSES = UNSIGNED.

SEND QUICKEST WAY POSSIBLE YOUR BEST PHOTOS FOR MOTION PICTURE TRYING TO
INTEREST SOMEONE IN YOU KISSES = UNSIGNED.

Friday

My dear *Blume,*

For a few days I've been without news from you; probably there was a letter from you yesterday but I didn't get it because of the move. I have moved into a very nice big hotel, a little like the St. Moritz. All rooms have a kitchen with a little dining room, bath, and dressing room. It was most sensible to move to a hotel at this point and not get tied down with an apartment, as long as I don't know what's going to happen. Nothing's going to happen with *Vogues.* The idiot won't say yes or no. And I won't go there anymore unless he calls me. Yesterday I was at Metro, and I'm going there again today to play my music for them, because they don't have the faintest clue. The agent thinks they'll offer me a six-month contract, but if they do, I doubt very much I'd take it. I won't if this thing with the Spewacks turns into something, because after a real Broadway hit I could make as much money with one film as I could now with a six-month contract.

Just now, Elisabeth Meyer (Florence's sister) called and asked me if I knew of a European actress (with an accent) for a role at Selznik [*sic*] International. Of course, I recommended you right away. She's seen you only once (at the Gershwins') and didn't know much about you.[1] I told them you were the Luise Rainer type, and just as good an actress; for certain things even better. They were thinking about Dolly Haas (who, however, is under contract elsewhere) or Franziska Gaal.[2] If they like your pictures, they'll have you come out for a *test.* I don't know if anything will come of it, but in general I'm convinced you have a good chance. If (now or later) you're here with me for a longer time, we'll make a good test and my agent will work for you. In any case send a *registered letter* (Cheryl should help you with it) to Goldsmith[?] saying you consider the contract with him terminated, since every contract automatically expires if the agent has not closed a deal within four months. But leave Jack Wildberg on the sidelines! Don't say anything to Florence.

Oh, gee, I have to go. It would be very nice if you could come here. Many, many little kisses,

Your *Mordspison*

1. *Welles reports that at one of the Gershwins' parties in New York, George had confessed to Kurt how much he liked the Telefunken recordings of* Die Dreigroschenoper, *except for the "squitchadicka" hillbilly voice of the leading lady; Lenya overheard the remark and never forgave him.*

2. *The Hungarian cabaret, stage, and film actress Francisca Gaal (1904–72) at one time was married to Felix (Joachimson) Jackson, the librettist of Weill's* Na und?

178 WEILL IN HOLLYWOOD TO LENYA IN NEW YORK, [5 APRIL 1937]

Monday

Dear Liiiiinerl,

It's just like you to have no pictures right at the moment you need one. I hope you get some very soon and can send them at once by *air mail special delivery.* I'll take them immediately to Madam Meyer when they arrive.

There's nothing new. I was at the Spewacks' on Saturday. They're really very nice people. They're furious with Wanger because he didn't engage me for *Vogues.* Of course he took the cheapest, lousiest "*songwriters*" he could hunt up.[1]

I believe my chances of finding another *job* here are very slim. I saw the musical director of MGM. He spoke about me in tones that made me blush like a virgin. I'm apparently somebody they need badly; I would knock out all the others because I'm definitely a "*heavyweight.*" (He knew everything about me through Sternberg, who actually had talked of no one except me for months.) But he doesn't know whether he can push me through with the producers, because I'm not well known enough yet and because they have a gigantic music department. When my agent said I was a very good friend of Luise's, the man said Luise was close to Wachsmann and had insisted that he write songs for her next film!!![2] The agent thinks that MGM might offer me a one-year contract at approximately $600 per week for forty or fifty-two weeks. This, of course, is not a good salary, but he believes I couldn't get more at this time unless a producer or director insisted on having me. It would be a very difficult decision if I were to get such an offer, because I absolutely want to do a show for New York, and my position here would be totally different if I had a real success with a "*musical*" in New York (the agent admits that). I would try to get it down to six months and start only in the fall, or two months now and four months in the fall.

My music is ready, and I'll use the time I'm still here to meet with people and take a look around the country a bit, especially since the weather is very beautiful now. If I don't get anything I'll drive back in about two weeks and will have to find someone to ride with me.

Today I got a *ticket* for running a *stop* sign. I'll pay a pretty penny for that.

Farewell, *Blume.* Be nice and behave yourself, even though it ain't easy for ya.

> Little kisses,
> Your *Birühmti*

Please always take a taxi when you go home late at night.

1. Vogues *(originally titled "Vogues of 1937," then "Vogues of 1938") starred Warner Baxter, Joan Bennett, and Hedda Hopper and featured music by Sammy Fain and Lew Brown, including the song "That Old Feeling."*

2. *German-born Franz Waxman (originally spelled Wachsmann; 1906–67) had settled in Hollywood in 1934 and studied*

briefly with Arnold Schoenberg. His numerous film scores include Rebecca *(1940) and* Rear Window *(1954), as well as* Sunset Boulevard *(1950), for which he won an Academy Award.*

179T WEILL IN HOLLYWOOD TO LENYA IN NEW YORK, 6 APRIL 1937
Western Union: telegram in German

AM ALSO LONGING FOR YOU AND WOULD LIKE TO SEE YOU SOON MANY KISSES = WEILL

179 WEILL IN HOLLYWOOD TO LENYA IN NEW YORK, [7 APRIL 1937]

Wednesday

My dear *Rosenblümchen,*

Your phone call was very nice. I can imagine that you often feel quite alone with me being gone so long. What do you think of the following plan: you take a three-week leave of absence from the show, come here next week, and stay with me for one week. If I get a *job,* we'll write Weisgal that you won't be coming back. If I don't get anything, we'll drive back together. Of course, I would love to make the trip back with you, because I know how much fun it would be for you to drive in that beautiful car and see the whole country. And the return trip would not cost anything because I get reimbursed for it, and for the cost of a railway ticket the two of us can comfortably go by car. When we get back, there are two possibilities: either they'll pay me my royalties, in which case it doesn't matter whether they take you back, or they won't want to pay, in which case they'll take you back in order to keep on friendly terms with me.

I think we shouldn't be too miserly. After all, when I get my money here, we'll have almost $9,000 in the bank. Chappell keeps on paying me (they've just sent a check), and in the fall I'll have one or two shows in New York. So there's no reason for you to keep performing if you're not having fun or if you want to join me here.

Things here are going very slowly, but it's no use getting upset. I now know quite clearly what the situation is like here. For background music they don't pay very much, and for *musical pictures* my name is not well known enough yet, and it's also too good. The best thing would be if one of the *producers* personally would be interested in me, like Milly, or several others as well. I haven't heard anything from MGM as yet. Of course, that's partly because the agents are so terribly slow. But I must definitely wait to see what happens with MGM before I leave.

It's very important that I not neglect the Spewacks. They are awfully nice to me. Tomorrow I'm going away with them for two days to talk about the play, somewhere in the desert. That will probably be very nice. Too bad you can't be with us. I'm almost certain I'll get the play from them when I go back to New York, and that would be the greatest opportunity for me. And I'm also certain that something will develop here for me in the course of this year, even if things don't work out right now. Therefore don't worry, *take it easy,* and if you like my plan, talk to Weisgal right away and come here soon. Take a *bedroom* to Chicago and from there a *compartment,* which costs approximately $150. And bring all the papers from Moses with you, so we can drive to Mexico and immigrate from there, in case we stay here.[1]

If this plan won't work, we'll have to wait and see what happens here. If I stay, you'll leave the *show* and come here; otherwise I'll go back. I hope very much that I know something by the end of this week or the beginning of next.

I could tell on the phone that you hardly speak German anymore, because you would always start up in English. That's great.

Many, many little kisses

from your Weillchen

1. At that time, immigration law required that anyone entering the United States on a visitor's visa had to leave the country again in order to apply for a permanent visa at any American consulate. Most of these "immigrant visitors" chose to apply for reentry in Mexico, Cuba, or Canada. To obtain a permanent visa, each applicant first had to have two sworn affidavits sent to the selected American consulate: one by a close relative and one by a well-to-do citizen who could guarantee that the applicant would never become a public charge.

180   WEILL IN HOLLYWOOD TO LENYA IN NEW YORK, [11 APRIL 1937]
Letterhead: Hollywood Knickerbocker

Sunday

Dear *Blümchen,*

I just spent two magnificent days on a ranch in the desert, the whole time regretting that you weren't there, because you would have liked it a lot. The Spewacks (who really are ever so nice to me) had invited me. It was one of the most beautiful spots I've ever seen (incredibly expensive), in the middle of the desert, surrounded by snow-covered mountains, a ranch with horses, a *swimming pool,* places to sun yourself, tennis, ping-pong, marvelous food, and small, very elegant *bungalows* with baths. Now that's really what one thinks of as "Hollywood." La Crawford and Franchot Tone were there and were terribly nice to me, and just as we were leaving, Astaire arrived.[1] Just for a few days, something like this is very interesting. When we're together again, we'll have to come here for a few days.

Everybody—without exception!—advises me against accepting a contract with MGM, because I'd be totally paralyzed there and would get three times the money if I had a musical in New York. Besides, I still don't have a definite offer; the agents keep dragging their feet, and there's no sense sitting around here waiting. Therefore, if nothing happens within the next few days, I'll be leaving at the end of the week. If you don't want to quit the show (because of the money), then Sam Spewack would probably drive back with me, which would be very nice, because I could work with him on the road. Now we have two ideas, one of which would be very easy to realize and would have great possibilities. In any case, they seem to be determined to do something with me, they have good ideas, and we understand each other wonderfully.—However, if you really want to come here and then drive back with me, you have to let me know right away. But today or tomorrow I'll probably have your answer to my last letter. In any case, we'll be seeing each other soon, either here or in New York. I've written a very strong letter to Nizer. But that's a hopeless situation.

With my next letter you'll get a lot of snapshots, and today a kiss from

Knuti

1. *Joan Crawford (1904–77) had established herself as an international star in* Grand Hotel *(1932); from 1935 to 1939 she was married to the wealthy socialite Franchot Tone, once a leading man with the Group Theatre. Fred Astaire, born Frederick Austerlitz (1899–1988), had played a small part in Crawford's* Dancing Lady *(1933) and was now himself becoming a star in many of the great Hollywood musicals, including* Top Hat *(1937).*

181 WEILL IN HOLLYWOOD TO LENYA IN NEW YORK, [14 APRIL 1937]
Letterhead: Hollywood Knickerbocker

Wednesday

Dear *Mistblume*,

For several days now I've been without news from you, and I'm a bit nervous on account of that. You haven't responded to my proposal to come out here and then drive back with me. In the meantime Spewack has decided not to drive back with me, because he has to stay here for a few more days and then take the train back. But he's offered to let his chauffeur go back with me, and maybe I'll take him up on it, although it's not so very interesting to drive around for a week with a Filipino. The other possibility is to take Paula [Miller] along. I intend to leave Monday, and I think I can make it in approximately seven to eight days.

Jed [Harris] is here. He's mad as a hatter, but very nice. And he has a really brilliant idea for a new musical. He's flying back today. This week I'm trying to make up for all the *social life* I've neglected, but it makes me nervous to see so many people. Yesterday I was at Button's for dinner; today Spewack's; tomorrow lunch with Elisabeth Meyer, *dinner* with Gottfried [Reinhardt] and "wife" [Salka Viertel]; and Friday lunch with Sidney Howard, dinner with Paramount producer Lewyn, whom I met at Cliff's the other day—he knows every note of mine by memory, is a great admirer of yours, and wants to bring you to Paramount (he's a very important man, was the closest collaborator of Thalberg's).[1] Sunday I'm giving a farewell party in a Russian restaurant with the Group people, Milly, the Reinhardts, Litvak. It would be much nicer if you could be there— but *"Vielleicht ein andermal, wenn's wieder Mai wird"* [perhaps another time, when May is here again].

Milly is the only decent person here. Just now he called; he had heard that [Max] Steiner was leaving Selznick, and he immediately called Selznick, and tomorrow he'll go there with me. It's the best position that would be available here, because Selznick makes the best movies, and there's no mass production.[2] It could possibly mean I'd be doing a movie right away (*The Prisoner of Zenda*, with Colman), which of course I would like.[3] If that should come to pass (which, of course, isn't very likely), you'd come out here at once, wouldn't you?

Up to now Nizer has not answered my letter, and Friday I'll discuss what steps should be taken with Sidney Howard, who is president of the Dramatist Guild. My patience is at an end with this bunch of swine. I'm totally convinced that Weisgal and Nizer are putting a few thousand dollars aside for themselves every week.

Were it not for this Selznick matter, I'd be very glad to go back to New York, to our nice apartment, to a real city with people who are alive—and to you. I have many plans for the theater, some of which will surely materialize. And I've laid sufficient groundwork here that I will probably soon be called back. Everyone knows and talks about my having written a *thrilling score* for Wanger, and Wanger himself does a lot of promotion for me.

I'm curious to hear from you what's new there. How is Paul?[4] I wrote to Cheryl.

If you write me a *special delivery* letter, I'll still get it by Sunday, and I'll wire to tell you where you should write me then—or whether I'll be staying here.

> Many, many little kisses,
> Knuti

1. The playwright and screenwriter Sidney Howard (1891–1939) is best known for his play They Knew What They Wanted, on which The Most Happy Fella was based. The producer and director Albert Lewin (1894–1968) rose to second-in-command at MGM; after the death of artistic director Irving Thalberg (1899–1936), he joined Paramount as a producer.

2. David O. Selznick (1902–65) was one of the most brilliant and successful of Hollywood producers; his credits include Gone with the Wind (1939), Rebecca (1940), and Duel in the Sun (1947).

3. The British actor Ronald Colman (1891–1958) was a popular leading man in Hollywood during the 1930s and 1940s.

4. The reference to "Paul" is ambiguous. Lenya and Paul Green had been carrying on an affair since 1936. Included in the cast of The Eternal Road, however, was Paul Mario, with whom she would be involved later during the production of The Firebrand of Florence (Weill also cast him in the chorus of Lost in the Stars). Although he was an unreliable singer, involved with drugs, and once even attempted blackmail, Weill would not allow him to be fired. Lenya recalled that he attended Weill's funeral.

182T WEILL IN HOLLYWOOD TO LENYA IN NEW YORK, 15 APRIL 1937

Western Union: telegram in German

WHY DON´T YOU WRITE YOU *MISTFINK* DEPARTING PROBABLY MONDAY LITTLE KISSES

182 WEILL IN HOLLYWOOD TO LENYA IN NEW YORK, [17 APRIL 1937]

Letterhead: Hollywood Knickerbocker

Saturday

Dear *Blümilein*,

It's a terrible mess here, and I have an irrepressible urge to toss everything away and leave town. But I'm afraid that would be sheer insanity, and I have to stick it out for a few more days. It's clear now how smart I was to see nobody here all this time, and what a good life I had. Now, after seeing people for a whole week, I'm so tense that all the relaxation I've had has gone to hell.

It's certain that if I were to stay here and carry on this kind of life, all kinds of *jobs* would come through for me. But I don't believe that such *jobs* are worth these spasms. If I could quickly make a movie now and earn another $7,500 and finally get a start in films, I'd probably do it, although I'd rather leave. The immediate movie opportunity would be the *Prisoner of Zenda* at Selznick. I had a long talk with Selznick (in his house) and Milly (whose behavior is terrific). The result was typical Hollywood: he would like to have me but he doesn't know enough of my music, and he wants me to compose, orchestrate, and record a scene from the movie as a test, after which he'll decide. That's a hard nut to crack. But I'll try to do it, if I can be sure he'll give me an orchestra and good collaborators. It would take one week altogether, and I think it would be worth it, because it's one of the year's biggest movies, and Selznick is the great up-and-coming man here. Of course, it's a big question whether I can do anything under these conditions that will give him a sense of what I'm capable of—but that's the way they do it with everybody. I'll go there once more and talk it over. If it doesn't work out, I'll leave right away, because for the first time I'm really totally fed up.

I would like to try to be in New York before the 28th, because Terry [Helburn] sent me a telegram and also wrote that she would like me to speak with Charell before his departure.

Things with the Spewacks are going well. They talked with Max Gordon, who was enthusiastic about the Spewack-Weill combination and wanted to draw up a contract right away. This, of course, reassured them. It would still be *all right* with the Spewacks if I were to do a fast movie, because they will need several weeks anyhow to get settled on their farm near New York.

I saw Fritz Lang. He definitely wants to do a movie with me (which would not be uninteresting, because he's had some tremendous successes).

The announcement that *The Eternal Road* is closing was a big surprise. It's an unbelievably dirty deal. To judge from your letter, you too seem to be quite worn out, and if it should work out that I do the film, I would want you to stop performing right away and come here and get a good rest, go swimming, horseback riding, etc. Otherwise I'll come home quickly so you're no longer alone.

Now farewell, my *Blümchen*. Don't be impatient, since in any case we'll see each other soon.

Many, many little kisses

from your *Schnübchen*

Letterhead: Hollywood Knickerbocker

Saturday

Dear Linerl,

Many thanks for your letter. Once again they can't make up their minds here. Three days ago it looked as if the thing was absolutely certain. Then suddenly complications with Lang's contract at Paramount turned up, which haven't been ironed out yet and might make the whole thing collapse. Aside from that, this Russian Jew, Boris Morros, found out about our negotiations, and he's beside himself with anger, because for the first time a composer is negotiating directly with producers and simply bypassing this gangster. Now he's told the producers that they shouldn't pay me more than $600, but of course I'm insisting on $1,250. But for the time being the negotiations are stalled altogether until Lang's contract is settled. And so it's getting later and later, and if they wait any longer, I won't be able to do it at all anymore. The Spewacks left for New York yesterday (perhaps they'll call you; please be very nice). Practically everything for the show is set. Max Gordon will produce it, and we've found a brilliant *lyric writer*, with whom I'm already working here.[1] This is, of course, the most interesting and important work, and a tremendous opportunity. We've definitely settled on my coming to New York at the very latest in about six to seven weeks, so that we can open the show in the fall. It's questionable whether I can do the Lang film within that time span. Of course, I would love to do it, because it offers me the best collaboration, and we could really create a new form of musical film. But the question is whether I would be able to combine it with the show, which is why this sitting around and waiting for a decision makes me so insanely nervous. As of now, the plan is that I prepare the script with Lang for about six weeks, composing the main body of music so that he can then get ready to start shooting the film, after which he'll have me come back for just a few weeks if he needs me. It would be great if that could be worked out.

I think it would be too difficult to rent out the apartment at this point, because we don't know where we stand. I'll most likely be in New York during the summer and would not like to be living in that Hotel Belvedere you love so much.[2] Besides, it would be difficult to sublet our rooms, because the furniture doesn't belong to us; I'm sure Bess [Eitingon] wants her furniture back, and we'll have to return it to her when she gets her *house in the country* ready. I don't know what to do about the apartment in the fall. It would be nice if we could arrange to keep the two rooms, because they're so beautiful. But if that doesn't work, we just have to get out. It wouldn't be the first time.

I'll tell the WPA people here they should prepare a score for the WPA there [Chicago].[3] That's the only thing I can do about the matter.

All of a sudden my chances here are very good. You just have to sit around as long as it takes, and suddenly offers come in from everywhere. Selznick still wants me for that movie (and without having to submit to a *test*), 20th Century has asked if I'm available, Marlene [Dietrich] is telling everybody that she will be doing her next movie with me and that she's jealous because Lang is stealing me, Cliff and his producer definitely want to do a musical with me, and Henrietta[?] calls every day and asks whether I'm available. If I stay here now, I might get very busy. But the play is more important, and I don't want to settle down here. Greetings to Cheryl. Much love,

Schnube

1. *Weill is referring to E. Y. (Yip) Harburg (1896–1981), who went on to write the lyrics for* Finian's Rainbow *(1947), as well as* The Wizard of Oz *and* April in Paris.

2. *The Belvedere Hotel, at 319 West Forty-eighth Street, was a popular trysting spot, with rooms that rented by the hour.*

3. *After it closed on Broadway after just sixty-eight performances,* Johnny Johnson *was produced by the Federal Theatre Project of the Works Progress Administration. It opened a six-week run at the Mayan Theatre in Los Angeles on 28 May 1937.*

183T   WEILL IN HOLLYWOOD TO LENYA IN NEW YORK,
24 APRIL 1937
Western Union: telegram in English

NO DECISION YET DONT RENT APARTMENT BEFORE HEAR FROM ME = LOVE.

184   WEILL IN HOLLYWOOD TO LENYA IN NEW YORK,
[29 APRIL 1937]
Letterhead: Hollywood Knickerbocker

Thursday

Dear *Blumi*,

I got quite a shock when I heard your story about the fire. I can imagine how shaken up you must have been when you landed in the street; but your being such an authority in criminal matters stood you in good stead this time. When I had recovered from my initial shock, I had to laugh when I pictured you bounding down those stairs. But it's terrible about the girl who burned to death. Considering that things like this probably happen every day in New York, one begins to realize what kind of danger one lives in at every moment. Well, I'm glad you got away with just a scare. It's so typical that something like this has to happen to you, who are forever imagining and describing just such things.

From day to day I'm waiting for a decision in the Fritz Lang matter. As it stands now, Lang's contract—which ten days ago already was as good as settled—still hasn't been signed. He thinks it will be settled this week, but I'm not so sure if they actually want a contract with him at all or if they just got scared because he's notorious for being totally crazy and difficult to deal with. Of course I'd like to do this movie, because Lang is nuts about me and will do anything I say. He treats me like a sacred totem. But it's awful that it's getting to be so late. Naturally the Spewacks want to open the show in the fall, and I worked hard to persuade them to make it their first project. Now I can't leave them in the lurch because of a movie job, so I'll have to be back in New York by the beginning of June at the latest, in order to have the piece ready for rehearsals in August. They sent me a telegram upon arrival to say that they couldn't get into their house yet and would first go to Bermuda. But I don't want them to lose interest or think it was I who wrecked the project. Also, this play is much more important because it could become a tremendous success, and then it would be easy as pie to have all that I'm now fighting tooth and claw for. If the movie becomes a reality, I would work four to five weeks on it now and try to finish the script and the greater part of the music during that time; then I'd go to New York to work on the show and—if they need me—come back here for another two to three weeks. Even if the Lang contract becomes a reality, there are still all kinds of difficulties with Boris Morros, who is furious that I went over his head and negotiated with his *bosses* and who still wants to pay me a lousy salary. But I'll be watching all of this with great calm. That's really not what makes me so nervous; it's rather the very monotonous and irritating atmosphere, about which everybody seems to feel the same way.

I'm now working every morning with the lyricist of the show ["Yip" Harburg], and we have great ideas and have started to work out several numbers. That's a lot of fun. Besides, I've written a long and very good essay for *Modern Music*.[1]

If you see the Spewacks, please try to convince them that working with them is more important to me than any movie deal and that I'll certainly arrange to begin work with them by the end of May or beginning of June—and by then I'll most likely have done the most important musical numbers.

I spent an evening with Sylvia Sidney, who is very nice.[2] Otherwise I have not seen many people this week.

Now I'm off to see the Fritze [Lang], that lunatic. Write again soon; many little kisses, your

Schnubi

---

1. *"Oper in Amerika," published as "The Future of Opera in America,"* Modern Music *14 (May–June 1937): 183–88.*
2. *Silvia Sidney (b. 1910), a stage and screen actress, was married to Luther Adler; she had starred in the 1931 film of Elmer Rice's Pulitzer Prize–winning play* Street Scene.

185 WEILL IN HOLLYWOOD TO LENYA IN NEW YORK, [4 MAY 1937]
Letterhead: Hollywood Knickerbocker

Tuesday

Dear Linerl,

There's still no decision in the Fritz Lang matter, since his contract has not been signed yet. In the meantime, it's getting so late that I doubt whether I could still do the film. These things just take terribly long out here, because the people who live here and don't want to do anything but movies have a lot of time. I doubt very much that anything will be decided this week, but if I don't start work until next week, I see no way to come to New York at the beginning of June, which means all my plans for the theater would collapse—and naturally I don't want that to happen under any circumstance.

Therefore, I'm planning to leave here next week. That way I could still see Charell, who is leaving for Europe on the 19th. Terry wired me that she'd be happy if I spoke to Charell before he leaves. They still seem to be keen on *Liliom*.

I've laid the groundwork for several things here, which will give me the possibility of returning in the fall to do movies. The work with the lyricist is moving along quite nicely. He's very talented, and we already have some first-class ideas for songs.

Yesterday I got a telegram from Bel Geddes asking me when I'd be back, because he's preparing a revue for this fall.[1] Also, the *New York Times* has sent a telegram asking about my plans with the Spewacks and *Liliom*. I sent a telegram to Heugel saying the publisher should no longer license *The Eternal Road* if they don't immediately pay *royalties*, and he wired back that he's sent a cable to Weisgal with that message.[2] I've let that bunch of pigs drag me around by the nose long enough. They now owe me over $3,000, a fact they just keep ignoring, as if I didn't even exist. In the Sunday *Times* there was a long article with tremendous publicity for Mr. Leftwitsch[?]. I'm not the least bit interested in what Mr. Weisgal's family has already sacrificed for the show. He'd treat his family, as well as me and all the others, like shit. Three months ago Jed's idea would have been good; now it's of no use at all.

Otherwise there's little news. Saturday I spent the whole day with Cliff and Luise, who now are getting along with each other much better. It was very nice. In the evening I went slumming with Lang and Sylvia Sidney. Sunday I was at Lang's for lunch with Marlene, who was again very stupid and superficial. I spent the evening with the Group people. All this is rather *boring*.

How are you? Have you recovered from the shock of the fire? If we could sublet the apartment for the summer, I would love to rent a small house in the country near the Spewacks, because—once again—I'm thoroughly fed up with living like a vagabond. But we can talk about that when I get back.

Today much love from your

      Knut

Are you still staying at the hotel?

---

1. *A distinguished set designer, Norman Bel Geddes (1893–1958) began his career at the Metropolitan Opera. He then turned his talents to Broadway, where his work was seen from 1920 on, in such contrasting productions as* The Rivals *(1922) and Max Reinhardt's spectacle* The Miracle *(1924). His sets for* The Eternal Road *(1937) had required a structural overhaul of the Manhattan Opera House and caused the postponement that required Weill and Lenya to stay on in the United States.*
2. *Jacques Paul Heugel (1890–1979) led his publishing firm until 1944.*

186   WEILL IN HOLLYWOOD TO LENYA IN NEW YORK,
[8 MAY 1937]
Letterhead: Hollywood Knickerbocker

                            Saturday

Dear *Blume*,

It looks very much like the Fritz Lang movie at Paramount will work out. They've agreed to pay $10,000 for the whole *job*. I would have to work about four weeks on the movie and try to do as much as possible within that time. At the same time I would have to write the most important numbers for the show. Then I would be in New York around 10 June and could work for three months on the show. During this time Lang will prepare the movie and begin shooting, and I'll come back only when he needs me. If I'm unlucky, he'll need me just when the *show's in rehearsal*. That could get very unpleasant. But somehow it will work out. One of the two projects, the movie or the show, will most likely come to a halt somewhere along the way. Paramount insists that Lang's contract will definitely get signed on Monday, and my contract automatically kicks in with his. They have Sylvia Sidney and George Raft for the leads, and I think it can turn out to be a very interesting movie.[1] It certainly won't be an easy nut to crack with Lang, who is a really miserable guy (although for the time being he is nice as pie to me), and we'll have the craziest fights.

Things look very good with the show. It's absolutely definite that [Max] Gordon will produce it. I had a long letter from the Spewacks, who are still in New York. When I eventually go to New York, I would like to have a small house with a piano in the country close to them, because most likely I will have to work on the film as well as the show.

Blumi, we want to be very careful with money, because all I'm doing right now will ultimately be justified only if I can save enough to enable me finally to do something really significant again, by my former standards. I don't want to make the mistake everyone here makes (Cliff and all the others)—to spend all the money one makes and then be forced to take on another *job* and little by little become a complete slave to Hollywood. I know this is your point of view as well. If we're careful we could have approximately $16,000 dollars in the bank by this fall, when the movie is done, and could rent a small house near New York, have a maid and a car, and give up this gypsy life, where you never get a chance to collect your thoughts. It will be much better for you also. Of course, you can buy yourself whatever you need, go horseback riding, play sports, etc. But please be careful in choosing your acquaintances, so that not just anyone will take advantage of you again. Don't be angry that I tell you this, you know how I mean it. We are both of an age now that we have to shape our lives so as to get the most out of what we can possibly achieve. If money has any use at all, it's to give us independence.

In last Sunday's *Times* there was a report from Vienna that [Bruno] Walter performed my symphony there. It was the first time that Toscanini went to another conductor's concert.[2] The article says the audience reacted more positively to the work than to any other modern one.[3] That makes me happy, especially as I sit here in Hollywood fighting with Boris Morros.

I spent one evening with Stokowski, who was very nice to me.[4] I will send you a telegram as soon as everything has been decided.

Many little kisses

from your *Schnubi*

1. Warner Brothers' biggest gangster star, George Raft (1895–1980), specialized in suave underworld characters (Scarface, Each Dawn I Die); the white tie on black shirt and nonchalant flipping of a coin became Raft trademarks, often imitated by actual professional gunmen.

2. Conductor Arturo Toscanini (1867–1957) became artistic director of La Scala at age thirty-one and served in the same role at the Metropolitan Opera (1921–31). During the last twenty-five years of his career he centered his activities in New York, particularly as conductor of the NBC Symphony.

3. The 2 May 1937 issue of the New York Times reported in detail Toscanini's visit to Vienna, but not quite the way Weill summarized it: "The news that Toscanini was coming to the last regular Philharmonic concert of the season caused a great craning of necks and much searching with opera glasses of remote corners of the Musikverein Saal. Yet when the concert was over nobody was found who had laid eyes on the master. It transpired that he had occupied a seat on the podium, somewhere in the shadow of the organ, as secure as possible from prying eyes. The program he heard offered Kurt Weill's symphony, which Walter brought out in New York two years ago; Strauss's "Don Juan" and the fourth Brahms. The Viennese received the Weill novelty with a good deal more equanimity and good-will than they usually extend to things of the sort. But all told, it hardly seemed to me one of Walter's better days."

4. Conductor Leopold Stokowski (1882–1977) had given the American premiere of Weill's Der Lindberghflug in April 1931 with the Philadelphia Orchestra. He resigned as that orchestra's music director in 1936 and thereafter appeared in or conducted a number of films, including Disney's Fantasia (1940).

187T   WEILL IN HOLLYWOOD TO LENYA IN NEW YORK, 13 MAY 1937

Western Union: telegram in English

JUST CLOSED PARAMOUNT DEAL MOVING TOMORROW INTO LITTLE HOUSE 686 SAN LORENZO DRIVE AT SANTA MONICA CALIFORNIA LOVE KISSES = *SCHNUBI.*

187   WEILL IN SANTA MONICA TO LENYA IN NEW YORK, [14 MAY 1937]

Letterhead: Hollywood Knickerbocker

Friday

686 San Lorenzo Drive
Santa Monica (Calif.)

Dear *Blume,*

After going back and forth for days, the agreement with Paramount was finally closed with a handshake on Wednesday evening. The contracts are being executed today or tomorrow. I'm getting $10,000 and can go to New York in between "if it does not encroach upon my work on the film." I'll get the money in four installments, one right now, one after five weeks, one after three more weeks, and one at the conclusion of the work. Boris Morros was called in, and he was told by his superiors that I'd been engaged. He was as nice as pie. That was another small triumph, because up to now nobody has been able to bring such an arrangement off.

I moved first thing yesterday, and by nine o'clock in the morning we'd already started work at Lang's. I have a very small house right near Lang and the ocean, with a big living room, two small bedrooms, bathroom, kitchen, garage, and a little garden. It's very expensive ($200 a month!), but I couldn't have stood it in the hotel anymore, and it's already become very hot in the city. It's so wonderful to be outside the city again and to have peace. I'm glad this movie has worked out, although it is difficult to be working with this puffed-up Lang, but for the time being he's really listening to me and behaving quite decently. If we're lucky, it could turn out to be a very good movie and a very good basis for further Hollywood work for me. Of course, I have to do all I can to fit it in with the Spewack show, because it's at least as important. I've written the Spewacks that I can come to New York anytime in the beginning of June if they want to work with me. But I think I'll have to stay here until at least 10 or 15 June. This will be an expensive month for us, since you won't be earning anything more (Francesco told me you haven't been paid for weeks, and it's a mystery to me why you've kept on performing). But we'll save over the summer instead. Chappell won't pay anything during the time I'm working for Paramount, because Paramount has its own music publishing company. I hope he [Max Dreyfus] will give me a leave of absence.

I found Francesco more repulsive than ever. I'm simply flabbergasted that this amateur has the nerve to produce *Die Dreigroschenoper* in Paris again. It will be a tremendous flop, to be sure. He is completely without talent and only cares about gossip; his main concern in casting is whether whoever is picked likes him personally, etc. Unfortunately I can't forbid it, since Aufricht is having him come over, and he bribes Aufricht for that. But Brecht will be there and spoil it all anyway. In any case I've wired the Société des Auteurs that they should not license it if my royalties will not be paid in France.

Yesterday afternoon I was at the Gershwins' for a short visit. They live in a palace with a *swimming pool and tennis court*. But George has gotten even more stupid than he was before. They were very nice to me.

Now I have to go to work. I'll have a lot to do in the near future, since I also want to work on the show on the side. Write me soon about what you're going to do.

Kisses
Schnubi

Did you have to get money from the bank, and how much?

188 WEILL IN SANTA MONICA TO LENYA IN NEW YORK, [17? MAY 1937]
Letterhead: Hollywood Knickerbocker

Monday morning

Dear *Blume*,

Many thanks for your letter. First of all, I want to answer the various questions. It's difficult to say whether you should play Lucy in Paris. I'm convinced this whole thing will be a total disaster because Francesco, who has never been able to do something like that, now seems completely decrepit, and Aufricht's bulb is none too bright either. Besides that, you don't speak French, and you know how chauvinistic they are in Paris, especially in that regard. Therefore, I'm rather inclined to advise you against it, but we can still wait to see how the whole thing develops. Personally, I'd like to stay out of this thing as much as possible, so I can retain the option to stop it if it gets to be too awful.

As far as your teeth are concerned, you certainly won't need to have the work done on account of Hollywood, because here you'll get a chance only if this or that producer or director is really interested in you—i.e., your talent—and somebody like that wouldn't give a hoot how your teeth looked, because he'd know they could be fixed. If anyone here gets interested in you, the work would be done at the studio's expense, and I'm convinced that such things are done better here than anywhere else in the world. The Group Theatre people have had all kinds of cosmetic surgery done, with brilliant success and at the expense of the studio. Therefore, it doesn't make sense to undergo such a strenuous ordeal for the vague possibility of a movie. Regardless of the movies, I [FIGS. 53 & 54] don't even know whether it would be right for your face, because your teeth lend character to your face just as they are and certainly enhance your personality on stage. And since it isn't even sure this thing will really materialize, I'd advise you to wait on all this until you come here sometime in the future and I get you together with some movie people to determine what your chances are here and whether they think the dental work is necessary.

You'll find the address of the *Immigration Office* or *Immigration Bureau* in the telephone book under either name. It's somewhere *downtown* on Fifth Avenue. But I really hope I can be there during June in time to get the papers before 10 July, which is getting more and more urgent, with the danger of war in Europe growing day by day.

I haven't heard anything from the Spewacks, and of course, I'm constantly afraid they'll give up the whole thing. I know too well how it goes if you don't keep after these things constantly and pour all your energy into getting something like this done. I already have some very good numbers worked out for the show.

We're working day and night on the script for the film. We hope to have the story to the point where we can start working on the details, and I can start concerning myself with the songs.

The house is nice and, best of all, completely quiet. I have a cleaning lady who comes every other day. I'm not eating at home but mostly at Lang's, where we always work because for the time being we don't have to be in the studio. We had *lunch* with Boris Morros. He's buttering me up, but I don't trust the truce.

What are you doing all day long now that the show has closed?[1] I'm surprised that the Spewacks haven't called you. Cheryl seems be to very *busy,* since there's something about her production in the newspapers every day. Tell Charles [Alan] that I'll write him as soon as I have a free minute. Write again soon. My telephone number is Santa Monica 28430.

> Many little kisses,
> Your Knuti

1. The Eternal Road had closed on Saturday, 15 May, after 153 performances.

Friday

Dear Linerl,

You really surprised me with your sudden trip. I hope you're having nice weather and a hell of a good time too. To judge from your telegram you seem to have left in a great hurry, and I don't quite understand how you can manage a long trip like that in just two days. Are there any horses for you to ride? I hope you'll have a good rest.[1]

I'm working day and night with Lang on the script. We've finished the first draft and—after the Paramount people have talked it over in detail—I'll start on the songs with a *lyric writer*.

I guess I'll have to stay here until at least 15 June. I haven't heard a thing from the Spewacks, and I'm scared to death that they've forgotten the whole thing or somehow lost their enthusiasm. I wrote them today that they should let me know just when they'd want to work with me. If they want to start on 15 June, I'll probably take the train back so as not to lose too much time. Then it would hardly be worth it for you to come out here, seeing as you won't be getting back to New York until the end of the month. As soon as I hear from the Spewacks, I'll write you.

Otherwise there's little to report. The weather is bad today. But in order to get some exercise I've started to practice every morning with a tennis teacher. When the weather's nice, I also go swimming in the ocean sometimes; it's so close to my house. Last night there was a big birthday *party* for Litvak at [Miriam] Hopkins's house. Today I'm going to have dinner at the Reinhardts'.

Now farewell. Much love from your

Frosch

I wrote you at the New York address about the immigration office.

1. *Lenya had impulsively driven to Texas with her current amour, Billy Jones, to whom she refers as "wild animal Bill" in later letters.*

Saturday

Dear *Blume*,

This has been a terribly strenuous week, because besides the work on the movie I had *story* conferences, petty arguments with the agent about the contract, etc. I also had two performances in *downtown* Los Angeles; I had to put up with the California auto traffic for three quarters of an hour each way. Thursday we did *Der Lindberghflug* in the Antheil Gallery with just a few singers and two pianos.[1] It's amazing how good that music is and how fresh an effect it still has after almost ten years. We also showed the *Dreigroschenoper* film, but we could get only the French version, which is rather poor and—in contrast to *Der Lindberghflug*—unfortunately feels quite old-fashioned already, which proves that it never was any good in the first place. Everybody in Hollywood who's interested in modern works was present: the Gershwins, Miriam Hopkins, Litvak, the Milestones, Lang, Luise and Cliff, and many more. Gershwin behaved obnoxiously, but this bumpkin is just too dumb even to bother with.[2] Yesterday was the Los Angeles premiere of *Johnny Johnson*. I went to a few rehearsals and helped them a little bit. It's the biggest project the WPA has undertaken up to now; of course, it has inferior actors—but a charming, very young Johnny (the play works quite differently with a young Johnny), a big (lousy) orchestra and chorus, and very interesting *sets*. That the second act received the strongest reaction by far demonstrates how greatly the performance differed from the New York one. They included the "French Wounded" chorus and did the "Dance of the Generals" in its entirety, which proved most effective. At the premiere last night everything was still very rough and not quite ready, especially musically, but it was definitely a great success; the people reacted marvelously—they laughed a lot, were dead silent during the "Gun Song" (which got lots of applause, as did all the other songs), and gave a tremendous ovation at the end. The press, too, seems to be good. They'll play it for six to eight weeks.

The work on the movie is progressing. We're finished with the *story*, and my musical ideas have been accepted. Now I'm beginning to work on the songs, and I hope to have enough preparatory work done that I can leave here around 20 June. I got a very nice *wire* from the Spewacks. They've settled everything with Max Gordon, and he hopes to open on 15 October. They're moving to their farm on 10 June, but they tell me I don't have to come before 15 July. However, I'd like to go earlier in order to have the play ready as soon as possible, because I'll have to come back here late in the summer (which I don't want to tell them yet). So if you want to come over, you'll have to make up your mind very soon; otherwise it wouldn't be worth it anymore. You don't seem to be very eager anyway. Of course, I'd be delighted if you would come. If you do, I will try to arrange to go back by car. If not, I'll probably take the train and ship the car.

I got a letter from Cheryl. They're going to the country on 1 June already. Unfortunately she wasn't able to sublet the apartment, so we'll have to pay for the whole summer. But I'm glad that Dorothy is well again. Should you wish to come here, I'll ask the Spewacks to look around for a small house in their vicinity for us. If you see them, tell them how much I'm looking forward to the work, that I'm more and more enthused about the idea of the play and am burning to get started.

I can't tell you how much I'm looking forward to going back to New York. This Hollywood is no picnic, especially when the weather is as bad as it is now and has been for weeks. Lang makes you want to puke. Nobody in the whole world is as important as he imagines himself to be. I completely understand why he is so hated everywhere. He's still trying to be very nice to me, because he knows that I don't need him, and I always let him know it too. He really can get on your nerves terribly, but I must stay on good terms with him so he'll let me leave.

That's enough schmoozing. Decide quickly if you want to come, and let me know. A thousand kisses from your

Schnubi

Charles is coming here. He's leaving New York on 2 June. Write a few words to Hans [Weill] if you have time.

1. *Universal Edition had published George Antheil's English translation of the work in the second edition of the piano score. Aaron Copland recalled that on a visit to Hollywood in June 1937, where he was testing the waters himself at MGM and visiting his friend Harold Clurman, "George Antheil and Kurt Weill came by to take me to dinner" (Copland and Perlis, p. 270).*

2. *Although still undiagnosed, George Gershwin was already showing in his erratic behavior symptoms of the brain tumor that would claim his life on 11 July.*

191T WEILL IN SANTA MONICA TO LENYA IN NEW YORK, 2 JUNE 1937

Western Union: telegram in English

IT MUST BE QUITE BORING FOR YOU IN NEW YORK AND I THINK YOU SHOULD COME HERE AS SOON AS POSSIBLE LOVE = KNUTI.

191 WEILL IN SANTA MONICA TO LENYA IN NEW YORK, [6 JUNE 1937]

Letterhead, used for second page only: Hollywood Knickerbocker

Sunday

Dear *Blume,*

I already had a hunch you'd give me the cold shoulder again in response to my invitation to come out here. I had figured it would amount to about the same thing in terms of expenses, since I would have gone back by car with you, which is much cheaper. Now I'll take the train. It costs $100 to ship the car. But we'll need a car when we're in the country. Well, I'll see if I get done in time, and if I can find someone to come along, I might still go by car. I'll also try to get a $500 advance from Max Gordon to cover the travel costs, because of course Paramount won't pay. My contract still has not been signed, because I'm insisting it include permission to do the show. This is such an unusual request that it has to pass through all the various channels. But they've agreed to it.

Chappell has paid me another $750—although they had to give me a leave of absence for the film. They'll probably skip the next *check*. But I'll still get a few hundred dollars from *Johnny Johnson,* so we'll have more than $2,000 in the bank. With that we can live comfortably this summer and save the money I'm earning here. You can send a total of around 300 schillings to Mariedl [Hubek, Lenya's sister] and Max [Blamauer, her brother]. Max can have some more later on.

When I come, we have to take care of the immigration business right away. With the always acute danger of war, it's high time we do it. Make sure Moses has all the papers, recommendations, press clippings, etc. ready, so he can draw up the applications as soon as I let you know the exact date I'll be leaving. Going to Cuba would take too much time for me. We'll drive to Canada instead.

The Spewacks move to their farm on 10 June and are probably busy with the move. Perhaps you can write a few nice words to them and offer to help. Address: Bella and Sam Spewack, 14 Walnut Place, Newdrop, Staten Island, N.Y. Once they are there, you should drive out and look around for a small house or a nice apartment in their neighborhood. The farm is on Windybush Road, Newhope, Pennsylvania. They'll probably invite us to stay with them, but I wouldn't want to accept, because the house is probably too small, and I can work better when I'm alone. When you see them, tell them I already have five very good songs and a lot of material for the show, that I'm very much looking forward to it and believe in the show more and more.

Of the five songs for the movie I've already written three, but without words as yet. Again the lyricist is terribly slow, and I have to squeeze everything out of him.[1] Provided he doesn't leave me in the lurch, I could be ready to leave in two weeks. I would rather leave sooner than later, because most likely I'll have to be back here by the end of August, when the movie is being shot. But for the time being I don't want to say anything about that to the Spewacks.

Otherwise there's nothing to report from here. The weather has been bad for weeks; today the sun is shining for the first time. I went to the ocean early this morning (because I can't play tennis today), have worked for six hours already, and now have to see Reinhardt, who is already sore that I haven't been to see him for quite some time.

Write soon again and accept many kisses

from your *Schnubi*

1. *Weill is referring to the composer, author, lyricist, publisher, producer, and recording artist Sam Coslow (1902–82), who went on to win an Academy Award in 1944 for* Heavenly Music.

192T WEILL IN SANTA MONICA TO LENYA IN NEW YORK, 10 JUNE 1937
Western Union: telegram in English

DID NOT HEAR FROM YOU ALL WEEK AM WORRIED ABOUT YOUR HEALTH PLEASE WIRE HOW YOU FEEL LOVE AND KISSES = KNUT.

192 WEILL IN SANTA MONICA TO LENYA IN NEW YORK, [11 JUNE 1937]

Friday

Dear *Blümchen*,

Isn't chicken pox the pits! Now you see what a *Doofi* you still are, because here you are getting chicken pox at this point, even though you always insist you're already grown up. After your previous letter I thought this thing would be over with by now, but when I didn't have any news from you for several days, I surmised you weren't feeling well and was very worried until finally your letter arrived today. *Blumi*, please be very careful with this sickness; get a very good doctor and do everything to get over it. I'm so sorry you have to be alone with this thing in the heat of New York, and therefore I'm very anxious to get away from here. Unfortunately I had to take another *lyric writer,* since the one I was working with got another *job.* But now I have a better one, actually the best one I've found up to now.[1] But it's questionable whether I'll have all the *lyrics* together by the end of the week, and it could be I'll have to stay on a few more days. I can hardly wait to get away from here. I feel as though I'll be coming back to life after having been in some other place, most likely hell. I'm also looking forward so much to seeing you again at last. You know I didn't mean anything by that remark in my last letter. It was just that I was so disappointed that you weren't coming, after I'd been looking forward to it so much and had told everyone you were coming. But I do realize that you really would have liked to come.

Please don't overdo your thriftiness as far as your personal needs are concerned, and in particular do everything you have to for your illness. After all, I'm earning pretty good money now, and the worst that can happen is that we'd have a little less money in the bank. It's just that I don't want to be as stupid as all the others and sell my soul (because that's exactly what one does out here) and still not really get anything for it. Life here in Santa Monica and being with Lang, who never goes to a restaurant that's less than three dollars per person, costs me a lot of money. But that's going to stop now. So don't think too much about money. Knock on wood—we haven't had it this good in a long time and with some more luck, we'll be as well off as in former times (only here we can enjoy our money more).

It's not a bad idea to take the little Ford for the summer (I would even pay him a little something, since I don't know the man) and leave my car here. Write as soon as possible telling me whether that was a serious offer, and if so I'll arrange to leave my car here. Do you think you can accept this from that gentleman? In the next few days I'll try to get some more information; there is yet another railroad line on which neither the trip nor the shipping cost for the car is as expensive as on the Santa Fe.

Please, *Blümchen,* send me the following telegram in the next few days: "Moses advises that we definitely have to take out our First Papers [citizenship application] by the end of the month, otherwise extension of residence permit is very questionable." I can show that to Lang so he'll let me go.

My contract has been signed, I got the first *check.* They're deducting 10 percent for taxes, and the agent gets another 10 percent. But as a result I'll have less to pay in taxes at the beginning of next year, so the money really isn't lost.

Now I must go to see that lunatic and listen to his nonstop nonsense. Farewell, *Kleene,* be nice, and behave yourself so you don't have any more pox when I get back.

A thousand kisses from your

> *Schnübchen*

Enclosed, a few little flowers for the *Blümchen* (from my little garden).

1. *Weill's new lyricist was Johnny Burke (1908–64), who wrote hit lyrics for numerous Hollywood films but was best known for his collaboration with James Van Heusen for the Bing Crosby film* Going My Way.

193T WEILL IN SANTA MONICA TO LENYA IN NEW YORK, 12 JUNE 1937

Western Union: telegram in English

PLEASE BE VERY CAREFUL STAY IN BED AND DO EVERYTHING TO GET OVER THE FEVER STOP I AM SO GLAD TO SEE YOU SOON WRITING TOMORROW THOUSAND KISSES = KURT.

193 WEILL IN SANTA MONICA TO LENYA IN NEW YORK, [17 JUNE 1937]

Thursday

Dear *Blume,*

Many thanks for both of your letters and telegrams. Just now I got your telegram that the Spewacks can't get into their house until 10 July. Did they write a nice letter? Now I won't have to push myself so hard, but I'll still try to get away from here no later than the end of next week. Anyway, it will take until 10 July for us to get our immigration taken care of and get back from Canada. The only thing I'm still wondering about is whether I should try to find someone to drive back with me. It's much cheaper, especially considering that we could then return by car as well. In that case we could also drive to Canada, which would be another savings. And it doesn't seem right about that other car, since I wouldn't want to have anything at all to do with Francesco. (When he was here, he disgusted me more than anyone I have ever had anything to do with, and I've never seen anybody as low-down and dirty, inside and out.)

I'll still consider that car trip. I wouldn't drive by myself. If I find a good driver, the two of us could do it in five or six days.

It's a good idea not to take a house in Pennsylvania yet. Once the Spewacks are settled out there, we could still easily find something nice and take it for four to six weeks. The way things look now, I don't think Lang can start shooting before 15 August, which means I wouldn't have to be back here before the middle of September. He really hates to let me go, because apparently he never got along with anyone else as well. But he isn't making any trouble, knock on wood.

I'll take care of the matter with old lady [Agnes] Meyer. I hope she'll do it. I'll invite Elisabeth [Meyer] for dinner and talk about it with her.

Now I'll try one more time to squeeze a few lines out of one of those *lyric writers.* But I think I'll have a few very good songs *after all.* They're really excited about me at Paramount.

Be careful, and take good care of yourself so you'll have clear skin by the time I get there!

Lots of love,

Knut

194T WEILL IN SANTA MONICA TO LENYA IN NEW YORK,
23 JUNE 1937
Western Union: telegram in English

WORKING VERY HARD HOPE TO BE IN NEW YORK MIDDLE OF NEXT WEEK MRS MEYER IS
IN EUROPE KISSES = KURP.

Yip Harburg's recollection of the plot of the planned Spewack musical differs somewhat from Weill's description to Lenya (Letter 175). In Harburg's account the theater troupe has had to leave the score behind in Germany and thus must try to reconstitute the music from memory, but the climactic waltz resists recollection until the finale. One of the other songs, Harburg said, took the form of a letter from one of the singers to the Aryan occupant of his apartment back in Germany, asking how all his old possessions were doing (Sanders, pp. 260–61).

Shortly after his return to New York, Weill wrote Universal Edition: "My position in America has become so secure that I am now able to contemplate making my earlier works better known here than they have been up to now. . . . I have been receiving inquiries from many different quarters about my earlier orchestral and stage works. . . . I have now completely settled down and feel absolutely at home. As you know, it is hard going in America, especially for someone who speaks his own musical language, but for theater the situation is still more favorable here than anywhere else, and I'm sure I'll reach the point where I can carry forward here what I began in Europe" (W–UE, 28 July 1937). He and Lenya would stay; having originally entered the United States on a temporary visitor's visa, on 27 August they reentered from Toronto, Canada, on an immigrant's visa, thus taking the first step toward citizenship. Meanwhile, Weill's lease on the apartment in Louveciennes had expired, so Madeleine Milhaud arranged for his belongings to be shipped to the Weills' new duplex apartment at 231 East Sixty-second Street in New York.

The Spewack project was postponed indefinitely, never to be resumed. In August Weill visited Paul Green in North Carolina and planned a patriotic musical pageant, The Common Glory, *for the Federal Theatre Project, of which Green was a board member. Weill couldn't make much progress on the music until they had a finished libretto, and meanwhile Burgess Meredith had convinced the composer to attempt a musical adaptation of H. R. Hays's* The Ballad of Davy Crockett, *also intended for the Federal Theatre Project.*

194 WEILL IN CHAPEL HILL TO LENYA IN NEW YORK,
[7 OCTOBER 1937]

Thursday

Dear *Schnübenblümchen,*

Many thanks for your letter. What you write about the new apartment *sounds very exciting to me,* and I'm already quite excited about my room. The weather here is nice now, and for the last few days I've played a lot of tennis with Paul Green, Jr. This tennis playing is wonderful for me. The work is going extremely slowly. Paul is hyper-hysterical; he has no ideas, no pep, no enthusiasm, no courage; he reads and reads and gets more and more confused, because he can't absorb all he's reading. And he's always asking me how this or that happened in [American] history. Of what we have so far,

80 percent is mine. He wants me to stay until the end of the week. If I could only have the *story outline*, I'd beat it. It's highly questionable that he can write it the way I want it. I'm living here in his house. But at the end of the week, they'll have guests again and they have only one servant. I think I'll leave here on Saturday evening and get to New York on Monday morning. I'm looking forward to being in the apartment and working on the other piece [Davy Crockett]. I haven't heard a thing from Charles [Alan].

Things are looking terrible again in Europe.[1] I'm glad we have our immigration papers.

Don't work too hard, you little bee, and be careful. Many little kisses from

Kurti

1. *On 30 January 1937 Hitler had proclaimed in the Reichstag that Germany was withdrawing from the Treaty of Versailles. At the end of May, Neville Chamberlain succeeded Stanley Baldwin as Britain's prime minister. Hitler had been cultivating Mussolini, and on 25 September 1937, Mussolini finally paid his first visit to Hitler in Berlin. After a parade demonstrating the results of four years of German military buildup, the visit climaxed on 28 September with a gigantic crowd gathering to hear the two fascist dictators' inflammatory speeches. A month later Mussolini and Hitler would sign the Anti-Comintern Pact in Rome.*

1938

On 13 December 1937, unable to delay his return to Hollywood any longer, Weill left New York and rented a house on Ocean Front Drive in Santa Monica. Lenya went with him this time, her first visit to the West Coast. They stayed until early February, then both returned to New York.

Green had made little progress on The Common Glory, *and although Weill managed to complete a draft of some forty-five minutes of music for "Davy Crockett," Charles Alan could not find financing for a production. Meanwhile, however, Kurt and Lenya had been spending more and more time with Mab and Maxwell Anderson, whose* What Price Glory? *Weill had seen in Berlin and whose* Winterset *was the first serious play the Weills had attended in New York. When Anderson showed him* High Tor *in 1936, Weill felt it an ideal subject for a musical play and started trying to persuade him, then the foremost American dramatist, to collaborate on a musical play. Early in 1938 Anderson agreed and suggested an adaptation of Washington Irving's* Knickerbocker History of New York.

On 11 March Hitler invaded Austria. In early April Weill had to return to Hollywood for the final editing and dubbing of his music for Lang's film, now titled You and Me. *Lenya stayed on in New York, where she was appearing at the Ruban Bleu nightclub.*

[FIG. 55]

195   WEILL IN HOLLYWOOD TO LENYA IN NEW YORK,
19 APRIL 1938

Tuesday, 19 April 1938

Dear *Blümchen*,

I'm writing you just a few lines, because I'm hungry and tired. I have a very nice room with bath, dressing room, kitchen and dinette, all for $75 a month. It's on Franklin Avenue, near Hollywood Boulevard and Vine Street. Yesterday afternoon I went to the studio, had dinner with Fritz [Lang] and his goat (I can hardly talk to them anymore, and she's more impudent than ever, but it just bounces off the surface of my deep silence).[1] This morning at 8:30 Fritz showed me about two thirds of the movie. It's very beautiful, at times excitingly so, but *zu lang* (i.e., too long and too Lang), often very draggy and very German, but of a much higher standard than anything they're doing here. The songs are definitely the highlights, and one could just cry (or laugh) to think that in this movie all my ideas have again proved to be right and new and exciting—and nobody will ever know they were my ideas. "The Right Guy" is terribly effective; "Song of the Lie" [which was ultimately dropped] comes through much better than I had thought. The best thing is the *cash register* in the beginning, but of course they won't understand it (except for Lang), and I'm sure they'll cut it. Oh well, I've decided not to get upset, and I'm more convinced than ever that it isn't worth it getting irritated, because you're dealing with the lowest human scum. I've asked that Boris to his face what happened with Wanger, and from his stammering it became very clear that he had his dirty fingers in it. When it comes to making a real *Schweinerei*, then they all band together. I'm more disgusted with this place than ever, and I wish I didn't have to deal with this bunch of swine anymore. Of course, I'll have to try to do as good a job with *You and Me* as possible, but the question is whether they'll let me do anything they can't understand with their pig brains. At Paramount they've brought in a herd of cows for one of the movies, and one of these cows gave birth to a little calf this afternoon, right next to the music department. I arrived about five minutes after it happened. That the Lord God should allow something like that is really the end!

Now I'm meeting the Spewacks to get my car, and we'll have dinner together. Ann [Ronell] is very busy with the movie I got for her [*Blockade*], on which she now works in heavenly peace with the other gentleman (they've thrown out all my music!).[2] We have to forget our standards of ethics and decency.

I'm happy, my *Blümchen*, that things at the nightclub are going well and that you've gotten used to it and are getting good audiences. Everyone here knows you're a success.

Farewell, *Schnübchen*, I'm off to stuff my face.

Your Knuti

1. *Lang's companion was Lily Latté (1901–84).*

2. *After work on* Castles in Spain *ceased, Walter Wanger had commissioned a new screenplay from John Howard Lawson. Weill's score for that script, "The River Is Blue," was discarded after a piano audition for the new director, William Dieterle; a new one was commissioned from Werner Janssen (b. 1899), the husband of film actress Ann Harding and conductor of the Baltimore Symphony. The film was finally released in 1938 under the title* Blockade. *The composer Ernst Toch had introduced Weill to Ann Ronell during his first stay in Hollywood; she had hoped to become George Gershwin's protégée and was supporting herself by writing English lyrics for productions of European operas and operettas.*

Letterhead: 231 East 62nd Street / New York

Wednesday

My dear *Sonnenblumi,*

Thanks for your two telegrams. I'm glad you had a pleasant trip. No doubt you got a swelled head from all the *papers.* I got a nice write-up in the *Times* (Sunday): *engaging young Lady* (I don't put much value on the "Lady" part). Jacobi was in seventh heaven.[1] Yesterday it was so crowded again that you couldn't breathe. I'm really good now (after Charlie [Alan] read me the riot act on Sunday about everything I was doing wrong, and he was right, too). I sing "The Right Guy" very softly now, and it's a big success every time.[2] Last night they were really crazy about me. A lot of acquaintances were there, friends of Geddes's. He himself hasn't come. Tomorrow night is that gala evening at the Gladstone, which Jacobi had mentioned in the beginning. Otherwise there's nothing new on my part. Tonight I'm having a dinner party! Elsie Huston, Marie Eve with her girlfriend, and George Davis. Pretty fancy, huh? I'm rather tired, never get to bed before 4:00 A.M., and Saturdays are still awful. But at least it's going well now. I hope you're doing OK. Is it very warm? Here it's been stifling hot for two days. If it stays like this, I'll fix up our *roof.* I went to take care of the taxes, had to pay $7.50 more in state tax. How's it going with Fritz? Is he nice to you, or is the dear little bitch busy making a stink again? I hope, *Blumi,* you're not getting irritated and are taking it as *easy* as possible. And go play tennis and don't give two hoots about your arms. You can't even see it [the rash] when they get a little tan. Cheryl called and was surprised that you'd already left. She's going to write to you. Her *show* is not doing well. Sandy Meisner told me.[3] On Monday I went to *A Doll's House* with Sofie [Messinger, Weill's cousin]. It was more like "A Dull's House." About as boring as watching your fingernails grow. Like a *slow motion movie.* Everything so profound—enough to make you puke. And this Ruth Gordon can drive you to despair.[4] A very unpleasant evening. Eleonora [von Mendelssohn] has gone to Hollywood with [Rudolf] Forster, of course without seeing me perform or even just saying goodbye. A disgusting bunch. I always have the feeling she's afraid somebody will snatch her true love [Max Reinhardt] away from her. I'm really curious how they'll make out in H. They and the "*Countess*"[?] will make a fascinating trio. That old Soscha Kochanski[?] has already come to see me three times, and she always brings people along. I find that very nice. Yesterday Mrs. Korff[?] (whose husband worked for the *Berliner Zeitung* and recently died) came. She's very nice. Well, *Blumi,* do you notice how all I talk about is that dive? I'm all alone at home. I'm not in the least afraid. It's almost *daylight* by the time I come home. Then I snooze until Vera [the maid] comes, and by then the day is almost over anyway. Now my *Bitrübelchen,* write me when you have the time. You probably don't have a lot to spare. Get a little rest and be loved by your

Blümchen

Regards to Ann [Ronell] and the others

1. *Herbert Jacoby (1898–1972) was the artistic director of the Ruban Bleu nightclub, which was then located at 4 East Fifty-sixth Street. Jacoby had known the Weills in Paris, where he had operated the famous nightclub known as "Le boeuf sur le toit"; Lenya had performed there, as had the dancer Marie Eve. Together with Max Gordon, he later owned another club in New York, "The Blue Angel" (1943–63); then "The Red Garter," a banjo bar in Greenwich Village; and finally "Wheels," a discotheque.*

2. *"The Right Guy for Me," with lyrics by Sam Coslow, was one of Weill's songs for* You and Me; *it was published by Famous Music Corp. in 1938.*

3. *Sanford Meisner (b. 1905) had been a leading actor with the Group Theatre. Cheryl Crawford suffered five failures in a row: an unnamed play by Lewis Meltzer that never opened after a disastrous run-through;* Yankee Fable, *starring Ina Clair and directed by Otto Preminger;* All the Living, *directed by Lee Strasberg, which had fifty-three performances;* Family Portrait, *with Judith Anderson, banned by the Catholic Church after a run of three months; and* Another Sun, *by Dorothy Thompson and Fritz Kortner, which opened and closed quickly.*

4. *The stage and screen actress Ruth Gordon (1896–1985) played Nora in the 1937 Broadway production of* A Doll's House. *In 1955 she would play Dolly Levi in* The Matchmaker; *in 1968 her portrayal of a "Manhattan witch" in* Rosemary's Baby *was nominated for an Academy Award; in 1971 she starred in the film* Harold and Maude.

197 LENYA IN NEW YORK TO WEILL IN HOLLYWOOD, [21 APRIL 1938]

Letterhead: 231 East 62nd Street

Thursday

My *Schnübchen,*

Your letter just arrived. A thousand thanks. I'm glad you've found a nice room. I hope you've stopped upsetting yourself over these pigs. They are the scum of humanity, otherwise they wouldn't have been able to stay on top all this time. I hope that Lang edits the movie well. I'm convinced the music is beautiful and will bring the film up to a high level. Whether they will understand it is another matter. I never had any doubts that that dear little Ann is quite a con artist. But one has to be fair. Naturally she doesn't want to pass up this chance, for which she has waited a really long time. But the bounds of decency can be moved by the slightest stirring of the wind. See to it that you get away again soon. I called the agent about our apartment, and she thinks it's possible to sublet it for the months of June, July, and August. Well, we'll see.

Bravi [Abravanel] called this morning; he's on his way to Hollywood. Don't be shocked. If you can't find anyone better, you might have to drive back with him. My party yesterday was nice. I took them all to the People's Theater in the Bowery. Then we all went to our dive, which again was packed to the last seat. Meyer Weisgal was there. Enjoyed himself and was as proud as if he had given birth to me. Julian Fush (does this still mean anything to you?) was also there, with his American bride, a horrible, ugly Yidina (who came over—no later than with the Mayflower—last year from Poland). But they were very enthusiastic. It now seems very strange how it's beginning to crystallize and people are simply going along with whatever I do. They love the German songs. The "Kanonen Song" is always a big success, during the "Pirate Ballad" they're as quiet as little mice. Actually, all of it goes well. They're really showing off with me now. Jacobi is behaving extremely well. He helped me get through my initial period of nervousness and now beams when all that he'd been telling me to do from the start proves successful. On Saturday I only have to sing very little. Now I'm just curious to see whether he will pay punctually again today.

Tonight is the gala evening at the Gladstone. There will be a big dinner. I've been invited by my *boss* with Marie Eve. Well, *Schnübchen*, that's about all I can tell you about me. Jed [Harris] called last night. I've sent Ruth Gordon a soft-soap telegram; *the hell with the truth*. He's been meaning to come for days but is always too tired. Well, we won't hold our breath waiting for that one. *Blumi*, wouldn't "Die Ballade vom Räuber Esteban" from *A Kingdom for a Cow* be something for me? And where is the music? Maybe Phoebe Brand has it? That time at the *camp* [Group Theatre in Nichols, Connecticut] she was learning it.

Now farewell, my *Schnübchen*. The Sohns are coming at five. Don't get annoyed, but rather think how nice it'll be when you're here again, and the little Max too. Little kisses,

Your *Blumi*

198 WEILL IN HOLLYWOOD TO LENYA IN NEW YORK, 21 APRIL 1938

Thursday, 21 April 1938

Dear *Pflänzchen*,

I thought I would have a letter from you by today. I'm curious as to how things are going at the club. I told Henrietta[?] she should write to Sam Lyons [Arthur's brother] again so that he does some *publicity*. She, too, says the main thing is that as many people as possible hear you; that's the best publicity. Have you arranged it so that you sleep late in the morning? I hope you won't get too bored all alone in the house. And I hope you aren't getting too uppity.

I'm already in the midst of doing the *underscoring*, but it's rather boring work. I've gotten the *cash register song* accepted. They were all ready to cut it; then they showed it to someone who is very important *(executive)*, and he was enthused. Now they all act as if they had always thought it was wonderful. A second triumph was that the *publisher* said in front of everybody that he thinks "The Right Guy" is definitely a hit. Yesterday I went with Boris to Lucey's for lunch, where Fritz was waiting for us. Guess who was sitting there? Wanger with Joan Bennett.[1] He got up right away and came over to me. I was terribly brash and took full advantage of the opportunity of having all those rogues together. They all maintained that they had tried to get me to come here, and all the trouble was Allenberg's fault. That *gangster* has not shown his face at all. Wanger was awfully embarrassed, and La Bennett laughed her head off at the shameless things I told him (*"I am not angry, but I think you are a fool. The trouble with you is that you have too much money, etc."*)

Last night I met with Henrietta. She showed me the Kingsley contract (which is completely idiotic).[2] Then we met Miriam Hopkins and Tola [Litvak] (who already have all kinds of marital fights and problems; I believe we're the only married couple without problems) and went to hear Maxine Sullivan, who is here and whom I find (without the New York orchestra, the New York mise-en-scène, and the New York snobs) completely insignificant.[3] But we had a very nice evening. Today I left the studio at four and played tennis with Lester[?]. Now I'll go eat, and in the evening I'll work. On Sunday the local Lyons brother will give a garden-*lunch-party* for Forster. I've been invited. His "sweetie" is here, too.

That is, I believe, everything I have to tell you today. Actually, all this time I have really been thinking only about my play with Max [Anderson]. I wrote him a long letter on the train. May God grant that he write it. Today I had lunch with Russell Crowse. He's tremendously excited about the *White Wings* idea and says he'll do it with me right away.[4] He leaves for New York on Saturday and will go hear you.

Now farewell, my *Schnübchen*, and accept a little kiss from your

Knut

1. *Joan Bennett (1900–1990), a member of the famous Bennett acting family and a star in her own right, was Wanger's third wife.*

2. *The playwright, director, and producer Sidney Kingsley (b. 1906) was president of the Dramatists Guild; he was married to the actress Madge Evans.*

3. *The singing star Maxine Sullivan (1911–87) appeared in the film* St. Louis Blues *(1938), the stage musical* Swingin' the Dream *(1939), and an African-American version of* A Midsummer Night's Dream *with Louis Armstrong as Bottom.*

4. *Initially a press agent for the Theatre Guild, Russell Crouse (1893–1966) had collaborated with Howard Lindsay (1889–1968) on the rewrite of* Anything Goes *and* Red, Hot and Blue! *Subsequently they wrote* Life with Father, Call Me Madam, The Sound of Music, *and* Mr. President. White Wings *was a failed comedy from 1926 about a street cleaner who rebels against the advent of the automobile, by Philip Barry (1896–1949), who in 1939 wrote* The Philadelphia Story.

199 LENYA IN NEW YORK TO WEILL IN HOLLYWOOD, [24 APRIL 1938]
Letterhead: 231 East 62nd Street

Sunday
9:00 P.M.

Dear *Schnübchen*,

I just got back from the country. We (Marie Eve, Jimmy Daniels, the two pianists, and our *boss*) had been invited for lunch by the Meyers, a wealthy Jewish family. We were picked up in a fancy car at one o'clock. Last night it was easy. He let me sing only two songs in one of the shows! It was so smoky and crowded. He let Jimmy [Daniels] and the Fat One [Hope Emerson] sing for almost the entire evening.[1] On Friday the Sohns came with Sofie [Messinger]. They were terribly enthusiastic. I sang "Surabaya," and Jakobi said I had never been as good. You won't believe what kind of people are coming and requesting songs. Yesterday someone wanted to hear the opening song from *Anna-Anna* [*Die sieben Todsünden*]. I'm enjoying myself now, and I'm glad I accepted this gig. I'm learning a great deal from it. I know how to grab an *audience* now. Sometimes they're loud, but they are with Elsie [Huston] too. I also got my money (except for ten dollars). I've gotten a few facials, which aren't cheap (but so necessary because of all that smoke). Today the people were very nice. A lot of people. Of course we had to sing. The "Barbarasong" was again a big success. *Blumi*, I think you must want to throw up hearing about the club again and again. But it's just my job.

I'm glad you're taking it *easy* with people like Wanger. I think one can't be brassy enough with his ilk. Is Fritz being nice to you? I hope the *publisher* will do something with "The Right Guy." There's nothing new here. Is it warm there? What are the Spewacks doing? Are they finished with the play? . . . I'd be happy too if Max [Anderson] would write that play. But who knows how badly he'll be torn by doubts again when he's by himself. *Blumi,* my writing is a little scribbly. I'm a bit tired. I'll stay in bed until showtime. I'll try to take a little nap. Tonight it won't be so *hot.* At least I hope not, because my stomach isn't quite right. Now farewell, my *Schnübi.* How was the *party* with the "sweetie"? I suppose all those "dear ones" will have gotten together for it. Play tennis if you have time. How is that stocking device working?

Farewell, *Blumi!*

1. *The character actress Hope Emerson (1897–1960), whom Lenya calls "die Dicke," later played Mrs. Jones in the original production of Weill's* Street Scene *and then went on to a successful career in motion pictures. In his autobiography Virgil Thomson writes: "It was on one of these trips uptown, at a small joint where Jimmy Daniels (1910–84) was just starting out as host and entertainer, that I turned to Russell [Hitchcock], realizing the impeccable enunciation of Jimmy's speech-in-song, and said, 'I think I'll have my opera* [Four Saints in Three Acts] *sung by Negroes' " (p. 217).*

200 LENYA IN NEW YORK TO WEILL IN HOLLYWOOD, [26 APRIL 1938]

Tuesday

Dear *Schnubchen,*

It was nice talking to you on the telephone. I'll talk to Jacobi again tonight. That remark he dropped so casually on his way out yesterday was really unclear. But I'm under the impression that neither he nor I can get any more out of this. You can't do much more in a *nightclub.* You can see that with Elsie Huston, who still has the biggest and surest success every night. She hasn't received a single offer from anywhere else. I don't know how he figures he can leave me out for a week and then later put me back in again. I think that's completely idiotic. He claims to have such big *expensies.* I went to see [Arthur] Lyons. Unfortunately he wasn't in. I talked to his secretary and she, too, thought it wouldn't make any sense to stay on after 1 May. There aren't any more important people coming, either. It's too late. If I had done this during the winter, it probably would have been more useful to me. My program isn't substantial enough, either. Actually, I always sing only the [Marc] Blitzstein song,[1] "Barbara," "Surabaya," "Pirate Ballad," and sometimes also "Bilbao." Plus "Kanonensong," almost always, and "The Right Guy." But it was good to have tried this. I've learned a lot. You know, *Blumi,* this Elsie has quite a bag of tricks. She has it a lot easier. With all those *drumms* and strange instruments. Then people think it's really something. My things are all so straightforward. Marie Eve told me that this Oswald has again had an enormous success in Paris.[2] She specializes in communism and sings only revolutionary songs now that she has milked *Die Dreigroschenoper* dry. She knows how to pull it off. And I believe that Jacobi had counted on a sensation. And I was anything but that. Well, *the hell with it.* I did the best I could. He's closing soon anyway and will probably keep only Hope

Emerson for the remaining time. Marie Eve leaves on 4 May, Jimmy Daniels on the 15th. There's no news at all, *Blumi*. I hope you can get away soon. And then we'll have ourselves a nice summer. There's another insolent letter from your parents. They "acknowledge" that you're trying to help the family now, that I have a "good" engagement. The rest is all about their problem finding ways to while away their idle days in the most pleasant way. I gave it to Ruth, who will answer it because Leo has to do something about their promissory notes. Not once do they ask what all of us are doing here and how the Sohns are managing to subsist. Your parents are really too sweet. Yesterday [Alfred] Strelsin came to the club again with several girls. That guy is especially repulsive. There's no hope of help for Leo from that corner. But Leo is quite happy and is quietly looking around some more. Otherwise I haven't seen anyone. Jed [Harris] never showed up again. Charlie [Alan] is busy with his exhibition. It's very beautiful in New York right now, and just wait until the Max finally gets here! I'll put an ad in the paper. Maybe someone will show up for the apartment. [Stella] Adler has not been able to sublet hers, either. If you drive back with Bravi, *take it easy, Blumi*, and don't let him drive if he can't drive well. Under no circumstances let him drive without a *license*! Now I'll go eat, and then I'm going with Marie Eve to a concert Elsie is giving tonight in a private home. That's how the time flies. Now farewell, my *Blümchen*. I'm upset about what's going on in the world. Four Nazis here attacked a Jewish newspaper editor in his office in the middle of the day and made a mess of him. It really makes you sick to think that all that may start up here too someday. Many little kisses, stay well, and don't get annoyed.

Blumi

1. *It is not clear which song Lenya is referring to. She had made her U.S. radio debut in Marc Blitzstein's radio cantata* I've Got the Tune, *broadcast by CBS on 24 October 1937, singing the part of Suicide. Among Lenya's papers was a seven-page holograph copy of a song for voice and piano by Blitzstein, entitled "Few Little English" and dated 15 July 1936. It is now in the Weill/Lenya Archive at Yale University.*

2. *Marianne Oswald, née Alice Bloch Kahn (1903–85), had played one of the Salvation Army girls in* Happy End *in 1929 at the Theater am Schiffbauerdamm. In 1933 she fled to Paris, where she established a remarkable career as a cabaret and recording artist. Milhaud accompanied her first appearance, Cocteau wrote monologues for her, Honegger composed songs for her. Cole Porter called her "completely unique"; one critic aptly described her voice as "not pleasing to the ear, sometimes nasal, sometimes throaty, bereft of any musical timbre; she doesn't sing but exhales a sort of monotonous recitative which doesn't allow one to tell the difference between one tune and another" (quoted in O'Connor, p. 12). Her first recording of Weill's music coupled "Kanonensong" with "Surabaya Johnny," which she eventually recorded three times. She spent the war years in New York and then returned to Paris, where she became a friend of Albert Camus's and was active in cinema and television.*

201 LENYA IN NEW YORK TO WEILL IN HOLLYWOOD, [28 APRIL 1938]

Thursday, 4:30 A.M.

Dear *Blumchen*,

Tonight was one of those noisy nights again. Even Elsie stopped right in the middle, because it was so loud she couldn't go on. But I have a sense of humor now, and that seems to make it go better. Last night I talked to Jacobi about my eight days off, and he was terribly nice (he really is sympathetic); he simply goofed up with a previous engagement. As of today he has hired a gentleman who accompanies himself on the guitar ("[La] Paloma"), because he thought that Marie Eve was going to leave. But now she's staying until the 4th. Of course, his program is now much too long and too expensive. I told him it would be very bad for me if I had to stop for eight days and then come back. I'd rather stop altogether. He didn't want that. Now we'll do it like this: tonight Hope (the Fat One) will take two days off. Saturday and Sunday I will (which suits me very well), and then Marie Eve is going to leave and we'll see how it goes from there. On Monday I'll sing again. Of course, he has to change the program more often now, because the good people all go away after 1 May, and then come the provincial hicks. He won't be able to stay open much longer anyway. It will close as soon as it gets warm. He's really nice and puts great emphasis on not being looked upon as just a manager. Last night Marlene [Dietrich] suddenly showed up! She looked marvelous and was unbelievably nice to me. When Jacobi announced me (it was the second performance; she came at 1:30), she said quite loudly, "*how wonderful,*" and applauded like crazy (which, of course, made a great impression on everyone, including Jacobi). I sang "The Right Guy," "Surabaya Johnny" (I sang that one for her), and "Pirate Ballad." She brought me over to her table. Well, you should have seen all the others. The Fat One almost turned green with envy. But it helped me a lot, because afterward I had that talk with Jacobi. But I thought the way she acted toward me was awfully nice.

And tonight Cole Porter was there. He sat with Horst, the photographer from *Vogue.*[1] I was the only one they invited to their table, which again was good. Cole Porter liked me a lot. He said I had *wonderful diction.* It really is all the same to me, but showing off to people is important. He can hardly walk, is on crutches, and still seems to be very sick. You see, *Schnübchen,* this is New York's nightlife. It's a very nice atmosphere, and we all get along quite well except for the Fat One. But there's no stopping a hurricane.

Otherwise there's nothing going on. Today the owner invited us to a great dinner down in the club. We all had champagne. The real high life—you see, *Blumi,* how your *Schnübe* is living? And what about my *lila Schweinderl?* I thought I would get a little *letter* today. *But nothing.* I know you have to work a lot this week; the main thing is that you'll be finished soon. Have you heard anything from Max Anderson? But he is not one to write letters. The telephone hardly rings anymore since you've been away. Not a word from anyone. And I don't care, either. Surprisingly, I got my *money* already today. I wrote ten dollars' worth of checks (I made one payment for you, six dollars or so!). But most likely this is correct. *Blumchen,* this letter from Germany came in an open envelope, forwarded by the Group Theatre. I think you should give another address, or have the mail come here, it's *safer* than the Group address.[2] Saturday I'm going to see *On Borrowed Time* [Paul Osborne]; I'm already looking forward to that. And George Davis has invited me to see Tallulah Bankhead in *Circle* [Somerset Maugham] next week. It's a huge success for her. And now, my *Blümchen*, you should see my poor eyes; they're already half closed. Good night, stay well, and come soon.

> Much love from
> your wife,
> Lollie

Your telegram just came. *Blümchen*, don't worry about writing. And don't get annoyed. See that you get everything behind you quickly and try to part in peace with those people. You never know what's going to happen and how you may need them again. Be a *Klugi*! Now farewell,

> *Schnüb*

1. *Horst Paul Albert Bohrmann (b. 1906).*

2. *It's unclear whether Lenya's advice was intended to avoid Nazi censorship of letters from Germany, minimize identification with the "communistic" Group Theatre, or maintain confidentiality for Weill's extramarital relationships (such as Erika Neher).*

202 WEILL IN HOLLYWOOD TO LENYA IN NEW YORK, 28 APRIL 1938

28 April 1938

Dear *Schnubenblümchen*,

Many thanks for your letters. I'm glad you don't seem too upset about the nightclub. I'm certain that it's been good for you, even if you have to stop now, and that you can't get much more out of it anyway. So see to it that you recuperate a little bit from all that strain. It would probably be nice for you to go to Chapel Hill for a while. It must be beautiful there right now, and the Greens would be happy if you went, and the kids would see to it that you won't get bored. You can tell them you'll take a room in that pretty little hotel (Carolina Inn); it's not expensive at all.

I'm in the midst of fighting all the mess that surrounds this Boris Morros. He really is the end. Now they're trying to twist things so that someone else would collaborate on the *score*, because time is so short. For now I have flat-out rejected this, but most likely they'll just do it anyway without asking me. The whole thing is so deeply immoral and vicious that it's impossible to retain any enthusiasm, and I have only one desire: to finish up and never see these miserable little con men again. Fritz, of course, is on their side and anyway is repulsive enough in his own right. But the movie could turn out to be very good. They say we'll begin recording the music in a week, and you can imagine how much work I have to do before then. Please tell Charlie (who sent me a wire today) that I don't believe Boris Morros will fly to New York to see his show, but if he decides to, I'll enlighten him about Charlie.

Please do send the records to Max [Anderson], if you haven't done so yet (New City, N.Y.). And please send the enclosed letter to Hoffman Hays; the address is in the little telephone book.[1]

I've written a terribly nasty letter to Cheryl, because she wrote to Ann [Ronell] (and not to me!) saying she had bought *White Wings*! She, too, wangles through life quite nicely.

Don't you want to call Mab Anderson and meet with her when she's in town? She's very important for me, to keep his interest alive.

Now farewell, *Blümchen,* and be kissed by your

> *Schnüb*

---

1. *The author and translator Hoffman Reynolds Hays (1904–80) collaborated with Weill on a musical version of Hays's play about Davy Crockett; it was never finished. Later he supplied one of the affidavits in support of Brecht's immigration to the United States. He translated* Mutter Courage *in 1941, and Brecht suppressed recognition of his work on* The Duchess of Malfi *(which premiered on Broadway in 1946, starring Elisabeth Bergner, adapted by W. H. Auden, with incidental music by Benjamin Britten).*

203 LENYA IN NEW YORK TO WEILL IN HOLLYWOOD, [2 MAY 1938]

Monday

My dear *Blümchen,*

I've just come from the record shop (and Liberty). They don't have any more of your recordings. I could only get a French one with Lys Gauty. With Oswald they have only "Kanonensong" and "Surabaya," but those you certainly would not want to send to Max. I listened to the Oswald records. The police should ban them. Therefore I'm sending the Klemperer record (which we have at home) and the French one. We must ask someone to bring us all the records from Paris. I believe you can still get them there.

Otherwise there's nothing new. Kurt Riess[?] sent me some beautiful roses and thanked me for the invitation to the club. The flowers came a week after he had come to the club, but I suppose he didn't have any money before that. I found that so touching. Yesterday evening (Sunday) I sang anyway. Jimmy [Daniels] wasn't there. Edward James came with Julien Levy.[1] He was very nice. Strangely quiet. I think he's completely crazy now. He's staying only a few days and then will come back in July. I'm very tired and am looking forward to your coming back here. I've bought a few little trees for our *roof,* and now I'll buy a few more chairs. I think it'll be very nice. I'm so happy about the news that Max is going to write that play. If only something would work out for once. I'll be glad to call Mab, only I doubt that she'll come into town. It's already so hot.

I'm so glad you'll be leaving H.! Did you know that Cole Porter is going to do *Serena Blendish* [*sic*] with a *collerd cast?*[2] Jimmy will have a part in it. That's how I know about it. Tonight I'm going to the Mercury to see *Heartbreak House* with George Davis.[3] The press so far is fifty-fifty. Have you seen *Harper's Baȝaar?* The two *Schnüben!*[4] *It made a big impression on Jacobi. I have a very good write-up in the Hollywood Reporter of April 25. "Swell singing comedienne."* Of course, Sam Lyons is not doing a thing. He promised to bring W. Winchell here.[5] But that's hopeless.

Now farewell, my *Blümchen.* Don't drive yourself too hard. The Sohns are coming for dinner on Wednesday. Charlie is fully occupied with his *show*. Many little kisses from your

Blumi

1. New York art dealer Julien Levy (1906–81) owned the Julien Levy Gallery, which specialized in imported neoromantic and surrealist paintings.

2. Serena Blandish, Sam Behrman's play based on Enid Bagnold's novel about a wide-eyed innocent in Mayfair, had originally been staged in 1929 with Ruth Gordon. There is no published account of Porter's involvement in a musical adaptation.

3. In 1938 Orson Welles produced Shaw's play and played the part of Shotover, dressed to resemble George Bernard himself.

4. On page 100 of the May 1938 issue of Harper's Bazaar, a photo feature captioned "Entertainers" included one of Louise Dahl-Wolfe's (now familiar) photographs of Lenya and Weill taken in 1935. The accompanying text explained: "Lotte Lenya's talent manages to be both endearing and sinister at the same time, her wistful childish voice echoing the dramas of the gutter and the underworld. Her husband is Kurt Weill, who first won fame with his Three-Penny Opera, and who is now composing in and for Hollywood. Lenya is singing his songs, among others, at Le Ruban Bleu, the new night club on 56th Street, tremendously popular with the same international crowd that patronized the boîte with the same name in Paris."

5. Walter Winchell (1897–1972) was the most influential and controversial columnist and radio commentator of the time.

204 LENYA IN NEW YORK TO WEILL IN HOLLYWOOD, [4 MAY 1938]

Wednesday

Blümchen,

I haven't had any news from you for days, but I can imagine that you're terribly busy. Several people have already been here about the apartment, and I'm quite certain we can rent it. Now you only have to tell me whether you really want to do it and where you think we should get a house. Charlie thinks Connecticut is much more beautiful than Pennsylvania. But if you want to be near Max, we have no choice. There are no lakes whatsoever in that neighborhood. I called Mab; she doesn't ever come into town. If we decide to go to the country, I would ask her to look around there a little bit. Margret has sent you a chest with twenty-four drawers for music.[1] Buss [Burgess Meredith] had bought it some time ago. It's very beautiful and stands in the corner where the bench was. [Stella] Adler wants to know whether we're keeping the apartment, because if not she'll have to look around. Otherwise there's nothing new. Miriam [Hopkins] and Grace Moore (a horrible goat) came to the club and all of us were rather awful that evening.[2] It was a repulsive audience. But they still heard "Pirate Jenny," and they liked it very much. Gr. Moore had to leave after half an hour because of her shitty voice. It was so smoky. Last night Lubitsch, Tilly Losch, Cheryl, [Jack] Wildberg with his wife, and Mady Christians (who's really very nice) were here.[3] Tilly was especially *sweet*. Lubitsch is really nice. They didn't stay very long, either. You just can't expect people to sit there for three hours to hear a few songs. I'm so tired, *Blumi;* I'm glad it will be over soon. The bank sent a statement. There was still $229 in the account. We really haven't taken out much this month, except for writing a few checks. Everything else I pay with my money as far as possible. There's hardly ever anything left over. I'm not earning big money, *Blumi*. But it does help just a little bit. I hope to hear from you soon. Now farewell, *Blümchen;* be nice. How are all the lunatics? You'll be happy once you're back here again; it's so wonderful in one's own home. I got a long letter from Vienna. They seem very much in favor of the new regime, because Ernst got work right away.[4] Well, that's the most important thing for them. They don't understand anything else anyway. I'm glad that at least there everything is going OK. Jacobi is nice all the time. Today I took Marie Eve (the dancer) to the boat. Practically everybody is sailing on the *Normandie*. From Tchelitchev on up and down.[5]—If Marie Eve were not aboard, I'd wish it would all go down—man and beast. Now farewell, *Schnubi;* I hope you'll come soon.

> Much love and many little kisses!

1. *Margret Perry (b. 1913) was the second wife of Burgess Meredith. Her mother, Antoinette Perry (1888–1946), was chairman of the board of the American Theatre Wing. In 1947 the Wing's annual awards for excellence in the theater were named after her and are now popularly known as "Tony" Awards.*

2. *A glamorous star of the Metropolitan Opera and motion pictures, the soprano Grace Moore (1901–47) had been nominated for an Academy Award in 1934 for* One Night of Love.

3. *The Viennese-born actress Mady Christians (1900–1951) was appearing as Gertrude in Maurice Evans's* Hamlet; *in 1944 she would play the central figure in* I Remember Mama.

4. *Although at some point Lenya's mother left Blamauer and cohabited with another abuser, Ernst Hainisch, it is not clear whether she officially divorced and remarried.*

5. *The Russian-born painter and set designer Pavel Tchelitchev (1898–1957).*

205 WEILL IN HOLLYWOOD TO LENYA IN NEW YORK, 5 MAY 1938

5 May 1938

My beloved *Schnübchen,*

I'm taking advantage of the first free minutes I've had to write you a few lines. For over a week I haven't slept more than four hours a night: I've been working until three, then up again at seven. Just working wouldn't be bad, because I always enjoy that, but it's these annoyances, these squabbles, and this horrendous stupidity and lack of culture I have to struggle against, and on top of that the secret conniving of Boris and, of course, our beloved Fritz, who opposes me at every opportunity and is so incredibly unmusical it makes you want to tear your hair out. I've found there is only one remedy that's effective here: to be incredibly brazen and tell them all to their faces what is on your mind. It's suddenly going much better since I started using this technique; they have more respect for me than for anyone else they've worked with up to now, and I was able to force through all kinds of things the way I wanted them. I did it without giving a thought to any future *jobs*, because the most important thing at the moment is to establish who I am, for that is the only thing that impresses them—and in this I've succeeded. Tomorrow we start to record the music, and we'll be finished by the middle of next week. After that (let's hope very soon) the first *preview* will take place, after which I might possibly have to make a few small changes. Therefore, it's entirely possible that I'll be finished within two weeks.

Many thanks for your nice letters. I'm glad it's going so well in the nightclub and that you enjoy it. Why don't you ask [Sam] Lyons whether he thinks you should hire a publicist for one or two weeks? I will also talk with Henrietta about that. Did the $500 *check* from Hungerford arrive?[1] If not, please call Charles and say they should send it. The picture in *Harper's Bazaar* is rather tiny, and I sure look funny among those *entertainers*. But it's a very nice picture of you. I was very happy about what you wrote about Marlene. I sent a telegram to Max [Anderson] telling him how enthusiastic I am. I'm keeping my fingers crossed that it will come to pass. He said the letter I wrote him on the train has so inspired him that he began to write right away and is making good progress. He might even be finished already by the time I get back. I ought to try to negotiate with an actor here. [Guthrie] McClintic will do the staging. Don't tell anybody; I haven't told anyone here, either.

Now farewell, my *Blumenblümchen*. I'm looking forward so very much to being back and with my *Pflänzchen*. I have not seen a single human being in one week, except in the studio. Today I will, for once, go to bed early and sleep.

Many little kisses,

Your *Schnub*

1. *Edward Hungerford (1875–1948), the author of many publications dedicated to the history of the American railroad, planned and wrote the "fantasia on rail transport,"* Railroads on Parade, *for the 1939 New York World's Fair. Weill had been commissioned to compose an extensive score for soloists, chorus, and orchestra for Hungerford's pageant.*

206 WEILL IN HOLLYWOOD TO LENYA IN NEW YORK, 7 MAY 1938

7 May 1938

Dear *Schnübelein,*

I'm sorry you were worried because I hadn't written for a whole week. By now you must have gotten my letter and telegram. It's just as well that your *night club* is over and done with so you can take a good rest now. Yesterday I had my big triumph. It was the first day of *recording*, and we did two pieces, which I had worked out all by myself (the two *sequences* of "The Song of the Lie"). Of course, everybody was ready to let me have it. But instead, you should have seen their jaws drop when that orchestra started to play. Once they heard for the first time what came over that microphone, they were simply bowled over and readily had to admit that this was better than anything they'd ever done before. As soon as they realized they had something here that most likely would cause a sensation, they were all falling over themselves, each one claiming that some part was his own doing. Oh well, that's really unimportant. But I now realize just how much I could achieve in motion pictures, if only they would let me.

Allenberg thinks I can leave once all the music has been recorded, which should already be by the end of next week (around the 14th). But I might have to stay until the *preview*, which takes place around the 18th. In any case, it won't be much longer now. Perhaps you could go to Paul [Green]'s, and I could pick you up there in the Max.

As far as the apartment is concerned, there are several possibilities. I don't know whether we should sublet it before we've found something in the country. I think we could look around in Connecticut, which really is much more beautiful, and where we could perhaps find a little house near the water (some lake or the ocean). Perhaps Bess [Eitingon] knows of something. It's not more than two hours by car to Max [Anderson], and if I want to work with him for a longer period, I can, of course, always stay with Buzz [Meredith]. So if we could find something nice for around $100 a month, I would be inclined to sublet the apartment for three months. Do you think it would be possible to sublet it for only two months (July and August)? During those two months we really should be away from New York; you remember how awful it was last year, and I absolutely insist you take good care of your health this summer. Of course, another possibility would be not to sublet the apartment but to take the car and go away every *week end*, and go to the ocean for four weeks (to Cape Cod) during the hottest period. That would probably be more expensive. Think about these various options. I would hope we could get along on $400 a month during the summer. But if the thing with Max really materializes, and I can also get the play with Hays, "Davy Crockett," on its feet, we do have some pretty good possibilities for next season. So don't worry, and buy yourself some *Sächelchen* for the summer, and this time we will really have ourselves a nifty summer, won't we?

Many little kisses for you.

La Adler should wait until I come back. If you have time, try to find out how the prices for apartments *down town* are—like the one Jed [Harris] has.

207 LENYA IN NEW YORK TO WEILL IN HOLLYWOOD, [8 MAY 1938]
Letterhead: 231 East 62nd Street

Sunday

My beloved *Schnübchen,*

Finally your letter that I've been waiting for has arrived. I'm firmly convinced that the way you're telling these idiots off right to their faces—regardless of any future job (which you would no doubt get as soon as you have a show running on Broadway)—is the right attitude to have. Most of all, you don't want to get involved in their lame-brained schemes, which in the end won't do any good anyway, so it's better to speak up and show them at every opportunity that you're far more capable than all the others, and that it's their own fault if they don't understand this. It's such a shame—but you see it happen time and again—that decent behavior gets you nowhere. I've noticed it once more with Jacobi, toward whom I've really acted decently, but if I had been La Oswald, everyone else would have been fired and not me.—

Thursday was a very good evening for me. This Mrs. Morris[?], whom we'd met one Sunday afternoon at Jed's, came with a big group, and they liked it a lot. Afterward Jacobi came and asked me if Friday could be my last night ("People are getting tired of hearing the same songs over and over again"). He thought it was enough, and that all the people who wanted to hear me had now heard me. He mumbled something about engaging me again next winter, when I would have a new program. He wants to bring over La Oswald, whom he considers a genius, so there's nothing that can be done about it. I was very nice, saying yes, I understood, but in that case I wanted to quit right away. He agreed to this. It would not have salvaged anything to sing for one more night. Besides, I most likely would have been very bad the next evening.

So, that's that.—It didn't do me any harm, and I've learned a lot, but so far it hasn't done me any good, and I hated it more than any previous work. (Now I can tell you this quite calmly without making you nervous.) Many people liked me very much, and if I'm in a *show* next fall, I'll be able to tell what good it did to have sung here. My program was somewhat *limited* after it turned out that a few of the songs I had on the program did not go over. Lately I'd always sing only Blitzstein, "Pirate," "Barbara," "Kanonensong," "Right Guy," "Surabaya." That is, of course, not very much for a longer *run*. The other songs didn't do so well. But I've kept my spirits up and have proved once more that I can get a bunch of drunks to shut up for some minutes (but not to applaud). If nightclubs were my only ambition, I would be totally content. But thank God I've got other fish to fry. So, *Blümchen*, you won't hear anything further about New York nightlife in the near future, and I will snooze again like a normal human being. I slept from 10:00 P.M. on Friday right through to Saturday at 3:00 P.M. (That's the "Ameisgasse" in me.)[1] I feel like a new person.

I've bought little trees for the *roof*, some chairs, and a reclining chair for the *Hollywoodpflanze* when he comes to sunbathe. It will be very nice. Nobody has come for the apartment, and unfortunately yesterday Vera forgot to put an ad in the paper. When I thought of it, it was too late. Now I want to put one in the *Post* on Saturday and one in the *Times* on Sunday. Something will come along. In the meantime Buss's butler will be looking around for houses in their neighborhood. There's still enough time. But first I have to see whether we can sublet our apartment for $175 (I don't want to give it away for much less; a room like yours with a *roof garden* alone goes for $80–100 in New York).

Imagine, *Blumi*, I got the entire *Dreigroschenoper* set—four records—in a Nazi store on Eighty-sixth Street and sent it on to Max right away. The Nazis are pressing the records again after a three-year suspension.[2] There was such demand (perhaps because people have all heard the songs again now) that Telefunken is reissuing them. Isn't that funny? And not even expensive—four dollars for the whole set. One of your records in the same shop costs two dollars.

And Leo [Sohn] is close to getting a job with a bank. It's almost a sure thing. Isn't that wonderful? They're very happy; they've taken a new apartment and move in on Friday. They got a letter from your parents. Hans and Bissie are going to visit them in Palestine.[3] Well, they're so completely mixed up that they don't seem to know what the hell they want.

Otherwise there's nothing new. *Our Town* won the Pulitzer Prize (but you'll get all that news in your little gazettes). Jed [who produced *Our Town*] has never called again.

As usual. I pray God that Max will write the play. It would be wonderful if McClintic could stage it. That would offer such a good, wholesome atmosphere and a great opportunity at the same time. According to my horoscope, which I once had done in Austria, 1938 should be a very good year, in all. Well, we shall see. *Blümchen*, this is a long letter, and I'm going to make some coffee now. And then I'll go play pinochle. I hope you'll come soon, *Schnübchen;* otherwise the time will drag on. Now farewell, my *Sonnenblume.*

      Your *Schnüb*

1. *Ameisgasse was the street on which Lenya lived as a child.*

2. *An article in* P.M. *noted that "Weill's* Threepenny Opera *can be bought in Yorkville, where it's being imported from Germany. Although the Nazis have banned Weill's music for local consumption, they export it—for the money" (unidentified clipping in* Railroads on Parade *production file, Weill-Lenya Research Center, ser. 50A). In 1938 songs from* Die Dreigroschenoper *were included in the Exhibit of Degenerate Music in Düsseldorf; so many people crowded into the room where they were played that the songs were soon withdrawn.*

3. *Weill's niece Hanne Weill (b. 1923) is the daughter of Hans and Rita Weill. Because of her fragile frame and leanness, her family nicknamed her "Bissie," derived from the German* bißchen, *"a little bit."*

208 LENYA IN NEW YORK TO WEILL IN HOLLYWOOD, [10 MAY 1938]

Tuesday

Dear *Schnübchen*,

I'm going to be brief. I still have to write a letter to Rita. Hans is leaving Europe on 31 May. He can't decide yet whether to stay over here. I have a funny feeling they'll squander all their money in celebration of finally leaving Germany for good. Rita is in Geneva, and Hans is driving around (Belgium, France, Holland) looking for a job, when he should be packing up everything and coming over here and building a new life as fast as possible. But I think they should be old enough to know that themselves. In any case I'll answer as well as I can. Ruth [Sohn] has moved to her new apartment at 215 West Ninety-second today. I went there and took little Eve [Sohn] out for lunch. Just now Charlie called; that check of Hungerford's has gone to 231 East Sixty-second in Hollywood because of a secretary's mistake! They've asked for it to be sent back by airmail. I just wanted to have it to pay back Leo for the $25 he put out this month for your parents and Nathan. I still have some of my club money left for Vera and the household. I'll try to sublet the apartment for only two months (or possibly three: July, August, September), but there will still be time for that when you are back here. It's still a bit uncertain whether you'll have to see Max and when, and I don't want to rush things, so that we don't end up paying two rents. We'll still be able to find something in the country in July, and we won't perish here until then. We have the Max and can always drive somewhere. Let's proceed calmly. I'm terribly happy you're in such good shape with Hollywood. I hope it will stay that way. The movie really has great possibilities. Last night I went to see *The Girl of the Golden West* (only because of Jerome Kern's music).[1] Well, *Blümchen*, it's really meager. It has a nice little waltz, but after that it's a real wasteland. With just a bit of luck, if they don't cut and ruin too much of your work, it will be a really big break for you. So I think it's very important that you wait for the first *preview* and then make the necessary changes yourself. Don't get nervous now; it might really turn out to be a success for you, and in any case it will attract attention. A small box with some matzo (a little piece) arrived from Madeleine [Milhaud]. I didn't send it to you because that's too complicated. It first went to Ocean Front [Weill's previous address in Santa Monica] and then came here. That's all for today. Your parents have also sent a letter of "desperation" to Hans. They still aren't satisfied. Ruth said it was unbelievable, because so far they're still doing very well. They have a wonderful apartment, and they aren't going to starve to death yet, either. But you really can't get involved in all that. Now I'm going to stop, *Blümchen*. Tonight I've been invited to a *party* at G. Platt Lynes's,[2] and Friday I'll have dinner with that Ho-ho-Wiesengrund at the home of some Jews from Frankfurt. I'm only going because I might meet people who could be important for Hans or Leo. After dinner they'll perform an abortion on some music.[3] It'll be frightful. Love

Schnubi

1. The film, starring Jeanette McDonald and Nelson Eddy, featured music by Siegmund Romberg, not Jerome Kern.

2. The famous photographer George Platt Lynes (1907–55) was a friend of George Davis, who would marry Lenya in 1951. In 1938 Lynes photographed Lenya—glamorously dressed all in black, with a stylishly molded, brimmed hat (reproduced in Spoto, Lenya: A Life).

3. Lenya's original German "nach dem Dinner wird Musik abgetrieben" cleverly plays on Musik treiben (to make music) and abtreiben (to abort).

209 LENYA IN NEW YORK TO WEILL IN HOLLYWOOD, [12 MAY 1938]

Thursday

My beloved *Schnubschen*,

Today I have some very pleasant news for you. Helen Deutsch called this morning to ask for her two lamps back, which Cheryl had given to us and which belong to her, for her *country house*.[1] She came here and said that Max had read the first act of your play to her! So he actually seems to be writing now. She said it was "*the funniest thing she ever heard.*" Unfortunately, she seems to have irritated him somewhat with stupid remarks like "*Kurt can't write so silly music,*" etc., so that he—as she tells it—stopped for a while. You know how easily Max can be influenced. I hope he'll keep on writing. But you can't say anything against Helen, because they're such good friends, otherwise he wouldn't have read it for her. Maybe he just read one scene to her. She talks so much nonsense, I don't know whether you shouldn't write a few lines to him, telling him you're so pleased and that you hope he is having fun at it too. Helen said he'll include a humorous role for me! Isn't that wonderful? It's probably because of Mab. I was very nice to Helen. She gave me her address, and I told her we would come to visit her when you got back. She has definitely given up her *job* with the Guild. The Rodgers and Hart premiere [*I Married an Angel*] was yesterday. I'm curious to see how it went. Yesterday I had lunch with Charlie, who complained again that he has no money at all and let me pay for his lunch. There's nothing you can do about that. That's just the way he is. He says the Gershwin-Swift song is so terrible that everybody at the *Worlds Fair* agrees.[2] That serves them right. Then I saw Paul Green, who's here. He's so idiotic that he gets on your nerves. He's written a book. Probably something for "posterity" again.[3] He reacted somewhat sourly when I said, half jokingly, that I could go to Chapel Hill now. Well, OK then, I won't. I can do without that, too. He'll be staying here a few days; he's come from Washington. He really is a hopeless case. *Blumi*, just look at this telephone bill. I don't know how this could happen. I hardly use the phone. Can I take $100 from the *special account* if the check from Hungersford doesn't come this week, and pay that bill as well as the $25 to Leo? I just spoke to Ruth on the phone. This thing with Leo still seems to be dragging on. But we know how that is. It's never as smooth as one would like. The *party* at G. Platt Lynes's was awful. A hundred gays and one *girl*. But I met Orson Welles's wife [Virginia Nicolson], who's very nice. Marc [Blitzstein] seems to make a lot of publicity for me in these circles. But apart from that, it was frightful. Now I have to go to the *hairdresser, Blumi*. I hope you're feeling well and can get out of there soon. Please drive carefully, *Schnube*. I'd rather not call Mab again. It's much better to leave her alone. Otherwise they'll think I'm after them too much. Apparently I'm also not supposed to know anything about that role, but Helen, discreet as she is, peddled the red-hot news immediately. *Blumi*, can you write me what *Ave.* the Boises live on in your next letter? I only know Franklin, but the cross-street I don't know. Something that begins with *W*, but not Wilcox. It could also be something entirely different.

Now farewell, my *Blumi*. Many little kisses,

Linerl

1. *The press agent Helen Deutsch (b. 1906) represented Maxwell Anderson; she founded the New York Drama Critics Circle, whose first awards for best play went, not coincidentally, to Anderson's* Winterset *and* High Tor, *in 1936 and 1937 respectively.*

2. *The late Gershwin's erstwhile romantic interest and amanuensis Kay Swift (1905–93) had adapted with Ira Gershwin the chorus of one unpublished tune and the verse of another as "Dawn of a New Day," the official march of the 1939 New York World's Fair.*

3. *One of Lenya's favorite stories that she related to Lys Symonette described an incident from the period when Weill was studying counterpoint with Busoni's assistant, Philipp Jarnach: "Once [Weill] arrived too early. Waiting for the master, he started to play the piano in the living room downstairs, when Mrs. Jarnach entered. 'Not so loud,' she said in a hushed voice. 'Don't you know that the master is working upstairs? He's creating for posterity* [er schafft doch für die Ewigkeit].' *Weill responded with a double-entendre: 'I hope he makes it* [hoffentlich schafft er's].' "

210 WEILL IN HOLLYWOOD TO LENYA IN NEW YORK, 12 MAY 1938

12 May 1938

Dear *Schnubelinchen*,

Many thanks for your very nice letters. Everything is OK here. Last night we recorded until 3:00 A.M., and tonight we'll be completely finished with recording. Tomorrow Allenberg will settle everything for me. Everybody is wild about the music for the movie; they all claim it's the most original and unique music they've had up to now. Also, the way my name appears in the opening credits is very good, just me and Boris Morros. If I'm lucky, this could become a success for me. Perhaps I'll hire a publicist in New York for a few weeks before the premiere. But I don't know whether that'll be necessary, since the music in itself is so conspicuous, and anyway after a few minutes everyone will know it's mine.

As far as my leaving here is concerned, here's what I think I'll do: if the *preview* takes place before the middle of next week, I'll wait for it, but if not, I'll leave on Monday or Tuesday, since I don't think it's worth waiting too long for that. There's not much they could spoil anymore. I'll know in the next few days when the *preview* will be and decide accordingly. I'm going with Bravi, but I'll have to do all the driving, since he has no *license*. Well, I'll take it *easy* and would rather drive an extra day than rush myself to death.

I've played tennis with Lester a lot this week, and I'm in good shape. Now I want to work as much as possible on the railroad show, which has to be ready by 1 June. And by the way, I'll be doing a bit of socializing. One never knows how one can make use of them.

I'm free this afternoon and will drive around a bit with Ann. Sunday I spent the whole day with the Reinhardts and the Sokoloffs; it was very nice. I talked him into letting me do the Thornton Wilder play if he gets it.[1]

Now farewell for today, my little *Blümchen,* and be loved by your

    Schnüb

1. Reinhardt had introduced Weill to Our Town *playwright Thornton Wilder (1897–1975), hoping they would collaborate on a musical adaptation of Johann Nestroy's* Einen Jux will er sich machen *(1842). Wilder doubted his ability to write lyrics, so Reinhardt directed it as a straight play in December 1938,* The Merchant of Yonkers. *It ran for just thirty-nine performances. In 1955 Tyrone Guthrie directed a revision of the farce, now entitled* The Matchmaker, *which in turn was adapted as* Hello, Dolly! *in 1964 by Jerry Herman.*

211 WEILL IN HOLLYWOOD TO LENYA IN NEW YORK, 15 MAY 1938

15 May 1938

Dear *Blume,*

I'm quite worried by the things you wrote me about Helen Deutsch. I've been afraid all along that she would find out about my work with Max and would, of course, intrigue against me. Remarks such as she has made are extremely dangerous, and if she drives out there once or twice and makes a stink, she can louse up the whole thing, since there's no one there to counter the stink she raises while I'm gone. I'm only too glad I had foreseen all this and talked with Mab about Helen, so let's hope they won't take her scheming too seriously. I wouldn't be surprised if she's already brought little Blitzstein out to Max. I wrote Max right away that I'd be back around the 25th; naturally I mentioned nothing about Helen but just wove in a few crafty remarks, saying how important it was that the music in this play be humorous, etc. I hope I can still set things right when I get back. Of course, it would be just horrendous if I couldn't get Max's play either, since I put all my money on it and haven't made the slightest effort to get another job here. Hays has written a letter full of excuses; he hasn't worked on a single line for the play since I've been gone. But he writes that he's rented a little *cottage* five miles from New City, with a *swimming pool* in the neighborhood. The name of this place is Congers (N.Y.). If Max continues to work on the play, it would probably be best if we actually took something in the neighborhood there, so that I can have both authors by the neck. Kingsley, too, will be in the vicinity, so perhaps I'll manage to get a play out of one of these sluggards.

It's all right about the telephone bill. If you deduct the cost of the call to Hollywood ($13.75), it's just a normal telephone bill of $20.

I'll write Hungerford to hurry up with that *check*. If you need money in the meantime, you'll have to take something out of the *special account* and then pay it back again. If I'm careful with money during the trip, I'll bring approximately $550 back with me.

The *preview* is supposed to be on Wednesday, and since I couldn't leave before Tuesday anyway, I'll wait for it and leave on Thursday, I hope. I think I'll be on the road for about six days. The weather here is horrible all the time, and it's uglier than ever. The Boises' address is Havenhurst Apartments, Franklin Ave., corner Whitley Ave. Yesterday I saw the Spewacks. They are neurotic and idiotic. I haven't once seen Lang in private. He behaved atrociously. I'm under the impression that all of them here hate me, because I'm more than a match for them. Farewell, *Schnube;* today I'll work on the *railroad show.* Little kisses,

    Knut

212 WEILL AT THE GRAND CANYON, ARIZONA, TO LENYA IN NEW YORK, 21 MAY 1938

Picture postcard

Blumchen,

The Grand Canyon is really wonderful. The car has new tires and runs beautifully. I'm looking forward to seeing you. Many kisses,

    Schnub

After the first dubbing sessions for You and Me *in spring 1938, Weill's score underwent ruthless surgery. What remains in the final cut evinces nothing of his original formal conception for what he had hoped would be a genuinely new type of musical film. Starring Sylvia Sidney and George Raft, the film was officially released on 8 June 1938, to largely unfavorable reviews.*

When Weill returned to New York in May 1938, he and Lenya rented a cottage on the Eastman Estate outside of Suffern, New York, and throughout the summer Weill and Maxwell Anderson worked together on Knickerbocker Holiday. *The play premiered in New York on 19 October, after tryouts in Hartford, Connecticut, and in Washington, D.C., where Franklin D. Roosevelt attended and laughed at the barely concealed barbs aimed at him. With Walter*

Huston and Ray Middleton heading a cast conducted by Maurice Abravanel and directed by Joshua Logan, Knickerbocker Holiday *enjoyed modest success as the Playwrights' Producing Company's first musical, running for 168 performances. It showcased "September Song," which would in time become Weill's first standard in America.*

During the winter Weill completed a commission from the 1939 World's Fair for the incidental music to a spectacular pageant about the history of railroads in America, Railroads on Parade. *Elliott Carter praised Weill's forty-five-minute score for soloists, chorus, and orchestra: "Weill has used all kinds of American tunes . . . with fine taste, intelligence and showmanship" (p. 239). Anderson and Weill also started work on a musical play entitled "Ulysses Africanus," intended for Paul Robeson, and Weill completed incidental music for Sidney Howard's* Madam, Will You Walk? *and Elmer Rice's* Two on an Island, *as well as a fifteen-minute radio cantata with Anderson,* The Ballad of Magna Carta, *which Burgess Meredith narrated on CBS in February 1940. By then Germany had invaded Poland, and Britain and France had declared war on Germany.*

Part II

LETTERS IN THE
ORIGINAL ENGLISH

• • • • • • •

Speak low when you speak love;
Our moment is swift,
Like ships adrift,
We're swept apart too soon.
Speak low, darling, speak low,
Love is a spark,
Lost in the dark.

Ogden Nash, "Speak Low," One Touch of Venus *(1943)*

Weill and Lenya at the piano in Brook House, 1942.

1941

Early in 1940 Weill and Moss Hart had decided to do a show together; after enlisting Ira Gershwin as lyricist for his first stage venture since George's death, the collaborators recruited Gertrude Lawrence to star as Liza Elliot. Lady in the Dark *tried out in Boston before opening at the Alvin Theatre in New York on 23 January 1941. Weill's letters are by now almost exclusively in English; Lenya soon follows suit.*

[FIG. 57]

213 WEILL IN BOSTON TO LENYA IN SUFFERN, NEW YORK, [JANUARY 1941]

Letterhead: The Ritz-Carlton / Boston

Blumi,

I'm just thinking that, in case you don't want another sheep dog you could get one of [Sidney] Kingsley's police dogs. He will be glad to give you one. Moss [Hart] was very nice and said immediately he would send you another one.[1] He wanted to send you a wire but I told him that I had talked to you. I suppose you got already the new dog from Raimond[?].

Morris Jacobs talked to Ira [Gershwin].[2] They have awful troubles with tickets for the opening night. He said that Elmer Rice has ordered 3 tickets. So you'd better call him (Jacobs) CI 6–6787 and tell him that we have 3 tickets for Elmer.

We are doing terrific business. Tonight Atkinson will be here, Watts on Saturday.[3] —Do you think we need the hotel room till Thursday? Well, we'll see. *Lebe* [farewell], *Schnübchen. Sei niedelich* [be nice] and take care of yourself.

Viele Knüsschen [many little kisses]

    Trrräubchen

1. *Hart's sheepdog had birthed seven puppies in August 1940 while Weill, Gershwin, and Hart were working at Hart's Bucks County farm. Apparently a mishap befell the first puppy Hart had given the Weills; a subsequent gift, "Wooly," became a beloved canine addition to the Weill family after they moved into Brook House.*

2. *The first pre-Broadway tryout performance of* Lady in the Dark *took place in Boston on 30 December 1940. Morris Jacobs was the general manager of the production.*

3. *Fearing that the length of the show would prevent critics for morning papers with early deadlines from seeing the end of the play when it opened in New York, Moss Hart paid the expenses of the four most prominent New York drama critics, including Brooks Atkinson and Richard Watts, Jr., so that they could attend a preview performance in Boston. The show played to standees each night in Boston.*

Indeed, the "musical play" Lady in the Dark *was a huge success in New York, with nearly unanimous critical raves. It ran for 467 performances before touring and then returning to New York for a limited run, all 777 performances with Gertrude Lawrence in the leading role. Paramount paid the highest sum in history for the film rights; Weill's share enabled him to purchase Brook House, a charming 150-year-old farmhouse on seventeen acres abutting Maxwell* [FIGS. 58 & 59] *Anderson's property on South Mountain Road in Rockland County, New City, New York.*

[FIG. 60] *That same year Lenya played the role of an Austrian maid that Maxwell Anderson had written just for her in his new play* A Candle in the Wind, *starring Helen Hayes. The first performance was at the Colonial Theatre in Boston on Monday, 15 September 1941, coproduced by the Theatre Guild and the Playwrights' Producing Company. It went on to open in New York on 22 October and ran for ninety-five performances. Brooks Atkinson wrote in the* Times, *"Lotte Lenya plays the part of a continental servant with the patient weariness of experience."*

214 WEILL IN NEW CITY, NEW YORK, TO LENYA IN BOSTON, 17 SEPTEMBER 1941

Sept. 17, 1941

Trrrräubchen,

Here are a few reports from Boston in N.Y. afternoon papers and the *Boston Traveller* with some nice things about you. Madge told me on the train she had a long talk with Helen's mother;[1] the whole Hayes family seems very depressed about the play and they say Helen will not take it to N.Y. unless they fix it. She is very disappointed that the Playwrights didn't help Max and she seems to doubt if he will do the necessary cutting and rewriting.[2] I'm afraid the situation is more serious than Max and Mab realize, but I don't think you should say anything. They will find out in a few days. I tried to make a few suggestions yesterday, but Mab turned them flatly down and Max didn't say a word. If you see in a few days that they don't make drastic changes, I will write Max a letter and say everything I have to say. Madge, the glamour girl, got sick on the train and slept most of the time. Our car looks beautiful and glamorous like Victor Mature.[3] 14 bucks. Norman Corwin was very enthusiastic about my idea and wants to do it, but he is completely tied up with radio for another 6 weeks.[4] Then he wants to start. I have a feeling he would be fine to work with. He is a real poet and very much on my line and full of ideas—but it will be hard to get him away from his other projects.

The house is lovely as always. Quentin [Anderson] says Wooly cried all the time because he was lonesome for us. Peter Broye[?] sent the bill: 204 in addition to the 250 which he got already (454 together). That's alright. I send him the check.

I just talked to Charlie [MacArthur]. He said he gave Helen some very good suggestions which they are working on now and he thinks it will be alright. He doesn't like the play (between us!), but he thinks it will be a success if they fix it. Well, take it easy, kid.

Good bye, *dumme V . . .* (V not for victory)[5]

Kurt

1. *The well-known stage and screen actress Madge Evans (1909–81) was married to writer Sidney Kingsley.*

2. *The Playwrights' Producing Company, also called Playwrights' Company, was a producing collective founded in 1938 by Maxwell Anderson, Sam Behrman, Sidney Howard, Elmer Rice, and Robert E. Sherwood, all established dramatists who were dissatisfied with the modus operandi of the Theatre Guild, on which they had previously relied for production assistance. Weill was later taken on as a member, along with the lawyer John Wharton, the producer Roger L. Stevens, and the writer Robert Anderson. The Company was dissolved in 1960 with only Behrman (who had resigned) and Rice still living and few new playwrights interested in participating.*

3. *Victor Mature (b. 1915) had played the role of the glamorous movie star Randy Curtis in the Broadway production of* Lady in the Dark *during its first season.*

4. *Weill had composed* The Ballad of Magna Carta *for Norman Corwin's (b. 1910) CBS radio series* The Pursuit of Happiness *in 1940. In February 1942 Corwin would direct the NBC radio production of Weill and Anderson's* Your Navy.

5. *"Silly V" is an allusion to a joke that was very popular during the war years: an immigrant "lady" is sitting in the subway on a hot summer day, with the fan blowing her skirt up to reveal that she is not wearing panties. Across the aisle, a man grins and says, "Ah! V for Victory!" But she replies, "No! V for Velcome!"*

215 WEILL IN NEW CITY TO LENYA IN BOSTON, 18 SEPTEMBER 1941

September 18, 1941

Schnäubi,

Sheila[?] called up yesterday to tell me that she had talked about you for Pilar [in Hemingway's *For Whom the Bell Tolls*] with the William Morris office. They found out that the part is not cast yet and they are very interested. They will send one of their directors (Mr. Joe McGee) to Boston on Saturday to see the show and to talk to you. I told her that your part is quite different from Pilar and she said they realize that.

You know the William Morris office is an agency. They will probably try to sign you up first and then to work for you. Please don't sign anything. Tell them (if they ask) you would take them as agents if they get you the part, and if they are too urgent you always can say they should get in touch with me. All they can do is to suggest you (as agents) to Paramount and the most they can get for you is a test. But if they want to do that let them go ahead, but don't sign anything.

That's all to-day. I was at Burgess' last night. He was in bed, exhausted. Now I am driving into town, lunch with [Max] Dreyfuss, then meeting at 21 [posh restaurant], to-night I go to the show.

Bye-bye, my darling. Kisses,

Kurt

All Broadway talks about <u>your</u> wonderful notice in "Variety." I met Sidney [Kingsley] and Madge [Evans] at Sardi's.[1] They invited me for dinner Saturday. What are you doing all day? Are you bored? I'll call you up one of these days (probably Sunday). Our show had standees Wednesday matinee.[2]

1. *Sardi's, a restaurant in Shubert Alley in New York, was a favorite of theater people, who usually congregated there to await opening-night reviews.*

2. Lady in the Dark *had reopened in early September after a three-month hiatus stipulated in Gertie Lawrence's contract. Weill's report of standees was good news indeed, for it meant the show was regaining its momentum at the box office.*

216 WEILL IN NEW CITY TO LENYA IN BOSTON, 25 SEPTEMBER 1941

Sept. 25, 1941

Dear *Trrrräubi*,

Just a few words for you. There is not much news here. Monday at the meeting I met Ben Hecht. He said he would send me his play [*Lily of the Valley*] in about 10 days and that it needs "all kinds of Kurt Weill music." He had the *3 Groschen Oper* records going all the time while he wrote it. Well, we'll see. I made the picture with Tallullah [Bankhead] who is a very stupid and malicious person (She hated "Lady in the Dark," of course).[1] Tuesday night I met Moss at 21 and we had diner with Lillian Hellman and Shumlin.[2] Moss told them about you. Lillian asked: is your wife an actress? and Shumlin said: she is one of the greatest performers of our time. How do you like that?

I spent all evening with Moss. He was full of apologies because he wants to write a play before he would do another musical with me—and if he writes another musical he would do it only because he wants to work with me. He told me his idea for a comedy about Garbo which seems a little thin, but very amusing and sure fire. He has a Valentina part in it which he thinks you should play.[3] But I am not sure if it would be the kind of thing you should do next. We are going to build up your career very carefully.—Well, Moss is out for me at the moment—and I am not sure if I am not glad about it. Irene Sharaff said the other day, that Moss can only write about himself—and this Garbo play is certainly about Moss Hart again.[4]

All this is strictly confidential! How was your trip back?

[*Komm u. sei mein Passagier, ficke ficke fick mit mir*]

[Come and be my passenger, fuck, fuck, fuck with me]

How about Sunday? *Knüsschen*

    Kurt

---

1. *Weill had written incidental music for an anti-isolationist pageant by Ben Hecht and Charles MacArthur,* Fun to Be Free, *which was sponsored by Fight for Freedom, Inc., and performed on 5 October 1941 at Madison Square Garden. Tallulah Bankhead, Melvyn Douglas, Burgess Meredith, and Franchot Tone narrated.*

2. *Herman Shumlin (1898–1979) directed and produced most of Lillian Hellman's (1905–84) important plays, including* The Little Foxes *in 1939.*

3. *Valentina (Nicholaevna Sania Schlee, 1904–89) had designed the costumes for* A Candle in the Wind. *Born in Kiev, she had immigrated to the United States in 1923. Her designs often incorporated elements of Russian folk dress.*

4. *Irene Sharaff (1912–93) and Hattie Carnegie (1886–1956) had designed the costumes for* Lady in the Dark.

217 WEILL IN NEW CITY TO LENYA IN BOSTON, [LATE SEPTEMBER/OCTOBER 1941]

Wednesday

Darling,

Here is a letter from your family. The Ben Hecht affair is settled. He called in the morning and I explained him that a score would only hurt his play (which I'm convinced is true). Of course, he agreed completely. Then I offered him to help with whatever little accordeon music he needs. I said I don't want any money, but I also don't want my name on it. He was very flattered and very nice. I'll see him on Friday before he leaves.

Harold [Freedman] called about "Madame will you walk" and said it depends completely on me. If I really want to do it he will get me the rights. I feel it is still the best thing I have and the easiest to realise—if I find a collaborator. I am going to work on that now.[1]

Buzz [Burgess Meredith] comes for dinner tonight. Tomorrow I go to Gabriels,[2] Friday dinner with Moss. I am a real busy-body this week.

So long, my little jewel! *Knüsschen*,

    Kurt

---

1. *In 1939 Weill had written incidental music for a scene of Sidney Howard's play* Madame, Will You Walk?; *produced after Howard's death, with George M. Cohan in the cast, it was poorly received in Baltimore and Washington and therefore closed before coming to Broadway. Weill admired the play and contemplated a musical adaptation. Howard, who died in a farm accident in 1939, did not live to see Frank Loesser's musical adaptation of his Pulitzer Prize–winning play* They Knew What They Wanted *(1924) as* The Most Happy Fella *(1956).*

2. *The journalist Gilbert W. Gabriel (1890–1952) was a frequent contributor to* P.M.; *his wife's name was Ada.*

1942

After the bombing of Pearl Harbor on 7 December 1941, the United States had finally entered the war. Lenya toured with A Candle in the Wind *during much of 1942. She then started writing her letters in an idiosyncratic mixture of English and German.*

218 WEILL IN NEW CITY TO LENYA IN PHILADELPHIA, 16 JANUARY 1942

Jan. 16, 1942

Dear *Schnäubi,*

Thanks for the letter which I found last night when I got home. I hope you got over that cold now and feel fine and dandy. I had an interesting day yesterday. I met those two guys from Cechoslowakia. They look like two real comedians and I had a very good impression. They speak English perfectly and have made a real study how to adapt their theatre (which is very much like 'our theatre') to Broadway. Now, after 3 years, they are writing their first show here (they always write their own shows) and they offered it to me. It is the best idea I have heard in a long time—exactly on the line of what I am looking for (fantasy with a biblical background). They will come out to the house for a whole day next week.[1] Then I went to the Freedom-show meeting [Fight for Freedom] and got that started. I left with Ben Hecht and spent the evening with him (diner at the Plaza). We had a real "heart-to-heart" talk and I liked him very much. He wants to do a show with me and we talked about a lot of ideas. He wants us to see a run through of his play Monday at 2.

Well, maybe I will have a play after all . . .

Pauker wrote me that Pascal wants to make a contract for one picture. I see him on Monday.[2]

Tonight I have the Andersons for diner. Tomorrow I drive over to Moss for lunch and see you in the evening. You call me at diner time. New Hope (Pennsylvania) 606.

Lebe Schnäubchen!

Kurt

1. *The famous comedy team V & W, Jiri Voskovec (in the U.S., George Voskovec; b. 1905) and Jan Werek (in the U.S., Jan Werich; 1905–80), had founded the Independent Theater, where until 1938 they staged satires and political revues attacking middle-class values and fascist ideology.*

2. *In 1937 George Bernard Shaw had granted the film producer Gabriel Pascal (1894–1954) exclusive film rights to his plays. Weill had met him in Paris, and Pascal assured Weill that he was first choice for not only* Caesar and Cleopatra *but all the Shaw films that Pascal planned to produce. The war intervened and the series ended with* Caesar and Cleopatra— *with a score by Georges Auric.*

Jan. 26, 1942

Trrrräubi,

If you would be here you would probably yell: "pretty bad! pretty bad!" when you would look out of the window. It is snowing—and it looks like the real thing. I don't even attempt to get the car out. Jules [the butler] went into town last night with Hans and Rita [Weill] and will be back tomorrow morning. I'll stay home all day. It is a little lonesome without the *Schnübe*—but I am working on the Mac Leish song and another Walt Whitman.[1] I guess I'll invite myself for diner at Mab's. Tomorrow I'll try to go into town (by bus, of course) to see V & W [Voskovec and Werich]. I will try to get [Russell] Crouse and [Howard] Lindsay interested in that show.—Charlie [MacArthur] called yesterday in the morning and apologized for his getting drunk. He was very nice and said it wouldn't happen again (??) and he felt awful about it. Please don't mention it to Helen [Hayes]. He is quite a problem child. I still believe he has talent and a brillant mind and a certain sincerity and warmth. But he is completely frustrated and confused and bitter. I would have to get the Nobel prize for psychology if I would get a play out of him.

"Lady in the Dark" is a year old in New York and Gertie [Lawrence] celebrates "First Anniversary Week" by giving away defense bonds every night. Business is still picking up and we might stay here the rest of the season.

I agree that you should get out of the show at the end of the Chicago run. But don't say anything about it. It is too early. In the meanwhile take care of yourself. I am sure the time will pass much quicker from now on. *Lebe,* my *Schnübchen,* and many kisses for our wedding anniversary!

Kurt

Meg & Quentin [Anderson] were here for diner last night, with Hans & Rita. We ordered seeds for the vegetable garden. I'll get a garden hose through the Offuts [neighbors]. I invited her and Florence [Meyer] for diner Feb. 6.

1. *A two-time winner of the Pulitzer Prize, the poet and novelist Archibald MacLeish (1892–1982) was serving as Librarian of Congress (1939–44), and Weill set his "Song of the Free" as a morale booster in the war effort. It was included in a revue that opened at the Roxy in New York on 4 June 1942. Weill had presented the first of his Whitman songs, "Oh Captain! My Captain!", to Max and Mab Anderson for Christmas. He completed two more in January 1942.*

Letterhead: The Pittsburgher / under Knott Management / Diamond St. and Cherry Way / Pittsburgh, Pa.

Tuesday 27th

Well Darling,

This is Pittsburg. A gray, smoky unfriendly town, which would be ideal for a Minstrel show! You dont have to blaken your face, it does it automatically. The trip from

Philadelphia was alright. We all stayed in the company car. Evelyn [Varden] said, it isn't worth while to take a compartment. So between diner and cards, the time passed fairly quickly. The hotel is o.k. I took the best room $30 on the 18th floor corner room. Whatever view you can get here, I have it. I open my eyes and look at a big signe, which says: The commonwealth Comp. A <u>friendly</u> bank, friendly underlined. That is so far the friendliest thing I have seen in this town. My stommac is terribly upset from the water, they say. It's full with clorine and tests awful. I cant drink it. The food is medium, wherever you go. Last nights opening, was pretty awful. A very cold caughing audience. Charming old theater with nice big dressing rooms, tremendous stage. (Good for the "Lady"). After the performance, we had a little broadcast. Evelyn, Tonio, Borell, Wengraf and I.[1] Helen isn't allowed to do anything on the air according to her tea-contract. Everybody made a little speech. Evelyn was very "schmart." Thank God, the time was almost up, when Wengraf spoke. So he could only say, that he was born in Vienna, his father was Austrian, his mother, Parisian–? his name is flamisch and his grandfather was british. Then the microphon started to vomit (and we too) and everything was over. He is really the most awful guy I have ever met. In the car on Sunday he took out a big comb and started to comb the inside of his motheaten fur coat. So one of the actors asked him, whether he is going to feed him too. He is interested in 3 penny opera he says and asked me for an English translation. Well, he got the right answer, you bet. Darling, the Lauchheims or Lochheims are not in the telephon book. But I think, I wont do anything. I am always so tired in the evening, I go right home and to bed. And the time passes pretty fast. I am reading "Ondine" with Madam Bourani and this is great fun.[2] We leave on Sunday at 10:30 A.M. and arrive in Rochester [N.Y.] at 6:30 P.M. That is pretty long. Today I'll go to look for payamas for you. Maybe I find some. Well [tiny flower drawing] that's about all so far. What are the

[FIG. 61]

news in N. City. How was the "Watch on the Hudson"?[3] Please write. *Nun lebe* [now farewell] *Schnäubi*. I'll write soon again.

love yours truly and sincerly

Karoline Weill

[how is Wooly?]

One nice thing here, you hear the boats from the river like in Louveciennes

1. *Evelyn Varden (1893–1941) had the role of Maisie Tompkins. Tonio Selwart (1896–?) was playing a French resistance fighter, whom Helen Hayes's character tried to rescue from a Nazi concentration camp. Louis Borell (1906–73) played Raoul St. Cloud. John Wengraf (1897–1974) played a German officer, Colonel Erfurt.*

2. *Ondine is a play from 1939 by Jean Giraudoux (1882–1944). Michelette Burani (1888–1957), a fellow cast member, gave French lessons to Lenya while on the road.*

3. *Weill had volunteered as an air warden, scouting the skies for enemy aircraft. Lenya and Max and Mab Anderson also took their turns at this Civil Defense activity.*

Jan. 28, 1942

Schnäubi,

It is a miserable day here, changing from snow into rain and back, and the roads are "pretty bad." I have to go into town later for a "Fight for Freedom" meeting and then I'll have a drink with Moss and probably see Ben Hecht in the evening (his play got bad notices, as I expected).[1] I have a cold, but it didn't come out yet and feels badly in my throat. I drank hot tea with rum last night and took aspirin, so it is a little better today. I went into town with the Spring Valley bus yesterday and met V. and W. They were very nice about my criticism and suggestions, surprisingly not very stubborn. The only thing is that they would like to get the show on as soon as possible because they are starving. It would be wonderful if that show could be done right away and open in spring. I'll talk to Moss today and will try to get him interested. If he is negative I'll go either to Cheryl or Bobby Lewis (who would be very good for this kind of show).[2] Cheryl, by the way, has a big success with "Porgy and Bess."[3] It is selling out.

I sent you some Rumpelmayer [chocolates] because you are very *niedelich* [nice]. When I bought it and wrote your address the girl said: "Oh she is playing the maid! Gee, is she wonderful!" You see, what a *Berühmti* [famous one] you are!—At Sardi's I saw Preminger who said he wants to talk to me about some material for a revue which he would like to do in the spring and he is thinking of having you in it.[4] I will see him next week and find out what his idea is. If he would have good material for you, and if he would feature you—it might be a good opportunity to get back!

Hans called up and asked if Rita could come out for a couple of days. She fainted in the subway and seems to be quite sick. She looks awful. They invited me for diner and then I drove out with Rita in Hans's car. I guess she will just stay in bed for a few days. On Sunday I'll have a big party coming out for lunch: Stonceks, Bravi, the Marquise Casa-Fuerte and Rieti.[5] Sunday night at four I go to the watch tower with Max (it has been postponed).

I am finishing another Whitman song (Dirge for two Veterans) which I think will be the best, and I started working on the MacLeish song.

Well, take it easy, baby. I hope you have a little fun with Aline.[6]

Be good. Love,

Knut

There is a letter for [Richard] Révy (I think from the Lunts) to be forwarded. What is his address? The plombers were here today and fixed the pump. It runs now pianissimo—for a few days, I guess. Jules is cleaning and pressing my entire wardrobe today. He doesn't seem quite to agree with the way my suits are made. But he certainly is a pearl. By the way, Vera was here on Sunday. She still cannot walk and she says herself that she couldn't work for quite a long time. She hopes to get money from an accident insurance. We had a very nice little talk and then she left with her things.

1. Hecht's Lily of the Valley *had opened on 26 January and ran for only eight performances. Brooks Atkinson wrote in the 27 January* New York Times: *"The loose ends are dyed in bold colors, but they are never tied into a coherent play."*

2. The actor-director Robert Lewis (b. 1909) had been a member of the Group Theatre.

3. Cheryl Crawford had been an assistant stage manager for the Theatre Guild's 1927 production of the spoken drama Porgy. *In 1941 she produced a streamlined version of the opera at her Maplewood, New Jersey, theater; it featured a smaller cast and orchestra, had spoken dialogue instead of recitative, and was thirty-five minutes shorter than the 1935 production of the opera, but it retained most of the original principals and the original conductor, Alexander Smallens. With the backing of the Shuberts, it opened at the Majestic Theatre on Broadway on 22 January 1942, played 286 performances, and then toured for eighteen months. It was much more successful than the original production.*

4. The Viennese-born actor and director Otto Preminger (1906–89) went on to direct such outstanding films as The Man with the Golden Arm *(1955) and* Advise and Consent *(1962). Weill and Preminger took their oaths of citizenship at the same ceremony in 1943.*

5. The cellist Morris Stonzek (1902–85) served as the contractor for many of Weill's Broadway shows and became a close friend. The violinist Yvonne de Casa-Fuerte played in several of Weill's shows; a friend of Virgil Thomson's from France, she also contributed criticism to Modern Music. *Vittorio Rieti (1898–1994) immigrated to America in 1940; he and Weill had met in Europe.*

6. The actress Aline MacMahon (1899–1991) had a career on stage, screen, radio, and television for over fifty years; she was instrumental in getting Weill to participate in various support groups for the war effort.

222 LENYA IN PITTSBURGH TO WEILL IN NEW CITY, [28 JANUARY 1942]

Letterhead: The Pittsburgher

Wednesday after the show

or 12:30 P.M.

Darling,

Thanks so much for your letter. I was waiting anxiously for it. I would have forgotten our wedding anniversary. But Darling, this town almost makes you forget, that you are alive. What a town for [Eleonora] Duse, to die in! I am happy to hear, that everything is fine in the house. Jules seems to be a real find. I would have been very worried with Vera around you. Of course, I wont anything say to Helen. But it is a pitty for Charlie and I dont think, it's worth the effort, you would have to make, to get a play out of him. How did Ben's play go. Helen said, it got terrible notices (she said it, not without a smile, I guess.) But it is a shame. Ben probably is very discouraged and I really do think, he is a great talent. Maybe he just cant do it alone. I wish you could work with him. I think, you could get more out of Ben, than of Charlie. He is a better worker and doesn't drink so much. I hope, you got something startet with V. and W. That's probably your best bet. Yes, I will try to get out of this show after Chicago. It's such a dismal thing to do. Of course, it has a little bit to do with the play too. Because you can feel it all the way through that the audience doesn't like it at all and it is only pushed through by Helen. But it is a unhealthy child. It doesn't go too well here. I am very happy to hear, that our "Lady" is still doing good business. I think, it will be surefire on the road. I feel much better now. I dont drink a drop of water only milk and tea *no* coffee either. I didn't try to find Aline. I wasn't well this week (after 3 weeks delay!) so I stay in bed, whenever I can. I have dinner with my Madame [Burani] (she was married to a french flutiest George Barrere? do you know him?)[1] and the rest of the time I am alone and like it too. Yes, from now on, time will pass quicker. We have some long trainrides between. I stay at the Statler Hotel in Buffalo. We stayed there, coming from Toronto. I bought you 3 pair of payamas. I got the sleeves and trousers shortened and they ought to fit now. They'll be probably still a little big, but the shrink in the loundry. Well, *Trräubchen*, that I bought from the money I saved. And the dressing gown for you (which I liked very much). Did you ever get the statement from Macy? And how are you coming along with only one car? Did you go to the tower? How is Max and Mab? I am furious about the English in Lybia.[2] 150 miles they lost in 4 day's. I am sure you'll laugh about me, but I <u>am</u> reading *die Paperchens* [the little papers]. Pretty bad I mean, those Pittsburgher paper's. We had a Mateneé today. We dont go to Louisville, we go to Fort Wayne instead. What the hell, doesn't make any difference to me. Jackie and Guy disappered.[3] They are way up in Helens ass [circle drawing]. And H. is still trying out things. It's too funny for words. Dont tell Max. I dont care. I would have been angry for 89 $. But for 130 $ I dont care. Now, I am going to bed. *SCHNEEPELN* [snooze] and tomorrow I have a french lesson and then I'll go to a Movie. Good night my Angel! Drive carefully in that snow. I wish we had some here instead of that rain. Darling you better write to the Theater, I dont know, which Hotels we get for the one night stands. Buffalo I know. *Lebe mein Blümchen* [farewell my little flower]. 15 years we have already now lets see, whether we get that silver medal.

    love and *Knüsschen*

Dein [(your); drawing of a flower and birds]
    das sind Schwalben [these are swallows]

I send the payamas today.

    1. Georges Barrère (1876–1944) was a world-renowned flautist who had a profound influence as an exponent of the French style of flute playing.

    2. Although Erwin Rommel's forces had been driven back by the British in North Africa in the last months of 1941, in January 1942 he recaptured half the territory he'd lost and had the British army reeling back toward the Egyptian border.

    3. Jacqueline Page served as "Girl Friday" to Helen Hayes, and actor Guy Monypenny left the profession, eventually becoming the editor of House Beautiful.

223   LENYA IN PITTSBURGH TO WEILL IN NEW CITY,
29 JANUARY 1942
Postcard: "The Pittsburgher, Pittsburgh's newest, busiest hotel."

Darling,

    I just recieved the chocolate. Pretty good, pretty good. Thanks ever so much. I just came back from a little walk. What a city! Well two more day's and then of to Rochester, Syracuse, Ithaca, and Buffalo. *Knüsschen* [drawing of eight circles] Linerl

[On front of card]: That' me! [room circled] Near the sky! Pretty Good! *Lebe!* [flower drawing]

Letterhead: The Pittsburgher

Friday 12:15 P.M.

Darling,

I got your letter this afternoon. *Sehr niedelich* [very nice]. I hope, you are careful, when the roads are so bad. And watch your cold. You know, I had a terrible cold in Philadelphia and my troubles here I had with my stomac was a leftover from that cold. So stay *im Betti* [in bed] for a day or two and let Jules take care of you. The chocolate is *primi* and that the girl remembers me from the show, doesn't surprise me at all. I am used to that. *(Den trick hab ich aus der Bibel)*.[1]

I hope Moss gets interested in the V & W show. He would be so good for it. With Cheryl is that awful Wildberg. If you could keep him out (which I think is rather difficult) it would be alright. But I doubt it. I talked to Helen a little bit and I think, she is just waiting that you should get Charlie to work. Maybe if you and Ben with Charlie get together on a show, that could be very good. Or dont they work together any more. I am sorry for Ben, because he has done more than Charlie and deserved better notices. But *die Wege der Kritiker* [the ways of the critics]. It would be swell, if Preminger would do a show. What about "Reigen" with him?[2] (There you could use V & W.) Or is that too crazy? I'll write you now, because tomorrow I have no time and on Sunday we leave so early. But thank God, we go. This town is really dreadful. I am reading with astonishment about your social life. Casa-Fuerta seems to be almost sadistic. But Jules will be in Heaven.—Of course Rita can stay. I hope, she gets some rest. Give her my love. I bought myself warm slippers (*richtige Wollbeine* [lit., real wool legs]—) and some bubbles for my daily bubblebath and lots of wool for a lunchonset I am going to crochet. As soon as I have finished that red cross sweater, I am going to start one for my [drawing of grapes] *(das ist ein Träubchen)*. There are no news from here Darling the same old sh...t. I am reading "Ondine" with Madame. It's lot of fun. And then we always have dinner together. Everybody is trying to avoid everybody. What a lovely company. Révys adresse is: 768 Glenmont Av. / West Los Angeles. Dont give any money away. I went to see "Suspicion" this afternoon. Very good cast and a fairly good picture. I wonder, how much is from Sam Rapaelson.[3] Has Ben's and Sam's play closed already? And is it true, that "American Way" is sold to the movies for 270,000 $?[4] I just cant imagine what Moss would do with all that money, now the wing is finished.[5] Well, *Blümchen*, that all for a cuple of day's. I'll write you from Buffalo.

> *Viele Knüsschen* and *lebe* [many little kisses and farewell]
> *mein* beloved [flower drawing]

1. "I learned this trick from the Bible," one of Mr. Peachum's lines from Die Dreigroschenoper.

2. Reigen, by the Austrian playwright Arthur Schnitzler (1862–1931), was first performed in Paris in 1900 as La Ronde.

3. Playwright and screenwriter Samson Raphaelson (1896–1983) was the coauthor of Alfred Hitchcock's Suspicion. *His play* Jason *had opened on Broadway on 21 January.*

4. *Moss Hart's 1939 patriotic spectacle about an immigrant family.*

5. *The sale of the film rights for* Lady in the Dark *had enabled Hart to add a wing to his Bucks County farmhouse and Ira Gershwin to pay off the mortgage on his Roxbury Drive house in Beverly Hills.*

225 WEILL IN NEW CITY TO LENYA IN ROCHESTER, NEW YORK, 31 JANUARY 1942

Jan. 31, 1942

Trräubi,

Thanks for the wonderful dressing gown which arrived yesterday (the pyjamas come separately, I guess). That was a real surprise and I needed it badly because the old one went to peaces. It is a real beauty, but now stop spending your money for me and buy some *Sächelchen* for yourself!

It is a dismal day here—rain, sleet and a gray sky. My cold is in full bloom, but I guess it will be over by tomorrow. Rita wanted to leave yesterday, but the weather was too bad for driving. So Hans comes today to get her. I guess she was bored. I stayed in my room all the time and saw her only for meals—and ping pong. Tomorrow Bravi was supposed to come for lunch with the Stonzeks and Marquise de Casa Fuerte with Rieti. But I hope the weather will be too bad and they will cancel it. Schwarz just called up.[1] He has been accepted for the Air Corps and is very proud. I told him he should come for diner before he leaves. Maybe I'll invite him Friday with the Offuts.—I called Macy's on Wednesday and they sent the statement yesterday.—I was at the meeting for the Freedom show and found out that [George S.] Kaufmann and Harold Rome had taken and used all my ideas.[2] The whole thing seemed rather small and uninteresting (I think your instinct with Kaufmann is right. He seems very ordinary and commercial). I had a drink with Moss (who is much nicer). I don't think he understands the value of V. and W., but he is interested because I am, so V. & W. & I have diner at his house Monday night. Monday lunch with Howard Dietz.[3]

Well that is about all, I guess. Do you think I should come to Buffalo next week end? *Lebe, mein Blümchen.*

> *Knüsschen*
> Kurt

I was at Ben Hecht's Wed. evening. No Dorothy any more. Rose [his wife] has taken over and takes him to Hollywood today—beaming that the battle was won for her. Ben a little embarrassed, but very nice.

1. *Howard Schwartz was Lenya's current lover; in fall 1943 he was killed in an airplane crash. She usually referred to him as "Schwarzie" or "Schwartzie."*

2. *Harold Rome (1908–93) wrote many Broadway musicals, including the long-running revue* Pins and Needles *(1937),* Destry Rides Again *(1959), and* I Can Get It for You Wholesale *(1962).*

3. *The lyricist Howard Dietz (1896–1983) often teamed up with composer Arthur Schwartz; Weill set Dietz's "Schickelgruber" for one of the "Freedom" shows.*

Letterhead: Hotel Syracuse / Syracuse, N.Y.

Tuesday 6:30 P.M.

3rd

Darling,

I just talked to you and that was a real treat! It's so good to hear your human voice after so much stage talk. This is a very nice hotel. Your dish. We left Pittsburgh (which is exactly like Bitterfeld [industrial city near Dessau] and smells like it too) Sunday 10:30 A.M. and arrived in Rochester 6:30 P.M. That was a long trip and the diner missed the train, so one couldn't get any food except sandwiches. That was "pretty bad," but it's not the worst. In Rochester (which is a lovely town) I went with Madame to the hotel, then we had dinner and after that, I went for a little walk. (5 inch snow!) That was refreshing. Next day, I went in the afternoon to see the movie "the man who came to dinner" [Kaufman and Hart]. It's amazing, how well that kind of comodie goes with an audience. And I myself laughed very much. It's much nicer, than on the stage. Then evening performance in a tremendous house. I got your letter there. Thanks very much! Next morning (I mean this morning) we left at 10:30 A.M. for here. Only 1 hour and 20 minutes. The dressing rooms are terrible and the whole thing looks a little bit like Sing-Sing [state prison]. With galleries and so on. I went for a walk with Helen before the matineé. She talked about poor Darling Charlie and how she wished he would write a play with Ben! and you. And she talked about Charlie, how timid and uncertain he is of himself and that she doesn't know anymore what to do with him and finally she said, she is in a way happy to be on the road to escape all his troubles! (That was the moment when the "american woman with mother in the background") came in. So poor Charlie can drink himself to death and she will go on to be "the womens club" Darling. No wonder, he is full of complexes. *Nicht niedelich, wie ein gewisses* [not nice, like a certain (flower drawing)]!! Well it's her life not mine. (Darling, I just had a delicious! diner. Excuse me, talking about diner but's the only real thing on this wander-circus trip.—) You know, the only real disgusting poeple in that company are the Europeens! Weingraf is just so awful, that one could spit every time he opens his mouth. And that louse Borell is just too dumm for words. The rest is ashes—ashes.—But, I dont care. I hope, I learn a little french. That's all I can do. And knit and crochet and read. That book "Darkness at noon" is very interesting.[1] The only discouraging thing is, that the methods of the Russians are so similar to the ones of the Germans. I hope, democracy will survive! I am worried about my poeple in Vienna. If you talk to Rita again, ask her if she could find out at the "red cross quarter in N.Y." whether it is possible to send through the red cross foodpakages to civilians. That would be of some help. She has time to do that for me. Well my love, that's about all from here. Now I am going to sleep for an hour and than back to the factory. I am looking forward to Milwaukee! Try to stay for a cuple of days. It's a nice change for you too. Maybe Max would like to come along. *Lebe mein* [farewell my] [flower drawing]. I am doing allright. I hope, we stop after Chicago!

1,000,000 and 5 *knüsschens*
Kneubchen Träubchen Schleubchen Läubchen that' all! *handkuss!* [kiss on the hand]

1. Darkness at Noon, *by the Hungarian-born Arthur Koestler (1905–83), had been published in German in 1940 as* Sonnenfinsternis. *It deals with the arrest, trial, and imprisonment of N. S. Rubashov, who lived in an unnamed country under a Stalin-like dictatorship. Dafne Hardy's English translation, published in 1941, was to serve as the basis for Sidney Kingsley's 1951 play of the same title.*

227 WEILL IN NEW CITY TO LENYA IN BUFFALO, 5 FEBRUARY 1942

Feb. 5, 1942

Träubchen,

Snow, snow, snow. It is coming down fast today. But I don't have to be in town today and tomorrow. So I just stay home and take it easy.—Well, the V & W combination with Moss is off. Moss was terribly nice Monday night. He is really a swell guy. When I told him the idea of the show he was immediately interested because it is on the line of what we want to do. Then when they told him the story in detail he made exactly the same criticism that I had made and some excellent suggestions for changes. He liked the boys very much and we stayed till three. They acted a little dialogue for him (it was the first time that I saw them acting), and I was rather disappointed. It didn't seem funny to me, some sort of imitation of old fashioned american slap-stick comedy which was new for an audience in Prague, but not to an american audience. But Moss was very nice to them and said they were wonderful. The next morning he called me and said that he couldn't say the truth to them because they are so nice, but he didn't think they are good enough for us—and then he said exactly what I had felt. I will try to get them into the Freedom show so that they can make a little money and can be seen by people.

Yesterday I saw "Porgy." They have done quite a good job. It is much more of a show now and less of an opera. They have a wonderful cast and the whole thing is very alive and refreshing. The songs are still magnificent, but the rest of the score pretty bad. I listened to the first dream of "Lady" in the evening and decided that it was much better music.

Then I met Howard Dietz. He was crazy about the tune I wrote for "Schickelgruber" and he is finishing the words now.[1] It might become very popular. I doubt very much if he will do a show. He is very busy with his job as publicity chief for MGM and they've just made him Vicepresident. So here I am, still without a show. Well, something will come up suddenly, I guess.

Now I am working on the MacLeish song and a song which St. Clair McKelway wrote (for the show).[2] The three Walt Whitman songs will be printed and I will try to get Paul Robson to sing them first.[3] Elmer Rice called me this morning. He was very nice when he told me that he has married Betty and that they want to see me.[4] I'll probably go for diner to them on Saturday night. Maybe Betty has rejuvenated him enough that he would write a show for me. He sounded like seventeen on the phone.

I took the Suffern bus yesterday and dropped in at Schwarz's shop. He wasn't there, but his father told me that they didn't take him to the Air Corps because he is too old. He had faked his age and they had found out about it. He is just too dumb for words.

I looked up your first papers. Your nationality is German. So you have to get the registration.

Well, my darling, that's about all. I'll leave the car in the garage today and tomorrow. Tomorrow night I have the diner party (Offutts and Kennedy's). After diner we go to the "Penny Sale" for the defense depot. So it is a short evening.

> *Lebe, mein Schwänzchen.* [Farewell, my little tail]
> Many *Knüsschens,*
> Kurt

I ordered the cookies for you. Jules made them. I ate at Gigi's Mexican Restaurant last night.[5] Pretty awful! My new coat looks *primi* and all the *dämen* look after me!

---

1. *Anna Maria Schicklgruber bore an illegitimate son, Alois, in 1832; Johann Georg Hiedler eventually legitimized the boy, while at the same time changing his own name to Hitler. Alois's son Adolf was born in 1889.*

2. *St. Clair McKelway (1905–80) wrote the lyrics for "One Morning in Spring" for the* Lunch Time Follies.

3. *The foremost African American singer and actor of the day, Paul Robeson (1898–1976) had played Joe in the 1932 revival of* Show Boat. *Anderson and Weill had tried unsuccessfully to interest him in their "Ulysses Africanus."*

4. *Betty Field (1918–73) launched her Broadway career in George Abbott's comedy productions of the late thirties. Of* Mice and Men *(1940) established her reputation as a film actress. Elmer Rice, to whom she was married from 1942 to 1956, was the first of her three husbands.*

5. *Lenya had met Gigi Gilpin (b. 1919) at Benno Schneider's acting studio. Gilpin had appeared with Burgess Meredith and Ingrid Bergman in Molnár's* Liliom. *Weill and Lenya often stayed at her apartment at 200 West Fifty-fourth Street when they had to be in New York City.*

228 WEILL IN NEW CITY TO LENYA IN BUFFALO, 7 FEBRUARY 1942

Feb. 7, 1942

My sweety-pie,

An awful rain is pouring down today. I'll take the two o'clock train from Haverstraw and go to see Aufrichts in the afternoon and Elmer [Rice] in the evening and then I take an 11 o'clock train back. It was very *niedelich* to talk to you on Thursday night. That Willkie story is a scream.[1] Those things happen only to you.—Well, my diner party last night was a great success. Jules has made the best roast lamb I've ever tasted and everything was so nicely served and prepared—a real pleasure. He is definitely the best servant we've ever had. I hope they don't draft him to the army. I had invited Bessie, but she said: no, she has to work all evening.[2] We had just finished when she came through the kitchen, sat down at the table and Jules served her a complete diner. She is completely nuts.—After diner we went to Mab's "Penny Sale" at the school house, but it was so crowded that I said to John O'Malley: lets go to the movies. We saw "How green was my Valley" which I thought was one of the finest pictures I have seen in a long time. It has great style and at the same time great reality—and I know how difficult it is to get that combination. The little boy [Roddy McDowall] gives a deeply moving performance. And what a story for an opera! I will read the novel which it is based on.—[3]

Norman Corwin is doing for the government the biggest radio program ever produced, over 500 stations, every Saturday night. They want Max and me to write the program about the Navy, and we'll probably go to Washington early next week. That would be a very important job for me. I hope it works out.—We got 180.– for "Knickerbocker" performances, but at the same time the Dramatist's Guild has written that my weekly contribution from "Lady" (9.– a week) have piled up to 270.–! That is a bitter pill, but I knew it would come.

Guess who has bought the "modern house" next door? The McEvoy's![4] It has one advantage: they will have a tennis court! Well, good-bye, my love. Don't worry about me. I am a busy bee!

1,000,000 and 6 *Knüsschens!* from

Trrrrr—

1. Indiana-born Republican Wendell Willkie (1892–1944) had lost the 1940 presidential election to FDR.

2. Bessie Breuer (1893–1975) was women's editor for the New York Herald Tribune. Married to the painter Henry Varnum Poor, she wrote a roman à clef, Take Care of My Roses, in which thinly veiled characters based on Lenya and Mab Anderson appear.

3. The 1941 film was based on the novel of British author Richard Llewellyn (1906–84).

4. New City neighbor J. P. McEvoy had collaborated with Arthur Schwartz in 1939 on a musical about a "radical" playwright, loosely based on Marc Blitzstein, entitled Swing to the Left. In August 1942 McEvoy and Weill wrote "Russian War Relief," a sketch for Rockland Riot, a fund-raiser for the Russian relief fund.

229 LENYA IN BUFFALO TO WEILL IN NEW CITY,
8 FEBRUARY 1942
Letterhead: Hotel Statler Buffalo

Sunday

Darling

I am just about to leave for Colombus. The snow is 10 inch. deep and maybe we wont get through with the train. That would be some fun. Those three days here were very nice on account of the Theater. The dressing rooms were wonderful and warm and one had the feeling of being treated like a human being. Thanks for your letter which I will answer tomorrow. This review just gives you a slight idea, what I mean

when I say, that I am "pretty good." Now *lebe* mine

I'll write tomorrow. The cookies are so delicious, that I have only few left. But I stop now.

with much reverences and
[(*Knüsschen*)]

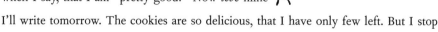

Letterhead: Deshler-Wallick / Hotel / Columbus, Ohio

Monday 6:00 P.M.

Darling,

This is going to be a "shorty" because nothing new happened. We had a nice train ride (I won 5 $ playing "stud" with the crew). When we arrived in Colombus, the Johnsons (Gigi's friends) were at the station and took Jackie [Page], Guy [Monypenny] and me home for dinner.¹ Tonight they give a big party for the cast. Helen is coming too. I am very sorry, that you cant find a book. But I dont know what to do about it. I think you are right with the V-W. It was probably good for Prag. You dont know, how your music is loved by everyone. They all here have your record. Mary Johnson's children sing My Ship and all the songs, the cat got the name "Jenny" in honour of "Lady." They are very nice poeple. Today was like a spring day, which was a surprise after that snow in Buffalo. I am looking forward to Milwaukee. I think you will like it. Take a sleeper so you can *schneepeln*. Did you see Cheryl? Or does she behave like the old Belasco after her success with Porgy.² How was the dinner with Mr. & Mrs. Rice-Field. I am going to write Hazel [Rice's first wife] tomorrow. And how was the evening with the Offuts and Sheelagh[?]? Rita wrote me a letter, telling me about her invention she made "the folding shopping bag." I hope, she can make money with it. Darling, it's a pitty, that I haven't an idea for a play for me. I am really a cinch for an audience. And I really shouldn't try to do anything else except acting. It's so easy for me. Maybe we can write a play together this summer and have it looked over by Max or Moss, when it's ready. I think, we could do it. At least, we could try. What do you think. I laughed very much on the train about Evelyn Vardens coloured maid. We talked about church (a favorite subjekt for coloured poeple) and she said 'Oh Miss Lenya, I love the church especially those "roman numbers" they sing' (she meant the latin choruses) and so on. Isn't that wonderful? She washes my loundry. Then the Johnson children told me a joke (not so good but I laughed—) Why does Hitler change his socks three times a day? He smells "defeet." Well Darling this is Colombus and you cant expect too much. The cookies are gone. *Primi!* I see, I dont have to worry about the house and Jules. I know he takes good care of you. The play is going very good. (hell—).

Well Darling that's very little and all I know. I hope, I get a letter soon. Next stop—12–13–14 Indianapolis English Theater. Then after that a solid week in St. Louis.

> *lebe* mine
> *Sch—sch—sch—sch—nubi*
> write soon. love [tiny flower drawing]

1. *Mary and Stanley Johnson were wealthy friends of Gigi Gilpin's who loved to entertain lavishly artists who visited Columbus, Ohio.*

2. *The American playwright David Belasco (1859–1931) was notorious for staging his life as carefully as his plays. He affected priestly demeanor by wearing a clerical collar, and he used a large supply of cheap wristwatches for temper tantrums that climaxed in his stamping on his own watch.*

Feb. 9. 1942

Good morning, *Trrräubchen.*

It is a beautiful blue sky, the sun is shining and it is very cold, but dry. We just carried some wood from the garage to the wood shag, to Wooly's great excitement. Yesterday I had a quiet Sunday and finished the MacLeish song. In the afternoon I took Max for a 2½ hours walk across the mountains—and did I feel my legs when I came back! Mab paid back 1000.– yesterday, the rest on March 1. She is frantically looking for an apartment in New York. Somehow I can understand that she gets nervous, sitting in that awful room day after day, and Hesper being in bed now for over 3 weeks and not getting better, and that old Teddy bear who cannot think of anything but his plays—and how he can make money. I think we Träubchens are much wiser!

Saturday I was at the Aufrichts who have some radio project they wanted to talk about. There was a man who made all the records in Paris [Borchardt]. He is starting a recording firm here and would like to make a Kurt Weill album (which I would like to do). My idea is to have some German, some French and some English songs of mine, the German and English to be sung by you.[1]—Then I had diner with Elmer, Betty and Peggy [Rice's daughter from his first marriage]. Elmer is very gay and very proud of being married to a movie star at last, Betty very pretty and very nice. Peggy very ugly and very dirty, but highly intellectual. We went to see [R. B. Sheridan's] "The Rivals," an excellent old English comedy, very nicely done by the Guild, with a wonderful co-median Bobby Clark.[2] Then we went to Billy Rose's Diamond Horseshoe which is ex-actly what we used to call "Gojim-Naches."[3] I am waiting for a call from Max if I have to go to Washington tonight. This Government broadcast which we are to do is sched-uled for end of February. I hope it will not spoil our Milwaukee plans. That would be *wiedelich* [terrible]! Well so long, *Schnäpschen* [little brandy]. Maybe I call you from Washington—if and when.

> *Knüsschen*
> Kurt

Mab asked why you never write her.

1. *Lenya and Weill indeed recorded six songs for BOST records (6-5017/9), two each in German, French, and English. They have been rereleased on compact disc (Capriccio 10 347). The BOST label had been founded by Herbert H. Borchardt (b. 1906), who worked closely with the Office of War Information and German-speaking artists after his arrival in the United States in 1941.*

2. *Bobby Clark (1888–1960) had appeared in the* Music Box Revues, Ziegfeld Follies, *and the 1930 version of* Strike Up the Band!

3. *Theatrical jack-of-all-trades Billy Rose (1899–1966) began his career as a lyricist, then turned to producing and purchased the National and Ziegfeld Theaters. For a time he was married to the actress Fanny Brice. In 1943 he would produce* Carmen Jones *and in 1944* Seven Lively Arts. *The Diamond Horseshoe featured his "long-stemmed roses," or leggy show girls. The expression* Gojim-Naches *was used by (German) Jews to mean that this kind of fun was so stupid that only a "goy" might enjoy it (Gojim means "goy," or gentile; naches, fun or amusement).*

Feb. 12, 1942

Darling,

Just a few words today because I am working with Max all day on the broadcast. I got your sweet little letter from Columbus, Ohio. I am so glad that you are in good spirits and I am sure that, in spite of all the disadvantages, this is a very good experience for you. You probably would have gotten awfully nervous sitting around all winter and listening to those eternally bad news on the radio, and you would have regretted it if you would not have gone on the road. There is no doubt in my mind that you can be a terrific success in this country if we only get the right play. I thought myself of sitting down and writing one. The only thing I couldn't do is to write a good dialogue—and there are very few people who can do that. But the rest we could do ourselves. Well, anyhow, we can try.

Cheryl called up after I had written her a nice letter about 'Porgy'. She wants to do a show with Marc Connelly and me, and we had dinner with him in her apartment last night. It was very nice and she got very excited about the Venus story.[1] But Marc is leaving for Hollywood today—it is always the same.

While I am writing I keep thinking: if I only could do a show with Walter Huston and you. "Caesar & Cleopatra" would be ideal. But how to get the rights? I will talk to Cheryl about it. And with Walter.

The war situation is terrible, and the picture we got in Washington was very depressing.[2] I am glad you are working so you can keep your mind off these things.—I have to be in town early tomorrow morning because some government official wrote me he has to talk to me between 9 and 10 about "an official matter." I don't know what they want.

I sent you a package yesterday to the Warren Hotel, if it doesn't arrive before you leave give them your St. Louis address, so they can forward it.

Lebe, mein Schnäubchen. Viele Knüsschens!

Friday morning. Just left the man from the State Department. He just had a few questions with regards to the visas for my parents—and a long inquiry: "How is it when you write music?" And for that I had to get up at 7!

1. The Tinted Venus, *a novel by F. Anstey (pseudonym of Thomas Anstey Guthrie, 1856–1934).*

2. *Rommel had launched a new offensive, the Japanese were invading Burma and the Dutch East Indies, and on 12 February the* Gneisenau, Scharnhorst, *and* Prinz Eugen *escaped from Brest; attacks by German U-boats soon intensified.*

Letterhead: Hotel Warren / 250 rooms / tub and shower / phone Riley 4562 / 121 South Illinois St. / Indianapolis, Ind.

Friday 13th 42

Darling,

I packed your last letter in the trunk so cant answer correctly. But as far as I remember, you didn't ask me any questions anyway. Well, this is about the ugliest town so far. An overwhelming monument in the heart of the city (very roman looking) makes it very clear, that this is definitely "the heart of the city." What I really love, are the different "stage doors." An almost tender feeling creeps into my heart, when I enter it. You know Darling, I think I start to like this kind of traveling. It's practically an "opening" every other day and still a little exciting. I just had to get used to it. And Helen is very nice now, I think that makes the whole thing look different now. And then I discovered my love for acting again. I had forgotten how much of an actress I am all those years sitting still. (That's sounds almost like Dorschka's letter's with the only difference, that I have talent.—)[1] Well anyway, those day's in Colombus were awfully nice thank's to the Johnsons. They really knocked themselves out to make it nice for us. And Jakie, Guy and Hagott[?] are very nice now, since they found out, that I dont want to become Helens busom friend. We are looking forward to Milwaukee to see the Lunts. They are coming for the opening. I wishes you could come, but of course, your radio job is really much more importent. I am very happy, you got it. And dont worry too much about another show Darling. I am sure something will pop up quite unexpectedly. It's much more importent now, to be in touch with those poeple in Washington. I am kind of worried, that you are all alone now in N.C. I think it's foolish of Mab to do a thing like that. What will she do in town. She hasn't got the guts to enjoy things. She just will run from Bonwit Teller to Bergdorf Goodman and that's all. And Max will hate it and she will be just as nervous as before. I can understand, that one get's tired of sitting in the country, but I just [don't] think, that going in to N.Y. for 2 months does the trick. Well why should I worry. Well Darling now my income tax (I feel very importent) has to be made. Please take my bills from the try out (they are in the little letterbox on my desk) and take it to Miss Stern and let her do it.[2] I dont know, how much one can deduct for travelling expenses and so on. But she'll know. And write. You are a lazy bone. We have now a ful week in St. Louis. I just sent [John] Steinbeck's a card. And the rest of the letters I have to write I'll do in St. Louis. Now *lebe* mine *Träubchen.* I saved already 100 box [bucks] and the 70 I had, when I left. *Primi* isn't it? I could have made more, but I bought *Sächelchen,* as you know.

By, by [little flower drawing]

love Linnerl

1. *Dorschka was the wife of Samson Raphaelson, Dorothy Wegman.*
2. *Rose Stern and her sister Henrietta were notaries and tax preparers with an office in the Great Northern Hotel on Fifty-seventh Street.*

Letterhead: Hotel Warren

Träubchen,

Save those notices for me. A letter is on the way, I just have to get some dates to
night for my income tax, which I want you to bring to Miss Stern for me. I'll send the
letter tomorrow.

> l o o o o o o o o o ve!
> Linnerl

Letterhead: Hotel Warren

Friday 11:45 P.M.

Darling,

This is the money I earned in 41. It includes rehearsal money and everything. That's
what the Guild will send to the income tax. You only have to take it and the hotel bills
to Miss Stern and she will do the rest.

I got a nice umbrella from Evelyn for a Valentine! I knitted her soks. You see, I am
very popular among the ladies. (less with the gentlemen—thank God.) I bought myself
a Jicky-Guerlain *parfümchen.* One of the last I could get. 9 buck. 15 buck I won this
week playing Gin rummy with Krueger.[1] Unfortunately he leaves the cast tomorrow for
Hollywood. There goes my income.—Sunday we leave at 12:00 for St. Louis. I'll be at
the Mayfair hotel with Evelyn. *Jetzt gehe ich schneepeln* [now I'm going to sleep].

lebe mein Trrrrrr dont send me any chocolate. I still have the Rumpelmeyers and I
got a large box in Colombus.

> *Kn ö ö ö ö ö schens!*

1. *Knud Kreuger played a German officer in* A Candle in the Wind. *Helen Hayes recalls that during the tour Lenya
"had a little thing going" with one of the actors playing a Nazi—either Kreuger or Wengraf: "I think Lenya was one of
those people who required male company, attention, and encouragement. I was a little startled by this little episode that went
on for the tour when it developed. She got involved with this young actor who played a Nazi in the play, they were a twosome.
She was with him all the time" (int. HEH).*

Letterhead: Hotel Warren

Saturday morning

Darling,

I just got your letter. It's very funny what you write about the road tour, because my
letter which I wrote last night is almost the same. Please tell Max about my good notices, because it is really very seldom, that province critics notice a small part like that.

Well Darling this is about all. I am having my breakfast now, orange juice, 1 *geboiltes* [boiled egg] and rolls, 1 glass of "Mountain Valley Mineral Water." The ordinary water one cant drink. It's like drinking loundry water with loundry soaked in it. Awful. By, by,

   Tülpchen

[Regards for Jules and how is Wooly]

236T   LENYA IN INDIANAPOLIS TO WEILL IN NEW CITY, 14 FEBRUARY 1942

Western Union: standard Valentine greeting

I KNOW I'M LUCKY BECAUSE YOU'RE MINE; YOU'LL ALWAYS BE MY VALENTINE = LINNERL

---

237   WEILL IN NEW CITY TO LENYA IN ST. LOUIS, MISSOURI, 15 FEBRUARY 1942

Feb. 15, 1942

Dear *Schnäubi*,

It is Sunday afternoon. Norman Corwin was supposed to come out today and that's why I had postponed again the long postponed visit of Bravi and his gang. But Norman didn't show up. So I have a nice quiet Sunday by myself and later I go to the McEvoy's for a cocktail party and cold buffet. His son who is a reporter came just back from Russia and probably has interesting things to tell. I got your Valentine wire yesterday. *Sehr niedelich* [very nice]! I hope you got my Valentine package and the airmail letter which I mailed Friday morning (to Indianapolis). I thought the powder bag with the big heart is very cute. You use it after the bath. That's what the girl at Saks told me with a very seductive smile. There isn't much to report today. I worked all day yesterday and finished both songs ("Schickelgruber" and the "Freemen's Song" by Mac-Leish). Both turned out very well. I am having a very good writing spell and I wished

I had an opera to work on. Well, anyhow, it is good to feel that my invention is still as strong as ever.

I'll have hard work for two weeks on the Navy Broadcast with Max which takes place on Feb. 28, at 7 P.M. on all stations. Max is going back to Washington tonight to work there and I will spend two days at the library in N.Y. to get my material together. Then during the second half of the week I have to write the score and next week orchestrate and rehearse.

Just coming back from McEvoy's. It was very nice and the son told fascinating stories from Russia and Japan. This war is very very serious. I registered yesterday for the draft.[1] Don't forget to get your alien registration, before the 28th! I do it this week. These two Valentine cards are from the Offut children for you. Good night, my love. Take care of yourself. I hope I can come to Detroit to see you.

>Thousand kisses
>Kurt

1. *In a letter to his brother Hans from 1917, Weill had responded to an earlier anticipated call to war by saying "I will never go unless they pull me by the ears" (W-HW, n.d. [June 1917], #202).*

238 LENYA IN ST. LOUIS TO WEILL IN NEW CITY, 16 FEBRUARY 1942
Letterhead: The Hotel Mayfair in St. Louis

Monday 16th 42

Darling,

Just talked to you. Thank God. I woke up trembling after that horrible dream. I finished that book last night "Darkness at noon" and I guess that was the cause of that nightmare. What a depressing book. Who is right? Getkin or Rubashow. They both believe in the same thing and still the one who knew so much more and had the much better brain had to die in the end. Is there any answer to such a story? I shouldn't read books like that without having you around me. I cant digest them alone. But I suppose, I am not the only one who doesn't know the answer in what to believe.

Well Darling, here I am again in another hotel room, in another city, which looks almost alike the previous ones. It was a short trainride only 6 hours but very exausting. I dont know why, the air was soo bad and the war news so terrible discouraging. What in the world is going to happen? And those English with letting those German ships go trough. It's just unbelievable.[1]

Darling nothing new here, its always the same. I dont know, how long the are going with that play. I think Helen just wants to make money now. And it's practically sold out everytime we come to a new town. We'll see what happend this week. One night and two seemed to be a cinch. But as a whole, it's very boring. But I dont see, how I ever get out of it and whether I should. It's still the easiest way for me to make money and for later if I want to go on playing (which I want more than anything else) it's better to have a clean reccord and be known as a good trooper. I know it's tough on you, but we'll talk it over when you come to Detroit. I didn't realize, that we are so far from N.Y. That traveling 6 to 10 hours between takes away the distance. We went last night to the old "showboat" down on the river, they played "The drunkard."[2] It wasn't as amusing, as I thought it would be. They took it too serious. They had a huge pictures of Gerty [Lawrence] there. When she was in St. Louis, she went down to see them and gave an interview about them afterwards. (Great girl.) I like her for that. I am going to see Dumbo this week and the Bergner movie [*Paris Calling*]. And then to the Zoo. It's a famous one here.

That's about all Darling. One just try's to kill time. That's why I like one nighters. Time flys then. I would hate to miss the spring in our house and hope it want run much longer.

Good by Darling

Come to Detroit and plaese let me know, the exact hour of your broadcast. We are an hour earlier or later here, (I dont know, but it's an hour difference.)

love and *knüsschens* [little flower drawing]

1. *On 11–12 February the British navy and air force had been unable to prevent two German battleships from slipping through the English Channel. The* London Times *reported that "nothing more mortifying to the pride of sea power has happened in home waters since the 17th century."*

2. *The Drunkard, or The Fallen Saved, a play in five acts by W. H. Smith (1806–72), had been revived in Los Angeles in 1933, where it ran for 7,510 performances.*

239 WEILL IN NEW CITY TO LENYA IN ST. LOUIS,
17 FEBRUARY 1942

Feb. 17, 1942

My *Schnäuben-Trräubchen,*

I had two very busy days and am glad to have a quiet evening at home. Yesterday I was at the library. Then I played the MacLeish song to Max Dreyfus who said it is a great song and might become very important. Then I met Aufrichts and talked about that recording project. Then I took Mab for dinner and to the theater ("Angel Street"—pretty dull play well acted).[1] That's how Mab's exciting excursions to New York end up: that I have to take her out and that she rushes from one shop to another and spends money like mad. She stays at the Pierre—that's her idea of great life. She talks as if she were just about to divorce Max—but that is just silly talk after one drink. I took the 11:30 train home and went in again this morning on the 10 o'clock train, back to the library, then audition for the Freedom show, lunch with Kaufmann, Moss and Bobby,[2] conference with Preminger, meeting with Moss etc. about "Lady." Then I drove out with Mab. Preminger wants to do that musical which Eddy Chodorov told me—and he wants to do it in the spring![3] It sounds pretty vague, but maybe there is a chance. So Preminger and Chodorov are coming out tomorrow afternoon and stay for dinner (Jules beaming!) I have to try everything. About "Lady" we have decided to take it out of town Easter. We have a wonderful offer to take it to California (4 weeks Los Angeles, 3 weeks San Francisco). So the idea is: 4 weeks Philadelphia, 2 Baltimore, 2 Washington, then California, then in the fall Chicago etc. Sounds wonderful, doesn't it?

Max is in Washington—I still haven't got a script for the broadcast and God knows when I can write that score till next Saturday.—If you have a chance to talk to Alfred Lunt alone try to talk about possibilities of doing a musical show for them. If he has anything he wants to talk about I might go to see him, maybe in connection with my visit at Detroit. Now good night, my darling. I am glad that you have a good time and like playing. Yours truly

      Trrrrrr.

My income tax man is doing your income tax too.—When I came home to-day Jules had waxed the kitchen floor!! Remember Vera?

    1. *The English thriller by Patrick Hamilton (1904–62) was first produced in London in 1939 under the title* Gas Light. *In New York it ran for 1,295 performances, making it the longest-running foreign drama in Broadway history.*
    2. *"Bobby" was Hassard Short (1877–1956), who had designed and staged* Lady in the Dark.
    3. *Edvard Chodorov (1904–88) and his brother Jerome (1911–81) were noted playwrights and directors. Edvard's* Those Endearing Young Charms *opened in 1943.*

240 LENYA IN ST. LOUIS TO WEILL IN NEW CITY,
18 FEBRUARY 1942
Letterhead: Hotel Mayfair

Wednesday 18th
between Matinée

Darling,

I just got your letter. Thank you. The package finally arrived. I love it. The *parfum* is wonderful and the powder I am going to use, when you come to Detroit—to beat the seductive smile of the salesgirl.—I am very anxious to hear the broadcast. I will borrow Helens radio to be sure to get it. I am very glad, that you have at least a little work. Dont be afraid, you'll write operas again. It's nice, that the McEvoy's took that house. I just had my pictures taken for the registration. Have the Anderson left for N.Y.? Thanks for the Valentine card. I'll send them a postalcard.

Nothing new from here. The play got very good notices. It's going fine. No reviews for the acters except Helen. So what.—I am taking still french lessons. What a language! I dont know, whether I'll ever get it. But it kills time and it's fun to learn. I saw "Dumbo" yesterday. That's the most beautiful thing, I've ever seen. I cried my eyes out. When that mother elephant takes Dumbo in her arms that's like a Boticelli madona. Just beyond words. And that beautiful pink ballett. Oh I could go on for ever.

You probably read that Lyons colum.[1] Anyway, the whole cast was saving the paper for me. On Sunday we have a tough ride. We leave here 11:55 A.M. and arrive in Madison 10:00 P.M. One and a half our stop in Chicago. It's very cold here. From Gigi [Gilpin] came a letter and from Dick McKay.[2] Nothing interesting. I am working on something very *niedelich* for your birthday. I hope, I'll get it ready in time.

How is the house and Jules? This is an awful town. Ugly. But that's the way, they all look. I am going to write a long letter to Mab tomorrow. That's what I am saying since Buffalo.—But I'll do it. Well *Träubchen*, that's about all. You must be bored stiff by my reports about this road tour. But that's all there is. That german guy with the riding clothes, got arrested here on account of his accent on the street. But they reliesed him, after coming down to the theater to find out, who he is. It's a miracle to me, that he got away with that outfit for so long.—

Good by my "sugarpie" am going to have dinner now with my understudy (called Madeline "the sauer puss") but she is allright. I suppose one gets that way if one is still a virgin with 45.

love and O°°°°°° *Knüschens* [little flower drawing]

1. *Leonard Lyons wrote a regular "Broadway gossip" column in the* New York Post.
2. *Dick McKay gave up acting to become an interior decorator.*

241 WEILL IN NEW CITY TO LENYA IN ST. LOUIS,
19 FEBRUARY 1942
Letterhead: Brook House / South Mountain Road / New City, N.Y.

Feb. 19, 1942

Schnäubi,

How do you like our new stationary? "*Sehr gilant*" [very elegant], isn't it? Max came back from Washington last night and just brought the script over. It is pretty dull and has very little opportunity for music. I am very disappointed because I had hoped I could do something exciting. But it is all talk and talk, just like a newspaper. So I am just writing what little music it needs. It is a pity that I had to give up my trip to Milwaukee for that. Max is very proud that he wrote the script in two days, and now he says Mab is probably right that he should be in closer contact with people and he is thinking seriously of selling his house and moving into town! If he thinks he'll write better plays in town he is greatly mistaken. But perhaps he'll write them faster—and that seems to be very important for him. It is all very stupid and depressing.

Preminger and Chodorov were here yesterday, and they had a wonderful time. Jules made the best diner I have ever had and Preminger said it was better than 21. Of course, we didn't get anywhere with the play. The idea is too thin.

I saw in a paper today that somebody had offered to the Lunts the Curt Goetz comedy "Hokuspokus."[1] As far as I remember it was an excellent comedy. Maybe that could be done as a musical for Lunt. I don't remember the play. Do you?

Loyd was just here, had a couple of drinks and told stories.[2] I was thinking of continuing the stone wall along the road instead of that old wooden fence. What do you think?

Well, that's about all today. I am thinking of taking the train to Detroit the night of the 28th after the broadcast. Then I would be in Detroit when you arrive. Jules is in town today. I make myself a cold diner. *Lebe, Schnäpschen!*

> *Hochachtungsvoll* [respectfully yours]
> *Trrrr.*

---

1. The German writer of comedies Curt Goetz (1888–1960) had a successful stage and screen career on both sides of the Atlantic; his The Talk of the Town *with Cary Grant was a hit in 1942.*

2. Lloyd Orser, a New City carpenter-mason, had inspired the character of the hero in Maxwell Anderson's play High Tor, *portrayed by Burgess Meredith.*

242 LENYA IN ST. LOUIS TO WEILL IN NEW CITY, [21 FEBRUARY 1942]
Letterhead: Hotel Mayfair

Sonnabend [Saturday] 1:00 A.M.

Träubchen,

I'll write you now, because today I'll be pretty busy. hairdresser, matinee and so on. This was a week of surprises. First the Valentine pakage, then yesterday the book and a letter and today another letter. *S - e - e - e - hr n - i - d - e - l - i - c - h !* I am glad that Dreyfuss likes the song. I am sure it's a beauty! You are right to try everything. But just dont be too unhappy Darling, if you dont find the right thing. It's so much better for you to wait (I know how hard it is for you). I am sure, you will get something. Just keep up the contact with everybody available, Cheryl and all those poeple. The "Lady" tour sounds teriffic. (I know it's written with two cc and one f—but I am too "hired.") They'll do tremendous business. You will see. Poeple are dying to see something gay. You get much more feeling for it, when you are in a play like ours. (It doesn't do bussiness at all, if we are in a town for a whole week.) It's only good for 2 and 3 day's. But all the plays like Arsenic and old laces and Panama Hattie, do terrific bussiness.[1] I hope, your income-tax man is good and get's your income down. (Mine want couse him much trouble—!

I am very disgusted with Mab. What a goose she can be. In a time like that, to be so foolish to look for entertainment and excitment. Isn't there enough going on in this world right now? Let them move into town. It'll be disastrous for Max. It wont do him any good. First of all, she wont be any help for him. You know, how poeple dislike her and she doesn't know how to make friends and keep them. That has to do with hospitality and cleverness how to treat poeple. And she certainly hasn't got any of those thing. They'll sit in town in their apartement and after a cuple of weeks nobody will come except us and the family. Ok, it's all so dumm and out of a little bourgois brain (nice but too stupid). I am sorry for you, that he turned in such a dull script. But Darling, I think he just cant any more. And his desire to write it fast! I'll see dark for his future. It'll be hard for him, to find a star after Candle. I will talk to the Lunts. Of course. I dont remember at all "Hokuspokus." If you cant find it in the library Tonio Selvart gave me the name of Edyth Isaac, editor of "Theater Arts" monthly, and she probably has all german plays. If you write to her, you can mention Tonios name. He know her quite well, as he said. Maybe you can read X.Y.Z. by Klabund, Spiel im Schloss by Molnar, the great bariton (Basserman played it wonderfully). I dont know who wrote it and then I would read "Sorina" by Kaiser.[2] That's really very funny. I'll find out, maybe the Lunts have an idea. It's really a pitty, that you cant come, when I am there, but you can always visit them, in case they are interested. That's all I remember about german comedies. It's not much help I am afraid. I am so pleased, that Jules works out so wonderful. Waxed kitchen floor! I almost forgot, that things like that exist! Vera was really incredible. I am glad we got rid of her. I cant wait for Detroit. I'll know the hotel next week and we arrive on Sunday. I'll take a double room, so if you arrive earlier then I, you just go there and get the room, which I will have reserved for us. And then we make *finelebe!* [we'll live it up] *Schneckidibong!* I bought defense stamps. (Only one dollar!) But it'll be more soon.

How is Moss? What is he doing. Hasn't he got an idea? This was a dreary week. I am glad to get out of it. I went to register today. It's really amazing, how nice they are in cases like that and what a conglamorate of nations are rallied on one bench. And that is really democratic the way they handle things like that. I bought a beautiful french dictionary (more for you, because you like good books). Here is a nice story for you. Pompadour walks in her park and a husky soldier slaps her on the behind. He is thrown in jail for that, so he writes her a little note saying: Madame! *"si votre coeur est aussi dur que votre cul—je suis perdu!"* [if your heart is as hard as your ass, I'm done for]. She answers, Sir, *si votre queuqueu est aussi dur, que votre main venez demain* [if your cock is as hard as your hand, come and see me tomorrow].—That's what I've learned so far. Well, *Träubchen,* now I have to pack my trunk, wash my laundry and then go to bed. I gained 5 pounds (dam it) 122 ! ! ! So my *cul* wont be a disappointment.—

Thanks for everything and with my most severe *handkuss* I'll remain eternally yours.

> Misses Karoline
> Wilhelmine
> Charlotte
> Weill

Darling, I dont think an all stone wall is pretty. It's so nice a gate with green on it and much higher. You couldn't have a stone wall that high. Wait for me! The brookhouse paper is very *gillant!*

---

1. Arsenic and Old Lace *by Joseph Kesselring opened in New York in January 1941; Cole Porter's* Panama Hattie, *starring Ethel Merman, had premiered in October 1940.*

2. *Molnár's* The Play's the Thing *(1927) had become a worldwide hit. Albert Bassermann (1862–1952) had appeared in Frank Wedekind's* Der Kammersänger *(The Great Baritone; 1899) at the Deutsches Theater in Berlin. Georg Kaiser had written* Die Sorina *in 1909.*

243 LENYA IN MADISON, WISCONSIN, TO WEILL IN NEW CITY, [24 FEBRUARY 1942]

Letterhead: Hotel Loraine / Madison / Wisconsin

Tuesday

Darling,

This is a lovely little town. I just came back from the theater Lee Simonson built last year. It's for the students. Next production is "Jorney to Jerusalem."[1] They planed "Knickerbocker" but cant do it this year too many students are in the army. That's really a charming theater "very modern." That's all the news from Madison. Tomorrow we leave at 12 and we arrive in Milwaukee at 2:30. So that's a "shorty." I'll stay at the "Hotel Wisconsin." In Detroit "Hotel Fort Shelby." Alfred [Lunt] will be at the theater tomorrow. So we are all excited! I finally wrote that letter to Mab. Then please give me Ritas adress. I want to write her too. It's cold here and I dont feel so well today (I get my business—I guess). Those pictures were 10 cents a piece. Taken here in the hotel after 10 hours train. Not so bad I think. The turban is new! 25 cents at 5 and 10. Very becoming, they say. Well *Schnäubschen*, this are only few lines. But I ran out of messenges. Next time more.

I'll see you soon. Thank God.

> *lebe*
> [flower drawing]

---

1. *The successful designer Lee Simonson (1888–1967) was one of the founders of the Theatre Guild. Maxwell Anderson's 1940 play* Journey to Jerusalem, *which wrestled with the problem of preserving faith in a world threatened by Hitler, ran into legal barriers posed by a little-known New York law prohibiting the representation on stage of the deity; Anderson thus named his central character Joshua instead of Jesus.*

244 LENYA IN MILWAUKEE TO WEILL IN NEW CITY, [25 FEBRUARY 1942]

Letterhead: Hotel Wisconsin / Milwaukee's largest independent hotel / Milwaukee / Wisconsin

Wednesday 11:30 P.M.

Dearest, dearest most dearest [flower drawing] ! ! ! ! !

It's over again! It was like an opening night with Alfred (<u>very</u> fat) in the audience. Lyn [Fontanne] went to N.Y. (Dentist, maybe she droped her teeth—) It was fun. I never saw so much <u>underplaying</u> before. Just too, too divine!—I saw him only for a moment after the show. He invited me Jackie, Guy and Tonio for Friday for an early dinner. He sends the car at 2:00. It's an hours drive. Helen and Evelyn are staying in his house.[1] So I hope I get a chance to talk to him. I was expecting a letter as you told me in your wire. But nothing for me. I send Meg [Anderson] a wire. For the Baby. Madison was very dreary. Bad house. They advance sale is so good here, that they have to take the orchestre pit out and put 6 more rows in. When Mab goes to town again, she can take a suit in the Ritz-tower.—It was only a 2 hours ride from Madison. Sunday we leave for Detroit at 11:15 A.M. arrive in Chicago 1:15. 3 hours lay off, leave Chicago at 4:15 and arrive in Detroit 10:00. Schmart isn't it? If you come to Detroit, go to the hotel I dont think, you would like to get me at the station, when the "circus" arrives. Fort Shelby is the hotel and there is a double room reserved for Mrs. Lenya and hobby. (That's you!) I'll listen to your Broadcast on Saturday at 6:00. We are an hour earlier, I think. I'll find out to make sure. Well *Bläumchen*, there is so little news from here. It's always the same. I heard to night, that this tour is going up to June 1st! ! ! I am horrified. We have to work out something, so I can get out sooner. It would be too awful, if I had to stay that long. They go way down to Texas and Arizona! Can you imagine. I cant stand this heat and practically all one night stands. How is everything in the house. Well *Träubchen*, I go to bed now and I'll see you on Sunday I hope. We probably have one week lay off Easter. Then I can go home. That would be wonderful!

> Now *lebe Du Schwänzchen*
> *Dein Plänzchen*

---

1. *The Lunts' permanent home was located in Genesee Depot, Michigan. Carol Channing described Genesee Depot as "to performers what the Vatican is to Catholics."*

245 WEILL IN NEW CITY TO LENYA IN DETROIT, 25 FEBRUARY 1942

Feb. 25, 1942
Wednesday morning

Schneubi,

This has to be a short letter because I have to go into town. I have worked hard since last Friday and I think Max's script and the whole broadcast is greatly improved now—with all my ideas in it. It is the same old story with Max: once he has written a script (which is always a first draft) he doesn't care any more. This time he depended entirely on me. Norman Corwin came out on Sunday and I had Max & Mab for diner. Monday morning I drove into town with Norman, talked to the conductor and had a meeting for the Freedom show.[1] They are all crazy about the MacLeish song. I'll bring it along to Detroit. Yesterday I worked all day on the score. Today I have a rehearsal. Tomorrow I'll work all day on a song I am writing with Hammerstein for which I had a good idea, a song about China with the title: The Good Earth.[2] Friday all day rehearsal, the same Saturday. Then, Saturday night, off to Detroit. I'll find out about my trains, also I have to get the travel permit.[3] It will be wonderful to see you and I am full of expectations regarding the 122 pound *cul*.

> So long, my love! 10000000 kisses.
> Kurt

Broadcast is Saturday at 7 on all stations.

6 P.M. I got my travel permit from Mr. Werner and made my reservation (bedroom) on

the train 10:40 P.M. which arrives in Detroit Sunday at 12:30 (noon). I'll wait for you at the Hotel. I hope you made reservation at the Cadillac Hotel because that's what Mr. Werner wrote into the permit. But if necessary I can change it in the travel permit. I hope you will be in Detroit Sunday afternoon so I don't have to wait too long. Anyway, let me know when you arrive.

1. *The conductor of* Your Navy *was Donald Vorhees.*

2. *Oscar Hammerstein II (1895–1960) was the most successful lyricist of his generation, beginning with Romberg's operettas, then* Show Boat *(1927) with Kern, and finally teaming up with Richard Rodgers for* Oklahoma! *(1943).*

3. *All "enemy" aliens had to be fingerprinted and registered; they also had to request permits to travel and, in California, had to observe nightly curfews.*

Fredric March and Douglas Fairbanks, Jr., narrated the broadcast on NBC Radio of Your Navy. *Weill's score has not been found. Weill was devoting more and more time to the war effort, which faced increasingly darker news as the Axis powers prospered. German U-boats sank British and American ships, and Rommel was victorious in North Africa. The Japanese occupied Bataan.*

246 LENYA IN DETROIT TO WEILL IN NEW CITY, 6 MARCH 1942

Letterhead: Book-Cadillac Hotel / Detroit, Michigan

Friday 5th [6th] 42

Darling,

Life looks different now, since you came. And the cake is gone too. Finally. It was very good, with coffee. Well there is nothing new, except Helen keeps on talking about "the Darling." She said, maybe Claire Boothe could write it.[1] I said, I wouldn't know, I saw only "the Woman" which I didn't like and Helen didn't either, but she said, she talked to her before she left N.Y. and Claire Boothe told her the story of her new play "Happy Mariage" and that was a very subtle and tender story. Of course, if Moss or Paul Osborn would do it, it's much better. But she seems to be so keen about it. So please, do what you can about it. She loved the songs (so did I—I think the are the best songs you have ever written. They are the most effortless (at least that how they sound) songs, you ever wrote. I'll sing "my captain" all day, the other ones are too difficult to remember after one hearing. I am sure, you didn't read that [Brooks] Atkinsons article. But it was on our board, so I got the paper. *Primi* isn't it? My new radio is wonderful. I really did need it. Now everything seems fine. The only hope I have, is that the shorten the tour after those 3 one night standers. Now *lebe* mine *Schnäubchen.* I hope, you dont feel lonely. Give my love to Moss. I'll use the Sunday to finish your sweater and write some letters. The rest we play cards

love and *büsschens* [(little kisses); little flower drawing]

I didn't hear about the suit, but Harry Esex[?] will call them tomorrow.

1. *"The Darling" is a short story by Anton Chekhov (1860–1904). Clare Boothe (1903–88) was married to the publisher Henry Luce and served as the U.S. ambassador to Italy (1953–57) under Dwight D. Eisenhower. Her most successful play was* The Women *(1936).*

246T LENYA IN DETROIT TO WEILL IN NEW CITY, 7 MARCH 1942
Western Union

SEND MUSIC AND LYRICS HOW CAN YOU TELL AN AMERICAN[1] TO CINCINNATI STOP HELEN WANTS IT FOR RECORDING STOP WRITE TO FORT SHELBY MR MOOR THAT BUTLER PACK THE SUIT THEY ARE STILL INVESTIGATING THATS ALL DARLING IS EVERYTHING OK. HERE TOO LOVE AND A PLEASANT SUNDAY = LINNERL.

1. *"How Can You Tell an American?" is a song from* Knickerbocker Holiday.

247 LENYA IN TOLEDO, OHIO, TO WEILL IN NEW CITY, [9 MARCH 1942]
Letterhead: Commodore Perry Hotel / Toledo, Ohio

Monday 6:00 P.M.

Darling, [outlined by a heart]

This is an awful town. We left Detroit at 1:15 and arrived here at 2:40. I went to the best hotel and it's a dreary place. Smells like they just fumigated the rooms. I went right down to the theater (which is a movie house) the pictures still was on, so I saw Veronica Lake in "Sullivans Travel" by Preston Sturges. A phony picture, but she looks so pretty. I go and have dinner now and then back to the theater. Yesterday was nice. It was pouring, a real hurrikan. So we went again to the movies and played cards afterwards. Darling maybe Max could change a little bit the lyriks for the american song. I dont think, Helen could do anything like "he want go to heaven he won't go to hell" on a reccord and then "free of govermental snuping" it wouldn't be the right thing to say right now. But I think Max could easely change those few lines. It would be such good publicity for you if she would do one of your songs. Did you talk to Moss about the "Darling"? And what is going on in N.Y. I am glad, if we get to Chicago. *Schnäubchen*, there is nothing new I can tell you, so I better stop and wait of news from you. By, by, *Blümchen* and write soon

love
Linerl

248 WEILL IN NEW CITY TO LENYA IN TOLEDO, 9 MARCH 1942

Monday, 3/9/42

My *Trrräubi*,

It was very *niedelich* in Detroit and it seems so long since I came back. The trip back was very nice. I had a wonderful train this time and slept quite well. Then I had lunch with Dreyfus and dinner with Moss. I gave him "The darling," but I don't think he will like it. We saw the première of an English anti Nazi picture "The Invaders" [1940]—pretty bad. They announced [Laurence] Olivier, Leslie Howard and [Raymond] Massey as stars, but Massey didn't appear. Finally a lot of Indians came on horseback and I said: "Now Massey cannot be far away." Moss laughed his head off. On Friday I went into town late in the afternoon and saw Hammerstein. Then to dinner at the [John] Whartons—very nice, but not exciting. On Saturday Hans and Rita came out and stayed over night. On Sunday Bravi came with Yvonne Casa-Fuerte, Rieti and Morris Stonzek and [his wife] Lee. That was an awful combination and not very entertaining. Those French people insist on speaking French, just like the Germans. We had a buffet lunch (Virginia ham and baked beans, *primi!*). At 6 I threw them all out and today I am glad to be alone. Max is in Carolina in a soldiers camp to make studies for the soldiers play which he will write with Alan [his son?](!!). (But that is a secret!). He is nuts. She [Mab] is dying of jealousy because Steinbeck's book about Norway got rave notices and the play will probably be a smash hit.[1] I'll get the book for you.—I send you 2 lovely letters from MacLeish (very important), a letter from Brecht and my answer. Send them all back! The tax man has done a good job. He has brought down the taxes to 12,000, but it is possible that we have to pay another 4000. And of course his salary, but anyway it will be under 20,000—so we have saved 10,000.—MacLeish wrote Max: "Weill's score was the best radio music we have ever heard!" Saturday I am invited for dinner at Atkinsons. Mab has paid back all the money. "Lady" closes definitely April 25. It is in the papers today.

I think this is about all. You'll have another letter in Cincinnati. *Lebe, mein Schnäpschen, und sei hochachtungsvoll gegrüsst von deinem ergebenen Affenschwanz* [be respectfully greeted by your devoted monkey tail].

1. Steinbeck's dramatized novella The Moon Is Down *concerns the Norwegian resistance to the German occupation.*

Prior to the letter from Brecht that Weill enclosed with his own to Lenya on 9 March, Weill and Brecht had had almost no direct contact since 1939, when Brecht inquired from Weill, "What are the real chances for Die Dreigroschenoper *in America?" Weill answered, "One could risk it, of course, only with a completely new adaptation (which must be done by someone first-class) and with one of the best Broadway producers" (Bertolt-Brecht-Archiv 1646/08, n.d.). In March 1941 Elisabeth Hauptmann had solicited Weill for a contribution to support Brecht's immigration to America with his family. Weill sent one hundred dollars to Brecht's bank account in Finland; Brecht arrived in Los Angeles in July 1941 and contacted Weill with veiled allusions to plans for an all-black production of* Die Dreigroschenoper—*even though Brecht was already deeply involved in negotiations. The entry in his diary for 22 November 1941 reads: "The Negro Clarence Muse has done an adaptation of* Die Dreigroschenoper *and wants to put on an all-Negro production." Brecht's letter to Weill in early March 1942 had been preceded by a telegram of 5 March from his new agent: "Negotiating between Brecht and Clarence Muse for musical version Dreigroschen Oper. Please wire immediately your share in stage royalties and motion picture rights." A casual explanatory letter from Brecht himself arrived the next day:*

Some Negroes are very interested in a production of *Die Dreigroschenoper*. Clarence Muse (who, I think, produced *Run, Little Children* here [a musical play by Hall Johnson and Lew Cooper first performed at the Lyric Theatre in New York on 1 March 1933]), together with Paul Robeson (who is helping him to start a National Negro Theater; for the time being he doesn't want any prominence, but in New York, if the play makes it there, he might play Peachum), wants to produce it here with Katherine Dunham as Polly. Muse has made an adaptation, almost nothing changed except the setting (now Washington, with the inauguration of the president instead of the coronation). They want to do their own instrumentation of your music for their band. . . . I will send the contract on to you as soon as I get it. (BB–W1, 5 March 1942)

Weill answered Brecht on 9 March with a two-page, single-spaced typed letter in German:

It's a shame that you didn't give me the opportunity to advise you at an earlier stage of negotiation. I believe I could have advised you better than most people in Hollywood, especially since in the matter of an American revival of *Die Dreigroschenoper* I am sort of an "expert," having been engaged with this problem continuously during the last seven years. Because of the overall nature of American theater, it is very tricky to revive a play that has failed once before, even if it has as good a reputation as *Die Dreigroschenoper*. But no doubt we will have a first-class revival of *Die Dreigroschenoper* if we wait for the best combination of translator (for the play and, what is especially difficult, for the lyrics), director, producer, and actors. In recent months I've had many negotiations with Charles MacArthur, one of the best young dramatists in America and a long-time collaborator with Ben Hecht. He was very interested, and my plan was to get a really first-class American adaptation either from him alone or together with Hecht, with whom I am very friendly.

Weill also reminded Brecht that he had already been working for years with an American writer on an all-black version of Die Dreigroschenoper, *but there were real problems to be solved: "It became apparent that the idea of having American Negroes perform a German adaptation of a seventeenth-century English ballad opera was so 'sophisticated' that it would totally bewilder the audience. We then attempted to rework the piece so that the problems became the genuine problems of the Negro—but that meant we'd have to write a whole new play." Weill did empathize with Brecht's position:*

It goes without saying that I can very well understand that you're eager to get something going here and also that your financial situation makes a quick theatrical success desirable. But I had hoped you would find a start in film through your friends in Hollywood so that we could wait with *Die Dreigroschenoper* until we could really take advantage of the best prospects this "property" holds for us. But you will probably say this is a typically capitalist viewpoint. . . . I can well imagine how my music would turn out if I were to agree to the theater's desire to do its own instrumentation. I have always, especially here in America, insisted that my music be played only in my own orchestrations in the theater, and I must hold to that principle in this case as well. (W–BB, 9 March 1942)

249 WEILL IN NEW CITY TO LENYA IN CINCINNATI,
11 MARCH 1942

March 11, 1942

Dear *Schnäubi*,

Here is your income tax return. Sign it at the bottom of the first page where you see the pensil cross, in presence of a notary public and have him notarize it. Then sign the check which I include (just to be signed, not notarized), put the paper and the check together in the envelope which is enclosed and which has already the address and everything, and mail it by airmail, not later than Saturday night. *Vastehste* [you understand]? And don't get scared that you have to pay over 5000 because we have made a partnership between you and me so that you pay half of my income tax. (If that goes through it saves us about 4000).

I was in town yesterday, had lunch with Hammerstein and told him the story of "The Pirate."[1] He said it was surefire if the Lunts would do it. Do you think there is still a chance of their doing it? Maybe now after "There shall be no night" they would be very glad to [do] a light show like that.[2] I could try to get either Moss or George Kaufmann to write it, with Hammerstein's lyrics. I'll talk to Moss about it, and maybe I'll write a letter to Alfred, or perhaps, if Moss is interested, we'll talk to Lynn here.— Then I saw the Aufrichts. They seem to go downhill very fast, live in a terrible apartment and everything was so poor and miserable that I decided to give them some more money. I'll also try to get a job for him. In the evening I saw "Ladyinthedark." Schwarz was there and said he would drive me home. Then he showed up with some jewish girl and said we would have to drive her home first; she lived way out in the Bronx and it took me about 3 hours to get home. He is an awful guy, loud, bragging all over the place and unbearably jewish. He said: "I went to see John to show him my latest works." I said: "John who?" He: "Steinbeck, of course. I talked to Gwenn [Gwyn]." I said: "Do you know them?" He: "Well, I met them in your house." I was furious. Well, it's too late now to do something about it, but I am glad that I didn't let him come to the house any more. He says he has been accepted for the airforce and is waiting to be called any day now. It is a lovely spring day here today. Jules went into town this morning. I have a lot of letters to write and then I'll go for a walk with Woolley. Louise Rainer's play opened yesterday and got awful notices.[3] I suppose it will close Saturday. Tola (Litvak) just called. He is in town for a few days and I'll probably go in and have dinner with him, and see "Lady."

How where the one-night-stands this week? Did you pick a nice hotel in Chicago? Good-bye, *Trrräubchen*. Next time I'll write to Chicago.

Knüsschen,
Kurt

Moss doesn't think there is enough material in "The darling" for a play. He is going to write Helen about it and I told him to write her that we would try to do something else for her. Maybe I'll get in touch with Paul Osborn. He might be interested because it is more on his alley than on Moss's.

1. *Ludwig Fulda's (1862–1939) comedy* Der Seeräuber.

2. There Shall Be No Night, *Robert E. Sherwood's 1940 play about the war between Russia and Finland, won the Pulitzer Prize.*

3. *The play was* A Kiss for Cinderella *(1916), by James Barrie (1860–1937), the English playwright best known for* Peter Pan *(1905). It was produced by Cheryl Crawford.*

250 LENYA IN CINCINNATI TO WEILL IN NEW CITY, 12 MARCH 1942

Letterhead: Netherland Plaza / Cincinnati

Thursday 12th

Darling,

Thank God I am here. These 3 days were very depressing and tireing. Detroit, Toledo, Fort Wayne, train, sleeper (for 5 hours) buss rides and filthy hotels (everything is just overcrawed). But it's lovely here, I got a wonderful room on the 21st floor. *Sehr elegant.* What the hell. Helen is really a terrific draw on the road. In Fort Wayne we broke the record! 5000 one night. Max can be very grateful to her. I got your letter just now. I am so happy, that your music was such a success. I'll show Helen the letter. It's so important. Helen ask me whether you would help her on her reccords. I said, I am sure you would, if the company pays you, the trip and the expenses. Because you would have to stay a whole week in Chicago. So I dont know, what she will decide. I hope, I did right. I can imagine, how boring that french party was. But anyway, they saw the house.—I hope you find some one for "the Darling." Charlie [MacArthur] comes to Chicago on Sunday. I hope, he doesn't talk her out of it. It's wonderful about the income tax! I am glad for John [Steinbeck] that he has such a success with his book. Max is an old gaga. To write a play with Allan! Well, what do we care. Brechts letter is typical. Please Darling dont do anything! Your answer is just right. That would just be up his alley, to spoil your carefully built up good name. He'll live without *3groschenoper.* I have no pitty or sympathy, they are too mean that german bunch (Kaiser included.) They just use you, whenever they need you. Nop! Let him spell his name—you have to do the same. He's got enough "friends" out there. They'll take care of the "genius." I've got a letter from Ruth Page.[1] She invites me for dinner on Monday to meet the first critic in Chicago. But I dont believe in meeting critics before an opening. I fear their "objectivity," not to mention one, if they know you. I'll call her and try to get out of it and arrange something for after the opening. Not that it is so important but, I did so well so far and get such good notices every where, that I am superstitius (I cant spell that "superstitious," is that right?). We stay definitly 3 weeks in Chicago. I still havn't got the list for after that. But I'll get it. It's a wonderful day and I am longing for New City. It must be wonderful in spring. But that Texas tour sounds so exciting. New Orleans, Charleston, down to the mexican border. I still think they wont go further and just make those 3 weeks one nighters. I feel kind of sorry for "Lady." But it probably was the right thing to close. If you dont come to Chicago, I'll try to come one Saturday night and try to take Monday of. That would give me one Sunday and Monday. I could leave Monday night. I think, I get that out the stage manager. Well Darling, I have to stop, it's 1:30 and I have to eat. Write again soon! love and love and love!

Linerl

I'll send you the MacLeish letters with my next letter. I'll show them to Helen tonight.

1. *The pioneering American dancer and choreographer Ruth Page (1905–91) was married to the prominent Chicago attorney Tom Fisher, who acquired a dubious reputation because of his handling of several famous gangster cases.*

251 WEILL IN NEW CITY TO LENYA IN CINCINNATI, 12 MARCH 1942

March 12, 1942

Darling,

Just a few lines today. I had your letter from Toledo yesterday. Please tell Helen I am sure that Max would change those lines if she wants to do the song and that I would make a special arrangement for her, maybe using a small men's chorus. These men could throw in little remarks, for instance:

Helen: It isn't that he's short or tall
Chorus: No!
Helen: It isn't that he's round or flat
Chorus: Certainly not!
Helen: It isn't that he's civilized or aboriginal
Nor the head-size of his hat,
Chorus: Ain't it true!
    etc.

Sometimes they would ask the questions and she would give the answers and vice versa. It could be worked out this way, almost like another "Ballad for Americans"—and I am sure Max would do it.[1]

Tell Helen also that I will try to get in touch with Paul Osborn about "The Darling." He is in Hollywood and I will get his address from Josh.[2]

I had dinner with Tola last night and saw the whole "Lady in the Dark" (which I hadn't done in over a year). When you sit right in the audience you realize how they love every minute of that show. Gertie was wonderful. She is quite a gal. Tola, Bravi and I went to the Stork Club (!). What a dreary place that is!

I called Charlie MacArthur today, and he is coming to dinner tonight with Bemmelman.[3] Jules is busy. We'll have roast lamb, hashed brown pitatos and chocolate roll. I told Jules [that] Litvak and Tyron Power may come out for lunch Saturday.[4] He said: "Now Mr. Weill, you get me all excited."

Today they have fixed the fence, at last. Pete [Broye] was here yesterday. He will make an estimate for painting both houses. He thinks it will be about 200 and he will start in about a month. I'll send you color samples. He thinks we should leave the doors blue and paint the shudders rost read.

That's all, *meine Träube. Hochachtungsvoll,*
Kurt

I just got a check from Dreyfus for 215.16 from the sale of music from Lady in the Dark. That's the first time in this country that I get anything out of [printed] music. *Primi*, isn't it? That pays for painting the house. It means that he has earned back the 1250 advance which he had paid me. That's a nice feeling.

1. *Earl Robinson (b. 1910) wrote* Ballad for Americans *in 1938 for the revue* Sing for Your Supper, *and it became well known nationally.*
2. *Joshua Logan (1908–88) had directed* Knickerbocker Holiday; *he went on to become one of the great forces on Broadway with* Annie Get Your Gun *(1946),* Mr. Roberts *(1948), and* South Pacific *(1949).*
3. *Ludwig Bemelmans (1898–1962) was an Austrian-born author of whimsical books with his own illustrations.*
4. *The actor Tyrone Power (1913–58) made his Broadway debut as Mercutio in* Romeo and Juliet *in 1935. During the forties he was one of Hollywood's most popular leading men.*

252 LENYA IN CINCINNATI TO WEILL IN NEW CITY, [13 MARCH 1942]
Letterhead: Netherland Plaza

Friday 11:30 P.M.

Darling,

I send the incom tax. Gee, that sounds good. I hope, he gets it through. Helen showed me your wire. She seems to be very excited about the idea to have you for the reccords. They'll call you. I gave her your telephon number. I hope they pay you the trip and expences. We got very bad notices here. They play I mean. They cast was hardly mentioned. Please by all means, talk to Lynn [Fontanne]. They have nothing and are dying to find a show. They are probably both in N.Y. You can get their adress through the Guild. Helen said something very funy about them after she stayed 4 day's in his house. He is really very dumm, doesn't know anything what's going on in the world and is just a good actor. I am sure that's true. If you talk to them just be very sure and dont treat them too carefully. He hasn't got much mind of his own and you can talk him in to anything. I think especially now. I'll be very happy if you would come to Chicago. And I think it's good to do a thing like that and have your name on the reccords.

Evelyn saw the list of the tour after Chicago. Well they are going to Canada. Here is my chance!—am glad, I wrote that in the contract. Isn't that wonderful! I dont know yet, when they go, but there are 3 towns in Canada on the list. That means at least a week off. *Primi!* Dont get angry about Schwartz, he is a fool. I am sure, he didn't even get to see John and John is probably used to things like that. Maybe the army knoks some sense into him. Today was a fire in our hotel, just when I was going to lie down around 4:30 I heard the fire engine stop on the street, crabed my bag and down I went. But the fire was in another part so I went up again. I saw "Goldrush" this afternoon. What a wonderful picture after 17 years. Chaplin himself speaks the narator.[1] See it, if you get a chance. It's really beautiful. I just wrote Ruth Page a letter. I think I'll go there for diner. What the hell it's not that important. Darling here is the list of thing, I wanted you to bring me if you come to Chicago. Then I'll send my big trunk home. It's a nuissance for all those one nighters. I feel sorry for the Aufrichts. He probably is unable to learn the language. You know how long it took him to learn french. I hope you find some kind of a job for him. I'll write them a letter. What's his adress? I'll go to the Sherman Hotel in Chicago. It's right across the theater. Helen goes to the Ambassodor East. But it's far from the theater and each taxi is 75 cents. Too much for 3 weeks. I'll get a nice room at the Sherman. High up. This hotel here is beautiful. But very loud. They all are.

Now good night *Blümchen*. Things look very nice now with you coming to Chicago (maybe) and then Canada off!! I was very pleased about Cheryl's flop. And Luischen [Rainer] looked like 5 Cinderellas. Too cute for one life. Good night Darling. It's awfuly warm and sticky outside. Schpring! I guess.

Träubenknüsschen

1. *Weill and Lenya knew Chaplin's* Gold Rush *in the silent version from 1926; it had exerted a big influence on* Mahagonny, *as well as the dancing banana scene in* Der Silbersee. *It was rereleased with music and voice-over by Chaplin in 1942.*

253   WEILL IN NEW CITY TO LENYA IN CHICAGO,
16 MARCH 1942

Monday morning
3/16/42

Trrrrrr ——

It was very *niedelich* to talk to you last night. I am afraid it will be pretty expensive for a little moneymaker like you, so I am sending my contribution to the phone call (which is also your 10% from the Dreyfus money). *Damit du dir deinen Wiener Popo massieren lassen kannst, du Pflänzchen* [so that you can have your Viennese tush massaged, you little *Pflanze*].

I forgot to ask you if you got the special delivery letter with the income tax papers and if you did everything as indicated and mailed it back because it has to be in the mail not later than tonight. I am a little worried because you didn't say anything about it. I mailed the letter Thursday evening Airmail Special, so it must have arrived at the Taft Theatre before Saturday night. Well, I hope I will hear about it in your letter which I probably get this afternoon.

The Victor people just called. They don't seem to know exactly what they want, and I told them my idea, but added that I have no objection if they want to do it their way. I told them, they'd have to pay all expenses and give me credit. They want to record next week so that I would be in Chicago the coming week-end, if it works out. They'll call me this afternoon.

It is a lovely spring day again and it has been that way for almost 3 weeks—which is good for the spirit and for the oil-bill.

Everything else I told you on the phone. Maybe I'll be in Chicago soon. *Dann werde ich dir zeigen was eine Harke ist* [then I'll show you what's what].

So long, my love,

Kurt

The hotel will cash the check.

Afternoon: The Victor people called again. They want me to do it and they'll pay all expenses. They will postpone the recording a week. So it looks as if I will be in Chicago a week from Friday. *Primi?*

254 LENYA IN CHICAGO TO WEILL IN NEW CITY, 17 MARCH 1942
Letterhead: Hotel / Sherman / Randolph, Clark, Lake and La Salle Streets / Chicago, Ill.

Tuesday 17th

Well Darling,

Here is the first part of the *"Hinrichtung"* [execution]. It's going to be longer. But I think not much more will come after that. I had diner on Monday at Ruth'es house. It was quite nice. I meet Cecil Smith (a nice fairy) and the whole thing was *kurz und schmerzlos* [short and painless].[1] Ruth and Tom are kind of envious that we have a house and he tried several times to make some craks about it like: those "central Europens come here and the first thing the do is, to buy houses"—. So I told him, as long as we dont buy oilwells it's alright. He is a rather cynical guy. But I would get bitter too in an apartment like they have. In a huge apartment house, ful with modern *"mief"* [stuffy] painted dancers on all the walls, bad food, very gloomy. They saw the show, liked it, as they said . . . and they went home. That's all. They play got the worst and most intelligent notices (I wish Mab would read them—) but the house is sold out for the first two weeks on subscription and the last week has a good adwance sale. Please save those notices for me. I went to a massage place today and I'll go 3 times a week. They weather is terrible. Fogy and rainy. But I dont care any more. I just hope, that time will pass and I can go home. It's too long. I hope they go to Canada, so I can stop and not return. Have you thought of anything for next weekend? I want to go home on Saturday night and go back Tuesday night. Not this Saturday. Next. I hope, I can manage. Helen didn't say anything about the reccords. But Charlie is here with her adopted son [James MacArthur]. So one cant talk to her. And I wont say anything as long as you are not so anxious anyway. It would have meant only, that you would be here for a week and that I would have liked. But maybe it still works out. You see Darling if you want to come for Easter, that's about when we leave. So that wouldn't be so good. And after Chicago, I cant see you anymore for at least 2 Month. That's bitter [flower drawing]! Did Rita get my letter? I invited her, to pay her staying here if Hans pay's her the trip. But she didn't answer. And what's the news in N. City. Dont you have to invite the Atkinsons? John and Gwenn [Steinbeck] would be a nice combination. What's Moss'es adress. I want to send him a card. I bought you today a bedspread for your bed. I have it send. It's nice. White with *püncktchen* [little dots]. Please tell Jules to write me down the adresses, where he stayed over night in all those southern towns, (if he still can remember them) for Evelyn's maid. I have a very nice room here and right across the theater, which is very pleasant. Darling, I have a feeling like that tour will never end. It's awful. I am sick and tired of it. But good. But I dont see, how I ever could leave. Write soon. Anything just to get a letter from you. *Lebe Blümchen*, one day it just has to end. Did you see those wonderful Kippling pictures in Life with his "Caroline." That's how we will look if we live that long. And those terrible pictures with those 5 Russians hanging on a tree. It's too depressing.

Well by by Darling. I hope I'll see you before I leave.

1. *Music critic Cecil Smith (1906–56) taught at the University of Chicago, edited* Musical America, *wrote for the* Chicago Tribune, *and authored* Musical Comedy in America *(1950).*

255   WEILL IN NEW CITY TO LENYA IN CHICAGO,
19 MARCH 1942

March 19, 1942

Schnäubi,

I was just sitting down to write you a letter when your letter arrived. The notices are awful for Max, but very good for you. Well, that road tour is something! I can understand that you have a kind of *"Katzenjammer"* [hangover]. If I only knew how you could get out of it. Do you think I should talk to Terry [Helburn]? The way they have worked out the tour, it looks as if they are planning to go to Canada after May 16 because they are coming back to Illinois. (I was afraid they would go on to the West coast from Texas, and that would have meant at least another four weeks, but thank God, that seems to be out). So if they go to Canada you quit and come home and get good and sick here, with a nice letter from [Dr.] Heller. Or do you think you could get sick in Chicago?

The Victor people said on Monday they want me to go to Chicago and they would pay the expenses. Yesterday they called here while I was in town and left a message that the recordings take place the 30th and 31st, so that seems to indicate that they still expect me to go. I'll probably hear from them today or to-morrow and settle it definitely. In that case I will be in Chicago probably from Friday March 27 for about 5 or 6 days. But if you would rather come home I can cancel the whole thing and stay here. Anyhow I will see you before you go on the tour. I'll call you to-morrow (Friday night). By that time I hope I have talked to the Victor people.

There isn't much news here. Yesterday I was in town, saw Cheryl who has some excellent ideas with regard to "The Tinted Venus" and also a wonderful idea for a Negro play. Then I had dinner with Moss. He was very nice again and I gave him a brand new idea for a show which he liked. He is going to Florida for two weeks the end of next week. We saw "Café Crown" a very charming little play with a wonderful performance by Sam Jaffe with whom we had a drink later.[1]

"Lady in the Dark" is not going on the road in the spring because Washington doesn't allow children on the stage. So we stay here as long as we have an audience (which may be all season, it is picking up this week) and go on a long tour next season—which is just as good—or better. The Fight for Freedom show is definitely off (no money). MacLeish didn't answer my last letter in which I offered to come to Washington to show him the song. I see in the papers that he is in New York today, but he didn't call. So this beautiful song is lying around in my drawer—with all the others. And no show in sight. It is just as depressing as your road tour. But we shouldn't complain, I think. I hope it will never be worse in our life than it is now!

Please, *Schnäubchen*, don't be too depressed. If you want to, I'll get you out of this tour. And anyway I'll see you next week, either in Chicago or here, and then life will be beautiful again.

Lebe, mein Schnäpschen, und viele viele Busschen auf deinen P . . . [farewell, my little schnapps, and many, many little kisses on your tush],

dein ewiger Gatte [your eternal spouse] Kurt

Die Zeichnung im letzten Brief war typisch für eine Sinnenpison [the drawing in the last letter was typical of a sensual person]. Do you think I should ask Victor Samrock's advise if and how you could get out. I am sure he would treat it confidential and give his honest opinion.[2]

---

1. Cafe Crown *is a play by Hy Kraft (1899–1975). The film and stage actor Sam Jaffe (1891–1984) had played the role of the Adversary in* The Eternal Road.

2. *Victor Samrock (1907–95) was the general manager of the Playwrights' Producing Company.*

256 LENYA IN CHICAGO TO WEILL IN NEW CITY,
23 MARCH 1942
Letterhead: Hotel Sherman

Monday 11:30

Darling,

Here is the list. I think Jules will find it. I feel a little better this morning, but still drowsy. It'll be over by Friday. I am curious what Vic will say about leaving the show.

It would be such a relief for me but I doubt it whether it can be done. It's a shame with Behrmann. And *dieser Versteller* [this hypocrite] Lunt must have known it.[1] Well, what can one do. Wait for something to come up. I am so anxious to get home. I am not very bright this morning Darling but this cold got me this time. So *lebe!* and Friday in a suit! Eligant.

   love from Madame Weill

Ask Jules about those adresses he stayed overnight on his road tour. Does he still remember them?

1. *Sam Behrman (1893–1973) was one of the five founding members of the Playwrights' Producing Company. He had adapted Ludwig Fulda's* The Pirate *as a straight play for the Lunts.* The Pirate *was a romantic satire, set in the tropics, about a wife who dreams of being carried off by the mysterious pirate who controls the surrounding waters. Her fat husband turns out to be the pirate.*

Weill went to Chicago at the end of March to work with Helen Hayes on Mine Eyes Have Seen the Glory: Four Patriotic Melodramas for Speaker, Chorus, and Orchestra, *recorded on 30–31 March by RCA. That he was able to orchestrate the music on such short notice was typical of his facility after years of working in the theater. He arranged "Battle Hymn of the Republic," "The Star-Spangled Banner," and "America"/"Pledge to the Flag" as melodramas and made an arrangement of one of his recent Whitman songs, "Beat! Beat! Drums!" for speaker instead of singer. The 78s were released as a two-disc set.*

257   LENYA IN CHICAGO TO WEILL IN NEW CITY,
[3 APRIL 1942]
Letterhead: Hotel Sherman

                  Friday
Darling,

 Mr. Weiss[?] (and wife "Frankie") called me yesterday and we had lunch together. Then we went to hear the reccords on a wonderful "Capcheard" (oh—how do you spell that) machine. They sound wonderful. "Beat, beat, drums" just lifts you right out of your sit. I am sure Weiss will do it over again with Tibbett or Thomas.[1] He is grazy about you! Well, that's that. It was worth while coming up here (besides seeing me— which was very very *niedelich* for me too.) I am glad to get moving again. It means, we are getting closer to the end. I send my trunk to Spring Valley (collect—excuse me, but they didn't know, how much it will be 3 or 4 bucks, that's all). Jules should brush everything and then put it away. I'll send you back the check you gave me. I really dont need it Darling. Spent it for the house. I dont want to carry too much money with me. I have enough. I get my travelling permit tomorrow. What a nuissance. I started the Steinbeck book. It's almost a play the way it is. Strangly enough, it reminds you on what Max has to say in "Candle." But I guess as soon as one deals with Nazis, there is only one thing to say. But it's a beautiful written book. My little manicure case is sheer delight. I used it the first time today. "Very pritty." Tomorrow is closing night. Thank God. Sunday 2:15 Evansville and then good by with glamour. Just train and dirt. I am very happy about the reccords and Helen seems to be too. I hope I'll get a chance to talk to her about your plans. Well Darling, that's all for today. How did you get home? Alright? Schwarz wrote me a very nice letter. He is just a little fool but he means well. He is so happy about his coming job. He thanked me for everything, I ever did for him. He is alright. I wonder who gave him the address. He probably read it in the papers where we play. Well Darling, I dont think I'll be able to write you much from now on, but I'll write you postalcards. And take care of yourself and have a good time. It want be so long anymore than I'll be home. The worst part is over.

> *Viele Knüsschen of Deinen bobo* [many little kisses on your behind] and love!
> *Deine "Blüte"*

1. *Lawrence Tibbett (1896–1960) and John Charles Thomas (1891–1960) were leading baritones at the Metropolitan Opera. In 1945 Weill considered both as strong candidates to play Cellini in* The Firebrand of Florence.

258 WEILL IN NEW CITY TO LENYA IN EVANSVILLE, INDIANA, 5 APRIL 1942
Letterhead: Brook House

April 5, 1942

My darling,

I guess you are on the train and you'll probably arrive tonight in one of those awful Midwestern towns. It is a lovely day here! I have worked with Hans in the garden, cleaning out all the dead branches. Your willow tree is full of little buds and everywhere little green points are looking out of the ground. Max came back this morning. He has an idea for his play now and doesn't want to go south right now—thank God! He wasn't quite happy when I told him that Sam [Behrman] had done an excellent job with "The Pirate" and that it probably will make a million dollar (which I think it will). I had lunch at Sam's yesterday and Alfred [Lunt] was there. He asked about you and I told him that you are feeling fine and that you like touring like a good old trooper. Sam said: I guess she would rather be home in her beautiful house. Alfred (almost hysterically): No, no, she wouldn't leave the show! An actor should never leave a show!—He would have hated you for the rest of your life if you would have quit the show.

They were both flabbergasted about my criticism of "The Pirate" script, because it was the most exact and most constructive criticism anybody had made (it needs work in the 2nd act, but it can be the best play the Lunts have had in years). Alfred wants music "all through the play" and he said: "By the time you get through with it, the music will be just as important as the play." That means they realize that they have to pay me royalties (I'll ask 2%). It will be a much more interesting job than I expected because I will have 7 negro musicians *on stage*, playing, singing, dancing etc. and that is something I always wanted to do. It is a difficult job because it has to sound like improvisation and I have to find a new style, half spanish half negro. If they really want to do it in the spring I'll have to work like mad—but that's o.k. with me. Alfred was nice—but so stupid! Well, I think it will be a very nice thing for me to do next just because it is not a musical, and something original and high class. And would I be glad if this waiting period would be over.

A wire from Brecht: "Could you come to Hollywood. We could settle Pennyopera and some new thing as well." Ha ha! And a letter from —— Wiesengrund, of all people! pleading I should give the rights (a completely idiotic letter).[1]

Haven't got your letter yet, but am very glad that you like the records. Here are some samples for the cushions for the terrace-chairs. I think either the rost-red or the green is right. Pick out one and send it back.

I guess that's all today. I'll write once more to Atlanta. I had a lovely time in Chicago and I thought you were very *niedelich*—as usual! Don't get impatient with the road tour. You'll have to stick it out and it will pass quicker than you think. Mab wired Max from Miami after 2 days that the whole trip seems "imbecile." I suppose she will be back soon!

Lebe, Schnäpschen. Viele Knüsschen. dein Trrrrr.—

1. *Weill's cool response to Brecht's first letter precipitated a torrent of telegrams and letters from Brecht and his agent, reiterating their confidence in the project and emphasizing Brecht's dire financial straits. On 31 March, Theodor W. Adorno sent Weill a letter supporting Brecht's position: "The ideological situation in America could not be compared to the German one of 1929; America was not yet ready to accept the authentic* Dreigroschenoper, *which is so inseparably tied to a climate of crisis" (TWA–W). He proposed that a faithful rendition of the score be abandoned in favor of a sociological refashioning, which could be achieved by "allowing a Negro jazz ensemble the greatest and most radical improvisatory freedom" with the score—a most unlikely proposal from Adorno, who scorned jazz as a decadent product of the "culture industry."*

259   LENYA IN EVANSVILLE TO WEILL IN NEW CITY, 6 APRIL 1942
Postcard: New Ohio River Bridge, connecting Evansville, Indiana, and Henderson, Kentucky

Monday
6th 42

Darling,

I walked along this beautiful Ohio-River and spring was in the air. I felt quite homesick—but as the fools say "the show must go on."—I hope you are well. Give my regards to Jules. We leave tonight at 11:30 stay in train until 9 A.M. Not so bad. Love as always Linnerl

260   LENYA IN LOUISVILLE, KENTUCKY, TO WEILL IN NEW CITY, 7 APRIL 1942
Novelty postcard with jackass illustration: "I'm out on a h—— of a time! In Old Kentucky"

Louisville 7th 42

Darling,

This was a little tough leaving at 3:00 in the morning arriving here at 9 A.M. Went straight to hotel and slept. Matinee now. Tomorrow "Well well" CHATANOOGA, a long trip. Leaving at 1:00 arriving 2:00 P.M. *heiteres künstlervölkchen* [merry band of artists] . . . LETTER from ATLANTA! Love [little flower drawing]

Letterhead: Hotel / Lakeland Terrace / Lakeland, Florida

Tuesday 8th 42

Träubchen,

This is like being on the road again. Only the hotel is so much better. Have a wonderful room overlooking the lake and it looks like the rivierra. The trip was awful. The train was so filled with soldiers and sailors, that it was impossible to get near the dining car. So no dinner. Only a sandwich and beer. But I slept wonderful, as usual in the train. I arrived here, with 1 hour delay and found a message from Sch[wartz] to come out to the airfield at 4:00. They put on a great show, all those little planes going up like moskitos. It's almost incredible, that one can learn to fly in such a short time. At 7:30 they came out and had a little party at the officers club which lasted until 12:30. Then they had to drive to the camp in a truck. You wouldn't recognize Sch. He is quiet, nothing of that showing off business any more. Just one in a million. Sunday morning he came at 11:30. Then we went swimming all day. At 12 P.M. he had to be back. Sunday morning I found out about the beach. It's pretty far away, the nearest is St. Peterburg. It's beautiful here, so I think I'll stay here and go swimming in the lake and take sunbath on the roof. It's raining every afternoon since I am arrived. They call it rainy season. But I think I will get a little sunburn and get rid of that cough, which still sounds like T.B. It must be more, than just a cough, because it's so persistent. I am worried about you and the house. Do you make your breakfast and lunch. And does Lynn Baker[?] clean up? Please do write about it. I would like to stay this weekend, but if you do need me, I'll come back before. I dont have to make a reservation for the sleeper. I get it on the train. I asked. So if you need me, I can come any day. This is a pretty little town. Filled with soldiers all sorts. It's monotonous. We have to think Darling what to do, to keep you out. It's no fun. I can see that now. One has to be very young to stand that. It's like living with cattles. They are never alone, just thrown together. It's impossible for you. Oh Darling, I just got you telegram. I knew, I shouldn't have gone. Now what is the matter. Did you get a cold? Please stay at the Dorset. As long as we have no servant. I'll try, to call you tonight. I sent you a nighletter yesterday. But they probably tried to call the house and nobody answered. Did you call a doctor? And what was it? Please wire, how you feel. You know, I have no quiet moment, if you are not well. I rush to the post office. love *Schnubi*

Two picture postcards of stalactite formations in Lookout Mountain Caves

Darling,

Helen took us to see those caves (*Tropfsteinhöhlen* [stalactites and stalagmites]). It was wonderful. It's very warm already but lovely. We have no time for a hotel today, but tomorrow we'll clean up in Atlanta, where I hope to find a letter of yours. It must be wonderful in N.C. Good by Darling, more tomorrow. love [little flower drawing]

Letterhead: Brook House

April 8, 1942

Träubi,

Your trunk arrived Monday, but they didn't charge anything. Jules is just unpacking it. We had a real summer day yesterday and everything is green in the garden, full of violets and yellow flowers. Morris and Lee Stonzek came out and put on the curtains in the kitchen. Very pretty. Loyd [Orser] came over and caught a trout which I'll eat for lunch today. I'll go over to Burgess' house today and ask his gardener if he would work for us once or twice a week. The Brown's [neighbors] are also looking around for somebody.—

MacLeish wired that he expects me Thursday at 6 at his house. Hans thought he would drive to Washington with me in his car, but Rita just called and said Hans has a stone in his bladder and can't go. I could have his car, but I think I'll take a train and come right back.—

The Playwrights had a meeting yesterday about the Lunt show. The Guild is trying again to grab it away from them, but they will not give in this time and Sam will withdraw the play if the Guild insists on producing it. It is entirely the fault of Sam and "Sleeping beauty" [Harold Freedman] that this situation came up. Sherwood is furious and the Lunts refuse to play in a Guild production.[1] Quite a mess! (All this strictly confidential!) I'm afraid these negotiations will drag on for weeks, then suddenly they will decide to do it right away. So I'd better start preparing my material.—

Clarence Muse, that poor old negro fellow who wants to do 3-Gr.-O. [*Dreigroschenoper*] wrote a desperate letter.[2] I am sick and tired of this whole affair and wrote him I would be willing to make a contract for a production in California only, but that I don't allow to show it outside of Cal. unless I have seen and passed it. That would be completely harmless for me because nobody cares anyhow what they are doing out there. If they don't accept this, to hell with them! But at least I have shown my good will. Muse writes me that Brecht had told him last summer he had written to me and I didn't answer! The good old swinish Brecht method. Well, I wrote Wiesengrund a letter which he won't forget for some time. I wrote him: It is a shame that a man of your intelligence should be so misinformed. Then I explained him that the American Theatre isn't as bad as he thinks and in the end I said: "maybe the main difference between the German and the American theatre is the fact that there exist certain rules of 'fair play' in the American theatre. Three cheers for the American Theatre!"—[3]

Here are a few *Blümchen fürs Blümchen* [little flowers for the little flower] (from your garden). Next letter goes to Birmingham, Ala.

> So long, my honey-pie!
> thousand kisses,
> Kurt.

I'll take the records along to MacLeish. I forgot the most important news: Arthur Kober is crazy about "The Tinted Venus" and wants to write it.[4] (You know, he is one of the

5 Lillian Hellman-suitors, which is good for the critics!) We are trying to get the rights now and will start working in June, probably with Ira. Cheryl will produce. It is a nice set-up. If I could do the Lunt show now and then this one, I would have 3 shows running next season! Poor Virgil Thompson!⁵ Max just called, Mab is coming back tomorrow, after exactly one week! Bye-bye!

1. *Playwright Robert E. Sherwood (1906–55) had won Pulitzer Prizes for* Idiot's Delight *(1936),* Abe Lincoln in Illinois *(1938), and* There Shall Be No Night *(1940). He had also translated Jacques Deval's* Tovarich *and was one of the founders of the Playwrights' Producing Company. He is credited with the doggerel: "If you want a play to run many a munt / Get Lynn Fontanne and Alfred Lunt."*

2. *The singer-actor Clarence Muse (1889–1979) had moved from vaudeville to film in the late 1920s and frequently played Uncle Tom types. He collaborated on several scripts and in 1973 was honored as one of the first inductees to the Black Filmmakers Hall of Fame.*

3. *Weill's letter to Adorno has not been traced. Adorno's to Weill is in the Weill/Lenya Archive, along with the two reviews of books about jazz that Adorno enclosed with his letter.*

4. *The Austrian-born Arthur Kober (1900–1974) was a minor playwright whose only claim to success was* Having a Wonderful Time *(1937), which Harold Rome adapted as a musical in 1952.*

5. *The eminent American composer and music critic Virgil Thomson (1896–1989) was best known for his collaboration with Gertrude Stein on the opera* Four Saints in Three Acts *(1934). In his position at the* Herald Tribune, *he was for years one of the most prominent (and feared) American music critics. His obituary of Weill in that paper was one of the most insightful at the time: "Every work was a new model, a new shape, a new solution of dramatic problems."*

264 LENYA IN ATLANTA TO WEILL IN NEW CITY, 10 APRIL 1942

Letterhead: Hotel Georgian Terrace / Peachtree Street and Ponce de Leon Avenue / Atlanta, Georgia

Friday, 9th [10th]

Darling,

Thanks so much for your 2 letters. There are so many news in it, that I have to go slowly answering. I am very glad to have those 3 days rest. It was very exausting those 3 nighters. Awful trains, hot, bad food. But it's nice here and whole Sunday for a good rest. We leave Monday 9:00 A.M. for Birmingham. I got a beautiful handbag (Elisabeth Arden) for Easter from Helen. It was more for you, I guess (she is in love with the Weill family—as she said). In Chatanooga she took me to those caves. That was beautiful. 15 billion years old stones! I felt very little and not so important.—Well now to your letters. I think, you're right to do the Lunt show. I hope, they are not too stingy, to pay you 2%. It will be a very big job, as you know. Those plays with music are much tougher to do, than a straight musical. You have to find a new style and then to have negros, that means music! I hope, they have nothing to do with the Guild, it's so much nicer to work for the playwrights. Where does the Guild come in, in the first place? The whole project sounded swell and I wish it would work out. First it's an interesting job for you, 2ⁿᵈ the Lunts! (that means if it's a success—2 years touring [—]keep me out of it—) and it always was an amusing idea. I am sure you gave them wonderful ideas. I hope Alfred is not too stupid.—Why is Sherwood *beese* [angry]? Because Sam got the Lunts? I am very excited about the Kober project. That's such a fresh amusing story. And you would have the whole Hellman clique (which isn't from *pappe* [is nothing to sneeze at] either.—) If you start in June, then I would be home thank God! That would be a swell summer if all the things you planed would work out. I keep my fingers crossed.—

The whole Brecht schit—is just too funny for words. "Could you come to Hollywood." Good God! Sounds like in the good old days when he tried to keep your name off the program. And this *"blasse flammende Arschloch" dieser* Wiesengrund [paleface flaming asshole, this W.]. It's just beyond belief. I am so happy, you wrote him the right letter about American theater. But please Darling insist, that they are not allowed to show it outside Hollywood. Dont give in. The hell with them. You know, what they will do, if you would give in. Cut the music to pieces and make the whole thing cheap and ridiculous. And this stupid Brecht, this chinese-augsburg *Hinterwäldler* [backwoods] philo-so-pher. It's too much already, that letters from him, soil our mailbox.—

I am sorry, that Hans couldn't drive with you to Washington. I am anxious to hear, how MacLeish liked the song. How was John's play in N.Y. [Steinbeck's *The Moon Is Down*]? That frightened [Luise] Rainer child almost made me vomit. Darling, I think, the green cushions would be nice. It's such a gentle green. Oh I cant wait now, to come home. Trout! how did it taste? Goodi? This is a pretty town Atlanta. But it's pouring rain. I am kind of shaky. Still havn't got my business . . . which was due on the 28th. Maybe it's change of life. Well, if it doesn't bother me more than it does until now, it's o.k. with me. But I think, it'll show up again. It's probably this constant change of *clima*. This hotel is typical southern. Looks like a Sanatorium for T.B. Zauberberg [*The Magic Mountain* (1924), by Thomas Mann]—No one is under seventy. How do the doilies look I made for your bedroom? I am glad, you dont have to go south with Max. Mab is pittiful funy. Well Darling, this is all. (Ruth Page send me that write up, which I hadn't seen—naturally—.) Thanks for the *Blümchen*. And write soon again. It's so nice to find a letter from you! Love *mine Schnäubchen von Deinem* [(from your); little flower drawing.] It's blooming here too.

S – C – H – P – R – I – N – G

(Did you get in touch with Tom Fisher about the Auditorium?) They all talk like Elisabeth Green with terrific speed . . . [1] The "High Tor" picture is very cute, I'll send it back. I am afraid to loose it.

1. Paul Green's wife, née Elizabeth Atkinson Lay (1897–1989), was the daughter of an Episcopal minister. She graduated from the University of North Carolina in playwriting in 1919 and worked as an administrator for the Carolina Playmakers.

265 LENYA IN ATLANTA TO WEILL IN NEW CITY, [11 APRIL 1942]
Letterhead: Hotel Georgian Terrace

Saturday

Darling,

I just bought in an antic store [John A. Locknit Antiques], a nice little lampe for my dressingtable (closetroom) and a 1000 eye glass platter to use for serving cake. It's a little chipped on the edge, but hardly noticable. Has a lovely green collar and hard to find. If Katz[?] comes around, give him the lampe and he should screw on a top for the bulb. The wire for the pluck runs outside the lamp. That's all *Träubchen*. I got the package insured, in case it arrives in pieces, you get the money back from the postoffice. You only have to pay the package due, the rest I paid here. It's a beautiful day and tomorrow is big "cleaning" day. My arm hurts like mad in this damp weather, but they promised me it'll get worse further south. So I have something to look forward to.— We leave Monday 9:00 in the morning. Nothing new Darling same old sh... Maybe I find nice things, for the house down in New Orleans (we probably stay 3 day's. Beaumont [Texas] is out) Good bye *Schnäubchen*. One week less! Hurrah.

266 WEILL IN NEW CITY TO LENYA IN BIRMINGHAM, ALABAMA, 12 APRIL 1942

Sunday, April 12, 1942

My *Träubenträubchen*,

This will be a short letter, but I am writing again tomorrow. Bravi [Abravanel] is here today and we had lunch with [Dr.] Heller at the house of Mrs. Ormos, the psychiatrist who lives in the little house where Loyd used to work last year. Then we went over to the Andersons and now it is so late already, I am driving into town with him and go to hear a spanish-negro singer to study background for the Lunt show. But I want to be sure that you have a letter in Birmingham, so I write you in a hurry.

My visit in Washington was extremely successful. When I had played the song MacLeish sprang up and said: That's what we've been waiting for all the time. He was in extasy, and so was his wife. He is going to do everything to get a big start for the song, probably he will write himself one of the "This is war" programs around the song.[1] I also played the Helen Hayes records. He thought they are absolutely unique, and they should be spread all over the country, in schools, factories and private homes. He raved about Helen, said that she spoke these words so completely american, as they've never been spoken before and that he could listen for hours and hours to her reading. About the music he said it was miraculous what I had done. Well, all this is very important and very promising. He is [Franklin D.] Roosevelt's closest friend, and a wonderful man.

My two shows which looked absolutely sure two days ago, don't seem so sure today. The Lunts refused flatly to do the show with the Guild, Bob Sherwood says he will dissolve the Playwrights Comp. if the Guild would do this play—and the Guild insists on producing it. Alfred and Lynn called me yesterday and told me that the whole is off for the time being, but it didn't sound quite convincing to me. We'll see. About the "Tinted Venus" we found out that it had been done into a play and into a picture around 1920, so we have to clear the rights first which will take a time, I'm afraid. But I don't get excited about these things anymore.

Well, these are all the important facts of the last few days. Details follow to-morrow when I'll have more time.

Pardon the hurry, Good-bye, my angel, I hope I'll have a letter from you tomorrow, but those little postal cards every day are very very *niedelich—und du auch* [and so are you].

Dein dichliebender Gatte [your spouse who loves you], *Schnube*

1. *"This Is War!" was a series of thirteen weekly radio broadcasts carried by all four national networks. Beginning on 14 February 1942, it reached an estimated audience of twenty million each Saturday night. Norman Corwin hosted this pioneering effort at wartime propaganda, which aimed to elucidate the government's policies and rally the support of the population.*

267 LENYA IN MONTGOMERY, ALABAMA, TO WEILL IN NEW CITY, 13 APRIL 1942

Postcard: "The Whitley Hotel, Montgomery's largest hotel."

Darling,

It looks pretty, but it ain't. It's a very southern town already, with poeple standing on corners and having "so" much time. "Did I do" is what you hear, when you ask for a street.

love L [little flower drawing]

268 WEILL IN NEW CITY TO LENYA IN BIRMINGHAM, 13 APRIL 1942

Monday, April 13, 1942

Darling,

I wrote you all the news yesterday, but here is another letter. Last night, after I wrote you, I drove into town with Bravi and we went to the concert of those negroes from Martinique and Trinidade. It was absolutely enchanting and you would have loved it. They are French negroes, quite different from Haarlem, much more intelligent, full of charm and grace, almost like Chinese. That woman (Belle Rosette) will be a big hit. She has been picked up by the Shuberts and follows Carmen Miranda in "Suns o'Fun."[1] Musically it wasn't very interesting, but that woman who arranges these concerts, Louise Crane (a rich Lesbian who is crazy about Negroes) took us to a spanish-negro place in Haarlem where we heard a good orchester. Then, at 2 A.M., we had a very good Ravioli in 116th Street. Today I had to be at the watch tower from 12 to 4 P.M., but it is a lovely spring day and the river looked beautiful.—I talked to Philip Barry on the phone this morning. He loved my new idea for White Wings and said it is exactly what he wants to do this summer. He is leaving for Florida today, as usual. So, there is another project.—This enthousiasm of MacLeish for me is most important. His wife said to me: "You don't know what it means to my husband to have at last found a composer who can do with poetry what you are doing."—The Lunts are awful fakers. When I talked to him, she took over after 2 minutes and told me, that Alfred was very upset, but she thinks it will work out. They don't work with the Guild—which I understand. I wanted them to come to that concert (it would have shown them what could be done with "The Pirate"), but they are soooo busy with the Canteen, and it is soooo wonderful at the Canteen and so on—just *verlogenes Gequatsche* [twaddle packed with lies].[2] Interesting news about Virgil T. [Thomson] in [Walter] Winchell's column: it seems that the FBI has investigated him because of his connections with sailors! Bravi met him in a party and Virgil started to talk about me after dinner and talked till 5 A.M.! He says he would call the music for "Lady" a masterwork if I had not written it, because he always thought the 3 most interesting European composers were Debussy, Satie and Weill. What is really wrong with me is that I have no character (!!) and I had behaved very badly to him in a personal matter.—Well, I must be pretty good if the great Thompson talks all night about me. It seems to bother him!

The willow tree is getting all green, and the big tree next to the brook is full of red buds. I am trying all the time to find a gardener, can't find anybody.

The write-up about you in Chicago is very impressing. You didn't tell me that you gave an interview. We are two real *Birühmtis!*

Moss seems still to be away, and I couldn't talk to him about the Auditorium. But Gertie [Lawrence] told me she found out that a theater next to the Erlanger (Grand Opera House) which they always said was too small, has sent a carpenter and proved that it can easily take the show. There we could probably stay half a season—or more.

You should have seen Alfred L.'s face (at Sam's house) when I told him how wonderful Helen's records turned out. He suddenly interrupted me: "Excuse me when I change the subject, but we wanted to talk about Sam's play." *Hi! Hi!* [hee, hee!]

The doilies look very handsome. The whole house looks like a jewel, Jules rubbs and shrubbs and cleans. He reminds me of our Erika in Berlin.

So long, my darling. Next letter goes to Memphis. Take care of yourself.

    100000000 kisses!

Hans had a terrible case of kidney stones and was in the hospital. I couldn't take the car to Wash. because it was snowing. Took the train and came right back. Gigi [Gilpin] sent a letter for you which I sent to Memphis. I met Dick [McKay] at Offutt's.

---

1. *The Shubert brothers—Lee, Samuel, and Jacob—were theater owners and prominent Broadway producers, especially of musicals. The 1941 revue* Sons o' Fun *starred the comic duo Olsen & Johnson. The flamboyant Portuguese entertainer Carmen Miranda (1909–55) appeared in Broadway shows and Hollywood musical films, usually adorned with fruited headdresses.*

2. *Prominent actors and actresses entertained and mingled with servicemen at the USO's Stage Door Canteen.*

Postcard: The Tutwiler / Birmingham's largest and finest / One of the Dinkler Hotels / Dispensers of true southern hospitality

It's just one of those tiny little places with <u>not one</u> quiet room in the whole cottage! My sleeping hours are reduced to 4–5. Pretty bad! But N.C. will do the trick. I called the Ackermans.[1] I cant see them. No time. But I talked on the phone. Good by Darling

love Linerl

1. *Weill's cousin Rosie Ackermann (b. 1902) was the daughter of his mother's twin brother, Emil, who was killed in World War I. She married Ernst Blum and the two immigrated via Cuba, settling in Birmingham, Alabama.*

270   LENYA IN BIRMINGHAM TO WEILL IN NEW CITY,
15 APRIL 1942

Letterhead: Dinkler Hotels / Dispensers of true southern hospitality / Written from the Tutwiler Hotel / Birmingham, Alabama

Wednesday
15th

Darling,

Well what a surprise! One letter when I came to the theater last night and one special delivery during the performance. That's the way to do it Mr.! I wanted to answer last night, but I was really exausted and just sunk in to my bed. It's not so *"schnecki"* [sluggish] anymore. Leaving at 8:15 A.M. tomorrow at 7:15, that's not so good *für eine Schniepel pison* [for a sleepyhead] like me. I showed Helen the part in your letter about the reccords (the rest I covered—) and she said "Good God that Kurt, not enough that he helped me so much on those reccords no he's showing them around." She was so touched, she actually had tears in her eyes (but not Lunt's tears—) After the performance, she said—show me again what MacLeish said.—But with her, it's really no fake, she is just so excited about it. Charlie [MacArthur] wrote her, that the best is "Beat, beat, drums"—that's a knock out, then the battle hymn and so on. Well *Schnäubchen*, I think you did a pretty good job there. The Lunts are awful. But really Darling, they are just stupid. They'll do the show, I am sure, but they have to fuss. I wish, you could find something for Helen. I didn't have a chance yet to talk to her. But dont loose Charly, call him once in a while. Maybe something can be done with the idea he had for her. She has so much confidence in you now, that she's not afraid of music anymore. Who handles the "Tinted Venus?" I hope not *Dornröschen* [Sleeping Beauty: Harold Freedman]. And that Phyl Berry! That would be so wonderful now, a show like this. Your nightlife in Harlem sounds very exciting. Are those french negros callipsos singer? I am just so afraid of the Lunt's. You'll write a beautiful score and I dont know, whether they'll understand. It want be easy Darling you know that, I hope. I didn't give an interview. That's the one you wrote out for me (years ago—in N.Y. when Bill Fields sent that girl down to the theater)[1] it finally got into the papers in Chicago! Didn't you know Honey, that it is a long way to Tipperary? VERY INTERESTING that V. Thomson business. F.B.I. behind him. I like that! That hurts him more than he can realize at the moment. Especially because it's the truth. *Das Lavinchen fängt an zu rollen* [the little avalanche begins to roll].—What he said about you, would be very interesting material for a campagne against him, calling the score of Lady a masterpiece—"if only somebody else would have written it." But you have no witnesses and Bravi isn't very reliable. Unfortunate. Well if that what Virgil has, is called "character" then it is just ducky that you aint got it. And where that personel bad behavior comes in, we know that. But as you said "it seems to bother him" and that's more than good. The F.B.I. will do the rest, I hope. I am glad, that Gertie is so anxious to get that show going. You saw that house next to the Erlanger didn't you? It's a big thing. And I am sure Lady would run in Chicago for a long time. If only Moss would be more interested to get that show going. It's a gold mine on the road, I am sure. This is a tremendous theater here, 2500! and a lovely town. It's a pitty that one is so tired, that you dont see anything. I got that card from one of your relatives. I'll meet them after the matinee. I dont remember at all, who the are, but what can I loose.—I am looking forward to New Orleans. We stay 3 days. Beaumont is out. That means, one free day in N.O. *Primi*. If you dont find a gardener, maybe you can make some arrangements with Nick[?]. Or does she[?] need him every day (now that they have money—). Dilts will be too expensive I fear. I really would love to be home now, but *die Kunscht* [Art]! Darling, dont let a cedar closet be made by Lyod [Lloyd Orser]. It's too expensive. You can buy it at Bloomingdales. Much sheaper and just as good. They come readymade. Jules should go and have one send out. He knows the size we need. I am sorry about your suit. By the way, did you hear anything from the "Fort Shelby" about your suit? If not, let the lawyer write again. Well Darling, that's all. 7 more weeks and than everything is over. And no fried chicken, no lamb chops no cole slaw for a long while—.

das ist der Schpring!
love

1. William Fields (1899–1961) was the director of publicity for the Playwrights' Producing Company. Previously he had represented the Ringling Brothers circus.

April 16, 1942

Blumi,

It is all settled with the Lunt play. Sam had invited me for lunch yesterday because he wants to talk about "Zuleika Dopson"[1]—but every time he tells Lunt that I am coming Lunt says: o.k., I will be there. So he came again—very happy that they got rid of the Guild. The Playwrights will produce it. Everybody agrees that it needs a lot of music and possibly a few songs. Alfred wants Sam, Joe Mielziener and me to come to Genesee for a week early in May.[2] I sold him the idea to open the play on the West Coast in August—and that is what they are planning to do. I am glad about the whole combination. It will be lots of fun. Alfred was very nice and funny. He is all excited about his cooking class. He raved about you again ("she is absolute perfection," he said).

Did I write you about that negro dancer and singer from the Westindies (Belle Rosette) whom I saw Sunday? Well, I am trying now to get those 6 colored girls who were with her, for the show and have Belle Rosette act as a kind of choreographer. I really should be my own producer. . . .

I met Hammerstein and we finished the song "The Good Earth" which is definitely a hit. We'll try to sell it to the movies. Then I went to [attorney Howard] Reinheimer who is getting the rights for "The Tinted Venus"—with the usual slow motion tempo. So I put some pressure behind it and made him cable to London. Then I had dinner with Gil Gabriel and Ada. They are awfully nice. He told me that one day he was working with John Steinbeck in the Sherwood office and a man came in and talked about the propaganda broadcasts to France, Germany etc. which are under the direction of John Houseman.[3] The man said: "what we need most is a great song." Steinbeck said: "Why don't you talk to Kurt Weill." The man said: "I mentioned him the other day and Houseman answered: I don't want this name mentioned any more!" It seems those pansies will never forget that I turned them down with Mahagonny![4]—He also knew details about Virgil Th.: He was found by the FBI in a Nazi place where sailors are being paid for giving away informations. Gil thinks, he might lose his job, if the Tribune finds out.

Tonight I am having dinner with Moss. On Saturday the Atkinsons are coming for dinner, but they don't stay over night. I am trying to get the Steinbecks (they live in Sneeden's Landing) or the Gabriels and of course I have to invite Max.

And how is my *Träubchen?* Did your business show up at last? I am sure that all the travelling has caused this irregularity.

Here is a letter from Brecht which came yesterday. It sounds very pitiful and I feel sorry for him. Maybe we are a little injust with him. He probably went through so much that his nicer side is on the surface again. I just hate to triumph over somebody who is down on the floor, and I don't want anybody to feel that I am cruel or inhuman or egotistic. I would rather have the reputation of being a sucker than of being greedy or stingy or *"kleinlich"* [petty]. He knows now he cannot play ball with me, and I think I can afford to be nice to him. I am inclined to offer him some financial help (something like 50.– a month for a few months). What do you think?[5]

Well, this is a long letter again, my darling. Now I have to do some work.

One million and three *Knüsschen*, Kurt

I just found a gardener, a wonderful old man. Everybody told me he is the best gardener here, but he wouldn't work any more. So I went over and talked to him, and he agreed to come once a week. His name is [Bill] Beaubelle.

1. *Gertie Lawrence owned the theatrical rights of the novel* Zuleika Dobson *by Max Beerbohm (1872–1956).*

2. *Jo Mielziner (1901–76) was an American set designer whose credits included work on both the play and opera versions of* Street Scene.

3. *The Russian-born, English-educated writer-producer-actor John Houseman (1902–89) founded the Mercury Theatre with Orson Welles in 1937 and directed radio specials, including the* War of the Worlds *broadcast in 1939. Late in life he enjoyed success as an actor, winning an Oscar for* The Paper Chase.

4. *In 1936 Virgil Thomson and A. Everett "Chick" Austin had hoped to produce* Mahagonny *in Hartford. When plans to produce the whole opera collapsed, Weill acquiesced to a double bill of the Paris version of the* Mahagonny Songspiel *and* Die sieben Todsünden. *He withdrew from the project when those plans also failed to materialize. But thirty years later Thomson wrote in his autobiography that "we took Weill there to see the theater, and I even played through the score with him for setting tempos. But quietly the project was dissolved." Thomson asserted that "one came to understand that Weill's working association with Bertolt Brecht, as part of a possibly communist-tainted past, was to be buried" (p. 253).*

5. *Brecht's undated letter of mid-April included a lengthy apologetic account of the history of his involvement with the Muse project. It concluded: "I write at such length because I realize you could easily misunderstand all of this, since I always write only out of extreme necessity, and then too briefly. I'd like to suggest that we take up our collaboration again and simply erase all the misunderstandings and longstanding semi-quarrels, which so easily arise out of these troubled times, separation, etc. Till now I have lost none of my friends, and in our work we've always had so much fun and made such progress" (BB–W2).*

272 LENYA FROM NASHVILLE, TENNESSEE, TO WEILL IN NEW CITY, 16 APRIL 1942

Postcard: "The Hermitage of Andrew Jackson."

Darling,

That [the hermitage] looks pretty nice (no time to see it—the rest is Ashville—lets all fall down—) tomorrow up again at 6:00 arriving at 3 P.M. in Memphis. *Ja- ja- wie man sich bettet*[1] but it's becoming —— *für die Kleene!*

1. *"As you make your bed," from Jenny's act 2 aria in the opera* Mahagonny.

272T LENYA IN MEMPHIS TO WEILL IN NEW CITY, 17 APRIL 1942

Western Union

CONGRATULATION TO NEW PROSPECT I AM VERY HAPPY FOR YOU WILL WRITE YOU SUNDAY TOO TIRED NOW VERY HOT HERE DONT SEND MONEY TO BRECHT ILL EXPLAIN STAY HERE TILL MONDAY 815 AM HOTEL PEABODY LOVE = LINNERL.

April 17, 1942

My darling,

I just came back from a meeting of all the air observers in Haverstraw and before
I go to bed I'll write you a few lines so that you find a letter when you get to New
Orleans. I hope you'll find some time to look around in that beautiful city. Today I had
your letter from Birmingham, and 2 postal cards. That's nothing *für eine Schniepelpison*
to get up at 7:30 in the morning.

Last night I had dinner with Moss. He is through now with dentist, but now he says
he has to push the analist, so he is going 1 hour in the morning and 2½ hours in the
afternoon. So he won't do any work and I am glad I have some other show projects
and don't depend on him. We went to see "Priorities of 1942," the Shubert vaudeville
show which is next to Sons o' Fun the biggest success in town.[1] It is what we used to
call *"zusammengehauen"* [thrown together] and I don't think they have spent more than
25.– dollar for the whole show. But it is funny in parts, especially a wonderful Jewish
comedian Willy Howard. Today I have started to write some music for the Lunt show
[*The Pirate*]. Schwarz came and I invited him for lunch. Jules gave Wooley a bath because he was stinking dirty. Tomorrow is my dinner party and Jules has his great day.
He cleaned the whole house and the silver and bought a turkey and flowers—all because he says we have to be very nice to a critic. I drive in for lunch with Alfred, Sam
and Joe [Mielziner] and then I take the Atkinsons out and the Gabriels come later with
the bus, I couldn't reach Steinbeck. Charlie [MacArthur] called today, was very nice.
And that's about all for the moment. I'll write again to New Orleans.

> *Lebe, mein Träubchhen. Knüsschens,*
> Kurt

1. Sons o' Fun *had opened on 1 December 1941 at the Wintergarden, where it ran for 742 performances.* Priorities of
1942 *opened on 12 March 1942 and featured the jazz pianist Hazel Scott, the modern dancer Paul Draper, and the comedians
Willie Howard and Lou Holtz, all of whom presented their own material.*

Sunday morning.

Sweetie,

Just after I had wired you last night that I had written a letter yesterday to New
Orleans, I found same letter in my pocket. *"Typisch für ein Doofi"* [typical for a little
dummy], you will say.

Well, my party last night was not a smash hit. It started out very nicely, but then
before dinner Oriana (that is Mrs. Atkinson) got awfully drunk, and she is terrible when
she is drunk. He was furious at her, she attacked him and Max, the Gabriels tried to
keep her down, dinner was good, but he [Jules] was awfully slow—well, just one of

those evenings which only you can handle—I can't. Mab didn't come—she had to go to a birthday party of an old woman and, of course, the Atkinsons and Gabriels didn't think that was very nice. She just doesn't know how to behave.

My lunch at Sam's was very nice. Alfred is full of ideas for the play—and very good ideas too. He is a great theatre talent and ideal for this type of play. He loves all my ideas. Sam keeps talking about "Zuleika Dopson."

I guess you are right with Brecht. Mr. Marton sent a "contract" yesterday which is so incredible that I didn't believe my eyes. They disregard completely my demands and the whole thing is as crooked and *"ausbeuterisch"* [exploitative] as only contracts with communists can be. I cannot even get angry about it because it is so idiotic. But I certainly cannot waste any more time with it.[1]

Afternoon. Hans and Rita came out and we had a wonderful lunch (*reste* [leftovers] from last night) and a big ping pong. Gil called up to tell me how awful they all felt about Oriana's behaviour last night. It seems she collapsed completely on the way home (Jules drove them home.) What a party!

That's all, honey-pie. Have a nice time in New Orleans and take care of yourself.

Love K——

1. *Weill's reply to Brecht's agent George Marton on 20 April sizzled: "This is the most shameful proposition that ever has been made to me. My agent and my publisher did not find one paragraph in this document that would serve as a basis for discussion" [W–GM]. Marton then suggested that Weill send a draft agreement of his own; Weill did not respond. Instead, he wrote to Brecht that he could not "waste any more time on this ridiculous affair" and pointed out that under the terms which Brecht had accepted in February he had ceded worldwide rights for* Die Dreigroschenoper *in all media in perpetuity to Muse, for which Brecht would have received 5 percent of the adapter's share of royalties, a sum Weill estimated at ten dollars per week, providing he donated his own share to Brecht as well. After a brief lecture on the complexity of the American theatrical system, Weill closed by reciprocating Brecht's offer to collaborate again: "I too would like to avoid, without fail, having any misunderstandings come between us, since I always recall our collaboration with great joy and hope that we will soon find the opportunity to resume it" (W–BB, 20 April 1942).*

275 LENYA IN MEMPHIS TO WEILL IN NEW CITY,
[19 APRIL 1942]
Letterhead: Hotel Peabody / Memphis, Tennessee

Sunday 9:30 P.M.

Darling,

I just came back from the station. Howard [Schwarz] has left. He came yesterday evening and stayed over night. That was a tough job, to cheer him up. He was terribly depressed and unhappy and I am just the wrongest person in the world for cases like that. As you know, I am so flexible and adaptable to everything, that it is a great effort for me to understand somebody who is on the verge of comitting suicide just because he has to peel potatoes three times a week. So I took Madeline (my understudy) to help, and she was just wonderful in jeering him up. So when he left, he felt quit happy. It was a beautiful day and we walked along the Mississippi, which is the most beautiful river I have ever seen in my whole life. It is very hot already and it isn't going to be any cooler. But it'll be alright. This is now the pritty part of our journey and much more interesting than the middle west. Now let me go back to your letter. I cant tell you Darling, how happy I am about the new show. I'll think it'll be great fun for you after that long pause. You think Mielziner will do a good job? You probably will end up some day as your own producer. I hope, you get those six colored girls. (Yes you did write me everything in your previous letter.) I am thoroughly disgusted about those dam pansies like Housmann. What a mean bunch. But it want do them any good. They cant stop you. But it is a pitty that a guy like that, has such an importent position. No wonder, Sherwood never answered your letter.

I am very happy about the new song. Helen told me they cant find a name for her reccords and she said, poor Kurt, he probably has to think of a title too.—I am glad, *Dornröschen* [Freedman] doesn't handle "Tinted Venus." He is a little better (Rhinheimer I mean). I wonder, how your dinnerparty with the Atkinson turned out. I read notices about Steinbecks play. I think Atkinson was right about it in his second write-up in the Sunday times. How does the play go? [Paul] Munis play [*Yesterday's Magic*] didn't do so well, I hear. But that doesn't surprise me. He is such a dreary actor.

I wish, you could have seen the house we played in Nashville! An old church, the worst house I have ever seen. Alfred knows it. They played "Idiots Delight" there.[1] 3000 poeple! I felt like Mickey mouse on the stage.

Now to Brechts letter, which is a sympathetic one, but I am very much against it, to send him money. I belief to a certain extent, what he writes about the procedure of that 3 penny opera project but I dont trust him at all. I never believe, that he ever can change his character, which is a selfish one and always will be. I am sure he went through a lot of unpleasant things, but not so unpleasant, that it would change him. I know Darling how easely you forget things but I do remember everything he ever did to you. And that was plenty. Of course he wants to collaborate with you again. Nothing better could happen to him. But I am convinced after few days, you would be so disgusted with him, I just could write it down for you what would happen. Think of poeple like Moss and John Steinbeck and Max and all the rest we know and compare them, than you know it's impossible for you to take up that relationship again. It's not surprising that somebody gets nice and soft when they are down and out, that's the natural way, but just let him be a little successful again and he'll be the old Brecht again. No Darling, I dont believe in changes like that. I dont give a dam, whether they call you selfish and stingy. I hate to think of all the things they called you in Germany and you where not any different from what you are now. But I always believed in dicency and a certain fairness. And Brecht hasn't got much of it. So please Darling, dont waste much time of thinking about what they will say about you. It's not importent. Let him do 3 p. Opera if he thinks, he gets something out of it and it helps him but stay away from that crowd. Write him, that you are working on a new show now, but if he has any new ideas he should tell you about it and you'll see what you can do. And dont think, that I am unjust, you know I have a natural gift of being a sucker, but not when it involves you. *"Die sieben Winter und die grossen Kalten" und die ganzen Gemeinheiten tauchen for mir auf.*[2] *Nein, nein.*

Swell, that you found a gardener. Did that little lamp and the tray arrive I'll sent from Atlanta? And Darling, I gave Howard 50 $ and he left me that check. Bring it to the bank. If it makes you feel better, send Brecht 100 $ but dont send him anything monthly. It's very hard to stop it and one cant go on doing it. My business still didn't show up. The hell with it. I feel fine. Rita wrote me a long letter. I am sorry, that Hans feels so bad. Gigis letter is so dumm that's an effort to read it through.—

We leave tomorrow at 8:45 arrives at 2 and leave after the performance for New Orleans. I am looking forward for your letter. Now *Träubchen*, I have to pack and then I'll sleep. They woke me up at 8:00 this morning to bring me your wire. But that was a nice awakening. Give Ada and Gil my love when you see them again.

> *Ich küsse Ihre Hand* [I kiss your hand]
> Monsieur and remain
> yours truly and
> very lovable Missi.

(They colored poeple here are very different from the northener. Much more real and much darker. And sooo slow!!!)

---

1. *Robert Sherwood's three-act comedy* Idiot's Delight *had run for 299 performances on Broadway in 1936 starring the Lunts.*

2. *" 'The seven winters and the great cold' and all those dirty tricks come to my mind again" (the quoted phrase comes from* Mahagonny*).*

276 LENYA IN NEW ORLEANS TO WEILL IN NEW CITY, 21 APRIL 1942

Postcard: Wrought iron balcony in the French Quarter, New Orleans

Oh Darling,

What an enchanting town! We have to come down here together. I just got a room, which is almost as hard to get as in old Moskau. But it doesn't matter. Palm trees! I am delighted. Now I go to get your letter from the theater.

> love and love Linerl

277 WEILL IN NEW CITY TO LENYA IN HOUSTON, TEXAS, 21 APRIL 1942

Tuesday, April 21, 1942

Darling,

I was in town yesterday, had lunch with Irene Sharaff at Sardi's where I met Dick Rogers, Dwight Wiman and Josh [Logan],[1] all coming from the rehearsal of the new Rogers and Hart show [*By Jupiter*]. In the afternoon I got things settled at Chappel's [music publisher] and then I went to see Goldrush which is still a great work of art and entertainment at the same time which is quite an achievement.

When I came home Max called up and told me: there was a Playwrights meeting yesterday and Max (I had never asked him to do it) brought up the question of my royalties for the Lunt show. They all said they didn't know what my contribution to the show would be and it is up to Sam. Sam said he was afraid that I was writing a lot of music and the Lunt would cut it out—and it all meant that he doesn't want to pay me royalties. I am furious. He lets me come to meetings all the time, I give them a lot of ideas, and at the same time he is thinking only how he can get his full 10%. I am sure that Max meant it well, but he had no business to do it, and you know he does these things like an elephant. But Sam's attitude is really incredible. He is just such a weakling that he never opens his mouth and he always creates confusion because he cannot make up his mind. I tried to call him yesterday, but he seems to have again one of those periods where he disappears into the air because he thinks that is the way to avoid issues. Today his secretary said he is "out of town." *Dornröschen* is "out of town," as always when you need him. So again I have no idea where I stand, and of course, I stopped working. My first instinct was to tell them to go to hell. But I am already very much interested in this work, and I think it could be a very interesting job. I told Max, if Sam wants to do it as a straight play, he should say so, but that I am convinced it will be just another one of those fair successes that run only on account of the star names— whereas it would have a chance of a smash hit if they would let me do what I want to do with it. But they are so conceited with their plays and they don't want to admit that music or anything else is necessary to make successes out of their plays. They say, Lunt always talks of "music all the way through" when he starts, and then he abandons it.

But they forget that Lunt is completely sold on my idea of the seven negro musicians and the six colored girls whom I have found. And how can they cut out the music if they have seven musicians and six dancing girls on the stage? Well, I will have a heart to heart talk with Sam and Alfred, and if possible I'll have John Wharton there. I'll tell them exactly how I feel about it and will ask them to make up their mind right now before I go any further. I will make them a very decent financial proposition, because this show is more important for me as a prestige matter than as a source of income. What I want to get out of it is to try again something new in the theatre, and to have my name again connected with a big success. "Lady in the Dark" is all set for the road from the end of September until May, and it looks very much that I'll have another show anyhow, and the more money I make, the more taxes I have to pay. So I would be satisfied if I would make about 200 a week with this show. And if my contribution isn't worth that much to them, it will be much better to take my ideas back and stay out of it. I am sure Lunt will be furious when he hears what is going on, but I don't expect any help from that *"Versteller"* [hypocrite]. What a mess! Thank God, I am *"abgebrüht"* [hard-boiled] against those things by now. I am not going to break my neck for that job. But I have to be very diplomatic because I want to get "Zuleika Dopson" out of Sam.

I wired Mr. Marton a flat refusal of that ridiculous contract, and I wrote Brecht that I cannot waste any more time on this nonsense.

The new gardener, Mr. Beaubelle, a wonderful old Frenchman, came yesterday and started cleaning out. He did a first-class job and gets only 4 (against the 11 which we had to pay Dilts). I will investigate the matter of the caretaker which I talked to you about. I think it is an excellent idea and will save us money because he can do everything that Loyd would do. I'll talk to him first and then I'll write you about it.

I was so glad that you were in such good spirits Sunday night. Don't worry about your "business." [Dr.] Heller will fix it again, when you come back. I'll probably write another letter to Houston, and then one to Dallas. I guess you will see Bill [Jones] down there.

Lebe, mein Trrrrrräubchen. Knüsschens,

Kurt

1. Richard Rodgers (1902–79) was the most successful composer for the American musical theater in the thirties and forties, collaborating first with Lorenz Hart and then with Oscar Hammerstein II. Dwight Deere Wiman (1895–1951), heir to the Deere manufacturing fortune, had studied drama under Monty Woolley at Yale and was soon attracted to producing, often investing his own money.

278 WEILL IN NEW CITY TO LENYA IN DALLAS, 22 APRIL 1942

Wed., April 22, 1942

Darling,

I wrote you yesterday to Houston, Texas, but am not sure if I wrote the right address and if you got the letter. I told you that Max had told me about a Playwrights meeting where Sam said he was afraid I would write a lot of music and Lunt will cut it out again—and Max seemed to have the impression that Sam was hesitant about making a royalty agreement with me. Sam has disappeared, but I called Alfred today and when he asked if I am working I said that nothing seems to be settled and that the Playwrights did not seem to be sure if the play needs music. He said the play would fall apart without and he was sure I wouldn't have any difficulties with the Playwrights. Well, anyhow I worked today and wrote some very good stuff. I want Alfred to learn just a few notes on the clarinet (he is crazy about it, of course) and I write a Rhumba when this same little phrase comes back all the time, while the other instruments play in between. That will be very funny.

It was a lovely day here. I mowed the lawn and the garden begins to look pretty, but there is still a lot of work to be done. Schwarz brought a huge trout, so Jules will make it for dinner and I invited Schwarz. He just came. I had your letter from Memphis today. The lamp and the tray arrived too, both very pretty.

Evening. The fish was delicious and we went to see "Kings Row" in Haverstraw.[1] What a bore! John and Gwenn [Steinbeck] called up. They just came back from New Orleans and are in Sneedens Landing now, will probably stay there all summer. They were awfully nice. Moss gave them a poppy and they called him Willy.

So long, *Schnäpschen. Ich verbleibe in ausgezeichneter Hochachtung dein ergebener Affenschwanz* [I remain in extraordinarily high respect, your devoted monkey tail].

1. The 1941 motion picture, based on a novel by Henry Bellaman, starred Ronald Reagan and Betty Field, with music by Erich Korngold.

Letterhead: Dinkler Hotels / Dispensers of true southern hospitality / Written from the St. Charles Hotel / New Orleans, Louisiana

Thursday

Darling,

Thank you very much for your letter. It was nice to talk to you on the phone. (It was a bright idea of mine, to call you!) Dont worry about your dinnerparty. That can happen and she is known for getting very disagreeable, when drunk. Mab is really incredible. She knows, that I am away, but no help from her side. Well, she'll need me again and then I'll do the same. I am so glad, you feel the same about Brecht. It's really no use, to try to be nice to them. Dont send any money please. I cant tell you how happy I am about your new show. At last! I am getting very restless now and I want to go home. We left Memphis (where I had a lovely room) at 8:40 Monday morning and arrived at Jackson at 2:00, left Jackson on a sleeper and came to N.O. at 8:50. The Hotels are so crowded that we had to wait until 6:00 P.M. to get rooms. I got mine earlier, but what a room!—It doesnt matter. Darling, you cant imagine, what a beautiful town this is. You come to the french quarter and you are in the heart of south of France. Just breathtaking. Beautiful old houses, lovely squares, one just doesn't know, where to look first. I took a "sideseing" buss (if I do things like that, then it really must be worth it) but it is. I missed you so much. You would love it. Half of the town consists of the old part (which is the french quarter) and the other half is modern (very ugly naturally). But for just this town, it was worth to make that tour. And one cant see everything, it's too much. The have a market here one goes at 4:00 A.M. and eat donnats [doughnuts]. But that's too much for me. And then Darling, those antic shops!! You can loose your head. I could go on for hours to talk about this town. We have to come down together. I came to a antic store and bought a beautiful table lampe—bright red, old english. The owner (a hungarian—as most of them—) said to me "You look so familiar to me I must have seen you before. Well we agreed on 3.G.O. [*Dreigroschenoper*] which he saw in Berlin and which he adored. Then I bought, two curtain holders (for the big window in the livingroom) and a big old porclain flower vase which hangs! on the wall and I'll probably put it on that ugly wall where the hidden staircase is. It'll look just wonderful in that room. Today I am looking for a silver set (which I have to charge to you in case I find one). But I'll be careful Darling. One could buy old gardenfurniture gallore here, but it isn't worth it, the transport cost to much, to send those iron benches and chairs. No furniture, very little, mostly silver, porcelain and jewelery. I bought a little victorian silver cigarette case for me. Very pretty. I wrote a blank check for the lamp (35.–) because, I didn't have enough money, had it in the trunk and couldn't get to it. Anyway, it's for the same family.—Take it of from the 50.– I send. And be careful when it arrives, with unpacking. Oh, *Blümchen*, I wish I could walk with you trough all those lovely, lovely old streets. Monsell[?] appeared yesterday! God knows, what they are cooking up. Well, I leave on the 30th. Maybe they close earlier. But I dont think so. The play goes alright. It's not sold out but the houses are too big.

And I dont give a dam whether [it] is full or not. I hope, Wolly is O.K. Well Darling, that's all. We leave tonight at 11:00 for Huston. We have to leave Tonio [Selwart] behind. He had a severe kidney attack last night during the performance and was send home with 103 temperature. The understudy had to take over. But he'll be alright for San Antonio. That's the news out of the factory.—Helen is fine. Kind of restless too. Wants to be home like I.—I cant wait for my livingroom. I have everything figured out. Very pretty! And Darling! Maybe we shouldn't paint the shutters red. I again saw here, how pretty that bluish gray is, we have on the garden doors. I am afraid, the red will look so new. Rather have the garden furniture bright. Talk it over with Peter. We cant go fail on the blue. And here is the rest of the tour. That's all for today my love. It want be so long now. And maybe I see you, when you go to Genesee. And if you see Alfreds house, (love it) he is so proud of it. It's awful in parts. Done by a fairy.—

We have one of the loveliest houses, that I saw again, walking through this town. By by my *Blümchen!* Write soon.

280 LENYA IN HOUSTON TO WEILL IN NEW CITY, 25 APRIL 1942
Letterhead: Rice Hotel / Houston, Texas

Saturday, 25th

Darling,

I got your two letters and the wire. I hope, everything works out with Sam. It's a shame, that one always has to fight for the money. As long as Alfred wants it, it will be O.K. in the end. But one never can tell with him. It's true, that he always has the idea "music all the way trough" but when it comes to it, little is left. I think, they had the same with "Teaming of the Shrew." But maybe this time, he means it. The most important thing is to get him so involved, that he cant see the play at all without music. And that seems to be the case already. Your idea letting him play few bas [bars] on the flute sounds charming. He'll like that. I think, the both are dying to show, that they can do something with music. Lynn practised all the time a "striptease" ever since she saw Gertie doing "[The Saga of] Jenny." Sorry, that Max jumped into it. He surely meant well but he is too clumsy. I hope the Playwright know that. It's perfectly enough if you get 150–200 every week out of the play. If it is more it only goes to the income-tax. We just need a little support. I'll be very economical when I get back.—Now Darling back to New Orleans. The last day I found a little silver set cream pitcher and sugar bowl on a little stand. Very cute. Waterbottle and glass (beautiful bohemien glass—red) for the guest room, a wounderful foldingtable (English) for the living room behind the maulberry coach. Then I bought an iron table (oldfashioned) for the garden. A little table to put coctails on it. Alltogether, I wrote a blanc-check for 77 dollars. I could have paid it myself but I had my money in the theatertrunk and couldn't get to it. Then a 15 dollar check for the old italien flowervase. We will have a beautiful livingroom.—I hope, you get that man Florence [Meyer] talked about and I hope, he is good, because it would be much sheaper to do it without that expensive Lyod. I can help a lot. There was a charming, old french dressingtable (like your writing table in your room) same stil [style], which would look lovely in my bed room inspite of the different stil. 65.–. I didn't dare to buy it without asking you. But I still can get it, if I write to that woman in N.O. It's not essential for our house, but a very pretty piece of furniture. Now good by N.O.—

It was terrible on the sleeper. I got my bussines and didn't feel too well.—But I am glad it came. I really thought, it was that dam "change of life" and I felt already 20 years older without it.—But now, I am pretty again and a "young actress to watch!" Last night after the performance, Bill [Jones] stood there! Unchanged, a little thinner still. I was very glad to see him. After two minutes he told me he had a Baby girl! 6½ month old. So I went with him to his room and there was the mother and the baby. He is not married but he lives with that girl (whom I knew from N.Y. she was a salesgirl at Stern's brother.—A jewish girl about 30 talks like Helen Deutch. The baby is just wonderful. Blond as a cornfield and the biggest blue eyes. Very cute. Bill is working the first week. They are very poor and live in a terrible 1 room. So I had Lunch with her today and gave her a little money. The invited me for a little diner after the show. I am going. Tomorrow I leave at 9:15 A.M. for San Antonio. I am glad to get out of this terrible damp city. And so ugly after N.O. Well, that was Bill. It was kind of sad to see that wild animal tied down to a normal life. But he loves the baby. 5 more weeks and then I'll be home. Time goes fast now. Will I be happy when that is over. But it was nice and I dont think I'll regret it. I have seen a lot and learned a lot. I am glad, you got rid of Brecht. It made me sick to think that you would get mixed up again with that "Belege" [voucher] bunch. Dont invite Schw. too often, otherwise he gets on your nerves again. But I always liked him. He is such an honest guy and anhänglich [devoted]. He means well just doesn't know, how to behave. Where should he have learned it? Well Darling, now I'll have dinner with Madeleine (my understudy, a very nice person) and then back to Madison Square Garden—. San Antonio is supposed to be a lovely old spanish town. I haven't talked to Helen in days. She is "nervous" again.—O.K.

By by my beloved *Träubchen*. I'll be seen you soon. Dont write to Fort Worth. They say, it's impossible to get mail there. Why, nobody seems to be able to explain.

"*Grützi*" [greetings] my

[FIG. 62]

Saturday, April 25, 1942

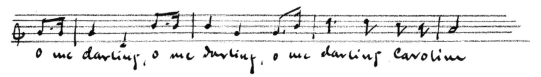

O me darling, o me darling, o me darling Caroline

If you think that only you have nice and warm weather you are mistaken. We are having lovely spring weather here and Jules and I are busy all day long in the garden. Jules cannot wait to start the vegetable garden. He knows everything about it, studies all kinds of books and is all excited. We are still waiting for the man with the horse to plow the field over before we can start. Yesterday we had great excitement. We wanted to use the new garden hose and when we came to the cottage to get it we discovered that it had been stolen. We spent hours looking for it, finally gave up and bought another one. In the evening Mr. Brown came and brought his garden hose as a present. The garden is all in bloom, the myrtle is covered with little blue flowers which look like violets. I had Mr. Wickes, the tree expert, here. He will spend a whole day here, cleaning out all the dead trees and brushes. That hasn't been done for years and the whole place will look better. Today I am going to buy roses and other plants so that the gardener can plant them on Monday. The annuals we put in in May. And so it is going on all day, and I haven't done any work all week. But I couldn't have done much anyhow because there is a complete stagnation with the Lunt show. The Lunts say they don't sign a contract before Sam has made the necessary changes. I think they are right, but the Playwrights don't like it that one of their members should work more than 4 weeks on a play and get less than 10%. I had lunch with *Dornröschen* and found out that my first impression about Sam's attitude was right: he doesn't want to give away any of his royalties. It seems he wants the Playwrights to pay me a flat sum, because he told them Sam Barlow (!) got 2500.– for the incidental music in Amphytrion.[1] Strange how well informed that distracted genius suddenly is when it comes to money. Now I understand why he always talks about "Zuleika Dopson." That's just a *"Köder"* [come-on]. Well, I told Harold, the ideas which I gave them already are worth the royalty I'm asking. The whole thing is deeply disgusting. I am not sure if I shouldn't tell them to go to hell. I am pretty sure it will be awful to work with Alfred and that bitch Lynn who runs the whole thing. They'll make me work all summer, and then they'll cut out most of the music. Well, I guess I just have to be diplomatic and wait and see what happens in the next Playwrights meeting when Harold tells them my conditions. That coward Sam has disappeared. In the meanwhile those 6 colored girls will be picked up by other producers, and, of course, I cannot do any work on the show. What a mess! I always think how wonderful Moss is compared to those people. No wonder that he is more successful. He is much more honest and more efficient and a much better worker. Cheryl is back in town, but I haven't seen her yet. I saw Kober and he is still very excited about

Venus. We wait to hear from England about the rights. Phil Berry wants to do White Wings now, but he wants to do it all himself, lyrics and all (for royalties, of course). That's another tough baby. And another wonderful idea wasted because of the conceit and greed of a playwright.

Well, maybe it will all find a very simple solution. I got my questionaire from the draft board and I may be in the army instead of writing shows. I wouldn't mind.

I got your card from New Orleans. That must be a charming town and I wished I would have been there with you. The next 3 weeks will be hard for you because they are all one-nighters. But then a beautiful new painted house and a vegetable garden and terrace furniture and *eine Trrräube* expect you for real *Feinlebe* [the good life].

> Loads of love,
> Kurt

1. *Samuel Barlow (1892–1982) composed his score for Jean Giraudoux's play in 1938. Barlow had reviewed* Lady in the Dark *for* Modern Music: *"Something first-rate has gone third-rate, which is a loss for everyone who cares deeply for an art, beyond any prejudice or timeliness or mode" (p. 192).*

282 LENYA IN SAN ANTONIO TO WEILL IN NEW CITY, 27 APRIL 1942
Postcard: The Alamo

"And Davy went down to the Alamo!" This very interesting this old mission. The rest of the town looks a little bit like Albuquerque. Tomorrow Austin. Short trip 3 hours. I hope everything goes well back home.

> love Lottie!

283 LENYA IN SAN ANTONIO TO WEILL IN NEW CITY, 27 APRIL 1942
Letterhead: The St. Anthony / San Antonio / Texas

Monday, 27

Darling,

Thank God, we are out of that awful town Huston. I didn't go to see Bill after the performance. I had lunch with the girl he is living with and that was just enough. It's too dismal and not very interesting. So that's that chapter.—I just came back from the old mission and saw pictures of Davy Crocett and the other heros of the Alamo. All together a not very exciting town after N.O. The population is very mixed. Mexican, Negro and very blond children. The town is overcrowded with soldiers (as everywhere) mostly flyers! It's an ugly town they seem to have a passion for painted *"totenköpfe"* [skulls] green, purple, red. Very peculiar.—Tomorrow I'll take a taxi and drive to the Mexican part of the city. We leave at 2:00 P.M. and it only a 3 hours ride to Austin. I bought a little present for you today and will send it tomorrow. Nothing importent. I am very anxious to hear, how everything worked out with Sam. I hope, it want be too difficult. I wonder, how you'll like the things I bought in N.O. But they'll look very pritty, if the living room works out as I have it in mind. Now *Schnäpschen, lebe.* This is not much of a letter, but just saying hello and showing you the "eligant" Hotel I am living in since the experience in "Fort Shelby." Did you ever hear from them?

> Well *lebe Pfläumchen* [little plum] and take care of *dein Bäumchen* [little tree]—
> *Dein* [your]

with matches to play and
to add two then it makes

(*arschi* [little ass, synonymous with *Popo*]—excuse me
4 month touring—.)

284 WEILL IN NEW CITY TO LENYA IN SAN ANTONIO, 27 APRIL 1942

Monday, April 27, 1942

My darling,

Today I had your letter from Houston, Texas. I am very glad that you bought those lovely things in New Orleans. They all sound very exciting. Two packages are already in Spring Valley and I go tomorrow to get them. Your notices in Houston are wonderful, and I am sure that this whole road tour was very good for you and that you will feel much better because you have worked for more than nine months. These last weeks will be pretty tough, but pretty soon the whole thing will be over.

Well, here is my daily report. Hans came out on Saturday and we worked in the garden all afternoon, got the sprinkler going on the lawn and watered the flowers. In the evening we went over to the Poors [Henry Varnum Poor and Bessie Breuer] because the Steinbecks had dropped in at our house before dinner and told me that they will be at the Poors. It was very nice. He said, the critics were right about his play [*The Moon Is Down*], it wasn't very good. Later we went to the depot where Mab had a big poker game going. On Sunday we cleaned out the alley in the woods. Hans loves to work in the garden, and so do I. I forget completely about all my problems and worries, and that is very good for me. And you have really the feeling that you have something accomplished after five hours work in the woods or in the garden. Rita came out for lunch, and in the afternoon my two lesbians (Miss Crane, the rich girl who manages all those negroes and her girl friend) came out and brought Belle Rosette with them. She is a wonderful woman, extremely intelligent and a violent defender of her negroe rights. She tells very interesting story from Trinidad and the hypocritic English colonial policy. I had the idea that it would be wonderful to take the finest negroe entertainers (singers, dancers etc.) and do a negro musical like Porgy, but the whole thing about the negroe question; the whole problem of race oppression combined with great entertainment. I'll talk to Moss about it. Belle Rosette opens in "Sons O'Fun," in place of Carmen Miranda, on May 5. But she agreed to give an audition for Alfred and Sam on Wednesday, with her group. So I told Max that this is the last chance to get those people. He called Sam this morning and Sam called me back and said he would come. Then I called Alfred and he got Lynn's permit to come to the audition. And now I must see that I get those girls together. Alfred asked if I was working on the score. I said no. He asked why. I said: because the whole thing is too vague. Maybe I get it going this week.

Today I was up at 7:30. The gardener came and cleaned out the rock garden outside of the living room. He is really wonderful. We planted morning glory around the door—for you. Loyd came and we drove to Spring Valley and bought a garage door. Of course, it takes him two days to fix it. He is very amusing, but too expensive. I worked with him all afternoon. We fixed the stone steps in the rock garden in front of the porch. Then I went with Florence to see old Bill [Beaubelle] who is working on a place over in Mount Ivy. He is a very nice man, a perfect carpenter, knows all about gardening, chickens, plumbing and automobiles. He is making 50.– a month now and he says he has to make that much because he has a son who gets money from him. If I give him a room and 20.– a month, he would have to make another 30.– outside. I'll talk to the McEvoy's if they would take him for 2 days a week, and if he gets one more day a week outside he could swing it and we would have him four days a week which is plenty. If he does any extra work like building a fence or any other building etc. we would pay him a little extra (not more than 1.50 a day). I think he would be just the right man for us.

Tonight I went to see Max and we went over to see little Martha [granddaughter] who is very cute; looks just like a real Anderson. Tomorrow I go to the Authors' League meeting. Wednesday lunch with Sam, audition, cocktail party at [Norman Bel] Geddes', and in the evening I take Irene Gallagher, Dreyfus' secretary, to the Circus.

That's all today. Now I go *schniepeln. Viele Knüsschen aufs Warschi* [many little kisses on your little ass],

Schnubi

Wooly was all day at Miss Dingman's. She clipped him and gave him an injection for the ears. He looks beautiful.

285 LENYA IN FORT WORTH, TEXAS, TO WEILL IN NEW CITY, 29 APRIL 1942
Postcard: "Fort Worth's hotel of distinction, The Blackstone."

Thanks for letter. I'll answer tomorrow in Dallas. Put bycicle in attic otherwise it get's stolen too. Put nightlatch on tool house and put everything in there. I am exausted from heat and lack of sleep. I'll be better tomorrow.

Love Linerl

Thursday, Apr. 30, 42

Träubchen,

Yesterday I had your letter from S. Antonio. The things that have arrived from New Orleans so far are lovely. The red lamp is a real beauty, the silver set is very sweet and so is the red water bottle and glass. That's all that has arrived. I have paid 35.– for the lamp, and there is a check of 77.– from "French Quarter Shop" at the bank. I begin to see how you are planning our living room. I am sure it will be beautiful by the time you get through.

I had lunch with Sam yesterday. He has finished rewriting and sent a script to the Lunts. Alfred called him up and said, he didn't think it was improved. Then Sam, for the first time, got furious and told them that is all he can do and they can take it or leave it. Half an hour later Alfred called back and said he had read it again and thinks now it is very good. They are absolutely awful, those two old fakers, and she is definitely the greatest bitch I've ever seen. I had arranged the audition and explained to them who Belle Rosette was etc. Then she sang and Lynn kept saying: "What a charming costume!" Then Belle Rosette did a number which is a take off on an old woman gossiping (a wonderful performance). Lynn said: "She would be very good as an old woman in the chorus." When I explained again that this woman will be the star of "Sons o'Fun" next week, she didn't even listen, went over to Alfred and repeated: "Wouldn't she be good as an old woman in the chorus?" And so it went on. She was tired, soooo "overworked," had to eat dinner early and lie down an hour before a radio rehearsal. And he is so dumb and so egocentric! He reminds me of [Otto] Klemperer all the time—the same fake voice and the same stupid chicken-eyes. I have the feeling I'll save myself a lot of trouble if I stay out of this show. Life is too short to be bossed around by two old hams—and the results are too meager. Anyway, I won't make another move now. If they want me they have to get in touch with me. That's the only way to deal with them. I talked to Cheryl. "Venus" situation is quite good and we may start on that pretty soon. Gilbert Miller called and said he is interested in "Davy Crockett."[1] Had dinner with Irene and then to the Circus. It was very nice, but too much of it. The Elephant Ballet very bad, the Stravinsky music terrible (everybody says so).[2] I think he has lost his talent. At eleven I was exhausted and left to make my 11:30 train. Out here it is lovely today. Nick came in the morning and plowed the little field, and Jules is starting his vegetable garden. The lilacs are in bloom, and many other things, Peter starts painting this week—slow as usual. I discovered that there is a cess pool on the lawn, right under the terrace. It is filled up and I get it cleaned and a new cement top put on (35.–). The garage door was 20.– and Loyd spent two days fixing it (12.–). That's how it goes. Well, we cannot make more than 25,000.– —anyhow—the rest goes to taxes. Today I go with Mab to get some plants. Tonight we have blackout test and I have to play victim. Tomorrow I have dinner with—Kätchen [Rudolf Kommer] who called yesterday. We figured out today that you will be home 4 weeks from Sunday, so there is a lot of work to do to get everything nice and clean before you come.

Well, good-bye now, *mein Pflänzchen*. Take care of your *warschi*
Bussi [little kisses],

Kurt

Did you get my letter in Fort Worth and Dallas?

1. *Gilbert Miller (1884–1969) was a prestigious producer in London and on Broadway. Weill and Hays never finished "Davy Crockett."*

2. *Circus Polka, a ballet for fifty elephants and fifty girls, featuring Old Modoc and Vera Zorina, was directed by George Balanchine, with costumes by Norman Bel Geddes, and was first performed in Madison Square Garden on 9 April 1942 in an arrangement for band by David Raksin. Stravinsky completed the orchestra score on 5 October 1942.*

287 LENYA IN DALLAS TO WEILL IN NEW CITY, [2 MAY 1942]
Letterhead: The Baker Hotel / a Texas institution / Dallas

Saturday 9:30 A.M.

Darling

I wanted to answer your two letters last night after the show, but then when I got home I was so tired, that I fell in my bed and slept 8 hours, which is enormous. It's a problem to sleep in these noisy hotels. But anyway I feel much better and it's a little cooler too. Darling, I wish you would take the whole Lunt-Sam setup a little easier. Of course it's disgusting the way Sam behaves. *Im ausbeuten sind sie alle gross* [they're all great at exploiting others]. That's their mother milk. But you have to get used too it. You're a little spoiled by Max and Moss. And you know (I hope) that you cant trust Alfred from one inch to the next. He is no help so ever. All he wants is a play and new ideas and your music of course. But if it comes to fight for it, he want do it. They are probably convinced if the Lunts play it, it'll be a success anyhow. They all want a "Lady" success, but the dont want to pay. What a miserable bunch those literats are. I wouldn't give in Darling. You will write a beautiful score and then they'll cut it down (that you know too) and at least you have your royalties if they ruin your score, which you never know with that "Everest of character"—Alfred. I am very curious, whether they will engage those wonderful negros. With that old bitch Lynn one never knows. She is probably jealouis of everything. Just dont get too excited about it Darling otherwise you'll be too disapointed, if it doesn't go through. It's really the most disgusting thing, that you have to fight for royalties after "Lady in the Dark." Sam should be slapped for that, that idiot.

The reports on the "house and garden" sound very good. I am so happy that you like gardening. It's so good and relaxing for you. It's a pitty that they stole the hose. (who could it be?) Was the cottage locked? I am afraid, one of these days they'll steale the tires of the cars. We have to get good locks for every door. Has the new garage door a lock? They will steal anything from now on. I hope, we get that old man Bill. He sounds just right for us. I know Lyod is amusing, but not "that" amusing to be so expensive. And you know, when he starts trout fishing in the midde of a mantelpiece—.

But we have to take him if we dont get somebody like Bill it would be bad if we take somebody else instead of Lyod. I feel like jumping on the train and go home. I am soo tired now. I just wanted to see N.O. which was a real treat. But the rest now is ashes.— And I am angry, because I havn't saved much money. But it's not possible. Those one nighters are very expensive. And the hotels are very expensive too on account of the war. They are all overcrawded. One has to be happy to get a room. I hope, you'll like the things I bought. We will have a beautiful house, when it's all done. It's a pitty, that I miss all the flowers. One doesn't see anything on a tour like that. You sit in a train practically all the time and when you get out you dash to the theater and the rest of the time one tries to get some sleep. But as you say, I will have worked 9 months and can take it easy when I come back. I have to wait six month anyway. Well Darling, I hope, your show works out. It would be wonderful for you to work again. The records of Helen come out in July. The title will be "They have seen the glory" (or something like that, as Helen told me yesterday.) In San Antonio, Helen invited me for a little party after the show and I met "General Kruger."[1] One of the few generals of the american army. Very impressive all those stars and stripes. Before we left I put on his cap and said "you mind general—if I take over." He laughed like hell. (*Sehr niedelich*—) He saw the play and picked out one guy, who has nothing to say, just stands still during the concentration camp scenes. He said, that's the "real" nazi type. Well— he picked the only real "irish" man in the whole cast. I hope, his strategic jugment will be a little better:—In the same party was a conel and a liutenent, with all the wives. That's a world of it's own. There is a wonderful comodie burried. After the war of course. I like [Wendell] Wilkie better.—Darling, these coming 4 weeks will be tough as you know and I want have time to write much. But I'll keep up my postal card system. How do you like the chain? It's not much but I guess it'll look nice. Well my *Blümchen lebe* and I think you are a wonderful housekeeper, *mit einem klugen Köpfchen* [with a clever little head]. Well of course, you learned a lot in living with me.—*Du warst eine dünne rübe* [you were a thin turnip] and now you are a very intelligent *spargi* [little stalk of asparagus]— 🗝 .

Ich küsse the hand monsieur and *vibleibe* [remain]

truly yours.

    Caroline

---

1. *Walter Krüger (1880–1967) was born in East Prussia and came to the United States in 1889. He served in France during World War I and commanded the Third and Sixth Armies in the Pacific during World War II.*

288 WEILL IN NEW CITY TO LENYA IN TULSA, OKLAHOMA, 2 MAY 1942

Saturday, May 2, 1942

Dear *Schnäubi*,

I have a cold, on my chest, but otherwise I am feeling alright. The bank statement came today. Last month I had spent only 350.– for living expenses. So I didn't watch it this month and it went right up to over 500.–, apart from taxes and other expenses. There were three blank checks from New Orleans: one for 35.–, one for 15.– and one for 77.–. The one for 35.– is from Kaplan & Co., but the package from Kaplan that arrived last week (with the lamp) was C.O.D. and I paid again 35.–. Is this a mistake and did they charge us twice for the same thing, or is it correct? I am sending you the receipt from the Railway Express and also the blank check. You can check it. If it is a mistake you can write them, but don't send these two papers, because they are our *"Belege"* [documentation].—There is another package at the Railway Express today. I'll get it later.

I wished you were here and could see the garden. You remember we always complained last year that there was nothing blooming in our garden. Well, you should see it. It is just covered with flowers now, and it smells like heaven. All the ivory [ivy] has little blue flowers like violets. Then since yesterday there are everywhere lovely purple flowers, so many that Jules filled our vases with them. Right under the porch there is a big appletree in bloom, also the cherry tree and the peach tree. Now the lilac is starting, and the "Judas tree" is covered with buds. Then there is an almond tree full of pink flowers. Everything looks much better than last year because we are taking care of it. But it seems that there are more flowers in the spring in this garden than later. That's why I'll plant lots of annuals later in May, so that we have flowers all summer. Jules has started the vegetable garden and will write you about it. I am taking care of the lawn which looks very pretty this year.

Complete silence from Sam and from the Lunts, and I don't call them any more. It's funny, but I just don't trust Sam. I am sure he means well, and he is very nice and sweet, but out of pure weakness, he is lieing all the time and does things that aren't correct. I invited Kätchen for dinner last night. He was awfully nice. Sam had given him the play to read, and Kommer who had no idea that I was connected with it, told Sam right away: this play needs music all the way through. And sweet little Sam still didn't mention that I was working on the score! That proves again, what I always suspected, that he really doesn't want music and that he is just too weak to say so. I am sure the only thing for me to do is to sit back and wait what happens. In the meanwhile I'll make sure with *Dornröschen* that they are not allowed to use any of my ideas if I am out of the show.

Tom Fisher and Ruth [Page] called up yesterday. They had lunch at 21 with Billy (Mrs. Bobby [Hassard] Short) and I met them after lunch. They were here only for a day. I met Phil Barry at 21. He said he wants to do "White Wings" if we get a producer. The Fishers took me later to cocktails at the house of a rich woman who is on the board of directors of the "League of Composers," but also an ardent admirer of "Lady in the Dark"—so I could do some nice little undermining work.[1]

Today it is cloudy here and rather *betrübelich* [gloomy]. Tomorrow Hans is coming out with Bravi and perhaps Cheryl and Dorothy [Patten]. Tomorrow night I am on the watch tower with Max.

And that's all and there isn't any more. So long, my pet.

> *Knüsschens fürs Pfläumchen vom Glätzchen* [little kisses for the little plum from the little baldy].

I wrot you to Little Rock. Next letter to Kansas City. I suppose you'll see Charles Alan there.

1. *The League of Composers published the journal* Modern Music, *for which Weill had written "The Future of Opera in America" in 1937. Weill was serving on the "composers' committee" of the League; his name appears on the roster at the front of each issue of* Modern Music, *sandwiched between Edgard Varèse and Stefan Wolpe. The only women on the executive board of the League at this time were Claire Raphael Reis (1888–1978), the executive director of the League for 25 years; the composer Marion Bauer; and the editor Minna Lederman. But the "auxiliary board" and "associate committee" comprised predominantly women; the identity of the "rich woman on the board of directors" therefore cannot be conclusively determined. On 4 December 1942 Weill corresponded with Claire Reis about the birthday concert of the League.*

289 LENYA IN LITTLE ROCK TO WEILL IN NEW CITY, 4 MAY 1942

Letterhead: Hotel Lafayette / Little Rock / Arkansas

May 4th

Darling,

I just got your letter from Thursday. Yes I got also your letters to Dallas and Fort Worth (which I answered if I remember correctly—). Well I am not a bit surprised about what you write about the Lunts. She is a bitch. And never in a million years, I believe, she would allow anyone as good as Belle Rosette seems to be in a show, where she is in. And he is just as dumb as your description. Chickeneyes! that's what he is and has. Dont make too much an effort Darling to get that show. You will go trough hell with them and no securety so ever, that in the end, they wouldn't cut down your score beyond recognition. It isn't worth it. You waited so long for a show, you can still hold out. There was never anyone real good in a Lunt show. They just want do it. Black or white. They are scared to death, maybe some one would steal a little glory. They are two old "Possarts."[1] I would be of iron in negotiations with them. And if you make a contract, have everything in it. The right billing and every little detail. That's the Agents job! I am glad you like the things I bought! 1 table (english), 1 iron garden table, 2 curtain tiebacks, 1 flower vase (which should have arrived with the red lamp) it will come, and 2 golden vases, which I just found in Little Rock, are still coming. It will be very pritty. I send you a check here for 100.– which takes care of the 77.– and 35.– (almost) 15.– are still to be paid for the flowervase. I had the money in the trunk. I bought for about 100.– shoes for me and some little things, blouses and so on in Dallas (famous store). Did you get the shirts and ties I bought for you? I hope, you like them. The blue shirt is for your blue slaks and the green and jellow one for your brown slaks. Well it sounds like the house will look like a jewel when I get back. With everything cleaned out and painted. Did you decied on the blue shutters? or the red ones? It must be lovely now. I just refuse to think about these last 4 weeks (no 24 days), they are too awful. I took a train yesterday Sunday at 5:00 and arrived here at 12 midnight. The company left 6:20 this morning! I just didn't do it. So I got a good nights rest and prepared myself a little bit for the sleeper this night. (They should call those trains "Waker"—not Sleeper—) But it'll be over soon.

Well Darling take it easy too. Life is really too short to fight with the Lunts.

> *Viele Träubchen*
> *Knüsschen*
> *Deine* Madame

---

1. Ernst von Possart (1841–1921) was a distinguished German actor and stage director who eventually became general manager of Munich's Royal Theaters. His fame as an actor had rested upon his resonant voice, his distinguished appearance, and most of all his shrewd handling of every possible theatrical effect.

290 WEILL IN NEW CITY TO LENYA IN KANSAS CITY, MISSOURI[?], 6 MAY 1942

Wed. May 6, 1942

My Sweetie-pie,

That was a wonderful little surprise when I got the silver chain yesterday. It is very beautiful, but I'll have to get some more keys to put on. Very very *niedelich!!* I just sent you a little wire which you will get at the matinee today. I can imagine how tired you must be. For *eine Schniepelpison* like you it is "very bad" if you don't get enough sleep. Well, the only consolation is that it will be over soon. By the time you read this letter it will be only three more weeks. "Lady in the Dark" closes the same night as "Candle . . ." May 30: Gertie will sign a 20 weeks contract for next season, but she will play the whole season if nothing unforseen happens.—On Sunday Hans and Bravi came out, and Schwarz came for lunch with a girl (Miss Mitchell), but they left after lunch. Then later in the afternoon [Anatole] Litvak came with William Wyler (a very nice guy).[1] Jules made a very good improvised dinner, and we had lots of fun. In the evening we all went to Max, then at midnight I went to the watch tower with Terry [Terrence Anderson]. Monday I worked with the gardener, started to put in annuals. I also cleaned all the dead wood out of the vine over the terrace. Pete is working every day. I told him to paint the shutters with the same slightly faded blue-gray as the doors, according to your latest instructions. If you are not definite about it please let me know right away. Yesterday I was in town. Talked to Freedman. It seems the Lunts still haven't signed. I don't do anything unless they call me. I had lunch with Max Dreyfus. We are getting the Whitman songs ready for print. In the afternoon I went to see "Fantasia"— at last. It has wonderful things, but too much of it, and without a great idea to hold it together, it seems rather artificial. Then I had dinner with Moss, nice as always. He wants to give you his last poppy, 3 months old, female. She could have poppies with Wooley later. Please let me know if you want it, but think it over. I would say, if we get a caretaker, like Bill, we could do it. Otherwise we'd have two big animals to worry about if we have to move into town in the winter. Of course, it would be fun, and I guess you would like it. So let me know. I talked to McEvoy today. He would take Bill for three days a week, so that he could make his 50.–. I go over to talk to Bill today. But something else occured to me. It looks as if we won't get enough fuel oil next winter to heat the house and we might want to live in the cottage which has a coal furnace. On the other hand, we might live in town for the three cold winter months, especially if I have to do some kind of war work. In that case it would be better to have Bill on the place. I don't know. But I first have to find out if we get Bill.

I went with Moss to Belle Rosette's first night in "Sons o' Fun." That is the noisiest, rowdiest, dirtiest thing I've ever seen. It has nothing to do with theater, but it is very funny and people are having a wonderful time, with girls in the audience, people being dragged on the stage and undressed, an auction sale etc. Poor Belle Rosette was completely lost with her highly sophisticated Calypso songs. It was as if you'd want to sing "Seeräuberjenny" (in German) at the Circus in Madison Square Garden. She had picked the wrong songs and was very badly advised—and a complete failure.

Well, I guess that's all, honey. I'll stay out here the rest of the week. It is so beautiful. Jules has put big lilac bushes in all the vases, and the whole house smells like paradise. The porcellain-vase from N.O. arrived today. What a lovely piece for the living room! *Primi!* Don't try to save money. You have to live as well as you can on this tour.

Now take it easy, *mein Schätzchen. Mit dem Ausdruck meiner ausgezeichneten Hochachtung verbleibe ich ergebenst* [with the expression of my most extraordinary respect, I remain, your most devoted]

Kurt Julian W.

Did you ever write Moss? 461 E 57th St. N.Y.

Just got your letter from Little Rock, with the check. You didn't have to send the money now. Well, it goes all in the same pot. The Steinbecks are just coming for a little visit.

1. *William Wyler (1902–81) had worked his way up from a propman to one of the motion picture industry's most distinguished directors.*

291 LENYA IN WICHITA, KANSAS, TO WEILL IN NEW CITY, 7 MAY 1942
Letterhead: Friendly Hotels / Allis Hotel / Wichita, Kansas / Hotel Connor / Joplin, Missouri

May 7th 42

Darling,
Thanks for your wire and letter to Tulsa. I wrote to Kaplan and Comp. and I think in the meantime they've discovered their mistake. If not, we have to write once more. I'll send you back those 2 *"Belege"* in case Mr. Gold c/o Kaplan a. Comp. N.O. Royal Street sends the money back and writes for the recipts. Please let me know, what things have arrived already, so I can check them. I am so sorry I cant see the garden in its full bloom. I wonder whether those pionies I planted last year, start to come out. I dont wont to say anything about the tour anymore. It's really very tireing now and the whole company gets slowly but surely hysterical. But it'll be over soon. Helen wrote you a letter, she told me. She was kind of upset about that Lunt show, but I told her, that is an old 3 year old project and it's not even sure, that you'll do it. That seemed to relief her a great deal. She is really very anxious to do a show with you and so pleasant

to work with. I just hope, you find the right thing for her. In the diningroom in Tulsa, a man came to my table to greet me. I didn't recognize him but he turned out to be one of your most ardent enemies Mr. Sam Barlow! Well anyway, he sat with Helen after the show and Helen asked me too. He is a little unsecure lous, works for a russian relief fond. Tries to get money from rich poeple. Not a word out of his *"briefkasten"* [mailbox] mouth about my performance. You think I'll live?—I am glad you did a little undermining with that Lady from "the league of Complotters—"

Sam is really something out of this world. I wonder, whether Kätchen really didn't know anything about it. Maybe he just wanted to show how brilliant he is, to know, that the play needs music. Dont do anything anymore Darling, you are really to good for it. They will come for you if they really want you and need you.

How do the shirts fit? No money left anymore. Just enough for comfortable living and a little pokerplaying in those endless train rides. Well, *mein betrüblichen Pfläumchen* [my saddened little plum], *lebe recht wohl* [fare thee most well] and I'll be seeing you very soon. *Sei intelligent* [be intelligent] like *Dein unvigessliches Blümchen* [your unforgettable little flower] and *nehme meine gewaltige Hochachtung vollwertig entgegen* [accept my most immense esteem].

Dein Weib

292 WEILL IN NEW CITY TO LENYA IN DES MOINES, IOWA, 8 MAY 1942

Friday, May 8, 1942

Darling,

We've had rain for two days, and we needed it badly. But today was a nice day. I went for a ride with Max and Terry and mowed the lawn in the afternoon.

There is a complete standstill again in all my enterprises. That nice trio Sam-Alfred-Lynn continue to behave in the strangest way. I didn't hear a word from them. Sam didn't send me the script of the revisions. No word of reaction to the negro audition. Wednesday evening *Dornröschen* called up which is, as you know, a rare event. He stammered something that everything is settled and they had worked out a statement. I smelled a rat and asked what they had announced about me. He said he didn't know. Next morning it was in all papers . . . "incidental music by K.W." At 10 Jules came back from town. He said Lynn had asked her maid (who is a friend of Jules') if Jules would pack Alfred's luggage (I am sure they are trying to get Jules away from us). Jules went there at 7 A.M. and Alfred sent a message through Jules (!!!) how sorry he was that he couldn't see me before leaving and he would write me a letter. Later I called Bill Fields and asked how it got into the papers without asking me and why they used the expression "incidental music." He spilled the whole soup: Sam was afraid that people would think it is a musical and insisted on "incidental music." I think my original impression was the right one: Sam is the one who is working against the music, partly because he is afraid of it, partly because he doesn't want to pay. Well, he won't get away with it. I will force an issue and I am not afraid of a possible break with Sam because, if he is afraid of music in this little comedy, he certainly would never do a real musical with me. The whole thing is deeply disgusting, and I have the feeling that I am wasting away my time with those little unimportant quarrels instead of doing something really worthwhile. I am in the mood to throw away all this show business and get a real war job or join the army or go into a factory. I make a last try with the Arthur Kober project. At least he is young and I can try to do something fresh and amusing. If that also falls through I give up. (Of course, you know that's not true and I'll never give up).

The house has the first coat of white paint now and looks terribly pretty. We tried out some blue colours for the shutters today. We have to paint them a shade darker than the doors so that, when they fade, they look just like the doors. I'll get new screen windows because the old ones would look awful on the new painted house.—I got our sugar rationing card at the street school. Mab was the official and filled them out. She had to ask for your age. I said *(ohne mit der Wimper zu zucken)* [without batting an eyelash]: 34. Mab said: "Isn't it silly of Lenya that she never told me her age. She is younger than I am and I thought she is much older because she didn't tell me her age." A little later she said: "Lenya was only 18 when you got married." So don't forget: you were born in 1908.

The gasoline rationing will be quite a problem. We'll probably get only 6 gallons a week which means that we can just drive to Spring Valley and back once a day. I wonder if I should buy another little car because then we would get another 6 gallons. I saw a little Ford today for 185.–, but I cannot make up my mind if I should spend the money.

Thanks for the lovely shirts and ties. The shirts came very handy and are very pretty (although I cannot wear them without a jacket because my elbows are very bad.)

Helen has announced in the papers that she has bought the play about Harriet Beecher-Stowe which she had talked to me about. You remember that I suggested to her to combine this story with a kind of ballet of the "Uncle Tom" story. I will try to see Charlie [MacArthur] these days and try to find out if there is a chance that they would do it with my idea. How much more I would like to work with Helen than those old ham actors!

On Sunday I have an all girls party: Cheryl with Dorothy, Miss Crane with her girl friend and Belle Rosette. I am getting over all these invitations so that you don't have to bother with it when you are back. I am trying to get Paul Green to come out because he is supposed to be here on Monday.

Your next week will be very tiring. All one nighters. I hope you'll get some sleep and don't get too run down. I am leaving now (11 P.M.) because I sleep at the depot tonight (night watch). I'll write some more in the morning. Good night, my love!

Saturday morning. Just came back from the depot. It is raining and I wonder if my guests will come tomorrow. I hope I have a letter from you this afternoon.

Lebe, mein Schnäubchen.

Three weeks from tomorrow you will be here and *Feinlebe* begins again.

    Knüsschens!

I think in Cedar Rapids we stayed over night, coming from the Lunts, in a very noisy hotel.

Please sign the sugar card at x and send back.

293   LENYA IN DES MOINES TO WEILL IN NEW CITY,
[13 MAY 1942]
Letterhead: Hotel Fort Des Moines / Des Moines, Iowa

Wednesday
Des Moines

Darling,

    I just got your letter. I cant write much, I am so dogtired (not well—) I haven't got more than 3–4 hours sleep in a long time. It's just impossible to get any rest in those terrible overcrowed, terrible noisy hotels. I really cant wait any more to get home. It's alright touring, but not under 2000.– a week. Otherwise is suicide. But it'll be over soon. I am so thoroughly disgusted about that trio Lunts-Sam, that I almost wish you could just tell them: to go to hell. But I am very much afraid, they will use your ideas and you want hear from them anymore. I dont know, what to say. I have the impression, that they are terribly afraid of you. I am almost sure, they would be happy, if you wouldn't do it after they got out of you on ideas, what they could. That would be just like them. It's just incredible that Alfred disappeared without talking to you any more and sends you a message trough Jules! Darling, it's hard for me to tell you, to forget about the whole thing, nothing good will come out of that "poison-factory," because I know, how you would like to work again. But think it over. Even if everything will be straightened out, do you think, they'll let you do, what you really want? If Sam insists on "incidental" music doesn't that show you already very clearly, what he is up to? And those two old *"verstellers"* [hypocrites] they wont help you a bit. They are just as afraid as Sam is. I wish, Helen would get something. She wrote you a letter. You must have gotten it by now. If there would be a chance for you, I would just not do the Lunt show. I hope, Jules stay's with us. If not, we will have a hard time to get somebody good. But I am not running after anybody any more. If he wants to leave us, let him go. Something will come up again. Dont buy another car Darling. Even if we cant go more than 3 times a week to Sp.V. We will get along in some way. You know, how it is with an old car. We will have more trouble in winter than use. We probably will have to move to town for a few month if you work. If we dont get enough oil for the house, we can always arange in this way, that we close the upper part of the house, you take the living room for your studio and we have my bedroom together. The diningroom we can keep warm with wood, that would use up very little oil. I am sure, that would work out that way. It only gets really cold 2–3 month. I dont think, it will be a problem. The shopping we can cut down to twice a week. And there will be still some kind of delivery. So dont worry about that too much. After all, there are more poeple in the country. It will work out. I am so glad, that Gertie signed a 20 weeks contract and is willing to stay longer. That show will do enormous business. I know that now. I hope, the transportation will work out. With all the children and that big cast. Now Darling with that new poppy. I dont think, we should have it. Even if we get Bill. It'll be too much. One should try to simplefy everything around and in the house. And a poppy is too much of a *risico* [risk] with distemper and all that. Wolly is enough. Tell Moss, I dont dare any more after 2 death in my house.—It would be alright if one could drive quick to the doctor and all that. But not now. I am sure, he'll understand. I am anxious to hear, whether we get Bill. It would be a great help, if he is really a good carpenter and all that. I am so afraid of Lyod. I dont want to spend any money on the living room. Just try to do it all by ourselfs. Which can be done, with a little carpenters help. We have a lot of furniture already, which we can use and the piano helps a lot. I cant tell you Darling, how happy I'll be in Youngstown! I picked up *Filzläuschen*'s [crab lice] probably in one of those filthy trains. I got some stuff in a drugstore. They are gone now. But it was depressing. But it's no wonder. Those trains are filled with soldiers and they are just dirty beyond belief. And those terrible houses we are playing in now. That has really nothing to do any more with theater. That's just wholesale.—I am sorry about your elbows. Maybe some vitamin would be good for you. When I come back, we'll start to treat them a little bit and the sun will do the rest. Dont get *nervös* Darling. We will have a nice summer. Show or no show. But dont let them upset you. 15 more day's and then, *das "fine lebe"* beginns. This *"Berlin v. damals"* [Berlin as it was] sounds like an Eisler evening. I dont think, I would be interested in spite of the Saga of ADOLF.—I found two lovely handblown bohemien vases (dont be afraid, that the living room will be only furnished with vases—) but they are lovely and very sheap 5 !!- (I have them send) 5 Dollar both. And all those little details will make the room. I hope, that English table has arrived by now (if not I have to write imidiatly). Did you hear from Kaplan about the 35.00? If not I have to write again. Well Darling, that's all for the moment. We have all 1 nighters this week, 1 sleeper on Friday, and 4!! sleepers next week. But after that, the worst will be over. I hope, you had a nice party on Sunday. Or did it rain? What's the world hero *Nr.* [no.] 1 Schwartz doing. Still home? If he is still around tell him, he should leave me his fishing rod, before he leaves for the army. He wont have time for fishing. But only if he comes around. Dont call him.—

Well my *Träubchen*, I wanted to write a short letter, but I have so many things to say.

Lebe Darling and in 2 weeks !!

love—love—love—

Linerl

Friday, May 15, 1942

My *Trrrrräubi*,

This has to be a quick one because the mail carrier is coming in 15 minutes and we always give him the mail now because we cannot drive much any more. We are getting about 8 gallons a week (gasoline). That means we just can drive to Spring Valley and back or New City or Haverstraw once a day. No driving to New York at all. You'll have to take the train or bus! *Hi hi hi!*

It was nice to hear your voice the other night. I can imagine how tired you must be. Well, It'll all be over soon. On Wednesday Jules made a wonderful dinner (very excited) for Buzz and Paulette and they loved it.[1] We had drinks on the terrace, with the new furniture. She is a very nice girl (surprisingly), very intelligent and much prettier in life than on the screen. The kind of girl you like, very simple and natural. It is a big affair with Buzz, and I think it is the real thing. I told him to hold on to her, she is just right for him, after all those society girls. I went to see "Candida" yesterday. Burgess is excellent, but the rest rather disappointing after those rave notices. I just cannot stand that female impersonator Cornell.[2] But what a lovely play! How far superior to anything that has been written since for the theatre!

Last night I had dinner with Gil and Ada [Gabriel] and we went to see Russell Crouse. Today I have to make my questionnaire for the draft board. Tomorrow night Max and I are going to Washington to confer with Frank Capra and Tola [Litvak] about the picture for the War Department.[3] We will stay until Monday or Tuesday.

Yesterday I had a long talk with Jack Wilson.[4] He was very nice. He thinks it is sure that the Lunts want me badly, and he himself thinks nobody else could do it. But he warned me: working with the Lunts is hell, they are just thinking of themselves, nothing else counts, they consider everybody just at their service, they treated Bob [Sherwood] exactly the way they are treating Sam—but the results are worth it. I said: yes, if you get a royalty. He said the Playwrights are making quite a mess. He himself is supposed to coproduce the show, but he has no agreement and nobody makes any effort. Lunt expects me at Genesee the end of next week. Well, I wrote Victor [Samrock] once more today and made my point absolutely clear, so that no more misunderstandings will come up. And now I wait without excitment. Let them fight it out.

I hope Helen got my wire. I'll write her a few lines today. Of course, I would love to do a show with her, and I don't think the Lunt show would interfer—if I do it at all, which seems doubtful. Maybe I can arrange to come and see you and Helen on my way to Genesee, so that I know what Helen has in mind.

Well, sweetie pie, I better finish here.   I see you sooooon!

> *Viele Liebesknüsschen auf den Bobo* [many little love kisses on your fanny]
> *Glätzchen*

A package came with two wall ornaments (like lamps), very lovely.

1. *Paulette Goddard (1911–90), a film star of the 1930s and 1940s, had been married to Charlie Chaplin. Weill wrote a march, now missing, for her wedding to Burgess Meredith.*

2. *Before* Lady in the Dark *became what he termed a "veritable* Traviata," *Moss Hart had intended his play, then called "I Am Listening," for Katherine Cornell (1893–1974), perhaps Helen Hayes's nearest rival on the legitimate stage. George Bernard Shaw's* Candida, *about a woman who must choose between a visionary and a practical socialist, enjoyed more American revivals than any other Shaw play, and most of the revivals were led by Cornell, who had first played the part in 1924. Richard Bird was her first Marchbanks, followed by Orson Welles, Meredith, and Marlon Brando.*

3. *Frank Capra (1897–1991) directed* It's a Wonderful Life *and* It Happened One Night, *among other films. In his autobiography he described his room at the Carlton Hotel in Washington as "some days occupied by as many as three shifts of sleepers." He quotes an account by the* New York Post *columnist Leonard Lyons of Marc Connelly's visit on this same occasion: "In Capra's office he met Kurt Weill, the composer, and Maxwell Anderson, the playwright. . . . 'Capra was thoughtful enough to reserve a little room for me,' Connelly told Weill. 'Were you able to get a reservation, Kurt?' . . . 'Yes,' the composer replied, 'I'm in Room 308, at the Carlton.' 'But that's the room I'm in,' said Connelly, 'and I suppose that bag I saw in the corner of the room was yours'. . . . 'No, it isn't,' Weill added. 'That bag is Maxwell Anderson's' " (Capra, p. 337).*

4. *Jack (John) Wilson (1899–1961) spent many years as a stockbroker before his friendship with Noel Coward led him into the theater, where he became a successful producer and director; he was married to the actress Natalie (Natasha) Paley.*

295   LENYA IN SOUTH BEND TO WEILL IN NEW CITY, 18 MAY 1942

Letterhead: Hotel Oliver / South Bend, Indiana

Monday 18th

Darling,

I just got your letter. You'll be in Washington today and I hope, you'll have some interesting things coming up there. What Wilson say's about the Lunts is a known fact—that's exactly why everything should be worked out very carefully, before you start. You know Darling, how it is with you. You get so interested and involved as soon as you start to work and then you dont care so much anymore. So be clever and have everything on paper, before you start. I am sure, it wont be easy with them and I dont think, they wont anybody like Belle Rosette in their show either, but on the other hand, they are very good themselves and I think you can do a lot with them. It wont be as easy, as with Gertie (Gertie will become a Saint—compared to Lynn) but maybe you can handle them. Get that royaltie business set, so at least you get something out of it, in case they ruin your score, which one cant be sure at all. I dont mind taking a train to N.Y. after all that travelling 1 hour train will seem like nothing now. I dont think Darling it's a good idea to talk to Helen now. She is dying to get home. I thinks it's a better idea, to go and see her in Nyack after a cuple of days (sh'll be probably bored soon—) and than it's the moment to get her. Dont you think so? She is too hysterical now. I tried to find out about a sleeper from Youngstown on the 30ᵗʰ after the show. But there is none. One leaves at 10:34 which I cant make, the next leaves at 1:15 A.M. arrives in Buffalo at 5:40 A.M. leaves at 8:00 A.M. and arrives in N.Y. at 6:00 P.M. Well, that doesn't make sense. So I go with the company car on Sunday and will be in N.Y. probably around 10:00 in the evening. But that's allright. I'll be home then. I got a good nights rest here, in a very nice and quiet !! hotel. Thank God. So I feel fine today. I am glad the curtain tiebacks arrived. They are really old and rare. They will look lovely on the big window in the living room. I sent a wire to N.O. for the table. But I am sure it will come. Everything just takes time now. I hope they dont take you in the army. Dont want to be "alone."—I am afraid, that new romance of Burgess wont last. But we will see. Last night we went to see "the son of Frankenstein" [1939 film starring Boris Karloff]. I never laughed so hard in my whole life. I didn't buy anything for Mab on this trip. But I think, I dont have too. They made enough money now.—I wrote to Jules. Did he say anything about leaving us? It dosn't matter, if he does. We'll find somebody else. Not so good, I am afraid, but what can we do.—Well *Schnäubschen*, that's all, nothing new as you can imagine. 2 weeks from today and I'll be home. Those last 4 weeks were the longest.

Lebe mine Pflänzchen and be clever with the Lunts.

[love for / from]

296 WEILL IN NEW CITY TO LENYA IN CLEVELAND, 20 MAY 1942

May 20, 1942

My *Betrübelchen*,

You must have a kind of *"Veitstanz"* [St. Vitus Dance] now from travelling all around the Middlewest, round and round. This is probably the worst week, with all those awful industrial cities every day—but it is the last. Next week in Cleveland you will catch your breath and then it is only three more days—yippee! Maybe you can catch a night train from Youngstown and get here Sunday morning. I am saving gasoline that I can come with the car and call for you in style.

I came back from Washington last night. It was very interesting and very amusing. That Hotel Carlton is like the Beverly Wilshire and I saw during breakfast, lunch, dinner and at the bar the following people: Capra, Tola, Wyler, John Huston, Olivia de Havilland, Burgess, Paulette, Marc Connelly, John Gunther, MacLeish and some others.[1] We had long conferences with Tola & Capra about the picture and it depends now on Max—and you know what that means. If it would work out I would have to go to Hollywood for about 10 days during the summer. Of course, I would love to get into this kind of work because it would be my best contribution to the war effort. If I had my citizenship I could apply for a commission in this department and they probably would make me a captain (Tola will probably be a major). But I'm afraid Max will write again one of his "fast jobs" and will mess up the whole thing.

At MacLeish's office I arranged that the song ["Song of the Free"] will be used on "United Nations Day," June 14, in several mass meetings and on the radio.[2]

I called Harold [Freedman] last night to find out what happened in the Playwrights' meeting on Monday. John Wharton decided the play needs only some incidental music and they cannot pay royalties. Bob [Sherwood] was in complete agreement with him. Bob said he talked to Alfred and he also agreed with them. What a bunch of hypocrits! They act just like the Shuberts. All the ideals go out of the window when it comes to royalties. It seems that Jack Wilson is going to be the producer and he will tell me I shouldn't look at it from the money point-of-view, a Lunt show is important for everybody concerned and that kind of shit. I will answer him what Jed Harris answered Irving Thalberg: "How much do you get? I want the same!" I have an appointment with Victor [Samrock] and [Jack] Wilson on Friday. I would love to tell them to go to hell, but I am afraid they'll steal my ideas and some louse like [Marc] Blitzstein will get the credit. If I only knew how serious Helen is about her show and if she has something that would be really interesting.

Troubles with "Lady in the Dark." The fight between Moss' ego and Gertie's ego came to a clash and Moss wants to call off the road tour altogether just to punish Gertie. He is quite a problem boy now since he goes to the analyst twice a day. It is all about the transportation difficulties. Gertie wants to take the show to Chicago and stay there (which is the right thing to do) and Moss says she has no right to "run the show." So I have to try to straighten it out again, but it seems doubtful if we'll have a road tour. *Zum Kotzen* [enough to make you puke]!

The iron table is in Nanuet. We'll get it tomorrow. Here is a letter about the other table. No news about the 35.— Schwarz just came to say goodbye. He is leaving Friday for Maxwell Field, Ala. The place looks lovely, full of iris. I brought Gertie a big bouquet on Saturday. This afternoon I am going to fix screen windows with Pete. He is quite a good carpenter and we might fix the living room with him alone. Bill does not come, he stays at the place where he is now.

Well, honey, that's all I can think of right now. I just wired you to call me tonight. *Lebe, mein vitrauliches Blümchen* [farewell, my discreet little flower].

A bientôt, mon amour!

Kurt

---

1. *The director, screenwriter, and actor John Huston (1906–89) was the son of Walter Huston, the star of* Knickerbocker Holiday; *Olivia de Havilland (b. 1916) had played Hermia in Max Reinhardt's stage and screen productions of* A Midsummer Night's Dream; *the journalist John Gunther (1901–70) was the author of a series of books (*Inside Europe, Inside Asia, *etc.). After Hollywood and Broadway had come under attack as luxuries expendable during wartime, many people in the entertainment industry demonstrated their loyalty and defended their calling by participating in the war effort.*

2. *United Nations Day celebrated the signing of the declaration by twenty-six nations.*

May 23, 1942

Dear *Roadschweinchen,*

It looks like a rainy week-end here. But the house looks very very pretty, with the new shutters on. You will be surprised when you see it. I did some carpenter work myself, fixing screen windows. Pete showed me how to do it, and it was fun. More fun than the Lunt show.—Before I went to see Victor and Jack Wilson yesterday I talked to Kätchen. He told me that the Playwrights now blame the whole thing on me and say that I am difficult (!!). Have you ever seen so much dishonesty and hypocrisy in one place? They are all so dishonest to each other that they consider anybody who tries to clear things up as difficult. Of course, I had to be very careful because I don't want to get that reputation. Max had told me that he got a report from the meeting and that they had decided to offer me 1500.—He was furious and advised me not to go to see Victor. But I didn't want any more *Stunk* [underhanded gossip]. Victor was very nice and said they all feel that I should continue to be the musical adviser and composer for the Playwrights, but they all (including the Lunts!!) agreed that this play doesn't need much music and I should do it for them. I suggested Jack and Sam should go to see the Lunts and then tell me exactly what music they all want for the show, and I will tell them if I want to do it or not. That was satisfactory for them. I also suggested to them they should just get a band of calypso singers and let them improvise, and I would be glad to help them. That stopped them completely. Well, anyhow, I have stalled them now and can wait 'til Helen is back.

Very nice lunch with Phil Barry. He is very interested in doing White Wings now. We are negotiating with Guthrie McClintic.

Tuesday I went in to straighten out "Lady." At Sardi's I met Gertie and invited her for lunch. She was in uniform and looked like 28, very pretty (you see, you don't have to worry about age). Everything is settled now for the road tour and she has signed. She asked me about doing another show for her. I told her about "Zuleika" and "Alice in Washington." She loved both ideas, and I'll have dinner with her after the show closes.—One more week, and my *Träubchen* will be home! Hurray! Take it easy now the last week. Thousand kisses!

Two vases from Sioux City arrived, also the iron table which is wonderful with the garden furniture.

Tuesday, May 26, 1942

Sehr viehrtes [most revered] *Schnäubenträubchen,*

This will be just a little letter so that you are not without any word from me all week. It was *sehr niedelich* to talk to you on Sunday. I was in the middle of a gin rum-mey with Hans. Monday morning we drove into town with Max in Hansens [Hans's] car (he still had some gasoline). Max and I had lunch with Tola. Max asked Tola to postpone the picture because he wants to finish a play—as usual. But later Tola told me that Capra was very impressed with me and I could do any picture I want. Tola wants me to do with him a short about China. John Gunther is writing it.

All afternoon I worked at Chappells on the MacLeish song. I want to do everything to give it a big start. So I went over to the Roxy Theatre and played for the director. He was crazy about the song and said: this is what we've been waiting for. They will do it as a big number, with flags of all the United Nations, in their stage show. That's a good start. Tomorrow we are sending the song to 75 radio singers.[1]

Later in the afternoon I met Tola again. We saw some chinese pictures and had dinner with Kendall Milestone[?] at 21.

Today Jules is in town. I just made myself a little dinner (*Brattoffi* [fried potatoes]). Charlie just called up if he can drop in tonight with Bemmelmann [Ludwig Bemelmans]. Geddes announced in the papers that he is doing a musical with Charlie, Bemmelmanns and me, but nobody seems to know anything about it. Anyway, who wants to work with those drunkards?

Tomorrow I go into town. Tomorrow night I am on the tower with Max. Friday night I sleep at the depot. We are saving gasoline all week so that I can drive to town when you arrive.

Ta ra ra Tsching tsching tsching! Wiedisehn, Pflänzchen!

Dein Glätzchen

1. On 9 June Weill reported to MacLeish: "As you probably know, our song is a very big success at the Roxy. I went to see it yesterday and I must say it has a very stirring effect on the audience, although the singer [Bob Hannon] is far from first-rate and the production is typical Roxy" (W–AM).

299 LENYA IN CLEVELAND TO WEILL IN NEW CITY, [26 MAY 1942]
Letterhead: Hotel Carter / in the heart of Cleveland

Tuesday

Darling,

Thanks for your letter. I am glad, that you are out of the Lunt show. I dont think, it ever would have worked out. It's just disgusting the way, the Playwrights behave. I think, it's all that John [Wharton]. And as you say, as soon as it comes to pay royalties! 1500.– to offer you! This is really incredible. But I knew, that Lunt wouldn't do a thing for you to fight it out. He has no character so ever. I talked to Helen. I told her about that 1% and she was furious. She said, she never heard anything like that. I thought, it's much better to tell her frankly, before she hears it trough somebody else. She thought, you would get 10%! (At least her secratary thought so, and that's the same.) Well anyway, let them do it without your music, but you are not going to help them either. You'll be very busy, when it comes to that.—I am sure, they will steal all your good ideas. But there is always one good thing about it. That no one except you can do the right things with them. I am sure they just want a little *"Gepinkel"* [tinkling around] backstage, like they had in Amphytrion. That was pittiful. I am glad, Gertie is setteld. By the way, she really would be a wonderful "Suleika." I am sure, that something will work out during the summer about transportation for roadtours. They need it for the moral of the poeple too. They cant let them be without shows. I am terrible restless those few days. I wonder, what kind of job I will do in that war. I dont want to do anything in the country. I wouldn't like Mabs job. What is Gertie doing, that she wears a uniform? Oh, yesterday morning around eleven o'clock, Schwartzi! called from Loui-ville Ken. He knew, I was in Cleveland, so he asked the operator to give him the best hotel and he got me. He was on his way to the camp and said goodby. Of course, I was so touched, that I cried like hell. I am getting soft—. But he seemed to like it and he is looking forward to get started. But I think, this enthusiasm wont last very long (we talked to many soldiers) he will realize after a while, what he is in for. But he said, they would have gotten him anyway which is true. I told him, I'll come and visit him, when he gets too lonely. He said, if I promise him that, then he feels lonely already. Well, there goes another of my friends. I sent my trunk home today. It'll arrive probably with me. I cant send the key, the same key fit's my handbag. I bought a travelling makeup case for me yesterday (20$) Very pritty. I had to do something yesterday. I felt kind of unhappy after that call. It brought the war a little closer and then my window is over-looking a cemetary which isn't so good either. I want to be home now. I have enough.—

Darling, we probably have a chance to leave Saturday night. But we have to take a taxi and drive 15 miles to another station. So Helen, Evelyn [Varden], Helen's secratary, Tonio and myself, we split a cab and try to reach that train. I would have to pay the difference to the pullmann and the birth. But that's allright. That would mean, I'll be in N.Y. Sunday around noontime. I hope, that works out. I send you a wire. Now *lebe mine Träubchen*. I'll be home in no time now. And leave something for me to do in the house.

The [Leonard] Lyons story, I had read already in the papers. Very cute.—

300 WEILL IN NEW CITY TO LENYA IN ERIE, 27 MAY 1942

May 27, 1942

Darling,

It is wonderful that you can get a night train. But I am not sure if I can come to the station. I just got notice that I am having my physical examination for the draft on Sunday at 2 P.M. and I have to be there exactly on time. If the train is a little late (which happens quite often now) or something else happens, I couldn't make it. Hans offered to be at the station and to bring you out with his car. But if you don't want them out here the first day I would send Jules to pick you up. I am very sad that I cannot be there, but what can you do? This is war—and we are all in it now. I was quite surprised that they called me already for the examination because nobody else has been called yet. But here in the country the draft boards are working much faster because they have less people. Of course, that doesn't mean yet that they take me, and there is nothing to worry. Dr. Glass makes the examination. If I pass the examination I would immediately try to get into Frank Capra's outfit in Washington.

Now hurry home, *mein Schnäubchen*. The iris, the poppies and the yellow wild roses are still in bloom and I hope they will be still there on Sunday.

I cannot wait to have you back. Thousand kisses from your buck private

Kurti

5 · NEW CITY, HOLLYWOOD: 1942–1944
Letters 301–366

Weill and Lenya in Hollywood, possibly in September 1944.

1942

Shortly after Lenya's return to Brook House, Cheryl Crawford agreed to produce Weill's proposed collaboration with Sam and Bella Spewack on a musical adaptation of F. J. Anstey's novella The Tinted Venus, *which Weill described to Ira Gershwin as "a first-rate idea for a very entertaining and yet original kind of opera comique on the Offenbach line" (W–IG, 13 Nov. 1941). By September, Gershwin had declined to collaborate, Ogden Nash had agreed to write the lyrics, Weill had drafted some songs, and the title role had been offered to Marlene Dietrich, who insisted on seeing something of the work.*

On 21 September Weill left for Hollywood by train with act 1 of the script and seven or eight musical numbers. During their discussions Dietrich performed for Crawford and Weill on [FIG. 63] *her favorite new toy, a five-foot-tall musical saw, on which she would accompany herself while singing various songs, including "Surabaya Johnny." While there, Weill also talked, in his role as chairman of the production committee, to members of the Hollywood Writers Mobilization on the need for material for* Lunch Time Follies, *an organization that entertained workers in war-related industries.*

In Weill's absence, Lenya attended the Boston tryout of Maxwell Anderson's The Eve of St. Mark, *produced by the Playwrights' Producing Company.*

Letterhead: The Ritz-Carlton / Boston

Friday morning

Schnäubchen,

Here I am in "the old villa." Madeleine and I had to share a room it's packed other-wise.[1] The play [*The Eve of St. Mark*] is a great success. A real healthy one. The audi-ence went grazy. And I must say, Lem Ward [the producer] did a beautiful job. It's so funy all the way through it really is like "What Price Glory." They still have to do some work on it. The dream scenes are not quiet right yet and the end of the play has to be shortened. But it's really very little, almost nothing. The first farm scene is so touching, that poeple started to sob right there. For my feeling, the charactor of Marion is completely wrong and unreal, but that's my private feeling and I wouldn't say it be-cause, they would jump on me. And it doesn't matter anyhow. The rest of the cast is perfect. So it looks good. The notices are raves. We are all happy and "Papa Suder-mann" talks already about movie rights and big money.[2] That's O.K. with us. And "Se-cret Agent"[?] is here of course and keeps on asking about you and your new show. And since Max told him how wonderful the story of "Tinted Venus" is (and he really seems to like it) he just makes all the effort to come in on it. But I know from noth-ing,—so he has to wait for you.—And then Elmer [Rice] was here, biting his nails over that very visible success of Max's. Well Darling, that's all about here. I am going back on the one o'clock train, because I want to get home. When I picked up the MacEvoys [neighbors] the evening you left, she had an enormous trunk with her (they are really impossible), it took us ½ an hour to squeeze it in the car. Then in the very last moment the paid the brigde. Hesitatingly.—I passed trough Sp. V. [Spring Valley] and Mrs. Brown [neighbor] picked up the score 15 minutes later.—So Bravi [Abravanel] got it. I wanted to sleep long in the morning but no chance. At 8:00 I was wakened up by a terrible crash. I went downstairs and run over to the garage. [Bill] Beaubelle fainted behind the car and rolled down the driveway and crashed through the door of the maidsroom. He cut his nose, his car was shmashed and so was the door. Pete was there, so he drove him home. He is alright now. Pete doesn't think he fainted, he thinks he just lost control over the car, otherwise he would have driven in the brook, if he really would have fainted. Well, there went my morning sleep. So I washed all the loundry and ironed it in the evening. Next morning I wanted to take the 9:50 train to N.Y. to make the 1:00 o'clock for Boston and overslept! Woke up at 10!! So I had to take the car. I'll save the gas next week. Then we came up here, had dinner with Max and the rest you know already. Today, we have the door fixed, Pete and Charlie[?] will do it. Lyod (who is a terrible vicious guy[;] Pete told me a lot about him and his repu-tation[—]Ku-Klux-Klan-er!!) it's better not to have him in the house anymore. Just keep him gracefully out of it. That's why I wanted to get home. I leave in an hour. Tomorrow I am going to Philadelphia for the dressrehearsal [*Lady in the Dark* tour]. I talked to Maurice [Abravanel]. I take a nighttrain back and stay at Gigis [Gilpin]. Sunday we drive out. Hans and Rita. So Darling, that's all. I hope, you had a nice trip and got a good rest on the train. And I hope, you come home with "Marlene *im Rucksack*" [in your knapsack]! I dont think, we have to worry about an apartement in town. Gigi will help me, she knows a cuple of good hotels. But there is no great hurry. It's so beautiful in the house now, that I hate to leave it, as long as the weather is so nice. Well Darling I better stop. You havn't got the time, to read a long letter like that. I made "budget" for this month. We are up to 4500 $. But with all those taxes. I hope, I get my curtains, so I can finish the living room before we move. Pete is an angel and really a help in the house. Now *schnabuliere* [eat heartily] good *Blumi* and take it easy. *Alle mine hochachtung and grosse Knüschen* [all my respect and great little kisses]

> *Deine* Madame
> Karoline
> Wilhelmine
> Charlotte

1. *Madeline Sherwood was the wife of Robert Sherwood (one of the founders of the Playwrights' Producing Company). Her first husband was Marc Connelly.*

2. *"Papa Sudermann" is a satiric reference to Maxwell Anderson, who, like the German playwright Hermann Sudermann (1857–1928), specialized in verse drama. By the time of his death, Sudermann was considered old-fashioned, his plays seen as dated imitations of Ibsen's.*

302 WEILL IN BEVERLY HILLS TO LENYA IN NEW CITY, [26 SEPTEMBER 1942]
Letterhead: Beverly Hills Hotel and bungalows / in Beverly Hills, California

Saturday morning

Trrräubi,

My trip was quick and uneventful, except that something got into my eye and it got so bad that I had to go to a doctor yesterday, as soon as I arrived here. He took it out—a typical Beverly Hills "private clinic." They'll probably charge 50 box.

Cheryl was already here, feeling awful after her trip. Marlene had already called several times and came over from the studio to say hello. She stayed until Jean Gabin came to pick her up and then we went all together for dinner.[1] She is a swell girl—and she seems very enthousiast about going to Broadway. Tonight we go to her house to read the play and play the music. She is trying to arrange the curfew business for me today [see letter 245, n. 3]. If it cannot be arranged I'll have to stay in her house for a few days.

This is a lovely hotel. Everybody seems to live here—from Luise Rainer to Simone Simon.[2] I haven't called anybody yet. Cheryl thinks we'll have to stay till Thursday or Friday which means I won't be home before Sunday or Monday.

Thanks for your wire from Boston. Max's play opens here in Pasadena Monday. If I get a permit to leave the hotel at night I'll go and see it.

Lebe, Schnäubchen,

Kurt

1. *The French stage and film star Jean Gabin (1904–76) had taken refuge in Hollywood after the German occupation of France; his long affair with Dietrich was well publicized.*

2. *The French movie star Simone Simon is best known for her glowing performance opposite Jean Gabin in Jean Renoir's* La bête humaine *(1938) and her romance with George Gershwin.*

303 LENYA IN NEW CITY TO WEILL IN BEVERLY HILLS, [28 SEPTEMBER 1942]

Letterhead: Brook House

Monday evening

Thank you for your letter Darling. I hope, that your eye is better. Please be careful! I went to Philadelphia on Saturday. They have a good new cast. Gertie was in great form, overacting like a berserker, but still very amusing. The orchester was fairly good, but Bravi gets a 3 hour rehearsal on Monday, so I guess it will be allright. Moss was very hysterical, all about Gertie again. The only very puzzling thing is, that the advance sale was extremly bad. Far from being sold out for the opening. They cant explain that. They hope, that the notices will be good and that will bring them in. It's strange, the way it is. Moss seems to be very worried about it and so was I. I will call Bravi tomorrow and find out how it went and how the notices are. If I get him on the phone I'll will write you in this letter. Nothing new from here. I came back from Phil. at 3 A.M. Sunday and stayed at Gigi, got few hours sleep in that terrible noisy apartment. Then I called Rita at 12 but they didn't want to come out with me, so I went home alone. It was pouring but I was so tired, I didn't want to stay in town. So when I got home, I cooked myself a little dinner and went to bed. Today was a beautiful day. We got the garage door fixed, the chandelier came, we messured the bookshelfs and Pete is going to make them as soon as he finishes the gate. The curtains will be up by the time you get back. In the afternoon I went down to Beaubelle, got coffee and cake and he is coming tomorrow. We put the glass table and chairs away. It's very cold already and we wont them use anymore. Tomorrow I am in the depot and Thursday tower. Wednesday I'll probably go into town, but be out in the evening. I want to see the doctor to get an injection. I went over tonight to Meg [Anderson], we pickeld tomatos. I probably have a girl by Monday. Luellas Sister. She came today and looked very nice and clean. So I dont need her this week for myself. I told her to come back on Monday. I'll try her out for two weeks. That's what I told her. So everything will be O.K. when you get back. I hope, you want have to much trouble to get Marlene. Your letter sounds good about her. Pete is very nice and fixes everything. I am not afraid to be alone in the house. It's nice in a way. I miss *mine Träubchen* but it want be long. Dont fly Darling. You are not in such a hurry. So I am looking forward to see you soon. A lot of mail came, but all nonsense. So I sent you only, what looks interesting. *Jetzt gehe ich sneepeln* [now I'll go take a snooze]. Good night my Darling. *Mit ehrfurchtsvollem Handkuss* [with a reverential kiss upon your hand]!

Dein [(your); little flower drawing]

Letterhead: Beverly Hills Hotel

Sept. 28, 1942

Trrräubi,

Thanks for your letter. I am glad for Max that the play is a success. When you see those guys like Marc Connelly and [Arthur] Kober out here you can learn to appreciate and like Max again.—

Well, we had a 6 hour session with Marlene yesterday. When I read the play on the train I knew that we would have difficulties with her because Bella [Spewack] had written all other parts much better than hers. Marlene found that out immediately. She was extremely intelligent about it and put her finger right on the wrong spots. She also was very constructive with suggestions how to improve the play. I am glad about it because it will break down Bella's stubbornness in certain points which I always tried to get from her. We called her today and hope that she will come out immediately. That means that I will have to stay here until Friday, probably even Saturday or Sunday. I hate to have you alone so long, but it is no use to rush back without getting this thing settled one way or another. Marlene liked the music, but started that old business about the different quality of my music here in America. I cut it short by saying: "Nevermind those old German songs—we are in America now and Broadway is tougher than the Kurfürstendamm." That stopped her.

Ira called yesterday and they came over for dinner with Marc because I cannot go out after 8. They are awfully nice. Lee [Lenore Gershwin, Ira's wife] is furious that Ira didn't do the show with me. She wanted to call me in N.Y. to tell me I should tell Ira: Yes or no. He wanted to do it more than anything, but was too lazy to make up his mind. They have a charming house. The night before I went for a few minutes to a [Lewis] Milestone party for Tola [Litvak] who is going "oversea." One of those dreadful Hollywood parties—[Ernst] Lubitsch, [Charles] Boyer, Miriam [Hopkins] etc. Today I worked for the Lunch Hour Follies, tomorrow movie sale Knickerbocker, Wed. auditions, Thursday Bella. I'll try to see Brecht. Take care of yourself and stay in town during the week. *Lebe Schnäpschen u. viehrungsvolle Grüsse* [farewell, little schnapps, and adulatory greetings]

    Knuti

Tuesday noon

Darling,

I just called Bravi. It looks like Philadelphia stands on its had. The critics write "Lady" is a show, which one sees once in a lifetime. The rave about the music! I guess, after that they will start to sell out for the rest of the 4 weeks. Lets hope. I told Bravi, as soon as you come back we come up to see the show. I have to see Dr. Glass in the afternoon. I rushed to the phone at 9 o'clock this morning, half asleep and bumped my toe. I hope it's not broken. Hurts like hell. I just got your wire. I am very happy, that Marlene makes suggestions. That shows that she is really interested. Dont worry about me Darling. I dont mind at all staying in the house alone. Time passes very quick. It's a lot to do here. Pete and *die* Beaubelle are working on the fence. It's a beautiful day but very cold. My fingers are blue! Now I am going to the unemployment to get my 18$ again. That idiot Osterman[?] was on the phone at 9 in the morning. That's all. So take it easy Darling. It looks after that what Bravi told me, that we can "eat" again. All my love.

Yours truly

    Wilhelmine

306 WEILL IN BEVERLY HILLS TO LENYA IN NEW CITY, 1 OCTOBER 1942

Letterhead: Beverly Hills Hotel

Oct. 1, 1942

Schnäubchen,

I hope you are not too much bored all alone. I am pretty much bored here and can't wait to get back. They are all so busy with their silly pictures and they cannot talk of anything else. And those dreadful agents! Well, it will be over in a few days.—Marlene had tried to get me free from the night curfew. The result was that I was called to the Police station where they told me I had no right to come to the military zone and I should get out in 48 hours. That was fine by me and I made train reservation for Friday. Of course, it was a misunderstanding and Marlene is arranging now that I can stay until Sunday or Monday, because we should have a few sessions with Bella whom we expect today. So this morning an army official called me this morning and gave me permission to stay till Monday, but I cannot go out after 8. Yesterday I was free for a few hours and called [Richard] Révy. He came to see me, but he talked so much nonsense that I threw him out. Then I met Brecht. He was just as dirty and unshaved as ever, but somehow much nicer and rather pathetic. He wants badly to work with me and the way he talks about it sounds very reasonable—but you know how long that lasts. Anyhow, I will try to see him once more before I leave.

Bella arrived today and we had a long session with Marlene. There are still a lot of problems to solve with that show, but Marlene is more and more interested and seems definitely set to do it. Well, we'll see if she signs a contract. Last night I had a long session with Edw. Justus Mayer (a first class writer) and Ira about Nell Gwynn.[1] I got a wonderful idea for that show and they are very excited about it and want to do it. It would be a perfect set-up. If I don't have to go in the army I think I will do a show with Brecht <u>for you</u>. He has enough money now for 2 years and could come to N.Y. We will leave Monday noon and arrive Grand Central Thursday 9 A.M. on the "Twentieth Century." I hope it is nothing serious with your toe. *Widisehen, mein doofi* [bye-bye, my little dummy]!

1. *In late summer 1942 Weill had outlined to producer Russell Davies plans for an operetta based on the life of the seventeenth-century English actress Nell Gwyn. As a performer in Dryden's plays and a mistress to the king, she was to be the central figure in a satire on monarchs and imperialism.*

1943

Weill returned to New York, but work on the book of "The Tinted Venus" with Bella Spewack stalled. In February 1943 she withdrew from the project, and Cheryl Crawford commissioned a new book from S. J. Perelman, while Nash revised his lyrics and wrote new ones to accommodate the switch from an operetta set in Victorian London to a musical comedy set in New York. But Dietrich found the new treatment "too sexy and profane," and she withdrew from the enterprise, leaving the team without a star.

During the winter Weill had stayed at the Hotel Ambassador to avoid commuting from New City while working with Ben Hecht on the Jewish memorial pageant We Will Never Die, *dedicated to the "Two Million Jewish Dead of Europe"—one of the first dramatic attempts in America to call attention to the Holocaust and to aid the four million more whom Hitler had promised to exterminate before the end of the year. With a cast including two hundred cantors, two hundred rabbis, four hundred actors, and the NBC Symphony, the pageant was presented to forty thousand people at Madison Square Garden; it was then restaged in Washington, Philadelphia, Chicago, Boston, and Hollywood, and also broadcast on radio.*

In May 1943, Brecht (with Ruth Berlau) visited the Weills at Brook House, and Weill and Brecht planned musical collaborations on The Good Soldier Schweyk *and* The Good Person of Szechwan. *Weill requested well-placed government officers to expedite his citizenship papers so that he could enter war-related factories in his capacity as chairman of the production committee of the Lunch Time Follies. In June Weill went to Hollywood to work on the film versions of* Lady in the Dark *and* Knickerbocker Holiday.

307 WEILL IN BEVERLY HILLS TO LENYA IN NEW CITY, [28? JUNE 1943]

Letterhead: The Beverly Wilshire Hotel / Beverly Hills, California

Monday

Darling,

Just a few words before I go to dinner with Bravi. I had a very nice trip. In the train from N.Y. to Chicago I met Bretaigne Windhust (you remember he came to our [house] with Josh [Logan] that afternoon when the Carey's were there).[1] In Chicago breakfast with Ruth Page and Tom Fisher. Then to the other train—and who was standing there? Tilly [Losch] with some old lady-chaperone, on her way to California. And not enough with that—the compartment next to mine was occupied by Barbara O'Neill.[2] So, surrounded by beautiful gals, I crossed the country. But it was fun. Anything was alright as long as it wasn't Lunch Time Follies. The air-cooling on the train didn't always work and it was very hot, but the food was wonderful and I slept a lot.

Here is everything as usual. I had to take an apartment with Windhurst, but Lee [Gershwin] called and begged me to live at their house. I might do it. Ira and Eddie [Mayer] are dying to do that show with me and it is very hard to turn them down.

They would be terribly offended. Tonight we meet Jed [Harris]. I saw some agents. Didn't call Marlene yet, waiting for Gadget [Elia Kazan]. Hear a lot about a girl who sings now in St. Louis; might have to go there on the way back.

That's all for the moment. Take care of yourself.

Love

Trrrrr. . .

1. *Bretaigne Windust (1906–60) was a movie director. The Careys are probably Harry Carey (1898–1947) and his wife, Olive. Harry Carey had acted in* You and Me.

2. *The character actress Barbara O'Neill (1909–80) had played Scarlett's mother in* Gone with the Wind.

308   WEILL IN BEVERLY HILLS TO LENYA IN NEW CITY, [3? JULY 1943]
Letterhead: Mrs. Ira Gershwin / 1021 North Roxbury Drive / Beverly Hills, California

Saturday

Darling, just a little *Morgengruss* [morning greeting]. Agnes de Mille and Gadget are coming to work at 9.30.[1] I haven't had a free moment since I came here, but at least I jump into the swimming pool twice a day. The weather is lovely, and I have a beautiful room here at Ira's and Lee who both are so sweet to me that I just cannot refuse to do that show with him. He had turned down a big movie deal with Kern to work with me (Lee is the one who insists that he should do a show with me especially since they heard the Nash lyrics!)[2] I haven't signed any contract yet, but I am working with Eddie Meyer on the story.—Marlene is out. She is a stupid cow, conceited like all those Germans. I wouldn't want her if she would ask to play it. But I have found a new upcoming singing star, a young Grace Moore who everybody is raving about. She is singing in St. Louis and I'll go there on my way back, the end of next week. Ogden [Nash] & Sid [Perelman] saw her in N.Y. and think she is the best we've found.[3] MGM, after hearing the new score, wants me to do a picture. I said: next year, maybe. They were completely overwhelmed.—I haven't heard from you since Tuesday, hope everything okay.

Love to Brookhouse, Wooley, Pete, Elisabeth [Meyer?] and my *Trröpfchen.*

Knut

Unser Häuschen is viel feiner [our little house is much nicer]

1. *A niece of Cecil B. DeMille, the choreographer Agnes de Mille (1905–93) staged the ballets for* One Touch of Venus. *Her major credits include choreography for* Oklahoma! *(1943), which launched her Broadway career, and* Carousel *(1945).*

2. *Ira Gershwin did collaborate with Jerome Kern in 1943 on the score for* Cover Girl, *starring Rita Hayworth, Gene Kelly, Eve Arden, and Phil Silvers.*

3. *In his note of thanks to the Gershwins, Weill reported that "the girl in St. Louis was a disappointment—too young and inexperienced. So it will be either Kitty [Carlisle] or [Vera] Zorina for Venus" (W–IG, 12 July 1943).*

After Vera Zorina and Gertrude Lawrence both declined to play Venus, the authors approached a young actress who had sung "My Heart Belongs to Daddy" in a small role in the Porter/

[FIG. 64]

Spewack musical Leave It to Me!: *Mary Martin. Following tryouts in Boston,* One Touch of
Venus, *as it was now called, opened at the Imperial Theatre on Broadway on 7 October 1943,
directed by Elia Kazan, conducted by Maurice Abravanel, with choreography by Agnes de Mille.*

[FIG. 65]

*The cast included Kenny Baker, John Boles, Sono Osato, and Paula Laurence. It was an instant
hit and ran for 567 performances in New York.*

*In November Weill returned to Hollywood to begin work with Ira Gershwin on an original
film musical,* Where Do We Go from Here? *No correspondence from this period has survived,
as Lenya accompanied him; they rented a house at 881 Moraga Drive. Friends recall that
sometime during this period Howard Schwartz was killed in a plane crash, and Lenya was
inconsolable, "unable to eat or sleep for days." Lenya reported to Rita: "I think, time will pass
quick. I hope. There is nothing much I can do, except driving Kurt to the studio. But that's all
I want. I need a good rest. I am still having a tough time—but dont want to talk about it again
you had enough of that Darling and you were very sweet & helpful to me, the rest I have to do
myself" (L–RW, [3 Nov. 1943]).*

1944

*After returning to New York in early March 1944, Weill continued his war efforts, chiefly by
writing the score for* Salute to France, *a propaganda film produced by the Office of War
Information. Meanwhile, Gershwin and he had decided to collaborate on a musical version of
Edwin Justus Mayer's 1924 play* The Firebrand, *based on the life of Benvenuto Cellini. In
June Weill returned to Hollywood to work with Gershwin on the operetta and supervise the
recording sessions of the score for* Where Do We Go from Here?

309 WEILL EN ROUTE TO LOS ANGELES TO LENYA IN NEW CITY, 25 JUNE 1944
Letterhead: Santa Fe / The Chief

Sunday, 6/25,44

Trrräubi,

It is Sunday afternoon, it is pretty boring here on the train and I think I'll write you
a little letter to inaugurate the new typewrite ribbon, with red lettering! (it was very
niedelich when you had bought a whole box of typewrite paper to take along to Hollywood, the city of typewrite-paper. *Du bist übihaupt sehr niedelich* [you are altogether
very cute]).

Well, I slept from ten to eight the first night. I was a little sad, as I always am when
I leave you, and you looked very pretty at the gate in Grand Central Station. So the
next morning I sent you a little wire from Chicago, got a very bad hair-cut, met Ruth
for breakfast at ten and walked back to the station where I boarded the Chief at noon.
I exchanged the drawing-room for a very nice compartment; I just couldn't stand the
thought that I would occupy a room with three beds while other people have to sit up
all night. I'll never make a good capitalist.

I read all afternoon "The autobiography of Benvenuto Cellini" which I bought in
Chicago. It is quite a fascinating book, full of intrigues, jealousies, fighting and f.... He

was a real big-mouth, bragging, lieing, cheating, but with a great feeling of independance and an utter disregard of any authority. The amazing discovery is how little life and manners have changed in those 400 years. It is obvious from this authentic book that Cellini was quite unsympathetic, that Eddie's characterisation is very good and that Cellini should possibly not become the romantic hero and should not get the girl at the end. (He never wanted to get the girl in the first place).

In New City it is four o'clock now. S'ppose you are taking a little nap, or s'ppose you are playing gin with your sister-in-law [Rita]. Our train is two hours late and we won't get to Albucerque before 6. I am feeling fine. That four weeks' rest is showing now. I am much more quiet and relaxed and I am determined not to start worrying again. If the show is not ready for Christmas I won't break my neck.

Here is Las Vegas. I'd better go for a little walk and try to get some cherries.

No cherries, no nothin'. So I went to the dining car, had a salad and fresh rasberries, and now I lay me down to sleep.

So long, *Schnapspison, Knüsschen*

Schnubi

310T LENYA IN NEW CITY TO WEILL IN BEVERLY HILLS, 26 JUNE 1944
Western Union

DARLING I HOPE YOU HAD A NICE TRIP LETTER ON WAY BLUE SLACKS STILL AT CLEANERS LOVE = LINNERL

310 LENYA IN NEW CITY TO WEILL IN BEVERLY HILLS, 26 JUNE 1944
Letterhead: New City, Rockland Co., N.Y.

Monday

Tröööpfchen,

I s'pose you arrived this moring after I s'pose a nice and comfortable trip. Thanks for your wire. That was "awfully" sweet. After you had left, I went back to the apartment and took a bath. Then I went over to Gigi and waited for about an hour. Finally she arrived, ashgray.—We had diner together and then I went to see "Follow the girls."[1] Well, we dont have to talk about the "show" but I was very enthusiastic about Gertrude Niesen. She is a mixture of everything: Merman, Fany Brice and mostly May West.[2] Sings beautifully with a very deep voice and completely relaxed and like a fish in clear water. Maybe the "most" american girl on the stage. With a wonderful sense of comedie. The music is not worth spending a drop of ink, there is one song she sings: "I want to get married" which is kind of pattern song and which she does with really great stile and charm. So it was a very pleasant evening. You know, how exited I can get, when I see something good on the stage. But I saw also, how very, very different it is, when they sing songs. I dont think I ever can learn that. Or somebody would have to teach me. There were two exellent exentric dancers in it. And: Miss Baranowa![3] If I would have the power, no russian dancer would ever appear in a show on Broadway and speak lines. And she looks exactly like a too blond *Berliner Pfannkuchen* [doughnut]. Terrible. Has no appeal so ever. Well any way after the show, I thought of seeing Bravi, but then I decided to drive home. There was a terrific thunderstorm during I was in the theater and when I got on the highway the fog started and got so bad that I got home at 2:30! I drove about 5 miles an hour. On Saturday Gigi came out on the 5 o'clock train and we went over to Nancy [Anderson's] and played cards with R.H. [Rita, Hans?] and we. Nancy went to the movies with Hanne [Weill] and her girl friend. And yesterday (Sunday) afternoon, Kathrinn Deming had a big party for her 2 boys.[4] So we went over at five Gigi and I. Before we went, Bessie [Breuer] called up to ask me to come over to see the Steinbecks. But it was already time for the party, so we met down at the Demings. He was nice, but Gwen was all "Mrs. Steinbeck" and the pregnant Mrs. Steinbeck! So I didn't make much effort to remind her, that she once spent a weekend in our house. The hell with them. They stayed only few minutes and didn't even say good bye to me. So who cares. But one could see, Bessie did a good job.—They party started out terribly boring. But then Gigi started to dance as usual— and I went home to get some Bogie Woogie reccords and it turned out to be very nice. We stayed until 12:30!! At eleven, they all went down to the pool and swam. I didn't, on account of my shoulder. But Henrie [Varnum Poor] went in and all the boys and the high tor shop girls (who are very nice and gay) and Gigi of course. But it was nice and everybody had fun. Gigi of course grabed the youngest of the Deming boys (Bimmi) and left for the stables.—Nobody exept me saw it. So it was alright. Max Mab & her sister who is a fat image of Mab were there and Max told me about his play. Oh Darling it sounds awful. I am afraid he hasn't the guts to write a comedy. *Jetzt wird es wieder auf "Bedeutung" zurechtgestutzt* [now it will be pruned back again to give it "meaning"]. Well we see. Well Darling this is all the news since you left. Now we'll see what you have to tell. At the present moment Lester[?] is turning the hay. It was a rainy weekend. Today it is beautiful and I'll be a little neighbourly. Tomorrow Tuesday I'll go in for my routine singing, massage and Dr. And we all meet for the 5:30 train. No important mail. [Fritz] Stiedry's letter I answered. Do you want me to send you Leahs weekly statements?[5] Or shall I put them away. Horowitz got his letter.[6] Marc Conolly send 25.– for the dead Fish (I hope) dead.[7] Now good by Boy, take it easy for the first few days so your bloodpleasure stays normal and if you see the Revy's tell them, I'll write eventually.—Give my love to Ira and Lee and Gigi sends hers to them too. And *viele Knüsschen für Dich von Deinem* [many little kisses for you from your]

Weib

1. The *"burlesque musical"* Follow the Girls *starred Gertrude Niesen and opened at the Century Theatre on 8 April 1944.*

2. *Ethel Merman (1909–84) was the first lady of the musical stage, from her debut in* Girl Crazy *(1930) to* Hello, Dolly! *(1971), which was written with her in mind. Fanny Brice (1891–1951) starred in various editions of the* Ziegfeld Follies, *specializing in comic numbers. Mae West (1892–1980) appeared in several Broadway musicals before becoming a bawdy Hollywood star in the thirties.*

3. *The Russian-born ballerina Irina Baranova (b. 1919) had been engaged by Balanchine as one of the three principal dancers for the Ballets Russes de Monte Carlo.*

4. *Katherine and Harold Deming were neighbors in New City. They had three children, Barbara, Mark, and "Bimmi."*

5. *Leah Salisbury (1892–1975) was the authors' agent for* One Touch of Venus; *at this time she was attempting to negotiate a sale of the smash musical's film rights.*

6. *Jack Horowitz (1896–1962) was Weill's accountant.*

7. *Congressman Hamilton Fish ((1888–1991) had taken the German side during the years leading up to World War II and made a much-publicized visit to Germany as the guest of Hermann Goering. In 1944 New York's congressional districts had been redrawn, and Fish's new district added Rockland County. Maxwell Anderson led a campaign against Fish, which culminated in his defeat in the general election.*

311 LENYA IN NEW CITY TO WEILL TO BEVERLY HILLS, 28 JUNE 1944

Letterhead: New City

Wednesday the 28th of June 1944

Darling,

I got your very nice letter from the train (very cute). I thought, you couldn't stand it in that drawing room, I couldn't either. This morning I got your wire. I am so happy for you, and I hope, you can work well with Eddie. It's terribly hot right now and I didn't go in on Tuesday. I got sick and stayed home. Tomorrow I go and see [Dr.] Adler. Everything seems fine now. Yesterday I had the family for dinner. We had a nice coctail first and a nice Pinocle afterwards. Today I took it easy and stayed mostly in the house. There is very little new Darling. There was not one call for you, since you left. They must have all read in the papers, that you are gone. Rita was in "Venus" Monday with Friede Lustig[?] and they had to stand. it was sold out! in that enourmes heat. It wont stay that way "but it feels good." I took care for two hours of Alan. Then I visited Eden she is a very nice girl.[1] She is sick, can hardly walk. Max seems to tell everybody that he doesn't know, whether he can write the new play. He said it to Nancy, to Meg, to Eden. I dont know why he does it. Why for God sake does he have to write it at all. It's getting so boring. I havn't seen Meg since Sunday, when she came to the party. She seems to be busy with her sister. I am reading "Fair Stood the Wind in France."[2] I like it very much. There would be some nice material for the great poet.—Of course, I haven't heard anything from Speiser about rain.[3] I really dont care Darling. It's too much of a head ache. I will call Moss after the 4th of July. Maybe he is free for an evening. In case you do see Tonio Selvart, dont say anything too good about his room.[4] Tell him, it's a lovely room, but no good for you so ever, because you cant sleep there. It's too noisy. Just in case you do see him some where. I'll try to get rid of it as soon as I can. I really dont use it at all. The radio is in the dining room again. I can use it more in summer downstairs. Did they give you a nice room? I was afraid, you would have troubles. And how is Lee + Ira? We will have a long weekend. Hans stays out here from Friday till Wednesday. So you can easely imagine, what that means.—There was no mail except those two letters. When you are through with the Cellini book, I would like to read it. You think, you can send it? Hanne doesn't change. She is still "atrociously, heavenly" desinterested in nature. But that seems to be the stile of those girls. Her girlfriend was out here, almost exactly the same. They talked like a sister act. Well, what do I care. I care only for my *Träuby*. And because I care so much for my *Traubi*, I will help myself to bed and will have a divine sleep with heavenly dreams and heavenly *arschjucken von so viel* moskitobites [ass itching from so many mosquito bites]. You know Darling, when I answered Stiedry in German, I spoiled about four pages before I got those few German lines together. That's good. Now *lebe mein Schnäpschen*. I am looking forward to your letter. Love & nothing but love. Yours truly!

    Träubi

1. *Alan Anderson Jr. (b. 1943) was Alan and Nancy's son. Eden Friedman was Bessie Breuer's sister-in-law, the wife of her brother Julian Friedman.*

2. *"Fayre stood the winde for France" is the first line of the "Ballad of Agincourt" by Michael Drayton (1563–1631); Lenya is probably referring to a very successful novel of that title by H. C. Bates.*

3. *Maurice J. Speiser was a prominent Philadelphia lawyer;* Rain *is Clemence Randolph's 1922 drama adapted from Somerset Maugham's story "Miss Thompson." The musical version entitled* Sadie Thompson, *by Vernon Duke and Howard Dietz, originally was to star Ethel Merman; she dropped out of the cast and was replaced by June Havoc. It opened to mixed reviews on 16 November 1944.*

4. *Because Brook House was an hour's drive from Manhattan, during gas rationing and late-night rehearsal periods Weill and Lenya had rented a room from Selwart, who had been a member of the cast of* A Candle in the Wind.

312   WEILL IN BEVERLY HILLS TO LENYA IN NEW CITY, 28 JUNE 1944
Letterhead: Beverly Hills Hotel

Wednesday
6/28, 44

Träubi,

    I just came back from my first tennis lesson (8 to 8.30) with Harvey Snodgrass[?]. He was very satisfied with my "form." (Don't you like my "form"?). So you see I have started that old *fine-lebe* again. I had quite a time getting a room. I came to the hotel at 2 on Monday. There was no room free. I waited around for 2 hours, finally they gave me a little hole of a room, half furnished, without bath. It was hot and uncomfortable that I couldn't sleep at all and thought all night how stupid it was to have our "little grey house in the one street town."[1] Well, next morning I raised hell and got a very nice room, facing the garden, very quiet and pleasant. On Monday I had dinner at Ira's and a long talk with Eddie. He still has 2 weeks on the picture, but we can work every evening and week-ends. Ira, of course, is still trying to stall, but he has good ideas and I like his integrity and his knowledge (after Sid and Ogden!). He says: lets make this a "classic," not a one season show for Broadway but something lasting—and you know that goes down like honey with me. So I'll keep fighting his laziness because it is worthwhile. Yesterday, after having moved into my new room, I had lunch with Eddie. I told him about you. He said he doesn't know you as an actress, but as a "very charming girl" and if Moss & I think so, it is o.k. with him.[2]

    Now I go after Ira which will be more difficult. But I'll get it. In the afternoon I was at Ira's. He didn't want to work, so I swam and sunbathed. Then I had dinner alone at the hotel—and who comes in but Nannerl [Walter Huston's wife]. She seemed in very good condition and quite normal. We stayed together till 10, then I went *schniepeln.* Today I'll see Perlberg, then lunch with Joe [Alma "Jo" Révy] (she is very busy because Thomas has the mumps), afternoon Ira, evening Eddie.[3] Real busy-body, but don't worry, I take it easy.

[FIG. 66]

And how is my *Tröpfi?* How is everything in the house? Did you get the chain on the door? Do you feel alright? How are the singing lessons? You (and Pete) did a first class packing job. When I unpacked the big valise, I thought: *"Als sie aber ausgestattet waren . . ."*[4] The "Reporter" reports today that Ethel Merman has signed for "Rain," but Lee tells me [Rouben] Mamoulian left only Monday for New York and won't be there until Thursday. I told the Gershwins that you had been offered the part, but they say it sounds like something to stay away from.

Well, honey-pie, I'd better get dressed and get a taxi to the studio. I'll write again before the week is over.

Take care of yourself and watch those curves on the road!

Yours, for keeps!

     Knut

P.S. The weather is awful here. Cloudy, no sun. Of course, that's all Roosevelt's fault.

If you find the belt that goes with the brown gabardine slacks please send it.

---

1. *Weill is quoting the first line from "The Little Grey House," a duet intended for* Ulysses Africanus, *the musical that Anderson and Weill left unfinished in 1939.*

2. *Weill intended the role of the Duchess in* The Firebrand *for Lenya, but she was ill-suited for it, thus prompting considerable resistance to her being cast.*

3. *William Perlberg (1899–1969), the erstwhile personal assistant to Harry Cohn at Columbia, went on to produce many successful films, including* Song of Bernadette, State Fair, *and* Country Girl. *He produced* Where Do We Go from Here? *for Twentieth Century–Fox.*

4. *"But after they had been properly fitted out" is a quotation from "Stolz" (Pride) in* Die sieben Todsünden.

313 WEILL IN BEVERLY HILLS TO LENYA IN NEW CITY, 1 JULY 1944

Letterhead: Beverly Hills Hotel

Saturday, July 1, 44

Good morning, my darling. I had my second tennis lesson this morning (not so good), then *primi* breakfast (cranshaw melon, toasted rolls, *milade* [marmelade] and *Böhnchen* [fresh-ground coffee]), then a shower and now I want to talk to my *Blümchen* a little before I go to work.

It was only a week yesterday since I left New York, but it seems like much longer. On Wednesday I went with Eddie downtown to see that musical show "The Song of Norway" that made such a sensation here. It is a kind of *Dreimäderlhaus* about the life of Edward Grieg, with Grieg music—and too much of it.[1] It has all the elements of the theatre which I despise—including the Russian ballet. After the show we went to Ira's and met Marc and Minelli.[2] They are all very nice. On Thursday Ira and I spent all afternoon with Bill Perlberg at the studio talking over things for the picture.[3] It seems that Ira as well as Bill got terrific reactions to our score for "Where do we go from here." It has become what they call "the talk of the industry." Bill played for us the Rodgers-Hammerstein movie score which they wrote for him ("State Fair"). It is very weak and Ira was refreshingly frank about it and told Bill that he didn't like it. Bill finally admitted that our score is "in a class by itself."

In the evening I told Eddie and Ira in so many words that I didn't come to California to swim in the pool and that I want to start to working, otherwise I would go back home. The result was Ira started working yesterday with me and Eddie will work all day today, all day tomorrow and all day Tuesday, and promised to finish the picture in 10 days. I think that is pretty good after 4 days.

Ira and I played a lot of 16th Century music (madrigals, italian folk-dances etc.) and got very good ideas for the style of the score. We are now really working well together.—I got in touch with Bobby Lewis and will see Susanna Forster in a few days.⁴ I didn't see anybody yet (thank God), except Joe with whom I had lunch. Talked to Milly [Lewis Milestone] on the phone. He was almost dead two weeks ago—only Sulpha-Drugs saved him.

Leah sent a wire to call her which I did. It seems I was right again about that movie deal which [Cheryl] Crawford–[Jack] Wildberg wanted. It was a complete fake. Now it seems that the Stromberg deal is going through after all—which would be a triumph for me, and a much better deal too.⁵ In the meanwhile I got a new offer here by a producer who wants to outbid everybody. I am seeing him today. Also working on the financial and movie set-up for "Firebrand," but Ira and I decided to let [Arthur] Lyons handle it.

Hotel situation pretty bad. They'll throw me out here after two weeks and I don't know yet where to go. But something will show up.

Had a very sweet letter from my *Träubchen* on Thursday and was very happy to see that you take it easy and seem to have a nice time. That Deming party sounded like fun. I hope you have some guests for the long week-end which starts today.

The hotel is very comfortable and I have a lovely room on the first floor and very quiet. Tilly [Losch] is here at the hotel, but I haven't seen her—and have no intention to see her anyhow. I'll have to work very hard with Eddie and Ira because we all want this to be really good. I am trying to sneak in a swim in the Gershwin pool every afternoon.

Lebe, mein Schnäuzchen. Viele Knüsschen von deinem

Boy

1. Edwin Lester's production of Song of Norway *originated in Los Angeles and subsequently opened in New York at the Imperial Theatre on 21 August 1944. Das Dreimäderlhaus, with music by Franz Schubert, selected and arranged by Heinrich Berté, was first produced in Vienna in 1916; in 1921 it was staged in New York, with music arranged by Sigmund Romberg, under the title* Blossom Time.

2. Vincente Minnelli (1913–86) was active on Broadway in the thirties before becoming one of Hollywood's most successful directors of musical films.

3. Gershwin and Weill had finished the score for Morris Ryskind's screenplay of the musical film Where Do We Go from Here? *in January 1944, although the film wasn't released by Twentieth Century–Fox until May 1945.*

4. *Susanna Foster (b. 1924) had a modest career in film musicals, and at one time was married to the musical actor Wilbur Evans.*

5. *Hunt Stromberg (1894–1968) was one of Hollywood's leading producers; at MGM he made many films with Jean Harlow and Joan Crawford.*

314 LENYA IN NEW CITY TO WEILL IN BEVERLY HILLS, [2 JULY 1944]

Letterhead: New City

Sunday evening

Well Darling, I think I gave you a full report up till Thursday. I went in [to New York City] Thursday morning for my usual routine. You cant imagine <u>how</u> hot it was. I took Mimi[?] out with me and we met Hans on the train. Friday was quiet, nothing special. Saturday afternoon Margot Aufricht came for weekend. He couldn't come. We digged out a little swimming whole under the tree and today we all took a dip. It was wonderful. Last night we, Meg, Nancy, Hanne and myself went to a Red Cross party at Zukor's.[1] Of course, Mab and Bonnie in full dress were there for dinner already and we all felt quiet forlorn in that awful crowd of East Side New Yorkers, dancing like mad (one of those evenings were one could leave the place and be violently antisemitic).[2] So we all (I mean we four girls in one Buik) left and went up to Hans and had a drink. Mab behaves awful. I am not going to lift my little finger.—Last night, Dick Holliday called![3] As sweet as Maple syrup. Asking how you are and how you are getting along and so on. I said fine and that you are very happy with the new show. He told me, that Daly-rumpel [publicist Jean Dalrymple] is out. Finally after 10 month. I didn't say much about it and let him talk. Then I asked how the show is going and he said in that *arschficker* [butt fucker] voice of his: very baaadly. They evidently had a bad matinee and of course the heat does a lot of damage. But Mary [Martin] feels fine inspite of a severe laryngitis she kept on playing. I told him, I would come and see the show and he was begging me to let them know, so we can have dinner together. They dont seem to be overrun with offers—otherwise he wouldn't have called me. That old taktic not to give a dam, seems to work eternerly. Well Darling you see what's going on here on the place. Next weekend Florence Meyer-Homolka who called me comes out for weekend. She is having her second Baby in 2 month. I am very very happy to hear, that Ira is so enthusiastic about the show. Yes, I think it is worth while staying there and trying everything to make a classic out of the show. It certainly has everything in it for doing so. Dont do too much with your tennis. Take it easy Darling. I sent you your blue slaks and the brown belt. The blue belt is still at the cleaners. The other day I just cought my car in time. There was not a drop of oil in it. I bought a new stamp. 5 dollar. And Hans showed me bookkeeping. So I am so stingy now, that I dont want to spent anything any more. This afternoon Hans came down with Ritas friend (one of those glamorboys), Dr. Bernard[?]. It's really terribly, what she picks up. I have to stop that. I dont want them here on our place. Last night at Hanses, Dr. Brown[?] and Dr. Blankstein[?] came with Ritas niece. She got stuck in Sp.V. [Spring Valley] and Rita told her she should go to the Browns. So he grabed the chance and brought her home. He was very cool to me just told me, we have to come to the wedding next June! So I said, well we have still a little time left to talk it over. That would be a blessing, if she would get married. Tomorrow morning I drive it with Nancy, who goes for a week to Cape Code. I have a lesson at 12:30 then I'll see the Dr. and go back on the 3:50 train to stay out until Thursday. Well Darling, this is my report. Nothing exiting. I am waiting for your letter. You pro-bab-ly have much more goings on than I have here. *Und du wirst Dich auch ganz schön dicke tun* [and so you'll really lay it on thick].

Yes, Ethel Mermann has signed for "Rain." Speiser wrote me a letter. So what. But it was diplomatic to tell Ira, that they offered me the part. But Darling please, dont get yourself in trouble with Ira, if he doesnt see me in the part of the Duchess. I want you to be entirely free and unburdned when you work. And give Nannerl my love when you see her again. To Joe I'll write these days. And now my *Tröpfi*, *lebe* and write soon. Your letters are very *niedelich!*   *Knüsschens* oooooooooo   Yours for ever [flower drawing]

the five kittens are very cute and are fat and the eyes are open!

1. *Adolph Zukor (1873–1976) was one of the founders of Paramount and one of the most influential people in the film industry.*

2. *Bunny Caniff was the wife of Milton Caniff (1907–88), the creator of some of America's most beloved comic strips (*Terry and the Pirates, Steve Canyon*). They were close friends and neighbors of Weill and Lenya's in New City.*

3. *The producer Richard Halliday (d. 1973) was Mary Martin's husband at the time.*

315   WEILL IN BEVERLY HILLS TO LENYA IN NEW CITY, 3 JULY 1944
Letterhead: Beverly Hills Hotel

Monday, July 3, 1944

Träubi,

[FIG. 67]

I have been working two full days with Eddie and we have made great progress on the Firebrand story. Eddie is much better to work with than I expected. I thought he would be slow and unimaginative, but just the contrary—once we got into it he became quite excited, full of ideas, witty and very easy. And what a relief, after those amateurs I have been connected with lately, to have somebody who has that enormous experience, who knows how to construct and how to write a scene. We found a wonderful opening: a marionette show in the market square of Florence, showing the adventures of Cellini—and right in the middle of the marionette show we introduce Cellini himself. We are working out the story on the line of your suggestion (after having tried a few others, less good): we make Asconio, Cellini's young apprentice, a young man who is in love with Angela and who gets her in the end. It is not as easy as it sounds, but I think it will work out. The whole thing looks quite exciting and it looks as if it could develop into one of the most interesting projects I've worked on. It probably will become almost an opera because I hear music almost all the way through, except for the comedy scenes. Ira is still trying desperately to stall and to stay away from everything that smells like work. But as soon as I am through with Eddie, he'll have to start. I am trying to find a quiet working room, either at the studio or at the hotel, because I want to do a great deal of work on this score by myself so that when I go to Ira I have definite musical ideas. That seems very important in this case because the show depends to a great extent on the beauty of melody and on musical inspiration. Arthur Lyons says he can get me a room for any length of time at the Beverly Wilshire Hotel. I don't like that place too much, but the rooms are larger and I might find something where I can move a piano in and really work. I also heard about a small new hotel in Bel-Air which the Kobers are investigating for me.

Well, I started working on Ira and Lee about your playing the Duchess. I was alone with Lee and Minelli when I told them first. Minelli said immediately: well that seems to solve one of your casting problems. Lee asked me if I really feel you could do it since she never saw you on the stage. So I told her that I am convinced you are better for the part than anybody we could find etc. and also what Moss said. She was kind of non-committal about the whole thing, and Ira reacted about the same way when I talked to him. But they didn't protest or anything like that. So I think the thing to do is for me just to go ahead and bully them into it. I don't think they will seriously object to it and I can just use my power to force the issue since I am convinced that the first time they will see you in one of the scenes they will be entirely in your favour. For the next few weeks I will not talk much about it, now that they know what my intention is. Of course, they were both very much impressed about Moss's talking to Max Gordon etc. So I am very hopeful in this matter.

[FIG. 68]

I had dinner at Ira's Saturday and Sunday night. They are really awfully nice to me. I am still not quite accustomed to the climate here and a full working day like the last two days make me so tired that I have to go to bed early (which I am doing) and sleep about 9 hours. Today Joe takes me to the beach for a few hours before I go to Ira in the early afternoon. Tomorrow I work again with Eddie all day.

Leah wrote me that Cheryl had prepared a newspaper ad announcing the critics' award for Mary and me, but Dick Halliday objected and demanded that Mary's award has to be advertised alone!! So Cheryl will run separate ads, one for Mary and one for me.[1] That guy is getting more and more impossible. I wonder if I shouldn't write him a letter and tell him what I think about it. Jean Dalrymple is arriving here today and I will try to work out an ad for me without Mary, even if I have to pay for it.

Hans wrote me that the Insurance Company has accepted me. So it seems I am alright. And how is my *Schnäuzchen?* I expected a letter today, but s'ppose the mail is very slow now because of the holidays. S'ppose you're having a nice time tomorrow celebrating 4th of July as an American citizen.[2] Tell Max I got some more money here for Ham[ilton] Fish. Kurnitz sent him a check, also Marc and Ira.[3]

Now Good-bye, my love. Take it easy, and work on that voice—you'll need it.
Yours trrrrrruly,

Kurti

---

1. The advertisement reads: "Winner! New York Drama Critics' Award / Kurt Weill / 'Best score of the season' / One Touch of Venus."

2. Weill had taken his citizenship oath on 27 August 1943 and Lenya hers on 5 May 1944, so this was their first Independence Day as genuine "Yankee Doodle Dandies."

3. The screenwriter and playwright Harry Kurnitz (1909–68) wrote novels under his own name and detective thrillers under the pseudonym Marco Page. He wrote the screenplay for One Touch of Venus.

316 WEILL IN BEVERLY HILLS TO LENYA IN NEW CITY, 5 JULY 1944

Letterhead: Beverly Hills Hotel

July 5, 1944

Hello, me darling Caroline,

In a few minutes Mr. Jameson[?] will bring me a car, same Plymouth, same prize. Then I start on my daily routine: lunch with Eddie, afternoon Ira, evening both Ira and Eddie. I am glad I am getting a car; it makes it much easier. Lee told me there will be dinner for me at her house every night if I want it. (She has a bad cook now, but still it is better than that restaurant routine).

Well, Monday I went to the beach with Joe and within two hours I got a nice sunburn. I am feeling fine and healthy. We made great progress with the work the last two days and even Ira got more excited than I have ever seen him. Yesterday I got the idea to make Angela's original lover not an apprentice in Cellini's shop (like Ascanio) but a wandering street singer who sings ballads at street corners as accompagnment to the puppet show. That will give us a lovely ending when Angela goes off with the puppet show and leaves Cellini and the Duke behind. Another few days like the last two, and we'll have the whole story outlined and can start writing. I hope by then I'll get settled somewhere with a piano, probably at the Beverly Wilshire. Then I will work by myself in the morning, with Ira in the afternoon and evenings with Eddie.

On Monday walking home from Ira to the hotel a car passed me and stopped and who was in it? Burgess [Meredith]. I'll have dinner with him and Paulette [Goddard]. At lunch at the Beverly Wilshire I met Paul Green. They have a house on the beach and will call me. Another day at lunch I saw the whole Adler family including Stella and her daughter (an oriental beauty), and Kazan with Constance Dowling.[1] John O'Malley called today. I don't think I'll have time to see all these people once I have started writing. I told Ira that I don't want to stay longer than about 8 weeks and that he'll have to come to New York in the early fall, and he seemed to agree. Well, at the moment the show looks so exciting that it is worth while spending some time here on it. I wished I could transplant my nice working room from South Mountain Road.

Darling, what happened with oil for the furnace? Is everything okey in the house? Did you get your chain on the door?

I have to run now. Just wrote to Hans, Sid, and Ogden. Good-bye me darling.

Viele Knüsschen

Kurt

1. Constance Dowling was a minor actress, the sister of Eddie Dowling, a well-known stage actor, director, and producer.

Thursday morning

Darling,

I wanted to write you this morning before I go into town, but I got up too late and now I am in a huuuuury. So I have to leave it for tonight. I am having dinner with Bravi at Sardis. The rest tomorrow. I am very worried about your hotel. Will you get an other room? And then I am worried, that I dont get any statements from Leah now that I am doing all the bookkeeping. It's discourging.

Mit Handkuss und Beinkuss [with a kiss on the hand, and on the leg]

Dein
[flower drawing]

Written at the top of the letter: "(no mail for you)"

Friday the 7th of June [July]

Darling,

I found your letter from Monday, when I came home last night, after a terrible hot day in town. I had dinner with Bravi at Sardis and went to a movie (2 girls and one Sailor—very stupid and boring after those terrific notices it got.) So your letter sounds very good and interesting and after I read those "famous" last words: "it's one of the most interesting projects I've worked on" I knew you are in the groove again.—Of course I am very proud, that you even consider my idea to make Ascanio her real lover, but I honestly feel, you need that, because, then you have much more freedom to make Cellini as crazy and unreliable as he probably was. I cant tell you how happy I feel about Eddie. I was afraid too, that he would be dry and worn out by Hollywood. Ira is no problem for you anymore. You can handle him alright. I dont think it matters that he and Lee were non comitted about me, so were the Lunts and Guild before they knew me. I am not afraid of that. As soon as my feet hit the stage—I am safe as you know. I just have to get there. I am very pleased with Gauthier.[1] She is intelligent. I only should go more often for the beginning. I will do that, as soon as that terrible heat has ceased. Then I had a long talk with [Dr.] Adler and he understood very well. He said he doesn't intend to keep me for ever, he only knows, that those injections do me a lot of good and keeps a woman young especially in that critical age. After a month, I have to go there only once a week, which I will do, as long as we can afford it. It will help me for later years too. After all, I look like 30 and that's quite a accomplishment.

Bravi had nothing to report, except that Mary didn't have a cold, she did recordings and was tired. He gave her hell and she is alright now. Bravi thought it was very funy too, that there was no mentioning in the ads about you getting the awards. Please be nice to Dalrymple, she can help you to get publicity which you need more than anything. I was so mad, when they gave Carmen Jones the Bilboard award for the best score.[2] Those snobs. Especially what the did with that score. It makes me furious to think, how little they know about you. But maybe after the war you will have a chance to write operas again and then see what will be left of that Hillbilly show "Oklahoma."[3] That music sounds dummer and dummer every time I hear it. There is something about tradition and it cant be pound into poeple. It has to grow trough centuries. Evidently. So lets be patient and be grateful for the little white house we got out of spite of them not knowing your real value.

I hope, you get settled and find a nice room where you can work. Dont think about money Darling, do everything for your comfort. Will you please. There is only you and me and we always will have enough. There is nothing new from here. On the 4th of July, Bessie had a big party. So we all went. It was alright. Henri is nice. And she is just an old bitter woman. No wonder one gets bitter if one looks like her. I looked very pretty that day. All in white. Henry gave a fencing lesson. He was a champion. I didn't know that. Naturally I got it in no time and they all told me, how beautifully it looked when I did it. Good old ballet training.—After the party, Milton, Bonnie & Mab came to my house and we played Gin until 4 o'clock. I lost! 22 dollars to Mab. Thank God. She was so happy about it that she almost put it in the local papers.—She broke down and invited Hans, Rita and Hanne for dinner! Well, well. He [Maxwell Anderson] left the party. He is sick. His beard is growing and as his beard grows longer his dullness grows with it. I feel sorry for him. He is just a victim of his concit. He doesn't seem to get along with his play. How could he! He has nothing to say, what a good laxative couldn't do. He is a little bit like Darious [Milhaud]. The way he can *cack* [shit] music Max can *cack* plays. Did you know, that Quentin [Anderson] has been going to a pshychiatrist (I looked it up) (I dont know how to spell that) but you know a guy: 20 buks a throw since a year. Nancy told me. Well the result is pathetic. He cant talk at all any more and is frightened of poeple. What a healthy neighbourhood! I am eternally grateful to be born *in der Ameisgasse*. That takes care of everything.—

So Darling, you can see. I am doing fine. Tomorrow Florence comes out. I am busy. <u>Real</u> busy. How is the Revy family? Give them my love. I am glad you go to the ocean with Joe and have some fun besides working. (As long as it stays in the limit of not forgetting your [flower drawing] you know what I mean—)

I am driving to New City now to mail the letter, so you will have it by Monday. Nannerl send me a wire this morning saying: "I know, who is Duchess." *Ihr Wort in Gottes Gehör* [her word into God's ear]—

By by Darling, take care of yourself, you know you are essentionell for my wellbeing.—

love Linnerl

1. The Canadian-born soprano Eva Gauthier (1885–1958) specialized in unusual Lieder recitals, often including George Gershwin's songs on her programs.
2. Carmen Jones was Oscar Hammerstein II's adaptation of Georges Bizet's Carmen, with the action transferred to present-day America. It had opened on 2 December 1943, with Muriel Smith and Muriel Rahn alternating as Carmen.
3. As late as 1942 the Theatre Guild was still considering Weill to write the music for Oscar Hammerstein II's adaptation

of Green Grow the Lilacs, *which in the end became* Oklahoma! *(1943), Hammerstein's first collaboration with Richard Rodgers. Lenya and Weill both resented that* Oklahoma! *went on to outlast on Broadway both* Lady in the Dark *and* One Touch of Venus *and to usurp Weill's claim to originating the "musical play."*

319 WEILL IN BEVERLY HILLS TO LENYA IN NEW CITY, 7 JULY 1944

Letterhead: Beverly Hills Hotel

Friday, July 7, 1944

Darling:

On Wednesday I was just about to mail my last letter when your letter from Sunday arrived. I am so glad that you have week-end guests and that you are having a nice time. Don't bother about Mab. She probably means well, but she is tactless, cold and egotistic. In the end she suffers more than the others from her unability to make friends and to have a warm feeling towards people. Max is probably sweating out that so-called comedy of his. What makes it so hard for him is his dishonesty towards himself. He wants to be the great poet-playwright, but at the same time he wants to imitate the success of "The Voice of the Turtle," and he doesn't realize that one cannot write a "Voice of the Turtle" if one doesn't believe in it just as much as he believes in verse-drama.[1] But he is shrewd and a good technician and, God knows, he might put together another success play. But then—who cares?

I was very much amused by your report of Dick Halliday's call. In the meanwhile you got my letter in which I told you that he refused an ad featuring Mary together with me. Of course, he called because he wanted to know if we knew about it. They are scared stiff of me, and that's how it should be. I think you should go and have dinner with them one night and use your old trick which you play so well: to be friendly and disinterested at the same time. After all, we want her to play the show for a whole season more. The only way to treat those people is to use them just as they use us.

Here things are going very slow at the moment and I had to raise hell yesterday. On Wednesday night we decided that the Ascanio story is too pedestrian and that it might be better to try another way to make the love story between Cellini and Angela the main story because we are afraid of too much plot for an operetta. So I wanted to work on this idea yesterday, but Eddie is busy with his picture and doesn't make any attempt to finish it, and Ira doesn't want to work as long as Eddie doesn't. Lee who is very nice about the whole thing told me that Ira definitely wants to do the show, but that he is also a little irritated by Eddie's attitude. I am seeing Eddie for lunch today and I am going to tell him that I will give up the whole idea and go back to New York unless he finishes his picture next week.

There are more complications concerning the movie rights for Firebrand. This is again Eddie's fault. He should have [had] them ironed out before he asked me to come out here. We had a long meeting with Arthur Lyons yesterday and we have made a new proposition to Twentieth Century who own the rights. But there is always a possibility that they turn it down altogether. All this is quite depressing, but thank God, I am not getting excited and take entirely the *"leck-mich-am-Arsch"* [kiss-my-ass] attitude. If the whole thing blows up it has the one advantage that I can go back to my *Trrräubi* and my little grey house.

I still don't know if I get a room at the Beverly Wilshire next week. Lee insists that I should move to them if I don't find anything and I might have to do that although I would rather not. In the meanwhile I'll talk to Bill Perlberg today about a working room at the studio.

Sid and Ogden wired that they have found an unknown Anstey story (I had told them to read Anstey) which they are very excited about. I showed the wire to Ira and it made quite an impression. I wired Sid to let me know more about it.

Yesterday at last I got in touch with Susanna Forster. She was very cute on the phone, said she was dying to do a show and she has a kind of commitment for a show with [Sol] Hurok. I am having lunch with her on Tuesday.

I am having dinner at the Gershwin's practically every night. Tonight I am at the Milestones. I am having a car now which makes life easier. [Erik] Charell called and invited me for a cocktail party on Tuesday. He wants to tell me an idea. I wanted to go to the beach this afternoon with Joe and Thomas, but the weather is bad.

Now good-bye, my sweetie-pie. How are the voice lessons coming, and the massages? What does the doctor say? I hope you're having a nice time with Florence.

Much love and many *Knüüsschen* from your busy-body

Knuti

Ich bin auch geizig mit die Geldies, brauche fast nichts ausser hotel und car [I'm also pinching the pennies; I'm spending almost nothing except for hotel and car].

---

1. *The three-act comedy* The Voice of the Turtle, *by John van Druten, had opened in December 1943 and went on to run for 1,557 performances. It was the first small-cast play (just three characters) to become a smash hit.*

320 WEILL IN BEVERLY HILLS TO LENYA IN NEW CITY,
10 JULY 1944
Letterhead: Beverly Hills Hotel

July 10, 1944

Darling honey,

One advantage of this hotel is that I get mail on Sunday, So I got your long letter from Friday yesterday and had a good time reading it. I am so glad that you're feeling fine. I am feeling much better when I know that everything is alright with you and that you are having a good time. Please, by all means, continue with your cure at [Dr.] Adler's. I am sure it is good for you and you shouldn't even think of money in connection with your health.

Well, I spent two full days, Saturday and Sunday, with Eddie. I was in great form and so full of ideas that Eddie had a hard time digesting them as fast as they came. We had decided earlier in the week that we would cheat the audience if we would give the girl to another, minor character at the end (like Ascanio). The audience will rood for Cellini and Angela to get together, but the difficulty was how to do that without destroying the humour and satyr of Cellini's character. Well, I found it. We build in the first act to a real love story between Cellini and Angela with a real climax in the first act finale when he takes her away from the balcony. Then in the second act he is cooled off, more interested in his work, treating her badly, finally giving her to the Duke just where the play ends now. But then we play a last scene, one year later, at the Court of Fontainebleau where he is working for the King of France. It is the day of a reception for the Duke and Duchess of Florence. Cellini was unable to work since he had given away Angela. Now he finds out that the Duke didn't get anywhere with Angela who has become a friend of the Duchess. So the lovers meet, he promises to be good and faithful, but just before the curtain comes down he starts again fighting and flirting. And Angela exchanges an understanding smile with the Duchess.

We worked out the whole thing, then we went over to His Highness Ira Gershwin and got him a little more excited and finally told him that he has to start working today. He agreed with everything. The only time he got upset was when we mentioned that he has to come to New York with us at the end of August. That will be a tough job to get him out of that house! Well, that's a later worry.

My housing problem is still unsolved. Several people are working on the hotel here to let me stay, and so far they didn't tell me to get out. The Beverly Wilshire would take me if they had a room available. I just talked to Tola's secretary (he is in Russia!!), asked her about his house. She said it is for rent, but he wants 800.– a month and I would have to pay for the maid extra. Of course, it would be an ideal place to work in, but it is crazy to pay that kind of money. Sheilagh[?] and John[?] are just coming for lunch. They know about a little house I can have for a few weeks. Well, I'll find something. Don't let it bother you.

After lunch. Sheilagh and John told me their whole saga. It sounds like The Grapes of Wrath. This is really a terrible place for somebody who hasn't got a lot of money. We saw the little house Sheilagh had in mind for me, but it is free only for 2 weeks. I told the Lyons office they'll have to find a place for me where I can live and work, other wise I go back home and To hell with the show—just to put some pressure on them.

Lots of trouble with the movie sale of "Venus" which has been completely messed up by that stupid Leah. Bay the way, she is sending the statements here directly (last week was under 30.000.–). If one statement arrived after I left please send it to me so that I have them all together.

Friday I had dinner at the Milestones, last night at the Revy's. Both very nice dinners.

Now I have to go to work. Leah sent the ads for Mary alone. They look awful. Today they are supposed to have ads for me alone.

Good-bye *Pflänzchen*. Take it easy in this heat. Here we have continuously bad weather, cloudy and cool and stinking.

Viele Knüsschen,

Knuti

Please give Hans these papers.

321 LENYA IN NEW CITY TO WEILL IN BEVERLY HILLS, [11 JULY 1944]
Letterhead: Brook House

Tuesday morning (yes Sirie morning) 6:15

Darling,

It's going to be a hot day again, and we (Florence, who goes into town with me today) went to bed so early. I got your letters from the 5 & 7 of July the same day. It's the usual up and down. I think it's a wonderful idea to introduce a puppet show and I liked the idea of a wandering street singer very much but it might burden the love story too much. But on the other hand does Cellini have to be so much the center. Couldn't there be 4 parts equally importent? Be a little patient with Eddie. It might not only be that he is still busy with the picture, he might need time to get used to work again for Broadway and all that or do you think it's only because he hasn't finished his pictures? I hope, you soon get your room and piano. I would go to Ira for dinner, but dont stay up too long Darling and dont smoke too much. That's the idea, to get a car. I knew, you couldn't be without one. Drive carefully. It sounds absolutly frightening to meet the whole Adler family on one lunch. I am courious about Paulette and Burgess. Dont tell me, that Paul Green is doing the Rickenbacker pictures?[1] I never would talk to him again. Florence, who lives in California as you know, gave me quite a picture of that Sam Goldwyin organisation. That's no joke. And I dont trust *diesem Tiroler* [that yokel] from North Carolina *nicht ganz* [not entirely]. So, be careful. I am curious, how you like Susanne Foster and what chances there are to get her. Dont rush around to see all the poeple you know in Hollywood. It's just a waste of time anyway. I had quite a week-end. Mimi was here since Friday. She left yesterday. Florence came on Saturday as big as the "Musa Dag."[2] I thought of the story *"auf die Dame die beim einsteigen in den Wagen denselben umwarf"* [about the lady who tipped the car over when she got in].— One more month to go. She is awfully nice, intelligent and surprisingly well informed. It's fun to have her around. Saturday evening Kathrin Deming and Barbara came up after dinner and we played all the music from the movie, which they liked very much. Sunday Barbara Deming, who is a very nice girl came to play croket with us and stayed and stayed for dinner. We cooked, Lissy[?] was off and after dinner went all to Mab for a crabb game (which was very very boring!) Max came for dinner last night. Mab stayed in town with Bonnie. *Die sind beinah wie die beiden Ayax'n* [they are almost like the two Ajaxes]. He was very nice, you know nice and dull. He gave up the idea to write a comedy. So now he is looking for something else. He is reading Pushkin!—Not a bad idea. *Da haben shon andere davon gelebt* [others have already made a living off that]. So we listened to "information please" at ten o'clock to Mr. Swing and I felt myself married to Max at least 30 years.[3] In the afternoon Eden & Julien [Friedman] had a cocktail party. First wedding aniversary! It's utterly ridiculous and I am going to built a high stone wall sooner or later to keep *das spiesertum* [the philistine domain] away.—Darling, dont worry about the house. How can anything go wrong as long as Pete is around? At the present moment he is fideling in the garden, putting the tomatoes up on sticks and painting the sticks green! so they match with the landscape! One tire is worn out. I have to get a new one. I will go over tomorrow and talk to Viola[?]. I paid Dr. Atshley's bill. 60.– dollar. That wouldn't be much. But maybe there comes a hospital bill afterwards. Dr. Glass send a bill 20.– dollars. So I paid everything off. Darling will you please send Tonio a check of 50.– from the Hollywood bank. His address is: Tonio Selvart Hedges place 8540 Hollywood for June. But dont forget and I try to get rid of it by August. So for July we have to pay too. But as long as it is so hot, it's pleasant to go there and wash up during the day. 750.– I paid for the New City war bond. Max seems to feel awfully lonesome. I feel sorry for him. He is so *sture* [stodgy]. Does one have to get that way? He wrote another poem in the New Yorker, but it's all done without any emotion and real exitment for the course. It's written *wie am laufenden band* [as if on an assembly line]. (A propos *"laufendes band"*) stay away from Brecht. Life is too short. Well my Darling, that's all for today, this coming weekend will be a quiete one. No guest. Only Gin with Rita. So lets see, what your news are. Yes, I will have dinner with Mary one of the less hot day's. Because 95 degree and Dick Halliday *dash isch zu viel for 'nen einzelnen* [that's just too much for a single soul].

By by *Tröpfchen* take it easy take it easy

> yours
> [flower drawing] pretty?

1. *American war hero and airline executive Edward Vernon Rickenbacker (1890–1973) was an ace pilot in World War I, then headed Eastern Airlines.*

2. *The Musa Dagh is the mountain in the title of Franz Werfel's 1933 novel* Forty Days of Musa Dagh.

3. *The journalist Raymond Gram Swing (1887–1968), formerly a foreign correspondent, was a news commentator on foreign and political affairs.* Information Please *was a well-known radio quiz show.*

322 WEILL IN BEVERLY HILLS TO LENYA IN NEW CITY, 12 JULY 1944
Letterhead: Beverly Hills Hotel

Wednesday, July 12, 1944

My *Träubi,*

I suppose I'll have a letter from you later today or tomorrow. In the morning mail I got a clipping from the N.Y. Times Monday edition with a very nice advertisement for me. I think I told you that Leah has messed up the movie sale to such an extent that Stromberg has withdrawn his offer and we are now without any serious offer. It is alright with me because I couldn't keep the money anyhow, but it just shows again what I got my high blood pressure from.[1]

Well, I am just on the verge of getting Ira to start actual working on the score. I thought we would start yesterday, but we both didn't feel well (I had a slight cold; the weather is just awful here). Today I am fine and dandy. Monday night we had a very good working session at Ira's. It looks more and more as if "Firebrand" might become what you and I have been waiting for: my first Broadway Opera. Ira who keeps comparing it with Rosenkavalier, is getting really exciting every time I tell him that this show could be an entirely new combination of first class writing, music, singing and acting. You know how ambitious he is, and the aspect of writing the first real Broadway Opera exites him to no end. Of course, the step from this excitment to settling down to real work is not easy with him, but I think today or the next day I'll get him to the piano. The main problem with him is to get him out of that chair in his living room and to come to New York. His argument is, of course, that he spent 5 months in N.Y. for "Lady in the Dark," so it is alright if I spend some time with him here on this show. Several times in the last days I got very impatient about this attitude and said to myself: why don't I go home and forget about the whole thing. But then I had to admit that I would have a very hard time to find another subject like "Firebrand" and another combination of collaborators on my level like Eddie and Ira. So I suppose I'll stick it out. I am sure it will all be much easier once I have solved my housing problem. On Saturday I have to move out of this hotel. If I don't find anything else I'll move to Ira's. But there is a chance to get a room at the Beverly Wilshire or to find some Bungalow where I could work. I told Lee, Ira and Eddie that I will try everything to arrange good working conditions for me, but if I find after some weeks that I cannot work I would go back home. In the meanwhile I use my Linnerl's *Leitspruch* [motto]: take it easy, *lass es an dich herankommen* [sit back and let it come to you] and pipe down.

Yesterday I had lunch with Susanna Forster. You were right: she seems full of talent, youth and enthousiasm. She is very excited about my offer, but she has certain committments, and I'll get Max Gordon to start working on it. For Cellini we want definitely a singer to match her. We are thinking of [Lawrence] Tibbett, Nelson Eddie, James Melton.[2] If we can get two great voices for Cellini and Angela we can cast the other parts with singing actors.

Yesterday I went to Charell's cocktail party. It was very nice; I talked to Bemmelmans and Mimi all the time. Charell has a wonderful collection of paintings and drawings. He wants to talk to me about an idea. I get a new offer every day. They definitely offered now the Gaxton-Moore show to Ira and me.[3] Today I am having lunch with Arthur Kober and Granowski's brother who has an interesting idea, tonight dinner with John Huston.[4] In the late afternoon I go and see Burgess and Paulette.

So, you know everything now, my sweet, and I have to run.

So long, *Träubilein*. I kiss you,

How is Wooly? And Pete? And Polly? Who is mowing my lawn? Any vegetables? Love to all!

1. *Weill's tax problems were not finally resolved until 1948, when he and Lenya were allowed to establish a "collaborator partnership" for tax purposes. Because Weill's current income was then quite high, most lump-sum additional income, such as that from a film sale, would have been taxed at a very high rate.*

2. *Nelson Eddy (1901–67) was Hollywood's all-time favorite leading man in operettas, with limited experience on stage. The tenor James Melton (1904–61) had made his debut at the Metropolitan Opera in 1942.*

3. *William Gaxton (1893–1963) and Victor Moore (1876–1962) had played Wintergreen and Throttlebottom respectively in Of Thee I Sing; thereafter the comic duo teamed up again for Let 'Em Eat Cake (1933), Anything Goes (1934), Leave It to Me (1938), Louisiana Purchase (1940), and Hollywood Pinafore (1945). The last, an adaptation of Gilbert and Sullivan's HMS Pinafore by George S. Kaufman, produced by Max Gordon, closed after only seventeen performances on Broadway.*

4. *Alexis Granowski (1890–1937) was a screenwriter and film producer. Nothing is known about his brother.*

323 LENYA IN NEW CITY TO WEILL IN BEVERLY HILLS, [14 JULY 1944]

Letterhead: New City

Friday noon

Darling,

I just received your letter from July 10th. Of course I am worried about your housing problems. How can you get down to work and do a good job, as long as you dont know, where you will be. I dont think, it is a good idea for you, to take a house by yourself. Then you will have a hard time to find a maid to clean and all those things. Try to stay in a hotel and if you cant, well then maybe it's still the best to move to the Gershwins. I dont think it's worth while for me to come out it would make it even more complicated. And I wouldn't like to quit Gauthier. I dont see yet any progress in my voice, but I am sure a few more weeks will show something. It's a pleasure to work with somebody that intelligent. And she evidently has fun with me too. I am sure, you are wonderful (as usual) on the line out of the story and will work out something beautiful. I think you are right about Angela & Cellini, that an audience wants them together in the end. I only hope, Ira gets really hot about it. We played the music from the movie, as I wrote you before and I played it again, when Florence was here and it's surefire. You are a very good team. There was nothing out here this few day's. I went in yesterday and met Max on the train. Of course, [Howard] Rheinheimer told them finally about capital gains. He was very philosophical about it. They only thing he is concerned about is, where to find an idea. I told him about a wonderful artikel I just had read in the new Harpers Magacin about "Middeltown" Music—there is a whole play, going bak to the story of the five brother Ball, the founder of the city, up till the present war. A real calvalcade. But he said, that's a familiar story to him, coming from the middlewest, that he cant even read anything about it. Well there is nothing one can do about it. Hesper is in a camp and that seems to upset his system. One cant thing of all those thousand of children in Europe, homeless, without parents and here sit's that Elephant and worries about his daughter in camp which is expensive enough to support a family of 5. It's stupid. Well anyway, I went through my routine, then met Mimi who took me to Lùm Fang for dinner and I took her after wards to Venus. I bought two tickets, I wanted good seats. Well Darling, this show is in better shape than I have ever seen it. First of all, it was a very responsive house, not sold out, of course not, it's just too too hot, but an audience who really enyojed every minute of it. And so did I. The new cast is exellent. The two comidiens very funny. Ben Cutler is ever so much better (naturally not perfect after Kenny) and the new dancer for Sono is wonderful.[1] Does the walse much better then Sono. She doesn't look so beautiful in the Crippen ballet but is very very good in the bachanale. So that is a "capital gain." Maurice [Abravanel] (who didn't know, I was in the show) did a beautiful job. I didn't go backstage, because I looked awful after all day in town, hot and dirty and I would have had to say hello to Mary too, so I didn't go. But I talked to Nick Holdi and the idiot [Jack] Wildberg.[2] He said, I should tell you about the show, how they keep it up and all that crap. Nick seemed very confident about the pick up of the show and told me, that other show are way down. I believe it. Mary was in good form and they got about 8 !! curtains in the end. And you know what that mean. That means, they really like it. We got an Ascap check for 748.94 cts, which I will deposit in the Sp.V. [Spring Valley] bank, where we have only about seven hundred dollar left. I saw Aufricht yesterday too and we went up to the Bost studio to listen to the Greta Keller album.[3] Very good. Viennese Songs. This weekend will be quiete. The Baker-Reeves children are home (one can hear them through the woods) so I will be busy.[4] That's about all *Trrrrröubi*, dont worry a moment about me. I am getting "along famously." Boles was really exellent.[5] I wish it would be cooler soon, I cant stand that moist heat. Gigi has left and is on her way to California-Pacific. She'll call you.

Give my love to Lee Ira and Eddie. (I will look around, maybe I find something nice for Lee)

> By by Baby
> dont cry Baby
> your Linnerl's well off—in the little house
> Love [heart and flower drawing]

1. Ben Cutler (b. 1904) had appeared as the voice of God in The Eternal Road *and now replaced Kenny Baker as Rodney the barber in* One Touch of Venus. *Baker (b. 1912) was a regular soloist on Jack Benny's radio show. The dancer Anita Alvarez replaced Sono Osato (b. 1919), who had left* Venus *for a role in Leonard Bernstein's* On the Town.

2. Nick Holde was the general manager for the Broadway production of One Touch of Venus.

3. *Viennese-born Greta Keller (1905–77) was one of the leading cabaret stars during the 1930s. She recorded popular songs in different languages and appeared in a few films and on Broadway.*

4. *The fabric designer Ruth Reeves (1892–1966) had been the recipient of a 1941 Guggenheim fellowship for her studies of Inca art in Peru, Ecuador, and Bolivia. She lived near the Weills with a younger companion whose surname was Baker.*

5. *John Boles (1895–1969) had leading roles in Broadway and film, exploiting his good looks and rich voice. He played Whitelaw Savory in* One Touch of Venus.

324 WEILL IN BEVERLY HILLS TO LENYA IN NEW CITY,
14 JULY 1944
Letterhead: Beverly Hills Hotel

Friday, July 14, 1944

Darling,

I just put in a telephone call to you and while I'm waiting for it I'll write you a little letter so that you have some news from me on Monday. Yesterday I got your letter from Tuesday. *Sehr sehr niedelich.* I am glad you had a nice time with Florence and I laughed a lot about all the little *Witzchen* [witticisms] in your letter, especially that you felt you were married to Max for 30 years. That social life on South Mountain Road is almost like Hollywood, except that I prefer everything on South Mountain Road, even the people.

Well, the show is getting more and more exciting and I feel I have accomplished a lot these first 2½ weeks. We have now a complete story outline, and a very good one. Yesterday I had the first good working day with Ira. Of course, we didn't write anything yet, but we did a lot of eliminating, determining what not to do and we got much nearer to the style of the score. We decided now definitely to treat great parts of the score in real opera style, without any attempt to write American popular songs. The part of Cellini will be treated in a kind of grandioso arioso style and, as I wrote you before, the whole thing might very well become an Opera for Broadway—and you know how I would like that. I was so pleased with Ira yesterday. He knows so much about style in words and music and he plays up to all my ambitions as a musician. The next thing I have to do now is to find a musical style for this score which, if I find it, will be quite different from anything that I or anybody else has done.

—I just talked to you. Gee it was good to hear your voice. Well, I told you everything and tomorrow I'll wire you about the apartment. Darling don't worry about the part. The operatic music will be limited to Cellini and Angela. The Duke and Duchess will be written in comedy style. For the time being I don't want to talk too much about it. When the time comes I'll put my foot down. Of course, the question will come again when we start writing material for the Duchess. In the meanwhile I hope you'll see Moss, and make sure that he talks to Ira about you when he comes out here. That would be very important. Even if Ira doesn't believe me he will believe Moss.

Here is Eddie to take me to dinner. I'll cross my finger for that apartment. It is a lovely house up in the hills, more like South Mountain Road than Bel-Air. I would be all alone with a butler and could work all the time. And that's what I'll have to do if we want to write that show for a Christmas opening.

Good-bye darling. Thousand kisses from your eternal husband

Knuti

325 WEILL IN LOS ANGELES TO LENYA IN NEW CITY, 17 JULY 1944
Letterhead: Beverly Hills Hotel

10640 Taranto Way
Bel-Air
West Los Angeles 24, Cal.

Monday, 7/17/44

My *Träubenträubchen,*

Well, here I am in my house in Bel-Air and I think I've been damned lucky to have found it because in many ways it is an ideal arrangement for me. It is a lovely place on a hill side in Stone Canyon (which is the Canyon in back of Bel-Air). 2 acres of a steep hill, landscaped completely in South Mountain Road–style, covered with *"Efeu"* [ivy] (I cannot think of the English name), Azeleas, Rhododendrons etc., very much like our garden. The house is the most comfortable I have ever seen, even for California. It was built by a rich man for himself. He died some time ago and his sister (*eine mechuggene brazilianische Jiddenne* [a crazy Brazilian yenta]) is trying to sell it. Rudi, the Gershwin's gardener, asked her if she would let me live in the house until she sells it, and she was so impressed when she heard who I am that she agreed. She wanted 600.– a month, but when I told her that I need only one room (a large combined bed- and living room, wood pannelled, with cedar-closets and a wonderful shower) she said I can have it for 300.–. This includes the service of an old Viennese butler, a very nice guy, slightly drunk all day long, who makes my breakfast and cleans. He lived alone here in the house and is very happy that somebody is living with him now. The piano which I get tomorrow, will be in the lower living room which I can use as a working room. Doesn't that seem ideal?

The first day (Saturday) it was a little lonesome. You know: "wenn man an einen fremden Strand kommt" . . . [1] and I would have loved to pack up and go home to me darling Caroline. But then the next morning the sun was shining (the first time that we had sun in the morning here) and everything looked very nice and clean and the breakfast was beautifully served and I felt very elegant. So you can stop worrying. It will work out fine, and tomorrow I start writing music.

Of course, the day when everything went topsy-turvy (Saturday) Gigi showed up at the Gershwins with a 15 hour furlough, looking pretty awful, but very gay and amusing. I took her for lunch to Romanoff's, but then I had to leave her at the Gershwin's because I had to move out of the hotel to the new place and make all the arrangements. Later in the afternoon I went to the beach with the Révy's. It was too cold to swim, but I played with Tommy who is awfully sweet and my newest pal and then we all went to a fish restaurant for dinner. Yesterday I worked with Eddie and had dinner at the Gershwin's with the usual company which bores the s... out of me. Lee told me that Gigi went for dinner with Marc (who had already invited one of his glamour girls), then they all went to a chamber music concert (!!!) at the Kurnitz' where Gigi got drunk, as usual, Marc was busy with his girl, Lee took Gigi home and they talked until 5.30, then she went to bed. That's how she spent her last furlough. She is really a sucker.

Gee, darling, that Ascap check is terriffic. That means we are getting now 3000.– a year (250.– a month) from Ascap, and that ain't hay. The royalties from the show have gone down to about 1000.– on my part (500.– for tax account and 500.– for general account). I was very happy about what you wrote me about the show.

I am going to have a showdown with Ira today about you. On Saturday morning we had a conference with Arthur Lyons, just Ira and I, and talking about cast, Arthur (as we all had expected) suggested his sweetheart Kitty Carlisle for the Duchess.[2] Ira said: yes she is very possible, very good, very possible etc.—and that after he, Eddie and I had for weeks made fun of the Lyons-Carlisle affair and were all prepared if the name

Kitty Carlisle would come up, to turn it down. I was so upset and depressed that I didn't sleep all night. Of course, I didn't want to make a scene in front of Lyons, but I am going to tell him something. I talked to Eddie about it yesterday who was also quite upset, not only because he is all in favour of you, but because Kitty C. is so impossible for the part. I will tell Ira today, that we might just as well give up right now, if that is the way he wants to cast the show. I am determined to fight this thing through, and please don't say I should not. You know I wouldn't do it if I wouldn't be convinced that you are ideal for the part. If Ira wants to be bitchy in this matter, I am just in the mood to oblige him. But this point has to be cleared before we start working. I'll let you know what happens—and please don't worry about it. Eddie who is completely on our side is sure we can bully Ira.

So long, *Blümi*. It was wonderful to talk to you the other day and we do it again soon.

Thousand kisses,

Kurti

---

1. *"When one arrives on a foreign shore" is the opening line of No. 5 in act 1, scene 3, of* Aufstieg und Fall der Stadt Mahagonny.

2. *Kitty Carlisle (b. 1915) appeared in the thirties musical productions* Champagne Sec, White Horse Inn, Three Waltzes, *and* Walk with Music. *She also sang at the Metropolitan Opera and appeared in films, including* Phantom of the Opera. *She would marry Moss Hart in 1946.*

326 WEILL IN LOS ANGELES TO LENYA IN NEW CITY, [17 JULY 1944]

Monday 6 P.M.

Darling,

Just a word in connection with the last paragraph of my letter of this morning. I had a long talk with Ira. First I gave him hell that he agreed to Kitty C. He said he just wanted to be nice and it doesn't mean anything. Then I told him that he is the only one who doesn't seem to agree with you. He said he was sure that you would give an excellent performance and that it would be "exotic" and interesting casting, but that he has never seen you on stage and that he has always been reluctant with relatives and close friends for parts in his shows. So I told him that I am the same way, but purely as a showman I could assure him that it would be an enormous asset to the show and would give class and distinction. I was very firm and made him feel that he had to expect a fight with me about this point—so, of course, he backed down and said, it is up to Gordon. That's exactly what I wanted. I told him in so many words: that I had been waiting to find a part for you for years, that I was sure this is the part and that I am determined to have you play it.

I feel much better now since I had this open and frank talk. I am pretty sure we won't have much trouble with Ira any more. Maybe Lee, but that I can handle.

O.K. That's that! Now go on with your voice lessons, massages, hair treatment and beauty parlors!

I am waiting for Eddie to go to dinner. Am starved! Just rented a piano. Steinway of course, like a big shot!

So long, Duchess!

Knüsschen from your admirer

Kurt

327 LENYA IN NEW CITY TO WEILL IN LOS ANGELES, 18 JULY 1944
Letterhead: New City

Tuesday 18th 44

Darling,

It was so nice to talk to you on the phone. Now I am glad you found a house. I only hope, you havn't any trouble with keeping it in order. Is there any one in the house—who takes care of your loundry, breakfast and so on. You can see, how my worries keep on. But you are such a *döfchen*. And are you eating enough and do you sleep enough? I am asking that for later. You will need all your strenght when it comes to the orchestration and rehearsels. So please be economical with your health. I went to a 14th of July [Bastille Day] (what an idea) party to the Reeves in back of us, and spoiled my stomach with some kind of punch they mixed and I havn't been well since. Last night before dinner I had an awful attack of cramps so I had to go to bed right away. Now this morning it's all better and I am going into town with Julie and come back on the 5:30 train.[1] Our *kleiner arschficker* [little butt fucker] Dick called Saturday, to ask me whether he could write you a letter about the situation of Peter Pan.[2] Disney wants to sell now for the nice little sum of 250.000$. Nothing is worth that money. "He can take the motion picture bussiness"—He was, what we in Germany called: *"betro-petzt"* asked how you are getting along and so on.[3] I told him, I saw the show and apologized for not saying hello to Mary. Of course he asked me imidiatly how I like the new dancer, luckily enough that evening I was in, she got a real ovation, so I could tell him with a good conscience, how wonderful she is and how silly it is, (and that was said on purpose as you easely can imagine) to think that one cant be replaced, that this change of poeple keeps the theater alive and that the show is in better condition I have ever seen it. Well, he had to agree. I didn't have the feeling, that Mary was overrun by offers.—I am glad you liked S. Foster. I think she would be wounderful and a real discovery. (Of course, there is always Margie Brown[?]—) I am dying to see the open-ing of May West's show [*Catherine Was Great*] on July 27th and I have to ask Nick whether he can get me a ticket. I got the car creased and it needed a new batterie. The old one was gone. Tomorrow night I am going out with Florence (who has the pecu-liar desire to go to all low down night clubs—in her condition) so she asked me and a friend of hers Jonny Brighton? (a detective writer) to accompanie her.[4] I am not very keen about it, but it's only an evening. She comes out here on Thursday & Friday and I am going with her to Mount Kisko until Tuesday morning. I'll try to get some gasoline from Laiso [neighbor], so we can take the Yonkers Ferry and it's very near from there.

I think we will have a nice weekend. So Darling you see, it's *fine lebe* here too. The family is alright and it's alway lots of traffic in my ice box because theirs is too small to hold all the food for Ritas priceless collection of "glamorboys." Our morning glory came out and looks beautiful. Saturday evening I went to the Sloanes for dinner. Couldn't eat the lovely duck they had. Very bad. Lee wrote me a very sweet letter and a very funny one about the Speawaks [Spewacks]. They really should name themselves *"Spie-wachs"* [spit-wax]. Yesterday one of our little kittens died. The prittiest one. I brought her to Dr. Goebels in the afternoon, but there was nothing doing. Something wrong with her intestionel. So, Polly will have 5 more in no time. I havn't heard from Max & Mab. She went to the camp to visit Hesper. She'll call.

Darling, did you send the Money to Tonio Selvart. We have to pay 2 months. June & July. I will write him a letter and try to get out of it by August. If not, then we have to keep it for an other month. But maybe we should keep it anyway. It's cheap and you might need it. Or do you think, it's too unconfortable to work in there. I think so. But anyway, we have to pay those 2 months. So Darling you know, where I am over weekend. Saturday, Sunday, Monday. I am glad to get away a little bit from So. Mountain Road. I think, I wrote you everything. Our tomatoes are coming along fine, we had stringbeans from the garden, green peppers and you will come back just in time for the new potatoes. I havn't written to Joe & Richard. But it's an effort I am afraid to answer a Bedekker [Baedeker]. It's 8 A.M. now and I have to get dressed. Good by Honey, Sugar—take care of yourself! love

Linnerl

1. *Julie Sloane and her husband, the publicist William Sloane, were neighbors of Weill and Lenya's.*

2. *Evidently Dick Halliday was attempting to obtain the rights to adapt* Peter Pan *as a stage musical for Mary Martin, for which Weill would write the score. Disney made an animated film in 1953, and a year later Martin played Peter on Broadway in a version by Comden and Green, with music by Mark Charlap and Jule Styne.*

3. *Betropetzt is not a known German word; it may be of Yiddish derivation, meaning "upset, agitated, wrung out."*

4. *Johnny Bright (1908–89) wrote screenplays as well, including Mae West's* She Done Him Wrong *(1933).*

328 WEILL IN LOS ANGELES TO LENYA IN NEW CITY, 20 JULY 1944

Letterhead: Beverly Hills Hotel

10640 Taranto Way
W.L.A. 24

July 20, 1944

Träubi,

Here I am now well established in my new place and feeling really swell for the first time since I came out here. It is an ideal place for working, completely quiet and nobody around except Joe the butler who is working in the garden all day long. Yesterday I worked all day long and wrote some very good music for the show. Today I am doing the same, except that I have a tennis lesson at 1 P.M. Well, anyhow, there is nothing to worry about me. As long as I can stay in this place I am in perfect condition for working.

I wished Ira were in the same condition. He is trying every single trick to keep from working. At the present he pretends to have a cold, so every time before I go there he takes a medicine which makes him "dopey." You know those old Ira-tricks. But I'll get him to work in a few days. At the moment I have to work by myself for a few days to get a style for the whole thing. I must say that so far I have done about 95% of the work on the show. Last night again I had a long session with two tired old men, but I was so full of ideas and energy that they just had to come along. I had a wonderful idea for the first entrance of the Duchess, carried through the street in a sedan-chair

[FIG. 69]

("Sänfte"), preceded by a little band of negro boys; that's how she plays the first scene with Cellini. Good? By the way, I am using a new trick to make sure that you get the part. I am trying to get Walter Slezak to play the Duke—which means that they would need a European actress for the Duchess.[1] I also had a brilliant idea for Cellini: Don Ameche.[2] He looks just right, sings well and is not a bad actor.

As far as my social life is concerned, it is shrinking considerably since I started working. I was at a little party at the Revy's, but I didn't get there until 11 and it was nice and harmless. Friday I am supposed to be at the Kobers, Saturday at the Elmer Rice's, but I'll probably cancel both.

Just got your letter from Tuesday. So you know now that there is nothing to worry about me. The butler takes care of the laundry, suit pressing, breakfast and everything (all this included in the 300.- per month which is much less than I have to pay for a hotel room). I am eating very well, sleeping *primi*, swimming almost daily in the Gershwin pool and resting afterwards, and I think my blood pleasure is down to normal—at least that's how I feel. And you better watch out a little with what you're eating so taht you don't get any cramps, you *Schweeeeinchen* [little piiiiig]. Dick's telephone [call] is very interesting indeed. I suppose they are getting frantic for a new show. And that's good.—I am glad you are going away for the week-end, it will do you good and I am sure you'll have a nice time in Mount Kisko.—I sent Tonio's money yesterday for two months. But I do think we should get rid of it because we need a nicer place for me to work in when the show is in rehearsals. The contracts are being drawn for a Christmas opening, so you can imagine how I'll have to work. I would tell Tonio that he is free to rent to somebody else and we would pay him until he has rented it. That is fair.

I am so happy that you are having a good time. *Wahrscheinlich spielst du dich gewaltig auf ohne mich* [you're probably really showing off without me], but that is good for you for a change. All best to the family, Pete, Lissy, Wooly, Polly, Max, Mab, the brook and the bridge and a sweet kiss for my *Träubchen,*

Kurt

---

1. *Walter Slezak (1902–83), son of the great heldentenor Leo Slezak, was a very fine character actor on stage and screen.*

2. *A popular leading man of stage and screen, Don Ameche (1908–93) had just appeared in the Lubitsch film* Heaven Can Wait *(1943).*

Letterhead: New City

Friday 7/21/44

Darling,

I got two letters in a row. Which is pretty good for a busy body like you. Of course I am very happy about your housing arangement and 300.– is a cinch. And that old viennese butler sounds exactly right for you. And by now you are fully accostumend to viennese mentality—so there shouldn't be any problem. I am sure, you feel pretty important in the morning having your breakfast served by a viennese butler. I was very amused what you wrote about Gigi. Yes, she is the eternal sucker and a hopeless case. She is monotonous and *ein gefundenes fressen* [an easy prey] for Lee. Yes, the Ascap check was quiete a surprise for me too. In the meanwhile I keep the expenses down as much as I can. I'll send you a statement by the end of the month. I had to pay a lot of Dr. bills. But that will stop now. I will talk to Dr. Glass about my injections and I am sure, he can do exatly the same what that Royal Highness Adler does. He is such a prima donna and full of crap. He is away till end of September. Thank God. Now Darling, I am really upset about you, not sleeping a whole night just because Ira agreed with Lyons on Kitty Carlilse. What in the world did you expect of him? That he should take a stand right there in the office? Darling to push me through will need a lot of fighting and arguing but you have to do it without any emotion. If you have a sleepless night every time that question comes up, you wont get any sleep at all. I am fully prepared for fights. I mean Ira should talk about relationship in the theater. What the hell does he call it, when Lyons suggest his sweethart? So take it easy, he'll come around. I got your yellow letter this morning. I am glad you talk to Ira. He is such a weakling. He'll be probably the first one, if I turn out all right, to say, he always wanted me. And Lee shouldn't be difficult for you. I am having dinner with Moss coming Thursday (if he doesn't change it on account of M. West's opening, the same evening). He was very nice on the phone, but Charles [Alan] told me, he is feeling awful, going to the Dr. every day. It's really pathetic. I tried to get a ticket for the West show through Nick, but one has to by a warbond with the ticket. So sh-- I'll go later. I am very anxious to know, what kind of music you will write for the show. It must be wonderful for you to do something so different after Lady-Venus (which by the way is picking up beautifully). Whenever I think of Firebrand, I think of Hoffmans *Erzählungen* [*Tales of Hoffman*]. That has the same flavour for me. Bravi just called. I gave him your number, he wants to call you. He got an offer, I dont know what and wants to talk to you. Wednesday, we, Florence, Jonny Bright (he wrote the first May West picture which was based on "Diamond Lill" you remember?) a nice guy, one of those typical american talents— drinking like hell, crazy about "hot" music and weak as hell the same time. One of those "toughies."—So we started out at the Gladstone in Florence's room, where they ordered 3 martinis for each to beginn with. I drank one (Glass forbade any alcohol). Then we went to Cafe Society uptown for dinner and Jimmy Sava.[1] (Pretty boring.—)

From there we went to 52nd Street to hear all those blasting negro bands which bores the sh... out of me after 3 minutes. Then down town to down town Cafe Society! But that was worth while hearing Josh White (Libby Holmanns accomponist) singing a song called "strange fruit."[2] Beautiful! I was sober from drinking coca cola and Flo and Jonny had glasy eyes.—It's amazing how primitiv those americans are in their way of having fun. Well. at 4 A.M. the party was over and I slept at Mimis place to get up at 11 o'clock to take my singing lesson. In the afternoon, that was yesterday, I took Florence with me and today we will spend a nice quiet day and tomorrow we drive to Mt. Kisko (with Dr. Laiso's help—whom I bribed with two tickets for Venus—). We come back here Monday afternoon and go into town Tuesday. Then I'll will take 3 lessons a week now I got rid of Adler. My stomac is almost cured except a slight rash on my skin, which takes a few more day's to clear up. Well Darling this is about all. The pictures were taken at the night club around 3 A.M. They look it too. Now my beloved Darling *Tröpfi*, dont get exited, take things as they come, "be firm" though. You just have to hammer it in to their brains. What does a guy like Ira know so much about acting. It's not nesseccaraly my foult that he never heard about me.—But he is nice, just weak. So let's use his weakness.—

> by my honey, love and more love
> Linnerl.

---

1. *The comedian and mime Jimmy Savo (1896–1960) was particularly famous for his rendition of "River Stay Away from My Door" in the 1942 show* Wine, Women, and Song.

2. *Libby Holman, née Elizabeth Holtzman (1906–71), was one of the most celebrated torch singers of the 1920s and early 1930s. She also appeared in several Broadway shows. Joshua White (1915–69), accompanying himself and others on the guitar, was a popular recording artist. The song "Strange Fruit" was based on the novel by Lillian Smith (1897–1966)— a love story of a girl of mixed race whose life is ruined by tragic events in the South.*

330   WEILL IN LOS ANGELES TO LENYA IN NEW CITY,
23 JULY 1944
Letterhead: Beverly Hills Hotel

10640 Taranto Way
W.L.A.24

Sunday night,
July 23. 44

Darling,

The world news have been so exciting these last days that everything else seemed awfully small and silly compared with the events in Germany and Japan. For more than 10 years we have been waiting for what is going on in Germany now. There is no doubt that this is the real thing. I don't believe that there was an attempt on Hitler's life. He staged another Reichstagsfire to give himself a shabby excuse for the biggest mass murder in history. A desperate madman killing blindly. He might get away with it for another few months—and that is good for us because the greatest danger—a peace with the German generals, is now out of the question. I saw a picture by the Army

Signal Corps "Attack," photographed entirely in battle. It is about the war in the Pacific, the invasion of New Britain. It is incredible what these boys are going through, carrying with their hands their battle equipment through jungle, through kneedeep mud, always under enemy fire—quiet, modest, without fear or emotion. In seeing that one feels that one should stop complaining and worrying about the little difficulties as long as one has the privilege of continuing his normal life and work.

I had a showdown with Eddie yesterday, told him I would cancel the whole project and go home if he does not get out of the picture and starts writing the show. Ira is slowly starting to work, with lots of complaining and kicking. I have written some very good melodies, and the story is getting better every day. Today I went to the beach with Joe and Tommy, but it was too cold to swim. Dinner at Ira's, now to bed. The house is ideal to work, the butler very nice and I am a different person since I left the hotel. How was your week-end at the Meyer's? Gosh, wouldn't it be wonderful if Hitler were dead and the war over before I get back. What a party we will give! Good night, baby, and much love

     Kurt

Darling, in my wall closet where all my papers are there is a file "Contracts." Please take out of this file the contract between Cheryl Crawford and me for "Venus" and the agreement between Sid, Ogden & me and send me both. Also put the slip which came with the ASCAP check in the file "Ascap."

331   LENYA IN NEW CITY TO WEILL IN LOS ANGELES,
24 JULY 1944
Letterhead: New City

Monday 7/24/44

Well *Tröpfchen,*

That was quit a trip to the place where the sun of the republicans shines in full glory. We left Saturday at 10:30 (after we got our car filled up at Laiso's, no points—) drove down to Yonkers ferry (Tarrytown ferry takes only passengers) crossed the Hudson and arrived after an hour and a half at the "marble palace" of *"derer von Meyer"* [of the Meyer dynasty]! I didn't remember it as that pompous and old fashioned. Florence has developed into a very nice and human being. Homolka must have a good influence on her.[1] She has changed completly. You would like her very much now. Her father is an old tired man, whos main argument against Roosevelt is the fourth term. No matter who gets in as long as Roosevelt gets out. And she [Agnes] is a facist bitch. It was so silly after a while that we just stoped talking. I dont know anything about politiks anyway but they dont seem to know much more either. At least I have a good instinct. He is really an old gaga. Florence got so stewed up, that she started to cry at the table on Sunday and I had to take her upstairs. Nice going for a weekend! They wanted us to stay until Tuesday but we scrambed out right after lunch today. They are crazy about me, probably for the simple reason, that I dont give a damn for their money and gave witty answers when he talked about [Thomas] Dewey. So Flo stays with me until she has to go to the hospital. Coming to this place here was like entering the Paradise after those 600 acres of shit.—And then, there was a very nice letter from my *Träubi* with a wonderful idea for the entrance of the duchess. Wouldn't I like that? (The english word for *Efeu* is ivy.) Don Ameche is "the perfect" cast. He was wonderful in that last Lubitch picture with Gene Tierney (I cant remember the name) something with "Heaven".[2] He is a very capable actor with a good director. Slezak would be very funy for the Duke and good for me. I am afraid he is too tied up in movies. Have you heard anything about S. Foster? I dont think, this part is so difficult to cast even if you dont get her. If you get somebody like Ameche for Cellini you only need a good looking girl with a voice. And I think that can be found. I am really disgusted with Ira. For God sake, what is he waiting for. I can imagine, how difficult it must be to get those two "racehorses" going. Thank God you are rested and have enough energie to push them out of their lethargie. Your house sounds perfect and I am glad you eat and swimm and get some excercise with your tennis, (I hope not too much—). I am having dinner with Moss on Thursday. I still dont know, whether I get tickets for the May West show. We'll see. Darling there is nothing new on So.M.R. Can you imagine, I havn't seen Mab in 2 weeks. She never calls. The hell with it. It's just too boring. So Flo and I have a good time playing all the music we have, reading "strange fruit" and Thechow [Chekhov] short storys. The weather is still very hot and the garden pretty dry. But Pete, looking like Napoleon of St. Helena, with a sun hat and *"Gieskanne"* [sprinkling can] looks after every tomatoe. He cut some old branches of trees, cuts the lawn and is as useful as ever. Watches that his "little Madame" doesn't hurt her little feet. (he thinks I grew up in a palace and walked on velvet all my life—) So you see, "everything is going my way."[3] If I hear that stupid song once more, I am going to scream. That music always reminds me of that guy in Tirol, when our car didn't get up that hill and that Tiroler said—*"äh."* You remember? I wrote Tonio a nice letter about his apartment. I am sure, he'll understand. I wrote him, you cant sleep there on account of the noice and when you start to work on your show you need a quieter place. I wonder, how long you have to stay. Sometimes I feel lonesome for my *Träubi*, but it isn't bad. I hope, you dont love Thomas more than me. I am jalous. (But that you know—) Next week, we start to paint our living room. I am pretty exited. I am sure this time it's going to be nice. Hans and Rita are O.K. They always have lots of poeple. *Einer ist immer schöner wie der andere* [one is always more beautiful than the next].—Well Darling, it's now 11:30 and I better move into my beddie. I slept with Florence in one room because there wasn't any room in that 30 room house.—We laughed like hell. So tonight I will sleep fine. And that's my *Tröpfi*, who sees that I have a fine bed. Good by my *Blümchen*. I am down to 117 pounds. Very slim! Good night Darling. yours

Jenny Lind[4]
Lenya

1. Florence Meyer's husband, the Austrian-born actor Oskar Homolka (1901–78), had played Bill Cracker in Happy End *in Berlin (1929) and went on to a successful career as a character actor in Hollywood.*

2. *Gene Tierney (1920–91), an exotic, strikingly beautiful debutante, had a major career in Hollywood, financed by a family-owned company. Her most important roles included* Laura *(1944) and* Leave Her to Heaven *(1945); the film Lenya is thinking of is* Heaven Can Wait *(1943).*

3. *The penultimate lyric of "Oh, What a Beautiful Morning" from* Oklahoma!

4. *Soprano Jenny Lind, "the Swedish Nightingale" (1820–87), toured America in 1850 under the sponsorship of the circus showman P. T. Barnum.*

332 WEILL IN LOS ANGELES TO LENYA IN NEW CITY, 26 JULY 1944

Letterhead: Beverly Hills Hotel

July 26, 1944

Darling-honey,

Just after I had mailed my last letter I got your letter from Friday. I am so glad you are having a nice time with Florence. She was always one of the nicest American girls and lots of fun. Your trip through the different Café Societies sounds like fun too. I think Johnny Bright is the boy who wrote a very good play which Gadget was supposed to produce while we were working on "Venus" and he is supposed to be a very talented guy. The picture looks very three-o'clock-in-the-morning-ish, but your eyes are very bright and gay and full of pepp. Josh White sang for me many times in the "Lunch Time Follies" and his "Strange Fruit" is an old favorite of mine. I am very pleased that you are going out and that you spend week-ends with friends and get away from South Mountain Road a little. A propos South Mountain Road, Harry Kurnitz told me yesterday that all Hollywood is laughing their heads off about Bill Sloane having sold Hargrove's book, one the biggest best-sellers of the last 50 years, for 12,500.– to the movies.[1] It seems that he has also messed up a very big radio deal which would have assured a big income to Marion for years to come. He is known to be a very stupid guy and a horse's ass.

Well, yesterday was a red letter day: my threat to withdraw from the whole Firebrand project had finally success. Ira started working and we wrote in one session an opening chorus which sets the character of the whole play. It is a song of the hangmen, preparing the gallows for Cellini, written in a kind of Palestrina style. Here are the first lines:

When the bells of doom are clanging
For a man awaiting hanging
We face the facts without misgiving
One man's death is another man's living.

Doesn't that sound like Dreigroschenoper? That Ira is really talented. I think my capacity to get the best out of people will bring out an entirely new side of his talent this time. Eddie has been ordered by me to stay home on Sunday and write a complete outline of the first scene. He came through beautifully. What a pleasure to work with a real writer! I am sure he will write my next opera; he has everything for it. Well, you see, *Träubi*, "Here I go again." I am working very hard now and with great gusto.

Getting up at 8, working here by myself all morning, grabbing some lunch on the way to Ira where I start at 2 and mostly stay through dinner, then in the evening Eddie or Ira and Eddie. The working conditions are perfect as long as I can stay here at the house. The next problem will be to bring Ira to New York. I am working on that through Max Gordon who calls about twice a week. I want him to put in the contract that we have to be in New York not later than September. That will be the biggest fight with Ira.

Dick Halliday wrote me about "Peter Pan." It looks now quite possible that we can get the rights. His letter was nice, but a little reserved, which is alright by me. Not a word from Sid and Ogden. T' hell with them! The movie sale of "Venus" is a complete mess and I have given up the idea that it will be sold at all.

The weather continues being terrible. It is quite cold at night and in the morning, the sun doesn't come out until noon, then it is hot for a few hours and at 5 it is cold again. Maybe you could send me another sweater with long sleeves for the house (the blue one), also another pyjama (laundry is very slow) and if there are some panties left. And please put in the piano scores of "Johnnie Johnson" and "Silbersee."

Another thing: could you call Rose Bogdanoff[?] at the Lunch Time Follies (I think Bryant 9-8180). I left in one of the drawers the piano score and parts of the orchester score of "Eternal Road" (at the L.T.F. office) and I think some other music. Please make an appoinment with her to get it back.

Now to work! Good-bye my honey-chil' and all my love,

Knuti

1. See Here, Private Hargrove (1942), the best-selling novel by Francis Marion Hargrove (b. 1919), was produced as a film in 1944.

333 LENYA IN NEW CITY TO WEILL IN LOS ANGELES, 27 JULY 1944
Letterhead: New City

Thursday
7/27/44

Darling,

I just got your handwritten letter. I was supposed to go in to town for my lesson, but I simply couldn't. It's so muggy and hot and my stomac still isn't quiet cleared up. I still have a rash which itches the Jesus out of me and makes me nervous. So I stayed in bed and tried to relax. At six o'clock I take the car and drive in to meet Moss for dinner. We go to Chodows [Edvard Chodorov's] for dinner. I am sure, it's going to be nice. And on the way home tonight, I'll pick up Flo who'll stay until Monday. Glass will come tomorrow to put me on a diet to get rid of that *"Nesselfieber"* [hives] (that's what it is. I had it for years when I was a "pickenini" child.) Your letter was very interesting for me, because you are so right in what you are saying. At the Meyer's was an very interesting french man. Dr. Winkler[?] (a hungarien of course) but he knew a lot about inside Germany and he said exatly what you say. That Hitler tries to save time and that whole atempt on his life was a faked one. The only good thing is, that the kill of so many generals and officers. The more, the better. I stayed in town on Tuesday, had dinner with Barbara Deming (a very nice girl), went to a movie "The Great McGinthy" a Preston Sturges picture (early one) very good, then I stayed in her house (old Herald [Harold] Deming Palace, on 19th Street). Next morning she took me along to see movie shorts (she works at the Museum of Modern Art in the Film Division) and we saw the "Birth of Lilli Marlene," that war song which was taken over by the British from the Germans. A very interesting short. I saw Lucy Mannheim in it, singing Lilli-Marlene in an English studio. An old jiddish Mamme. You see, there only girls around me and that is good and so peacefull. No troubles. (If you know what I mean.) Darling, I hope, you dont knock yourself out with Eddie and Ira. It'll work out eventually. You know. And it will be such a good show. I am dying to hear the music. Moss is very eager to hear about the show and how it's coming along. He called last night to make sure the dinner. He seems in a very bad state. I will hear tonight. I hope, those are the contracts you are asking for. Now goodby Darling. I have to get dolled up, which is quiet a curageous entertaking in this hothouse heat. Not a leave moves and the brook is so low, that the trout are almost taking a sunbath on the stones. I'll write you tomorrow again. Love, all my love to you

  my *Tröööööööööpfchen*

Bravi called me to give me your greetings Thanks Honey

334 WEILL IN LOS ANGELES TO LENYA IN NEW CITY,
28 JULY 1944

Friday, July 28, 1944

My *Träuben-Spatz*,

 Your report about the trip into the republican camp was very funny and I had a wonderful time reading it three times over again yesterday. I told the Gershwin's about it at dinner and they found it just as amusing as I. Isn't it strange how little all these people, with all their money, really get out of their life. They live in a continuous fear to loose their possessions, and that doesn't leave them any time to enjoy themselves and to "Live." I am very glad about what you write of Florence and how she has devel-opped and that she is staying with you. That is a splendid idea. When does she have to go to the hospital?

 Well, we are really working now and I got Ira pepped up to an extend as I have never seen him before. He said yesterday: if we keep the show on the scope of the opening scene it can become the greatest thing Broadway has ever seen. And you know what that means coming from him. We finished the Hangmen's song, wrote a very good scene of street-venders, selling "sweets and tarts" and "souvenirs of the hanging of Cel-lini" (I invented a wonderful street-cry, musically) and yesterday we wrote a chorus about "Florence" with the refrain

Ev'rything warrants
Our singing of Florence,
So Florence, we're singing of you.

It all has terrific "gusto," tempo and elan.

Yesterday I had lunch with Slezak. He looks perfect for the Duke and I think we have a good chance to get him. He is a nice guy—and a natural comedian, with a good natural singing voice and good old Viennese musicality. I will urge Max Gordon to sign him as soon as possible. I don't think we can do better for that part.

I am feeling wonderful now that we actually working and things are going so well. Many times these last weeks I thought of packing my things and going home, but I always felt that this could become a very important piece, much more than "Lady" and "Venus." Now I am glad that I stuck it out. Eddie is definitely finishing his job today so that the three of us can work together. It is a terrific job we have to do and I am not quite sure if it really can be done for a Christmas opening, with orchestration and everything. The score will have the size of an opera. Max [Gordon], at my request, wrote Ira a letter asking him to come to N.Y. with me and work there. Of cours, Ira refused flatly, and I must say in all fairness, from his point-of-view he is right. He can work much better here and he is afraid of the heat and his mother. But he is willing to come, as soon as we have definite production dates. So we decided to work hard for four weeks. By that time we will see if the show can be done around Christmas and accordingly make our plans for coming East. If I have to stay much longer after these four weeks you might make a little trip on the "Superchief." On the other hand, if we decide to postpone the show I'll come home in September.

I am lonesome for you too, many times. But those little separations have always proved to be very good. I am thinking of you all the time. You know how everything I am doing, thinking, working is closely connected with you, and I know it's the same with you. I thought it was sweet of you to say you are jealous at Thomas. It's the same as if I would say I am jealous at Polly. You know how utterly disinterested in people I become when I am working. I don't want to see anybody and the great advantage of my house here is that it is so isolated and nobody really knows where I am. Some times, on my way to Ira, I am having lunch with Joe and about once a week we go to the beach. She is nice and quiet and doesn't bother me when I want to be alone. Oh, by the way, when I came to my tennis lesson the other day Herr Fritz Lang was just finishing. He still plays a very bad tennis, still acting as if he were Tilden himself,[1] Micky [Lily] Latté still standing ready with the bathrobe so that the genius doesn't catch cold, he still climbing in his big open Buick car and she driving after him in an old Chevvy—*zum Kotzen* [enough to make you puke]!

Here I am spending all morning talking to you! Now I <u>have</u> to work. Good-bye, sweet, have a good time and thousand kisses

from your eternal lover

Kurt

---

1. *Bill Tilden (1893–1953) was one of the world's foremost tennis stars, a seven-time U.S. singles champion and a Davis Cup winner.*

Letterhead: New City

Saturday
7/29/44

Darling,

That was a rather gloomy evening with Mossy. We went to Jerry and Eddie Chodo-
row for dinner. They have a lovely duplex on 76 and Fifh. Av. Some funy lieutenant
fairy cooked a very good dinner, but some how the evening didn't come off. I looked
very pretty with my hair up, Moss said I should never wear it any other way. I myself
dont like it so much, but it looks very american—pretty-pretty and it's amazing, how
generalized their test [taste] is. We stayed until 11 and then Moss and I went to 21 for a
drink. That was nice. But he talked nothing else except about his troubles. He is in an
awful state. I am more than ever convinced, that this Dr. of his, is a great faker, if that
is [the] result of a seven! years treatment, I must say it's a crime to do that to a person.
He gets shocktreaments now every other day. That means he gets an injection, which
knocks him out completly and then his subconciouess starts to talk! Good God. It aint
human. I feel terribly sorry for him, but he believes so much in that guy that one has to
be very careful what to say.[1] He'll be here until the middle of Sept. then goes to Calif.
for 3 weeks. He asked me, whether I would come for a weekend to his place. I said
sure. So he'll call me again. Lissy leaves for a 2 weeks vacation on the 10th of August.
Around 1 o'clock we left 21 and I picked up Flo' in her hotel, then we brought Mossy
home. Flo bought me a pair of beautiful earings from Cartier! Lovely. Yesterday we
went to see Max who was in good spirit, because Dewey reputed [repudiated] H. Fish.
Mabs Mother was there.—Mab went to see Hesper so Max was nice and relaxed and
came down with us to play croquet. Tonight Bravi is coming out for weekend. So you
see *Träubchen*, not a dull moment. Yesterday afternoon Dr. Glass came and I had a
long talk with him. Of course he can give me those injections I got from Adler (10
buks a throw—) for much less and with out any fake. First he has to clear up my skin,
which looks like the last state of leprosy! Terrible. He'll be back Tuesday. In the meanwhile he put me on a diet and gave me pills to swallow. I am willing to swallow a
broomstick to get rid of that itch. We just had a nice little thunderstorm and the garden
looks nice and fresh. I made you a little statement about what I spend here the Month
of July. 665.21 dollars that includes 95.– Lissy, a telephone bill of 46.58, 80.– groceries,
Liquour bill and all those things. I think I did pretty well, Coming month I have to pay
100.– Dr. Adler and Pete about 60.– for all the things he buys for me continously. But
it wont be bad. Well Darling after this domestic excursion we move up to a higher
braket.—How is my boy? You know everything about the girly. Moss was very interested how your show is getting along, how Ira behaves, how you like to work with
Eddie and so on. I told him about Don Ameche and he thinks, he would be exellent. I
told him, how Ira felt, about "relatives" in a show and he said oh sh... I'll work on him
a little more, when I am out there for weekend. I do hope, we get him to direct the

show. I think, he will do it. I didn't say anything about it, because I dont know, how you feel about it. Darling, I have to finish, the family comes with the car and we got to Haverstraw shopping. Good by my honney child. Take good care of yourself and dont swimm out to far in the ocean. And dont be too fresh on land either.—

          many *knüsschen* yours for ever
          Caroline

*   1. Moss Hart was in analysis with Dr. Lawrence S. Kubie for most of his adult life. Kubie contributed the preface to the Random House edition of* Lady in the Dark *under the name of Dr. Brooks, the psychiatrist in the play. His scientific writings are reflected throughout the play, and he later listed its preface among them.*

336 LENYA IN NEW CITY TO WEILL IN LOS ANGELES, 31 JULY 1944
Letterhead: New City

Monday
7/31/44

Darling,

    I just drove Flo & Bravi to the 2 o'clock train and now I have a little rest. I mailed 2 sweaters, 2 pair of pyjamas, (panties you better buy in California, any of those mens store, your size is 32 waist) Silbersee, Jonny Johnson and Jasager. Flo is coming back on the midnight train. I had again to cancel all my lessons, I cant stand any clothes on my irritated skin. It takes so long to clear that up. Very boring. And it's so hot, that one can only lie around and do nothing. Your letters (one Saturday & one this morning) sound so good. And those first lyriks are unbelievable good "one mans death is another mans living" sound like: *Erst kommt das fressen* but less aggressive and much wiser.[1] It must be great fun for you now that it has started. And I am so happy about Eddie. What a relief after that sick Micky Mouse Sid. It all sounds almost frightening right.— Dont get nervous Darling about the time. No matter how long it takes, there is no time limit on that show. Any time will be right for it. It's no use to rush just because Max Gordon might get impatient. It's too an important show to rush. I am very happy, that you are feeling fine. I hope, you can stay in the house, as long as you need it. If you have to stay very much longer than September, I always can come out. I am really allright Darling and as soon as that terrible rash is gone, I will feel better. Your letters are so sweet and you keep me so well informed about everything, that I am practically with you. The only thing I hate to miss are those mornings when you sit at the piano and those wounderful tunes start to pop out of it. That always is for me one the most exciting time in the beginning of a new show. We always play your records from Venus [tryout] and nobody wants to listen to Marys records. Max [Anderson] called the other day and was very excited about H. Fish suing him and you all. He wants it so much. But he says, that bastard Fish want do it in the end. But he keeps on challenging him with wires. (I am only afraid, that he might get an idea for a play and will drop the whole business.) Mab appologized for not seeing me (like a kid fourth grade—) so everything is pink again. I showed Bravi & Hans the lyriks and they were crazy about it. I hope, you get Slezak. He would be so right and he should be Europeen. (Shouldn't he?—) I love the street scene with selling "sweets and tarts." I think Ogden and Sid will discover too late what fools they were. But I dont feel sorry for a moment for them. They need a flop more than anything. That'll be a life saver for them. But they wont even get that far. They simply wont find anything. I will call Rose (L.T.F.) [Lunch Time Follies] next time when I am in town, (which might be the end of this week) Every night, I am sitting on the "fence" waiting for Flo to scream—then I have to drive her to the hospital. She is expecting it by the end of this week. She is as big as a house and looks like she would get a whole regiment. But it'll be only one. They took x rays. In the meanwhile she eats an enormous breakfast, lunch, dinner, coctail, ice cream, beer, it's amazing to watch. I thinks, I'll be the one who will start with labor-pains.—Very funny what you wrote about Lang and Lattie. One dishrag taking care of the other. What a life. Our kittens are so sweet. One had a swollen face. Looked like a baby with mums. So Pete takes care of it. We havn't done anything yet with the living-room. We are still waiting for the tileman! They are all so busy. But we get to it even-tually. Darling, I better send you an other suitcase along. You will get in trouble, when it comes to packing. And we have so many here. I am not thinking about the movie sale anymore. I think, that "has lost it's glamour" and it's chances are really passée—[2] Doesn't make so much difference in our budget. Bravi told me, Mary is behaving alright and Dick keeps on *forzing* [farting] around and bla-blaing about everything. But nobody cares. And Ben Cutler seems to be a real tenor (just an octave lower—) Complains that Mary isn't proffessional enough. Aren't they all asses. I am glad for you being away for a while from that crap. I will call Cheryll and ask for the Haig & Haig [whiskey], just to give her a bad morning.—Sunday afternoon we went all to Quentin [Anderson] swimming. I couldn't on account of my skin. But the rest went. Waldo Pierce[?] was there. and he said it looks like in Deauville—it was so crowded. Well Darling *meine Äuglein* (*die* [my little eyes, which] right at the moment a little small are puffed up, like puffed wheat) *fallen mir zu* [are falling shut], so I'll say good night my love. Good night wherever you are and dont forget the girl you are found (or fond?) of—because you are the boy I am found of (very funy) but it's late Darling it's late—I'll drive to Sp.V. in the morning to go to the bank.[3]

Good night *Schweenchen* [little piggy]—*Dein*

Kleenchen—

---

1. *"Erst kommt das Fressen, dann kommt die Moral" (feeding must come first, then morality) is the famous refrain from the second finale in* Die Dreigroschenoper; *ironically, Brecht thought it his most memorable poetic legacy.*

2. *Lenya is paraphrasing the lyrics to "I'm a Stranger Here Myself," from* One Touch of Venus.

3. *"It's late, Darling, it's late" quotes from "Speak Low," also from* Venus.

Tuesday, August 1, 1944

Hello, girly,

I had two very sweet letters from you, one on Saturday (from Thursday) and one yesterday (from Saturday). You are a good girl with letter writing this time. I hope you got rid of that rash by now and I am sure Dr. Glass will do just the right thing. The last time I was in Hollywood without you for a longer period (in 1937) you had also a rash. Remember? *Weil du eben ein dooofi bist* [because you're just a little dummy]!

Thanks for sending the contracts. We just got the first draft of the Max Gordon contracts. Your financial statement is very *niedelich* and you certainly were stingy this month. Don't overdo it. The main thing is that you have a nice easy pleasant life. That's what we make money for. According to your statement we probably have saved some money this month. I wished they would tell us what's what with the taxes so that we know where we stand with money.

Poor Moss! I feel so sorry for him because I know how hard he is trying to snap out of it. I am a little worried it might take a bad end with him. But what can one do? The Chodorov party sounds kind of dreary, but I am sure you looked pretty with you hair up. I think it was awfully nice of Florence to make you such a beautiful present.

Well, Max is doing quite a job on the Ham Fish campaign. When you get this letter we'll know how successful he was, but he deserves great admiration for his courage and his capacity of being angry and doing something about it. Out here the newspapers carried big headlines about his fight. It was a very clever move of him to take [Wendell] Willkie as lawyer against Fish. The whole thing, besides being a very honest fight and a sign of great integrity on Max's part, is also terrific publicity—but I am sure that is quite accidental. It seems to be the American Way that you can do something good only with publicity. When I look at that eunuch Marc Connelly, spending his days between Badminton, Poker, Gin Rummy and movie houses, Max takes really the proportions of a giant.

Hurray! Eddie is though with Lubitsch and entirely free for the show. We are making very good progress and it's going to be a peach of a show. You will get an idea of Ira's enthousiasm when I tell you that he wants to work afternoons and evenings every day this week! You know what that means coming from him. And you also know how I like it that way. I am in perfect condition, sunburned and healthy and, I am sure with normal blood pleasure. Saturday I worked with Eddie all day and evening. Sunday afternoon I was at the beach with Joe and Thomas and had dinner at their house. Yesterday lunch with Arthur Lyons, then Ira from 3 P.M. to midnight. I have now worked out a complete musical scheme for the whole first act and we are trying to finish the whole first scene (15 minutes straight music and lyrics) by the end of this week.

I talked to Arthur about the movie situation of "Venus" and he will probably make an official offer. Then we talked about cast for Firebrand and I took the bull by the horn and told him that one of the reasons for my doing the show is that I want you to play the Duchess. He was awfully nice about it and got very interested when I told him who you are and that I want him to be your agent. So we have him on our side. At the moment it looks as if the only real resistance we'll have is Ira (and, maybe, Lee), but I got him to the point where he doesn't make any other suggestions for the Duchess any more. For Ira we need Moss and it is your job before Moss leaves for Hollywood to see to it that he will take a very strong stand for you here. In that case I have very little doubt now that you will get the part. What we are really fighting against is the American narrowmindedness in casting matters. When they hear the word Duchess they think of a big luscious woman with bosoms and they cannot imagine that a part can be played in ten different ways. But, as you know, once they see it they will believe it. So we have to get to the point where they see it. The rest is a cinch.

That's about all I can tell you today, my *Träubilein*. You are probably a busy body with the living room now and I hope you get yourself some invitation for the time when Lissy is away. Or would you rather stay at home? Oh, I bought myself two beautiful sport shirts yesterday, saw them in the window at Bullock's, Westwood, blue and baige, linen, with long sleeves (which they shorten), 10 bucks a piece! *Da staunste* [don't that amaze ya]! But I needed something like that for sitting around at Ira's. I spend very little money since I eat at the Gershwin's almost every day. My butler has always a plate with fruit in my room and I practically live on cherries, plums, figs and grapes— and you know how good that is for me.

Bye-bye, sweet! *Handkuss, gnä Frau* [I kiss your hand, gracious lady]

Your italian composer-husband

    Kurtio Weillissimo

338 LENYA IN NEW CITY TO WEILL IN LOS ANGELES, 4 AUGUST 1944
Letterhead: New City

Friday
8/4/44

Darling,

I didn't get a letter since Monday and I hope, nothing bad happened. Bravi just called me, his agent will talk to Billy Rose first and then he will write to you and let you know what Billy offers him. I tried to write a letter to Joe and Richard, but Honey, it's so hot, that we are dripping at 11 o'clock in the morning already. I stayed out here since last Friday and thank God I am feeling much better. I have no talent so ever for being sick. We Flo & I had dinner at Mab's on Tuesday, it was nice and thank God a little different on account to H. Fish. We listened to the reports coming in from Nyack. Well, it looks so, that he will be definitely defeated in the fall election. Those 3000 votes he was ahead of Benett dont mean a dam.[1] When Wilkie heard about the whole campaigne, he called up Max and said "hello Maxwell can I be your lawyer." He is quiet a showman too.—But Max is really excited about the whole thing. And of course, she [Mab] is practically moving in to the white house.—Florence cant stand her. She really did a lot of talking that evening. I just wrote a letter to Lee. She'll like it.—Dont worry about Moss Darling. I am sure, he will snap out of it again and I will do my best to stew him up enough, so Ira will have a hard stand to be against it. I just got your letter from Tuesday. Hurray. I am glad Eddie is free. If Ira wants to work afternoon and evening, that leaves me speechless. Well everything seems to go your way Darling and you know, how happy I am. Polly arrived yesterday with her family at the kitchen-door. For the first time. It was like a procession. Very sweet. She so to speak introduced them to the property. We will keep two and two Lissy takes for her grandchildren. I made a slight mistake in my statement. It's 168.– more, a [Dr.] Adler-check, which he evidently turned in later. I am not stingy Darling, but it should come down consider-ably. We really spent too much. Dont worry about your spending money on shirts ect. You have to look nice. And 10.– isn't too much. They cost here the same. I got a very nice letter from Tonio. Of course, he agrees. He wants me to use it without paying as long as he hasn't found anybody. I'll try, to find somebody. So we have one more Month to pay August. That's all. And I am sure, I will use the apartment in August, to change my clothes there, if that heat stays on. Flo is still waiting for the baby to arrive. We both wait and the car is parked in the yard, so we wont loose much time. If nothing happens until Monday, shell go to the hospital. Bessie [Breuer] called yesterday to an-nounce the arrival of a baby boy at the Steinbecks. She talked like she would have made it, produced it and the rest of it. She invited me for Sunday. George Davis is coming out. So I'll burry the hatchet and will see him. I always was kind of found of that old poop.[2] The family is fine. A little monotonous. But who isn't exept my boyly. As soon, as it get's a little cooler I have to get a few new clothes so I look nice in case I get the part. I am behind my singing lessons too. But I catch up, by the time you get here. Well my sugarpie, that's all for the moment. We went to the movies to see "Hairy Ape." Are they kidding?—By by, my love

       yours trrrruly
       [flower drawing]

(you will have to get a publicity man for Firebrand.   This time we must.)

---

1. *Augustus W. Bennet was Hamilton Fish's opponent and eventual victor, despite Fish's lead in the primary election. Shortly before the general election on 7 November 1944, Anderson sent letters to the editors of several Rockland County newspapers: "If we elect Gus Bennet to Congress a sigh of relief will go up all over the United States. For if we do that it will mean that the man who has fought tooth and nail against every advance toward international understanding . . . will at last be out of our national councils. . . . Hamilton Fish's name stands, and he has stood in Congress for twenty-four years, for all that is futile, silly, blundering, and inefficient. . . . He has been saying the Rockland opposition to him comes from Communists and pinks. This he knows is a lie" (reprinted in Anderson, pp. 190–92). On 26 March 1988 the New York Post published a photograph of Fish on his one-hundredth birthday, holding an Oliver North poster "in support of the indicted Iranscam marine."*

2. *Lenya had been a frequent visitor in the early 1940s at 7 Middagh Street in Brooklyn Heights, a big brownstone house that served as an experiment in communal living. Residents, in addition to Davis, included at various points Paul and Jane Bowles, Carson McCullers, Oliver Smith, Gypsy Rose Lee, Peter Pears, W. H. Auden, and even Thomas Mann's son Golo. Benjamin Britten described the housewarming in 1940: "Peter and George Davis were doing a ballet to Petrushka, up the curtains and the hot-water pipes—an impressive if destructive sight" (p. 899).*

Friday, August 4, 1944

Good morning, my darling Caroline, it is a lovely cool and sunny morning in Stone Canyon. As usual I got up at 8, showered, shaved, had my breakfast and read my *paperchen* [little paper] in the patio, now I want to talk to you a little, and then on to work. We had a very good working week, finished the big chorus number about Florence (a sort of Tarantella, italian and spanish at the same time), then we wrote the slow procession, a slow march à la Weill for Cellini's walk to the gallows (his first entrance). His enemy Maffio is singing:

> At this point no angel, devil or genie
> Can save the neck of Benvenuto Cellini.

Then Cellini's apprentices appear, carrying his sword on a platter, singing

> Our master
> has met desaster.

They are followed by 6 beautiful girls in black, singing

> We models of Florence,
> disciples of grace
> are viewing with abhorrence
> what's now taking place,

and the whole chorus sings pianissimo

> The fateful bell has rung
> And soon the trap is sprung.

Now we are working on Cellini's first Aria, with the title

> I have loved, I have lived, I have laughed,
> And now the time has come to say farewell.

It all shapes up beautifully. I am so happy that you liked what I told you about the opening. Of course you would like it even better if you would hear the music (what a silly remark!). I think we can finish the first scene early next week and then go right on to the second. We lost one day again with Ira's lazyness, one of those days when I had to sit around from 2 until 9.30 (!!!) before he started. So the next day I raised hell, and now he is alright again. Between us, the family life at the Gershwin's is worse than ever. Lee seems to be icecold to him, leading all by herself a kind of empty, superficial life without really enjoying anything except seeing those same 6 or 8 people every day and giving parties. Poor Ira! He really should be so grateful to me that I inspire him to do things he really loves doing. He should work all the time, otherwise he'll crack up. I have the feeling he is having a better time writing this show with me than he ever had in his life. Darling, I am so sorry that you still are suffering from that rash. Please be very careful and do everything Dr. Glass tells you. Look at me, what a *Klugi* [smarty]

I am with my health. I had to laugh thinking of you sitting and waiting for Flo's baby to arrive. That's so much like you, and very *niedelich*.

The papers out here reported only that Max had been sued by Fish, and I didn't know that we all are partners in it. Of course, I am very happy to be sued by Fish, and I wished we could drag him into court. I bought the New York Times from Sunday yesterday and found the whole story, with Max, me, Milton [Caniff] and Henry [Varnum Poor] being threatened by that bastard. The result of the primaries is very encouraging, but we'll have to put up a very stiff fight for November and I hope to take part in it because it would be a tarrible indication of the post-war world if we couldn't succeed to keep this hateful bastard out of congress. Please tell Max that the Hollywood Democratic league offered me a series of recording which they used in a similar case out here very successfully, playing them over and over on the Radio. I will hear them next week and see if we can use them.

I read to Ira the parts of your letter where you talk about his lyrics (I did it purposely, knowing his vanity) and it went down like honey and syrup, especially the part where you say that we should take our time and not rush it too much. He liked that. But it's good that he knows that you are not rushing me, just in case that he might have had that erroneous impression.

I had a long letter from Sid. You remember they sent me a very excitied wire and a letter from Ogden, saying that they had found a story which they were absolutely sure about and they were working like mad. Well, Sid now confesses that they gave up the idea after a few sessions and didn't work at all. The usual story, Ogden is only interested where they could have lunch and is having a wonderful time in New York. God, was I clever to grab the Fireband and to go ahead with it. Can you imagine how I would go crazy if I still would try to get a show out of those two windy brains?

Elmer called again and I had to accept the invitation for dinner tomorrow night. I am going with Eddie. On Sunday I'll probably make my weekly trip to the beach if the weather is nice. Today I take my landlady for lunch to keep up friendly relations so that I can stay in the house. I think she has secret hopes that we might buy the place which, of course, we won't do. She still hasn't taken any money from me for rent because her lawyer has to work out a paper. But she is so impressed that I am working here.

And now hail and farewell, my princess of pure delight,[1] and a *Knüsschen* on every spot without rash,

     Knuti

I went with Eddie to an exhibition of Eugène Berman who is a wonderful man for the sets of Firebrand. I wanted to buy for you one of his designs for Dreigroschenoper (Paris) but he didn't have any.[2]

---

1. "The Princess of Pure Delight" is a song from Lady in the Dark.

2. The Russian-born painter and scene designer Eugène Berman (1899–1972) is best remembered for his outstanding designs for ballet and opera, including four productions at the Metropolitan Opera (1951–62).

Monday, August 6 [7], 1944

Darling sweet,

I just got a letter from my *Blümchen* and I am so glad that you are feeling better. I was a little worried because I saw in the papers here the reports about that heat wave in the East. It's getting pretty hot here now during the day, but the evenings and nights are cool.

There isn't much to tell today. Eddie, that louse, is secretly still working on the picture, but I just force him to give us enough material so that Ira and I are not held up. These first two weeks I have been actually writing with Ira I got more work out of him than in 6 weeks last winter when we were working on the picture. And better too. So I gave him the week-end off, for his poker game. On Friday night Louis Shurr [agent] wanted me to see a performance of Traviata to hear a very good baritone from the Met (Alexander Sved) singing, as a possibility for Cellini. He has a beautiful voice and is not a bad actor, but I don't think he is young enough. Irina Greco sang Traviata, not bad at all, but the rest was terrible. I took Joe along who hadn't seen an opera in eight years. Saturday I spent all afternoon at the Gershwin's pool and got that bronze color which you like so much on me. In the evening dinner at the Elmer Rice's. Betty [Field] looks quite worn out, but is very nice. He is a nice old gaga, still telling the same stories about his travels in Russia. On the whole a pretty dull evening. Yesterday we were at the beach all afternoon. So you see, I certainly combine work with relaxation, just as I did it last winter.

Slezak invited me for dinner next Monday, with the Werfel's [Franz and Alma Maria]. He is not available for rehearsals until January, so, unless our show has to be postponed, we'd have to look for somebody else.

Darling, two things I want you to do. 1. we have to register for the November elections, so that we can vote. Please ask Max what has to be done. 2. Do you think you could send some whisky to the Gershwin's? If you would get all the bottles that must have piled up at the Crawford office and take them over to our liquor store and ask them to pack and send it. Or would the liquor store sell us a case and send it out? It would be a nice gesture because I am eating there so much. If it is not possible it doesn't matter. It was just an idea.

Very sweet what you write about the kittens. And everything else. I have to run now. Bye-bye, my Linnerl, and all my love,

Kurt

Letterhead: New City

Tuesday
8/8/44

Well my *Tröpfi*,

There are very, but very little news from the homefront. After a nice weekend, with Flo & Mimi (we had dinner at Jerrys [tavern?]) we drove to town yesterday and Flo went to the hospital. I just talked to her and the new citizien is on the way.—In the evening, I saw the May West show. What a stupid play. It's about the worst acting I have seen in a long time on any stage. And Howard Bay went to town on interior decoration.[1]—And that old warhorse May West is amusing for the first 10 minutes and from there on it's ashes—ashes. After her first lover (she has about 20) embraces her one fears the stagemanager has to come with a broom and picks up the pieces. She is all glued together. The house was full with an illustrous? audience—Billy Rose, Corbett etc. and one could hear the wind in the paper[2]—The whole thing looked like an old russian Operetta we had in Zurich "Fatinitza" some 20 years ago.[3] I had dinner with Bravi, who hasn't heard from Billy yet. But he doesn't care. And why should he? Mary fainted on Friday after the Westwind scene and the understudy had to go on. The ice for the cooling system came too late and it was 95° in the theater.—Cheryll was out of town.—Mary is still sick, I just talked to Bravi. The house was good last night. Arent you glad to be away from that mess? Nothing can be done with those asses. I hope, Cheryll has a good solid flop next year and disappears from Broadway. That would be a blessing. I want to get that letter in the mailbox before the mailman arrives. There came a form to be filled out for the incometax for 1941. Something happened there. They missled your application. So I have to go tomorrow and see [Jack] Horowitz about it. Dont worry (I hear him say). But dont really, it will be alright. He just has to check on it and send it again. I feel much better and go to town 3 times this week for my singing lesson. Lissy leaves on Thursday for a 2 weeks vacation and I might stay in town next week for a few day in Mimis apartment, who goes away for 2 weeks on Sunday. But I dont know yet. You know, how I hate to leave the house. The records are all in folders and look very pretty and neat.

By by my love! I hope, everything is O.K. on the western front.

yours truly

Karoline

1. One of Broadway's busiest designers, Howard Bay (1912–86) had created the sets for One Touch of Venus, *as well as* Little Foxes *and* Carmen Jones.

2. Possibly the British actress and comedienne Leonora Corbett (1908–60), who came to the United States in 1941 to appear in Blithe Spirit *and remained in New York until her death.*

3. Fatinitza *is an operetta composed in 1876 by Franz von Suppé (1819–95).*

Wednesday August 9, 1944

Darling,

Thanks a million for the package. The warm pull-overs came just in time because I caught a slight cold, have a head-ache today, not bad, will get it over in a day or so. I am now in a real working routine and making good progress. This week I had to raise hell with Eddie to get him to work. I feel just like a slave driver. Ira is functioning fine, because Lee is on my side, driving him to work.

Well, what do you say, they started recording the music for "Where do we go from here?" and will start shooting in 3 weeks. Of course, they don't want us to interfere. Perlberg's secretary called in the last minute to ask if we want to come over for the recording of "Morale," but we were right in the middle of working, so I said no. The show is more important. They will do anyhow what they want with the picture score. Bill [Perlberg], whom I called yesterday, told me it is one of the most thrilling numbers he has ever done. He had to make some cuts, but Ira and I have great confidence in him. But I wouldn't know where to start if I wanted to explain the abc of musical direction to Mr. Ratoff, that greatest fake of the century.[1] So we just have to hope that Bill will defend our score (which he will) and the material is strong enough to withstand the Ratoff onslaught.

Lee told me she got "a darling letter" from you and she talked awfully nice about you, and "that we have to do something about the rheumatism of yours." Richard told very sweet stories about you at the Zürcher Stadttheater, your activities as a flower [girl] in *Parsifal* and a page boy in *Tannhäuser*.[2] My favorite story was the one when you and some other *"Ballettratten"* [ballet apprentices] were sitting in a dark room with Révy and having intellectual conversations when an old employee of the theatre came in and asked "What's going on here" and you, *frech wie Oskar* [sassy as ever], said: *"Schwule Stimmung"* [fairy time]. *Sehr typisch für mein Pflänzchen* [quite typical of my *Pflänzchen*].

Tonight I am going for dinner to the Arthur Schwarz's in their new house.[3] Tomorrow I am giving a little party. I want Lee and Ira to see the German set for Tudor's "Romeo and Juliet" and I want to see "Fancy Free" myself which they play the same evening.[4] So I am taking the Gershwin's, Marc and the Revy's for dinner to Chasen's and afterwards to the ballet. Very elegant, ain't it? Next Monday dinner at Walter Slezak's (with Werfel's). I want to make sure that we'll get him if we have to postpone anyhow (which is quite possible).

Darling, I hope that heat wave has eased up a little and you're feeling better and got rid of the rash. Now I am going to lie in the sun a little while before I am going to Ira. I have been working since 8 o'clock this morning.

So long, *Schätzchen*.

> *Je t'embrasse mon chou-chou* [I kiss you, my pet],
> Kurt

1. *Gregory Ratoff (1897–1960) came to New York's Yiddish Theatre via the Moscow Art Theatre. In 1930 he went to Hollywood, where he was usually typecast as a foreigner with a thick accent. In the mid-1930s he began to direct. In 1939 he directed Ingrid Bergman in her first American film,* Intermezzo—A Love Story.

2. *Lenya recalled that the first "scandal" of her career was an incident during her apprenticeship at the Zurich opera house, when she pulled off the dead Titurel's beard in* Parsifal *by mistake.*

3. *The composer Arthur Schwartz (1900–1988) was best known for his "Dancing in the Dark," with lyrics by Howard Dietz, with whom Weill had collaborated on* Lunch Time Follies.

4. *The great British choreographer Anthony Tudor (1909–87) choreographed* Roméo et Juliette *for the American Ballet Theatre to selected pieces by Frederick Delius, particularly suited to Eugène Berman's splendid Renaissance sets. The New York City Ballet had premiered* Fancy Free *on 18 April 1944, with music by Leonard Bernstein, choreography by Jerome Robbins. It was then expanded into the musical* On the Town, *which opened on Broadway in December 1944.*

343 LENYA IN NEW CITY TO WEILL IN LOS ANGELES; 10 AUGUST 1944

Letterhead: New City

Thursday
8/10/44

Oh Darling,

What a show that promises to be. Those lyriks really sound like François Villon.[1] I havn't been so excited in a long long time. You will have to keep the doors locked, so no late comers can disturb that beautiful first scene. I love "we models of Florence" and "our" master has met desaste—and that aria "I have loved ″ ″ lived ″ ″ laughed" could be Don Giovanni. Boy-oh-Boy—Yes, my imagination gives me a slight hint, what kind of music you write and still, it will be a surprise even though.

Darling, dont fight too much for me. I dont want you to get too much distract. This all sounds so wonderful, that it will be exciting for me whether I am in or not. (I mean, if it becomes too complicated for you. You understand.) Moss hasn't called and I am afraid that means, he doesn't feel all too good.) But I will see him before he goes to Calif. which wont be before middle of Sept. anyway. Yes, it was the right thing to skip those two Ajax's for the time being. I never believed, they would find a story without your help. And I am kind of pleased, that they discover that too, as it seems. Ogden is really incredible and I think completly lost without you. The same goes for Sid. I am happy for you, it couldn't be better. And Darling, dont get nervous if Ira hangs around sometimes. Dont forget, that you are an exeptional case on vitality. You have to understand, that Ira is just so much slower. I dont even think it's laziness, maybe he really needs a day or two between lines.—So dont be impatient. I am sorry about their home-life. It sounds so dismal. I dont think Lee has discovered yet, how much fun it can be, to be alone in a house and read. There books printed for the purpose to be read. Doesn't she know about it? How dreary it must be, to see the same poeple over and over again. To live constantly on the suburb of one self, leads to utter emptiness. It aint my idea of happiness. They really should have the disency and seperat. It would be a blessing for both of them. But there is nothing we can do. I am sure, Ira knows how good you are for him. But he cant admit it, at least not often, it would be a sacrilage (I think that's the word) toward George. But you dont need it. I told Max about the records, but he thinks, he doesn't need them. He said, he wants to stick to facts. It's more impressive. And Darling, dont bother in finding a story for him and you. He told me, you wrote him about a book, you thought would be an idea for him. But he forgot already, what the book was. So, the hell with that.—He will find something which fits his idea of "religion & theater"—I am sure.—Well, Flochen [little Florence] has an other boy. 9 pounds and 3 ounces. Born Tuesday afternoon. I talked to her on the phone. She feels fine. I am going to see her Friday. I was in town yesterday and came out with Hans in the afternoon. Lissy left this morning and will be back on the 28th of Aug. which will be on a Monday. It will be quiet nice to be alone for a while. Dont worry Darling. I am all right. My rash is still with me and Glass will come today to look me over. I might have to go to a Hospital to get some tests made, to find out, what causes it. I am allergic to something and it's too difficult to find out with just not eating much. But it's complitely harmless and baby's can get it. So dont worry a minute. I called Horowitz and he'll take care of the letter. Well Darling, that's about all for today. I got a very nice letter from Nannerl Huston, with a long paragraph about: how unimportent life is and how wonderful death is. I dont know why, but I get terribly hungry, when I read things like that. So I went to the kitchen and made myself coffee and felt, there is nothing more beautiful than life. God has to agree with me on that. You think he will? So long Boyly—you are O.K. and I am not far from it. My sincerest devotion Sir, yours for ever

     Caroline

1. Brecht had based several lyrics in Die Dreigroschenoper *on German translations of the fifteenth-century French lyric poet François Villon. The translator sued Brecht for plagiarism, provoking a minor public scandal and winning a 2½ percent share in royalties.*

344   WEILL IN LOS ANGELES TO LENYA IN NEW CITY, 12 AUGUST 1944

Saturday, August 12, 1944

My *Blümilein,*

    I had two very sweet letters from you, one on Thursday and one today and I am so happy that you are so enthousiastic about the work I am doing. This score ought to be damned good because that is the only excuse for staying away so long from my Linnerl-*Weibi* [wife]. I am rather proud of getting out of Ira the sort of lyrics which I want and on a level which he has never reached before. I am doing the same with Eddie, and both Ira and Eddie are following me blindly—I really don't know why but it seems that I have become so sure now of my craftmanship, of my theater knowledge and of my taste that I would take a dominating position in almost any combination. You can see clearly from the little samples of lyrics which I sent you that this will be more "my" show than anything I have done so far—even though I don't get credit for anything but the music. But I am sure that Verdi or Offenbach or Mozart contributed as much to their libretti as I do without getting credit for it. This is a part of a theatre composer's job to create for himself the vehicle which he needs for his music.

We finished the whole first scene in two and a half weeks which isn't bad if you think that it is as long as the "Columbus" sequence in the picture which took us about 10 weeks. Ira is in full swing and we work afternoons and evenings most of the time. With Eddie I am having some troubles. He finally got through with the picture, but now he is tired. Yesterday he brought in a scene in which he just had copied the original play—so I tore it into pieces and gave him a detailed outline, almost word by word how to do it. As a matter of fact I had an idea last night of writing it myself (which I might do). Well, anyhow, Eddie was so overwhelmed by the accuracy and sharpness of my criticism that he accepted it without any hesitation. He really is an awfully nice guy—and so talented.

My little dinner party was very nice and Ira was very glad that, after lots of kicking, he came along to see the ballets. Darling, that "Romeo and Juliet" of Tudor's is a masterpiece. It was one of the greatest artistic experiences I've had in a long time. He has a way of expressing ideas and emotions in movements of the body which can only be compared with the effect of good music. The whole thing is sheer beauty. I want to see it with you as soon as we have a chance. The set and costumes by Berman are absolutely wonderful and I will make a great effort to get him for my show because I see my show in the same "Boticelli" style as he did the ballet. That much heralded "Fancy Free" is (what I suspected after those hysterical outbreaks of the critics) a phony. It has a charming idea and is, on the whole, rather fresh and amusing, but seeing it after "Romeo and Juliet" is like hearing "Oh what a beautiful morning" after the Mattheuspassion [Bach's *Passion According to St. Matthew*]. Well, anyhow, I got rid of my social obligations for a while. The dinner at Slezak's has been postponed, thank God, and I hope I won't have to see anybody next week. I don't remember if I wrote you about the dinner at the Schwarz's, with Arthur at the piano for 4 hours.

Today Ira and I are having lunch with Perlberg at Twentieth Century and will probably hear some of the recordings for the picture. Then we will work until Ira goes to the poker game and I want to go to bed early and probably stay in bed to-morrow because I am having a slight case of intestinal flue today which I want to get rid of as quick as possible.

Darling, I am a little worried about that rash and that it doesn't get better. I wished you would go to the same hospital where I was and get the same check-up. Will you please do it for me? I am pretty sure the rash itself is harmless, but the cause for it might not be. How do you look? Are you getting too thin in the face? I want to see those little *"Grübchen"* [dimples], don't forget.

Walter and Nannerl were sitting next to us at the ballet. They will call me next week. That is just like my *träubi,* to go to the kitchen and have a cup of coffee after that letter about death from Nan. I love your vitality, and your "lust for life," and I am sure God likes it too.

I'll try to call you this week-end to find out what the doctor said. So here is only a kiss from your religiously and indefatigably devoted husband

Knuti

Please tell Hans thanks for his letter and I'll write him as soon as I'll get a chance

Letterhead: Brook House

Monday
8/14/44

Darling,

Your telephoncall came just at the right moment. I was rather depressed all day long. I felt just plain lausy. We couldn't go outdoor all day long, it's just unbelievable hot. The garden looks like desert. And of course, that's part of the reason why that rash (which is worse than poison ivy—) doesn't clear up. You can imagine on the top of an inflamed skin, that heat. Well, I do what I can and so does Glass. But he is no sorcerer. But the whole thing is depressing. Hans & Rita were here all Sunday and at 10 o'clock at night, we went swimming down to Quentin. That was nice and nobody could see me with my leprosy.—Hesper is home and Mab is just as stupid as always. She loves Florence just for the reason that her father is rich. Oh, I get so mad and some day I am going to tell that middleclass fool, what I think of her. She is really exactly the opposite what I expect of a human being. I canceled my singing lesson today (an other honney-day 95°) and drive in the afternoon down to the Washington bridge to visit Florence (whom I havn't seen since the baby arrived) and come right back. I just got your letter. Darling I hope, your cold is gone. Be careful with intestional flues. Its a triky flu. Eat only toast (no milk) tea and vegetable. Avoid any greasy stuff. No salads with oil! Lemonnade. And no pork or veal. Lamb and Beef. So that's that. I hope, you got the pipe I send you and I hope you like it. It's incredible, how long it takes to get a package to Cal. I sent the sweaters weeks ago. I am glad, Lee likes my letter. (I knew, she would.) I wrote, she is the most perfect hostess I know, and it seems to be just as simple as that, to win her over.—I am very curious to know, how your dinner with the Werfel's was. And how that old bitch Alma behaved, with so much success in the backyard.[1] I hope very much, you get Slezak. I really dont see, how you can bring the show out before Xmas. And I dont see why you should hurry so much either. There will be so many musicals next season and I think it's much smarter to come a little late with something extrodionary. Let's get the flops out of the way first. Dont worry too much Darling about the movie. Bill is a swell guy, the only disappointing feature he has is—to have Mr. Ratoff direct.—No matter what you would try, it's lost with a guy like that. And Bill loves the score. So let's hope for the (worst.—) I saw "Dragon Seed."[2] I think I am still there (or did an ambulance bring me home? I wouldn't know.). It was so long and so middle western chinese and the audience took a nice long nap and so did I. But the theater was airconditioned! I hope, Richard is careful about those stories, so poeple

wont guess my age. I was that little   he should remember! Oh vanity thy name is W O M A N. So Darling, I am dripping wet. So let me take a shower and saddle my horse and drive into town. I got enough gas. (Laiso.—) By-by-Baby—My next letter will be a "cooler" one, I hope.

a million and ¾ *Knüsschen*

yours for ever!

Caroline

1. *Werfel's* Song of Bernadette *had been made into the hit movie of 1943.*
2. *Katherine Hepburn starred in the 1944 film* Dragon Seed.

346 WEILL IN LOS ANGELES TO LENYA IN NEW CITY,
14 AUGUST 1944

Monday, Aug. 14, 1944

Darling,

Just a few words to tell you that my stomach is alright this morning. I kept very quiet for two days and lived on tea and toast. That seems to have cleared it up.

But I am a little worried because you sounded kind of depressed yesterday on the phone. It is probably that awful heat that got you down, and it is a terrible feeling for me that you are suffering and swelting while I am so comfortable and cool here. Of course, that might soon be the other way round because we are in for some mighty hot weather here, but at least the nights are cool and I don't think it will ever get really hot up here on the mountain. I see in the papers this morning that the heat in the East is "easing up" a little and I hope that some relief in the weather will clear up your skin and your mind. Maybe a trip out here, purely as a vacation from that heat etc., might not be such a bad idea after all. I would ask my landlady if I could get that other bedroom for you, or, maybe, I would take a house on the beach for a month, maybe Litvak's house. How long I will stay? Well, Ira wants me to write the whole score out here, of course. But I figure this way: if the show will not go into rehearsals until the end of January, I might work here until the end of September and get as much done as possible, then go home and do the rest when Ira has to come East. If we stick to the original schedule (rehearsals in November) we'll have to go to New York in October anyhow. So, if you feel like coming out for a little while some time in September, I could talk to Vivian at the Lyons office about train reservations. Or shall we wait a little while before we make a decision? By the end of this month we should know pretty well where we're standing with the show. In the meanwhile I could work on a train reservation for you anyhow, so that we don't get stuck if and when you want to come.

Ira and I had lunch with Bill Perlberg. "Where do we go from here?" will be one of the biggest 20th Century musicals. They're spending 2½ million dollars. You remember that little Indian number which we wrote in one afternoon, just for fun? Well, they're spending 50,000.— just for costumes for this number. "Columbus" will cost 250,000.— etc. Bill has thrown out everything they have recorded so far because they didn't use my tempos. It will all be done over, with my tempos. So I think we are in pretty good hands there.

I just had a letter from Dick Halliday, with the news that Mary collapsed on stage and that her mother died suddenly. If you have a chance, as soon as it gets a little cooler, please drop in and say hello to her.

Darling, don't bother with the whisky for the Gershwins. They will get along without. I am doing enough by staying out here to work with him and I don't have to make presents on top of it. And we can use those few bottles of whisky ourselves, can't we, darling?

Hans writes that you're having a bad streak of luck in cards. Of course, that must be depressing too for *mein Blümchen*. Ira, in case that is a consolation for you, lost 709.– on Saturday night.

I am feeling fine today, had my tennis in the morning, then I met Miss Horner from the Lyons office to get my car fixed for another month, and had a talk with Arthur Lyons about casting, now I had a shower and a little chat with my Linnerl, and now to work! We will work very hard this week and I will be with either Ira or Eddie every evening.

Cheer up, my love, please. And thousand kisses for you from your old lover, friend, husband, composer and lawn-cutter

Kurti

My butler just put some freshly cut white gardenias from the garden on my desk and I put one in the letter. Maybe the smell which you like so much is still alive when you get it.

---

347 LENYA IN NEW CITY TO WEILL IN LOS ANGELES, [16 AUGUST 1944]
Letterhead: Brook House

Wednesday
1:30 A.M.

Darling,

I cant sleep, so I might use the time and write to you to thank you for your long letter. Dr. Glass that louse, didn't show up today. I just have to be patient, it's a weary thing. Abravanel's friend had the same thing 10 times worse and struggeld along for 3 month! I am on a diet (and what a diet—nothing but cereal, milk, toast, tea and one baked potatoe!) no life for an eagle! I dont think it's nesesarry to get that check up. Maybe later, when that rash is cleared up. So let's forget about it. I am sick and tired of it. I stoped my lessons for the time being. It's simply too hot and I am too exausted. But the show is so long off. I have time enough to catch up.

I am so happy about your work out there. Of course, I know that's you, who inspires those 2 guys. Whenever would Ira have written lyrics like he does now? In every line one can feel your influence. I wish we would find an <u>intelligent</u> publicity man, to

write about you and tell them, what should be told. But where to find one who understands that? On the other hand, if you want to tell about your contributions to book,
lyriks and the whole production, there wouldn't be much left of the other's and they
wouldn't like it. But something should be done. It's no use to think about it now. As
long as you get out of them what you want for your music—that's more importent.
And I still do think, in a few years you will write operas again for "overseas."— And
all those shows you are doing now, will be produced abroad, so you will be quite busy
in years to come. I hope. And that's why you have to be a *Klugi* with your health and
dont wear yourself out with the boys. I am sure Eddie is a very nice guy. Think of that
sourpuss Sid what you went through there. At least you are working with people in
your class. I saw the Berman sets of *3-Groschen Oper*.[1] Francesco [von Mendelssohn] had
them. They were wonderful. Of course, he is a first class guy and I hope, you get him.
And Tudor is <u>my</u> choise of a dance director too. I am sorry, I missed "Romeo & Juliet." But you remember how much we liked his "Pillar of Fire." And what a little
repetitous poop Agnes is next to him. I read somewhere (yes in the Times) they talked
about forthcoming productions and there was a line about her, quote: "and of course,
Miss de Mille will do the ballett, pretty soon we will need a rubber stamp for that line."
It wont be long and they will make fun of her. And that'll be the end of her. I am glad
your party was a success. They always are. No, you didn't tell me about the party at
Schwartz'es. But I can easely imagine—Hans will pick up the whisky and then Pete will
pack it. I think we get 6 bottles. So I will send them. It's a nice present. I hope, you
feel better Darling and your flu is gone. I lost weight of course, but everybody has in
that heat. I'll put it on fast, as soon as I can start to eat again: *Hühnchen, Hörnchen and
die kleinen gelben Honigkuchen*[2]—I hope, you dont have to see that *Genie* [genius
(Brecht)]—*die Dänin ist auch dort* [the Danish woman is also there].[3] Nice quiet family
life they will have. I called Rose L.T.F. [Lunch Time Follies] and she has the music.
When I drive in again, I'll pick it up. It's quite safe there. And Darling, a-pro-pos ballett—shouldn't I call [Maurice] Speiser and ask him about "Judgment of Paris"? I dont
see any reasons, why we should let them have that money. Tudor has nothing to do
with it.[4] I think, Speiser is just as big an asswhole as the rest is. Florence told me, he
lauses everything up for Hemingway. Write me, whether I should call him. I talked to
Bravi today, he was trying to call you. Did he reach you? Mab saw "Venus" again with
Hesper and her Mother and—she liked it much better than at the opening night. Isn't
she a bore. Anything for a conventional line.—Flo took those pictures. I look pretty
thin, but *die Grübchen* [the dimples] are still visible for you.—

Well my Darling, that's about all. I am sorry, I cant write you anything exciting. But
life on So. Mountain Rd. isn't very exciting as you know but compared with Dragon
Seed—it's an Inferno of excitment.—And please give Joe and Richard my love and
appologize for not writing. But tell them all my writing abilities are exausted in writing
to you. Now good night my honneychild, many *knüsschen* from your leopard (spotted
as I look)

Linnerl

1. Berman had designed the production of L'opéra de quat' sous *that opened at the Théâtre de l'Etoile in Paris in 1937, with a cast including Yvette Guilbert, Raymond Rouleau, Renée Saint-Cyr, and Suzy Solidor. Among the audience on opening night were Marlene Dietrich and Margo Lion.*

2. "Little chicken, bread swirls, and little yellow honey cakes" is a quotation from "Völlerei" (Gluttony) in Die sieben Todsünden.

3. The actress, journalist, playwright, and director Ruth Berlau (1906–74) was then staying with Brecht and his family in Santa Monica. She had met Brecht in 1933 in Denmark and became one of his devoted assistants, collaborating on plays, compiling production documentation, and administering his financial affairs. She accompanied him from Finland to Russia to the United States, and then to the German Democratic Republic after the war.

4. Tudor had used music from Die Dreigroschenoper *for his* Judgement of Paris *in 1938.*

348 WEILL IN LOS ANGELES TO LENYA IN NEW CITY, 16 AUGUST 1944

Wed. August 16, 1944

Darling,

This will be only a short letter. I had expected a letter from you today, but I suppose it was too hot to write. I study the New York weather reports every day to find out if my *Trrräubi* is getting some relief from that awful heat. It seems that Sunday was just about the hottest day in recorded history, and that you got some slight relief since then. It must be terrible on the train coming back from town, and I hope you don't go into town on those really hot days.

Bravi called yesterday and we had a long talk about the Billy Rose show [*Seven Lively Arts*]. I think he should take it if he can make sure that he can get out of it when my rehearsals start (which I don't think will be before the first of the year). Of course, he would be right on top of Broadway conductors if he would do the Billy Rose show and then Firebrand—and there is nobody who deserves more to be on top than he. I only hope he doesn't expect too much from the Billy Rose show. By the time that show opens it will be just another big review, written around Bee Lilly and Bert Lahr, with some ballet dancing—probably a very good review and something sensational.[1]

Bravi told me that he talked to you in the morning and that you were feeling a little more cheerful. He says that itching rash is so discouraging, and I remember in what an awful mood I was when I had that skin desease in France. Don't you still think a thorough check-up in the hospital would be good for you? On the other hand, Bravi told me that last week when he had dinner with you you looked more beautiful than he has ever seen you, and like a real glamour girl. He just kept raving about your looks—and that was sweet music for my ears, because I know when you look beautiful you are feeling well—and to know that you are feeling well is good for my spirits.

Nothin new here. I am working 14 hours a day. Monday night till 1.30 with Ira, last night till 1 with Eddie, tonight and tomorrow with both of them. We wrote a little Arietta for Cellini where he tells his exaggerated version of the Maffio murder. Very good. Last night, in working with Eddie, I got an idea for the Duchess' song in the sedan chair scene. It is a line in the play [*The Firebrand*]: "Great men make poor lovers."

Jack the Ripper Wildberg just called to tell me that Mary was back in the show last night and will probably be out again because there is no ice in the theatre. I have a slight suspicion that she is sabotaging the show. Strangely enough business was better last week with Jane [Joan?] Davis playing the part than the week before with Mary.[2] But if Mary continues behaving like a super–Gertrude Lawrence she can easily ruin the show for good. And that wouldn't be so good for her either. I hear that sweet little Dick Halliday is going to produce a show—maybe that will help. I had a letter from him about Peter Pan.

Well, sweety honey sugar pie, that's all I can tell you. No social activities this week, thank God. The war looks wonderful, doesn't it? Those week, feeble minded democracies are doing alright by Mr. Hitler.[3]

Good bye, my love.

Kurt

1. *Canadian-born Beatrice Lillie (1894–1989) became a popular comedienne in London before establishing herself as a comic character actress on Broadway in the late twenties. Bert Lahr (1895–1967), the Cowardly Lion in the film* The Wizard of Oz *(1939), began his career on Broadway in 1927 and appeared opposite Ethel Merman in* Dubarry Was a Lady *(1939).*

2. *The actress Joan Davis (1907–61) had a long career in vaudeville, radio, and films. She was known for physical comedy and raucous delivery. None of the programs for* One Touch of Venus *in the Weill-Lenya Research Center mentions a Jane or Joan Davis.*

3. *On 26 July, General Omar Bradley's American forces had broken through the German front at Saint-Lô, and a few days later General Patton's Third Army cleared the way to Brittany. On 30 July Hitler was notified by Field Marshal Günther Hans Kluge that the Western front had been ripped apart and the left flank had collapsed.*

349 LENYA IN NEW CITY TO WEILL IN LOS ANGELES, 18 AUGUST 1944
Letterhead: New City

Thursday
8/18/44

Darling,

I just got your letter with the still faintly smelling gardenia. That was very, very, very, *niedelich*. I feel much better today inspite of that blazing heat. I got an injection last night, went to bed at 10:30 and slept wonderfully until 10 o'clock this morning. And that rash will clear up eventionally. I didn't go into town all week (since last Friday.) Tomorrow I'll go to the hairdresser (that will help my morale—) and see Flo. In the evening I'll go and see Mary and the show. I am very glad, that you feel better. Yes, I think it would be wonderful for me to be on the ocean for a few weeks. If we could get Litwak's house for a month, that would be haven. But lets wait and see how things run with you and how far you get with your work. It's no hurry. If you are very setteled in your house it might be too much trouble to move into an other house and all that. I could just as well go swiming every day. But you'll see. As I say, there is no hurry. I am very excited about the picture. It would be wonderful if (and for the first time) your music would be treated right in a movie. You need that break very much as far as pictures are concerned. But isn't it silly, that they have to try first alone, with you there, and then have to do it all over again? Bill seems to be alright. But you could save him money. Evidently they have to spend so much before they are convinced it's really good what they got. But I am so happy that they really do it. I was so afraid, it was shelved for good.—And dont worry Darling, if your show comes out after Xmas. You still will have "Venus" running and the new show sounds so perfect, that one month sooner or later, doesn't make a bit of difference. Thank God, you have a producer. When I think of Cheryl *in der Nacht—bin ich um den Schlaf gebracht*.[1]

I am reading "Faust" and having a wonderful time. Here would be the perfect answer for Werfels letter:

> *Wenn ihrs nicht fühlt*
> *Ihr werdets nie erjagen.*
> *Wenns euch nicht aus der Seele dringt*
> *Und mit urkräftigem Behagen*
> *Die Herzen aller Hörer zwingt.*
> *Sitzt ihr einstweilen und leimt zusammen*
> *Braut ein Ragout von anderer Schmaus*
> *Und blast die kümmerlichen Flammen*
> *Aus eurem Aschenhäufgen aus.*—[2]

What a language. I forgot it can be so beautiful. I am sure, he [Goethe] was a good business man and liked to live well and didn't rely on Ascap.—Woolly is lying up here in my bedroom with his tongue hanging way out. He doesn't leave me alone for a minute. We have lots of tomatoes and very "cute" little potatoes. I am sorry Boyly—

Mab remains invisible.—But life strangely enough goes on just the same. Saturday night I play billard at the Christens [Bruce Christians]. Thats always nice. They are so simple and no showing of. It's too hot anyway. Unfortuanatly Glass forbid me swiming. The water is too dirty for my skin. So I am standing under the cold shower most of the time. So my *honneybär* I have to drive to N.C. to mail that letter. Maybe you will get it Saturday. Maybeen,

And now many *knüsschen* fon *Deinem gepünktichen getupferlten* [little double-dotted] Linnerl.

Darling, why dont you stop in to see Louise & Milly on your way to the beach in Santa Monica. They live, when you drive down the rampe, the 2nd or third house on the left with green shutters (The Norma Shearer house). I am sure, they would like it. Louise Carpentir is the name & Milly Monti[?] (just in case)[3]

---

1. *"When I think of Cheryl at night—I can sleep no longer" paraphrases Heinrich Heine's famous lines from "Nacht-gedanken": "Denk ich an Deutschland in der Nacht—Dann bin ich um den Schlaf gebracht."*

2. *Lenya appears to be quoting the* Urfaust *(lines 181–88) rather than* Faust *(lines 534–41). The English translation by Douglas M. Scott reads: "If you don't feel it, you can't chase it down, / Unless it forces itself out of your soul, / And with the satisfaction of elemental power / Compels the hearts of all listeners. / If you sit a while and paste things together, / Brew a ragout from the leavings of another's feast, / And blow the sickly flames / Out of your heap of ashes" (*The Urfaust: Goethe's "Faust" in the Original Form *[Woodbury, NY: Barron's Educational Series, 1958]).

3. *Louisa Carpenter (d. 1976) was the sister of Ruly Carpenter, the owner of the Philadelphia Phillies baseball team. The actress Norma Shearer (1900–1983) won the Oscar for her performance in* The Divorcee *(1930) and was nominated for five other films. MGM billed her as "the First Lady of the screen." She turned down the starring role in* Gone with the Wind.

Friday, August 18, 1944

My Linnerl darling,

That was a lovely surprise yesterday when the little package arrived. It is a beautiful Dunhill and I love the long stem with the small bowl. Of course, I took it along to Ira and tried it out, *"und es war gut befunden"* [and he saw that it was good], as they say in the bible. Thank you, *Träubi*. I appreciate it very much!

Well, another hard working week is almost over. We finished the Cellini Arietta. Then we wrote the first love song for Angela and Cellini—and it is a peach. Ira first was stalling with the love song (as always). So I got together with Eddie and worked out an idea for one which I took to Ira whom of course got all excited about it. So we lined out a lovely lyric, starting "I'm afraid, afraid, you're far too near me," and yesterday I wrote a tune which Ira calls one of the great waltz melodies ever written (!!). I am very happy about it because it is just tailormade for the scene—and also a great song. And that combination, a great song in the right spot, is a nice thing to have. We, the three of us, are continously working with great enthousiasm and are having lots of fun. There is nothing else to report from here. I haven't seen anybody all week, not even the Revy's, but I hope I'll be able to go to the beach one afternoon over the weekend. Ira wants to work Saturday too! Walter Huston called today. They want me to come up to [Lake] Arrowhead next week-end, and I would like to do it if I can get away Saturday afternoon. It would be a nice change.

Yesterday I had your letter from Monday, together with the pipe. I only hope that you are feeling better by now. I am thinking all the time how you must suffer with that rash, during that heat. The papers say that the N.Y. heat wave is broken. Here it is continously cool, only for about 3 hours during the day it is kind of warm. At this moment (11 A.M.) I am sitting in my room with the yellow sweater on!!

Today I am having lunch with Gottfried Reinhardt who wants to talk to me about something. Tomorrow with Jack Wildberg and Louis Shurr who are trying to make a deal for the movie sale of Venus.—I laughed about your worries that Richard could give away your age. There was nobody present except Joe and me when he told the stories. So relax! By the way, the combination Gershwin-Revy didn't work out so well and my little party would have been quite a flop if we wouldn't have gone to the ballet which made it a very short evening. The Revy's were so shy that they hardly talked, and confronted with Broadway-Americans, they are still quite european. The Gershwins, on the other hand, were a little impressed because I had told them that the R.'s have money and a wonderful picture collection. For me it was fun to watch.[1]

Well, I had my little morning chat with you, now I have to work. Just this minute Louis Shurr called. There is a chance of a very good movie deal for Venus, but we have to wait until Wildberg is out of town, then Shurr and I will try to make the deal.

Thousand *Knüsschen* for you,

Knuti

Greetings for the family and Pete!

1. *In his diary entry for 13 August, Richard Révy recorded that Weill had played and sung* Der Silbersee *after dinner at the Gershwins', and he noted, "Kurt Weill is so far away from the Americans that he would be terrified if ever he would become fully aware of it."*

351 WEILL IN LOS ANGELES TO LENYA IN NEW CITY, 21 AUGUST 1944

August 21, 1944

My *Träubilein,*

On Saturday I had two letters from you and, thank God, the second one, from Thursday, sounded a little more cheerful, after a good night's rest. The snapshots are very *niedelich,* especially the one where you drink from a glass—very pretty and cute. But, as I expected, you got thinner in the face which is certainly no wonder with that diet and the heat. Well, we'll fix that when the real *Klugi* takes over again. As soon as I get a more definite idea about my working plans, dates for rehearsals etc. (which I should get by the end of this month) I'll make definite arrangements to get you out here since the idea of spending some time by the ocean here seems to be attractive to you.

We lost almost 3 working days because Ira went twice (Friday and Saturday) to his poker game. But he went home at 6 in the morning (not, as usual, at 2 in the afternoon) so we could do some work at least. We finished the love scene and have started on the Duke's entrance song. Eddie who has been lazy again is coming to my house this morning to work. I expect him any minute, and I'd better hurry up with this letter.

We had some bad luck with casting. Wilbur Evans is not being released from Mike Todd because the Fields are writing a new show for him. Yesterday we found out that Alfred Drake has been signed by the Guild for a show.[1] Universal refuses flatly to release Susanna Forster. Well, we just have to keep on looking. I had to go [to] Slezak's dinner party last night. It was one of the worst gatherings of refugees I've ever gone through. A German language evening of the worst kind—because it wasn't even German but that awful mixture of Hungarian and Viennese. The main topic of conversation was gossip about the other refugees, and a long discussion about *"g'stürzte"* (a kind of Potato pankakes, it seems). The Werfel's were very nice. He is a sick man and she is an old fool, but strangely warm and *"herzlich"* [cordial] to me, and genuinely enthousiastic about "Lady in the Dark" which she saw twice. A movie and operetta writer Walter Reisch was leading the conversation. He ought to be shot right after Hitler. Ernst Deutsch is a nice old gaga who talks mostly about food.[2] I didn't talk more than 20 words all evening and left early. But I did find out that Slezak would like very much to play the Duke if we can arrange our dates to fit his picture commitments. That was worth the evening. What I don't understand is why Slezak who has been in this country for 14 years still surrounds himself with that crowd. I am sure he could have lots of American friends. I begin to think that we are almost the only ones of all these people who have found American friends and who really live in this country. They all are still living in Europe. Well, t' hell with them.

Saturday night the Revy's took me to see "Wilson" which is a lovely, warm, thoroughly American picture (the refugees last night didn't like it, of course).[3] On Sunday we had a few hours at the beach, then I went to Ira to work and dinner.

There was all kind of excitment with the picture sale of Venus in the last days, but I don't believe a word. Wildberg called from San Francisco yesterday where he is stopping on his way back East, to tell me that he has the biggest offer ever made, and that the people who made the offer would call me. Of course, nobody called. In the meanwhile that idiotic woman Leah [Salisbury] continues messing up things in New York. But all this leaves me completely cool. I am too deep in my new work. Thank God, the show itself (Venus) seems to be strong enough to withstand all attacks. If we lived through these last weeks we should be good for a nice long run in the winter. I am curious to hear what you have to tell about Mary and the show.

Darling, don't forget registering for the elections. Also, would you please ask Hans to call Horowitz and to ask him how the partnership negociations are coming along. If he drags it out much longer and loses it then, we'll have to pay a fortune in interest alone.—I don't think you should call Speiser. I want to get away from him, and if we have no business at all with him I don't have to pay him any more. The few dollars which I might get from the Ballet Theatre are not worth paying 300.— every quarter year to Speiser. The Lyons office is handling the new show for me, so I don't need anybody.

I could tell you complete details of the private lives of the [Emmerich] Kalman's, the Felix Salten's, the Alfred Neuman's, the Mann's (Thomas and Heinrich),[4] the [Mischa] Spoliansky's, [Albert] Bassermann's, [Emil] Jannings, and 200 other members of the *Mumienkeller* [cellar of the mummies] last night, but I don't think you care to know, so here is a sweet *Knüüssen* for my New City girl, and loads of love,

Kurt

1. *The popular musical comedy baritone Wilbur Evans (1908–87) was tied up in* Mexican Hayride, *which was produced on Broadway by Michael Todd (1907–58). Dorothy (1905–74) and Herbert Fields (1897–1958) wrote the book and lyrics for many outstanding musicals, including* Annie Get Your Gun *(1946). Alfred Drake (1914–92) had originated the role of Curly in* Oklahoma!

2. *The Austrian-born screenwriter and director Walter Reisch (1903–83) wrote the script for* Ninotchka *(1939) and the lyrics for many German popular songs. Ernst Deutsch (1890–1969) was a highly-mannered German character actor.*

3. *The Canadian stage and screen actor Alexander Knox (b. 1907) won an Academy Award nomination for best actor for his portrayal of President Wilson in the motion picture of 1944.*

4. *The Austrian critic and author Felix Salten (1869–1947) wrote historical novels but is best known as the author of* Bambi *(1923). The German author and dramaturg Alfred Neumann (1895–1952) had arrived in the United States in 1941. The German novelist Heinrich Mann (1871–1950) had arrived in 1940; the film* Der blaue Engel *was based on his novel* Professor Unrat.

Letterhead: New City

Tuesday 22nd of August

My darling,

I am a day behind with my letter. But I wanted to see Venus first and tell you about it. First let me thank you for your 2 letters. Everything out there, seems to be going the way you wanted it And it sounds like you have really fun for the first time (in a long time) on a show. "Great men make poor lovers" is very sweet (and true too—) but they dont have to be. I am happy about the waltz you have written. The waltz in Venus ["Foolish Heart"] is still one of my most favorite numbers. I was quite mad when I read in the Sunday Times about fall productions (Barnes) and he talkes about the "eminent" Mr. [Richard] Rodgers and puts "Firebrand" down the drain with some minor announcments.[1] But I suppose, he doesn't know anything about it and that's good too. So it will be quite a surprise for them when it'll come out. I loved Ogdens piece he wrote about you.[2] It sounded so adorable and true. Did you like it? And how did you like Mary's interview in the Tribune? I thought it was slightly exacerated to say: if Cheryl wouldn't have convinced her, she wouldn't be in the show.—Na.—Anyway, I went to see her last night before the show started and they were both a little *"kühle"* [cool]. But you know, how I meet those attempts. I was twice as nice and even *kühler.*—So she asked me to come back in the intermission and have a cigarette with her, wich I did. Then she was all changed and very nice. No Darling, she doesn't sabotage the show, if you would have been in that theater (on a not very hot day) you would have melted too. There was no air condition so ever. And the audience (almost sold out) was just sitting there and fanning themselfs with programs. I was dripping myself. And then she is very unhappy with Cutler. And I can fully understand it. He hasn't improved a bit and looks more than ever like Harry James.[3] Without the slightest touch of humor. I really felt sorry for her to hang around with that broomstick. The rest of the show is exellent, but of course the present audience is an awful one, I found, "Provinces" [provincial].—But they like it. So let them laugh on the wrong places. They have new posters on stations and Broadway. Very good one too. Yellow with Mary's figure (like the old ones) and no names except Mary's and Johns [Boles]. Did you agree on that. It's very effective for the show, but they should have asked you at least. Did they do it?

I had dinner with Bravi before the show and he is very happy that you agreed for him to do the Billy R. [Rose] show. He gets 500.– a week, same billing than Norman Bel Geddes (well he got some insurance there.—) and will be free for your show. That's good. They found an understudy for Mary Bravi told me. Why they let Joan Davis go is one of those military secrets one will know about it after the 3rd world war I suppose.—So next week, I'll send Mary some candis and that'll be just right. Now I am really curious, what will happen to the movie sale.

By the way, I think Mary will stick to the show for the very simple reason, that she needs the money. You know, how stingy they are and she has to take care of her boy now too and her family is quite large.[4] And she hasn't got anything so far. One can feel that. She wont find anything so quick either with that husband. I had the feeling, that she is waiting for you to come back. So she'll play it next season. I am glad, you liked the pipe. I thought it was a nice one too. I am sorry your little partie went almost to pieces. I can imagine the Revy's with the Gershwins. I think they'll never will feel at home with Americans. They have too many *Fröschels* around them.[5] We had some weekend. I invited Jonny Bright and he came on Saturday evening. He is a very nice guy and so typical american. Soft and drunk! After dinner (which I cooked!) he read me his play, the one Gaget [Kazan] was supposed to do about Mexican discrimination in California. A very disent play in it's attitude but I am afraid not very good. I was a little disappointed (after Florence raving about the play) as one always is, after expecting something better. But maybe, I am just very spoiled. He asked me to send it to Moss what I will do. At the present moment, Norman Bel G. reads it. It can be very effective in a good production, but it just isn't what I would call a good play. So we sat up until four o'clock in the morning, listening to all his problems, with him getting drunker and drunker and softer and softer and more sentimental than it is allowed, but still nice. So finally he staggered to bed to get up at 12 noon. In the afternoon the whole family came, with the Sonders and Sofie Messinger!![6] But then Jonny was really as nice as only an American can be. Told very funy stories about Hollywood and made drinks and was the center of the partie (what a partie—) and felt importent. Which was O.K. with me. After dinner we brought him to the station. That was our weekend. And yesterday, I started my routine again. It's a little cooler now, my rash almost gone and I feel like a human being again. Well my sweetiepie, that's all the news. I hope, you feel fine. I am struggling with fixing our living room. It's a problem child. But we will get it eventually.

Now good bye my angel. I am so happy that I feel better. It was too disgusting.

Meinen ergebensten diener [my most submissive kowtow] Herr Johann Strauss-Weill

von Ihrer [from your] Caroline.

---

1. *From 1943 to 1950 Howard Barnes was the first-string critic for the* New York Herald Tribune, *not the* New York Times.

2. *On 20 August 1944 Nash wrote in the* New York Times: *"After working some six months with Kurt Weill I still don't know where his music comes from. He has a piano, but he does not sit at it picking out melodies with one finger; he uses it for laying his pipe on. . . . He does not pace the floor in a brown study humming tum-ti-tum, tum-ti-tum until suddenly he claps his brow and his face is transfigured with ecstasy as another ballad is born. . . . He simply puts in a full day at the OWI [Office of War Information], gets on the Weehawken ferry, rides for an hour in a non-air-conditioned smoking car, gets home, goes to his desk and writes 'That's Him.' "*

3. *The trumpeter and big band leader Harry James (1916–83) was married to the actress Betty Grable.*

4. *Martin's boy, Larry Hagman (b. 1939), grew up to star in two hit television series:* I Dream of Jeannie *and* Dallas, *playing J. R. Ewing in the latter.*

5. *It is unclear whether* Fröschel *is intended as a diminutive of* Frosch *(frog) or as a reference to the jail warden in Johann Strauss's* Fledermaus.

6. *Alfred Sonder (1895–1931) was Weill's first cousin on his father's side, and Sofie Messinger was his second cousin on his mother's side.*

Thursday, Aug. 22 [24]

My darling,

I wanted to write my usual report today, but then I started working—and now it is already after one and I have only time for a few words, so that you have something from me for the week-end.

I am terribly excited about France and the liberation of Paris. Who would have thought that the whole German fake would blow up so quickly. They just have nothing left, no fighting spirit and no gasoline. But Hitler doesn't allow them to quit until they are completely destroyed—and that is just perfect. What an exciting week!. We will probably remember the events of these last days all our life. Of course, out here people are so complacent, nobody talks about it. It is all too far removed and their life is too easy and comfortable.

Your letter with the newspaper clippings just arrived. Ogden's article is absolutely charming and makes good for all his shortcomings. I thought Mary's article very nice too, and I am glad you went to see her. I talked to Kazan yesterday. He will definitely go to New York within the next few weeks and rehearse the show. Maybe we should still get rid of Cutler and get somebody else, but as I know Cheryl, he is probably the only one who has a run-of-the-play contract. I talked to Sid last night because I am working on two very good movie deals for Venus. The group which Wildberg had talked about really called me up (Mary Pickford) and they say that they mailed a definite offer, including a 50,000.– check to New York yesterday. It would be a wonderful deal and they want me to write the additional songs. I'll tell you more about it.

Gee, I am so happy that your rash is gone, that it is cooler and that you are feeling so much better. That is a burden from my chest. Your last week-end sounded like fun.

Darling, I have to run. I write again over the week-end. Bye-bye, my love *au revoir bientôt, je t'embrasse, bien le vôtre,*

Knuti

Letterhead: Brook House

Thursday
8/25[24]/44

Darling,

This will be a shorty. Pete is home to paint the living room, so I am busy—cant you see—I am very busy.—And there is nothing new anyway. There is a new hit in town. "Song of Norway." When I looked at the pictures, I thought it looked like "Zar & Zimmerman."[1] But the[y] evidently liked it.—I went to the Metropolitan Museumm yesterday and looked at the 20 Rembrandts they brought back, after hiding them from possible bombing. I bought a few of them and then I bought 2 Goya's, 3 Franz Hals and a Raphael.—So I had a wonderful time and felt like Rokefeller. (I would have them home) if my mother woudn't have had the ambition to mary a *fiaker* [coachman]. Anyway, it lifted my spirit considerably after all that "canning tomatoes and corn talk" on So. Mt. Rd. Hans & Rita will stay 1 more week in my house after the 1st of Sept. That will be nice. Hans hates to go back to the city, so I invited them.

I wonder, what my *Träubchen* is doing. I didn't get a letter today though it is my *"Donnerstag"* [Thursday].—But I s'ppose he is busy. Thank God it's nice and cool!!! Now *Schnäutzchen* dont get too fresh out there otherwise the transitions will be too hard for you when you get back home to your little xantippe. But I think, you'll make the switch easely. Good by Sir, *mit* [with] highly errecktem *Affenschwänzchen* [little monkey tail]

> your very devoted Carolinchen

1. *Albert Lortzing's* Zar and Zimmermann *had been a staple on German stages since its premiere in 1837.*

355 WEILL IN LOS ANGELES TO LENYA IN NEW CITY, 27 AUGUST 1944

Sunday, Aug. 27, 1944

Good morning, my honey chil'. How are you today? I had worked so hard these last days that I was terribly tired yesterday and went early to bed, had a wonderful schleep until 9 and feel fine and dandy now. We finished the Duke's entrance song yesterday which, I think, will rank next to any Offenbach or Guilbert Sullivan song of that type. We still haven't got the right idea for the Duchess' song. We got cold feet on the idea "Great men make bad lovers." We started two songs for the garden scene: a madrigal for Angela and the girls with the title "The little naked boy" (Cupid, you stupid), and a duet for the Duke and Angela where he always mixes up words like:

Duke: Come with me to that nozy cook.
Angela: My lord, you mean that cozy nook.

I have straightened out some important story problems this week, but we are having troubles with Eddie—the same old playwright troubles. He is so confused, and I have to remind him all the time of things he forgot from one meeting to another. He is so used working for the movies that he always thinks in terms of lines instead of scenes. Ira, more than I, is worried that the comedy might be a little dated, but that probably comes more from Lee who doesn't like what she calls sex comedy (probably because she hasn't got anything where other people have sex).

Yesterday I spent 4 hours at the studio. They were recording "It happened to happen to me" ["All at Once"] (with Joan Leslie who will be lovely in the part), and then I saw a rehearsal of the opening number ("Morale") and the Hessian Drinking Song ["The Song of the Rhineland"].[1] It looks terrific, real big production scenes, done with great taste and gusto, and the music comes out beutifully. If it works out the way it looks now, it will be a very important picture and a great thing for me. I am amazed how carefully they work. Every bar is worked out to the minutest detail. Yesterday they had a two hours debate about the interpretation of one line, with an orchester of 50 men waiting. Of course, they have no try-out and no two weeks out of town to straighten out things, so they have to do right then and there. But it is very interesting to watch how the whole thing is organized for the exploitation of individual ambitions. The dance director fights for his steps, the voice coach for his tempo, the orchestrator for his effects, the conductor for his interpretation—and everyone is trying to get the best for himself out of it—and if the producer is clever he uses all these burning ambitions for the best of the picture.

We are still having great difficulties casting Cellini. I tried to get Alfred Drake, but he is tied up with the Guild for a new show. Now I am after some other people, but I have to do it all myself and it takes a lot of time. I heard a girl who is a good possibility for Angela. She is 17 years old, lovely looking, a beautiful voice of the Susanna Forster type and highly talented.

Tomorrow I have a meeting with Slezak in Lyons' office, will try to sign him up. Max Gordon sent a wire that he has booked the Colonial in Boston for Christmas week. I wired him we can be ready if he can cast the show. Darling, I'll talk to Vivian tomorrow and ask her to get a reservation for you anyhow for sometime middle of September so that we don't get stock if you decide you want to come. If it looks that I can come back early in October or that you don't want to make the trip for some reason we can always cancel the reservation. I'll let you know what she has to say. It is very hard to get reservations. Eddie's former wife had a reservation to New York since 6 weeks— and ended up on a milktrain, 4 days to Chicago.

It looked last week as if the picture sale of Venus was near, but I haven't heard anything since. It's probably one of those things again. Tuesday I have a meeting with Jessie Lasky, that nice old man whom we met at one of the parties last winter, who made the George Gershwin picture.[2] Maybe I can get him excited.

Lebe, mein Schnäuzchen. Take care of yourself and rest a lot to recover from that awful time you had.

Kisses, kisses, kisses

Kurt

---

1. *Nineteen-year-old Joan Leslie (b. 1925) played the role of Sally, opposite Fred MacMurray as Bill Morgan, in the film* Where Do We Go from Here?

2. *The prominent Hollywood producer Jesse Lasky (1880–1958) was president of the short-lived Pickford-Lasky Corporation. Robert Alda played Gershwin in the film* Rhapsody in Blue, *which was not released until 1945.*

Letterhead: New City

Monday
9: A.M.

Darling,

I just got Lissy. She looks well and fat and full of "calamities" about her family. So I guess, the telephon will start to ring again and the house will be full of southern laughter and gaiety.—

This was a quiet weekend with no guests. Saturday Mab (yes dont faint) Rita and I played cards until 6 in the morning. I still have bad luck, but it's not as expensive plaisure then Ira's and less expensive than poker. The old man called around 1 o'clock for her to come home, (aint it disgusting), but she finally decided against his will—after a desperate struggle between him and pinocle. Pinochle won.—I am driving in with Hans & Rita this morning, they start to bring their stuff into town (they have to leave on Thursday, the Fabers[?] come back) but they'll stay with me until Monday. And that will be the end of summer. It looks already a little fall and our tree up in the field starts already to look red. Hans will call Horowitz, though he doubts whether it will have any affect. Pete left this morning for New York for a week, to work in the Deming house. He'll be back Sunday. We fixed the living room. And this time, I got it. Looks simply beautiful. I brought the little desk from the guestroom down, the walls are all white and Pete broke down and gave me a sweet reading lamp—for one of the blue chairs, so my *Träubchen* can read his *paperchens*. Only the fireplace has still no tiles. We cant get that man here. But it would be too perfect otherwise. We'll get him. Those are all the news from here Darling. Julie Sloane came down to tell me, that she is going to have a baby. She was pregnant for the last twenty minutes I sp'ose because she was in such a hurry to tell me. Saturday Mab is giving a big coctail party for the scoolteachers! She keeps on telling everybody how much she hates to give that party (nobody is forcing her) just to make poeple feel good, I guess. The old man came down here, bearded like Barbarossa—gloomy, depressed, with a bad stomac and no idea for a play.[1] Aint it sad? Hans & Rita gave me a lovely silver bread basket because they had such a lovely summer. Isn't that sweet? I went to see Flo last Friday at the hospital and met [Oskar] Homolka, who is very nice and witty. They'll live at the Ambassador when she gets out, which will be tomorrow. I dont know, whether I wrote you, that I visited Gwen Steinbeck too. She looked lovely and had a terrible hard time. Now to my California *Pflänzchen*.

That sounds like a perfect party you attended at the Slezaks. Yes thats how they live, just like at "Schwaneckes" [famous Berlin literati café]. I am afraid, I wouldn't be too interested in their private lives, maybe I would like to know more about the Kalmans (oh horseshit—). I was more afraid for you to go to the Werfels on account of her. I thought she sure would be nasty to you. But I suppose, you are too successful, that stopped her. I am glad you liked the pictures I sent you. Yes, I got a little thinner. But it doesn't matter. It looks alright, when I am dolled up. My singing lessons are pretty monotonous. I simply fail to see, how any one can spent a life time to make hi hi hi and oh-oh-oh for more than 2 month. I see Margie[?] there and she is what we call *eingeschnappt* [miffed]. Does that worry you? I bought more irish folksongs to study, just to get some pep into the lessons. Well my Darling Kurti, that's all for today. Coming weekend Bravi will come out with a friend from Australia. So Hans will sleep in your bed and Rita with me. I hope, the wheather will be nice. Now good by my *Tropfi*. I have to get dressed for the "family." They'll be here any minute. We drive back in the afternoon. "Take it easy as you can and if you cant, take it at as easy as you can" (irish saying—I was told.—*Knüsschens* and many of them for my composer!

Isn't the war exciting? that one really can see the end now! Dont worry about registering they'll let us know.

1. *Legend has it that the beloved emperor Frederick I (1152–90), called Barbarossa because of his long reddish beard, never died but just fell asleep in the belly of a mountain, where his beard grew so long it reached the floor.*

357 WEILL IN LOS ANGELES TO LENYA IN NEW CITY, 30 AUGUST 1944

Wednesday, Aug. 30, 1944

Linschkerl darling,

I had two letters from you, one on Monday and one today—and they always are the nicest interruptions. The last days I have been a little tired because I have been working so hard, but both Ira and I [are] so hot on this show that we keep on working every day from two in the afternoon until 12 or 1 at night. That wouldn't bother me if I wouldn't have had to attend to so much business in the morning these last days. But that will be over shortly, I hope, and then I'll have again a quieter life.

The business is all about the movie sale of Venus. Wildberg is pushing his deal because, as I found out, he gets a movie job for himself out of it. I would close his deal (which is not bad for us) if I don't find anything better. Yesterday I saw (out at Warners, at 107 degree in the shade) Jesse Lasky (you remember him from a party last winter, a charming old man whom you liked very much). I got him all excited about it, and he showed me a letter from Mamoulian saying that he wants to direct Venus if Lasky will produce it. I told him what offer we have, and he said he would let me know today at noon if he could make the same offer. He is the best and most reliable and honest producer in Hollywood, and he wants me to collaborate on the picture. I am very excited about this possibility because the man is absolutely first class. So I talked to Ogden this morning, and as soon as I hear from Lasky today, I will call Leah, Sid and Ogden and push this deal through—and wouldn't I have fun to snatch it away from Black Jack Wildberg in the last minute, just when he saw himself as co-producer of the Venus picture.

In the meanwhile I talked to Max Gordon several times. Slezak wants impossible terms and we might have to give him up. Yesterday in the afternoon Max called while I was at Ira's and insisted—thank God—that we should cast the show in New York. I asked him to tell that to Ira directly, and I finally got Ira to agree that we would go to

New York on October 15 if we can do the show for a Christmas opening. So we decided to work full steam ahead with these dates in mind. In the meantime, Vivian called to tell me that they have a reservation for you for Sept. 23 (that's the earliest they could get). So you can think it over quietly and decide what to do. We can cancel the reservation the last days if we want to. The reservation is on the "City of Los Angeles," a wonderful streamlined train, as fast as the Super Chief. So at least we know you can come if we decide so.

Well, the first act of the show is gradually shaping up. We finished the "nozy cook" song and are working now on a big Tarantella for the garden scene. It all looks swell.

On Sunday Alma Maria called and insisted I should come to see them in the afternoon. You know my incapability to think of a lie in a case like that, so I went there. It was the most luxurious gathering I've ever seen, all poor refugees, drinking french Champagne (in the afternoon) and eating the best cold buffet imaginable, with caviar of course. The language was entirely that mixture of Hungarian and Viennese which I like so much. Well, I talked to Bemmelman for half an hour and left, leaving behing me a storm of indignation which I still could hear 10 blocks away.

I had a very nice note from Mary which seems to comfirm your suspicion that she has nothing and is waiting for me. Kazan left for New York to rehearse the show.

Gee, it is 11.30 I have to run to be in Shurr's office when Lasky calls.

Lebe, mein Schätzchen,

Your old busy-body

Knut

358 LENYA IN NEW CITY TO WEILL IN LOS ANGELES,
31 AUGUST 1944
Letterhead: Brook House

Thursday
8/31/44

Darling-*Tröpfi*,

The Lyons office just called me, to tell, they have a reservation for me the 20th of Sept. bedroom on the 20 Century to Chicago and from there bedroom on the City of L. Angeles. Well, well, that was quite a surprise. It's very tempting just to hop on the train but is it right? It depends a little, how long you will have to stay. If you come back in October, I dont think, we should spend the money (from which I could buy very much needed clothes for winter.) There are no other reason for me to stay in N.Y. except my lessons. But with those I can always catch up, when we get back in taking one every day. So I think, you can tell best, whether I should come. I have to cancel the reservation soon, I was supposed to pick up my ticket coming Wednesday. So maybe you can send me a wire to tell me what to do. Hans & Rita move in today to stay after Labor day. We drove in to town yesterday to pick up the music & the whisky. (6 bottles). So I think, I send four to the Gershwins as soon as Pete is back (Sunday) to pack them properly. I got your long letter from Sunday last night. I am glad you feel good and not tired. You probably dont sleep enough. I am a little worried about the problem of casting Cellini. But maybe you really shouldn't try so hard to get a name. There must be young singers around and it just needs a little luck. The girl you found sounds wonderful. I dont exactly see what Ira means by saying, the comedy might be a little dated. Either it's good and funy and then it cant be dated. I dont think that Eddie would right something like that. That's one thing they do know in movies, how to write comedy. I wouldn't listen too much what Lee is saying. She is a freak and doesn't know anything anymore (if she has ever—). Of course it should be fresh and agressive comedy without being dirty. Especially because it's a play in custums. But Iras lyriks certainly have exactly the quality I am thinking about and your music has it no doubt. And that Madrigal with Cupid "you stupid" shows, that you treat Angela not just as a little sweetiepie. She should be innocent but funy and young. Think how thin the comedy is in Venus and I am sure Eddie does 100 times better than that. Lee doesn't know anymore theater in sitting out there and listening to the same jokes for years. And Darling, you with your knowlegde of theater, you certainly know, what's what. I will go and see "Song of Norway" which is surprisingly enough a big hit, just to see what kind of singers they got. There is no name except the woman Petina (from the Met).[1] It'll be quite a cacrifice to see that show. The book seems to stink to heaven. There is nothing new to report from here. Hans and I went to the Sloanes last Monday. They had a very interesting man there Ralph Bates, who worked for years in China for the Russians. But he didn't get a chance to open his mouth, because that authority on China Bill Sloane couldn't shut his trap for a minute. I never saw anyone talking that much. He is really an annoying citizien. It's wonderful cool now and I feel reborn.—I am having dinner with Bravi tomorrow in town (but I might cancel it, because he is coming out here with a friend Saturday night. The house will be quite full with Rita sleeping with me, Hans in your bed and the boys in the guestroom. I think, this will be the last weekend with guest. The Aufrichts might come out one Sunday, shortly before the end of the season. Moss called last night, but I wasn't home then. So I will call him today. But this letter has to go in the mailbox, so I cant tell you anymore, what he wants. So Darling, tell me how long you have to stay (in case you do know) and whether I should come.

    lebe and many *knüsschen*

    from *Deinem*

       Weibi

---

1. *The Russian mezzo-soprano Irra Petina (b. 1907) came to the United States in 1930; she sang at the Metropolitan Opera until 1950 and occasionally appeared on Broadway.*

Saturday, Sept. 2, 1944

My *Träubilein,*

That was very very *niedelich* to be awakened by the sound of your voice this morning, and I am in very good humor ever since. The pain in my arm is almost gone and
I will take it very easy for two days because I have been doing a little too much this
week, mainly on account of those negociations for the movie sale of Venus. We're getting 150.000.— (100,000.— this year and 50,000.— next year) as an advance against 10%
of the grosses which means we can make up to 500.000.— or, if the picture is a flop, we
got just 150,000.— I am getting my non-interpolation clause which means, they cannot
use anybody else's music unless I give permission. So that's pretty good. We, that
means you and I, are getting about 22,000.— out of this deal, about 15,000.— this year
and 7,000. next year. Then, in 1946 we could easily get another 20,000.— out of the 10%
of the grosses. And, of course, if they want new songs, they'll have to pay 2500.— a
week.

I am sending you here my estimated income for Horowitz. Please ask at the bank if
you can sign a check "Kurt Weill tax account." If not you pay the tax checks from the
regular account and I transfer the same amount from the tax account to the regular.—
By the way, you forgot to write me how much was the balance of both bank accounts
on August 1st. In the meanwhile you probably got the Sept. 1st statement too. I suppose
we must have saved a few thousand dollar in these two months.

Well, *Tröpfi,* who was a *Klugi* again? When you wrote me that the family is moving
into town I knew that you would get a little bored alone out there, so I called Vivian to
get a reservation for you, and they certainly moved promptly. I think it will be lots of
fun if you come out—and t' hell with the *Zaster* [mammon]. *Hammersch doch, könn-
mersch doch* [as long as we've got it, we can do it]. I am pretty sure I won't leave here
before sometime around Oct. 20, so that would give you 4 weeks out here. You can go
to the beach every day, play tennis etc. and have a wonderful time. I will probably
work like hell those last weeks, so you can have the car all day. That will be real *Feinlebe* for my Linnerl. So go and get your reservation. The City of Los Angeles is a
Union Pacific train, and you have to inquire, before you buy a return ticket if it can be
exchanged for a ticket on the Santa Fe in case we want to go back on the Chief. It
saves a lot of money to buy a return ticket.

As I told you we did a lot of work this week, and the show looks really good. We
have now a complete outline of the second act which shapes up beutifully. We expect to
have the first act finished in about two weeks. Ira started talking about the casting of
the Duchess again as if I had never mentioned you. There is a certain viciousness in his
complete disregard of my desire in this respect—and that is so strange because Ira is
everything but vicious. I begin to suspect Lee. Well, I made it very clear again that I
want you for the part, so he shut up again. I am sure it will be a real fight, but I want
to wait until we have finished the show.

A long letter from Ogden, very sweet and very pitiful. He has wasted his whole summer, in a hot New York apartment. They didn't get anywhere. He asks me if I still consider him as a lyric writer for me if he forgets about writing books too—and that's exactly what I wanted him to find out. I will write him that I will be very glad to work with him again as soon as I find the right book.

Well, darling, our letters will probably get shorter and shorter from now on, because pretty soon you will be here in person. Get yourself some nice things to wear here, and start buying your winter wardrobe. Or do you think you buy better out here?

The war is so exciting that one has to stay away from the radio if one wants to do any work. Who would have thought that the mighty German army would collapse just like the mighty French army collapsed four years ago! I think it will be over very soon, don't you?

Goodbye, sweet. See you soon.

Thousand kisses,

Kurt

360 LENYA IN NEW CITY TO WEILL IN LOS ANGELES,
4 SEPTEMBER 1944
Letterhead: Brook House

Monday
9/4/44

Darling,

So everybody is out of the house and it's quiet and nice. It's 6:00 in the evening, I have slept 2 hours and I feel fine. Bravi didn't come that skunk. Called up in the last minute on Saturday after we had done all our shoping—So Saturday afternoon, Hans, Rita and I went to Mabs coctail party (all the hillbillys from So. Mountain Road in one bunch—) with McAvoys back in circulation.—I stayed for half an hour and left. It was a jolly party.—Mab had only eyes for Helen Hayes (who looked like a little tree trunk with millions of wrinkles, but with a golden laughter in her throat). And Barbarossa [Maxwell Anderson] didn't show up at all. Was probably in his cabin, creating.—But Rita got all the gossip. Meg and Quentin are separating! I feel sorry for that. But it was inevitable. Nothing that scruy [screwy] can last. They try to rent the house for a year and they move into town on the first of October. I lost a little trak of your letters that means our telephone call got ahead of us. I am glad the movie deal is done, just to have it out of your way and mind. They money really cant mean so much, except pays our taxes. I can signe the checks for the incometax. And Hans will go to Horowitz and talk to him once more. It wont help much, but he says, he will try to figure out in case our partnership fall through entirely, how much interest you will have to pay. But really Darling, dont let that worry you too much. I am sure, Horowitz will get something. I am looking forward to jump on the train. I dont like to be here alone, when fall comes. And the leaves turn brown already.—And I simply cant take those mounteners [mountaineers] alone. As you know, I hate gossip and they are all full of it. So it will be wonderful, to get away and come back with my *Träubchen*. The summer was really nice with Hans & Rita around. Passed very quickly. And with all those lovely letters almost every second day and the wounderful war news. How lucky we were, to be here. One cant be grateful enough. That Werfel party sounds gastly. You see how importent I am just to be around you and make up those quick lies on the phone. Lissy is busy. Putting up our tomatoes, fallen aples for jelly and grapes for my *Blümchen* for jam. It all goes very fast and no big talk of the importense of caning! We order our coal for winter, fill the woodshak with wood, so it wont be so wet and get everything done for my beloved winter to come. The house really looks lovely. And the livingroom is <u>so</u> pretty. Pete came back yesterday and he acted like he would have been away for at least 10 years. With tears in his eyes and voice. Such a nice old gaga. I havn't told him yet, that I am going to California. But he'll live, I sp'ose. Well my honeyboy that is all. I will see Moss in town before I leave. He was very depressed on the phone. He is not going out to Calf. California comes to him in form of a cameraman with the picture to cut in the East. He likes that. I cant wait to hear the music as you can imagine. I read in the papers, that Max Gordon is casting Firebrand and trys to get Nino Martini.[1] Bravi told me, he is so bad. I hope, he doesn't signe him, without you hearing him first. Then Dick Holiday writes a show for Mary! Is he kidding? Well, you wont be in this one.— Now good bye my Angel, it's getting dark *und die Rübchen stehen auf dem Tisch* [the little turnips are waiting on the table] for dinner. I am half on my way to Cal. already. By by Darling,

     love Linnerl

---

1. *The Italian-born tenor Nino Martini (1905–76) sang at the Metropolitan Opera but was also in demand for films because of his dashing good looks.*

361 WEILL IN LOS ANGELES TO LENYA IN NEW CITY, 6 SEPTEMBER 1944

                Wed., Sept. 5 [6], 1944

Well, *Pflänzchen*,

    I s'ppose you are getting your ticket today. The Lyons office called me yesterday to tell me that your train arrives here Saturday, Sept. 23, at 9.45 A.M. That certainly is streamlined. As far as I know you have lots of time in Chicago because the "City of Los Angeles" doesn't leave until late afternoon. But I might be wrong about that. In case you want to meet Ruth Page you would have to write her at 973 Sheridan Road, Hubbard Woods, Ill.

    Not much news from here, except work, work, work. Ira has again one of those hypochondriac spells which are so irritating, but I disregard his complaints and go right on working. Thank God, the Queen of Roxbury Drive [Lee Gershwin] is going to Mexico for two weeks today. That might help. She is such a stupid cow. She tries to be helpful, but she is too dumb to understand the problems. And he asks her and her

G'schamster [kowtowing minion] about every line he is writing. But what the hell, as long as he turns out such first class lyrics, it is alright with me.

Terry [Anderson] arrived last night and is staying with me for 3 or 4 days. He is on furlough. Joe the butler said I shouldn't even ask the landlady, so we gave him the nice room with bath opposite mine, which will be your room when you come. I cannot offer him much entertainment because I am working all day long and every evening. But today I take him over to the Revy's and he can play tennis with Richard, and tomorrow I'll take him along to the Gershwin's, so he can swim in the pool while we're working. I like having him here. It is a piece of South Mountain Road.

Well, it seems the movie sale of Venus to Mary Pickford is all set. Jesse Lasky would have given us a better deal, but they were all in such a hurry, so I let them have their way. Now it seems that Lasky was so crazy about me after that one talk I had with him that he wants to sign me to do a picture with Ira for him some time next year. Well, we'll see about that.

Max Gordon called this morning. He had Wilbur Evans in his office who is dying to play Cellini and who, I think, would be our best bet. There seems to be a good chance to get him away from Mike Todd.

I got the statement for the second quarter 1944 from Chappell which contains the money from the record album of "Venus"—with a check for, guess how much— 3449.41. That ain't hay. So you see that a very nice *purtsitag* [birthday] present is coming up. I am enclosing the check here, please deposit it at the bank and at the same time transfer 1800.– from the general account to Kurt Weill tax account.

My rheumatism is gone. Lee gave me a bottle of Vitamine which I am taking every day (without any reason). I am feeling fine.

Well, so long, baby. I s'ppose you're already excited about the trip, and so am I. Take it easy *und strample dich nicht ab* [don't run yourself ragged].

   7777 *Knüsschen*,

        Kurt

I'll make reservations for us to go back on Oct. 20. That would give you 4 full weeks here which is probably all you want. O.K.?

362   LENYA IN NEW CITY TO WEILL IN LOS ANGELES,
7 SEPTEMBER 1944
Letterhead: New City

                                                              Thursday
                                                              9/7/44

Darling,

Today I am a "real" lazy bone. Last night I played pinochle with Mab & her mother (who is leaving tomorrow and I am going to the train—good girly?—) until 4:30 A.M. So, when Dr. Glass hunked his horn around 11:30 I was still sound asleep! I got my injection and feel fine. Tomorrow I am driving in—got a few gas stamps from Mimi.

Otherwise everything sleeps it's "*Dornröschen* [sleeping beauty] sleep" on So. Mountain Rd. I am going to have dinner with Bravi tomorrow and afterwards I [am] going to see the family. I called the Lyons office and the ticket can be transfered, but then it wouldn't be any saving on the return ticket which I ordered now. But we might go back on "the City of L.A." If we tell in time, I am sure, we will get the reservation. The incometax is payed. You have to signe the declaration and it has to be mailed on the 15th of Sept. or sooner. 15th is the last day. Dont get upset about it, just signe it and send it and the rest you do when you get back. Then you can go to Horowitz and change the whole set up. Nothing will be seteled until then anyway. I am sure, Max has troubles with his taxes too. But he doesn't seem to worry. I am glad about Ogdens attitude. He is a smart guy and evidently found out, that bookwriting is not his dish. And that's good. And Darling, forget about Ira. He is just silly. I will tell him, when I get out, that he shouldn't carry on that much about that part and me playing it. I have done more im-portent parts and succeeded pretty well and if he doesn't trust your judgment, he always can ask poeple like the Lunts or Helen Hayes and so on. That'll fix him. After all my succes in Berlin, Paris and London is quite a prove that I am very able to play a part like the Duchess. So, he should shut up and wait. It's too boring that attitude and so unorigional. So if he starts again, just ignore it. If he has no imagination, it's not our fault. After all, who knows him in Europe? I will be quite conceited, when I get there and leave my usual modesty at home. I am good and angry now. Well, *Schnäpschen*, that's all. I send you the statements you asked for. I did my best in saving but there is always some thing to pay. Did I spent too much? I do need a few things, and I'll go to my dressmaker tomorrow and see what I can get. It wont be too much. You know me.—

Well kiss *die Hand* Sir Weill

Your Lady Weill

got a nice letter from Gigi [Gilpin]. She is in India (New Dehli and studies Hindu-stan—poor India)

363 WEILL IN LOS ANGELES TO LENYA IN NEW CITY,
9 SEPTEMBER 1944

Saturday, Sept. 9, 1944

Darling,

I just got your wire and I am very glad that you get that check-up. It is so good to know in what physical condition you really are and to live accordingly. I am pretty sure that there's nothing wrong with you, *weil du ja immer eine ziemlich freche Pflanze warst* [because you always were a rather sassy city-chick]. Please let me know exactly what the doctors say. Your wire was telephoned to me and I couldn't quite make out for what you were thanking me (it sounded like zennia), but I suppose it is for the sweeties from the Viennese shop.

Well, Terry left this morning. I must say he is a tough proposition as a house guest. It takes him about 20 minutes to make up his mind to get up from a chair and go to the window to see how the weather is. It is difficult to take him to people (I had him one afternoon at the Gershwin's) because he is so shy and full of inhibitions that he seems rude and bad mannered to people who don't know him. But I think he had as good a time as he can have, and I think I heard something like "Thank you" when he left this morning—but that might be an exaggeration of my european over-emotional mind!

We didn't have a good working week. Ira was in a bad way all week and we got stock on the Tarantella which opens the garden scene. But we finally solved it. I had a long talk again with Ira about the Duchess and I am quite sure now that there is no viciousness on his part, and nothing personal. He just sees it in a different way, but he says he is not sure if he is right. So I keep on nagging.

I had dinner at the Revy's with the Thomas Mann's who were a very pleasant surprise,—two very sweet old people, wise, humourous, intelligent and far superior to all those intellectual refugees of the Brecht crowd.[1] I had a very nice time talking to them.

Well, *Schnäpschen*, by the time you get this letter, it is only a little more than a week until you hop on that train. I am so glad, especially after your last letter, that you get away from South Mountain Road and it will be so much fun to go back with you end of October.

It has been very hot here the last days, 104 or so. But it is a dry heat, and not bad at all.

> *Lebe, mein Träubchen,*
> Yours truly,
> Kurt

1. *The winner of the Nobel Prize for literature in 1929, Thomas Mann (1875–1955) was acknowledged as Germany's greatest living writer; his wife Katja was Jewish. He and his family left Germany in 1933, eventually settling in Los Angeles; after the war he returned to Europe and died in Zurich. As an ardent defender of the Weimar Republic and the leader of the generation of German writers preceding Brecht's, Mann became a frequent target of attack by Brecht and his circle.*

364 WEILL IN LOS ANGELES TO LENYA IN NEW CITY,
13 SEPTEMBER 1944

Sept. 13, 1944

My *Träubenspatz*,

This will be a short one because I am right in the middle of writing a Trio—and pretty soon you will be here anyhow and we will talk about everything.

Your letter about the tax payments arrived yesterday. Of course, Horowitz has done everything wrong. Where in God's name he got the idea that 8500.– of my taxes have been withheld, I don't know. Before I leave here I will talk with Ira's tax man who has a big firm in New York, handling a lot of people in my position. I will tell him everything Horowitz is trying to do and, if he seems alright, I will hand him over the whole bloody mess. By the way, the checks should have been sent together with the tax form. It will make a lot of confusion when they arrive seperately. I hope you made out seperate checks for you and for me and wrote them a little note what the money is for. Otherwise they will never find out where this money belongs.

Darling, I think you did fine with money because, according to your statement, we have really saved a few thousand dollars over the summer. So will you please stop saving money on your wardrobe! Get everything you need to look pretty and to feel well—you know that's how I want it. So don't be stingy, you *doofi*.

Did you get the Chappell check?

Do you think you should bring a little present for Lee? She is in Mexico now, and Ira and I are having a very nice time, being excited about the show all the time and having lots of fun. What is so good for me with Ira, is that he loves to do things that nobody else does, and that he (the only one) has the technique to do them. So for instance, when I had the idea yesterday of writing a Trio between Angela, Cellini and the Duke, where everyone of them sings something entirely different, he got all excited and we wrote the whole thing between 2 P.M. and 1 A.M. last night, and it is a peach. Now I have to write it out.

So long, baby. You'll probably have another little note from me before you leave. I talked to my landlady and told her that you are coming. She said it is alright with her, but she has to talk to the trustees who are in charge of the house. I suppose I'll have to pay a little more money which is alright with me. If they are too difficult we can always move to the hotel or to Ira or even into Litvak's house.

> *Mit ergebenem Handkuss* [with a devoted kiss on your hand],
> Kurt

That was a funny misunderstanding with the hospital. Can you bring some Odol [peppermint-flavored mouthwash]?

365 LENYA IN NEW CITY TO WEILL IN LOS ANGELES, [14 SEPTEMBER 1944]
Letterhead: New City

Thursday 11: P.M.

Oh Boyly,

I am behind with my letters. I got yours two, with the check (very *primi*) and the up and downs of Ira's laziness. But as a whole it sounds so good. And I think Vilbur Evans would be very good for Cellini. I am glad, that the Queen isn't there, when I arrive. She is such a, what we call in Vienna: *magazinbesen. Zerupft und zerzaust* [a push broom. Shabby and disheveled]. And that *Gschamster* of hers, is hard to take too.—That week went so fast, that I dont know anymore, what I did. Last Friday I had dinner with Bravi, first I met Mab in town and took her to Fried[?] (the painter) she always wanted to go. Of course, she didn't buy anything, because she has to wait for the income tax. I dont know, why she was in such a hurry then, to get there. Then afterwards, we had diner at Sardis (I had an apointment with Bravi—the Mab changed our table and ordered one for her, Bonni—Milton [Caniff] & Bruce [Christians], Bravi & myself) and nobody in her crowd made a move to pay the bill. Though they had champagne coctail and so on. Bravi finally paid. I felt very embarrased. I called Bravi later and appologized, but he said, he is used to that kind of rearrangments. Max went the same evening to the hospital. He has to have an operation. Nothing serious. He has a missplaced sto-mac, that presses towards the heart and gives him that unconfortable feeling and stomac ache [hiatal hernia]. So in about two weeks, he'll have it fixed. I think that's about all news! I havn't seen Moss yet. I will call him and ask him for lunch on Wednesday before I leave. I am taking very little with me. I have a whole day in Chicago. Train arrives 9:30 in the morning and leaves 6: P.M. No, I dont want to see Ruth. I will have breakfast, go to a hairdresser, Museum & movie. It'll pass. The trip will be fun. I am so glad to get away a little. I will make "real" *finelebe* on the train. I will arrive 9:45 in Los Angeles Sept. 23rd. I hope, my boyly will be able to come to get me. Call up first, whether there is any delay. I just wait there at the gate, in case you are a little late. I just got home from Julie. I had invited her and the kids to Jerrys [tavern] for dinner. But Bill, this *hochdramatische Arschloch* [highly dramatic asshole], called from town, they should stay home, because there was a hurrican anounced over the radio. So they were busy all afternoon, locking windows and preparing candles and all that crap. So I went up for dinner. We had storm and rain all day and around nine o'clock, the hurrican arrived on schedule. I liked it. Sitting in a stonehouse, what can happen? Thank God the light went out and we had to lit the candles, which made Julie happy, because it gave her a chance, to say once more, how clever her husband is and praise his sooth-saying qualities.—On the way home, a few trees (little ones) were lying on So. M. Rd. So I got out and cleared the road. Spectacular aint it? I think, I am pretty fresh at the moment. But very *niedelich*, with a new permanent (25.– cold wave—the newest—) and all curly! Cute.—Bravi is coming out Saturday night, I wanted Hans & Rita, but they forgot about the Hollidays [Rosh Hashanah and Yom Kippur]. So they stay in town. Tuesday night I'll stay in town and Pete comes in on Wednesday. I'll stay at Mimis place, I have a lot of things to do on Tuesday. We make a record in the after-noon with little Alan [Anderson] saying all his words he knows for his father for Xmas. It was my idea. And Nancy loves it. His first real sentence was: "I see a girl" so Lyod [Lloyd Orser] said: it'll be probably his last one too.—Mab is all love again, because I brought Hesper a siamese kitten (which I got through [Eva] Gauthier.) So, I am "ador-able" again. Isn't it disgusting how easy it is to buy poeples affections? Well my boyly, I wont write anymore. I hope, everything is O.K. with you. It wont be long now and I'll be bossing around in the house. No privacy any more. You still can think it over. I always can move in to the Beverly Hills. In case you "wont to be alone."

By by Boy. Here I'll go to bed and *schwitze* [sweat]. It's so hot in the house.

> With true affection
> yours
> truuuuuly   Linnerl

Sept. 15, 1944

Darling, just a word to tell you that it is pretty cool out here at the moment—so you'd better bring some suits and sweaters and coats along. But people say it might get very hot again—so you'd better bring some light things too. We even had some rain yesterday (the first since I came out)—and it made headlines in the newspapers.

When you get to Chicago you'll have to find out from what station the "City of Los Angeles" leaves. As you know, it is not Santa Fe, but Union Pacific. I think the name of the Station is Dearborn—but I am not sure. You have about 8 hours to find out. Take a taxi and bring your bags to the other station and deposit them—you *doofkopp* [dumbhead].

I will be at Pasadena at about 9 A.M. Saturday morning. So you'll have to scramble out of bed at eight—unless the train is late.

I think it is *primi* that you are coming. I only hope the weather will be better than it is now, so that you can go to the beach every day and spend some time at the Huston ranch.

So long, sweetie. See you soon. Take it easy and make *feinlebe* on the train.

> *Knüsschens,*
> Kurt

<u>Please, please</u>: don't forget to register us both for the elections. Don't put it off!!!! It has to be done now, otherwise we cannot vote in November, and I certainly want to vote this time!!!!

Lenya arrived in Los Angeles the following week. On 28 September she reported to her sister-in-law Rita Weill:

Well, I had a nice trip, the way I like it. No one bothered me—there wasn't anyone I would have loved to be bothered by—so I stayed most of the time in my aircondi-tioned (what a long word) compartment and by the time I arrived in Los Angeles, I was practically frozen. I found Kurt at the station, looking wonderfully and 105 de-grees in the shade. Nice ain't it? But it's the sort of heat one doesn't feel so much because it's dry. The house is nice as all Hollywood houses. Then in the afternoon we were to see . . . (the Swiss girl you know) and there is a little tragedy going on—as far as she is concerned. Kurt as usual—is far beyond the situation. It's nice to have some experience to be able to handle things like that right.—So dont be afraid Darling, you wont loose your sister-in-law. [L–RW]

In October Lenya and Weill returned to New York, as The Firebrand of Florence *was scheduled to go into rehearsal before the end of the year.*

6 · HOLLYWOOD, PALESTINE, HOLLYWOOD: 1945–1950

Letters 367–393

Weill, Lenya, and Wooly, the Old English sheepdog given them by Moss Hart, in Brook House, 1945. (Photo by Morris Engel)

1945

Weill's optimism about his new operetta was soon frustrated. Moss Hart declined to direct, leaving the task to John Murray Anderson, who excelled at spectacles rather than "intelligent, intimate operetta," as Weill described his show. Casting went equally awry, with Weill winning his battle for Lenya as the Duchess but being forced to settle for a poorly acting and light-voiced Earl Wrightson as Cellini, a poorly singing Beverly Tyler as Angela, and instead of Walter Slezak as the Duke, Melville Cooper in a role ill-suited to his British manner. Weill finished his piano draft in October and worked feverishly to complete the orchestration in time for the Boston tryout, which opened on 23 February as "Much Ado about Love." Reviews were scathing, especially for Lenya: "Someone else should be playing the Duchess, for the sake of all concerned."

Prior to its Broadway opening at the Alvin Theatre on 22 March, the play doctor George S. Kaufman tried in vain to salvage The Firebrand of Florence, *as it was now called. Despite some fine lyrics and inspired musical moments, the show closed after just forty-three performances. It was Weill's only full-fledged flop on Broadway, an especially bitter outcome because he had embraced the idea at first so that he could write a role specifically for Lenya. Lenya took more than her fair share of blame for its failure and sought solace in the arms of one of the baritones in the chorus, Paul Mario. In a letter to his parents, Weill took it all in stride:*

The last few months were full of agitation, because the dramatist who had written the libretto was a total failure, and I felt especially responsible because it was a very expensive show, and of course also because Lenya had appeared in it. . . . Apart from the momentary unpleasantness and irritation that is always tied up with things of this kind, the minimal success has not touched me very much. . . . Long ago I got used to the ups and downs of success, and I have been very aware that after two giant successes, a setback was definitely due once again. Somehow I am even content not to fall into the routine of a regulated successful career. As long as I am trying with each new work to do something fresh, which in many cases is ahead of my own time, I have to make allowances for such setbacks—which, of course, is that much easier because financially I can hold out; therefore—on to new tasks! (W–A&EW2, 30 April 1945)

Within three weeks of the premiere, Weill was back in Hollywood to work on the film version of One Touch of Venus, *which, he was determined, could not be allowed to be ruined—as both* Knickerbocker Holiday *(United Artists, 1944, with Nelson Eddy and Charles Coburn) and* Lady in the Dark *(Paramount, 1944, with Ginger Rogers and Ray Milland) had been, with little of his music and nothing of his musicodramatic conceptions surviving.*

367 WEILL IN LOS ANGELES TO LENYA IN NEW CITY, 11 APRIL 1945

Letterhead: Hotel Bel-Air / Los Angeles 24

Apr. 11, 1945

Mein *Träubentröpfchen,*

It was so good to talk to you yesterday. I had called the Dorset first (person-to-person), then I remembered that you went to Brookhouse. This continuous cold of yours begins to worry me. I think we'll have to do something drastic (like a vacation in the desert) about it. For the time being you just have to be very careful and get as much rest as possible. Well, here is my report: When I arrived in Chicago there was no reservation at all. I had to wait 3 hours at the station until they finally came through with the bedroom on the Superchief. Then I went to see Mary [Martin]—I told you about that. She definitely doesn't want to go on with the show. "Venus" in that huge opera house looks funny, like Mickey Mouse. Mary sang very badly, she has practically no voice, and she is quite mistaken if she thinks that she knows all the answers. But she talked very nicely about you—so she is forgiven.—Madge Evans was on the train, also Jack Kapp (of Decca)—but I didn't see anybody.[1] I have never slept like that in my life. Joe [Jo Révy] was at the station in Los Angeles. As soon as I saw her I knew that I was right with what I had told you: there is nothing for you to be worried. I have a great desire to be left alone, to take it very easy and if I have to see people I want them to be easy to be with (which means: American). I am very glad that the Andersons are here, right next to me. They are so nice and really friendly. Right after I had talked to you, Max came in—happy as a lark because he just got Ingrid Bergman's O.K.[2] Now he has an idea for a comedy and he might do a picture. So they'll probably stay for another 4 weeks and I'll see a lot of them. Hesper was so sweet when she saw me. I spent all evening with them. During the day I am at the studio. They finally signed another writer today and I start working with him tomorrow on the story outline. Today I had lunch with Tola [Litvak] because I would like him to direct the picture [*One Touch of Venus*] if and when he will be discharged from the Army. He is going to N.Y. on Friday and will call you because he wants to see the show and he also would love to spend a few quiet days in Brookhouse if it is alright with you. Sid [Perelman] called today, and I am having dinner with him tomorrow. Sunday I go to the beach with Max and Hesper. The hotel here is alright, except that I don't know yet if it is quiet enough to work. But that is a later question. Ben Hecht is moving in here on Saturday. So you see, there is lots of activity, but don't worry, I take it very easy, and I promise you I won't get upset about anything, and just try to have some relaxation and fun. Sid said on the phone today he hears more and more people saying that you are the most interesting thing in the show. Please darling don't get upset when the show has to close. I'm sure we'll find something else for you. Somebody in the studio told me that it is 87° again in N.Y. and [Louis] Shurr just called he had heard the show is closing on April 28.

I told him to raise hell with Max (he has 15.000 in the show). Good-bye now my sweet and write just a few lines once in a while to your old admirer, lover and husband.

1. Jack Kapp (1901–49) was one of the top record executives of the era, moving from Brunswick to American Decca as its president in 1934. He ruled the thirty-five-cent record world with sales of twelve million discs in 1938. He was known in the trade as "a man of no taste, so corny he's good."

2. In 1947 the Swedish actress Ingrid Bergman (1915–82) would star in the Broadway production of Maxwell Anderson's Joan of Lorraine *and thereby win a Tony Award. At this time she was married to Dr. Peter Lindstrom.*

368   WEILL IN LOS ANGELES TO LENYA IN NEW YORK, 14 APRIL 1945
Letterhead: Hotel Bel-Air

April 14, 1945

Good morning, my Duchie,

I had a wonderful sleep and feel fine today. The last days I had been tired from the change of climate and the President's death gave me a terrific shock. I was at the studio when the news came through—and I have never seen people of all kinds in such an emotion, everybody crying—office girls, executives, writers, actors—completely overcome by real grief. Everybody seemed to grasp immediately the enormous tragedy of the moment, to a man who, like Moses, was standing on a hill looking down on his achievement which he was not allowed to see through to the end, and to a world which probably lost its greatest man. It seems so meaningless, so senseless, this death of a great man at the moment when we all expected the death of Hitler. But then, when we think of the strange similarity with Lincoln's death, one begins to see a meaning. Maybe Roosevelt achieved through his death what he probably could not have accomplished alive. This is the optimistic standpoint. The pessimistic one (which most people here share) is that the coming generation will have to pay for this untimely death.

As far as we are concerned, an event like this helps a little to put things in their place and to look more philosophically at the strange ups and downs of life. I talked to some people who saw the Firebrand: the Hacketts (who loved your performance), Boris Aronson, Victor Samrock (who arrived last night)—and everybody agrees on one point: that the show was killed by production.[1] I begin to see myself pretty clearly what has happened and I learn my lesson. The only thing I really regret is that you were involved in it—but somehow I feel that the whole venture was not so bad for you as it looks. That's the optimist in me.

I got a lovely apartment here in the hotel now, right opposite the Andersons, very quiet, with a large living room looking out on a little brook. On Monday I'll get a piano. I started working with the new writer[?] on the script. He is quite good and I got already a lot of bad stuff out of the script. In about another week we'll be far enough advanced on the script to get started on the songs. I'm getting along very nicely with Pickford, and we spent an afternoon at Pickfair which is really a beautiful place and far superior to those silly Beverly Hills houses.[2] Thursday I had dinner with Sid and his collaborator, they read the show to me, I turned it down.[3] Most of my free time I spend with the Andersons. Today we all go to the ocean, with Victor and the Kingsley's [Madge Evans and Sidney]. Tomorrow I take Catherine and 2 soldier friends of hers to the beach.[4]

I hope I'll have a letter from you because I am always a little worried about your health. How do you feel? Do you put on a little weight? Do you take vitamins? I have a little " 'meride" [malady] myself now, not bad though. Darling, if [Jack] Horowitz calls you, don't do anything without talking to me. (He might pull one of his tricks and try to get money out of you). I'll write Hans about it so that you can discuss it with him.

> *Lebe, mein Schätzchen und sei hochachtungsvoll gegrüsst von deinem* [Farewell, my
> *Schätzchen* and be respectfully greeted by your]
> Knuti

1. *Albert Hackett (b. 1900) had collaborated with his wife Frances Goodrich (1891–1984) on the screenplay of* Lady in the Dark. *They also wrote the screenplays of* It's a Wonderful Life, Easter Parade, *and* The Diary of Anne Frank. *One of the theater's leading designers, Boris Aronson (1900–1980) began his career in the Yiddish Art Theater; in 1948 he would design Weill-Lerner's* Love Life.

2. *"America's Sweetheart" Mary Pickford (1893–1979) was married to Douglas Fairbanks, Sr.; together they built a mansion known as Pickfair. Before their divorce in 1936, they also founded United Artists with Charlie Chaplin.*

3. *Sid Perelman had started work on a new musical with the theatrical caricaturist Al Hirschfeld in 1944; it was first called* Futurosy, *then* Forty-Five Plus *and—after Ogden Nash had joined them as lyricist—*Sweet Bye and Bye. *Weill declined the offer to collaborate because he felt the topic required a "hot jazz" composer. It finally opened in New Haven in 1946, with a score by Vernon Duke, but closed shortly thereafter in Philadelphia.*

4. *Weill is possibly referring to the dancer and choreographer Catherine Littlefield (1908–51), who founded her own dance company in 1936 and choreographed for stage, film, and television. She was the choreographer of* The Firebrand of Florence; *the gossip during rehearsals was that she and Weill were "very close."*

Letterhead: Hotel Bel-Air

April 18, 1945

My Duchie darling,

It was very sweet to have a letter from you and I am certainly glad you got over that laringytis quickly. You know, you really never quite recovered from that grippe you had during rehearsals. You were very weakened then, and going back to rehearsals and through all that excitment your body didn't have a chance to gather strength. That's one reason why the closing of the show has its advantages too: because then you really can take a rest. Of course, you'll keep the room in town so you don't have to bother with household etc. And I do think, if Nan and Walter [Huston] come out here you should come with them and make a real vacation—unless by that time I am already coming back, in which case we would go to Maine or Cape Cod in the summer.

I am pretty much reconciled to the idea that the show will close on April 28. Looking back at what has happened from a little more distance it becomes quite clear what mistakes in taste and judgement have been made. Murray was the main desaster,[1] Eddie [Mayer] the second—and that, coupled with the lack of a director, Ira's laziness and Max [Gordon]'s foolishness is enough to destroy anything. The only thing I have to blame myself for is lack of toughness and taking for granted that Max is a great producer or Ira a good showman (which were both mistakes). My score and you are the innocent victims of these mistakes. But that's the theatre. It wouldn't be so much fun if it weren't so dangerous, so unpredictable. Of course, it is safer to work in the movies. But how dull, how uninspiring!

Not much news here. The new writer is quite good, but he is working with Hollywood tempo, trying to get as many weeks as possible out of a job. I am trying to get the new story outline out of him so that I know where the spots for the new songs are. I have arranged my life here very quietly to get some real relaxation, lying in the sun in my little yard, reading, talking to Max [Anderson]. Saturday I dropped in at the Gershwin's, but they were so depressing that I fled after half an hour. He looks like a ghost. But I cannot feel sorry, because all he is really worried about is the money he has lost—and how to pay for the new decoration of their living room. And I just cannot be mad at her because she is a very stupid woman. On Sunday I had a very gay time at the beach with Catherine and two friends of hers and I got all sun burned. The water was icecold, but very refreshing. Those American boys are really sweet and Catherine is a good sport—no demands and no problems. Monday had dinner at the Révy's and we went to see "A Tree grows in Brooklyn." That's an awful picture, so pretentious and so dreary. Yesterday Max took me out to Malibu where he wants to buy some land at the ocean to build a house after the war. He wants us to buy something together, but I don't think it is a good idea unless we'd find something to build two cottages in some distance from each other. And all we saw were rather small lots (one very nice one near where Louise Carpenter bought her land). Mab is pretending that she is having a wonderful time, but they are staying home every night listening to the news every hour on the hour. They have no friends. Florence gave a party for them before I arrived—with Thomas Mann, Feuchtwanger and Brecht.[2] Mab seems so desperate for entertainment that she even wanted to accept a lunch invitation at Brecht's—but he cancelled it. But in spite of all this they are awfully nice, and real friends (as compared to the Gershwins!). Max and I talked to Ed Wynn (who lives here) about the possibility of doing a modern version of Molières "Le médecin malgré lui" as an intimate musical.[3] I think it wouldn't be bad to do a show with Max now if we find the right idea. What do you think?

Cheryl wired that there is a possibility that Mary will play Venus a little longer, since the picture has been postponed anyhow. Darling, don't bother with Tola. He had asked about the house and I had to be nice, but I am sure he won't go there anyhow.

That's about all I can tell you today. Please take care of yourself, rest a lot and take it very easy

> Yours truuuuuly,
> Kurt

1. *The director of* The Firebrand of Florence, *John Murray Anderson (1886–1954) started out as a dancer and lyricist. Among the musicals he staged are* Dearest Enemy (1925), Jumbo (1935), Two for the Show (1940), *and the* Ziegfeld Follies *of 1943.*

2. *The German dramatist and novelist Lion Feuchtwanger (1884–1958) collaborated with Weill in Berlin and supposedly gave Brecht the title for* Die Dreigroschenoper. *He had left Germany in 1934.*

3. *Ed Wynn (1886–1966) was billed as the "perfect fool" in the* Ziegfeld Follies. *Later he was nominated for an Academy Award for* The Diary of Anne Frank.

370 WEILL IN LOS ANGELES TO LENYA IN NEW YORK, 21 APRIL 1945
Letterhead: Hotel Bel-Air

April 21, 1945

Träubilein,

There isn't much to write, and I'll talk to you anyhow tomorrow—but I don't want you to be without a letter too long, so I write a few lines. I had quite a lazy week, but the weather has been so bad all week that I couldn't go to the beach at all. Mornings I sit around with Max and Mab. He has an interesting idea for a musical for Ed Wynn with whom we spent 2 evenings. The picture outline is far enough advanced so that I can start on the music some time next week. I am almost sure now that they won't keep me longer than 8 weeks—thank God! There are 2 interesting show projects: Paul Robeson wired me that he has an idea he wants to discuss—and René Clair wants to do a show. I have dinner with him tonight. Last night dinner at the [Arthur] Schwartz's—Ira, Lee, Sid, [Harry] Kurnitz—nice and boring. I'll write you more about all this. Now only 3½ kisses from

> your hubby.

April 25, 1945

My Linnerl darling,

There is very little to report from here. The weather is continuously bad and life is quite dull, but I take it easy and try to relax as much as I can. Once in a while I make an effort to help them a little on the picture, but soon I find out that they really don't want any help and that they much rather pay me 2500.– a week for nothing before they would let me do some work on the script. So now we are waiting for that writer to come through with a two page story outline which he could have written down in two hours, ten days ago when I had worked out the whole thing with him. When we get this story outline I might be able to start on the music. On the other hand Pickford might find out in New York that we cannot get the technicolor cameras until fall in which case they'll probably ask me to postpone the whole thing. We'll see.

I am so happy that you were feeling better when I talked to you on Sunday. It must be quite a torture to go through with that show every night now, and in a way I am glad it will all be over in a few days—for your sake. I am firmly convinced (and that is the official stand I take) that my score and your performance were the only interesting things in the show and that it was our bad luk that everything else went wrong. So all we can do is to forget all about it. I had fun writing it and hearing the orchester and chorus. And you had fun rehearsing—and a lot of people saw you playing comedy like nobody else can play it. And that's all we got out of it.

What is all this anyhow when you think that the Russians are in Berlin and when you look at the photo which I enclose here. This is what we've been waiting for for twelve years. Isn't it fantastic how unprepared those Nazis were for defeat? They didn't believe to the last minute that they really can be beaten—otherwise why would they committ suicides by the thousands? I don't think that ever a nation has suffered such a desastrous defeat. "Götterdämmerung" has always been a romantic idea to their morbid minds, and now that it becomes a reality, they are too small to take it. What stupidity! What cowardice! What a "masterrace"! When you think of the courage and pride and confidence which the English, the Dutch, the Russians and, above all, the Jews have shown in the hour of their defeat, it fills you with deep disgust to watch this complete collapse of all human dignity. But stronger than this feeling of disgust is the feeling of "trust in all mankind" to see, at one of the great moments in history, how the human spirit is able to throw off a disease and to return to decency and to overcome the greatest danger to civilisation and progress.

Well, while I'm writing this the sun has come out and a little blue bird is taking a bath in the brook outside of my window—and life is beautiful.

Last night I had dinner at the Gershwin's. Fanny Brice made stuffed cabbage—and it was dull as always. I cannot stand the atmosphere in that house right now, and I don't think they'll see much of me, but I want to keep the surface. Max is having troubles with the contract for Ingrid Bergmann. He was so eager to get her that he promised her all kinds of things which the Dramatists Guild doesn't allow him to give away—and Ingrid's husband seems to be another Dick Halliday. It is slightly disgusting to see the great playwright running after a movie star, but, after our last experience I have full understanding for any author who is trying to protect his work as much as he can.

Now I have to go to the studio. Please darling, take well care of yourself, get your strength back and have a good time. I have the feeling I'll be back soon and we'll have lots of *"Feinlebe."*

> Thousand kisses from your devoted husband
> Kurt

372 WEILL IN LOS ANGELES TO LENYA IN NEW YORK, 28 APRIL 1945
Letterhead: Hotel Bel-Air

April 28, 1945

Träubilein,

This is the last day of the show. I am sad when I think about it, but I know it's no use getting upset again. I suppose you have an empty house this afternoon and you'll be glad when it is all over.—The weather is very lovely here the last few days. I'll go to the beach with Max who has taken a little cottage in a motel and is writing a new play (!!), this time a comedy for Helen Hayes. Tomorrow evening [William] Perlberg is showing the picture [*Where Do We Go from Here?*], so I'm taking the Perlbergs, the Gershwins and the Andersons to dinner at Chasen's. Wednesday I had dinner with Jackson and Deanna.[1] They are not coming to N.Y. Monday dinner at René Clair. Tuesday Walter. Burgess [Meredith] called up and wants to see me. I'll write more about all this. I didn't have a letter from you all week. Maybe I get one today. Good-bye now, my sweet, take it easy, relax, rest, eat well and try to get some injections.

> Yours lovingly
> Kurt

The news from Germany reads like the most exciting detective story—and it is the last chapter.

1. *After fleeing Germany in 1933, Weill's friend and collaborator Felix Joachimson Americanized his name to Felix Jackson. He married Deanna Durbin (b. 1922), who was very much a star in the 1940s.*

373 WEILL IN LOS ANGELES TO LENYA IN NEW CITY, 1 MAY 1945
Letterhead: Hotel Bel-Air

May 1, 1945

Hello, Duchie,

I just had my breakfast with the Andersons. We thought they would announce the end of the war in Europe today, but it seems now that all those peace rumors were a

German trick again. So we'll have to wait a little longer, but it might happen any day now. Did you see that picture of Mussolini's death? Isn't that exactly like a Goya? What a perfect "death of a dictator"! No Shakespeare could have invented it better. I wonder now what kind of death fate has in store for Hitler and his friends.

Thanks for the sweet letter which I got Saturday. I am so glad you are staying out in the country this week and get rid of that cold once and for all. I hope you rest a lot, eat well, take it very very easy and put on some weight!!! And that is an order! It is no good for you to get too thin.

Yes, I can imagine what nonsense you had to listen to all this time, and I'm glad it is all over now. Strangely enough I am feeling much better since the show has closed. It is a closed chapter now. I wrote Moss a long letter and gave him a very good analysis of what has happened. When I described Ira's helplessness in Boston I added: "—and Lee continuing her anti-Lenya campaign with a violence which only an analyst could explain."

I am still waiting for that screenwriter to come through with a story outline so that I can start on the score. Now he has promised it for today, and I hope [Sam] Coslow and I can start on the songs by tomorrow. I am feeling much better physically these last days, mainly because I have been at the beach and in the water several times.

My little dinner party at Chasen's was *"kurz und schmerzlos"* [short and painless]. Just the Andersons, the Perlbergs and the Gershwins. The picture [*Where Do We Go from Here?*] is excellent and comes over as something very fresh and completely original and utterly different from any musical they've made so far. The Columbus opera is really sensational and shows that it would be possible to do a film-opera. Of course, there are week spots in the picture, especially in the end. They cut out the Indian number and "It could have happened" but on the whole I was very pleased.

I tried to call Walter to ask him over for dinner, but couldn't reach him. My dinner with René Clair has been postponed. Max got suddenly all excited about the idea of doing an American version of Dreigroschenoper, laid in the Bowery around 1900, as a satire on Tammany and the election machin. We would use only a few songs from Dreigroschnoper and write new ones—and I wouldn't give [it] to Cheryl. I would rather work with the Playwrights.—A possible show with René Clair also sounds quite exciting. I suggested to him that wonderful French comedy "Le chapeau de paille" which I read last year at the Milhaud's.[1] It is a french classic, and Clair's first picture was based on it. He was very enthousiastic about the idea. Yesterday I had a letter from Paul Robeson, with 2 different ideas for an opera for him, and that's another thing I'll follow up because I feel more and more like writing opera again—opera for Broadway, of course. So you see, I am in no way discouraged and full of ideas.

> So long, baby. My love to Nan, to
> Pete, to the Brook, and above all to
> my one and only Linnerl,
> Kurt

If you could find in the living room library (or in my room) a little book (unbound) of John Gay's "Beggar's Opera", please send it.

1. *Un chapeau de paille d'Italie* (The Florentine Straw Hat) *was written by the French dramatist Eugène Labiche (1815–88); Orson Welles's adaptation,* Horse Eats Hat, *premiered at the Mercury Theatre on 26 September 1936 and was an enormous success. Weill and Lenya had met Darius and Madeleine Milhaud at the dock when they arrived in New York in 1940. They remained in friendly contact until Weill's death; Weill claimed that Milhaud was his only composer friend.*

374 WEILL IN LOS ANGELES TO LENYA IN NEW CITY, 8 MAY 1945
Letterhead: Hotel Bel-Air

May 8, 1945

Here is "Happy V-E Day!" for my Linnerl darling. I am thinking of you all day because this is the day we've been waiting for twelve long years, ever since that night when we drove to Munich, March 1933. You never gave up that firm belief that we'll live to see the end of this horror—and here it is. I can imagine how exciting it must be in New York today and I am sure that you are celebrating, probably with the Hustons. Out here one doesn't feel much of a celebration. They are much nearer to the Pacific war here, and that doesn't let a real spirit of armistice come up. I have been working at the studio all day. But when I got up in the morning (I heard Truman's and Churchill's speach at 6 A.M.) I realized, more than ever before what this meant—and when I drove down to the studio I felt like a million dollar because this happened at a time when we are still young and can enjoy what is considered the best part of our lives in a world without nazis. Lets hope that they'll be really tough with the Germans this time. I think they will because those atrocity stories that were discovered in Germany in the last weeks made a devastating impression on the public opinion here—and even America's sweetheart [Mary Pickford] said today she wants 70 million Germans to be sterilized.

The situation with the picture is quite confused, but I cannot bring myself to worry about it. They are trying to get Greer Garson for the part but I don't think they have much of a chance because she is Metro's biggest draw and why should L. B. Meyer give her permission to do an outside picture?[1] Of course, they will finally find somebody and they can always put it back for a year and do it with Mary [Martin]. But in the meanwhile they'll have to make up their minds what they want to do with me. I have been working on the story again all last week, hoping to get some kind of story outline which would enable me to lay out the songs, but I still haven't got it because that writer is stalling all the time—and who am I to urge him? So I'm just taking it easy. I suppose some time within the next few weeks we'll write a few new songs and then call it a day, for the time being.

With René Clair I didn't get very far. He is interested in my idea of doing a show based on "The Florentine Strawhat," but at the moment he is preoccupied with his plans for a trip to France. He will be in New York when I get back and I'll see him there. I'll also see Paul Robeson then and talk about his ideas.

Max is wooing Ingrid Bergman to sign the contract, like a lover. He is also working on a comedy for Helen Hayes. So the plans for Dreigroschenoper are a little vague. But I am not worried about a new show. I want to wait until just the right thing comes along—and I hope it will be an opera.

I have talked to the publicity people at Twentieth Century and I hope I'll get some nice publicity on the picture "Where do we go from here." From Chappell's I hear that "All at once" will be the most played song by the end of the week and will be on the hit parade in a few weeks. "Speak low" had quite a comeback lately and is being played a lot. Did Bravi ever make those records for Victor? And how about the album for Decca? I suppose they cancelled it. Darling, would you ask Bravi to have another copy of the piano score of "One Touch of Venus" made. Mary Pickford needs it and will pay for it. I'll keep after Pickford to get Bravi for the picture. But as long as the whole project is up in the air I cannot do much about it. I am getting along very well with Pickford and she listens to me.

Well, I'll take a shower now and change my clothes. The Gershwins and Florence are coming here to the hotel for dinner and I think I'll have Max and Mab over and will serve Champaign cocktails for victory.—We had a few nice sunny days, but now it is cold and cloudy again and no chance for swimming. [Harvey] Snodgrass' time is completely booked and so far I had only two tennis lessons and not much exercise. But otherwise I lead a very healthy life, rest a lot and keep my blood-pleasure down.

So long, baby. *Sei niiiiedelich, spiel dich nicht zu sehr auf* [be nice, don't carry on too much], take it easy, have fun, eat well, don't drink and smoke, and *schlipel dich aus und sei hochachtungsvoll ergebenst gegrüsst* [sleep a lot and be greeted with high devotion and deep respect]

> *von deinem Ehegatten* [from your spouse]
> Knuti

Mab is your real friend—she hates Lee. But who doesn't? Max said: I have the impression she doesn't always mean what she says. A typical Anderson understatement.

---

1. *The British actress Greer Garson (b. 1908) was hired by Metro Goldwyn Mayer to "replace" Greta Garbo and Norma Shearer; she won an Academy Award in 1943 for* Mrs. Miniver.

375   WEILL IN LOS ANGELES TO LENYA IN NEW CITY,
11–12 MAY 1945
Letterhead: Hotel Bel-Air

May 11, 1945

Linutschkerl,

On Wednesday I had big mail day. In the morning I had the letter you wrote on Monday (it took only a day to get here) and later I had those two envelops with all kinds of silly mail which I am answering now.

This is another one of those cloudy days here. But I played tennis yesterday and the day before, so I'm feeling fresh as a daisy. I decided yesterday at the studio that the story is far enough advanced for me to determine the song spots and write the new material which, I am sure I can do in the three weeks left until June fourth when my eight weeks guaranty expires. Pickford and Coslow agreed, so now we are working on the score, at last. We are keeping "Speak low," "That's him" and "Foolish Heart," and I am trying also to get the Barbershopquartett ["The Trouble with Women"] in. I have to write about four new numbers.

My little V-E day party was alright. We all had dinner here and then went to see the newsreels with the German atrocity pictures—which seems to me a good way of "celebrating" this victory. Last night I had dinner at the Revy's and we went to see "Wuthering Heights" which I had never seen. It is a very good picture—a woderful story for a romantic opera, but maybe a little too romantic for modern times. Revy wants to get a job in the Allied Military Administration for Germany. I think it is a very good idea for him, especially since they both would like to go to Europe as soon as they can. I asked Max to write to Elmer Davis, head of O.W.I. [Office of War Information] about him which he did.

Max read the Beggar's Opera (thanks for sending it), but he just doesn't understand this kind of negative humor and is always afraid of anything that is not on the line of straight idealism. He sees everything in the light of today's events, and he forgets that it is the privilege of the theatre to see the world in a mirror. By showing with biting humor what the world would be like if it were inhabited by crooks and hypocrits, the "Beggar's Opera" does more good than all the dramas of "noble souls." But I gues one needs the background of an old civilisation to see that—and of all American playwrights Max seems to be the closest to it. I think I'll get him to write a book for an opera for me some day. But I have to get the idea, as usual.

At the moment my show-plans are pretty vague. I read somewhere that Mike Todd is planning the "Bourgeois Gentil'homme" with Bobby Clark which sounds very good. So I wrote Dick Madden [literary agent] to find out if they would be interested in talking to me about doing it as a "comedy with songs." I haven't heard yet. You are right when you say that I have to be very careful with my next book. That's why I am anxious to get back and to talk to a lot of people like Paul Osborn, Arthur Kober, Ogden [Nash], Elmer Rice etc. Right now everything seems to be in a state of suspense. The aspect of a world in peace, wonderful as it is, opens up a carload full of new problems and nobody can even guess in what state of mind the world will be in during the coming years.

Saturday.

I had to interrupt yesterday because America's sweetheart called and I had to go to the studio. In the meanwhile I got a nice letter from my *Träubchen* (from Wednesday). I am so glad you are feeling well and enjoy yourself. A show for Walter would be wonderful. I'll get after Max, maybe we can cook up something. How long is Walter going to stay in New York? I want to talk to him, either in New York or here. It seems pretty sure that I can leave here the week of June 4.

It is raining here today. No beach. So I'll have a long talk with Max. Tomorrow I play tennis at the Gershwins and in the evening I am for dinner at Florences. Her father is coming from San Francisco conference. Thomas Mann and the Andersons will be there. Paulette [Goddard] just called and invited me for dinner a week from Sunday. Last night I had dinner at the Gershwins, in the kitchen. They have no cook and Lee made dinner (very good, by the way—may[be] that's her real profession).

Well, so long, *Schnäuzchen. Tu dir nicht so dicke* [don't be such a show-off].

> *Knüsschen,*
> Knuti

Darling, please ask the Aufrichts what I'm supposed to do with these papers since I am not in N.Y. and can therefore not appear in court. Also, in order to fill out this form, their dates and place of birth, address etc.

Venus is closing today—for good.

376 WEILL IN LOS ANGELES TO LENYA IN NEW CITY, 18 MAY 1945

Letterhead: Brook House

May 18, 1945

Darling,

There is nothing new to tell from here. I am working on some new songs now, and it is hard work because there is no excitment about it. I have been stuck on a melody for three days now and still haven't liked it—and, as you know, that puts me always in a bad mood. The toughest thing for me is to work with second rate people—I loose all my talent. And, of course, it is no help to work on a project without really believing that it will ever be done. Why, in God's name a silly woman like Mary Pickford should produce pictures is beyond me. She doesn't know anything—and she thinks she knows everything. Well, I am determined to take it easy and not to get excited. But I must say, I don't like the idea of getting 20.000.– bucks without delivering anything, exept a few songs. On the other hand, Irving Berlin gets 50.000.– for one song. So I do my job and get out of here the week of June 4, probably leaving here on June 7 or 8. Madeleine [Milhaud] is trying to get a reservation from San Francisco to N.Y. in which case I would go back via San Francisco. If she doesn't get it I would go to see them one of the remaining week-ends.

As was to be expected, Max's enthousiasm for a colored "Oedipus" opera died a very quick death. He didn't find a "meaning" in it. I tried to call Paul Robeson in Chicago, but couldn't reach him, so I'll see him in New York. Otherwise nothing interesting has shown up yet with regard to a new show. It will be a hard grind to find a book because it has to be darned good this time—and I'll have to find [it] all by mayself, nobody will give me an idea. I had lunch with [Otto] Preminger. He wants to do a show—but leaves it to me to find one. Then I had a long session with the head of the story department at Lyons'. They have a lot of properties, and I am studying some [of] them now. I also saw Brecht for a little while. He was nice, but awfully dull. The same old double-talk. He gave me his persian version of "Kreidekreis" [Chalk Circle], but I haven't read it yet. He is leaving for N.Y. today.

So [Richard] Rodgers "is defining a new directive for musical comedy." I had always thought that I've been doing that—but I must have been mistaken. Rodgers certainly has won the first round in that race between him and me. But I suppose there will be a second and a third round.—Yes, Saroyan would be wonderful. I'll try to get in touch with him.[1]

He and Thorton Wilder and Paul Osborn are the guys to work with, and maybe some new, young writers who come back from the war.

I saw two pictures. "The Clock"—a little thin, but charming in parts. "Diamond Horseshoe"—which should be called "Diamond Horseshit." A terrible picture. But they had pre-announcement of "Where do we go from here" with Ira's and my name in huge letters. It seems they base the publicity mainly on the names of the authors— which is alright for me.

This doesn't seem to be a very cheerful letter, but don't worry, I am perfectly alright. Physically I am feeling fine and very relaxed, and I am looking forward to coming home.

So long, *Träubilein*. It is fine that you gained 5 pounds and that you are having a good time. I know that you are just as restless as I am about your work. Why did they turn you down for U.S.O.? Did you tell them that you are a citizen? Maybe we should put a show together for the soldiers oversee? We'll talk about that.

> Bye-bye, and loads of love,
> Kurt

You never wrote me if Bravi made records from Firebrand.[2]

1. *Weill did indeed contact William Saroyan (1908–81) about a collaboration, but nothing came of it.*
2. *Abravanel conducted "You're Far Too Near Me," "Love Is My Enemy," and "Life, Love, and Laughter" for RCA-Victor with Dorothy Kirsten and Thomas L. Thomas.*

377 WEILL IN LOS ANGELES TO LENYA IN NEW CITY, 21 MAY 1945
Letterhead: Hotel Bel-Air

May 21, 1945

Darling,

Today I had your letter from Thursday. I have almost finished the work on 2 songs. Now I have to write 2 more during this and next week, so I'll have to work pretty hard which is a shame because the weather is really lovely now. But, after all, I have to do something for my 20.000.–

Saturday night the Andersons and I went to a big party at Paulette's—very Hollywood but nice. She is very amusing and really *"ausgerutscht"* [unconventional]. Clark Gable is an awfully nice guy.[1] The Danny Kaye's were there, the Milestone's etc.[2] Wonderful Chinese food. Burgess says he has written a show for me and I have a date with him next weekend. He wants to direct it. I also had a long talk with Jean Renoir.[3] He is interested in doing a film opera.—Last night I was sitting with Max & Mab and they told me about the story of a famous american actors family of the middle of the 19th century which George Cukor had given them.[4] Max thought it could make a play but I saw right away that it was wonderful material for a show like "Showboat," so I got them all excited and we talked till late in the night—and this morning he came to my room with a lyric he had written during the night. It is the best material I have heard in a long time, perfect for Max & me—and with a great part for Walter! We are going to talk to Cukor about it.

"Billboard" announces this week that Artie Shaw has made a record of "September-song" which has a chance to become a best seller[5] (His recording of "Beguine" started that song and sold 2 million copies). They write: "K.W.'s classical Septembersong, a beauty of a tune which has been a favorite for [a] long time."

Hans wrote me that Horowitz has some kind of a result, but I'll write Hans to tell him to wait until I get back.

I had a lovely letter from Mary [Martin] thanking me for the show. She writes: "It happens once in every lucky person's life—and you made it happen to me."—Darling, I am looking forward to come home, to see you and the house and the brook. I hope Lizzy will stay.

Please write again. Thousand kisses,

Kurt

Träubi, please don't give Horowitz any money without consulting me. He should wait with the whole thing 'til I get back.

1. *Perhaps Hollywood's biggest male star, Clark Gable (1901–60) was known as "the King."*

2. *The comedian Danny Kaye (1913–89) achieved stardom when he stopped the show with "Tchaikowsky and Other Russians" in* Lady in the Dark. *He was married to Sylvia Fine, a composer-lyricist who wrote much of his special material.*

3. *The famed filmmaker Jean Renoir (1894–1979) was the second-born son of the Impressionist painter. Weill and he had collaborated in 1944 on the propaganda film* Salute to France.

4. *One of Hollywood's most imaginative directors, Cukor (1899–1983), whose credits include* Dinner at Eight *(1933),* The Philadelphia Story *(1940), and* A Star Is Born *(1954), had been replaced by Victor Fleming as director of* Gone with the Wind *(1939).*

5. *The clarinetist and band leader Artie Shaw (b. 1910) was once married to Ava Gardner, who would star in the film version of* One Touch of Venus.

378   WEILL IN LOS ANGELES TO LENYA IN NEW CITY,
22 MAY 1945
Letterhead: The Ritz-Carlton

Tuesday morning

Darling,

I am excited. Max just came over and told me that he has pretty much made up his mind to do that show. We are having dinner with Cukor tomorrow and will try to get him to direct the show and then do it as a picture later. Doesn't that sound good? (I'll try to write a part for you into the show.)—Lets hope that it works out—it is a terrific idea. I cancelled my appointment at the studio and go to the ocean with Max to work on the story.

Bye bye baby. I'll call you in New City Sunday.

Letterhead: Hotel Bel-Air

May 26, 1945

Träubilein,

Here are the notices [for *Where Do We Go from Here?*] in the two trade papers. They are certainly raves for me and I was very pleased to see that the quality of the music seems to make an impression even on those tough guys. I have now finished 3 songs for Venus (2 good ones) and have one more to write. I am definitely through at the end of the 8th week which will be June 4th and will leave that week, any time between the 7th and 10th whenever I get a reservation. The project with Max is pretty cool again, after 2 days of enthusiasm. I'll tell you about that tomorrow on the phone. Yes. You are right: I'll feel much better when I get away from those grave diggers here. Tomorrow I'll spend all day with Burgess, who has a very exiting idea.

> *Lebe, mein Blümilein,*
> Yours for the asking
> Kurt

Please keep these clippings!

Letterhead: Hotel Bel-Air

June 1, 1945

My *Blümilein,*

I just came back from a tennis hour with Snodgrass (my tennis is getting very good), had a bath and breakfast and feel fine and dandy. Now I want to talk to you a little and then go with Mab for lunch with a woman editor of Photoplay who is a great fan of mine. In the afternoon I work with Coslow to wind up my business on the picture [*One Touch of Venus*] and tonight I work with Max.

As I wired you, we are making very nice progress on the show now, Max and I. Of course, I have to have all the ideas because he still has his mind on the rewriting of the Joan play—but at least I keep his and Mab's enthousiasm alive and he is more than pleased with my ideas, and he'd better be because they are very good. It can be a very exciting show. I want to get enough ideas so that we can talk with Cukor and Griffith and set up the whole thing before I leave.[1]

I have some more interesting ideas for shows. One of them is to do a musical based on "It happened one night." I am seeing Leland Hayward tomorrow to find out if he can get the rights for me.[2] Also I haven't given up my idea of an Oedipus opera for Robeson—even if Max doesn't write it.

"All at once" doesn't seem to go so as well as we hoped.[3] I have a strong suspicion that some dirty game is going on at Chappell's again—and if I find that out it will be definitely the end of my relations with [Max] Dreyfus.

Last night I went with the Révy's to a performance of "Volpone," mostly by Group theatre actors. It was very nice, terribly overplayed, but full of good ideas and very refreshing. And what a wonderful play!

This weekend I go to see the Milhaud's if I get a reservation. Just for one day. And next week I'll be on the train home—hurray! I'll let you know as soon as I know exactly what day I'm leaving.

Did you ever see the Spring issue of a magazine called "Stage"? It has a very nice picture of you. I'll bring it.

Now I have to run. Bye-bye, my little Duchie and loads of love,

Kurt

1. *Possibly Richard Griffith (1912–69), who had worked with Frank Capra on the wartime documentary* Why We Fight. *He went on to become curator of the New York Museum of Modern Art.*

2. *Frank Capra's* It Happened One Night *starred Clark Gable and Claudette Colbert. Leland Hayward (1902–71) was a prominent agent and producer married to the actress Margaret Sullavan (1911–60); he went on to produce the Broadway productions of* Mister Roberts, Gypsy, *and* The Sound of Music.

3. *"All at Once" was the ballad sung by Fred MacMurray in the opening moments of* Where Do We Go from Here? *Weill had long felt neglected by Chappell's "standards" department. After the publisher was unable to place* Street Scene *in European opera houses, Weill became more and more dissatisfied, eventually giving* Down in the Valley *to Schirmer.*

1945–1947

After Weill's return to South Mountain Road in June 1945, it was nearly two years before he left home again for any extended period of time; thus there is no correspondence with Lenya during a highly intense period of compositional activity. In the first half of the decade Weill had seemed to focus on establishing a successful career in both New York and Hollywood, largely to secure financial stability and a base from which he could again create what he deemed "really important works." As the war ended, Weill concentrated on projects that now seem highly personal in their commitment: the folk opera Down in the Valley, *intended as a pilot for a series of short radio operas that were to be based on a folk song or popular ballad; the "American opera"* Street Scene, *based on Elmer Rice's Pulitzer Prize–winning play about the microcosmic melting pot of a New York apartment building; a "Kiddush" commissioned by the Park Avenue Synagogue in New York and dedicated to his father; and incidental music for Ben Hecht's Broadway pageant* A Flag Is Born, *a "vision of the Jewish homeland experienced by three survivors from Nazi persecution" that opened at the Alvin Theatre on 5 September 1946.*

Most of his efforts were directed toward the creation of his long-planned "Broadway opera." Soon after his return from California in 1945, Weill and Maxwell Anderson began work on an adaptation of Rice's Street Scene, *even attempting to patch in some of the* Ulysses Africanus *material. Rice objected to Anderson's participation (both were members of the Playwrights' Producing Company) and decided to adapt the property himself. He agreed, however, to employ the Harlem Renaissance poet Langston Hughes as lyricist for the project. It took the team nearly eighteen months to complete work on the most daring piece Weill had attempted since his arrival in America—a self-conscious response to the example of* Porgy and Bess. *Cast with a combi-*

nation of Metropolitan Opera singers, Hollywood actors including Anne Jeffreys, and veteran Broadway singing actors, Street Scene tried out in Philadelphia, playing to terrible reviews and nearly empty houses for three weeks. After much doctoring, the production opened at the Adelphi Theatre on Broadway on 9 January 1947. "Seventy-five years from now Street Scene will be remembered as my major work," said Weill at the time (quoted by Sundgaard, p. 26). And indeed his profound belief in his work seemed vindicated by critical and audience response, although weekly running costs were very high, with dangerously little margin. During the gestation of the work, Weill himself had been elected to membership in the Playwrights' Producing Company, the first new member since 1930 and the only composer among the group. After the Firebrand disaster Lenya had all but given up on her career, and she seemed anything but content playing only Mrs. Weill and canasta offstage.

After the exhausting months of composition, rehearsal, and tryouts of his opera, the sudden death of Weill's beloved brother Hans at age forty-eight on 1 March 1947 precipitated what some family members termed a "nervous collapse." In April Elmer Rice's nomination of Weill to the American Academy of Arts and Letters, which Aaron Copland reluctantly agreed to second, was unsuccessful, whereas Paul Hindemith was elected to membership and Arnold Schoenberg was awarded the Distinguished Achievement Prize of the National Institute of Arts and Letters, "presented annually to a European artist residing in America." On 1 May Weill reported to Margarethe Kaiser more bad news: "I had a letter from Universal Edition with the offhand notification that all my full scores had been confiscated by the Gestapo. Of course, that is an unbelievable breach of a publisher's responsibility to its authors. I don't have a single full score of my European works, and therefore at the moment I can't say if one can procure them anywhere" (W–MK).

On 6 May Weill boarded the RMS Mauretania for a trip to England, France, Italy, Switzerland, and Palestine—his first return to Europe since 1935 and his first meeting with his aging and ailing parents since they had immigrated to Palestine. Weill had been planning the trip for a long time; in his first postwar letter to Caspar Neher, on 2 July 1946, Weill had told him of his hope to visit his parents and oldest brother in Palestine, and "afterwards come to visit you in Switzerland." Weill's letter communicates something of the emotion he must have felt during the trip:

What a joy to hear from you again after all those years—to know that you've survived these catastrophic years and that you are safe, can work again, and are beginning to make plans for the future. It's strange; when I saw your letters, it suddenly felt as if the eleven years since 1935 had dissipated, and it seemed like only yesterday that we said goodbye for the last time. And all those wild, ugly, unspeakably cruel things that occurred over those years suddenly seemed to have been wiped away, so that quietly our good old friendship could resume as if it had never been interrupted. You can imagine how disgusted I felt at the events in Germany during those years, and at those who threatened to rush headlong into the destruction of not only their own people but the entire world. This feeling—allied with a great sense of gratitude and affection for the new home I've found over here—created within me a kind of indifference and apathy toward the fate of the people I had once known in Germany. You and Erika were the only exceptions, and there was hardly a day when I didn't think of you in some context or other. (W–CN)

In a private note to Erika, Weill philosophized: "The world has become so small, and there is no serenity or harmony or peace or bliss—maybe a bit more here in America than in Europe, but here, too, life is unsettled and stressful. The solution Voltaire posits at the end of his Candide *still seems the best: planting potatoes and flowers on a small parcel of land somewhere, a few friends, a book, and—work" (W–EN2).*

1947

381 WEILL EN ROUTE TO PALESTINE AND IN LONDON TO LENYA IN NEW CITY, 8–13 MAY 1947

Letterhead: Cunard White Star / RMS Mauretania

Thursday, May 8, 1947

My *Träubili*,

I feel like talking to you a little although I cannot mail this letter until I get to England and you won't get it before the end of next week. You looked very pretty standing at the peer on Tuesday and I didn't like at all the idea of leaving you and felt pretty blue that first evening. Mr. [Otto] Halpern turned out to be a nice old jew from England, almost deaf and very talkative. But we have arranged things as pleasantly as possible under the circumstances. He goes to bed first, I follow later. In the morning he gets up early and leaves the cabin, I have breakfast in bed and take it easy. So I have slept very well the first 2 nights. Yesterday was a lovely day, I got a chair on the sun deck and got my first sunburn. The boat is completely quiet and smooth and most of the time one doesn't even know that one is on the ocean. It is kind of *vorsintflutlich* [antediluvian] to travel this way, with a lot of people who are typical middle class, even if they have lots of money. The boat is not finished yet and in some respects quite uncomfortable, food plenty, but without imagination. But it definitely is an ideal way of resting and getting away and being lazy—so that's what I'm doing and it's good for me. But I don't think I want another week of this coming back. By the way, I'm not the only one who has to put up with other people. They have built upper berths in all single cabins, and there is a lot of complaining about it. So I'm sure the same thing would happen on the return trip, and I guess I'd better fly and get a week earlier to my *Schmöckchen*.—We have movies every day—the first night "The guilt of Janet Ames," a complete steal from "Lady in the Dark," with Rosalind Russell giving one of the worst performances of the century.[1] Yesterday a very interesting, beautifully photografed english picture about a nun convent in India, "Black Narcissus," with Deborah Kerr who is quite lovely.[2] They are away ahead of Hollywood, better ideas, better scripts, better color, and much better acting. Last night I sat with the [Yip] Harburg's and some very nice English people. Mrs. Harburg is nice and intelligent. She asked when I was married, I said: in 1928. She:—but not to the same woman who was on the peer—I: Yes—She:—but she looks like 30! I (thinking fast): she was only 18 when we married—See! I always told you that you are a *schmucke Puppe* [pretty doll]! There were some wires in my room on Tuesday, from members of the cast [of *Street Scene*], Yvonne [Casa-Fuerte], Don Saxon[3]—and a large fruit basket from Hicks, sent by Mr. and Mrs. Max Dreyfus. It is very sweet of them, but what shall I do with all that stuff! And yesterday I had a nice surprise with your wire which I answered immediately. You probably read it right now. Well, I go to lunch now. So long, *Schätzchen*, I talk to you again tomorrow.

Saturday. Here I am again. The last days were cloudy and foggy, and I couldn't make use of my chair on the sun deck. But I feel fine, make long walks around the deck, eat very moderately and am alone most of the time which, as you know, is much less boring than to be with people. I talk sometimes to some very intelligent English businessmen, and I think I understand the English character better now than 12 years ago and have more respect for it—or maybe the English have changed quite a lot. They are, in a way, wiser and less hysterical than Americans and they look at things with a great sense of humor. Today we had passport inspection and Ben [Hecht] was, of course, all wrong when he thought they would ask questions. All they asked was: have you any other business in P[alestine] except seeing your family?—and when I said: no—they just accepted it, according to the Anglo-Saxon law which [Ferruccio] Busoni taught me, that nobody is guilty unless his guilt is proven.

Sunday. It is still very cool and I could have used the warm yellow sweater. Thank God, you insisted that I take the Camel coat. *Weil du eben ein grosses Klugi bist* [because you're such a big smarty]! And very *niedelich* too! You were so cute when you made a sort of *"Kratzfuss"* [deep bow, with foot movement] at the pier, when Harburg, from the boat, introduced you to the man in front of you. I think I'm just nuts about you!— Today I had a cable from Louis Dreyfus in London. They have reservation for me at Claridges in London (that's where Tilly [Losch] used to live,) and the Raphael in Paris. It seems we will arrive in Liverpool Monday and get to London Tuesday afternoon, so I'll go to Paris Thursday or Friday and leave there probably Monday. That gives me very little time in London and Paris, but if necessary I can stay on my way back a few days. If I fly back I'll be home around June 10th, and that would be very much alright with me. I don't see much of the Harburg's. They are communists of the real stupid kind and full of old crap—discrimination etc. and they act as if they had invented it and as if they had to convert everybody including those shrewd English businessmen. Well—who listens? Darling, tell Cheryl she should read "Aurora Dawn" by Herman Wouk.[4] It has possibilities for a small satyric musical. The running commentary could be done by a small chorus or quartett and a certain 18th century quality of the book could be preserved in the music. If she likes the idea she might contact the author (Wouk) and get him to wait for my return. Carly W.[?] is fooling around with it.— How are you coming along without me? Are you going to Dubarry again and how is *der kleine weisse Hintern, mehr wert als eine kleine Fabrik?*[5] Are you having a nice Sunday today? Is the lilac coming out already? Or are they waiting for me? Well, here is the dinner bell. You would scream if you would have to go [to] that dining room every day. But I started my own little rebellion and don't dress anymore. So long, *Schätzchen!*

Monday. Here we are outside of Liverpool. We will land this evening and I am trying to get a sleeper for tonight to London so that I have a full day tomorrow. You cannot imagine all these formalities one has to go through with visas, duties etc. You would go crazy. But on the whole the trip was pleasant and restful and I am full of expectations about the next phase. (My fountain pen just went dead). Good bye now, me darling. When you get this letter I'll be in Paris, but I'll write from London. Sweet kisses from your Knuti!

Tuesday. Here I am at Claridge's, just arrived 8 A.M. The taxi drive through London very interesting. The town is much more scarred than I thought. I can see already that this is going to be a very interesting (and strenuous) trip and I'll give you day-to-day reports. This one I want to send off now. So here is another sweet kiss for my sugar-pie—Kurti

---

1. *Rosalind Russell (1912–76) was a major Hollywood star in the forties and fifties, appearing in* Auntie Mame, Picnic, *and* My Sister Eileen.

2. *Deborah Kerr (b. 1921) was nominated for six Academy Awards, including her performances in* From Here to Eternity *and* The King and I. *The classic* Black Narcissus, *directed by Michael Powell and Emeric Pressburger, concerned a group of Anglican nuns who try to establish a school and hospital in the Himalayas.*

3. *Don Saxon was playing the role of Harry Easter in* Street Scene.

4. *The American novelist Herman Wouk (b. 1915) wrote* Aurora Dawn *in 1947; he went on to fame and fortune with* The Caine Mutiny *(1951) and* The Winds of War, *for which he won the Pulitzer Prize in 1971.*

5. *Cole Porter's* Dubarry Was a Lady *starred Ethel Merman. "The little white behind, worth more than a small factory" is a quotation from "Unzucht" (Lust) in* Die sieben Todsünden.

---

382 WEILL EN ROUTE TO AND IN PARIS TO LENYA IN
NEW CITY, 15–16 MAY 1947
Letterhead: Claridge's / Brook Street W1

May 15, 1947

My Linercherl sweetheart,

Here I am on the train to Paris, Thursday afternoon, it is difficult to write because the train rattles like mad. These 2½ days in London were packed with excitment and the only regret I had was that you were not with me. But we will definitely come here together next spring or earlier. I am very impressed with the English people, their quiet friendliness and their complete [lack] of that fear and hysteria which has become so typical of Americans lately. One of the main reasons for their stoic attitude seems to be that they have a better conscience about the war because they have really suffered and—they did not use the atom-bomb (which they resent deeply). The food situation is really incredible, even at Claridge's where Louis Dreyfus took me for lunch every day. That was, as you remember, the place where [Rudolf] Kommer had his table and only the biggest snobs of society were admitted. Today it is a very simply dressed crowd eating their one dish—and it is the kind of dish which we would send back if the waiter at Child's would offer it. Yet, nobody is starving and nobody complains and most people say: alright, we get less, but for the poor people it is more than they ever had. Everybody gets the same, and what they can buy is cheap enough so that everybody can afford it. Louis and his office were wonderful to me. I had a lovely room (real *Feinlebe Schniekedibong!*) at Claridge's with perfect service and they arranged all reservations etc. which is terribly difficult. Chappell's in London is a real european publishing house without any song pluckers [pluggers]! The man for whom I played the Street Scene records and who is going to work on it, had tears in his eyes when he heard it. He thinks it could be a tremendous success if it is done right and he starts negociating with one of the modern opera companies. There is also a chance at Covent Garden. So you see already, they have a different approach from Larry Spier![1]

Monday evening I spent in Liverpool after we landed and went to a "pub" and a music-hall and was amazed how "european" the whole atmosphere was. When I came to the train at midnight, a woman said to me: Are you Kurt Weill? I said: Yes, how do you know? She: I am a Dutch sculptor, I watched you on the boat, and when I saw your hands I said: this must be K.W.—I slept through till 7, took a taxi to the hotel where I met Burgess just going to the studio. In the afternoon I saw one act of Sam Behrman's play "Jane" (very weak) and had tea with Hubert Clifford, Maurice [Abravanel]'s friend who is [Alexander] Korda's musical director. He doesn't stop talking about Street Scene and he says Korda definitely wants me to do a "film opera." Then I had dinner with Burgess and Paulette, very nice (he even paid the dinner!) At ten I drove out to Frank Cahill's. That was rather disappointing. He has become sort of middle class–*Kleinbürger* [petit bourgeois] and is more bitter than the other people I have talked to (the eternal *Spiessbürgerproblem* [philistine problem]). They live rather poorly, with a son who is 6 ft 3, and a very pretty daughter—but they are still english in the old sense, and quite hypocritic.

I'm getting close to the white cliffs of Dover now. The english landscape is lovely in the sunshine and one sees very little destruction. (In London one can still see a great deal of bomb damage, sometimes whole blocks are down and they use them as parking plots).

Now I am on the boat and we will leave in a few minutes. To continue my report: yesterday morning I walked around a little. In the afternoon I saw Marc [Connelly]'s friend Ormerod Greenwood, a sweet young man who talks exactly the way he writes. He would like to write opera librettos and I think he might be very good.[2] Then I saw one act of an intimate review "Sweetest and lowest" (not too good). In the evening Clifford had arranged a little dinner for me at his club with some of his friends. There were some of the old-guard Weill-Lenya-fans and they all know about Street Scene. We talked until 2—movie, theatre, film, politics—the kind of evening one finds so rarely in America. Of course, I am sure that all this is only the first impression. I still prefer living in America especially in Brook House chez Linnerl! I had your sweet letter when I arrived. It made me happy—and lonesome for you. I hated to leave you alone, but I had to get this over with, I mean this visit to my parents. I'll try to be back soon. Sunday night I go by train to Geneva where I get on the plane at noon. The same evening I get to Cairo where I stay over night and in the morning I arrive in Jerusalem. I have cut down my stay there to exactly 2 weeks, will be back in Paris on June 4 for 2 days and I think I should [spend] another few days in London to finish some of the things I have started, especially St. S. [*Street Scene*] and the Korda picture. I also talked, this morning, to Ralph Hawks about my situation with Universal Edition and I think it can be cleared up.[3]

Now I am in the middle of the Channel, that little stretch of water which the great Hitler could not cross. The sea is quiet and nobody is seasick. In Calais I have to go through the French custom inspection and at 11 tonight I am in Paris where the French office of Chappell takes me over.

3 hours later. I am in train from Calais to Paris now. France looks very pretty and very much like New City. I had a nice dinner on the train, simple food, but so much more tasty than in England—and a nice bottle of Bordeaux. The custom inspections will be on the train. At dinner I sat with an english boy who was taken prisoner at Duncerque in 1940 and came home in 1945. Now he is going to Montreux as a waiter. So me Darling, I say Goodbye now, so I can mail this letter in Paris tonight. I love you dearly and I miss you all the time and I am already impatient to get home. So long, baby, take care of yourself and *sei geliebt u. geküsst von* [be loved and kissed by]

> *deinem* Kurt

Can you read this *Gekritzel* [scribbling]?

Friday morning. I am in Paris. It was too late last night to mail the letter. The taxi-driver explained to me in beautiful French that the red light is *"pour stopper les voitures"* [to stop the cars] and the green *pour aller* [to go], and went into a long explanation why it is more *"utile"* [useful] during the day than at night. What a difference from England! That old French charm is still there—*mais la vie est très dur ici. J'avais une longue conversation en français sur le train et j'étais étonné que je peux converser assez bien.*[4] Now translate this. It will keep you busy for a little while. The Raphael is a very elegant small hotel near the Ave. de Triomphe. I have a lovely old-fashioned room which you would love—soooo french. They just brought me *"le déjeuner complet"*—a little coffee, a piece of black bread and marmelade. So here is another kiss for you, my *Schätzi*.

---

1. *Spier was the song plugger at Weill's publisher in New York, the American branch of Chappell Music.*

2. *John Ormerod Greenwood (1903–49) was a British writer (*William Blake as a Prophet, The Quaker Tapestry*) who also wrote the libretto for an opera by John Gardner.*

3. *Universal Edition's Jewish owner, Alfred Kalmus, had immigrated to London in 1936, after terminating Weill's contract in 1933. Ralph Hawkes (1897–1950) was one of the principals of the firm resulting from the 1930 merger of Boosey with Hawkes, both of which had been music publishers as well as instrument makers. Weill was particularly interested in getting Boosey & Hawkes to represent* Street Scene. *Weill had had little or no contact with Universal Edition during the preceding decade, and he never forgave the firm for the cowardice and disloyalty its leadership had demonstrated by suspending his contract already in 1933, soon after Weill's arrival in Paris, and for what appeared to be the loss of all the orchestral scores and performing material of his European works.*

4. *"But life here is very hard. I was having a long conversation in French on the train and I was surprised that I can converse rather well." (There are, however, a few errors in Weill's French.)*

Letterhead: Cunard White Star

Geneva, May 17, 1947

My Sweetie-pie,

   This will be just a little note before I go on the plane. You can imagine what a rush those few days in Paris were. I did more in those 3 days than a Frenchman does in 3 years. I was twice at the theatre (an evening of Jouvet plays, and Hedwige Feuillière in Cocteau's idiotic play, both evenings terribly old-fashioned, empty and pompous).[1] I saw Marie-Laure [de Noailles] and went to see the Monnet's in the country (he is a Senator now). And I had negociations for "Lady" and Street Scene. Aufricht's friends are awfully nice, Blanquet[?] especially, and I will give them the rights although I am pretty sure that neither they nor anybody else will do anything in Paris. It is absolutely the atmosphere of a Balkan town, deeply corrupt and defeatist. One feels every minute what Hitler has done to a people that was weak and that went into all the pitfalls of an enemy occupation. I'll tell you more about all this in my next letter. Last night I took the train (*wagon-lit* [sleeping car]) to Geneva, slept well, arrived this morning in an oasis of peace and quiet and welfare which reminds very much of America because it is untouched by war—clean, charming as landscape and without all those tricks which make everything so difficult in France. Now I'm sitting at the Airport waiting for the plane which is 2 hours late. It is a perfect day and I feel swell, just had lunch with *primi Rösti* [fried potatoes] and *Schweinebraten* [roast pork] and excellent beer. *Das lebt* [that's living]! The snow mountains are right above the airfield and look beautiful. I wished you were here—but it would have been a terrible strain for you, the whole thing. Europe is not ready for travelling. Good-bye now *Schätzilein*. I love you and kiss you and miss you.

Thanks for wire and letters! Very cute!

   1. *The French actor and director Louis Jouvet (1887–1951) staged many of the plays of Giraudoux; in 1947 he directed Jean Genet's first play,* The Maids. *Cocteau's neoromantic love story* L'Aigle à deux têtes *dates from 1946. Edwige Feuillère (b. 1907) was one of the great French actresses of the day.*

Naharia, May 22, 1947

Mein Träuben-Schätzchen,

   So here I am in Naharia and I must say it is much nicer than we thought it would be. To tell from the beginning: after I wrote you in Geneva, the plane arrived and we left at 2:30. As soon as we were up in the air I just loved the flight and there is no doubt that it is the only possible transportation if one cannot take trains. One feels completely safe in those huge ships, especially when one watches those quiet, self-controled American boys who pilot the plane. We flew down the Rhone-valley, over Marseille along the Riviera, crossing Corsica and landed in Rome after 3½ hours. Then, after an hour in Rom we left and flew straight to Cairo in 6 hours. I had a nice time with a young guy from Hollywood and a girl from N.Y. who knew me and was on her way to Cairo to get married. Unfortunately, we had to stay over night in an awful hotel in Cairo and the plane did not leave until 11 the next day. So I arrived in Lydia at 12.30 Tuesday. Leni and Hannelore [Nathan Weill's wife and daughter] were there and we drove in 2½ hours to Naharia. This is really a lovely place, very much like California, and beautifully built up by German Jews—the whole thing very impressive. Even more than in London and Paris I am sorry that you are not with me. I'm sure you would like, especially the wonderful beach and ocean. The family is much more pleasant than we thought. The parents are amazing—no lamenting or complaining, but sheer happiness to see me. Father looks like a man of 60, swims with me every morning, mother a little *kränklich* [sickly], but nice and intelligent. Nathan is a swell guy, witty and more like me than anybody in the family. They are knocking themselves out, of course, to make everything nice for me. I live at Nathan's, eat *Mittagbrot* [lunch] at mother's, go to the beach all morning, drive around with Nathan in Arab villages (very interesting), and talk to all friends of the family—which is the whole town. There is a great feeling of happiness, of youth and gaity over this whole place. The papers are full of reports about my arrival and all theatrical and musical organisations want to give receptions for me. Next week I will spend 2 days to see Jerusalem and Tel-Aviv, probably speak at the Radio and make a "personal appearance" with the Palestine Orchester and the Habima [Theater]. On June 3 I fly back to Geneva, on the 4th I take the train to Paris, on the 7th to London and from there I fly home on the 11th—hurray! And how is my *Schnäutzchen?* I am anxious to hear from you and more anxious to be back with you. After the first impression here is over it will probably get pretty dull and I am glad that I limited it to 2 weeks only. In Paris I will see some of the translations for "Lady" when I get back, and in London I'll talk to Korda. Tonight we went to the movies, "Meet me in St. Louis." Darling, I think we wait with the swimming pool till I get back. I haven't heard anything about Street Scene and don't know if it is still running. I say good-bye now. In less than 3 weeks I'll be home again. *Sei niedelich und sehr geliebt und geküsst* [be nice and very much loved and kissed].

[FIG. 71]

> *deinem Freundchen*

Friday morning: just another *Knüsschen* for my Linnerl. Everybody sends his love.

385 WEILL IN NAHARIA TO LENYA IN NEW CITY, 27 MAY 1947

Tuesday, 5/27/47

My Linntchkerl,

This will be a short letter because it is late and I am tired and have quite a sunburn on my back and shoulders. For a week now I have been at the beach every day and got a nice rest although I had to see people all the time. They are all so hungry here to talk to somebody from another country that one cannot refuse. But you know how tiring it is to talk to people.

Thanks for your sweet letter. Of course, I was a little sad about Street Scene, but there is nothing one can do. I had a nice cable from Wiman, saying that he is very hopeful for next season.[1] Your wire to the cast was lovely and I am happy that you sent it. You are a wonderful *Träubchen.* Yes, I think Charlie Friedman is a possibility for a new show and it would be nice to have him in the [Henry Varnum] Poor house for a while.[2] I am glad that you are not driving out alone at night and stay with Rita. Please give her my love, also Marc [Connelly?] and the Liebersons.[3] I have no time to write. No, darling, I don't think a trip to California would be much fun for us, unless I get a job and can make some money. I really want to start on a new show when I get home. I would love to do one with Max, but I don't think he will work out there. When he comes back he will be burning to start working.

We had holidays here Saturday and Sunday and the place was full with people. Yesterday the director of the Habimah came to see me and today a man with an interesting marionette film project.[4] This man will take me on 2 days tour through the country tomorrow and we will spend the night in one of the famous collective farms and see a theatre performance there. Sunday morning I take the parents to Tel Aviv when I will be received by the Mayor at 11, lunch with Dr. [Chaim] Weizmann in his house (the greatest honor one can get here), at 5 press reception, at 8 a performance of Oedipus by the Habimah and after that a big reception with 200 people. Monday I'll spend in Jerusalem, Tuesday I leave, Wed. Geneva, Thursday-Friday Paris, Saturday London, following Wed. home—hurray! *Ich freue mich schon mächtig auf mein Schätzchen und auf unser Häuschen* [I'm already looking mighty forward to my little treasure and to our little house]!! It is only 3 weeks since I left you, but it seems like an eternity. Good night now, my Linnerl, take care of yourself, don't loose too much weight, *sonst versohle ich Dir das Warschi—und sei sehr geliebt und geküsst* [or else I'll tan your little behind— and be very much loved and kissed]

von deinem [from your] Knuti

1. *Dwight Deere Wiman had coproduced* Street Scene *with the Playwrights' Producing Company. Following the disastrous tryouts in Philadelphia, Wiman put up his own money in order to make a New York opening possible. After its initial run of 148 performances, he hoped to reopen the production on Broadway in the fall.*

2. *The director of* Street Scene, *Charles Friedman (1902–84), had also directed* Pins and Needles *and* Carmen Jones *on Broadway.*

3. *Goddard Lieberson (1911–77) was married to the dancer Vera Zorina; an Eastman-trained classical composer himself, Lieberson headed the Master Works catalogue before assuming the presidency of Columbia Records in 1956. He had courageously produced the original cast recording of* Street Scene, *and in the 1950s would release a series of recordings by Lenya crucial to the so-called Weill renaissance.*

4. *The Habimah Theatre had been founded in 1909 in Poland and revived in Moscow in 1916; it toured throughout Europe after leaving Russia in 1926 and settled in Tel Aviv in 1931.*

386 WEILL IN NAHARIA TO LENYA IN NEW CITY, 31 MAY 1947

Naharia, May 31, 1947

My *Tröpfilein,*

This is my last day in Naharia, and I want to spend it as much as possible at the beach. My trip through the country was very interesting but quite tiring because it was

as hot as Needles, California. Those jewish settlements are very impressive indeed—but
what fascinated me much more was the strangely beautiful, biblical landscape and the
completely oriental character of life and people, the mixture of colorful Arabs on their
horses or camels, monks and churches, Jewish farmers on their Ford tractors, ancient
and new, christian, mohammedanian, jewish—three civilisations together in a small
piece of land. We bathed in the sea of Galilei (Genezareth, where Jesus went) and spent
the night in an ancient town, Safed, and went up to the Syrian border the next day.
Thursday afternoon I came back and went to the beach where your voice came from
the loudspeaker singing the Pirate ballad ["Seeräuberjenny"]. That was very nice. I had
a letter from Victor [Samrock] with a description of the last night of Street Scene which,
he says, was something unheard of in the American theatre—an ovation of 10 minutes,
then everybody singing Auld Lang Syne and then the public going on cheering.—He
also writes that Max had asked him to write me that Danny Kay wants to do that show
with us in the fall and that he, Max, wants to start working on it as soon as he gets
through with the picture. How is my sweety-honey-pie? In less than 2 weeks I will be
back. I think I wrote you already my itinerary. In London I'll live at Green Park Hotel,
Half Moon Street, Piccadilly, arriving June 7. Sunday I have lunch with Muir Mattiesen
who is now musical director for [film producer J. Arthur] Rank. I'll cable you from
London at what time on June 12 I arrive.

Saturday evening. The mayor of Naharia gave a very nice garden party for me and
I got a present from the city which you will love. Now I have packed and go *schniepeln*.
Have to get up at 6. So *lebe, mein Schätzchen*. In Paris I'll probably have a little
Briefchen [letter] from you. I just got a long article with picture about me in a hebrew
paper. Here are some snapshots from the beach.   [FIG. 72]

So long, babe.

> Mit hochgehobenem
> *Affenschwanz dein* [with monkey tail lifted high, your]
> Knuti

---

387 WEILL IN GENEVA TO LENYA IN NEW CITY, 4 JUNE 1947

Geneva, 6/4/47

My *Blumenblümchen*,

Here I am back in Geneva, after 2 weeks during which I have seen so much that it
all seems like a dream at this moment. The last days in Palestine were very strenuous
and, of course, the last hours with the parents quite difficult because they were so brave
and tried not to show anything. Here is a little report of the events. Details *"mündlich"*
[in person] next week. Sunday morning the parents and I went to Tel-Aviv (a very ugly
city with a jewish-fascist population that makes you vomit). 11 A.M. reception at the
Mayor—*kurz u. schmerzlos* [short and painless]. 11.30 I met the Palestine Orchester in a   [FIG. 73]
rehearsal, got a huge ovation (the admiration for me everywhere was quite touching
and far beyond anything I ever dreamed of; it seems that, through my long absence,

I had become a sort of idol); I made a very nice speech to the orchester, followed by another ovation. Then every musician wanted to talk to me in person. But I was dragged away, put in a car (whose driver was the first "terrorist" I met) and drove out to Weizmann. After 2 minutes with him we were good friends and I felt right away that I was in the presence of a very great man of Roosevelt's caliber. He showed me his chemical laboratories which [are] tremendous, then we drove in his Cadillac, through a guard of honor, to his house which is definitely next to Brook House the most beautiful place I have seen. At lunch we talked about everything, but a great deal about the plan to bring the Habimah to New York. Back to Haifa. 5 P.M. Press conference for almost 2 hours (the usual *Quatsch* [chatter]). 8 P.M. a very interesting performance of Oedipus by the Habimah, then a big reception in the theatre.

Monday we drove to Jerusalem and after we arrived I walked around for hours in this fascinating town where old and new are right next to each other—*moshees* [mosques], temples, churches, greek, roman, jewish, turkish, camels and goats in the streets and always english tanks—and that beautiful *"Altstadt"* [old town], a Labyrinth of streets from Arabian Nights! I couldn't get enough of it. In the evening the Jewish Agency gave a big reception. Yesterday morning I spent with the parents until, at 12.30, I drove out to the Airport. The plane left at 5. We had a beautiful trip—the Mediterranian in moonshine, the first lights of the Italian coast, Napoli—then we arrived in Rome at 3.30 (night). To our surprise they decided to stop over night (they are extremely careful now), so we had to go through a long pass control [passport check] and arrived at 5 at a charming little Albergo in the center of Rome. I slept 3 hours very well. On the way to the Airport I saw all the old spots again which are so familiar, the Colisseum, the Capitol, the Via Appia etc. Then we flew to Geneva in less than 3 hours. In the plane I felt suddenly that I had a big piece of a tooth in my mouth which was broken off, so I called Nelly [Frank] and asked her for a dentist and go there now. Since I am a great *Klugi*, I ordered myself, 2 weeks ago, a sleeping car to Paris tonight. So I will sleep fine, and tomorrow morning I hope to find a letter from my *Träubchen*. Saturday I go to London, and then I cable my arrival. Gosh, I am glad to get home (and not to see jews in concentrated masses for a while).

Good-bye, honey. See you soon, very soon! Kiss *d' Hand (und das neue 100 dollar Warschi)* [your hand, and your new 100 dollar little behind]

Bye bye, *Schätzchen*
dein Kurti

1947–1948

During Weill's absence, Lenya had written Mab Anderson: "One forgets in time how much one has become a part of the person one loves, and to be left alone for a while gives you time to reassemble your feelings and thoughts and then you know again and are sure, that you wouldn't like to live without him" (Taylor, p. 311). Upon his return, Weill wrote to the Andersons: "Coming home to this country had some of the same emotion as arriving here 12 years ago.

With all its faults (and partly because of them), this is still the most decent place to live in, and strangely enough, wherever I found decency and humanity in the world, it reminded me of America, because, to me, Americanism is (or ought to be) the most advanced attempt to fill the gap between the individual and the technical progress" (W–M&MA, 22 June 1947).

That same month Weill received a Tony Award, in the inaugural year of the awards, for the score of Street Scene. *Over the summer he discussed a musical adaptation of* Aurora Dawn *with its author, Herman Wouk, and received an invitation from Brecht to write the music for the first production of* Schweik im 2. Weltkrieg, *which was to be presented in the Russian sector of Berlin. But by August Weill was committed to writing a new show with Alan Jay Lerner, then entitled* A Dish for the Gods. *In November he arranged the Israeli national anthem* Hatikvah *for Serge Koussevitzky and the Boston Symphony, in honor of Chaim Weizmann's seventy-third birthday.*

In April 1948, at the invitation of Hans Heinsheimer (then at Schirmer Music in New York), Weill reworked Down in the Valley *as a folk opera intended for schools and other amateur productions. After two performances in New Haven in September, the new Lerner-Weill show, now called* Love Life, *previewed in Boston. A chronicle of marriage and family through 150 years of cultural and social change in America,* Love Life, *subtitled* A Vaudeville, *was perhaps the most experimental of all Weill's works to date. It opened in New York on 7 October, with a cast headed by Nanette Fabray and Ray Middleton, directed by Elia Kazan, choreographed by Michael Kidd, and produced by Cheryl Crawford. Despite an ASCAP strike preventing exploitation of its music on the radio, the show ran for 252 performances; it is widely cited as one of the first "concept musicals."*

Shortly after the Broadway premiere, Weill again went to Hollywood to pick up the pieces after the release of the dreadful film of One Touch of Venus, *made by Universal after Pickford had abandoned it. Weill and Lerner tried to sell the film rights of* Love Life *and another film treatment and discussed the possibility of a long-term tie-in between the Playwrights' Producing Company and a studio.*

1948

388 WEILL IN BOSTON TO LENYA IN NEW CITY, 14–15 SEPTEMBER 1948

Letterhead: The Ritz-Carlton / Boston

Sept. 15th 1948
Tuesday night [14 Sept.]

Hello, Bibi-*Schwänzchen*,

Here is another notice [*Love Life*], and one that you will like!

I went to the park with Alan [Jay Lerner] after you left and we worked on a park bench. Then I went to bed and slept for an hour and Alan woke me up and read me this notice and he was really happy that I got such a good write-up. He <u>is</u> a sweet guy.

[FIG. 74]

Then we had a big steak dinner in his room and worked well until 10, walked to the theatre where everything went fine (they think we'll start selling out in a few days) and now I'll go to bed, so I can start working tomorrow morning.

You have been wonderful, as usual, and I love you more than ever.

Goodnight, my honey chile' *und viele Knüsschen auf dein süsses Warschi* [and many kisses on your sweet little behind]

Yours truly
Bibiboy

Wednesday. Good morning my *Träubi*. Alan and I are working on the ocean song ["Love Song"] and in between I orchestrate new stuff. It is all very pleasant and peaceful. I had a *primi* 9 hours schleep.

Send me a checkbook, so that I can write hotel bill checks on our check, for tax purposes.

So long now, baby. I'll talk to you before you get this.

Love————

389 WEILL EN ROUTE TO LOS ANGELES TO LENYA IN NEW CITY, 11 NOVEMBER 1948

Letterhead: Santa Fe / The Chief

Thursday, 11/11/1948

Good morning, good morning, how is my delicious today? How did you get home? How was Joan of Arc? And can you now relax for a few days? How did you think that Max's play [*Anne of the Thousand Days*] went? He said it went badly, was overlong (which I, a lonely cry in the wilderness, said at the New York run-through) and the audience got restless (that's why I begged them to take out those 2 scenes—now, of course, he is ready to do it). It is so boring to say: I told you so—isn't it? The root of the matter, of course, is that he has a lousy director [Bretaigne Windust]. I'll write him that and also that he should change director and stay out of town until it is right.

Well, I had another long sleep. In Chicago we went for a long walk, got on the train at 1.30, had lunch (cottage cheese, of course), slept in the afternoon, dinner (with wine), to bed at 10; this morning Alan came over to my room at 10 and we had breakfast, and now I got up. I feel already much more relaxed, but I feel now how tired I am (those 2 days in Philadelphia really knocked me out.) Alan is terribly nice and *rücksichtsvoll* [considerate]. We talk about plans for a new show, but without pressure. He is a little scared of the meeting with Marion, Middleman[?] seems to have warned him, not to fall for her tricks again.[1] But *"Der Geist ist willig, aber das Fleisch ist schwach"* ["The spirit is willing but the flesh is weak"]. Marion will meet him at the station with his brother. I have wired Lazar to come to the station.[2] I'm going to take it very easy. Tola, whom I called before I left, said he would be back on the 26th and I could stay in his house till then, but I don't know if I should accept it. I'll see how it is at the Bel-Air, prices etc. I also met Irving Shaw at the Algonquin who gave me the address of the house they had rented.[3] It must be very near from the house where we lived with Max. He says it is about 250.– a month (which wouldn't be bad). I'll look into it. I'm looking forward to my vacation with you because you are the sweetest and most delicious *Träubchenpison* in the world. I think, if it isn't really warm in California or if the rainy season starts already, we should rather go to Florida, or Cuba, don't you? Well, I will know more after about 3 or 4 days out there and then I will call you.—I hope I can make some kind of a movie deal to get a little more money. The show looked a little shaky when I talked to Cheryl on Tuesday. It seems to be a general business trend which might change any time. But the fact is that our advance sale is not good enough. Well, I don't worry and I feel already a little removed from it.

Gee, it is difficult writing on the train. Can you read it? Give my love to Mariedl and mother and for you a lot of *Knüsschens* and much more—your Bibiboy.[4]

1. *Marion Bell had created the role of Fiona in* Brigadoon, *which opened in 1947. Lerner fell in love with her, married her, and then divorced her shortly after* Brigadoon *closed. In July 1948, Bell sang the role of Jennie in the premiere production of* Down in the Valley *at Indiana University.*

2. *Irving Lazar (1907–94), known as "Swifty," was one of Hollywood's top agents.*

3. *The writer Irwin Shaw had just published* The Young Lions; *he is now best known for* Rich Man, Poor Man *(1970).*

4. *Weill had paid for Lenya's mother and sister (Mariedl Hubek) from Vienna to visit them in New City. They stayed until 20 November; Lenya would not see her mother again, as she died in Vienna two years later.*

[FIG. 75]

390 WEILL IN LOS ANGELES TO LENYA IN NEW CITY, 13 NOVEMBER 1948
Letterhead: Hotel Bel-Air

Saturday Nov. 13, 1948

My *Träubi*, my delicious,

Well, here I'm sitting on my own little patio outside of my room. This place is really beautiful and very quiet and restful and very "selected." The whole management was excited to see me back and showed me all kinds of rooms and I picked the least expensive (which is 12.–!! a day), but the difference is only that it is not right at the swimming-pool (which I prefer anyhow). It is terribly expensive, isn't it? Of course, I had a bad conscience first and told Lazar to look for something cheaper, but then I thought, what the hell, why shouldn't I be a little extravagant. It certainly is the perfect place to get the kind of rest and relaxation I need. The weather is perfect, warm and sunny, but very cold at night. Lazar was at the station, took me to the hotel, then we had lunch and later met Alan. So I had a full load of agent's *schmuss* [soft soap] and got a pretty clear picture of the situation here. This movie industry is practically dead, with those few executives and their relatives frantically holding on to the sinking ship. There are only 2 studios still making a few musicals. One is M.G.M.—there the ruler is Arthur Freed who said, after reading "Miss Memory": "this is no time for sophisticated stuff; what we need is meat and potatoes." The other studio is 20th century and there is a slight chance to get Zanuck interested.[1] At Warner's the "front office" liked the story very much and they are giving it now to their producers to read. But I am pretty doubtful about the chances, not only for Miss Memory, but for anything halfway good, in this town. Irving [Lazar] seems quite sure he can get a job for Alan because they always need writers. That would be okay by me. Alan, that softy, of course has a bad conscience, but I encourage him to do the picture if he can get one. He doesn't talk much about his relationship to Marion (he lives with her at the Leonard's), but I'm not very interested anyhow.[2] Last night I had dinner (saltless) at the Révy's. Richard is getting soft and rather nice and Thomas is very amusing and very "actory." I went home early, unpacked my bags (which were beautifully packed) and had a wonderful 9 hours sleep. Today I stay here all day, go in the pool a little later, at 4 Lazar comes over, and for dinner I go to Ira. So you see, I'm really taking it easy and take advantage of this time.

Just now I had your sweet *Träubchen* letter which makes this just a perfect day. You are completely right about Max's play and about Mab's bad influence. I'm so glad I could leave, because I could not have worked with Windy [Windust] and would have lost my temper. I'm glad Rex came through and I'm sure Joyce will too if they get a director.[3]—Darling, I was pretty sure that you would need at least a week after your family leaves. I know what a strain it is on you, and I think you are absolutely wonderful and patient with them and really manage to give them a good time. Now what our vacation concerns, if you have a week to get ready and about a week to travel, it would mean that I would have to wait about 4 weeks here till you come, and that, right now, seems a little long to me. But I want to look around here a little more. Lazar says we can have a house at the beach for 200.– a month, but it is foggy in December and too cold to swim. The place to go to at this time is the Desert, but you might not like that and prefer to go to Florida and make the trip with me. Well, we'll figure it out, one way or the other. I'll write again, soon. Good bye now, my sweetest, try to take it easy these last days with the family, write again. Much love and many *Knüsschen*

    Bibi

1. *Weill and Lerner had developed a treatment for a film musical entitled "Miss Memory"; a typescript of the treatment has survived. The producer, director, and lyricist Arthur Freed (1894–1973) was hired by Irving Thalberg to create the "MGM Musical" after the dawn of the sound era, and his name soon became synonymous with the glitter and high quality of the post–Wizard of Oz releases. Darryl Zanuck (1902–79) became the prototypical Hollywood mogul in the golden years of cinema.*

2. *The film director Robert J. Leonard (1889–1968) worked for MGM for thirty years, specializing in musical films starring Jeanette MacDonald and Nelson Eddy, as well as Fred Astaire.*

3. *The British actor Rex Harrison (1908–90) starred in the 1948 Broadway production of Anderson's historical drama* Anne of the Thousand Days, *opposite the British actress Joyce Redman (b. 1918).*

391 WEILL IN LOS ANGELES TO LENYA IN NEW CITY,
[16? NOVEMBER 1948]
Letterhead: Hotel Bel-Air

                                                    Tuesday
Hello, delicious,

It was very *niedelich* to talk to you, a little while ago. Now the sun came out and I'll go down to the pool. It is very quiet and restful there. Yesterday I was the only person at the pool, had a wide, comfortable lounge chair, lots of papers and books, swimming between—real *feinlebe*. At 3 Alan and Irving came to visit me, harassed from their tour through the studios, and I felt very good that I didn't go along, offering my services to Mr. Freed (I don't understand why Alan does it; I just don't believe that he needs the money, but it seems to be Marion's ambition that he should do a picture at M.G.M.—

and he is like straw in the wind). He hasn't any feeling of dignity which to you and me is so important—but he is young and will learn, that it is much better to keep distance.

At Ira's it was very nice. I like him because he is a real personality. He has 2 new hobbies: television and a pool table. The set-up is the same: Peggy[?] keeping house, Harry Kurnitz for dinner, Oscar Levant after dinner.[1] Of course, Ira went later to the Saturday poker game and Irving took Oscar and me to Romanoffs.

Tola's secretary called and said that he would be here at the end of the week and wants to talk to me about "Anything can happen."[2] That's a very funny, juicy story about a crazy guy from the Caucasus arriving in this country, his gradual americanization and how he marries an american girl. We read it some years ago, Behrman wanted to do it with me and Max also was interested. It might be a good possibility for Alan and me, as a play. Alan is coming around to your point of view that our next show should not be too experimental and also not a crazy satire like the cave-men idea. We have been talking a lot about Sidney Howard's "They knew what they wanted" for Walter [Huston] and Deanna [Durbin]. I called Walter at the studio, but he didn't call back. I'll call again tomorrow and will get in touch with Deanna too.

Unless something happens with a picture (which I don't expect) I think I'll start back next week. Maybe I visit the Milhaud's on the way back. In the meanwhile I'm really getting a wonderful rest here and I begin already to feel the result, getting much more relaxed and looking better. But the real vacation will be with you, in Florida or Cuba (or perhaps Nassau). Isn't it wonderful, the good news about the show, darling? The advance is over 220,000.–, building steadily, last week we did 40,000.–, with standies Saturday matinee, and a much improved Wednesday matinee. So it looks as if that baby will live and we can take it easy. I hope these last days with the family are not too strenuous for you. I think you should visit Mab for a little while, after they leave.

Well, here I go to the pool, will finish this letter later.

6 P.M. Those Californians are really *"wasserscheu"* [afraid of water]—not a soul was there and I had a nice time all alone with the "life guard," a very clever young man from Montana. I ordered myself a little lunch down there and went again in the water. The sun is mild and one doesn't get sunburned. Alan came at 4 for his daily visit and just left. He says there is a picture for both of us at Warner's and we'll know more in a few days. I doubt it, and anyhow, I'm not keen about a picture. Good bye now, my darling, *mein kleines Tröpfchen* [my little droplet]. *Grüss die Weaner Maderln* [greet the Viennese maidens] and *sei geküsst von deinem* [be kissed by your] hubby.

Irving Lazar will be here in a minute to take me for dinner.

1. *The American pianist and composer Oscar Levant (1906–72) had established his career as a performer by playing Gershwin's music; he also appeared in films (including* Rhapsody in Blue*), hosted a radio show, and published witty essays.*

2. *A novel by George and Helen Papashvily that was popular in the 1940s.*

Friday, 11/19/48

Me darling Caroline

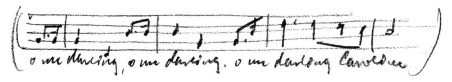

Here I'm sitting again in the sun by the pool as I have done every day since I came out. I feel and look definitely better than a week ago, have more energy and lost a little weight with swimming, walking and eating carefully. I didn't rent a car and walk over to Alan (about ½ hour) or to the village (45 minutes). The weather was rather cool for a few days, but there is always enough sun between 11 and 3 to go to the pool. Today it is lovely and warm and there are more people here, but, of course, nobody in the water.—I had your Sunday letter, with some very cute spelling mistakes which always make me laugh (it is a lawn, not a loan, which comes down to the brook, and Mab was not jeered but cheered, and you are not a "Xtippe," but a wonderful *Träubchen-Pisönchen*), and I am pretty bored without you and I don't think I can have any fun without you any more—and you know it too, you rascal.

I am so glad that you got your watch and very curious to see it. Were you excited when you got it? About the tires I'll leave all the informations when I get back. They are called super balloon (low pressure). I want to go to a good place where we don't get gypped. Maybe Fletcher[?] can take us, or we go with [Paul?] Mario direct to Firestone.—Alan is chasing around to the studios, going to parties with Arthur Freed and sitting around with those jerks in Commissaries. Maybe he'll get a job that way, but it ain't my way and I'd rather not get a job. He is terribly nervous, comes every day to "talk to a human being" and makes up all kinds of stories when I ask him why he is so desperate to get a picture. Last night Marion (who is getting more mannered and *verkrampft* [tensed up] by the minute) cooked spaghetti at the Leonard's—it is such a *spiessige* [philistine] Hollywood atmosphere over there, no wonder he is a nervous wreck. I'm trying to get him to go back with me Friday and he promised he would if he doesn't get a job soon. I go back anyhow at that time. If Alan doesn't go I might go via San Francisco and see the Milhaud's. Alan still thinks that we get a picture together, but I doubt it (no composer except Irving Berlin has worked here in 2 years) and I certainly won't sit around and wait. Here comes Alan now for his daily visit. So long, sweetie, I'll talk to you later.

10 P.M. It was wonderful to talk to you so long. I'm glad you are going to Philadelphia and I hope you'll stay over Thanksgiving day and have a nice time with Mab. I'm so glad they got rid of Windy. There was nothing anybody could do with the show as

long as that guy was there. I see in the N.Y. papers that they got H. C. Potter—he is an excellent director and I think he'll fix it.[1] I'll go to Baltimore Monday or Tuesday if they want me. Darling, I know exactly how you felt after seeing Moss's play, there is nothing more depressing than to think how they manufacture those slick, empty shows and how the critics go for them. I've been depressed ever since I read [Brooks] Atkinson's hymn about "As the Girls go"—but I just don't want to think of it.[2]

Well, I saw the Huston's for 3 hours, first Nan alone for an hour, then Walter came from the studio, and later on came in with a friend. Your ears must have burned between 8 and 9 your time because Nan and I talked about you a great deal. She is still crazy about you—and so am I, of course. She got the photo and I had to tell her all about mother and Mariedl. She seemed sort of in a daze when I came, out there she got warmer and almost normal. I don't think you are quite right when you say that it is all put on. My impression is that she has a terribly bad time with change of life, mixed with a full portion of good American neurosis. She says she is getting much better, the "attacks" are getting much rarer and she is quite sure, in about a year she'll feel better than she ever felt. She is going back to Mountain House tomorrow, and in about 3 to 4 weeks they'll come to N.Y. for the whole winter. Walter looks fine, but got much softer and older. He doesn't want to work much any more and is mostly interested in cooking. I didn't talk about a possible play for him, have to get him alone, without her. He is a swell guy and so is she. I liked them very much. John, elusive as ever, is going to Europe with Evelyn.[3] I asked him about Cuba where he spent a lot of time. He says, the place to go to now is Nassau. It is very quiet, not touristy like Cuba, has beautiful beaches, is warm, and only an hour by plane from Miami. It sounds wonderful. He said he would send me some addresses of hotels—but that's probably the last I heard from him.

Now I go *schneepeln.* Tomorrow I'll call Deanna and will probably see her Sunday. I feel fine tonight, having talked to you. Just found this review of Moss' play in the Los Angeles Times—well there is one critic who agrees with you.

Good bye now, my Linntschkerl.

Many *Knüsschens* from your Bibiboy

1. *The director H. C. Potter (1904–77) excelled at staging zany comedies, including* Hellzapoppin *in 1941.*

2. *Hart's* Light Up the Sky *opened in New York on 18 November and would run for 216 performances. Insiders considered the play's central character, a vain, effusive actress named Irene, to be a send-up of Gertrude Lawrence. As the Girls Go, a musical by Jimmy McHugh, ran nearly a year on Broadway.*

3. *In 1939 Evelyn Keyes (1919–91) had played Scarlett O'Hara's younger sister. She and John Huston were married for a short time.*

393T WEILL IN LOS ANGELES TO LENYA IN PHILADELPHIA,
22 NOVEMBER 1948
Western Union

DARLING PLEASE ASK FELIX [Jackson] WIRE ME HOW TO REACH DEANNA OR WIRE HER TO CALL ME. HOPE FAMILY ARRIVED SAFELY SEE YOU NEXT MONDAY LOVE = KURT.

Letterhead: Hotel Bel-Air

Thursday

My Linntschkerl,

I still haven't heard from you since Tuesday night, but by now it is pretty sure that you would have heard if something would have happened. My guess is that either they [Lenya's mother and sister] are grounded somewhere, or something happened to their cable. I hope I'll hear from you before I leave tomorrow afternoon.

I'm getting pretty bored here and am happy to get back to my delicious. Yesterday I had lunch with Deanna who definitely wants to do a show. Then some people who are doing Down in the Valley came to see me, and then Milly [Milestone] came out and we sent a cable to Korda about "Ghost goes West." In the evening I saw Alan who is more nervous than ever. He tells all kinds of stories about his different assignments, but it is impossible to tell what is true and what isn't. His latest plan is, since he "doesn't want to be seperated from us so long," that he would take a house here in January, have Otto and Anne[?] come out and invite us to stay with him. Well, you know his plans— but he is a sweet guy.

Darling, I'll arrive on the 20th Century (Roomette 13, car 2627) Monday morning 9.30, Grand Central. Don't get up so early. I'll call from the station and meet you when you get into town, I have to see Tola who is leaving that night, and Dreyfus.

Alles weitere mündlich [everything else in person]. I feel good and rested (except a little nervous about your family).

> *Knüsschen, mein Affenschwänzchen* [little kisses, my monkey tail]
> Your eternal hubby
> Bibiboy

I hope you get this before my arrival.

1949–1950

There is no further surviving correspondence between Weill and Lenya; they were not long separated again. In 1949 Anderson and Weill adapted Alan Paton's novel about apartheid, Cry, the Beloved Country, *as the "musical tragedy"* Lost in the Stars. *In July, Weill collapsed on the tennis court but convinced his partner, Alan Jay Lerner, that he was fine and never mentioned the incident to Lenya. As Weill looked forward to production of his latest work, he wrote to his parents in September: "All kinds of things have happened with my earlier works and it almost looks as if I could reap some kind of harvest after twenty-five years of heavy, indefatigable work—not in a financial but in a purely idealistic sense" (W–A&EW2, 6 Sept. 1949). In late October,* Lost in the Stars *opened at the Music Box Theatre to enthusiastic reviews, with Todd Duncan in the leading role, in a production directed by Rouben Mamoulian. Three days before it opened, Weill had reluctantly attended a performance of* Der Zar läßt sich photographieren sponsored by the Metropolitan Opera Studio; it was the first stage production in America of one of his European works that he had attended (there had been only a handful).

Brimming with ideas for new operas, including Moby Dick and one intended for Lawrence Tibbett, Weill and Anderson instead started work in January 1950 on a musical version of Huckleberry Finn. Exhausted, Weill had been planning a vacation to California, but Lenya feared that his long-term relationship there was becoming a real threat to their marriage. She gave him an ultimatum: if he went, she would not be at Brook House when he returned. He canceled his trip. In February he wrote his parents in anticipation of the upcoming milestone of his fiftieth birthday: "Don't let my birthday cause you any headaches. It's no special accomplishment to have reached the age of fifty. I don't feel like fifty at all—and the less fuss one makes, the better I like it" (W–A&EW2, 5 Feb. 1950). On his birthday he took to bed, complaining of an outbreak of psoriasis and flulike symptoms. On 17 March Lenya awoke to hear him gasping for air and clutching his chest. Diagnosed with a coronary attack, he was taken to Flower Hospital in Manhattan, where he rallied enough over the next fortnight to work on some Huck Finn songs. Expectations of recovery were dashed by his sudden death on 3 April.

Two days later family members and friends gathered at Brook House where Weill lay in state. Lenya had dressed him in his favorite white turtleneck pullover, and according to Maxwell Anderson's diary, "at three o'clock Lenya looked at Weill for the last time and the casket was closed and we started for the cemetery. Rain" (quoted by Sanders, p. 394). He was buried, without religious rites, at the top of a hill overlooking the Hudson River in Haverstraw. Mourners included Marc Blitzstein, Elmer Rice, Charles MacArthur and Helen Hayes, Marc Connelly, Rouben Mamoulian, and Arthur Schwartz. As a quiet spring rain fell, an unfamiliar black-veiled woman emerged from a limousine. When Lenya stepped away from the grave to allow her a moment alone with the casket, everyone knew that this was Kurt's special friend from Los Angeles. (Lenya had written her. "I told her that Kurt was very sick and if she wanted to see him she'd better come quick. But he was already dead when she arrived" [int. L3].) Maurice Abravanel recalled the moment: "Lenya took me aside and said: 'What do you say to that? You know, if she were a great beauty, I would understand that. What did he see in her?' And I couldn't tell her: 'Lenya, it's very simple. He found in her the qualities you don't have: the loyalty, the faithfulness, and so on' " (int. MA2).

Maxwell Anderson then read a brief eulogy:

[FIG. 76]

> For a number of years it has been my privilege to have a very great man as my friend and neighbor. I have loved him more than any other man I know. I wish, of course, that he had been lucky enough to have a little more time for his work. I could wish the times in which he lived had been less troubled. But these things were as they were—and Kurt managed to make thousands of beautiful things during the short and troubled time he had. . . . He left a great legacy in his music and in our memory of him. . . . But what he left must be saved, and we who are still here must save it for him. After a while, if we don't falter, the world's memory of him and of his work will be ours. (Quoted in Kowalke, p. 310)

As the group dispersed, Weill's brother-in-law, Leo Sohn, quietly recited the Kaddish over Kurt's grave. For the epitaph on his tombstone Lenya chose a quatrain from Anderson's lyric "Bird of Passage" in Lost in the Stars:

This is the life of men on earth;
Out of darkness we come at birth
Into a lamplit world, and then—
Go forward into dark again.

Burgess Meredith remembers that "after the funeral there were only a few people at the house":

Everybody talked in the way people do in these wakes. Lenya was holding up well with the courage that you would expect of her, being a very disciplined person when she wanted to be and very undisciplined when she wanted that, too. But doing it all with style. She was running things pretty well, and then she said an amazing thing. She said: "Burgess, sleep in Kurt's house tonight—in his bed tonight, so I won't be lonely." By this time I had quite a few drinks, but well, I said: "Of course" and went into the little room—they had separate bedrooms. (Int. BM)

Hesper Anderson recalls that in fact, for the next month "Lenya just couldn't be left alone. Either my mother or Bunny Caniff stayed with her every night, or she with one of them. And she cried, night after night after night. She just did not want to live" (int. HA). Coping with equally intense grief and guilt, Lenya finally realized that although her own survival would continue to depend on Weill, now his would also depend on her. She finally felt indispensable. In a letter to Manfred George, Lenya expressed (in German) her new resolution, a poignant one that ironically inverted Weill's own statement of priorities, "But Lenya, you know you come right after my music":

[FIG. 77]

It's been five weeks now since Kurt passed away and I haven't been able to take one step forward. The only thing that keeps me going at all is his music, and the only desire I still retain—everything I have learned through him in these twenty-five years—is to fight for this music, to keep it alive, to do everything within my power for it. Only a few recognize his importance, especially here, where only a part of his work is known. And I believe that I'll find my life's mission in making this music known. Everything is still very hazy, and I don't know yet where to begin. . . . Again and again I'm reminded of the last lines in *Der Silbersee:* "Wer weiter muß, den trägt der Silbersee" [whoever must go on will be carried by the Silver Lake]. . . . I hope that I'm choosing the right path by going on living for him, so he won't be forgotten too quickly within a time that has no time to remember what happened yesterday. (L–MG, 11 May 1950)

Epilogue

AFTER HE DIED

I hereby nominate, constitute and appoint my said wife,
KAROLINE WEILL, sole Executrix of this my last Will and
Testament and direct that no bond shall be required of her
as such.

I give, devise and bequeath unto my wife, KAROLINE
WEILL, absolutely and forever, all of the rest, residue and
remainder of my estate, whether real, personal or mixed
and wheresoever the same may be situated.

Last will and testament of Kurt Weill, 25 March 1944

In July 1950, the League of Composers again sponsored a Kurt Weill Concert—with the
New York Philharmonic conducted by Maurice Levine—this time "as an expression of
tribute to their late colleague, who made such a notable and lasting contribution to theatre
music of our times" (Kastendieck). Ten thousand people attended the event at Lewisohn
Stadium—as opposed to the 150 at the League's 1935 welcoming concert for Weill. Lenya
did not sing. Maxwell Anderson read a longer and more polished version of his eulogy,
and as if to prove Lenya's point that "only a part of his work is known" in the United
States, there was no performance or mention of any of Weill's European works. A few
months later, the appraiser of Weill's estate asserted in his affidavit that Weill's European
works had "no present value at all as they carry a very limited appeal." Conversely,
clippings of European obituaries sent to Lenya confirm almost total ignorance or incom-
prehension of Weill's American works. Lenya had her work cut out for her.

No one loved and understood his music better—possibly even more than she had loved
and understood the man himself. But she was unprepared for her role as the widow Weill.
Although she had been forced in Vienna and Zurich to become a woman long before any
child should, Weill somehow allowed (or enabled?) Lenya to remain the child-woman.
For most of their quarter century together, Weill had protected her from financial and
legal worries and responsibilities. If the Jennys in Weill's oeuvre continued to have autobiographical significance for Lenya, the one who "couldn't make up her mind" in *Lady
in the Dark* must have recoiled from the demands as executrix of the composer's estate:
copyright administration and renewals, performance rights, royalty statements, contractual

and legal disputes, tax problems, negotiations with publishers and collaborators and their estates, recording projects, authorization of arrangements, adaptations, and translations, and so on. Nevertheless, she rolled up her sleeves and tried to sort out the chaotic legacy of a "crossover" composer whose music continued to challenge or transcend publishing and performing establishments and norms—modernist/populist, European/American, "serious"/"light," evergreen/forgotten. And when Weill died, she no longer thought of herself as a performer. Not having appeared professionally since the *Firebrand* fiasco in 1945, she had few if any aspirations to fulfill her obligations as the Widow Weill as a firsthand interpreter of his music.

That was to change before Weill had been dead a year. Ernst Josef Aufricht, the producer of the original Berlin *Dreigroschenoper*, produced a "Kurt Weill concert" at Town Hall in New York in February 1951. Originally scheduled for one performance, it was repeated by popular demand twice more within a month. The second half comprised a concert version of *Die Dreigroschenoper*, sung in German and accompanied by two pianos, with Lenya singing virtually all of the female characters' music. In his review, Virgil Thomson referred to her as "the impeccable singing actress Lotte Lenya-Weill" and used the occasion to reassess Weill's legacy: while the American works were "thoroughly competent but essentially conformist," the German works had "made musical history" and "belong in the constantly available repertory." Lenya quickly took up the latter imperative as her agenda—but not on her own.

[FIG. 78] Six weeks after Weill's death, in a chance meeting at the home of a mutual friend, Lenya had renewed her acquaintance with George Davis, the erstwhile editor of *Mademoiselle* and the short-lived *Flair*, who had discovered and first published such literary talents as Carson McCullers and Truman Capote. By summer 1950, however, Davis was jobless and broke. He remembered their first meeting after Weill's death: "I scarcely recognized her. Her face was veiled by apathy. Here was a person who had lost interest in everything. She had abdicated from life" (quoted in Spoto, p. 185). Soon they were seeing a lot of each other, and although Lenya was well aware that Davis's sexual orientation had been exclusively homosexual, they became frequent companions. It was George who persuaded her to participate in Aufricht's concert, and he who calmed her down backstage as she sobbed, "I can't do it! I can't do it!" Maurice Abravanel noted, "The Lenya legend did not begin until after Kurt's death, when she emerged from his shadow under the gentle guidance of George Davis" (quoted in Spoto, p. 191). Another close friend characterized Davis as something of a benign Svengali: "When Lenya said she never wanted to work again, he forced her. . . . He began to shape and refashion her entire image" (int. MC). Lenya agreed: "George helped me out of the deep, deep depression I was in. He convinced me that I still had a place in the theater, and that the only way to work for Kurt Weill's name was to establish my own" (Lenya 1962, p. 43).

In July 1951 they were married in Maxwell Anderson's living room. "It was certainly not a love-match," cartoonist Milton Caniff recalled. "We were actually quite startled when they announced their marriage. But at that time George was absolutely broke and had no job potential. Lenya understood him, enjoyed his company, and didn't seem to mind that he really preferred the company of gentlemen" (int. MC). Lenya analyzed it differently: "George married me out of friendship, so I wouldn't be alone—it was a gesture of kindness, because I was so lost" (Chapin). One of Lenya's friends offered another explanation: "After Kurt's death, Lenya couldn't stop talking about him, so she married someone with whom she could do just that" (int. HIH). Even more conflicted and complex than her relationship with Weill had been, Lenya's marriage to George was grounded on a symbiosis arising out of their complicated circumstances: she was financially secure but frightened, lonely, and guilt-ridden; he was brilliant, but penniless, self-destructive, and undisciplined. Yet they shared two passions: Weill's music and Lenya's career. "He saw he could devote himself to the career of Lenya—not just for a year, but as a permanent occupation," their friend Paul Moor said. "George determined that she would be known as Lenya, not just the Widow Weill" (int. PM1). And a new Lenya indeed emerged, with the trademark Toulouse-Lautrec red hair.

But all was not well: soon George was introducing himself as "the husband of the Widow Weill." The underlying tensions generated by her tight-fistedness and artistic insecurities and his resentment and dangerous sexual adventures (he was hospitalized on several occasions after being beaten) often tested their arrangement. But under George's management and tutelage, during the next six years Lenya established herself as an international recording, concert, theatrical, and film star on a scale far higher than at any point in Weill's lifetime. In October 1951 she played the leading female role of Socrates' wife in Anderson's *Barefoot in Athens*, a part he had written for her. In 1952 Davis convinced her to allow Marc Blitzstein to finish his adaptation of *The Threepenny Opera*, and she sang Jenny in the world premiere conducted by Leonard Bernstein at Brandeis University. Thereafter, with Broadway producers and the New York City Opera vying for the right to produce the piece in New York, the problems she encountered as executrix required the diplomacy and judgment George could again provide. They gave the first production rights to a pair of young, unknown off-Broadway producers—Stanley Chase and Carmen Capalbo—who were willing to mount the play without alterations, even preserving Weill's original orchestrations. The producers insisted, however, that Lenya play Jenny; she refused, claiming she was too old for the part. Again George intervened and convinced her that her contribution as an "authentic" interpreter of the music was essential, for both the production and the larger Weill renaissance that it would launch, if successful.

The Theatre de Lys production that opened in March 1954 is now, of course, legendary. After an initial run of ten weeks, the production had to close because the theater had already been booked for the entire following season. Rather than move it uptown to a larger house, the producers put the production in storage and reopened in September 1955. It would then run for 2,611 consecutive performances, becoming the longest-running musical in history (at that point). During the run, Louis Armstrong, Dick Hyman, Bobby Darin, Frank Sinatra, and Ella Fitzgerald successively climbed the pop charts with renditions of "Mack the Knife," which became one of the biggest "hit songs" of the century. In January 1956 Lenya wrote to a friend: "The 'Moritat' has been recorded by 17 different companies. You hear it coming out of bars, juke boxes, taxis, wherever you go. Kurt would have loved that. A taxidriver whistling his tunes would have pleased him more than winning the Pulitzer Prize" (L–MD, 6 Jan. 1956). MGM's original cast recording—the first for an off-Broadway musical—sold more copies than any album except *My Fair Lady* and prompted the company to release a dozen Weill recordings (including a *Johnny Johnson* supervised by Lenya) during the run of the show. Lenya won the Tony Award for "best featured actress in a musical." By the time she left the cast for the last time (after several leaves of absence for various projects in Europe), she commanded a loyal New York following that clamored for her periodic concert appearances, at Lewisohn Stadium, Town Hall, and Carnegie Hall. Professionally George and Lenya made a great team; things were more difficult at home, as Caniff observed:

> She was one thing during the daytime and another at night, onstage. By day she was the purse-keeper, the woman who kept George on a tight budget and preferred that he be with her as a devoted companion. But at night she became the performer that he had virtually molded in his own hands. It was a very strange situation: half the time she was a Mama who saw to it that the line was toed, and then she became at night his creation. She had put herself in this apparently irreversible position, and she had to go on with it. (Quoted in Spoto, p. 209)

While they were waiting for the Theatre de Lys to be vacated in 1955, George coaxed, bullied, even tricked Lenya into making her long-dreaded and oft-postponed return to Germany. They first visited Berlin to do research for the biography of Weill on which Lenya and especially George had been working since 1952. It was a highly emotional homecoming for Lenya: "We toured the worst of the ruins, which literally sent Lenya to bed for days," Davis reported to Mary Daniel (GD–MD, 23 June 1955). Lenya herself wrote: "One could admire the determination to get on top again, if one would not be afraid that somewhere lurks another Hitler. But you can't seem to find a single Nazi in Germany! Nobody was one! It was all a dream!" (L–MD, 16 May 1955). Lenya visited Brecht in East Berlin but declined his invitation to join the Berliner Ensemble. He asked her to sing something for him; she did "Surabaya Johnny" a cappella, asking if it was still all right in light of his new theories of "estrangement" and provoking Brecht's memorable response: "Lenya, darling, whatever you do is epic enough for me" (quoted in Beams, p. 14). She also visited her sister in Vienna, while doing battle with Weill's first publisher, Universal Edition, to which she alternately referred as "those sleeping beauties" or "those old sharks." In June Lenya and George went to Hamburg, where she was to make the first of a series of recordings for Columbia Record's European affiliate, Philips, a project George had been negotiating for months but had kept secret from Lenya until the last minute. "Lenya's out rehearsing," he wrote to her friend, "and as always when she gets right on top of a job, very much in control, steady, no nonsense, the artist that she is. But boy! leading up to there, jumps, jitters, the vapors, yes, and even a rash" (GD–MD, 2 July 1955). The recording went better than even George had hoped; *Lotte Lenya Sings Berlin Theatre Songs by Kurt Weill* became an instant classic: it has never been out of print since its release.

At year's end, after reopening *The Threepenny Opera* at the Theatre de Lys, Lenya and George returned to Europe for the German premiere of *Street Scene:* "If only Kurt would know. He would be so proud. And that George running around and working on so many things at the same time that I get dizzy listening. He really has found a new function in life" (L–MD, 10 Oct. 1955). But such stress took its toll; while in Hamburg in August 1956, George suffered a heart attack—like Weill, at age fifty. He recovered sufficiently for Lenya to proceed with the recording of *Die sieben Todsünden* (in an unacknowledged lower-key arrangement commissioned by her) and then *Aufstieg und Fall der Stadt Mahagonny*. After both were in the can, Lenya convinced George to spend Christmas in Vienna: "I think George should know my birthplace too," Lenya wrote a friend. "He might understand my madness sometimes when he sees the house I was born in—and he might then also understand my fear of poverty" (L–MD, 9 Sept. 1956).

They returned to New York shortly after New Year's Day, and George immediately began negotiating for a recording of *Die Dreigroschenoper*. But at the end of March, Lenya reported to Mary Daniel that George had suffered another heart attack: "It's hell for me to find myself once more staring at an oxygen tent and it seems like yesterday that I was watching Kurt" (L–MD, 26 March 1957). But again George recovered, in time to help her record *September Song and Other American Theatre Songs* for Columbia in New York during August 1957. In September they left for Berlin to see the first (and to date only) postwar production of *Die Bürgschaft*. During her stay, Lenya received the Freedom Bell, West Berlin's highest cultural award. But George fell ill again, so Lenya went to Hamburg alone to make final preparations for the recording of *Die Dreigroschenoper*. As Lenya commuted between Hamburg and Berlin, he was in and out of the hospital. On 25 November George Davis died of a massive heart attack at age fifty-one. Paul Moor broke the news to Lenya:

> She collapsed in uncontrollable sobbing. She was utterly shattered, inconsolable. This was the man who had created her career, had carried forward what had only dimly begun with Kurt. . . . It was a repeat—it was the same cause of death as in the case of Kurt Weill. She was all too aware that George was responsible for her second career, and now he was gone. He was gone, furthermore, on the threshold of her doing the *Threepenny Opera* which he had been deeply involved in preparing. . . . She threw a scare into me the morning that George died by coming to me with Kurt's wrist watch. She said: "Kurt bought this watch when he had his first Broadway success. And then it belonged to George, and now I want you to have it." In other words, one, two, three. And that put me instantly on guard. . . . I think I actually managed the situation fairly well because I was able to salvage our friendship. (Int. PM2)

Moor needn't have worried, for in fact Lenya had just met the young British composer-critic David Drew, who would almost immediately succeed George as her personal and professional confidant, musical and contractual adviser, literary collaborator, and strategist for all matters Weill. Drew recalls that in the autumn of 1956 he had written to Lenya outlining his plan to write a book about Weill's music:

> Her friendly reply was followed by a long and enthusiastic letter from her husband, the American writer and editor George Davis, offering assistance of a kind I had not

dreamed of. For some while, Davis told me, he and Lenya had been collecting material for a biography of Weill. They now felt that the musical and critical questions which interested me were more urgent, and had therefore decided to renounce their project and offer me the material they had already collected. (Pp. 6–7)

Lenya described Drew to her friend Mary after their first meeting in Berlin in 1957: "He is a dream of a guy. Young, witty and extremely clever. I think we would have fun with him in the house for a few months. He has no money and one must think of a way, so he can earn a little. He was with me during the rehearsals, George not feeling too well and a blessing it was to have him with me, so I could rebel (musically—not reading a note as you well know—so he helped out there with his musicologist's brain) and we had fun too besides just raising hell" (L–MD, 24 Oct. 1957). For the next two decades, Lenya and Drew would collaborate not only on Drew's critical biography and catalog of works but also on Lenya's attempt at autobiography, as well as numerous recordings, productions, festivals, and performances. After *Die Dreigroschenoper* Lenya went on to record *Happy End* (1960); to perform in *The Seven Deadly Sins* with the New York City Ballet under Balanchine (1958) in New York, as well as in its German premiere in Frankfurt (1960); and to star in *Brecht on Brecht* (1961) in New York and London.

One of the most imposing critical intellects of his generation, Drew opened new vistas for Lenya, providing the philosophical and technical underpinnings for her own intuitive grasp of Weill's music. He brought the professional musical knowledge and perspective to the tasks initiated by Davis that would ultimately prompt Lenya to name Drew the European administrator of Weill's estate and Boosey & Hawkes to appoint him as their director of new music. While Drew worked on his Weill biography at Brook House, he also provided the companionship Lenya so desperately needed. But when the much younger man (b. 1930) decided to return to Britain in October 1958 (after spending a summer in New City) to pursue his own career, marry, and start a family, Lenya confessed her disappointment and loneliness: "David has booked his return to England for the 15th of October. That gives me plenty of time to get used to the idea, that he will be gone. By time my stormy heart will have quieted down too—I hope" (L–MD, 13 Aug. 1958).

She could no longer stand being alone in Brook House, so she rented a small apartment on East Fifty-fifth Street. Lenya yearned for a companion, even pursuing at one point Dag Hammarskjöld, the secretary-general of the United Nations. Her friend Gigi Gilpin saw how desperate she was:

She was sick in bed in her apartment on 55th Street. And there was a knock on the door and she said that she crawled on her hands and knees from the bed to the door and said to herself: "If it's a man, I'll marry him. I don't care what size, shape, color or anything. If it's a man, I'll marry him." And she got the door open, and there was Russ [Detwiler] standing, all shiny with little paintings to deliver. She had developed a real passion for Russ and his work, and she had bought several of his paintings. Frankly, I always thought she was much too young for him. He seemed like the old person, she the much younger. I think from the start she knew he was a heavy drinker, but it took a while for her to accept that he was an alcoholic. That didn't make him a very good companion, but as independent as she liked to consider herself, Lenya couldn't be alone. (Int. GG)

Russell Detwiler was twenty-seven years Lenya's junior. He had studied painting at Philadelphia's Academy of Fine Arts and had mounted a few exhibits of his own with no consequences. Blond, tall, and handsome, he was not only alcoholic but predominantly homosexual, and penniless—an unlikely prospect for anyone but Lenya. Caniff recalled:

We all knew she needed someone around, but we were afraid, when we met Russ, that here was another coat-holder, another dog-walker. He was very talented, but he was a terrible drunk. He was surely no match for Kurt or George, although he could be very pleasant and was obviously well informed. But when he wasn't sober, it was awfully difficult, and that was most of the time. (Int. MC)

On 2 November 1962, while appearing in *Brecht on Brecht* in London, Lenya married Detwiler. Despite the predictable agonies she endured because of his alcoholism, her years with him were among her most productive, with memorable motion picture performances in *The Roman Spring of Mrs. Stone* (1961), for which she was nominated for an Academy Award; *From Russia with Love* (1964); and *The Appointment* (1969). She also made several television films, returned triumphantly to Carnegie Hall in 1965, and played *Mother Courage* in Recklinghausen that same year (also broadcast on German television). In 1966 Harold Prince cast her as Fräulein Schneider in *Cabaret* on Broadway; over the next three years she appeared in most of its 1,165 performances. Lenya was again nominated for a Tony Award, this time as "best actress in a musical," but she lost to Barbara Harris in *The Apple Tree*.

Lenya had reached the pinnacle of her career, but her life at home was a nightmare that climaxed with Russ being committed to Bellevue, a self-described "zombie," diagnosed with "the severest effects of alcohol addiction, with episodes of paranoid schizophrenic behavior and hallucinations." During some of his spells and seizures, he had injured Lenya as well as himself. After intensive detoxification and psychiatric treatment in a private clinic in Connecticut, things improved, and Russ managed to stay sober on his own for a few months. But in April 1969, as *Cabaret* celebrated its thousandth performance, Lenya was again a victim of Detwiler's drunken rages; she wrote, "Sometimes I feel somebody is strangling me but not enough to kill me" (L–LS, 26 May 1969). In September the West German government conferred upon her the Great Service Cross for her contributions to the German and American theater. On 30 October, Lys Symonette, whom Lenya had asked to look after Russell while she rehearsed for an important performance at Lincoln Center, found him dead on the driveway of Brook House, his skull split open after collapsing from a seizure caused by alcohol and tranquilizers. He was buried at age forty-four, on their seventh wedding anniversary.

After the death of her third husband, Lenya's public appearances became less frequent, although her commitment to Weill's legacy was undiminished. "Strong women friends," one of her longtime male friends suggested, "surrounded Lenya and got what they wanted, materialistically and personally" (int. NF). Without either competent legal counsel or informed professional advice, she made a number of rash decisions. She later regretted most the assignment of the renewal term of copyright in all of Weill's European works to an American pop publisher eager only to have the prestige of "Mack the Knife." Although she received an advance of a quarter of a million dollars, the deal effectively buried Weill's "serious" music until the contract was renegotiated after her death.

In 1971 Lenya met the forty-four-year-old Emmy-winning documentary filmmaker Richard Siemanowski (a nephew of the famous composer), who had produced more than two hundred cultural films for television. Witty and genial, he was also alcoholic and homosexual. On the spur of the moment, Lenya married him on 9 June 1971. But unlike George Davis or Russell Detwiler, Siemanowski was quite independent in his own work and unwilling to give up his home and friends; he maintained a residence in New Jersey with his male lover. Thus Lenya and he never lived together, and few friends even knew that she had remarried. After Siemanowski was hospitalized for his alcoholism, Lenya took steps to protect her assets and then filed for divorce, which was granted in June 1973. When Siemanowski learned of the summary court action, he wrote Lenya that he was "shocked," but in any case had never liked being "Mr. Lotte Lenya."

Lotte Lenya was now seventy-five years old. She retreated more and more from public life, with only occasional appearances at exhibitions, art gallery openings, and television and radio interviews. She canceled her concert at the long-anticipated and highly visible Weill Festival in Berlin in 1975. She came out of retirement only as a favor for special friends or within the safety of an academic environment. She did accept a hilarious cameo part in Burt Reynolds's movie *Semi Tough* (1977) and made annual trips to Europe to visit her sister in Vienna and her friend Anna Krebs in Hamburg. In late 1977 she underwent surgery for abdominal cancer for the first time. After several severe accidents and some ill-advised cosmetic surgery, Lenya's malignancy recurred and metastasized.

Probably the happiest occasion in her later years was the Metropolitan Opera's first performance and national telecast of *Rise and Fall of the City of Mahagonny* in November 1979. The presentation of Weill's opera in one of the world's most prestigious opera houses seemed to be final confirmation of the long-term impact of her efforts on Weill's behalf. She symbolically passed the interpretive torch to Teresa Stratas, "her dream Jenny" and anything but an imitator, to whom she also entrusted a collection of unpublished songs, which Stratas then recorded as *The Unknown Kurt Weill*. Stratas and Lenya became devoted friends. In one of her final interviews, Lenya passed the mantle publicly: "When she sang Jenny and I met her after, I said, 'Teresa, here is my crown. I give it to you now; you are the one. So you carry on.' And now she sings Weill like he wrote it for her. The applause . . . it's a fading thing, you know, fame is so fading you know" (Vaughan, p. 14).

Her final months, up to the last days, were spent agonizing over the ultimate fate of Weill's legacy—the documents themselves, which she had put on temporary deposit at Yale in 1980, and administration of the copyrights after his death. She handpicked a board of trustees, including the editors of the correspondence at hand, for the Kurt Weill Foundation for Music and stipulated that it should be the beneficiary of the income derived from Weill's music.

Lenya died on 27 November 1981 in the apartment of Margo Harris, a sculptor who had become a close friend and adviser in an on-and-off relationship over the last decade. There was no religious service, and Mrs. Harris restricted the graveside party to a few invited guests. Lenya's friend and neighbor Martus Granirer recalled: "I've never seen such a grim and utterly uncathartic experience. Nobody cried, nobody even got to say they loved her" (int. MG). No one had been asked to prepare a eulogy. Several mourners tried to improvise as the rain poured down, but Lenya's own credo would have been most appropriate: "I love life and I believe in survival" (quoted by Wahls). She was buried next to Kurt Weill. [FIG. 79]

KRANICHE DUETT

Sieh jene Kraniche in großem Bogen!
  Die Wolken, welche ihnen beigegeben
Zogen mit ihnen schon, als sie entflogen
  Aus einem Leben in ein andres Leben.
In gleicher Höhe und mit gleicher Eile
  Scheinen sie alle beide nur daneben.
Daß so der Kranich mit der Wolke teile
Den schönen Himmel, den sie kurz befliegen
  Daß also keines länger hier verweile
Und keines andres sehe als das Wiegen
Des andern in dem Wind, den beide spüren
Die jetzt im Fluge beieinander liegen.
  So mag der Wind sie in das Nichts entführen
  Wenn sie nur nicht vergehen und sich bleiben
Solange kann sie beide Nichts berühren
  Solange kann man sie von jedem Ort vertreiben
  Wo Regen drohen oder Schüsse schallen.
So unter Sonn und Monds wenig verschiedenen Scheiben
Fliegen sie hin, einander ganz verfallen.
Wohin ihr?
      Nirgendhin.
            Von wem entfernt?
                  Von allen.
Ihr fragt, wie lange sind sie schon beisammen?
Seit kurzem.
            Und wann werden sie sich trenn?
                  Bald.
So scheint die Liebe Liebenden ein Halt.

CRANE DUET

See those cranes in a great circle wheeling!
   The clouds that ride beside them in the distance
Joined them when from their nest they first were stealing
   From their old life into a new existence.
At equal heights they fly, with equal daring,
   Each seems to give the other its assistance.
They fly, the crane and cloud together sharing
The lovely sky, through which their flight is fleeting.
   Neither dares lag behind and end their pairing
And neither feels a thing except the beating
The wind gives both. Each sees its partner quaking
As they fly side by side, their motions meeting,
   Letting the wind abduct them with its shaking
   As long as they can touch and see each other,
During which time they are immune from aching
   And can be driven from one place to another
   When thunder warns of rain and guns of danger.
So under sun and moon, each orb much like its brother,
They fly along, enthralled by one another.
To go where?
     Anywhere.
         In flight from whom?
           From strangers.
You ask how long have they been together?
Just briefly.
     And when will they be parting?
         Soon.
So love to lovers seems a strength and boon.

No. 14 from *Aufstieg und Fall der Stadt Mahagonny*. Music by Kurt Weill; text by Bertolt Brecht. English singing translation by Michael Feingold, amended by the editors. Copyright 1929 by Universal Edition A.G., Vienna; copyright renewed. Used by permission of European American Music Corporation and Universal Edition. All rights reserved.

AFTERWORDS

In 1945 I was hired to be rehearsal pianist, coach, and general understudy—"swing girl," they might call it today—for *The Firebrand of Florence*. I had been recommended to Weill by his close friend Maurice Abravanel, who suspected that I might be able to do the job, having been both a voice and piano major at the Curtis Institute of Music in Philadelphia. It took three days of sight-reading–transposing–improvising, as I accompanied countless hopeful auditioners, before a small man emerged from the darkened auditorium, walked up on the stage toward the piano, looked at me with a broad grin, and said: "I'd love to have you in the show. I'm Kurt Weill."

Born Bertlies Weinschenk in Mainz, Germany, I had the music of *Die Dreigroschenoper* and *Mahagonny* in my ears ever since I could remember and was in awe of Weill. But to the rest of the cast, musicians, and crew of *The Firebrand of Florence* he was just plain "Kurt," the show's amiable composer, whose two previous shows, *Lady in the Dark* and *One Touch of Venus*, had been big hits. He was always friendly and polite yet never involved himself in matters apart from the business at hand. Nobody in the cast seemed to have the slightest notion of who Lotte Lenya was. I was the only one familiar with her German recordings and her memorable performance in the Pabst film of *Die Dreigroschenoper*. Yet the first time I saw her playing the Duchess during a dialogue rehearsal, she looked completely different from what I so clearly remembered: her hair was now a yellowish blond, swept up high in tight curls, leaving her ears exposed—a style not particularly enhancing to her strong, angular features. She wore a fluffy purple dress and high-wedged sandals that looked extremely uncomfortable.

I was very busy during rehearsals and the Boston tryout and had very little chance to get to know Lenya better. But after *Firebrand* closed, Weill stayed in touch with me—and also with one Randolph Symonette, whose big, booming bass baritone he had so admired in the role of the Hangman. He said he wanted both of us, now a couple, involved in an opera he was working on. And so, sometime in the spring of 1946, he invited us to a first musical reading of *Street Scene* in the home of the director Charles Friedman. Weill played and sang all the male roles and asked me to sing as many of the women's as I could handle. The event created enormous excitement among the listeners, and Friedman (who had just had a huge success with *Carmen Jones*) agreed to direct. Thereafter Weill called me frequently to assist him in repeat performances in the homes of prospective "angels" on Park Avenue and elsewhere. It was extremely difficult in those days to raise money for opera on Broadway, and at times those "backers' auditions" were both annoying and humiliating—but that only increased my admiration for Weill, who took it all in stride.

Four weeks before the official rehearsals for *Street Scene* were to begin, Weill entrusted me with coaching the ensemble numbers in my studio on West Seventy-first Street. Occasionally he would drop in to see—or rather to hear—how things were going. By the time staging rehearsals started, in November 1946, everyone knew the music. I needn't go into the trials and tribulations of the infamous three-week tryout in Philadelphia. But it was during those dark days that I met Lenya again. The show was having tenor trouble. At the height of the crisis Weill called early one morning and asked me to come to the Warwick Hotel, where both he and Lenya were staying. When I got there, Lenya opened the door, and there was that face I had so vividly remembered: no makeup whatsoever, no fancy hairdo, and instead of floating violet silks, a simple bathrobe and comfortable bedroom slippers. She was equally concerned about whether I'd had breakfast and whether they could find another tenor. Weill said they had decided to send me to New York to coach one from *Show Boat* that they had in mind, but we had to wait for Friedman to show up to get his approval. Friedman did walk in shortly thereafter, with a face as grim as if he had just been crucified by the *New York Times*. When Weill saw him looking so dour, he turned to me and—with that typical ironic smile of his—said in Saxonian-flavored dialect: "Warum ist *der* denn schon wieder so beese?" (why is that one so angry again?). It was the only time Weill ever spoke to me in German.

Weill also engaged me for the radio version of *Down in the Valley* (1945), *Love Life* (1948), and *Lost in the Stars* (1949). During rehearsals for *Lost in the Stars* I noticed how nervously he asked whenever he entered the theater, "Where's Lenya?" I had never seen this kind of anxiety in him before. Indeed, she did come to rehearsals more frequently than she had in the past and often asked me to join them for lunch, sometimes with and sometimes without Maxwell and Mab Anderson. After the show opened in October 1949, I went off for a longish stay in Canada, where I married the Hangman. When I came back to New York in March, I called Weill to give him the news. I was shocked when a maid answered the phone to tell me that Mr. Weill was in the hospital. And a few days later a friend of mine called to tell me he had died! It sounded so unbelievable that like an idiot I ran down to Seventy-second Street to buy the *Times* and find out the *truth*. There it was.

Only a few weeks later Lenya telephoned me, her voice choked with emotion. Anderson was looking for another composer for the project he had started with Weill—a musical play based on Mark Twain's *Huckleberry Finn*. She said that Max had never heard any of the music Kurt had composed. (I knew that Weill had written "The River Chanty," which he intended for my husband to sing as Huck's drunken old father. Only much later did I learn that he had jotted down additional sketches during the three weeks he had spent in the hospital.) So Lenya asked me to play for Max whatever music there was; she would bring the manuscripts. I will never forget the three of them in my studio in New York— Lenya with her eyes swollen and red from crying, Max and Mab Anderson impassive, just waiting to get down to business. I managed to get through "The River Chanty" and "The Catfish Song," but when it came to the nostalgic ballad "This Time Next Year," it took me a while to compose myself before I could go on. The experience of hearing Weill's final musical thoughts for the first time under such tragic circumstances created a strange bond of solidarity between Lenya and me, a solidarity that, as I think of it today, evokes the image of Lenya onstage in Baden-Baden, in the final scene of the *Mahagonny Songspiel*, waving a placard with the slogan *Für Weill*.

This "for Weill" would become the leitmotif of our friendship. It lasted three decades, weathering many an onslaught. Over the years my husband had an operatic career in Germany, and we both participated in the German premiere of *Street Scene* in Düsseldorf; he taught at Florida State University, where Lenya (in her seventies) gave an electrifying performance as Jenny in a production of *The Threepenny Opera;* and I later taught at the Curtis Institute in Philadelphia, where Lenya sang "Mack the Knife" at the end of an all-Weill concert, to the delight of Rudolf Serkin. Our correspondence had few lapses, and whenever we could we would visit her, together with whomever was her husband at the time.

In the mid 1970s her health started to decline, but even after her first cancer surgery in 1977, she refused to believe there was anything seriously wrong. Blissfully ignorant of medical matters and largely disinterested in them, she always disliked people who talked about their doctors, pills, and operations. So when she had to undergo surgery again in 1978, she bore the considerable pain and discomfort with nonchalance, carefully avoiding discussions about the nature and possible consequences of her illness. She tried to resume her customary activities. She drove back and forth between her Manhattan apartment and New City, her car usually overloaded with leftovers, cats, dogs, books, magazines, and unanswered letters from all corners of the earth. Much as she loved routine household tasks—from sweeping the pine needles off the roof in New City to ironing her own blouses—Lenya admitted she just couldn't face her desk, which was now cluttered with stacks of mail. With her dilapidated Olivetti portable typewriter, she could no longer shoulder the heavy burden of an enormously complicated business and private correspondence. Thus, little by little, I began to help her with Weill matters.

I spent most weekends in New City, as well as those days I didn't have to teach in Philadelphia. We gradually organized all her documents in some forty-five "Leitz" filing boxes, which her friend Anna Krebs had brought from Germany. She labeled them in different colors: works, lawyers, producers, publishers, agents, copyrights, television, stage, screen, contracts, nuisances, and Brecht—this last one in red, of course! These colorful files were housed in what used to be Weill's studio on the second floor of Brook House, where, in addition, we sorted through boxes of newspaper clippings, programs, photos, piano-vocal and orchestral scores, sheet music, and orchestra parts. Weill's autograph manuscripts, however, had been deposited in a commercial Manhattan warehouse, referred to by Lenya as "the vault."

One day, while rummaging in a closet in the guest room, I came upon a bundle of envelopes, most of which were addressed to "Lotte Lenja Weill" in Weill's handwriting. I asked Lenya where the letters were. She said that David Drew had them in London, as he needed them for the biography of Weill he was still writing. After their return in 1976, I convinced Lenya that she couldn't let this invaluable set of documents just lie around the house, so she finally purchased a steel file cabinet for her bedroom and stashed the Weill-Lenya correspondence in the bottom drawer. On several occasions she shared a portion of them with me, but never those from the period of their divorce. The passage I remember most vividly even now was Weill's confession while en route by train to Los Angeles in 1944 that he couldn't stand the thought of occupying a room with three beds "while other people have to sit up all night." He said he'd never make a good capitalist (Letter 309).

Reluctantly at first but eventually with greater urgency, Lenya began to voice her concerns about the future of the Weill legacy and how the Kurt Weill Foundation for Music, which she had established as a (seldom-used) tax shelter in 1962, ultimately might be utilized to best advantage to preserve and promote Weill's music. Yet it was no simple matter to approach her with any practical suggestions; she quickly grew suspicious of anyone who recommended a course of action, referring to such people as "Gianni Schic-chis" (a reference to Puccini's character who unscrupulously alters the will of the deceased). I repeatedly pointed out the need to reorganize the Foundation, which up to that time had been active only sporadically and relatively informally, awarding grants to a few young composers and researchers. To my great surprise, one day early in December 1978 she asked me to accompany her to the office of her new attorney, Alfred Rice, who, it turned out, also represented Ernest Hemingway's widow. While she spent quite some time in his "inner sanctum," I waited for her in the reception room. Finally she reappeared, with flushed cheeks and shining eyes but saying very little, even as we were driving back to New City. Suddenly she broke the silence and said: "I've done it! I have settled my will for good! The Foundation will be the principal heir. Thank God, now I can relax."

The subsequent period of emotional and physical well-being was short-lived. In February 1979, she slipped on the ice in New City and fractured her shoulder so badly that she had to be hospitalized. A year later an automobile accident put her back in the hospital. Once more feeling vulnerable, she formulated a plan to revitalize the still very dormant Foundation. She composed letters, which I typed and she signed, inviting cautiously selected professional associates and friends to serve on the Foundation's new board of trustees. All the invitations were accepted. On 25 September 1980, at a meeting in Alfred Rice's office, Lenya and Milton Coleman, the other incumbent board member, elected Henry Marx, Harold Prince, Julius Rudel, Guy Stern, Kim Kowalke, and me as trustees of the Kurt Weill Foundation for Music.

I had first met Kim Kowalke at the commemoration of Weill's seventy-fifth birthday, at a concert I had organized with Curtis performers as the opening event for the Weill-Lenya exhibit at the Library of the Performing Arts at Lincoln Center. At the time he was working on his doctoral dissertation at Yale—a few years later to be published under the title *Kurt Weill in Europe*. A lively correspondence ensued; sometimes he addressed his inquiries directly to me, sometimes Lenya referred them to me for response. By the time he joined the board of trustees, Kowalke was teaching at Occidental College in Los Angeles. At the next (and last) meeting to be held with Lenya as president, on 2 April 1981, she asked Professor Kowalke to investigate possible institutional homes for the vault material, a decision she had agonized over and postponed again and again. Finally facing the fact that her terminal illness prevented further procrastination, she hastily deposited the most valuable archival material at the music library of Yale University, not permanently but rather "on loan" for a period of five years. She would not part, however, with one set of original documents: her correspondence with Weill. Those letters she still kept close at hand in her bedroom on the second floor of Brook House.

Having fought valiantly against the recurring malignancy, Lenya refused further hospitalization and decided to spend her final days in the apartment of her friend Margo Harris, almost as if familiar surroundings might be able to prevent the inevitable from happening. There, heavily sedated, dependent on intravenous feeding, and comforted most by her daily visits with Teresa Stratas (who had just returned from India, where she had worked with Mother Teresa), Lenya was allowed to see only those friends who appeared on Mrs. Harris's list of approved callers. Suddenly, just a few weeks before her passing, a new will and testament emerged from that apartment: her attorney, a real-life Gianni Schicchi, had done honor to his operatic model. Alfred Rice had even added a magnificently deceptive flourish: a bequest of Weill's own wristwatch to himself would allay any suspicions about the legitimacy or propriety of his role as executor. However, as good fortune would have it, though he had the foresight to bring his own notaries to witness the new will, he neglected to make changes to that portion of the document in which Lenya had made provisions for the Foundation and named her successors to oversee Weill's legacy. As she lay on her deathbed in November 1981, she summoned Kowalke from California to inform him that she wanted him to become president of the Foundation after her death.

During that brief visit, her last lucid moments were devoted to safeguarding the Weill-Lenya correspondence. She told Kowalke of their location in Brook House, instructed him to retrieve them (Mrs. Harris had a key), and asked him "to make sure the right thing would be done with them." Mrs. Harris refused to cooperate, however, and at the time of Lenya's death the letters remained in the filing cabinet in an unoccupied Brook House. Fortunately the burglars who broke into the house that winter and took some silver only rifled through the "worthless" paper contents of the filing cabinet they had pried open. The letters Lenya had safeguarded for half a century were found scattered across the bedroom floor. After a lengthy battle in probate court, in August 1982 the correspondence was determined to qualify as "archival material" rather than "house furnishings," so the Kurt Weill Foundation for Music was awarded ownership. The board of trustees decided that publication of the letters was a worthwhile project and assigned Kowalke and me to coedit the letters. During the subsequent decade of intensive work on Weill and Lenya's private correspondence, I have come to understand far better than ever before the two extraordinary artists with whom I had the privilege to work. By publishing the correspondence in its entirety and without abridgment, bowdlerization, or apologia, Kim and I hope that Lenya's final request has been fulfilled responsibly.

Lys Symonette
4 November 1994

ACKNOWLEDGMENTS

Active work on this project has spanned more than a decade, and therefore the risk of omission in expressing gratitude to all those who nurtured or abetted the endeavor is higher than usual. Although we editors initially assumed principal responsibility for preparation of the volume as part of our regular duties as staff members of the Kurt Weill Foundation for Music, it quickly became an extra-hours labor of both love and frustration, for in the absence of comprehensive scholarly biographies of either Weill or Lenya, annotating so wide-ranging a correspondence meant gathering almost as much material as would be needed for a double biography. Fortunately, our associates at the Foundation have made the enterprise a genuine institutional team-effort, thereby foreshortening its still lengthy period of gestation.

The various stages of work required to inventory, transcribe, word-process, translate, date, research, annotate, illustrate, and index the letters benefited from the assistance of several generations of staff members of the Weill-Lenya Research Center and the Foundation: secretaries James Lynch, Michael Hoexter, John Watson, Ed Buckley, Kathleen Finnegan, and Brian Butcher; office administrator Anita Weisburger; director of programs Mario Mercado; archival assistant David Stein and associate archivists Margaret Sherry and John Andrus; and associate director for business affairs Joanna Lee. Most recently Edward Harsh, associate director for publications, coordinated the final editing, proofreading, and correction of the typescript. Throughout the entire process David Farneth, director of the Weill-Lenya Research Center, has collaborated as an indispensable partner, placing the archives and his own knowledge of Weilliana at our disposal, advising us on research strategies and in the selection of pictorial material, and allowing the venture to claim priority over the demands on his own and other staff members' time. He has also been a valued editor of the volume editors' contributions.

At the University of Rochester, Carolyn Ratcliff, administrative assistant for the Music Program of the College of Arts and Science, not only word-processed with admirable accuracy a large portion of the correspondence but continually salvaged the project when technical emergencies threatened disaster. Her expertise and good humor made bearable many a hot summer day the editors spent in front of a computer screen in a non–air-conditioned office on the top floor of Todd Hall. Mary Frandsen and Michaela Harkins were able research assistants for several weeks during the summers of 1993 and 1995 respectively. Jean Caruso assisted in preparing the indexes. The doctoral research of bruce mcclung on *Lady in the Dark* and Tamara Levitz on Ferruccio Busoni's master class answered many questions raised by the correspondence. During 1993–94 Kim Kowalke enjoyed a sabbatical leave funded by the University of Rochester in order to complete work on the edition.

David Drew, Jürgen Thym, Christopher Hailey, Juliane Brand, and Guy Stern read the penultimate typescript and offered many valuable suggestions, corrections, and additional information. Queries were answered by Maurice Abravanel, Hannelore Bergman-Marom, Hanne Busoni, Milton Coleman, David Drew, Gigi Gilpin McGuire, Martus Granirer, Victor Carl Guarnieri, Mark Hammerschmidt, Helen Hayes, Stephen Hinton, Hanne Holosovsky, Pascal Huynh, Ulla Jablonowski, Horst Koegler, E. Anna Krebs, Tamara Levitz, Elisabeth Lürzer, bruce mcclung, Henry Marx, Burgess Meredith, Sofie Messinger, Patrick O'Connor, Jo Révy, Jürgen Schebera, Guy Stern, Victoria Stevenson, Arnold Sundgaard, Fritz Weinschenk, Richard Wollheim, and Norman Zelenko.

Our annotation benefited greatly from unpublished memoirs, oral histories, and correspondence in the Weill-Lenya Research Center in New York and the Weill/Lenya Archive at Yale University, including the Hans and Rita Weill Collection, the Eva Hammerschmidt Collection, and interviews and oral histories by Maurice Abravanel, Julius Ackermann, Stella Adler, Hesper Anderson, Quentin Anderson, Margo Aufricht, Phoebe Brand, Milton Caniff, Carmen Capalbo, Morris Carnovsky, George Davis, Agnes DeMille, Hans Dudelheim, Ronald Freed, Eva Hammerschmidt, Helen Hayes, Hilde Halpern, Hans Heinsheimer, Felix (Joachimson) Jackson, Irving "Swifty" Lazar, Bobby Lewis, Mary Martin, Burgess Meredith, Madeleine Milhaud, Paul Moor, Harriet Pinover, Harold Prince, Alan Rich, Ann Ronell, Victor Samrock, Tonio Selwart, Teresa Stratas, Virgil Thomson, Robert Vambery, Michael Wager, and Gottfried Wagner.

We are also grateful to the following archives and libraries for their resources and cooperation: In the United States, the Library of the Academy of Motion Pictures, Los Angeles; Aufbau Archive, New York; Leo Baeck Institute, New York; Bobst Library of New York University; Museum of Television and Radio, New York; National Archives and Records Service, Washington, D.C.; New York Public Library; New York Public Library of the Performing Arts at Lincoln Center; Sibley Music Library and Rush-Rhees Library of the University of Rochester; and State Historical Society of Wisconsin, Madison. In Europe, Akademie der Künste, Berlin; Bertolt-Brecht-Archiv, Berlin; Deutsches Literaturarchiv / Schiller Nationalmuseum, Marbach; Archiv der Genossenschaft Deutscher Bühnengehöriger, Hamburg; Österreichische Nationalbibliothek, Vienna; Österreichisches Theatermuseum, Vienna; Stadtarchiv Dessau; Stadtarchiv Lüdenscheid; Stadtbibliothek, Zurich; Theatermuseum des Instituts für Theater-, Film- und Fernsehwissenschaft der Univeristät zu Köln; Archiv der Universal Edition, Vienna; and Wiener Stadt- und Landesbibliothek.

For permission to publish photographs, we are grateful to the following individuals and agencies, who are credited in the relevant captions: Artists Rights Society (ARS); Irma Commanday; Morris Engel; Lotte Jacobi Archives of the University of New Hampshire; the Estate of George Platt Lynes; the Museum of the City of New York; the New York Public Library; the Man Ray Trust; Staley-Wise Gallery, New York; Ralph Steiner Photographs; Brigitte Taylor, London. Where no other credit appears, photographs have been provided courtesy of the Weill-Lenya Research Center, New York. Epigraphs excerpted from "There's Nowhere to Go but Up" and "Speak Low" are reprinted by permission of Warner/Chappell Music, Los Angeles. European American Music Corporation and Universal Edition granted permission to reprint "Crane Duet" from *Mahagonny*.

Kathy Robbins and her staff at the Robbins Office helped to place this book with appropriate publishers in each territory and language. We are especially indebted to James Clark and Doris Kretschmer of the University of California Press for their patience, guidance, and help in shaping the volume and their enthusiastic response to the result. But above all is our gratitude for the meticulous, imaginative, and rigorous editing by Rose Vekony, who deserves a place in line with the great collaborator-editors of the bygone days of publishing.

To our respective spouses and families we give special thanks for their support, forbearance, and encouragement: to Randolph and Victor Symonette, and especially to Elizabeth and Kyle Kowalke, who over the last six years spent many evenings and weekends alone in Rochester while editing progressed in New York and acted as hosts for "Tante Lys" when collaboration occurred in Rochester. Liz also gave us the benefit of her professional expertise, providing many psychological insights in her reading of the letters and ancillary material.

We dedicate this volume to the memory of four extraordinary individuals who died during its genesis but whose inspiration lives on: Maurice Abravanel, Milton "Chris" Blazakis, Henry Kowalke, and Henry Marx.

L.S. and K.K.

Appendix A

LIST OF PET NAMES AND PRIVATE EXPRESSIONS

WEILL'S SIGNATURES

Affenschwanz: "monkey tail"
Äppelheim
Bibi
Bibiboy
Birühmti: "famous one"
Boy
Bubü
Buster
Dany
Didi
Freundchen: "little friend"
Frosch: "frog"; Froschi: "little frog"
Glätzchen: "little baldy"
Hubby
Jésus; Jésus-Bub: "Jesus-Boy"

K———
Knudchen, Knut, Knutchen, Knütchen, Knute,
 Knuti, Knuuuuti, Knut Garbo, Knut
 Gustavson
Kurt, Kurti, Kurt Julian, Kurtio Weillissimo
Mordspison: "big shot"
Pünktchen: "little dot"
Schnub, Schnüb, Schnübchen, Schnube,
 Schnüberich, Schnubi, Schnubinchen
Schnutz
Träubchen, Trrräubchen: "little grape"; Trrrr,
 Trrrrr, Trrrrrr
Weili, Weilili, Weillchen, Weilli, Weillili,
 Weilli-Knut
Zappelfritz: "a fidget"

LENYA'S PET NAMES FOR WEILL

Bitrübelchen: "little woebegone one"
Bläumchen, Blumchen, Blümchen, Blumi: "little
 flower"
Boy, Boyly
Darling, Darling-Tröpfi
Döfchen: "little dummy"
Fröschlein: "little frog"
Glätzchen: "little baldy"
Herr Johann Strauss-Weill
Hollywoodpflanze
Honey, honeyboy, honneychild; honneybär:
 "honey bear"
Knutchen, Knuti
Kurtchen, Kürtchen, Kurti, Kurtili
Pflänzchen: "naughty boy"
Pfläumchen: "little plum"
Pi: "pal"

Schäpschen: "little schnapps"
Schnäubchen, Schnäubi, Schnäubschen
Schnäutzchen: "little snout"
Schnubchen, Schnübchen, Schnubschen
Schnube, Schnübi, Sch—sch—sch—sch—nubi
Schwänzchen: "little tail"
Schweenchen: "little piggy"
Sir Weill
Sugar
Sonnenblume: "sunflower"
Träubchen, Trräubchen, Traubi, Träubi, Träuby,
 Trrrrröubi: "little grape"
Tröpfchen, Tröööpfchen, Trööööööööpfchen,
 Tröpfi, Tropfi: "droplet"
Trrrrrr
Weilchen, Weili, Weilili, Weillchen, Weilli

LENYA'S SIGNATURES

Blümchen, Blumchen, Blumi: "little flower"
Blüte: "blossom"
Carolinchen, Caroline
Jenny Lind Lenya
Karoline, Karoline Weill
Kleene, Kleenchen: "kiddo"
Kneubchen Träubchen Schleubchen Läubchen
Lady Weill
Linderl, Linerl, Linnerl
Lollie
Lottie
Madame Weill

Missi
Nibbi
Pips
Plänzchen
Schnüb, Schnübe, Schnubi
Träubi: "little grape"
Tülpchen: "little tulip"
Weib, Weibi: "wife"
Wilhelmine
Zippi: "little tip"
Zybe

WEILL'S PET NAMES FOR LENYA

Ameisenblume, Ameisenpflanze: literally, "ant flower/plant," but probably better "flower of the Ameisegasse" (Lenya's address in Vienna)
Betrübelchen: "little sad one"
Bibi-Schwänzchen
Blümchen, Blumchen, Blümelein, Blumi, Blümi, Blumilein, Blümilein, Blümlein: "little flower"
Blume: "flower"
Blumenblümchen: "little flower of flowers"
Blumenpflänzchen, Blumenpflanze: "flowering plant"
Bubili: "little boy"
Darling, Darling honey, Darling-honey, Darling sweet; me/my darling Caroline
Delicious
Diden, Diderle, Didilein
Doofi, Doooofi: "little dummy"
Duchie
Girly
Honey-chil', Honey chile'
Kleene: "kiddo," dialect for "little one"
Lenja-Benja
Lenscherl
Liebchen,
Liebili: "dear little one"
Lila Schweinderl, Lila Schweindi: "little purple pig"
Lilipe Lencha: "dear Lenya," in Saxonian pronunciation
Linderl, Linerl, Linerle, Linnerl, Liiiiinerl
Linercherl sweetheart, Linnerl-Weibi, Linntchkerl, Linntschkerl, Linutschkerl, Linschkerl, Linscherl
Littichen
Lottchen
Mistblume: "dung blossom"

Mistfink: "dung bird"
Muschelchen, Muschi: "little mussel"
Negerkindl: "pickaninny"
Pflänzchen, Pflanze: in Berlin dialect, "fresh, sassy urban girl," "city chick"
Pilouchen: "little flannelette"
Pison, Pisönchen: "little person," "buddy," "pal"
Pfläumchen: "little plum"
Pummilein: "little plump one"
Rehbeinchen: "little deer leg"
Roadschweinchen: "little road hog"
Rosenblümchen: "little rose blossom"
Schätzchen, Schätzi, Schätzilein: "little treasure"
Schmöckchen
Schnäpschen, Schnapspison: "little schnapps," "schnapps person"
Schnäubchen, Schnäubi, Schneubi
Schnäuben-Träubchen
Schnäutzchen, Schnäuzchen: "little snout"
Schnübchen, Schnube, Schnübe, Schnübelein, Schnubelinchen
Schnubenblümchen, Schnübenblümchen
Schwämmi: "little mushroom"
Schwänzchen: "little tail"
Seelchen: "little soul"
Spätzlein: "little sparrow"
Süsses: "sweet"
Sweetie
Sweetie-pie, Sweety-pie, Sweety-honey-pie, Sweety honey sugar pie
Tobby Engel, Tobili
Träubchen, Trrräubchen, Trrrräubchen, Trrrrräubchen, Träube, Träubi, Trräubi, Trrräubi, Trrrräubi, Trrrrräubi, Träubili, Träubilein: "little grape"
Träubchenpison, Träubchen-Pisonchen, Träuben-Schätzchen, Träuben-Spatz, Träubenspatz, Träubenträubchen, Träubentröpfchen

Tröpfi, Tröpfilein, Trröpfchen: "little droplet"
Trrrrrr
Tütchen, Tüti, Tütilein: "little paper bag"; also,
   a playful colloquial term for someone slow to
   understand
Tüti-Pison

Weillchen: "little Weill"
Weilliwüppchen: "little Weill woman"
Wüllichen, Wülli
Zibelinerl, Zibelyne, Zybeline, Zybelienerl,
   Zybelinerl, Zyberlinerl: see letter 62 n.1
Zippi: "little tip"

PRIVATE EXPRESSIONS IN DIALECT OR INVENTED LANGUAGE

Affenschwanz: "monkey tail"
auf Wiedili, auf Wiiiiiiidisehn, Wiedi, Wiedisehn,
   Widisehen (auf Wiedersehen): "bye-bye"
beese (böse; Berlin dialect): "angry"
Berühmti, Birühmti (Berühmtheit): "famous one"
Bobo (Popo): "fanny"
büsschens, Bussi (Bußerl): "little kiss"
Feinlebe, finelebe (feines Leben): "the good life,"
   "living it up"
Gi, Gizette (Gazette): "newspaper," "tabloid"
gilant, gillant: "elegant"
G'schamster, Gschamster: "kowtowing minion"
Handkuß, ich küsse ihre Hand: "I kiss your
   hand"
Klugi (Kluge): "smarty"
Knüßchen, Knüschen, Knüüsschen,
   Kn ö ö ö ö ö schens (Küßchen): "little kisses"
Lebe (Lebewohl): "farewell"

niedelich (niedlich): "cute," "nice"
paperchen (hybrid English-German):
   "little newspaper"
Pison, Pi (Person): "person," "pal"
Poo'chen (Popochen): "little fanny";
   Popo: "fanny"
primi (prima): "first-rate"
Sächelchen: "trifles," "small items"
   (see letter 89 n.3)
schliepeln, schlippeln (schlafen): "to sleep," "to
   snooze," "to go beddy-bye"
schnecki: "sluggish"
Schneckidibong, Schniekedibong
schneepeln, schniepeln, sneepeln: see schliepeln
Schniepelpison: "sleepyhead"
Schweinerei: "mess"
Warschi, Arschi (Arsch): "little ass"
Zippi: "little tip"

Appendix B

A NOTE ON MONEY MATTERS

During the period 1924–32, the value of European currencies against the American dollar remained relatively stable:

CURRENCY	1932 DOLLAR EQUIVALENT	1993 DOLLAR EQUIVALENT
1 German reichsmark	.24	2.43
1 French franc	.04	.43
1 Austrian schilling	.14	1.42
1 Swiss franc	.19	1.92
1 British pound	4.85	49.08

During the period 1933–35, the dollar declined against European currencies:

CURRENCY	1933–35 DOLLAR EQUIVALENT (AVG.)	1993 DOLLAR EQUIVALENT
1 German reichsmark	.35	3.87
1 French franc	.055	.61
1 Austrian schilling	.17	1.88
1 Swiss franc	.29	3.20
1 British pound	4.50	49.73

The following are values for selected years from 1936 to 1950:

1 U.S. dollar in 1939 is equivalent to $10.32 in 1993.
1 U.S. dollar in 1945 is equivalent to $8.12 in 1993.
1 U.S. dollar in 1950 is equivalent to $6.15 in 1993.

BIOGRAPHICAL GLOSSARY

ABRAVANEL, MAURICE (1903–93)
Greek-born American conductor. His composition study with Weill in Berlin in the early 1920s initiated a lifelong friendship between the two men. Abravanel conducted performances of Weill's works in provincial German opera houses and later the premiere of *Die sieben Todsünden* in Paris, as well as *Knickerbocker Holiday, Lady in the Dark, One Touch of Venus, The Firebrand of Florence,* and *Street Scene* on Broadway. After immigrating to the United States in 1936 he conducted at the Metropolitan Opera. He left New York in 1947 to found the Utah Symphony and developed that ensemble into one of the leading orchestras in the United States.

ADORNO, THEODOR WIESENGRUND (1903–69)
German philosopher, sociologist of music, critic, and composer who was a central figure in the Frankfurt School for Social Research. A pupil of Alban Berg and a member of Arnold Schoenberg's circle, he began his career as a music critic, editing the prestigious periodical *Anbruch* from 1928 to 1931 and praising Weill's works with Brecht. He immigrated first to England and then to the United States, arriving at the New School for Social Research in New York in 1938, where he headed the Princeton Radio Research Project. He returned to Germany soon after the war. His *Philosophy of Modern Music* (1949) set up the dichotomy of Stravinsky and Schoenberg as the antipodes of modern music and laid out the central aesthetic precepts for Viennese Modernism. He fought against jazz, as well as any music intended for entertainment and pleasure, and was ideologically opposed to much of Weill's work after 1931.

ALAN, CHARLES (1908–75)
American set designer for MGM studios and, later, Warner Brothers. In the theater, he designed sets for Max Reinhardt's *The Miracle* (1924) and served as production manager for *The Eternal Road* (1937). In collaboration with Burgess Meredith and Weill, he later formed a company to produce ballad operas on subjects taken from American history, but no such projects ever came to fruition. He eventually became an art dealer, whose gallery showcased works of David Hockney, among others.

ANDERSON, GERTRUDE ("MAB"; 1904–53)
Maxwell Anderson's second wife, an actress with a short theatrical career but permanent social ambitions. She so effectively hid her Jewish background that her daughter Hesper learned of it only after her mother had committed suicide in 1953.

ANDERSON, MAXWELL (1888–1959)
Foremost American playwright of the 1930s, specializing in historical verse dramas. His plays include *What Price Glory?* (1924), the Pulitzer Prize–winning *Both Your Houses* (1933), *Key Largo* (1939), and *Anne of the Thousand Days* (1948). A founding member of the Playwrights' Producing Company, Anderson met Weill through Burgess Meredith, who had starred in Anderson's *Winterset* (1935) and *High Tor* (1937). The Anderson family and the Weills were next-door neighbors on South Mountain Road in Rockland County from 1941. Weill and Lenya grew close to the entire family: sons from Anderson's first marriage, to Margaret Ethel Haskett, Quentin (b. 1912, m. Margaret Elizabeth Pickett), Alan (b. 1917, m. Nancy Swan), and Terrence (b. 1921, m. Anastasia Sadowsky); and a daughter from his second marriage, to Gertrude ("Mab") Higger *(q.v.)*, Hesper (b. 1934; she went on to a career as a screenwriter). Although

Anderson and Weill finished only *Knickerbocker Holiday* (1938), *Ballad of Magna Carta* (1940), and *Lost in the Stars* (1949), they collaborated on several other projects, including "Ulysses Africanus" and a musical adaptation of *Street Scene*. They were at work on a musical play based on Mark Twain's *Huckleberry Finn* at the time of Weill's death in 1950.

ATKINSON, BROOKS, *in full* JUSTIN BROOKS ATKINSON (1894–1984)
Drama critic of the *New York Times* from 1924 until 1960. Educated at Harvard, he entered the newspaper world as a reporter for the *Daily News* of Springfield, Massachusetts. His post with the *Boston Evening Transcript*, where he began as assistant drama critic in 1919, immediately preceded his long tenure at the *Times*. An ardent admirer of Weill's American scores, Atkinson wrote several books on the theater, including *Broadway Scrapbook* (1947) and *Broadway* (1970).

AUFRICHT, ERNST JOSEF (1898–1971)
German theatrical producer who managed the Theater am Schiffbauerdamm in Berlin from 1927 through 1931. A son of a wealthy Silesian mine owner, he financed and produced a number of important new works—many of them featuring Lenya. The most prominent of these was *Die Dreigroschenoper*. At the Theater am Kurfürstendamm in Berlin he produced a fifty-performance run of the opera *Aufstieg und Fall der Stadt Mahagonny* (1931). Though he immigrated to the United States, he was unable to repeat his theatrical success and unsuccessful in reuniting Brecht and Weill in collaboration. He worked for the war effort in various capacities, including his production of the radio series *We Fight Back*. Aufricht and his wife, Margot (1899–1990), who had served as his assistant, returned to West Berlin after the war.

BEHRMAN, SAMUEL NATHANIEL (1893–1973)
American playwright, whose dramas include *Serena Blandish* (1929), *Biography* (1932), and *No Time for Comedy* (1939). In 1937 he adapted Jean Giraudoux's *Amphitryon 38* for the Lunts and the following year helped to found the Playwrights' Producing Company. He achieved success with his version of Franz Werfel's *Jacobowsky and the Colonel* (1944), as well as his rewrite for Lynn Fontanne and Alfred Lunt of Ludwig Fulda's comedy *The Pirate* (1942), which, though it was originally to feature music by Weill, was finally produced as a straight play by the Theatre Guild. In 1954 he and Joshua Logan collaborated on the libretto of the musical *Fanny*.

BEKKER, PAUL (1882–1937)
German music critic and theater director. After serving as chief critic of the influential *Frankfurter Zeitung* (1911–23), he became intendant of the Prussian state theaters of Kassel and Wiesbaden (1925–32). A prolific writer with many publications to his credit, he became one of the most energetic proponents of Weill's opera *Die Bürgschaft*. Bekker immigrated to New York in 1934, resuming his career as a critic in the local German-language daily newspaper *Die Staatszeitung*.

BERGNER, ELISABETH (1900–1988)
One of Berlin's most celebrated stars of stage and screen. A native of Drogobych (Galicia), she performed from 1916 to 1918 in Zurich, where she at times shared a dressing room with Lenya. In her memoirs, *Bewundert viel und viel gescholten* (1978), she recalls that phase in both of their careers. She immigrated to England and was one of the few German-speaking actors able to retain stardom. She also appeared in several successful Broadway productions.

BERTHON, MAURICE (1877–1953)
The Berthons (also spelled *Berton* in the correspondence) were the caretakers of Weill's residence in Louveciennes. Weill was especially fond of their son Emile.

BERTRAND, PAUL (1873–1953)
French music publisher who began his career in the publishing house of Alphonse Leduc. During World War I, Bertrand left Leduc to become manager of Heugel, which would sign Weill to a five-year contract in 1933 and publish his French compositions.

BLAMAUER, MARIE, *see* HUBEK, MARIE

BLITZSTEIN, MARC (1905–64)
American composer who studied piano with Alexander Siloti and composition with Rosario Scalero and Nadia Boulanger. While in Europe, he reviewed Weill's works for *Modern Music*. Sympathy for left-wing causes inspired his controversial agitprop opera *The Cradle Will Rock* (1937), dedicated to Brecht. Though in the late 1920s he dismissed Weill's *Die Dreigroschenoper* as "of no particular significance," his brilliant English adaptation (1952) did much to pave the way for the success of *The Threepenny Opera* in the United States. Leonard Bernstein, Blitzstein's lifelong friend, conducted the concert premiere at Brandeis University.

BRECHER, GUSTAV (1872–1940)
German conductor. After a brief internship under Gustav Mahler in Vienna, in 1903 he was named first conductor of the Hamburg Opera. Appointed music director of the Leipzig Opera in 1924, he conducted the world premieres of *Aufstieg und Fall der Stadt Mahagonny* (1930) and *Der Silbersee* (1933), as well as many other contemporary operas. Unable to escape from the Nazis, he and his wife committed suicide in Ostend, Belgium, in 1940.

BRECHT, BERTOLT, *orig. name* EUGEN BERTHOLD FRIEDRICH BRECHT (1898–1956)
Internationally renowned German playwright, poet, director, and dramatic theorist. His collaborations with Weill resulted in the groundbreaking *Dreigroschenoper* (1928) as well as many other notable works, including *Das Berliner Requiem* (1928), *Der Lindberghflug* (1929), *Happy End* (1929), and *Der Jasager* (1930). About his collaboration with Brecht, Weill remarked in 1929: "Music has more impact than words. Brecht knows it and he knows that I know it. But we never talk about it. If it came out in the open, we couldn't work with each other anymore." Brecht fled Germany in 1933; during his fifteen years of exile, he produced most of his finest plays, including *Mother Courage and Her Children* (1939), *The Good Person of Szechwan* (1940), and *The Caucasian Chalk Circle* (1945). Efforts to renew Weill and Brecht's collaboration in the United States were not successful, and Weill declined Brecht's invitation to write music for the Berliner Ensemble, the theater company Brecht founded in East Berlin after his return in 1947.

BRÜGMANN, WALTER (1884–1946)
German stage director who mounted the premieres of Křenek's *Der Sprung über den Schatten* in Frankfurt am Main (1924), Weill's *Mahagonny Songspiel* in Baden-Baden (1927), and then Křenek's *Jonny spielt auf* (1927), Weill's *Der Zar läßt sich photographieren* (1928), and *Aufstieg und Fall der Stadt Mahagonny* (1930) in Leipzig.

BUSONI, FERRUCCIO (1866–1924)
A brilliant Italian concert pianist and ardent proponent of modern music, who introduced many important new works in his concerts with the Berlin Philharmonic. His compositional activity included the operas *Die Brautwahl* (1912), *Arlecchino* (1917), and *Turandot* (1917), but he viewed most of his late works as studies for his opera *Doktor Faust*, left unfinished at his death. During the last four years of his life, he conducted a master class in composition at the Akademie der Künste in Berlin. His most successful students included Philipp Jarnach, Vladimir Vogel, and Weill.

BUSONI, RAFAELLO (1900–1962)
Self-taught painter and illustrator; son of Ferruccio Busoni *(q.v.)*. He and his first wife, Hide (1897–1931), were very close friends of Weill's early in the composer's career. Rafaello immigrated to the United States with his second wife, Hannah.

CHARELL, ERIK, *orig. name* ERICH LÖWENBERG (1894–1974)
German stage director, producer, and impresario. He had a brief career as a dancer before going on to become one of Berlin's most successful producers of extravaganzas (such as *Im Weißen Rössl* [1930]) and motion pictures (*Der Kongreß tanzt* [1931]). Proposed collaborations with Weill in both Berlin and London came to naught. After World War II, he produced one more smash hit, *Feuerwerk* (1950), in Switzerland, where he died.

CLAIR, RENÉ (1898–1981)
Famous French motion-picture director, whose classics include *Un chapeau de paille d'Italie* (1927), *Sous les toits de Paris* (1930), and *The Ghost Goes West* (1935). None of Weill's various proposed collaborations

with Clair, including a Paris stage production of *Der Kuhhandel* and a musical version of Eugène Labiche's *The Italian Straw Hat,* came to fruition.

COCHRAN, SIR CHARLES BLAKE (1872–1951)
The leading British producer of his era, he began his career as an actor in the United States, also serving for a time as secretary to Richard Mansfield. After moving to London (ca. 1902), he specialized in directing revues, some of them collaborations with Noel Coward. He penned several memoirs, among them *I Had Almost Forgotten* (1932) and *Showman Looks On* (1945). In 1934–35 Weill's hopes that Cochran would produce an English adaptation of *Der Kuhhandel* were unfulfilled.

CRAWFORD, CHERYL (1902–86)
Important American theatrical producer who began her career as one of the three founders of the progressive Group Theatre. She was instrumental in bringing Weill together with his first American collaborator, Paul Green. Her production credits include the 1942 revival of *Porgy and Bess,* for which Weill served as informal adviser. For a time, the Weills shared an apartment on East Fifty-first Street in New York with Crawford and her companion Dorothy Patten. Crawford also produced the original Broadway productions of *One Touch of Venus* (1943) and *Love Life* (1948).

CURJEL, HANS (1896–1974)
German art historian, dramaturg, conductor, and producer who served as Otto Klemperer's assistant at the Krolloper in Berlin from 1927 to 1930. He assumed the position of deputy director in its final season (1930–31). During this time he and his wife, Jella (pronounced Yella), were close friends to both Weill and Lenya. He immigrated to Zurich, where he became director first of the Corso Theater and later of the Stadttheater Chur. After the war he mounted *Mahagonny* in an expanded version of the *Songspiel,* as the musical material of the full-length opera was presumed lost.

DAVIS, GEORGE (1906–57)
American novelist and editor. Born in Ludington, Michigan, he left the United States at twenty-three to join the American literary circle in Paris. His first novel, *The Opening of a Door* (1931), made him an instant celebrity. As editor of *Vanity Fair,* fiction editor of *Harper's Bazaar,* and associate fiction editor of *Mademoiselle,* he discovered and nurtured the careers of many distinguished American writers, among them Truman Capote, Carson McCullers, and Richard Wright. Lenya and he became friends in the 1940s. In 1951 they married, and he guided her "comeback" career as well as the "Weill renaissance."

DEVAL, JACQUES (1894–1972)
Writer of light comedies in the tradition of French vaudeville. A Parisian by birth, he achieved his greatest international success with both the stage and film versions of *Tovarich.* His one collaboration with Weill, *Marie Galante* (1934), was made (without Weill's music) into a motion picture starring Spencer Tracy.

DIETRICH, MARLENE, *orig. name* MARIA MAGDALENA DIETRICH (1902–92)
German actress who became an international film star. Born into a Prussian military family, she pursued a career as a violinist until an injury to her hand motivated a switch to acting and singing. She appeared in several Max Reinhardt productions and Berlin revues before the film *Der blaue Engel* (1930) catapulted her to international fame. In 1934 she commissioned two songs from Weill, and she was the composer's first choice for the lead role in *One Touch of Venus.* Though none of the other projects she and Weill contemplated ever materialized, even in her later years she made plans to record *Die Dreigroschenoper.*

EISLER, HANNS (1898–1962)
Austrian composer, whose musical settings Brecht described as "the tests of my poems, what productions were to my plays." A student of Arnold Schoenberg from 1919 to 1923, Eisler quarreled with his teacher over his political views. By 1927 he had broken with the Second Viennese School and his music reflected his aspirations for the workers' movement. He was influenced by Weill's early collaborations with Brecht, and they shared the goal of shattering the "splendid isolation" of modern music. Eisler left Germany for Russia in 1936 but soon immigrated to the United States, where he found occasional employment scoring films in Hollywood. After the war, he was expelled from the United States by the House Committee on Un-American Activities. He returned to East Germany and worked closely with Brecht, providing the music to many of the Berliner Ensemble's productions. He also composed that country's national anthem.

ERNST, MAX (1891–1976)
German-born artist, generally recognized as one of the founders of surrealism. He immigrated to Switzerland and France, where he lived for several years before coming to the United States. His friendship with Lenya, begun in the thirties, endured after Weill's death and is documented in witty letters to her, which, along with Weill's, were among the only letters that she carefully preserved.

FONTANNE, LYNN (1892–1982)
One of the great actresses of the American stage, who met her future husband and future costar, Alfred Lunt (*q.v.*), in 1916. In the next three decades they appeared in a new play virtually every season, including *Arms and the Man, Pygmalion, The Doctor's Dilemma, Elizabeth the Queen, Design for Living, The Taming of the Shrew, The Seagull, There Shall Be No Night.* The principal offstage characters of *Kiss Me, Kate* are said to have been modeled on the Lunts.

FREEDMAN, HAROLD (1897–1966)
American literary agent and close friend of several members of the Playwrights' Producing Company. Weill nicknamed him *Dornröschen* (Sleeping Beauty).

GERSHWIN, GEORGE (1898–1937)
American composer who began his career in Tin Pan Alley and developed into a spectacularly successful songwriter for Broadway shows and Hollywood films. By the age of thirty he had established a new type of concert music based on popular models, exemplified by his *Rhapsody in Blue* (1924), Concerto in F (1925), and *An American in Paris* (1928). His opera *Porgy and Bess* (1935) made a deep and lasting impression on Weill. At thirty-nine, at the height of his success, Gershwin died of a brain tumor.

GERSHWIN, IRA (1896–1983)
American lyricist whose early career was largely a collaboration with his brother, extending from 1924 until George's death in 1937. Moss Hart and Weill persuaded him to start working again, with *Lady in the Dark* (1940). Ira and his wife, Leonore ("Lee"; 1900–1991), became close friends of Lenya and Weill's. In 1945 Gershwin and Weill also collaborated on the unsuccessful operetta *The Firebrand of Florence* and the musical film *Where Do We Go from Here?*

GORDON, MAX, *orig. name* MECHEL SALPETER (1892–1978)
Broadway producer who began his career as a press agent and later an agent for vaudeville acts. During the 1930s and 1940s he produced such hits as *The Band Wagon* (1931), *Roberta* (1933), *Jubilee* (1935), *My Sister Eileen* (1940), and *The Late George Apley* (1944), as well as Weill's only flop in the United States, *The Firebrand of Florence* (1945). He was well known for erratic behavior, once perching himself on a window ledge and threatening to jump if money was not forthcoming for a new production.

GREEN, PAUL (1894–1981)
Pulitzer Prize–winning American playwright. A native of North Carolina, he provided the Group Theatre with its first produced play, *House of Connelly,* in 1931. After working with Weill on *Johnny Johnson* (1936), he contemplated further collaboration with the composer on the musical pageant *The Common Glory* (1937), which he finished in 1948 without Weill's involvement. Green's wife, Elizabeth, contributed some of the lyrics to *Johnny Johnson.*

HARRAS
Weill's beloved German shepherd, who followed him into exile to France but not to the United States. He stayed on in Louveciennes with Weill's French housekeepers, the Berthon family, who took care of him and faithfully forwarded his latest photos to Weill in the United States.

HARRIS, JED, *orig. name* JACOB HOROWITZ (1900–1979)
Adventurous American stage producer and director. Born in Vienna, he was educated at Yale. His early successes included *The Front Page* (1928). In the 1930s he directed as well as produced, most notably *Our Town* (1938). He and Weill had met in London; they became friends in New York. Their hopes for a collaboration were frustrated.

HART, MOSS (1904–61)
Prominent American playwright and director. Born in New York and forced by poverty to drop out of school, he wrote his first play at seventeen. His first success was *Once in a Lifetime* (1932), written with George S. Kaufman. Hart's numerous other collaborations with Kaufman include *The Man Who Came to Dinner* (1939) and the Pulitzer Prize–winning *You Can't Take It with You* (1938). *Lady in the Dark* was his first solo Broadway play, written in 1940 at the urging of Hart's psychiatrist, Lawrence S. Kubie. In 1946 he married Kitty Carlisle. In the 1950s he directed the Broadway productions of *My Fair Lady* and *Camelot*.

HAYES, HELEN (1900–1993)
Known as the First Lady of the American Theater. Her long career began at age five in her native Washington, D.C., and lasted until she retired in 1970, after starring in a revival of *Harvey*. She scored her greatest triumph as Queen Victoria in *Victoria Regina* (1935–38), by Laurence Hausman. Although she won an Academy Award for her first Hollywood film, *The Sin of Madelon Claudet* (1931), she preferred to appear on stage. She and her husband, the playwright Charles MacArthur *(q.v.),* maintained a home in Nyack, New York, not far from the New City residence of Lenya and Weill. The two couples enjoyed a pleasant friendship and cordial professional relationship. Lenya had toured with Hayes in Anderson's *Candle in the Wind* (1941–42).

HECHT, BEN (1894–1964)
American screenwriter, director, producer, and a leading figure in activities on behalf of Zionist causes. He collaborated with Charles MacArthur *(q.v.)* on many plays and film scripts, including *The Front Page*. With Weill, he collaborated on *Fun to Be Free* (1941), *We Will Never Die* (1943), and *A Flag Is Born* (1947).

HEINSHEIMER, HANS WALTER (1900–1993)
German-born music publishing executive crucial to Weill's career in both Europe and the United States. The director of the opera division of Universal Edition in Vienna from 1923 to 1938, he immigrated to the United States and secured a position as director of symphonic and operatic music for Boosey & Hawkes (1938–47). From 1947 until his retirement, he served as director of publications for G. Schirmer, in which capacity he was responsible for the publication of Weill's *Down in the Valley* (1948). He authored several memoirs, including *Menagerie in F-Sharp* (1947) and *Regards to Aida* (1968). His correspondence with Weill is lengthier than the present one and critically important to an understanding of Weill's professional life.

HERALD, HEINZ (1891–1964)
German dramaturg and personal assistant to Max Reinhardt *(q.v.).* Meyer Weisgal described him as quiet and retiring in public but an articulate and persuasive adviser behind the scenes. His apparent humility did not prevent him from staunchly protecting the producer against "the playwrights swarming about with dreams of achieving that supreme distinction—a Reinhardt production."

HUBEK, MARIE, *née* BLAMAUER (1906–91)
Lenya's sister, referred to as Mariedl or Mariederl in the letters, resided her entire life at Ameisgasse 38, where they had grown up. Lenya consistently assisted Marie financially (she was an unskilled laborer); in her will Lenya set up a lifetime trust for her.

HUSTON, WALTER (1884–1950)
American actor of Canadian descent. He worked in vaudeville with his second wife, Bayonne Whipple, and subsequently achieved stardom on Broadway with *Desire under the Elms* (1924). The New York critical community honored him with a Best Actor award for his film re-creation of his own Broadway role in *Dodsworth* (1934). He starred in *Knickerbocker Holiday* (1938), and Weill wrote "September Song" with him in mind. He was the father of the director and screenwriter John Huston and the grandfather of actress Anjelica Huston. His third wife was the actress Nan Sutherland.

JACKSON, FELIX, *see* JOACHIMSON, FELIX

JAMES, EDWARD (1907–84)
Eccentric British millionaire who sponsored Les Ballets 1933 and commissioned for it *Die sieben Todsünden*, among other works, in a desperate but vain attempt to regain the affection of his estranged wife, the dancer Tilly Losch *(q.v.)*.

JOACHIMSON, FELIX, *later* **FELIX JACKSON (1902–92)**
German-born producer and writer. He studied piano and conducting before joining the *Berliner Börsen-Courier* as the second-string music and drama critic. Philipp Jarnach's recommendation that Joachimson study composition with Weill initiated a long friendship. They collaborated on the (now lost) opera *Na und?* (1926). Leaving Germany in 1933, Joachimson Americanized his last name to Jackson and achieved some success as a Hollywood producer and writer, with, for example, *Destry Rides Again* (1939). He recorded his recollections of Weill in *Portrait of a Quiet Man*, which remains unpublished.

KAISER, GEORG (1878–1945)
Foremost German expressionist playwright. The author of fifty-nine full-length plays, seven one-act dramas, two novels, and more than a hundred poems, he once had seven plays premiere in a single season. Kaiser provided the libretto for two one-act operas by Weill, as well as for the "play with music," *Der Silbersee* (1933). Persecuted by the Nazis, he immigrated to Switzerland in 1938, where his plays were still being performed. Weill tried to bring him to the United States, but the U.S. Consulate refused him a visa because his young son Anselm (1913–71) had been drafted and forced to serve in the German army during World War II. Kaiser died in Swiss exile. Kaiser and his wife, Margarethe (1888–1970), had introduced Lenya and Weill in 1924. The two widows remained close friends for many years and visited each other regularly after their husbands' deaths.

KAZAN, ELIA, *orig. name* **ELIA KAZANJOGLOUS (B. 1909)**
American film and stage director, nicknamed "Gadge" or "Gadget." A member of the Group Theatre in the 1930s, he organized the Actors' Studio in 1947, in cooperation with Lee Strasberg and Cheryl Crawford. He directed the original productions of Weill's *One Touch of Venus* (1943) and *Love Life* (1948).

KLEMPERER, OTTO (1885–1973)
German operatic and symphonic conductor. One of the leading conductors of his generation, he directed Berlin's short-lived avant-garde opera house, the Krolloper, from 1927 to 1931. There he commissioned Weill's *Kleine Dreigroschenmusik* and the all-Weill version of *Der Lindberghflug*. He reneged, however, on his commitment to mount the Berlin production of the full-length *Mahagonny,* and Weill never forgave his cowardice. In 1933 he immigrated to the United States and took a post as music director of the Los Angeles Philharmonic, and also appeared throughout the U.S. as a guest conductor. Returning to Europe in 1954, he conducted the London Symphony and the Royal Opera and recorded prolifically.

KOMMER, RUDOLF (1888–1943)
Rumanian-born adventurer, nicknamed "Kätchen." From humble beginnings as a cabaret performer in Vienna, he became first assistant to Max Reinhardt *(q.v.)* and served as such for the production of the Weill-Werfel *Eternal Road* (1937).

KORDA, SIR ALEXANDER (1893–1956)
Hungarian-born director, producer, and film executive. He began his career in 1916 in Hungary, then continued his work in Germany, Austria, and Hollywood until finally settling in England. He produced some of Britain's most successful films. As a director, he provided actors such as Charles Laughton and Robert Donat with roles that were to establish their careers.

LANG, FRITZ (1890–1976)
Important early twentieth-century German film director. Collaborating on screenplays with his wife, Thea von Harbou, he achieved great successes with his *Dr. Mabuse* series (1922), as well as *Die Nibelungen* (1924), *Metropolis* (1927), and *M* (1931). Invited by the Führer himself to direct and supervise Nazi productions, Lang feared discovery of his Jewish heritage and emigrated, first to Paris and then, in 1934, to the United States. He and Weill collaborated on the film *You and Me* (1938). Lily (Micky) Latté was his lifelong companion.

LAWRENCE, GERTRUDE (1898–1952)

British-born star of the legitimate and musical stage. She appeared in the United States in *Charlot's Revue* (1924) and *Oh Kay!* (1926), starring subsequently in London with Noel Coward in *Private Lives* (1931). She returned to New York in 1936 to appear with Coward in *Tonight at 8:30*. *Lady in the Dark* (1940) marked her triumphant return to the musical stage. A projected version of Sir Max Beerbohm's *Zuleika Dobson*, with music by Weill, never materialized. Lawrence affectionately called Weill "Chouchou." She died during the run of *The King and I*, in which she played Anna.

LERNER, ALAN JAY (1918–86)

American playwright and lyricist. He worked as a radio scriptwriter before teaming up with the young Austrian-born composer Frederick Loewe to write *What's Up* (1943) and *The Day Before Spring* (1943), both commercial disappointments. Their romantic fantasy *Brigadoon* (1947), however, was a huge hit, opening within a few days of *Street Scene*. Lerner's collaboration with Weill on *Love Life* (1948) was an important milestone in the development of the "concept" musical. Lerner scored his greatest successes with *My Fair Lady* (1956) and *Camelot* (1960), again in partnership with Loewe.

LITVAK, ANATOLE (1902–74)

Russian-born film director who settled in Hollywood in 1937 and became a friend of Weill's. One of his first films was Jacques Deval's *Tovarich* (1938). Several of his later films, including *Sorry, Wrong Number* (1948) and *The Snake Pit* (1949), won considerable acclaim.

LOSCH, TILLY (1904–75)

Austrian dancer and actress. She began her career at the Vienna State Opera from 1921 through 1928 before marrying wealthy Englishman Edward James *(q.v.)*. He financed Les Ballets 1933 for her, in which she created the leading role in Balanchine's *Errante*, as well as Anna II in Weill's *Die sieben Todsünden*.

LUNT, ALFRED (1892–1980)

American actor, considered by many the greatest of his generation. He made his Broadway debut in 1917; in 1922 he married Lynn Fontanne *(q.v.)* and rarely thereafter performed without her. They are widely recognized as one of the most formidable acting teams in the history of the American theater. Lunt also directed occasionally, his directorial credits including Maxwell Anderson's *Candle in the Wind* (1941). Weill was involved for a time in 1942 with the development of the Lunts' project *The Pirate*.

LYONS, ARTHUR (D. 1963)

Russian-born artist manager in New York and Hollywood. He and his brother Sam specialized in representation for the motion picture industry and were Weill's agents for a time. Arthur was also associated with David Loew's Producing Artists, Inc., a film production company.

MacARTHUR, CHARLES (1895–1956)

American playwright and husband of Helen Hayes *(q.v.)*. He was best known for his collaboration with Ben Hecht on stage and film productions such as *The Front Page* (1928) and *Twentieth Century* (1932).

MacLEISH, ARCHIBALD (1892–1982)

American writer, dramatist, and poet, who won a Pulitzer Prize for his 1932 work *Conquistador*, an epic about the conquest of Mexico. His many important posts included Librarian of Congress (1939–44) and Boylston Professor at Harvard University (1949–62). He collaborated with Weill on "Song of the Free" in 1942.

MAMOULIAN, ROUBEN (1897–1987)

Russian-born American stage and film director. Educated in Paris, he came to the United States in 1923 to become production director at Eastman Theater in Rochester, New York. He directed both *Porgy* (1927) and *Porgy and Bess* (1935) for the New York Theatre Guild, as well as that organization's most important musicals, *Oklahoma!* (1943) and *Carousel* (1945), both by Rodgers and Hammerstein. Weill tried unsuccessfully to persuade him to direct *Street Scene* (1947) but succeeded with *Lost in the Stars* (1949).

MARTIN, KARL HEINZ (1888–1948)
German producer and stage director. Founder of the Berlin Tribüne, he also served as director of the Berliner Volksbühne and the Hebbel Theater, which produced the first postwar performance of *Die Dreigroschenoper* in 1945. A central figure in the proletarian agitprop theater movement headed by Erwin Piscator, Martin directed Lenya in 1929 in Georg Büchner's *Dantons Tod*. He was married to Roma Bahn, the actress who played Polly in *Die Dreigroschenoper* when Carola Neher dropped out of the original cast.

MARTIN, MARY (1913–91)
Musical comedy star of stage and screen. Born in Texas, she worked as a dance instructor and nightclub entertainer until she was discovered for the Cole Porter musical *Leave It To Me!* (1938). Her rendition of "My Heart Belongs to Daddy" brought her notoriety, which led subsequently to her first starring role, in *One Touch of Venus* (1943). She went on to create the roles of Nellie Forbush in *South Pacific* (1949), Peter Pan (1954), and Maria in *The Sound of Music* (1959).

MAYER, EDWIN JUSTUS (1896–1960)
American playwright and screenwriter. He worked as a journalist and actor before succeeding with his play *The Firebrand* (1924), which starred Joseph Schildkraut as Benvenuto Cellini. Prior to the Gershwin-Weill adaptation for the musical stage, the play had been made into a successful motion picture with Fredric March in the leading role.

MENDELSSOHN, FRANCESCO VON (1901–73)
He and sister Eleonora were direct descendants of Moses and Felix Mendelssohn. A cellist of some accomplishment, he was a production assistant for *Die Dreigroschenoper* in Berlin, then unsuccessfully attempted to recreate that production in New York in 1933 and in Paris in 1938.

MEREDITH, BURGESS (b. 1908)
Versatile American stage and screen actor. He has played a wide range of stage, film, and television roles, from Shakespeare's kings (with Orson Welles) to Molnár's *Liliom* (with Ingrid Bergman), to the Penguin in the television series *Batman*, and more recently the trainer in the series of *Rocky* films with Sylvester Stallone. He also produced and directed *Ulysses in Nighttown* (1958) with Zero Mostel. He narrated the *Ballad of Magna Carta* (1940) and worked with Weill on the war documentary *Salute to France* (1944). He was Weill and Lenya's neighbor on South Mountain Road, and they contemplated further collaborations that did not materialize.

MEYER, EUGENE (1875–1959)
German-Jewish business tycoon who was a substantial investor in *The Eternal Road*. He had bought the *Washington Post* for $825,000 when the paper was sold at public auction in 1933. His wife, Agnes, was interested in financing a Frank Wedekind ballet (*Die Kaiserin von Neufundland*) for Weill during the composer's first years in the United States, but the rights could not be obtained.

MEYER, FLORENCE (1910–62)
The daughter of Eugene and Agnes Meyer, she had been a featured dancer in *The Eternal Road*. Married to the Austrian actor Oskar Homolka, she was a close friend of Lenya's in the United States.

MILESTONE, LEWIS (1895–1980)
Russian-born film director, nicknamed "Milly." Arriving in the United States at age seventeen, he started his Hollywood career in the cutting room, eventually working his way up to become one of the industry's most successful directors. He won Academy Awards for *Two Arabian Nights* (1927) and *All Quiet on the Western Front* (1930). In 1937 he was hired to direct "Castles in Spain," for which Weill wrote a score, but the film was never made. Beginning in the mid-1950s he worked frequently on television specials.

MILHAUD, DARIUS (1892–1974)
French composer. Early in his career, he was drawn into Cocteau's circle and was soon associated with a group of composers known as Les Six. His opera *Christophe Colombe* (1928), with a libretto by Paul Claudel, was a major success in Berlin in 1930. In 1940 he fled France with his wife, Madeleine (b. 1902), and accepted a teaching position at Mills College in Oakland, California. Upon his return to France in

1947, he retained this post while simultaneously serving as professor of composition at the Paris conservatory. Milhaud was the only major composer with whom Weill enjoyed a close personal friendship.

MORROS, BORIS (1863–1936)
Russian-born head of Paramount Studios' music department and film producer who worked with Weill on *You and Me* (1938). In the 1950s he was revealed to have been an American counterintelligence agent.

NASH, OGDEN (1902–71)
Author of light verse ranging from satire to the absurd. A native of New York, he worked in the advertising department of Doubleday, Page & Company prior to joining the staff of the *New Yorker*. The many collections of his poetry include *Free Wheeling* (1931), *I'm a Stranger Here Myself* (1938), *You Can't Get There from Here* (1957), and *Everyone but Thee and Me* (1962). At Weill's urging, he undertook the assignment of writing lyrics to *One Touch of Venus* (1943), his only successful venture into the theater.

NEHER, CASPAR (1897–1962)
Famed German stage designer and librettist. Born in Augsburg, he was a close friend of Brecht's from their earliest years. From the outset Neher defined the style of production that came to be known as "Brechtian." His set designs for *Die Dreigroschenoper* created a sensation, representing what was termed *Kaschemmentheater* (theater of the low dive). After the Weill-Brecht-Neher collaboration disintegrated in 1931, Weill and Neher collaborated on the tragic three-act opera *Die Bürgschaft*. The trio was reunited in Paris for *Die sieben Todsünden* (1933). Though he remained in Germany throughout the Nazi regime, he sustained a measure of artistic independence, collaborating, for example, with the exiled Carl Ebert at the Glyndebourne Festival in 1938. Neher wrote the librettos for Rudolf Wagner-Régeny's *Der Günstling*, *Die Bürger von Calais*, *Johanna Balk*, and *Persische Episode*. Up to Weill's death the two maintained a close friendship, something that had eluded Brecht and Weill. After the war, Neher resumed his collaboration with Brecht at the Berliner Ensemble.

NEHER, ERIKA, *née* TORNQUIST (1903–62)
Wife of Caspar Neher. She was born in Graz, Austria, the daughter of the university professor Johannes Heinrich Tornquist. The Nehers' one son, Georg, was listed as missing in action in Russia in March 1943. Close to Weill during his estrangement from Lenya, Erika often corresponded with him, sometimes under the pen name Luise Mattes (one of the characters in *Die Bürgschaft*). In that passionate correspondence Weill reveals innermost doubts and emotions absent from his contemporaneous letters to Lenya.

NOAILLES, CHARLES, VICOMTE DE (1891–1981)
Heir to one of the oldest and most prestigious names in the French aristocracy. Having become acquainted with Weill in Berlin, he helped to arrange Weill's triumphal first concert in Paris (1932). Soon after his arrival in Paris in 1933, Weill moved into Noailles's guest quarters and composed *Die sieben Todsünden* there. A draft of Weill's manuscript score of *Der Jasager*, dedicated to the Noailles, is now in the possession of their heirs.

NOAILLES, MARIE-LAURE, VICOMTESSE DE, *née* BISCHOFFSHEIM (1902–70)
Wife of Charles de Noailles; granddaughter of Laure de Sade, a direct descendant of the Marquis de Sade. Dividing her time among several residences, including the Bischoffsheim family town house on the place des États-Unis, she was determined to make a place for herself in Parisian society. She played patron to a number of leading contemporary artists, among them Salvador Dali and Jean Cocteau, as well as Weill, with whom she seems to have had a brief affair.

ODETS, CLIFFORD (1906–63)
American playwright closely associated with Group Theatre productions and one of the most prominent dramatists of the 1930s. His works include *Awake and Sing* (1935), *Waiting for Lefty* (1935), and *Golden Boy* (1937). He adapted several of his plays for the screen. The Viennese actress Luise Rainer *(q.v.)* was his first wife.

PASETTI, OTTO (1903–?)
Austrian tenor and adventurer. His passport identified him as Dr. Otto Pasetti-Friedensburg, a member of an aristocratic Austrian family. His marriage to Erna Marek (b. 1905) produced one son, Mario (b.

1930), before it ended in divorce in 1933. Prior to meeting Lenya in 1932, he had already recorded Weill's "Die Muschel von Margate" on the Paloma label (rereleased on compact disc, Capriccio 10 347). Pasetti sang the role of Jim in the Vienna production of *Mahagonny*. During the period of his involvement with Lenya, Pasetti's officially declared occupation changed from businessman and doctor of political economics to singer. His last official residency was reported in 1937 as Zurich. After the war, he campaigned for the denazification of conductor Herbert von Karajan.

PERELMAN, SIDNEY JOSEPH (S. J.; 1904–79)
American humorist. A contributor to the *New Yorker* magazine for some forty-five years, he was also a collaborating screenwriter for such Hollywood classics as the Marx Brothers' *Animal Crackers* and *Horse Feathers*. Throughout his multifaceted literary career he often collaborated with his wife, Laura, a sister of Nathanael West. His writings have been collected in many books, among them *Look Who's Talking* (1940), *Listen to the Mocking Bird* (1949), *The Ill-Tempered Clavichord* (1953), and *Eastward Ha!* (1977). The book for *One Touch of Venus* (1943) was his only successful effort for the lyric stage.

POLIGNAC, PRINCESSE DE, *née* WINARETTA SINGER (1865–1943)
Celebrated patron of the arts in France. The daughter of the American sewing machine inventor and manufacturer Isaac Merritt Singer (1811–75), she had inherited his vast fortune. Hardly a major composer of the time did not benefit from a commission from the princesse; she commissioned a symphony from Weill in 1933 (Symphony no. 2).

RAINER, LUISE (b. 1910)
Viennese-born actress who won Academy Awards for her work in *The Great Ziegfeld* (1936) and *The Good Earth* (1937). She married Clifford Odets *(q.v.)* in 1937 but divorced him only three years later.

REINHARDT, MAX (1873–1943)
One of Germany's most influential stage directors and producers. He directed the Deutsches Theater in Berlin until 1933 as well as the Salzburg Festival, where he initiated the famous outdoor performances of Hugo von Hofmannsthal's *Jedermann*. Although extremely innovative early in his career, he never gave up an illusionist approach to theater, and thus his style came to be regarded as dated. After his immigration to the United States he was never to regain the same preeminent position he had held in Europe. Still, he directed *A Midsummer Night's Dream* in Hollywood in 1934, staged *The Eternal Road* in New York in 1936, and established a distinguished Reinhardt acting school in Hollywood. His first wife was the actress Else Heims; his second, the actress Helene Thimig.

RÉVY, ALMA "JO," *née* STAUB-TERLINDEN (b. 1911)
Second wife of Lenya's drama teacher Richard Révy *(q.v.)*. The daughter of the Swiss art patron Alma Staub-Terlinden, she studied ballet with Trudi Schoop but had to abandon a dancing career because of the after-effects of a case of rheumatic fever. She studied and practiced costume design before marrying Révy. They had one son, Thomas.

RÉVY, RICHARD (1885–1965)
German stage director who had a decisive influence on Lenya's career and personality. He coached her privately and cast her in small speaking roles at the Zurich Municipal Theater, where he was the principal stage director from 1911 to 1921. He moved to Berlin in 1921 and staged major productions at the Deutsches Theater, Kammerspiele, Großes Schauspielhaus, and Volksbühne. A friendship developed with Georg Kaiser *(q.v.)*, to whom he introduced Lenya. Though neither he nor his second wife, Jo, was Jewish, they both immigrated to the United States in protest of the Nazi regime.

RICE, ELMER, *orig.* name ELMER REIZENSTEIN (1892–1967)
American playwright. He graduated from law school but abandoned that career for one as a playwright and novelist. His *Street Scene* won a Pulitzer Prize in 1929; Weill saw a production of it in Berlin in 1930. A founding member of the Playwrights' Producing Company, Rice experimented with novel dramatic structures in plays such as *The Adding Machine* (1923), but liberal idealism underlay all his efforts.

RONELL, ANN (1908–93)
American composer, lyricist, and conductor. A protégée of George Gershwin, she became the first woman to compose successfully for Hollywood films. Her best-known song is "Who's Afraid of the Big Bad Wolf." In addition to her musical projects, at Weill's behest in 1938 she adapted several of the lyrics of *Die Dreigroschenoper* into English, based on Weill's rough translations. She was married to the producer Lester Cowan.

SHERWOOD, ROBERT E. (1896–1955)
American playwright; one of the founding members of the Playwrights' Producing Company and one of its most prolific members. Among his many works are *Petrified Forest* (1935), *Idiot's Delight* (1936), *Abe Lincoln in Illinois* (1938), and *There Shall Be No Night* (1940). He also translated Jacques Deval's *Tovarich* (1936) for its Broadway run. He was the recipient of three Pulitzer Prizes.

SOHN, RUTH AND LEO, *see* WEILL, RUTH

SPEWACK, SAMUEL (1899–1971) AND BELLA (1899–1990)
American playwrights. Approximately a dozen of their plays reached Broadway, including the librettos for Cole Porter's *Leave It to Me* (1938) and *Kiss Me, Kate* (1948). Their comedy *Boy Meets Girl* (1935), an adroit satire of Hollywood in general and the work of Ben Hecht and Charles MacArthur in particular, was produced by George Abbott and ran for 669 performances.

STEINBECK, JOHN (1902–68)
American novelist, winner of both Pulitzer and Nobel prizes for literature. He was less successful as a dramatist, with only his own adaptation of his novel *Of Mice and Men* holding the stage. His second wife was Gwyn (Gwyndolyn), which Lenya frequently misspelled as "Gwen." They were friends and frequent dinner guests of the Weills in New City.

STEINTHAL, WALTER (1887–1951)
German-born publisher and editor. He knew the Weill family in his youth in Dessau. In his position as publisher and editor of the *Deutsche Monatszeitung* he discovered many important young writers. He took over the *Neue Berliner Zeitung* in 1922 and rechristened it the *12-Uhr Blatt*, a name it retained until 1933. He immigrated first to Paris, then to the United States, where he lectured in religious studies from 1940 to 1942 at Stanford University. Weill dedicated *Die Bürgschaft* to him.

STIEDRY, FRITZ (1883–1968)
Austrian conductor. A protégé of Gustav Mahler, he conducted Weill's *Frauentanz* in Berlin (1924) and probably introduced Weill to Georg Kaiser *(q.v.)*. He became the principal conductor of the Berlin City Opera, leading the premiere performance of *Die Bürgschaft* in 1932. He also conducted the premieres of Arnold Schoenberg's *Die glückliche Hand* and the Second Chamber Symphony. After a period in the Soviet Union he moved to the United States, where he conducted at the Metropolitan Opera and assumed the musical directorship of New Friends of Music in New York.

STRAVINSKY, IGOR (1882–1971)
Russian-born composer; with Arnold Schoenberg, one of the two most influential composers of the twentieth century. In *Expositions and Developments* (1959), Stravinsky recalled: "I saw the *Dreigroschenoper* in its first run in Berlin. I met Weill at this performance, and developed an acquaintance with him later, in Paris, at the time of *Mahagonny* and *Der Jasager*, both of which were performed, without staging, at the Vicomtesse Noailles'; and both of which I admired. I also saw Weill in Hollywood during the war, and I went on stage to congratulate him after the premiere of *Lady in the Dark*."

STROBEL, HEINRICH (1898–1970)
German music critic and administrator. He served as music critic for a number of leading German newspapers. The editor of *Melos* until that publication was suspended by the Nazis, he subsequently took up the editorship of the *Neue Musikblatt* (1934–39). He moved to France in 1939, returning to edit *Melos* after its revival in 1946. He was named chair of the International Society for Contemporary Music in 1956 and worked constantly for the promotion of contemporary music. His wife, Deta, was a friend of Lenya's in Paris.

VAMBERY, ROBERT (b. 1909)
Hungarian dramaturg and playwright. Born in Budapest, he was engaged by Ernst Josef Aufricht *(q.v.)* as dramaturg for the Theater am Schiffbauerdamm in Berlin. He created modern versions of Gaetano Donizetti's *La fille du Régiment* and Gilbert and Sullivan's *The Pirates of Penzance*. Weill's *Der Kuhhandel* was his first independent venture as a dramatist. Vambery immigrated to the United States in the late 1930s. In 1994 he attended the premiere of the reconstructed *Kuhhandel* in Bautzen, Germany.

VIERTEL, BERTHOLD (1885–1955)
Viennese cabaret performer, lyricist, and stage director. He moved to the United States in 1927 and wrote film and stage scripts. There were plans for him to collaborate with Weill on a *Kleiner Mann, was nun?* project. These plans did not come to fruition, but he did stage Brecht's *Fear and Suffering in the Third Reich* in New York in 1945. Returning to Germany in 1949, he worked as stage director for the Berliner Ensemble and Vienna's Burgtheater. He was married to Salka Viertel *(q.v.)*.

VIERTEL, SALKA, *née* STEUERMANN (1889–1978)
Polish-born screenwriter; the sister of renowned pianist Eduard Steuermann and the wife of Berthold Viertel *(q.v.)*. She collaborated on screenplays of several films starring Greta Garbo, including *Queen Christina* (1933), *Anna Karenina* (1935), and *Conquest* (1937). A close personal friend of Max Reinhardt's son, the producer Gottfried Reinhardt, she regularly entertained a circle of émigré artists in Hollywood.

WALTER, BRUNO (1876–1962)
World-renowned German conductor. A native of Berlin, he began his conducting career at the Hamburg Opera under Gustav Mahler, who exerted a lasting influence on him. He served as music director of the Munich Opera until 1922 and thereafter of the Berlin City Opera and the Leipzig Opera. In 1934 he conducted the premiere of Weill's Symphony no. 2 in Amsterdam and New York. Settling in the United States in 1939, he guest conducted with all the major American symphony orchestras and at the Metropolitan Opera.

WANGER, WALTER, *orig. name* WALTER FEUCHTWANGER (1894–1968)
American film producer. He joined Paramount Studios as a producer, later becoming production chief. His films ranged from ambitious undertakings to routine potboilers and included *Queen Christina* (1933), *Algiers* (1938), and *Joan of Arc* (1948). He commissioned Weill's first original film score (1937), but it was not used.

WEDEKIND, FRANK (1864–1918)
German playwright, singer, and cabaret performer. This multitalented artist collaborated early in his career on the antimilitarist satirical magazine *Simplicissimus* and even served one year in jail on charges of *Majestätsbeleidigung* (insulting His Majesty, the Kaiser). He became a member of "Die elf Scharfrichter" (the eleven executioners), a famous Munich cabaret team. His plays—in productions of which he often appeared as the leading man—foreshadowed many aspects of German expressionism. Among his best-known works are *Frühlings Erwachen* (1891), *Erdgeist* (1895), and *Büchse der Pandora* (1904), the last two the basis for Alban Berg's opera *Lulu*. Lenya appeared on stage with Wedekind in Zurich and was in a production of *Frühlings Erwachen* in Berlin.

WEIGEL, HELENE (1900–1971)
Austrian-born German actress; the second wife of Bertolt Brecht, whom she met in 1924. Following their marriage in 1929, she appeared in many of his plays, including *Die Maßnahme* (1930) and *Die Mutter* (1932). She left Germany with Brecht in 1933, eventually accompanying him to the United States. After the war she cofounded the Berliner Ensemble and played leading roles in memorable productions of Brecht's and other authors' plays. She continued as the director of the Berliner Ensemble after her husband's death until her own in 1971. Lenya's portrayal of Mother Courage was often compared unfavorably with Weigel's, and the two were, predictably, engaged in widow warfare for several decades.

WEILL, ALBERT (1867–1955) AND EMMA (1872–1957)
The parents of Kurt Weill. Albert Weill was born in Kippenheim in the Grand Duchy of Baden, the descendant of a long line of distinguished rabbis and scholars. At age twenty-six he became cantor in the small town of Eichstätt in Bavaria and published his first *Synagogengesänge*. In 1897 he married Emma

Ackermann of Wiesloch, whose brother Aaron had already published his own volume of *Synagogengesänge* in 1892. Albert Weill then took a position at the synagogue of Dessau, serving as both cantor and second-in-charge of its religious school. In 1920 he resigned the Dessau cantorship and moved to Leipzig to become the director of a home for children of divorced parents. The elder Weills immigrated to Palestine in 1936.

WEILL, HANS JAKOB (1899–1947)
Weill's favorite brother; married to Rita Kisch (1902–84). The two immigrated to New York and remained in close touch with Weill and Lenya. They had one daughter, Hanne Susanne ("Bissie") Weill Holesovsky (b. 1923).

WEILL, NATHAN (1898–1957)
Weill's eldest brother, sometimes called "Fritz" by family members; married to Helene (Leni) Frankenberg. They had one daughter, Hannelore (b. 1926). He and his family left Germany in 1933 to buy land in Palestine and settled in the small community of Naharia. A medical doctor, he learned to speak Arabic fluently and had many Arab patients.

WEILL, RUTH (1901–72)
Weill's only sister; married to Leo Sohn (1892–1969). They had one daughter, Eve Sybille Sohn Hammerschmidt (1925–79). Eve had one son, Marc Hammerschmidt.

WEISGAL, MEYER (1895–1977)
Polish-born theater producer who came to the United States as a young boy, growing up in Chicago and New York. A passionately committed Zionist, he became involved with theater in the 1930s, particularly with spectacles for Zionist causes such as *The Romance of a People* at the 1933 Chicago World's Fair. He also produced the Weill/Werfel *Eternal Road* (1937). Weisgal served as director of the Weizmann Institute in Rehovot, Israel, until his death.

WERFEL, ALMA MARIA, *née* SCHINDLER (1879–1964)
Significant figure in the Viennese artistic world; wife of three remarkable artists. The daughter of the Austrian painter and graphic artist Jakob Emil Schindler, she wed, in succession, the composer Gustav Mahler (1902), the architect Walter Gropius (1915), and the writer Franz Werfel (*q.v.;* 1929). Her relationship with Weill seems to have been friendly, as the two addressed each other with the informal "*du.*"

WERFEL, FRANZ (1890–1945)
Czech-German novelist and playwright; married to Alma Maria Werfel *(q.v.).* He lived in Austria and France before immigrating to the United States, where he was best known for *The Forty Days of Musa Dagh* (1933), *The Song of Bernadette* (1941), and *Jacobowsky and the Colonel* (1944). He authored the text for *Der Weg der Verheißung*, performed in the United States as *The Eternal Road* (1937), his only collaboration with Weill.

WHARTON, JOHN (1894–1977)
Prominent theatrical lawyer and partner in the Playwrights' Producing Company. He served as the attorney for Weill's estate and incorporated the Kurt Weill Foundation for Music in 1962 as a charitable organization for Lenya to utilize for tax-deductible donations.

WOLLHEIM, ERIC (1879–1948)
Polish-born theatrical impresario who moved to England in 1900 and worked in theater management with Sir Oswald Stoll at the London Coliseum. He brought Sarah Bernhardt, Sergey Diaghilev, and Max Reinhardt to London, and imported such productions as *White Horse Inn*, *Waltzes from Vienna*, and *Casanova*. He helped to get Weill's *A Kingdom for a Cow* produced in London in 1935.

WOOLY
The Weills' Old English sheepdog, a gift from Moss Hart. Apparently named after Monty Woolley, the American actor best remembered for his portrayal of the cantankerous Sheridan Whiteside in George S. Kaufman and Moss Hart's *The Man Who Came to Dinner* (1939). The name was pronounced, of course, "Vooly."

SOURCES CITED

ARCHIVAL SOURCES

WLRC   Weill-Lenya Research Center, New York
Yale   Weill/Lenya Archive, Yale University

The bracketed abbreviations that precede each entry are used to cite the source in the text.

Correspondence

FROM WEILL TO:

[W–MA]   Abravanel, Maurice. WLRC, series 40. Original in Marriott Library, University of Utah. German.

[W–M&MA]   Anderson, Max and Mab. WLRC, series 40. Original in Harry Ransom Humanities Research Center, University of Texas. English.

[W–BB]   Brecht, Bertolt. WLRC, series 40. Original in Bertolt-Brecht-Archiv, Berlin. German.

[W–FB]   Busoni, Ferruccio. WLRC, series 40. German.

[W–IG]   Gershwin, Ira. WLRC, series 40. Original in Library of Congress, Washington, D.C. English.

[W–MK]   Kaiser, Margarethe. WLRC, series 40. Original in Georg-Kaiser-Archiv, Akademie der Künste, Berlin. German.

[W–AM]   MacLeish, Archibald. Yale, series IV/A, box 47. English.

[W–GM]   Marton, George. Yale, series IV/A. English.

[W–CN]   Neher, Caspar. WLRC, series 40. German.

[W–EN1]   Neher, Erika. WLRC, series 30. German.

[W–EN2]   ———. WLRC, series 40. German.

[W–MR]   Reinhardt, Max. WLRC, series 40. German.

[W–UE]   Universal Edition. WLRC, series 41. Original in Wiener Stadt- und Landesbibliothek, Vienna. German.

[W–AW]   Weill, Albert. WLRC, series 30, box 7. German.

[W–EW]   Weill, Emma. WLRC, series 30, box 7. German.

[W–A&EW1]   Weill, Albert and Emma. WLRC, series 45. German.

[W–A&EW2]   ———. WLRC, series 46. German.

[W–HW]   Weill, Hans. WLRC, series 45. German.

[W–RW1]   Weill, Ruth. WLRC, series 30, box 7. German.

[W–RW2]   ———. WLRC, series 45. German.

TO WEILL FROM:

[BB–W1]   Brecht, Bertolt. WLRC, series 40. Original at Yale. German.

[BB–W2]   ———. Yale, series IV/B. German.

[TWA–W]   Adorno, Theodor W. Yale, series IV/B. German.

[UE–W]   Universal Edition. WLRC, series 41. Original in Wiener Stadt- und Landesbibliothek, Vienna. German.

FROM LENYA TO:

[L–MD]   Daniel, Mary. WLRC, series 43. English.
[L–MG]   George, Manfred. WLRC, series 43. Original in Deutsches Literaturarchiv, Marbach.
                German.
[L–CN]   Neher, Caspar. WLRC, series 30, box 1. Original in Österreichische
                Nationalbibliothek, Vienna. German.
[L–RR]   Révy, Richard. WLRC, series 43. German.
[L–LS]   Symonette, Lys. WLRC, series 39A. English.
[L–RW]   Weill, Rita. WLRC, series 45. English.

TO LENYA FROM:

[ME–L]   Ernst, Max. WLRC, series 43. German.
[EW–L]   Weill, Emma. Yale, series IV/F. German.

OTHER CORRESPONDENCE

[GD–MD]   Davis, George, to Mary Daniel. WLRC, series 37/II. English.
[EW–RW]   Weill, Emma, to Ruth Weill. Yale, series IV/F. German.

Interviews, Oral Histories, and Memoirs

[int. MA1]   Abravanel, Maurice. With Alan Rich, Kim Kowalke, and Lys Symonette, 26 August
                1979. WLRC, series 60. English.
[int. MA2]   ———. With Donald Spoto and Lys Symonette, 1985. WLRC, series 60. English.
[int. MA3]   ———. With Alan Rich and Kim Kowalke, 1987. WLRC, series 60. English.
[int. HA]   Anderson, Hesper. With Donald Spoto, 22 March 1986. WLRC, series 60. English.
[int. MA]   Aufricht, Margo. With Donald Spoto, Kim Kowalke, and Paul Moor, 24 March 1986.
                WLRC, series 60.
[int. MC]   Caniff, Milton. With Donald Spoto, 15 October 1985. WLRC, series 60. English.
[int. NF]   Fujita, Neil. With Donald Spoto, 16 January 1986. WLRC, series 60. English.
[int. GG]   Gilpin, Gigi. With Donald Spoto, 9 December 1985. WLRC, series 60. English.
[int. MG]   Granirer, Martus. With Peggy Sherry. WLRC, series 60. English.
[int. HIH]   Halpern, Hilde. With Donald Spoto, 25 November 1986. WLRC, series 60. English.
[int. HEH]   Hayes, Helen. With Peggy Meyer Sherry. WLRC, series 60. English.
[int. HAH]   Heinsheimer, Hans. With Donald Spoto, 1986. WLRC, series 60. English.
[int. L1]   Lenya, Lotte. With Robert Wennersten, 27 November 1971. Transcript of interview.
                WLRC, series 30, box 8, folder 16. English.
[int. L2]   ———. With Alan Rich, fall 1976. WLRC, series 60. English.
[int. L3]   ———. With Gottfried Wagner, summer 1978. WLRC, series 60. German.
[int. L4]   ———. With Hitzig and Landau, n.d. Transcript of unidentified interview. Yale,
                series X. German.
[int. L5]   ———. With George Tabori, n.d. Transcript of interview. Yale, series X. English.
[int. BM]   Meredith, Burgess. With Donald Spoto, 7 February 1986. WLRC, series 60. English.
[int. PM1]   Moor, Paul. With Donald Spoto, 24 March 1986. WLRC, series 60. English.
[int. PM2]   ———. With Donald Spoto, 18 August 1986. WLRC, series 60. English.
[int. RW]   "Kurt at School." Transcript of interview with Ruth Weill, 1954. WLRC, series 37.
                English.
[mem. FJ]   Jackson, Felix. "Portrait of a Quiet Man." Unpublished typescript biography of Kurt
                Weill, 1975. WLRC, series 30. English.
[mem. L1]   Lenya, Lotte. Unpublished memoirs. WLRC, series 34. English.
[mem. L2]   ———. Draft of "That was a Time . . ." [written with George Davis]. Yale, series
                VIII, box 69, folder 22. English.

PUBLISHED OR BROADCAST SOURCES

Writings and Printed Interviews by Weill and Lenya

Lenya, Lotte. "August 28, 1928." Foreword to Bertolt Brecht, *The Threepenny Opera*, translated by Desmond Vesey and Eric Bentley. New York: Grove Press, 1964.
————. "That Was the Time!" *Theatre Arts* 40 (May 1956): 78–80, 92–93.
————. "The Time Is Ripe." *Playbill* 6, no. 16 (April 16, 1962): 7–11, 43.
Osborne, Charles. "Berlin in the Twenties: Conversations with Otto Klemperer and Lotte Lenya." *London Magazine* 1 (May 1961): 44–51.
Weill, Kurt. "Aktuelles Zwiegespräch über die Schuloper zwischen Kurt Weill und Dr. Hans Fischer." *Die Musikpflege* 1 (April 1930): 48–53.
————. "The Future of Opera in America." *Modern Music* 14 (May–June 1937): 183–188.
————. Interview. *Brooklyn Daily Eagle*, 11 December 1938.
————. Interview with Ole Winding. *Aften-Avisen*, 21 June 1934. Reprinted as "Kurt Weill in Exile," in *Kurt Weill: Musik und Theater*, edited by Stephen Hinton and Jürgen Schebera, pp. 314–17. Berlin: Henschelverlag Kunst und Gesellschaft, 1990.

Radio and Television Interviews with Lenya

Adam, Peter. Conducted 19 April 1979. Broadcast on BBC-1 television, 24 May 1979.
Chapin, Schuyler. Recorded for "Skyline" on PBS television, 7 December 1978. Transcript in Yale, series X.
Newman, Edwin. "Speaking Freely." Broadcast on WNBC television, 24 October 1970. Transcript in WLRC.
Vaughan, Paul. Broadcast on BBC "Kaleidoscope" (radio), 21 December 1981. Transcript in WLRC.

Secondary Sources

Anderson, Maxwell. *Dramatist in America: Letters of Maxwell Anderson, 1912–1958*, edited by Laurence G. Avery. Chapel Hill: University of North Carolina Press, 1977.
Atkinson, Brooks. Review of *A Candle in the Wind*. *New York Times*, 23 October 1941.
————. Review of *The Eternal Road*. *New York Times*, 8 January 1937.
————. Review of *Lily of the Valley*. *New York Times*, 27 January 1942.
Aufricht, Ernst Josef. *Erzähle, damit du dein Recht erweist*. Berlin: Propyläen, 1966.
Barlow, Samuel. "In the Theatre." *Modern Music* 18 (March–April 1941): 189–93.
Beams, David. "Lotte Lenya." *Theatre Arts* 46 (June 1962): 11ff.
Bekker, Paul. Review of *The Eternal Road*. *Die Staatszeitung und Herald* (New York), 31 January 1937.
Blitzstein, Marc. "New York Medley, Winter, 1935." *Modern Music* 13 (January–February 1936): 34–40.
————. "Theatre-Music in Paris." *Modern Music* 12 (March–April 1935): 128–34.
Bordman, Gerald. *Oxford Companion to the American Theatre*. New York: Oxford University Press, 1984.
Brecht, Bertolt. *Brecht Briefe*, edited by Günter Gläser. Frankfurt am Main: Suhrkamp, 1981.
Britten, Benjamin. *Letters from a Life: Selected Letters and Diaries of Benjamin Britten II (1939–1945)*, edited by Donald Mitchell and Philip Reed. Berkeley: University of California Press, 1991.
Busoni, Ferruccio. *Selected Letters*. Translated and edited by Antony Beaumont. New York: Columbia University Press, 1987.
Capra, Frank. *The Name above the Title*. New York: Macmillan, 1971.
Carter, Elliott. "O Fair World of Music!" *Modern Music* 16 (May–June 1939): 238–43.
Copland, Aaron, and Vivian Perlis. *Copland: 1900–1942*. New York: St. Martin's Press, 1984.
Crawford, Cheryl. *One Naked Individual*. New York: Bobbs-Merrill, 1977.
Drew, David. *Kurt Weill: A Handbook*. London: Faber; Berkeley: University of California Press, 1987.
Geddes, Norman Bel. *Miracle in the Evening*. New York: Doubleday, 1960.
Halliday, Jon. *Sirk on Sirk*. New York: Viking, 1972.
Heinsheimer, Hans W. *Best Regards to Aida: The Defeats and Victories of a Music Man on Two Continents*. New York: Alfred A. Knopf, 1968.
Hess, Hans. *Dank in Farben*. Munich: R. Piper, 1957.

Ihering, Herbert. *Theater in Aktion*. Edited by Edith Krull and Hugo Fetting. Berlin: Argon, 1987.

Kaiser, Georg. *Georg Kaiser Briefe*. Edited by Walther Huder. Frankfurt am Main: Propyläen, 1980.

Kastendieck, Miles. "Weill Memorial Is Impressive." *New York Journal American*, 13 July 1950.

Kastner, Rudolf. "Kurt Weill: Eine Skizze." *Anbruch* 7 (October 1925): 453–56.

Kowalke, Kim. *Kurt Weill in Europe*. Ann Arbor: University of Michigan Press, 1979.

Lambert, Constant. Review of *Die sieben Todsünden*. *London Sunday Express*, 13 August 1933.

Levitz, Tamara. "Teaching New Classicality: Busoni's Masterclass in Composition, 1921–24." Ph.D. diss., University of Rochester, 1994.

Nash, Ogden. "Lines from a Lyricist at Bay." *New York Times*, 20 August 1944.

Newman, Ernest. Review of *Die Dreigroschenoper*. *London Sunday Times*, 10 February 1935.

O'Connor, Patrick. "Weill à la française." *Kurt Weill Newsletter* 9 (spring 1991): 10–13.

Review of *Aufstieg und Fall der Stadt Mahagonny*. *Dagens Nyheter* (Copenhagen), 2 January 1934.

Review of *A Kingdom for a Cow*. *Times* (London), 29 June 1935.

Review of *Lieber reich aber glücklich*. *Neue Zürcher Zeitung*, 19 August 1934.

Review of *Mahagonny Songspiel*. *London Evening News*, 19 July 1933.

Sanders, Ronald. *The Days Grow Short: The Life and Music of Kurt Weill*. New York: Holt, Rinehart and Winston, 1980.

Schebera, Jürgen. Interview with Stefan Krüger. *Kurt Weill Newsletter* 2 (fall 1984): 9.

Schiaparelli, Elsa. *Shocking Life*. New York: E. P. Dutton, 1954.

Shirer, William L. *The Rise and Fall of the Third Reich*. New York: Simon and Schuster, 1959.

Simon, Louis. "Up the Rungs from Opera." *New York Times*, 13 September 1941.

Spoto, Donald. *Lenya: A Life*. Boston: Little, Brown, 1989.

Stuckenschmidt, H. H. Review of *Aufstieg und Fall der Stadt Mahagonny*. *Die Scene* 20 (29 March 1930): 75–77.

Sundgaard, Arnold. "Portrait of the Librettist as Silenced Composer." *Dramatist Guild Quarterly* 16 (winter 1980): 24–30.

Taylor, Ronald. *Kurt Weill: Composer in a Divided World*. Boston: Northeastern University Press, 1992.

Thomson, Virgil. Review of Kurt Weill concert. *New York Herald Tribune*, 5 February 1951.

———. *Virgil Thomson*. New York: Knopf, 1966.

Toumanova, Tamara. Interview in *Balanchine's Ballerinas*, by Robert Tracy with Sharon Delano, pp. 51–53. New York: Linden Press, 1983.

Viertel, Salka. *The Kindness of Strangers*. New York: Holt, Rinehart & Winston, 1969.

Wahls, Robert. "Footlight: A Swinging Landlady." *New York Daily News*, 19 March 1967.

Weisgal, Meyer. *. . . So Far*. New York: Random House, 1971.

Welles, Benjamin. "Lyricist of 'The Saga of Jenny,' et al." *New York Times*, 25 May 1941.

For Further Reading

Kowalke, Kim H., ed. *A New Orpheus: Essays on Kurt Weill*. New Haven: Yale University Press, 1986.

Kowalke, Kim H., and Horst Edler, eds. *A Stranger Here Myself: Kurt Weill Studien*. Hildesheim: Olms Verlag, 1993.

Schebera, Jürgen. *Kurt Weill: An Illustrated Life*. New Haven: Yale University Press, 1995.

INDEX OF NAMES

All names appearing in the correspondence are listed by letter number below. Following the letter numbers, page numbers are given, in italic, for references to names in the Introductions, Prologue, Epilogue, Afterwords, and the narrative that joins groups of letters. Figure numbers are given at the end of the entry for individuals depicted in the photo insert. Persons whose names appear in boldface are identified in the Biographical Glossary; all others are identified in the first letter in which they are mentioned. First names, nicknames, and variant spellings found in the letters are cross-referenced to the main entry.

Hungerford, Edward, 205, 208, 209, 211
Hurok, Sol, 79, 319
Huston, Elsie, 196, 199, 200, 201
Huston, John, 296, 322, 392
Huston, Walter and Nan, 232, 312, 314, 318, 343, 344, 350, 366, 369, 372, 373, 374, 375, 377, 391, 392; *pages 269–70*
Hyman, Dick: *page 487*

Ibsen, Henrik: *page 19*
Ihering, Herbert, 15
Inkijinoff, _____, 91
Ira. *See* Gershwin, Ira
Irene. *See* Gallagher, Irene
Irving. *See* Lazar, Irving
Isaac, Edyth, 242
Ita, Frau _____: *page 15*

Jacobsen, Grete: *page 51*
Jack. *See* Wilson, Jack
Jackie. *See* Page, Jacqueline
Jackson, Felix. *See* Joachimson, Felix
Jacobi. *See* Jacoby, Herbert
Jacobs, Morris, 213
Jacoby, Herbert, 196, 197, 199, 200, 201, 203, 204, 207; fig. 56
Jaffe, Sam, 255
Jäger, _____, 76, 77, 90
Jakie. *See* Page, Jacqueline
Jakobi. *See* Jacoby, Herbert
James, Edward, 39, 40, 41, 45, 46, 49, 75, 81, 112, 144, 203; *pages 79, 81*
James, Harry, 352
Jameson, Mr. _____, 316
Jannings, Emil, 36, 351
Janssen, Werner, 195
Jarnach, Philipp, 15; *page 33*
Jed. *See* Harris, Jed
Jeffreys, Anne: *page 464*
Jessner, Leopold (Poldi), 97, 102, 105; *page 58*
Jessner, Lotte ("Lottchen"), 102, 104, 105
Jimmy. *See* Daniels, Jimmy
Joachimson, Felix (*later* Jackson), 12, 15, 17, 372, 393T; *pages 50, 51*
Jochi. *See* Joachimson, Felix
Joe. *See* Révy, Alma "Jo"
John. *See* Steinbeck, John and Gwyn
John (and Sheilagh) [surname unknown], 320
Johnson, Hall: *page 307*
Johnson, Mary and Stanley, 230, 233
Jones, Bill, 189, 277, 280, 283, 284; *page 4;* fig. 62
Jones, Grover, 170
Jouvet, Louis, 383
Jules [surname unknown], 219, 221, 222, 224, 227, 228, 230, 236, 239, 240, 241, 242, 249, 251, 254,

256, 257, 259, 263, 268, 270, 273, 274, 278, 281, 286, 288, 290, 292, 293, 294, 295, 298, 300
Julie. *See* Sloane, Bill and Julie
Juon, Paul: *page 29*
Jurmann, Walter, 159

Kaempfer, Walther, 14, 34
Kahn, Robert: *page 29*
Kaiser, Anselm, 21, 23, 24; *page 23;* fig. 8
Kaiser, Georg, 5, 20, 21, 24, 43, 61, 105, 115, 118, 173, 242, 250; *pages 1, 23, 34, 35, 36, 46, 50, 71;* fig. 7
Kaiser, Margarethe, 5, 21, 23, 24; *pages 23, 464;* fig. 8
Kaiser, Sibylle: *page 23*
Kálmán, Emmerich, 41, 173, 351, 356
Kalmus, Alfred, 31, 34, 54; *page 79*
Kaper, Bronislav, 159
Kapp, Jack, 367
Kardan, _____, 34, 50, 62, 66, 69, 73
Karloff, Boris, 295
Karlweis, Oscar, 57
Kastner, Rudolf, 15
Katayev, Valentin: *page 65*
Kätchen. *See* Kommer, Rudolf
Katz, _____, 265
Kaufman, George S., 75, 225, 226, 239, 249; *page 447*
Kaye, Danny and Sylvia, 377, 386; fig. 57
Kazan, Elia ("Gadge"), 153, 158, 160, 161, 166, 307, 308, 316, 332, 352, 353, 357; *pages 4, 195, 370, 475;* fig. 65
Keller, Greta, 323
Kennedy, Mr. and Mrs. _____, 227
Kern, Adele, 33
Kern, Jerome, 208, 308
Kerr, Deborah, 381
Keyes, Evelyn, 392
Kidd, Michael: *page 475*
Kiepura, Jan, 117
Kiki of Montparnasse, 105
Kingsley, Madge. *See* Evans, Madge
Kingsley, Sidney, 198, 211, 213, 215, 368
Kirchner, Otto: *page 22*
Klabund [Alfred Henschke], 242
Kleiber, Erich: *page 50*
Klemperer, Otto, 25, 69, 163, 175, 203, 286; *page 2*
Knappertsbusch, Hans: *page 31*
Kober, Arthur, 263, 264, 281, 292, 304, 315, 322, 328, 375
Koch, Friedrich Ernst: *page 29*
Koch, Karl, 20, 22, 25, 26, 33
Kochanski, Soscha, 196

327, 329, 331, 332, 333, 334, 335, 336, 337, 338, 339, 341, 343, 345, 347, 349, 352, 356, 369, 374, 375; fig. 51

Meyer, L. B. *See* Mayer, Louis B.

Meyer family, 199

Middleman, _____, 389

Middleton, Ray: *pages 270, 475*

Mielziner, Jo, 271, 273, 275

Milestone, Kendall, 298

Milestone, Lewis ("Milly"), 153, 154, 159, 160, 161, 163, 164, 165, 166, 167, 171, 172, 179, 181, 182, 190, 304, 313, 319, 320, 377, 393; *page 195*

Milhaud, Darius, 41, 58, 59, 123, 127, 318, 373, 380, 391, 392; *pages 7, 71, 191*

Milhaud, Etienne, 126, 127

Milhaud, Madeleine, 133, 175, 208, 376, 380, 391, 392; *pages 191, 248*

Milland, Ray: *page 448*

Miller, Gilbert, 286

Miller, Paula. *See* Strasberg, Paula Miller

Milly. *See* Milestone, Lewis

Milton. *See* Caniff, Milton

Mimi [surname unknown], 66

Mimi [surname unknown], 314, 321, 322, 323, 329, 341, 362, 365

Minnelli, Vincente, 313, 315

Miranda, Carmen, 268, 284

Mitchell, Miss _____, 290

Moholy, Lucia, 97

Moissi, Alexander: *page 19*

Molière, 369

Molnár, Ferenc, 162, 172, 173, 174, 176, 242

Moni, _____, 95, 97, 98, 103, 104, 105, 108, 111, 112, 113

Monnet, Dr. Henri, 59, 73, 75, 104, 111, 119, 120, 383

Monsell, _____, 279

Monti, Milly, 349

Monypenny, Guy, 222, 230, 233, 244

Moor, Paul: *pages 487, 489*

Moore, Grace, 204, 308

Moore, Victor, 322

"Mops," 95

Morris. *See* Carnovsky, Morris

Morris, Mrs. _____, 207

Morros, Boris, 161, 167, 171, 183, 184, 186, 187, 188, 195, 198, 202, 205, 210; fig. 55

"Moses," 176, 179, 191, 192

Moss. *See* Hart, Moss

Moszkowski, Alexander, 16

Motty. *See* Eitingon, Motty

Mozart, Wolfgang Amadeus, 50, 144, 344; *pages 29, 33*

Müller, Renate, 117

Multatuli, 56

Muni, Paul, 154, 275

Muse, Clarence, 263; *pages 306, 307*

Mussolini, Benito, 373

Nabokov, Nicolas, 40

Nan; Nannerl. *See* Huston, Walter and Nan

Nancy. *See* Anderson, Alan and Nancy

Napoleon Bonaparte, 331

Nash, Ogden, 308, 312, 316, 319, 330, 332, 336, 339, 343, 352, 353, 357, 359, 362, 375; *pages 362, 368*

Nathan. *See* Weill, Nathan

Neher, Carola, 25, 26; *page 65*

Neher, Caspar, 25, 26, 27, 28, 31, 32, 36, 37, 39, 41, 42, 43, 44, 45, 46, 47, 49, 50, 53, 55, 57, 60, 61, 64, 69, 72, 73, 75, 76, 77, 78, 81, 83, 89, 117, 133, 134, 135, 136, 138, 139, 140, 143; *pages 3, 57, 64, 65, 67, 77, 78, 80, 81, 464;* fig. 26

Neher, Erika, 25, 32, 41, 42, 47, 49, 77, 78, 83, 135, 136, 137, 138, 139, 140, 143; *pages 3, 7, 76, 77, 80, 464, 465;* fig. 35

Neher, Georg, 42, 143

Nelson, Rudolf, 88, 89, 92

Neppach, Rudolf, 37, 50

Nestroy, Johann, 45

Neumann, _____, 133

Neumann, Alfred, 351

Newman, Ernest, 108

Nick [surname unknown] (handyman), 270, 286

Nicolson, Virginia, 209

Niesen, Gertrude, 310

Nijinsky, Vaslav: *page 22*

Nikisch, Arthur: *pages 25, 29*

Nizer, Louis, 161, 169, 170, 180, 181

Noailles, Charles, vicomte de, 38, 51, 59, 122

Noailles, Marie-Laure, vicomtesse de, 38, 41, 45, 46, 49, 51, 59, 121, 122, 130, 383; *pages 71, 80;* fig. 38

Nostitz, Helene von, 14, 15

Nürnberg, Rolf, 67, 68, 70

Oberstein, _____, 158

Odets, Clifford (Cliff), 153, 154, 155, 158, 159, 160, 161, 163, 164, 167, 169, 175, 181, 183, 185, 186, 190; *page 195*

Offenbach, Jacques, 97, 344, 355; *pages 179, 362*

Offuts, _____, 219, 225, 227, 230, 237, 268

Olivier, Laurence, 248

O'Malley, John, 228, 316

Ondra, Annie, 130

O'Neill, Barbara, 307

Ormos, Mrs. _____, 266

Orser, Lloyd, 241, 263, 266, 270, 277, 280, 284, 286, 287, 293, 301, 365

White, Josh, 329, 332

Whitman, Walt, 219, 221, 227, 257; *page 316*

Wickes, _____, 281

Wiesengrund. *See* Adorno, Theodor Wiesengrund

Wiesenthal, Grete: *page 20*

Wildberg, Jack, 153, 155, 156, 157, 177, 204, 224, 313, 323, 348, 350, 351, 353, 357

Wilder, Thornton, 210, 376

Willkie, Wendell, 228, 287, 337, 338

Wilson, Jack, 294, 295, 296, 297

Wiman, Dwight Deere, 277, 385

Winchell, Walter, 203, 268

Windhust; Windhurst. *See* Windust, Bretaigne

Winding, Ole: *page 133*

Windust, Bretaigne, 307, 389, 390, 392

Windy. *See* Windust, Bretaigne

Winkler, Dr. _____, 333

Winter, Hugo, 34, 41

Wohlauer, _____, 49

Wolf, Theodor, 112, 114

Wolfy. *See* Aufricht, Wolfgang

Wollheim, Eric, 75, 78, 79, 106, 114, 115, 116, 117, 118, 119, 122, 124, 125, 127, 128, 129, 159

Wong, Anna May, 99

Wooly [Woolley] (dog), 213, 214, 231, 236, 249, 273, 279, 284, 290, 293, 308, 322, 328, 349; *page 447*

Wouk, Herman, 381; *page 475*

Wrightson, Earl: *page 447*

Wurm, _____, 21, 24

Wyler, William, 290, 296

Wynn, Ed, 369, 370

Zadora, Michael von, 5

Zanuck, Darryl, 390

Zemlinsky, Alexander von: *page 64*

Zimmermann, _____, 46, 53, 55, 57

Zorina, Vera: *page 369*

Zuckmayer, Carl, 143, 149; *page 192*

Zukor, Adolph, 314

INDEX OF WORKS BY WEILL

All works by Weill that are named in the correspondence are listed by letter number below. Following the letter numbers, page numbers are given, in italic, for references located in the Introductions, Prologue, Epilogue, Afterwords, and the narrative that joins groups of letters. Figure numbers are given at the end of the entry for works depicted in the photo insert.

INDEX OF OTHER WORKS

All works other than those by Weill that are named in the correspondence are listed by letter number below. Following the letter numbers, page numbers are given, in italic, for references located in the Introductions, Prologue, Epilogue, Afterwords, and the narrative that joins groups of letters. Figure numbers are given at the end of the entry for works depicted in the photo insert.

Designer: Barbara Jellow

Compositor: Impressions Book and Journal Services, Inc.

Text and display: Fournier

Printer and binder: Edwards Brothers, Inc.